American Society
A Sociological Interpretation

American Society

A Sociological Interpretation

by Robin M. Williams, Jr.

CORNELL UNIVERSITY

ALFRED A. KNOPF

NEW YORK

1952

Published July 23, 1951
Second Printing, May 1952

FOR *Marguerite, Bob,* AND *Nancy*

Preface

THIS BOOK is intended to provide a reasonably compact survey of the main cultural and social structures of American society. It is hoped that such a provisional synthesis will be of use not only in sociology and anthropology but also in related fields of economics, history, political science, and social psychology. The work has grown out of five years' experience at Cornell University in the development and teaching of a course on the structure and functioning of American society. Such a synoptic course was first suggested to the writer by Leonard S. Cottrell, Jr., who foresaw at the close of World War II a growing need for an analysis that would attempt to grasp and integrate the broad outlines of the society as a whole. Initial experiment showed that students of the most varied backgrounds and academic interests were eager to gain some systematic view of the total social structure. From the criticisms and suggestions of hundreds of these students the present work has immeasurably benefited.

The volume was designed originally to include a rather full consideration of social change in the United States. As the work developed, however, it became clear that more than a minimal analysis of the institutional structure and social organization would itself exceed the limits of a single volume. Accordingly the present treatment is largely, though by no means entirely, restricted to a cross-sectional view of the social structure. We are, of course, acutely conscious of the need for a comprehensive and rigorous analysis of the *processes* that are so rapidly transforming our institutions. Some hints regarding the social dynamics of our society are to be found below, especially in the last three chapters, but the exceedingly difficult analyses needed for an orderly synthesis must be reserved for a later time. Our more modest aim is to look at American society through the "wrong end of the telescope"—to make the main contours of its social topography appear in something like full perspective.

Every decision has its costs, and our attention to salient structures has meant a heavy loss of detail. The student is therefore urged to make full use of the supplementary readings suggested by footnote references, and of other references suggested by his instructor.

Such concentration upon America might, it is true, encourage myopia about other great societies of the West and East. Surely, however, one does not need in these times to stress the interdependence of our society with other national systems nor to deliver dicta concerning the hazards of extreme cultural parochialism. Solid work on a *comparative* sociology of the major cultures and national systems is, of course, greatly needed. As such studies appear, the present work will be seen in proper perspective as a single case study. In any event, it is surely worth while to seek now all possible clues as to what America is and what it may become.

ROBIN M. WILLIAMS, JR.

Ithaca, New York

Acknowledgments

THIS BOOK, like any other, is a social product to which many minds have contributed. Footnote acknowledgments in the text indicate the writer's awareness of numerous specific influences on his thinking, but such citations do not indicate all the contributions to the present work. Much, of course, is due to my former teachers. C. Horace Hamilton, of North Carolina State College, showed me that sociology could mean empirical search and hard thinking, and gave reality to the vision of a scientific sociology. As a student at Harvard University, I acquired lasting obligations to Gordon W. Allport, John D. Black, Robert K. Merton, Talcott Parsons, Pitirim A. Sorokin, and Carle C. Zimmerman. My colleagues in the Department of Sociology and Anthropology at Cornell University have contributed heavily to this book, although they perhaps will not always recognize their ideas here. Discussions with other members of the Cornell faculty have profoundly affected my thinking. In particular, Chapter 11 bears various marks of the discussions of the Cornell Values Study Group (Urie Bronfenbrenner, Stuart M. Brown, Jr., Leonard S. Cottrell, Jr., Mario Einaudi, Robert B. MacLeod, Morris E. Opler, Edwin P. Reubens, Edward A. Suchman, Gregory Vlastos, Robin M. Williams, Jr., and A. D. Woodruff).

A special word of appreciation goes to Melvin L. Kohn for his competent research assistance and perceptive criticism. I also wish to thank Mrs. Allen Clark and Miss Ruth Almond for their indispensable editorial assistance, and Mrs. Katharine Riegger and Mrs. Margaret Anagnost for secretarial aid in preparing a somewhat difficult manuscript for publication.

Contents

American Society
A Sociological Interpretation

1. Introduction

THERE are so many excellent books about the people and society of the United States that a new one aspiring to be of more than topical interest requires rather compelling reasons for being. A work on American society must aid our understanding, either by presenting new information, a new or more complete analysis of established facts, or, finally, a new synthesis and integration of the countless facts and interpretations that lie at hand.

The present work is a study in sociology. It is not a study in economics, although it often touches upon matters popularly termed "economic." Nor is it a historical work, although all of its data are in some sense "historical." It deals at times with political institutions, but it is not within the domain of political science. It cannot overlook conditioning factors of biological and geographic nature, but these do not constitute its central content or interest. Instead, it draws upon all these valuable domains of study for data and principles that will help it to describe and explain its own proper field: the social relations, and concomitant beliefs and values, that characterize the people of the United States.

The main focus in what follows will be upon analysis rather than upon description. In other words, we shall be interested primarily in *why* American society is the kind of society it is rather than simply in a detailed description of its present characteristics. For this reason, only so much descriptive material is presented as seems indispensable to a sociological analysis. This kind of selectivity is essential if we are to present anything more than a hodgepodge of facts interesting enough in their own right but largely without systematic scientific meaning. Some loss in vividness, concreteness, and color unavoidably results from this approach. But there are numerous excellent descriptive accounts already available to supply these qualities. What appears to be urgently needed is not another description, no matter how aesthetically pleasing or interesting, but a more complete analysis aimed at summarizing at least part of the existing body of scientific knowledge about the culture and social structure of the United States.

This is a sociological survey of our society; that is, it aims at a systematic analysis employing the tools, concepts, and theories of a particular social science. What these tools and approaches are will become clear in later chapters. In the introduction it is enough to indicate that the study deals with the facts relevant to *one* social science, and hence, that many things very important from other points of view will be omitted or given only passing attention. Every treatment of any subject is inherently selective—we never analyze all of the indefinite number of aspects that conceivably could be treated. The same human behavior can be described and analyzed in many different ways. This is not a cause for regret; on the contrary, such selectivity is not only inevitable but also one of the main roads to more useful knowledge of human society.

A study such as this necessarily has a certain detachment. Actually, there would be great advantages in having it done by an anthropologist from a radically different culture. It is impossible for a person brought up in a given society to get entirely outside all the presuppositions of that society and culture: there will thus always be blind spots in observation and analysis, and there will always be particular perspectives and evaluations implicit in the selection and interpretation of data. Still, it does not follow that everything is merely a "matter of opinion." There are facts about our society that can be agreed upon by all those who accept scientific criteria of fact. Furthermore, it is a cardinal principle of professional ethics in social science that the selection and interpretation of data be based upon *scientific* relevance, not personal wishes, political inclinations, ideological sympathies, and the like. We can perhaps never attain the objectivity of the proverbial man from Mars in looking at our own society. We can, however, do something very important: we can temporarily suspend our tendency to describe human conduct in terms of praise or blame, or judgments of desirability or undesirability, in order to make a disciplined attempt at scientific understanding of such matters as the regularities in social behavior, the interdependence of interactions within a social system, the causes and consequences of observed behaviors. Such will be the basic aim of this book. It is not designed to condemn or praise the United States or any particular group within it. There is, in any case, no great lack of such criticism and defense— as the daily output of the printed word abundantly testifies.

The analyses undertaken here are guided in part by the belief that some of the most prevalent errors of both public and private action in our day result from a failure to foresee the repercussions that may arise out of the total social system within which the particular acts take place. And often even a systematic analysis of various isolated parts of the social structure turns out to be highly unrealistic, if not simply fallacious, by reason of this same neglect of context. The present work is an attempt to sketch the broad structural features of American society in such a way that the total system can be visualized as a going concern. On the face of it, such an attempt is difficult—and it may well prove to have been foolhardy. Indeed, if one wished to go into any really considerable detail such a picture could not be drawn within the limits of any one work, no matter how extensive. Yet the student of American society now finds it difficult to obtain from available works the specific data and interpretations necessary to gain a view of the society as a whole. In this age of shrunken distances and planetary problems we must see things clearly and see them whole, and America is a good subject to start upon. This book cannot be limited to analyzing separately the various parts of American society, but must analyze the interrelated activities that maintain a going society as a whole. In so doing, one must be ruthlessly selective and parsimonious of detail. One can treat American social structure in only its broadest outlines, and therefore must decide what elements of structure and what interrelationships are most significant. Not only will analysis be in these general terms, but it will be seriously incomplete. Many vitally important questions simply cannot be answered yet for lack of reliable data or adequate theoretic and analytic tools. Nevertheless, these disadvantages, great as they are, may not outweigh the value of this modest foundation for later, more thoroughgoing syntheses.

For this task, we must use the fundamental method for understanding any human society: the practice of stubborn, repeated, questioning observation. If we want to comprehend how and why men behave as they do, we must look at what they do (and do not do), listen to what they say (and do not say). We must observe persistently, be alert to recurring patterns and far-from-obvious causal connections. For this we need a temporary and provisional detachment from the situations we wish to understand, sufficient for us to see them clearly and in their total context. This sort of analytic observation is one of the most difficult things in the world, but it is essential for adequate sociological knowledge.

The subject of this book is the behavior of the members of the social aggregate called "the United States of America." Our intention is to describe and analyze certain selected regularities in that behavior. For that task it is necessary to have tools of analysis; the tools chosen are the concepts, methods, facts, and theories of modern social science, particularly sociology.

Every specialized field of knowledge has its own concepts and methods. Each analyzes a portion of experience; none alone can encompass the whole. Our present task is an exercise in applied sociology, in that we will apply sociological concepts and principles to a specific national society as a whole; not social behavior in general but that found within a particular society is its subject. To analyze America as a social system requires a set of concepts with which to grasp the indefinite number of observable facts we confront. Thus a technical vocabulary is indispensable. Although there will be a minimum of jargon, a few technical concepts must be employed if we are to gain significant understandings.

Here is the basic problem: there are more than 150 million people inhabiting a vast territory and considered to constitute a nation. This collectivity has territories, outposts, and "spheres of influence" around the planet. For some purposes, the nation is thought of and treated as if it were an integral unit: in its name wars are fought, treaties concluded, agreements made; and its citizens abroad find that the label "American" means something to persons in other nations. Yet, internally it is evidently quite heterogeneous: the people are categorized into many occupational, racial, ethnic, and religious groupings; there are diverse interests; there are competing and conflicting groups of many kinds; there are marked regional and local differences in typical behaviors and values—and so forth. Yet for a social system to exist, for the word "nation" to have a concrete meaning, the behavior of millions of individuals in this bewildering network of crisscross group affiliations must somehow show considerable regularity and co-ordination. How is that possible? This is our bedrock question. How is it possible—concretely and in detail—that so many diverse human individuals manifest the predictability necessary for the existence of a society? The *fact* of this regularity can be documented as we proceed, but we shall also keep returning to the question of its *causes*.

We must also raise a second question: If there is an American social system, or a congeries of "systems," how and why does it change or remain the same through time? What significant changes in structure are discernible? How can we account for the changes we observe?

We thus have to study structure—the relatively definite and enduring social relations—and we have to study change. We shall begin with the most obvious influences upon this society, as upon all others—its location, its land and physical resources, its geographic habitat, and its population. Following this, there will be a brief analysis of certain major institutional patterns, groups, and other structural complexes of the society. Once this "morphological" description has been recorded, the analysis will turn to the functional interrelations of structural elements—or, to continue the analogy, the "physiology" of the system. Lastly will come a consideration of the changing structure of American society in a changing world. With a task of this magnitude before us, this is perhaps enough of a preamble.

2. Geography, Resources, and Population

WE START with the realities of the land and the people. We are seeking a sociological portrait of America. The facts of central interest here are therefore facts about human relations. Yet human relations do not occur in a vacuum, and if we are to grasp the nature of American society we will do well to glance briefly at the geography, the resources, the "material culture," and the gross population characteristics of the modern United States.

1. Geography

THE HISTORY of the United States and the nature of its present culture and social structure is the result, in part, of a unique combination of geographic circumstances. In the first place, the North American continent is a great land mass bounded to east and west by the great distances of the Atlantic and Pacific oceans. Especially in earlier days of slow overseas communication and transportation, the distance between the Atlantic seaboard and Europe was of momentous consequence. For example, it made possible, although it certainly did not completely determine, the emergence of a national consciousness out of an aggregation of varied and poorly integrated colonial provinces. It permitted, under the conditions of the times, the growth and organization of independent tendencies, culminating in the revolution that split the colonies from the British Empire. It interposed a formidable bar-

rier to extensive *direct* contact with European cultures and power
struggles during the formative years of the nation. It minimized
for most of the nation's history the danger of large-scale invasion
by a major foreign power. It thereby indirectly contributed to a
certain fluidity and "openness" in social relations and to the development of a decentralized, nonsecretive, nonmilitary governmental structure. Furthermore, the ocean barrier undoubtedly encouraged the feeling of alienation from Europe and attention on
American rather than European matters. The newness of the New
World and its self-consciousness of being somehow quite different
from Europe, instead of a transplanted part of western European
culture, rested to an appreciable degree upon the consciousness of
the Atlantic barrier.

With the work of Frederick Jackson Turner and his followers
before us we are no longer likely to ignore or minimize the significance of the frontier in American history. ("Frontier" has, of
course, had a meaning radically different in the United States from
that which is taken for granted in Europe.) We must also emphasize, however, the oceans and what they meant in military security
and economic advantage. From 1607 to World War I the Atlantic
served as a shield—partly in actual fact, partly in feeling—behind
which a Monroe Doctrine could be promulgated, national leaders
could speak of avoiding "entangling alliances," and an infant republic could dare to limit its standing army to eighty men.[1]

The barrier was, of course, also a highway. Although Americans
could believe in their military security because of their distance
from the great powers, the waters were potentially an unobstructed
road for immigrants or soldiers or goods. Much of the security attributed to the ocean distances in our early history was perhaps a
matter of the preoccupation of European powers with intramural
conflicts. When the social and economic situations permitted, the
"barrier" teemed with the movement of men and trade. Thus the
same geographic fact takes on sharply contrasting implications as
circumstances change. Perhaps we could ask no better example to

[1] This was the total regular Army at its lowest strength, in 1784. See James
Ripley Jacobs: *The Beginning of the U. S. Army 1783–1812* (Princeton, N. J.:
1947), pp. vii, 14.

illustrate the role of geographic conditions as "passive" agents, limiting or facilitating but not determining social behavior.

The United States as eventually constituted has had the great advantages of possessing ice-free ports on two oceans. Given the social and economic conditions of the nineteenth century, the possession of such ports meant that the United States had a prime requisite for development as a maritime power—and this without the heavy cost of conquest that many other nations have incurred in the attempt to gain access to the sea.

From the beginning, the bays and rivers insured that America, for all her vast heartland of arable plains, would not be a landlocked society. From the beginning she was geographically accessible. Even in early colonial days, Americans began to utilize not only ocean ports but also extensive inland waterways. The first settlements reached inland along the coastal indentations and the rivers, and when the footholds had been won, the rivers and their valleys formed the channels for the vanguards moving toward the mountain barriers.

A second prime geographic feature of the United States is the great expanse of contiguous land mass. The thirteen colonies that originally federated under the Constitution established a kind of beachhead on the fringe of a continent. Settlement could proceed as an advance on a broad front [2] and the continental mass offered the possibility of establishing an enormous contiguous area of free trade, mobility, and communication. In early periods, the varied geographic characteristics of different areas and the distances separating them contributed to provincialism and sectionalism and in other ways gave a loose and amorphous quality to the total society. But the political unification of the nation preserved the continental expanse as an enormous free-trade area for an expanding and developing industrial order.

The idea of apparently unlimited lands in the New World had

[2] In this as in many other instances, geography played the role it did only because of definite social conditions. One of the more important was the absence of well-organized, powerful, and technologically advanced peoples in possession of the territory. The settlers drove out or exterminated the American Indians (who would not take kindly to enslavement); they did not have to subjugate thickly settled peoples.

powerful social and psychological effects upon the American. Even a cursory reading of early American history tells of the preoccupation with the land, which went along with a vivid sense of room, of expansion, of great territorial sweeps to be mastered. Very early indeed the Americans began to act as if they had decided that this land was somehow *meant* for them to possess. And the sheer fact of the vastness of the land resources was highly significant in the early differentiation of American society from its European origins. Immigrants from tight, localistic, feudally-tinged societies met here abruptly with empty lands, with space, with abounding resources. What this experience did to the typical personality structure and social relations of the Americans is inevitably a main theme of any adequate social history of this country. For the society of western Europe in the early seventeenth century was still fundamentally rural, and the United States at the time of its emergence as an independent political entity was overwhelmingly agrarian. In such a society, the whole organization of human relations is closely bound up with the extent of land resources and the social conditions under which they are utilized.

2. Resources

THUS among all resources that of the land was first seized upon and became decisive for national development.[3] Within the present boundaries of continental United States are approximately three million square miles—an area exceeding that of all Europe. The successive waves of settlers from the first landing to the official closing of the frontier in 1890 were always pushing on to new lands. And these were lands so varied as to support nearly every major type of valuable plant and animal; they were largely fertile lands, unexhausted by exploitative tillage, relatively free from entrenched

[3] "The expanse of ocean and the expanse of land in the west have been two of the greatest geographical factors in molding the thought as well as the character of the American." James Truslow Adams: *The American* (New York: Charles Scribner's Sons, 1943), p. 227.

proprietorship. They worked a deep ferment among the land-hungry peoples and the venturesome promoters of Europe, and they furnished the foundation for that free-farmer society that Jefferson idealized and that has long been a major theme of the American ethos.

But land was only the first and most obvious of the natural resources that the territory offered to a people equipped to exploit it. The ocean, the land, and the forests could furnish the basis for an agricultural and trading society. The industrial civilization of the nineteenth and early twentieth centuries, however, was based directly upon two prime minerals—coal and iron. The United States had both, in easy proximity, together with the limestone for processing the ore into steel. The later hegemony of American industrialism was conditioned also by the emergence of petroleum and electricity as additional sources of vast inanimate energies. The United States now uses inanimate energy on a scale never before attained in any other society, for it has over half of the world petroleum supplies, nearly half of the coal, nearly half of the electrical energy and water power. Yet most of mankind even today must depend upon human muscles and draft animals for production. The tremendous utilization of energy from mineral resources in the United States is unique to a degree not always understood by its own people.

The resources available to this society are utilized by a relatively young and vigorous population, equipped with highly developed skills and technical knowledge and organized for effective economic production. One consequence is a level of material well-being above that of most areas of the world. Although international or cross-cultural comparisons of levels of living are notoriously difficult and treacherous, there is no question that in terms of food, clothing, shelter, transportation, and other physical necessities and comforts, American society as a whole is more favored than that of any other contemporary national area.

3. Technological Resources

To THIS panoramic view of the geography and natural resources of the society one must add a very highly developed technology and technological apparatus. America's giant industrial
plant is the epitome of the application of scientific technology to
production, and even its agriculture is mechanized and technically
rationalized to a degree undreamed of even in modernized Europe.

The bare descriptive facts regarding the technological resources
of the society would fill volumes; we will present a few salient characteristics most relevant to later analysis. The structure and functioning of the social system as such is basically affected by:

1. the presence of the elaborately developed industrial and
agricultural technologies and apparatus;
2. the existence of an extraordinary set of transportation
facilities, providing for extensive and rapid mobility of materials and persons;
3. the highly developed networks of facilities for both mass
communication and point-to-point communication.

For illustrative purposes, the last two items may be used to suggest
the sociological importance of the character of technological development.

The functioning of the contemporary United States as a social
system is greatly dependent upon the remarkable set of facilities
for transportation and communication. The network of railroads,
airlines, water routes, and improved highways makes feasible the
unprecedented ease and speed with which people and goods can
circulate over a large territory. As we shall see later, the great
mobility of the American population is one of its most marked characteristics and is intimately related to many other "typical"
features of American behavior. From earliest colonial days, this
has been a nation perennially "on the move." In our own time, the
facilities for movement over the face of the earth are unparalleled

anywhere else. This is a society with a rich store of "vehicles" [4] for the interchange of populations, communications, and goods.

Along with highly developed means of transportation, the United States has very elaborate and active communication systems. Telephones, telegraph systems, the postal system are facilities most Americans take completely for granted; yet the development of such a point-to-point communication system has never existed before over such a large area within a single political collectivity. The same can be said, perhaps with even more force, of the development of mass communication: radio, television, newspapers, magazines—one or another of these reaches nearly everyone. The American population is continually exposed to mass stimuli that present to large numbers of individuals simultaneously the same items of information and similar interpretations of the world.[5]

Clearly the social structure of the United States has a *permeable character*. Our society is very far removed indeed from the isolation of local communities that has been typical of most human societies throughout history until the last few decades.

4. Population

ANY comprehensive survey of the population of the United States would require more space than is available in this entire book; and the reader who is interested in securing a full population analysis will find available a number of excellent works. Fortunately, the most essential facts regarding population can be summarized quite briefly.

Perhaps the most striking demographic characteristic of the population of the continental United States is its *ethnic and*

[4] "Vehicle" has been proposed by Pitirim A. Sorokin as the generic term to designate all means for externalizing and communicating social values and meanings. See his *Society, Culture, and Personality: Their Structure and Dynamics* (New York: 1947), esp. pp. 48–63.

[5] Although the so-called mass media show much more diversity of views than can be found in societies with highly centralized governments. Cf. Alex Inkeles: *Public Opinion in Soviet Russia* (Cambridge, Mass.: 1950).

"racial" heterogeneity. America is a land of minorities, or as the title of Louis Adamic's book put it, "a nation of nations." To ethnic and racial heterogeneity must be added the varying religious affiliations of the people, since these affiliations often index more broadly cultural as well as purely creedal differences.

This mixture of peoples has been the result of three great waves of immigration. The first, during the 1840's and 1850's, drew chiefly upon the British Isles and northwestern Europe, including Germany; Irish immigrants, were, of course, prominent in this phase. The second wave of immigration occurred during the post-Civil War period of industrial expansion; it continued to draw heavily from northwestern Europe, but increasingly brought southern and eastern Europeans as well. The third wave, centering in the enormous influx of 1900–10, was made up largely of persons from southern and eastern Europe. Since the passage of restrictive immigration laws following World War I, a large proportion of immigrants have come from Canada, Mexico, and other parts of the Americas.

The successive "geologic deposits" of population have created a multiculture society in which nearly every nationality, race, or creed of the world can be found. "The American, that new man" of whom Crèvecoeur spoke, is a composite product of three centuries of contact and intermingling of diverse cultures within the same country. Again and again in later chapters, the multiple implications of this central fact will enter into our analysis.

The population of the United States is now *urbanized.* Most of the peoples of the earth in all eras have lived under "rural" conditions, and in America many of the most important attitudes and customs of the cultural heritage were formed in periods when the majority of the inhabitants lived on farms or in villages and small towns. Perhaps in part because of a certain nostalgic appeal lingering around the rural tradition, it is not always realized that the United States has now become a definitely urbanized nation. The 1940 United States Census reported 56.5 per cent of the population as "urban," that is, living in centers having 2,500 or more inhabitants. This figure considerably underestimates the size of the population that is sociologically urban. For instance, a very large proportion classified as "rural nonfarm" by the United States Census resides in unincorporated centers or in fringe areas around cities and has the essential social and economic characteristics of urban populations. In addition, even the population residing in strictly open country is increasingly subject to urban influences; the line between city and country becomes more and more difficult to establish.

Variation in the percentage of population from one state to another living in urban areas is very great, ranging from 92 in Rhode Island to 20 in Mississippi. The great region north of the Ohio and east of the Mississippi contains the most highly urbanized sections of the country. There are massive concentrations of population in cities like New York,[6] which are centers of economic and social influences that set their stamp upon the entire national life. The United States is very far indeed from the agrarian society that in its first census in 1790 recorded that only 5 per cent of its less than four million people lived in centers of twenty-five hundred or more.

We have, then, a heterogeneous people, an urbanized people. It is also a *mobile* people. The continent has been peopled by immigration and the long-continuing westward movement. More recently there has been an enormous farm-to-city movement: from the time when reasonably dependable data were first made available in 1920 to the postwar year of 1946 the sum of departures from farms is estimated to have been over 46 million persons. For the same twenty-six year period, the total migration *to* farms was nearly 30 million persons. Thus a ceaseless interchange of farm and city populations occurs, in which there is a large net balance in favor of the urban areas. In addition to rural-urban and urban-rural migrations, there is extensive mobility of residence within both urban and nonurban areas. Farm-to-farm mobility is high: in 1940 the average period of farm occupancy was only 12 years, and there are several hundred thousand agricultural workers who live as migratory laborers. For urban areas, there is ample evidence of even greater mobility.

As compared with the populations of western and northwestern

---

[6] In 1940 five cities in the United States had a population of more than a million, five more, more than 500,000.

Europe, the population of the United States is relatively young,[7] with relatively few old people and children and with relatively many young persons of working ages. There is thus a sense in which America at the present time is living off a fortuitous "unearned increment" in the form of an age distribution favorable to economic productivity.

Another important demographic characteristic of the American population is the *relatively high proportion of married persons*. The proportion of single persons is much smaller at all ages than in most other countries for which we have useful data; in 1940, only about 8 per cent of all persons who had reached the age of eighty-five had never married. Furthermore, Americans marry at an earlier average age than in most of the major countries for which data are available; and, in spite of high divorce rates, the married state is the normal condition for the great majority of adults.[8]

Urbanism as a way of life in the Western world has been associated with declining birth rates, and the United States constitutes no exception to the general tendency. The average net reproduction rate for the entire United States for the period 1935–40 was too low for replacement requirements; the urban rate in 1940 was such that with a continuation of the given birth and death rates for a period of a generation the city population would decrease to about 74 per cent of its current size.[9] A net urban deficit in reproduction has existed for a long time—the growth of the cities having been accomplished by in-migration.

Until recent years birth rates had been falling continuously in this country for over a century. Since the late 1930's there has been a reversal of the trend, although it is not yet clear how permanent this may be, nor to what extent the increase is due to "accidental" factors such as the unusually large numbers of marriages of women

[7] E.g., as compared with the British Isles, France, and Scandinavia. On the other hand, in comparison with the U. S. S. R., Latin America, or the great nonindustrialized populations of Asia and Africa, the United States has a relatively advanced age distribution.

[8] The essential facts are ably presented by T. Lynn Smith: *Population Analysis* (New York: 1948), chap. 6. pp. 132–52.

[9] Cf. Ibid., p. 210. Whereas a net reproduction rate of 100 is necessary to maintain population numbers, the rate for the United States in 1940 was 96 and for urban areas, 74.

in age groups most likely to manifest high reproduction rates. But the American population has a generally low fertility, especially in our cities. Early America was a highly familistic society, but today the childless couple is a common phenomenon. As is well known this situation is general among industrialized Western countries.

Mortality rates in America reflect the relatively high levels of nutrition, sanitation, and medical care. The "expectation of life" at birth is an index that summarizes the cumulative impact of mortality rates, and the United States exhibits a relatively high expectation of life, although the record is startlingly less favorable for the Negro population. The infant mortality rate, one of the most sensitive indications of physical well-being of a population, is also low.

In summary, the salient "demographic" characteristics of our population include its cultural heterogeneity, high mobility, urbanization, high marriage ratios, low fertility, and low mortality. Many other characteristics have been analyzed by students of population, including the relatively high educational status of the population. It is not necessary to go into any further details, however, in order to recognize in the facts already reviewed here the outlines of a composite, industrially advanced society. It contrasts sharply with the great agricultural populations of the technologically undeveloped regions of the world. To try to understand what kind of society has shaped and has been shaped by these characteristics is our difficult and challenging assignment.

3. The Problem of Analysis: Basic Concepts and Approaches

THIS, then, is the setting within which American society has taken its present form. No matter how much weight we must give to other elements in later analysis, we must never forget the factors of a high resources-population ratio, a geographic and climatic setting propitious for industrial and commercial development, and the fundamental demographic characteristics of the people.

Although American society cannot be understood without these factors, they are far from explaining even the most elementary sociological problems. From them we cannot predict very specifically about such matters as the American language, the forms of economic organization, the nature of religious beliefs or political ideology, or most of the other facts men wish to know about their society. For this reason we must begin to deal with factors that require truly sociological concepts for analysis. Ultimately, these concepts rest on the belief that human societies as they actually exist are not explainable by any sort of crude physical or biological determinism. On the contrary, societies are causal systems fairly independent of their bio-physical environments, especially when conditions do not press too severely upon human biological requirements for survival. Within the very broad limits of these requirements, there is wide variation in human cultural patterns—a fact noted by observant "tourists" from the most ancient times to the present. It has remained for social science to develop concepts for grasping more precisely and expanding this basic insight, and generations of workers have shaped the conceptual tools we need for understanding society.

In the remaining chapters recur such terms as "cultural structure," "social structure," "patterned behavior," "structural characteristics," "structural interrelations," "system," and the like. Those who think of human behavior as changing, highly variable, unpredictable, or "individualistic" may find it difficult to grasp this focus on "structure." Hence at the outset we shall outline concisely what structural analysis implies.

The basic logical and methodological questions on this point are similar to those found in the various physical sciences. In any field of inquiry a "structure" is a relatively fixed relationship between elements, parts, or entities, as, e.g., the structure of a house, an animal, or a plant, containing gross, observable parts that maintain a fixed relationship to one another for an appreciable time. We can easily see that some structures endure for very long periods, others are highly evanescent; yet a simple organism with a life-span of a few seconds has a structure, even as does the planet itself.[1] The ease or difficulty of observation is not an essential criterion of structure: biology has no hesitation in ascribing structure to a cell that no one can observe directly by his unaided senses. The "structure" of social action is no mere analogy, but a strict parallel. To demonstrate structure one need only show a recurrence of elements related in definite ways. In the interests of realism it is best to speak of the structure of social phenomena only where there is an *important* degree of continuity—where human activities are so patterned (recurrent) that we can observe a group standardization persisting, although changing, over a considerable time.

Human beings in society do exhibit complexes of action, thought, and emotion (1) shared by many individuals, (2) repeated in many successive situations, (3) definitely related to *other* patterns in the same social aggregate. This is essentially all that is here meant by "structure": an appreciable degree of regularity and relationship. There is thus nothing obscure or mystical about the concept, and

[1] Cf. Charles E. Merriam's paraphrases of Sherrington's conclusion from the study of cells: "Thus he arrives at the view that the only difference between structure and function in the constitution of the human organism is a difference in the speed of change." *Public and Private Government* (New Haven: Yale University Press, 1944), p. 40.

the question of how definite and enduring the structure is in any particular case is left open for empirical study.

Examples of structure in the present sense are not difficult to find. Perhaps the aptest instance for college students is the social structure of a university, a very elaborate patterning and co-ordination of the actions of many individuals. Streams of people move from room to room and building to building at appointed hours. Professors meet their classes, often with incredible regularity. Books are ordered and delivered, buildings lighted and heated, food served at cafeterias. Masses of people appear at athletic events, scheduled months in advance. Beneath this surface level of regularity, order and predictability take much more subtle forms. There are classroom rituals and subtle stereotypings of student-teacher relationships. Students form cliques and friendship constellations; they are graded in "generations" from freshman to senior; they are Greeks and barbarians. The university has a system of formal rules and expectations concerning the behavior of faculty and students and informal codes that supplement, modify, or counter the official structure.

The often repeated question whether human conduct is "really predictable at all" is answered every day that a society exists. Without some rough predictability as to what other people will do under given circumstances, there could be no continuing human association, no adjustment, no co-operation.

Along with the development of precise concepts, all science rests upon observation. Since sociology studies the behavior of human beings in association with others, its data consist of observations of what people say and do, and it assumes that it can infer from the data certain predictabilities. This assumption is tested by acting upon it; that is, by making predictions and then discovering the degree to which they accurately predict behavior *under specified conditions.*

Two crucial propositions have been asserted: (1) societies are not explicable solely in terms of bio-physical environment; (2) human interactions show structure, that is, they are in some degree recurrent or predictable. If so, it becomes fruitful to consider what conceptual tools are most useful in analyzing social phenomena.

The first conceptual tool is culture.[2] Most inclusively culture is social heredity—the total legacy of past human behavior effective in the present, representing the accumulation through generations of the artifacts, knowledges, beliefs, and values by which men deal with the world. It is the precipitate of *learned* human adjustments to the physical environment and to society. Thus, according to the famous enumerative definition of Tylor, culture is "that complex whole which includes knowledge, belief, art, morals, law, custom, and any other capabilities and habits acquired by man as a member of society." [3] A way of visualizing American culture in this broad sense would be to answer the question: What is "available" to be learned by all the infants born in the society today? This would emphasize the fact that culture comes down from the past, is not created by any one person or generation, and continues beyond the individual life-span, and the fact that culture is learned; it is no automatic or instinctive heritage, but must be won anew by each succeeding generation. It points to those common elements in behavior that are derived from individuals' having been reared in the same tradition.

This inclusive definition of culture is very useful in giving us a fundamental perspective on behavior: once the idea is grasped, one always sees behavior in relation to the pervasive social inheritance. Once its full implications are seen, it destroys the naive reliance on crude "instinct" theories of human behavior, explodes the myth of a fixed "human nature" apart from culture, and sensitizes the observer to aspects of social life he otherwise might not notice.

For this book, however, a more specific concept of culture is useful: culture as a normative structure, a system of what Linton has called "designs for living." [4] In this sense, culture is the "blueprint for behavior"—relatively standardized prescriptions as to what

[2] It is assumed that most students of this text already will be familiar with the use of the term in its technical senses. References on the concept include: Edward Burnett Tylor: *Primitive Culture* (London: 1913); Alexander A. Goldenweiser: *Early Civilization* (New York: 1922); Georges Gurvitch and Wilbert E. Moore (eds.): *Twentieth Century Sociology* (New York: 1945); Ralph Linton: *The Study of Man* (New York: 1936); Robert M. MacIver: *Society* (New York: 1937); and many others.

[3] *Primitive Culture*, Vol. I, p. 1.

[4] Cf. Ralph Linton: *The Study of Man*.

must be done, ought to be done, should be done, may be done, and must not be done. We face every day an elaborate network of "rules" saying that some behaviors are obligatory, some approved or permitted, and some disapproved or positively forbidden. "Rules" is in quotation marks because it includes not only the *how* of behavior but also the *what;* that is, culture includes a system of goals and values. Certain things are emphasized as pre-eminently worth striving for, others are matters of relative in-difference; some possibilities are ignored, others are defined as valueless, inappropriate, or evil.

The normative aspects include, furthermore, elaborate com-plexes of beliefs about the nature of man and the universe, typi-cally involving (a) valuational elements (good-bad, pleasant-un-pleasant, desirable-undesirable), (b) prescriptive elements (how one should act, think, feel), and (c) cognitive elements (what exists—what entities, sequences, causes, and consequences). The first two components have already been mentioned. We may call them respectively values and norms. The third component, cognitive belief, is exemplified by concepts of deities, after-life spirits, etc., as well as by cause-effect assumptions. By the cri-terion of scientific verifiability,[5] these cognitive beliefs fall into three categories: (a) those subject to scientific tests and refutable by those tests; (b) those outside the domain of empirical verifica-tion (e.g., the existence of heaven and hell, the superiority of American society to all others); (c) verified scientific knowledge (including various kinds of empirical knowledge that fall short of "perfect" scientific certainty). Applied to action, the whole body of empirical knowledge produces various *technologies* that are also a part of culture in the inclusive sense.

The present work focuses on those aspects of the culture that regulate *social relations*. It is a common misunderstanding to sup-pose that unless one is *aware* of cultural factors one is not in-

---

[5] This is, of course, an assumption that raises difficult philosophical questions. A work of the present character cannot deal at all competently with them. It is perhaps enough to say that for present purposes the distinction between positive scientific knowledge, ignorance and error, and nonempirical beliefs is a heuristic one—utilized because of practical convenience and claim-ing no "ultimate" validity.

fluenced by them. Nothing could be further from the truth. Participants in social groups are seldom fully aware of what determines their behavior, or of what results from it. Usually we do not know what we are doing until after we have done it, and often we remain unaware of causes and consequences even then. Probably no individual ever "knows" the total culture in which he is immersed. Most American parents, for example, certainly do not usually think of themselves as doing anything so formidable as "transmitting culture" when they deal with their children. They "just act." But their actions constitute in fact an important part of the transmission of culture. When little Johnny is told that "it's not polite" to hit the guest over the head with his baseball bat, or is admonished "don't be a bully," he is being introduced to the norms of his culture. Thousands of specific experiences with specific persons in particular situations comprise the "socialization" process. The individual eventually absorbs a complex and fairly standardized system of rules, perspectives, and valuations common to many other individuals in the society.

Culture, then, has these characteristics:

1. It is inferred from observation of behavior.
2. It exists prior in time to any given individual and continues beyond one's life span.
3. It is *acquired* by individuals and manifested in their behavior.
4. It includes rules or designs for obligatory, approved, permitted, disapproved, and forbidden actions.
5. It is never completely static and uniform.

It has been emphasized that culture includes definitions of events, objects, or behaviors as "good" or "bad"; it marks off the things to be sought or avoided. Certain *goals* or *ends* are thus prescribed as worthy of pursuit and others are discouraged or ignored. The core of any culture consists of those values and ideal-patterns widely regarded as obligatory. The term "cultural norm" refers to a specific prescription of the course that action *should* (is supposed to) follow in a given situation. Cultural norms therefore include both cultural *goals* and the approved means for reaching those goals. To be *cultural*, the norms have only to be acquired by learning and to be shared by individuals, but norms shade into one another in many complicated nuances. There is a continuous gradation from almost purely technical or cognitive norms (how to boil an egg, the most efficient way to manufacture TNT) to "moral" norms (thou shalt not kill). At the intermediate steps, one finds, among others, conventional norms ("custom," "etiquette," etc.) and aesthetic norms (standards of taste, of beauty, etc.). Any one of these types of norms may be further specified according to the degree of obligatory prevalence in a given social aggregate—in Linton's usage, whether it is a Universal or a Specialty, or an Alternative.[6] Although by the present definition norms always carry some prescriptive or proscriptive quality—some one of the many qualitatively different kinds of "shoulds" or "oughts"— there is an enormous variation in the *kind* of normative emphasis— for example, the conformity accompanying fashions and fads as over against the most deeply ingrained taboos and ethical precepts.

In empirical research cultural norms are discovered in two ways. Norms are inferred from *testimony;* that is, people either explicitly state the norm, or from their description of the approved and disapproved conduct for certain situations one can clearly infer an implicit norm. Or, aside from testimony, cultural norms may be discovered by observing spontaneous behavior in real-life situations, in particular, the meting out of socially supported rewards and penalties (social sanctions).

Thus "cultural norm" is a heterogeneous category including a very diverse universe of social prescriptions. Like culture itself, it points to an important *area* of problems, but requires further clarification in application to particular sociological problems. We shall sketch briefly some major dimensions of variation in cultural norms.[7]

1. *Prevalence* within the given collectivity.
2. *Enforcement* and imputed sources of authority.

[6] *The Study of Man*, chap. 16.

[7] There definitely are other modes of differentiation. See chaps. 10 and 11.

3. *"Formal characteristics"* of the norm itself, e.g., specificity, rigidity.

4. *Relation to other norms.*

Brief comments on each of these will suffice here, reserving more extended discussion until later.

The prevalence of any particular norm within a given social aggregate depends in the first place upon *how universally the norm is accepted as a valid guide to conduct.* It may be accepted by everyone without exception or only by a very small idiosyncratic sector of the population. The effective "constraint" of many highly prevalent norms comes partly from their near-universality. Thus, in an English-speaking society if one wishes to be understood, he must speak English, and his use of that language rather than another defines his social world in a particular way.

The extent of acceptance (consensus) is not identical with the *universality of application* of the norm. Certain norms are applicable only to special subsegments of the society, even though universally recognized as valid and binding. There may be high consensus upon the norms governing the status of parent and child, yet the norms for parents clearly do not apply to children. Special occupational codes—say, of a judge, a chief, a merchant—are widely accepted but are binding only upon those occupations. Although the prevalence of these Specialities (cf. Linton's usage) is undoubtedly relevant to the degree of consensus of a society, the two phenomena are different and must not be confused in analysis.

Furthermore, norms vary widely in their *modes of enforcement* and in their sources of authority. The source of authority has been variously imputed to divine revelation, the wisdom of ancestors, ideas of natural law and inherent rights, the magical or charismatic quality of a leader, and social expediency in terms of a taken-for-granted framework of ultimate values. Often the question of final legitimacy is simply not raised at all; a norm has "authority" from widespread practice, or "because it has always existed." Observe again the striking variation in the details of normative structure: many norms are axiomatically accepted—by "absolute social logics" (Warner)—others claim various kinds of derivative and elaborately rationalized justifications. Furthermore, the most immediate source of authority is often some definite social organization, and the purposes of the organization lend authority to the rule. Thus, the modes of imputed legitimacy are related to the mechanisms of enforcement.

First of all, an important distinction between norms enforced by the diffuse pressure of the total community and those enforced by specifically designated and publicly acknowledged functionaries is shown in the contrast between a small town, where nearly every member of the community acts to penalize violations, with the specialized and limited functions of the policeman, the military officer, the bureaucrat. Between extremes, of course, lie many shadings.

An obvious primary distinction in types of sanctions is that between rewards and penalties. There are intrinsic rewards for obeying social prescriptions that have become part of the basic personality structure; in fact, a perfectly integrated society may be defined as one in which everyone would want to do what he had to do. Short of that perfect integration, however, norms are supported by many specific rewards such as wealth, power, and social esteem and prestige. Similarly, violations of norms are met with an impressive array of penalties such as physical confinement, corporal punishment, physiological deprivations, exile and exclusion, removal of honors and "reputation," and the like. The *severity* of the negative sanctions constitutes a complex series, ranging from such conditions as socially disgraceful death, extreme physical torture, or complete social ostracism and condemnation, to various minor deprivations, mild ridicule, or group disapproval.

Besides the modes of variation already mentioned, there are great differences in the "formal" characteristics of concrete social norms. First, norms may vary in *explicitness* from those implicit rules or understandings rarely, if ever, verbalized, constituting the norms "everybody knows," or unconsciously accepts, to the vast body of verbalized (spoken or written) norms embodied in law, regulations, precepts, codes, etc.

Distinct from explicitness is a second dimension, *specificity*. A norm may be quite explicit though highly general and vague: love your neighbor as yourself. A norm may be implicit but definite: do not criticize the behavior of your host's children in his presence. Any society or group will have specific, minutely detailed norms as well as those highly generalized imperatives that apply to particular situations only by implication.

Finally, a norm varies in *rigidity or flexibility* from the requiring of exact conformity to wide latitude, and approximations to both of these extremes can be observed in our own society. Of course rigidity-flexibility is intimately related to other qualities. For example, it is easier to see "violations" of a specific rule than of a generalized precept—indeed, the certainty, promptness, and intensity of sanctions provide a practical definition of rigidity. An implicit norm is easier to modify or evade. Nevertheless, normative rigidity is to some degree an independent variable. That it is a real and important variable can be judged by anyone who has experienced the flexibility of norms between "friends" in contrast to the exacting regulations of military organizations or highly developed industrial, governmental, or educational bureaucracies.

Our next important concept is the central sociological idea of *institution*.[8] Among the various norms of a given society those that are *institutional* for any particular person are felt as "moral imperatives" closely identified with the individual's sense of self-respect, violations of them being followed by guilt, shame, horror, self-deprecation, etc. For a whole group *or* society, probably the best index to institutional norms is the occurrence of severe penalties for violations. Such penalties are truly institutional, however, only if supported by an effective consensus of the society. When severe sanctions are imposed by a small but powerful minority upon an unwilling population, what is institutional for the ruling group may not be institutional for the others. In addition to the test of social sanctions, therefore, it is desirable to have evidence of the degree of consensus with which the sanctions are accepted and supported. Institutional norms usually tend to be relatively stable,

---

[8] It is advisable to defer any further discussion of the modes of relations among various types of cultural norms to later chapters dealing with institutional interrelations, the problem of societal integration, and the analysis of socio-cultural change.

although permanence is a correlative rather than a defining criterion of their institutional character. Institutionalized norms tend to prescribe reciprocal rights and duties, and to be enforced through designated social functionaries; however, there are many exceptions.[9]

In summary, institutional norms differ from other cultural norms primarily in the intensity of social sanctions and in the degree of consensus with which they are supported. In other words, cultural norms are institutional in so far as they are really *obligatory* by effective social agreement. In operation, institutional norms are also likely to be relatively permanent, enforced through definite social organs, and reciprocally binding on the occupants of designated social positions. Institutionality is a product of these three factors. For example, there would be no doubt whatever that judged by these criteria the prohibitions of murder, treason, cannibalism, or rape represent institutional norms in American society.

The various specific "rules" are related to one another, not at random, but in definite patterns, which can be usefully classified and analyzed in several different ways. The approach followed here is to group norms according to the major "needs" or value centers they are most closely associated with, e.g., economic, political, religious, and so forth. Thus the term "institution" will refer to a set of institutional norms that cohere around a relatively distinct and socially important complex of values; for instance, American society, like any other, must somehow deal with sexual activity, the care of dependent children, and the social relations established by sexual unions and the birth of children. The institutional norms concerned with these matters constitute the *familial or kinship institutions* of the society. Similarly, there is in every society a set of

[9] See Pitirim A. Sorokin: *Society, Culture and Personality* (New York: 1947), chap. 4, pp. 69–91. Sorokin establishes the valuable concept of "law-norms," which are obligatory norms defining the rights and duties of the parties in a definite social relationship. Law-norms are both imperative and two-sided. Unlike a moral norm, which recommends but does not require a certain course of conduct, a law-norm establishes, on the one hand, a *right* to demand the specified behavior, and on the other, imposes a corresponding duty. In the most fully developed instances, law-norms specify the subjects and objects of both rights and duties, the source of the norms, the details of the required actions, and the sanctions involved.

functional problems centering around the coercion of some individuals by others. The problem of power is the central fact of political life, and it is convenient to group together the norms regulating power as the *political institutions* of the society.

Institutions regulate the modes of meeting important recurrent situations such as birth, death, marriage, acquiring economic goods, dealing with power relations, maintaining social consensus, and training the young, and at the same time help ensure that these situations will recur. By defining problems and approved solutions in certain ways, any particular institutional structure canalizes human experience along certain lines and ignores or prohibits other possibilities. It is a truism that the problems or evils of any society result partly from its most venerated institutions.

As will appear in more detail in Chapter 10, in a large and complex society the overt, publicly supported institutions fall far short of accounting for the facts of actual behavior. Cultural norms, as discovered by research, are statistical entities; that is, there is not a sharp line between normative and not normative, but a gradual shading from norms intensely supported by nearly everyone to those only casually accepted by a relatively few. Within such complex aggregates as modern nations many norms are effective only within limited subcultures, and there are wide differences in individual conformity and conceptions of the normative structure. Furthermore, minority power-groups can force certain standards of behavior upon dissenting groups. Finally, some norms are actually followed by considerable portions of the society, even though publicly ignored or disapproved. Some causes for these latent or counter-institutional patterns will be discussed in Chapter 10. Here it suffices to say that an analysis of the publicly approved institutions gives a selective and incomplete picture of a society. It is a necessary first approximation, but it requires supplementation to avoid oversimplifying the total social system.[10]

[10] Students are occasionally disturbed by finding the term "institution" used in different senses by different writers. Although the variant usage is perhaps unfortunate, there are several useful ways of defining institutions, and the particular concept chosen is largely a matter of convenience for the purposes at hand. "Institution" is sometimes defined, not as a complex of norms, but as a concrete social organization (church, school, etc.) or as a broad

Many of the so-called contradictions in a large, complex, heterogeneous society reflect *diverse levels of socio-cultural regulation*. Especially in societies with highly explicit ethical systems derived from religious authority, there is always a set of moral norms and values representing the "highest" aspirations of the moral culture. Such norms and values ordinarily are fairly loosely and unstably related to daily social action. First, they are "heroic" in their demands—are so difficult of actual attainment as to result in considerable nonconformity and in erratic movements, now toward rigor, now toward laxness. To love one's enemies, to turn the other cheek, to follow the Golden Rule, to be chaste, charitable, forgiving, and honest—taken literally are aspirations difficult to attain under the realities of living in most societies past or present. These imperatives are axiomatic, unconditional "ideals" of behavior. Even if the norms form a consistent, coherent system embedded in a stable social matrix—and these are stringent conditions— complete conformity of actual behavior to norms is unlikely, and in a complex, rapidly changing society such as the contemporary United States, still less likely. The cultural blueprint itself lacks unity and consistency. There are many varied, and often opposing, subcultures. Furthermore, the internal variety and the rapid change weaken the power of ideals to control conduct. Such influences are added to the inherent tension between the social action and "ideals"—which by definition are standards of conduct more difficult to actualize than the ordinary accepted patterns.

In addition, ideal norms are typically plastic and vague; they state a very general principle without specifying its detailed application. Where cultural prescriptions are so general, there can always be countless variant interpretations. Often the norm be-

---

field of activity ("making a living"). The present usage has been chosen both for theoretic consistency and because it facilitates the analysis of similarities and differences in various types of social organizations, e.g., the similarity of "bureacratic" principles in business and in government. Other usages are explained in the following basic references: F. Stuart Chapin: *Contemporary American Institutions* (New York: 1935); Joyce O. Hertzler: *Social Institutions* (New York: 1929); Constantine Panunzio: *Major Social Institutions* (New York: 1939); Talcott Parsons: *The Structure of Social Action* (New York: 1937); Sorokin: *Society, Culture and Personality*.

comes largely symbolic: what is enjoined is a state of mind (love thy neighbor as thyself) rather than a specific set of overt acts. Each group or individual can project its own needs and presuppositions into the rule and thus draw from it rather diverse implications for specific acts. In short, the meaning of the norm shifts according to numerous variations in time, place, emotional needs, intergroup and interpersonal relations, and situational pressures and interests of the most diverse kinds.

If we thus avoid thinking that the easy formula of "institution" is enough to explain all behavior, we certainly should not fall into the opposite error of assuming that institutions are fictional and make no difference in what concrete individuals do.[11] The obligatory norms centering around major social "needs" constitute the essential structure by which human behavior is channelized and given order and coherence. Society does not have definite institutional regulation of all activities, but society without some common institutional regulation would be a mere aggregate of human animals and not society as we know it. And, as later chapters will try to show, one can describe institutional norms from specific and objective data and systematically trace institutional interrelations.

There are three main problems in the study of social institutions. First, one must describe and analyze the normative structure itself: the existing patterns, their causes and interrelations, the sources and mechanisms of institutional integration, and consequences of the norms. Second, one must discover the processes of change in institutional patterns: their causes, mechanisms, and results. Third, one must study the relation of individual personalities to the normative structure; this is the area of "social psychology" dealing with culture-and-personality problems and facing the complexities of "social control" and of motivations for conforming, innovating, or dissenting.

In most of this book we shall deal mainly, although not ex-

---

[11] The latter error was common in much American social throught prior to the last few decades. Even as late as 1933 a prominent psychologist could write in terms that essentially denied the reality of institutions in the present sense. See Floyd H. Allport: *Institutional Behavior* (Chapel Hill, N. C.: 1933).

clusively, with structure and structural interrelations, focusing on these three questions: What institutional structures can be discerned in American society? What accounts for their characters, differences, and interrelationships? What consequences ensue for the total social life of the people? These questions are made scientifically meaningful only by asking what *difference* does it make that the institutional pattern is X rather than Y? All societies have institutions; the crucial question is, how do they differ? And this question can be answered only by comparison— either with other societies, or American society itself at some past period, or with some hypothetical standard constructed *ad hoc*. Thus any statements about institutional variation always imply a standard of comparison, explicit or implicit. If, for example, one says the separation of Church and State is an institutional pattern in American society, one implies a comparison with some society lacking this separation. The relations of individuals to their institutions can be studied intensively in small communities, but a broad comparative perspective is essential for adequate under-standing of the institutions themselves.

To recapitulate briefly, we have seen that culture in the most inclusive sense includes knowledges, skills, artifacts, symbols, technologies, and beliefs, as well as norms for conduct. Among the conduct-norms, we have concentrated on those regulating social relationships (rather than, for instance, the relation of man to nature or to the supernatural). Finally, we have examined briefly the special class of norms we call institutional.

So far we have discussed only the cultural structure, the normative patterns, but have not made explicit the idea of *social organization* as distinct from culture. The distinction hinges upon the normative quality of culture, that is, the fact that culture is not concrete behavior itself but contains the normative standard of behavior. The embodiment of cultural norms in concrete social relations marks the area of social organization. Social organization is not to be identified with any particular social groupings nor with highly formalized organization. Social organization refers rather to the actual regularity of human interaction, no matter what specific form the interaction may assume. There is organization precisely *to the degree that* the actions of individuals toward other individuals are recurrent and co-ordinated by the orientation of the acts of each to those of others. A newly formed unit of military conscripts will be oriented to a definite culture considerably before its actual social organization has come into full conformity with the normative structure. The practical test of organization is always *predictability*, hence *social relationship*. A social relationship exists to the extent that the interaction between two or more individuals is recurrent by virtue of the mutual orientation of the acting individuals to one another. The co-ordination of interindividual action through mutual concerns and expectations is precisely the measure of social organization.

Organization in this generic sense is clearly distinguishable from any specific organized "group." A group is a *specific aggregate of persons* within which there is organization; it exists only to the extent that the specific persons are in fact organized. A proximate, although inadequate, clue to the existence of a group is a greater frequency of interaction within the aggregate than occurs in outside relations; a group is an aggregate within which there is a special density of interaction, to use the phrase with which Chester I. Barnard has characterized "informal organization." A *formally* organized group is a specific aggregate of persons carrying out interrelated roles in explicitly defined positions. Actual social aggregates range from relatively unstructured and transient systems of interaction to the most highly formalized groupings, and the relative importance of "formal" and "informal" groups is important to study in attempting to describe any society.

We now have in hand the basic concepts necessary to begin our substantive analysis: structure, culture, cultural norm, institution, and social organization. Our approximate and incomplete model for the analysis of American society now includes the *organized activities* of a *population* that interacts in terms of a particular *culture* as it attempts to realize certain *normative goals* in relation to *other societies* and its *physical and bio-social environment*. All the terms in this statement are essential in the approach we shall employ. For the translation of these terms into useful analytic tools many diverse sets of data will be utilized. Every scientific fact is a statement about phenomena in terms of a particular set of concepts. Our "facts" must be objective, i.e., the operations by which they are derived can be described and publicly communicated so that ultimately they can be replicated and checked by any competent observer. At the same time, the multitudes of heterogeneous facts must be ordered and analyzed in concepts that are as clear and invariant as possible. The sources of information that supply our factual observation are initially illustrated in the following chapter on American family and kinship. They include statistical compilations, law codes, judicial decisions, historical records, observational reports, specialized research reports, and a variety of other materials. The present chapter tries to supply a minimal framework within which such data can be clearly arranged.

4. Kinship and the Family in the United States

1. Introduction

SOME kind of institutionalized *family group* is found in all societies and is fundamental to their social systems. In this chapter, we shall look at the American family and kinship systems as though we had never seen them before. Americans tend to regard the small conjugal unit of husband, wife, and children so characteristic in our society, as perfectly "natural"; but it is very special. In most simpler societies the kinship unit is a larger group, often including several generations and various collateral branches and having much greater family continuity than in our society. Again, Americans take for granted "dating" as the courtship pattern, but it depends upon very unusual features of our society. We observe Mother's Day or joke about in-laws without realizing how such behavior relates to our basic kinship system.

Kinship relations can be analyzed on two different levels: (1) institutional patterns (structure), and (2) the individual's relation to these norms and to the associated personal and social relationships. The latter study analyzes motives for conforming, as well as for resisting the nominally sanctioned relationships, rights, and duties; it may properly be called "social psychology." Mostly we shall focus upon *structure:* that is, the system of kinship statuses whose reciprocal cultural prescriptions define required, recommended, permitted, discouraged, or forbidden emotions and behaviors. Later (in Chapter 10), we examine "deviant" behavior of considerable structural importance.

Since this is an institutional treatment, our subject should be defined structurally. By "kinship system" we mean a *pattern of social norms defining interpersonal relationships relating to the facts of birth and the birth cycle.* A society is perpetuated only by new births, and the prolonged human infancy requires extended adult care—the central fact of all kinship systems. The social relations based on actual or potential births fall into four main categories: (1) the selection of marriage partners (courtship, arranged marriage, and so on); (2) the marriage bond—the relatively enduring, socially sanctioned union of one or more men with one or more women; (3) the immediate conjugal (nuclear) family; (4) the extended kinship relations beyond the immediate conjugal unit.

Our analysis centers on the last two categories, as fundamental to the social character of marriage and courtship.

For realistic description of a going kinship system we must treat systematically two elements outside the kinship system *per se:* age and sex categories, used to relate *any* individuals in the social system. To be young or old or to be male or female has a fundamental social bearing quite apart from kinship. Whereas kinship is a set of *relations*, a "family" is a definite *group* of persons united by kinship *and* by common residence (the household group), economic production and consumption, religious organization, or common recreational activities. *A* family is an actual group of persons in mutual familial relations. *The* family, on the other hand, is the over-all pattern of institutional norms and values that prescribe the familial roles within all particular families whatsoever.

For clarity, we must distinguish (a) the total kinship system, (b) the family system, and (c) the particular family unit. Even the simplified and truncated American kinship structure is much wider than the family system—strictly, a series of immediate conjugal units loosely linked; it includes wider affinal and consanguine relations and the even more general age and sex groupings.

Kinship relations are by no means a simple reflection of "blood relationships." The biological basis of kinship is, of course, birth or potential birth; individuals are related to others by being born of certain individuals, or by the possibility that births will result from marriage. But there is the further criterion of sex: the fact that the two parents are of opposite sex produces other relations, especially if both parents nurture the child. Thirdly, there is birth order; if older and younger children remain together for years, age tends to define relationships among them, and between them and other relatives. Seniority influences also the relations between an individual and relatives outside the immediate family. Thus, as Linton has pointed out, the culturally ascribed *roles* for various kinship *statuses* will be filled from a certain age-sex category: "Note the impossibility of adhering to the formal roles for an uncle-nephew relationship when the uncle is a child and the nephew an adult." [1] Finally, several children from the same parents makes the sibling group a potential subunit of the system.

These several biological reference points combine to give each individual a different position. "Children" are not merely children —they are male or female, older or younger, with other siblings or without. The sister of one's father is not in the same biological category as one's mother's sister, but both in our society are "aunt." Because of the complexity of the biological categories, no summary categorization of the *social* kinship system is adequate. This is clear for the American system, and anthropological observations demonstrate it in various other societies.[2]

Some of the "simplest" facts of human relations are the most fundamental. For instance, all known societies, past and present, have an incest taboo: all forbid sexual relations between persons in certain kinship positions. The taboo is universal, and violations of it typically arouse strong repugnance or moral revulsion. But the *line of prohibited intermarriage is drawn at very different points in different societies*. In the United States, the incest taboo applies with full force only to the immediate family group. In the traditional clan system of China, the prohibition nominally extended to a very wide group of relatives, many of whom were quite distant kin by contemporary American standards. Some societies prohibit

---

[1] Ralph Linton: "Age and Sex Categories," *American Sociological Review*, Vol. VII, no. 5 (October: 1942), p. 590.

[2] The outstanding summary of the anthropological evidence is given by George P. Murdock in his *Social Structure* (New York: 1949).

the marriage of cousins to the sixth degree; [3] in other societies the intermarriage of one type of first cousins is mandatory (cross-cousin marriage). There are many such detailed variations, each of which is considered right and proper in the society in which it occurs.

Yet some incest taboo is always the most persistent element in kinship structure. A brief examination of the social implications of this fact will introduce us to some of the distinctive features of the American system.

The various prohibitions against intermarriage of kin seem inexplicable on biological grounds. The doctrine of "instinctive aversion" ignores such evidence as inbreeding among animals, the widely varying degrees of kinship permissible for intermarriage in different societies, the actual occurrence of incest, and the frequent intermarriage of fairly close blood relatives in societies that do not forbid it. A second biological explanation rests upon the allegedly harmful results of inbreeding. But the scientific evidence of the biological effects of human inbreeding is by no means clear-cut; in general, it seems to bring out genetically recessive traits— good or bad. Yet all known societies have unequivocally prohibited marriage of close kin long before any definitive scientific evidence was available. Finally, Freud's contention that the taboo is necessary to repress sexual desires within a kin group seems clearly inadequate. Prohibitions against sexual relations with relatives seem in general to be more preventive than repressive; that is, they ensure that certain persons simply will not be regarded as potential marriage partners. In any case, however, this theory still leaves unexplained *why* the taboo should be necessary in the first place.

More promising is an explanation of the incest taboo as preventing potentially disruptive sexual conflicts within the kinship group. If family groupings are to exist at all—and there are important reasons for their universal presence [4]—internal conflicts must be

[3] For example, see David G. Mandelbaum: "The Family in India," in *The Family: Its Function and Destiny*, ed. by Ruth N. Anshen (New York: 1949), p. 97.

[4] Fundamental in this is undoubtedly the helplessness of the human being at birth and the prolonged period during which the infant needs adult care for survival.

minimized. Exogamy, furthermore, links together a series of internally solidary groups that would otherwise constitute a "mosaic" society of relatively small, closed segments. This function is especially striking in American society. Our society is made more diffuse and mobile by a marriage system tending to establish kinship relations cross-cutting segmentary local groups.

One more point should be made before we turn to the specific features of the American system. Kinship relations are among those learned earliest and most thoroughly. We "learn" them at first unwittingly, and they become integral to our personalities very early in life. They are implicit in the very language we are taught and are borne in upon us by countless experiences and injunctions throughout the most formative years of childhood. So completely and so early do we learn the system that we are seldom aware of ever having learned it. It seems completely "natural," to be taken for granted as a part of a fixed order of the universe. For this reason, and because we often have deep emotional blockages regarding some aspects of family and kinship relations, we often tend to make two untenable assumptions: (1) that the kinship system is "simple"—easy to describe by untutored common sense without rigorous analysis (actually, some features of our kinship system are so far from obvious that even prolonged and systematic study leaves many gaps in knowledge); (2) that American family roles reflect a constant "human nature," and hence that our unanalyzed concepts of "father," "mother," "uncle," and so on are directly applicable to other societies. Anthropology has shown, however, that kinship roles vary widely between cultures; a "father" in the Trobriands is certainly not the "father" of Freud's central Europe. Even in America a number of rather divergent family types are often found even within the same region, so we must proceed cautiously. Unless otherwise specified, "the American kinship structure" will refer to that prevailing among urban, middle-class groups, which tend to embody the "ideal patterns" toward which most other population elements are oriented. It is helpful to gain a clear picture of their situation before complicating the analysis with various deviations. Once we have examined the kinship structure of urban, middle-class America, we can consider its modifications among rural groupings, upper-class or lower-class groups, ethnic, racial or religious minorities, and so forth.

We turn first to American family law for certain clues as to the basic structure of the kinship system.

2. The Legal Norms of the American System: An Illustration of Evidence

THOUGH complex, vague, and various, American family law still exhibits a rather clearly defined core of principles about which the kinship system is built. The greatest uniformity and antiquity, mark the following as key points:

1. Violation of the incest taboo, which applies to the "immediate" biological family and to certain other relatives by blood descent or marriage, is one of the most fundamental breaches of the regulative order.

2. Marriages must be monogamous. All states prohibit bigamous marriages.

3. Marriage is more than an ordinary civil contract; it contains an element of *status* in the legal sense.

Marriage clearly differs from an ordinary contract, in that (1) it cannot be rescinded or its fundamental terms changed by agreement; (2) it results in a status; (3) it merges the legal identity of the parties at common law; (4) it is not a contract within the Fourteenth Amendment, United States Constitution, forbidding legislation impairing the obligation of contract; (5) the tests of capacity differ from those applied to ordinary contracts.[5]

4. Legal tradition gives the benefit of doubt as to validity to marriages that are marriages in social fact, although they

---

[5] An authoritative digest of American family law is contained in the series of volumes produced under the direction of Chester G. Vernier. The above passage is reprinted from Chester G. Vernier and Fred A. Weller: *American Family Laws: Introductory Survey and Marriage*, Vol. I (Stanford, Calif.: 1931), p. 51, with the permission of the authors and of the publishers, Stanford University Press.

might otherwise be null, void, or voidable on technical grounds of law.

Informal marriages based on mutual assent, without ceremony or officiant, have been considered valid as common-law marriages by a majority of states . . . notwithstanding criticism leveled at such informal marriages, they have been expressly repudiated by statute in very few states; and in many states such marriages have been held to survive even in the face of elaborate regulations governing licensing and solemnization of marriages.[6]

(The increasing instability of the marriage bond, however, causes this legal principle to be evaded and circumvented in numerous ways.)

5. There are many specific barriers to the dissolution of marriage; these reflect the basic presumption that a valid marriage should be maintained unless there is clear and crucial ground for its dissolution.

6. There are definite legal obligations incumbent upon individuals as a consequence of their kinship relations, irrespective of their personal wishes or "contractual" agreements.

7. There are vestiges of a surviving legal "double standard" that indicate an underlying conception of the male (husband or father) as the more powerful, responsible, and independent party to a marriage.

8. Women have a high degree of legal autonomy and freedom in marriage and kinship obligations; there is a strong tendency toward husband-wife equality. In some respects this represents marked individualization or "atomization" of the kinship unit.

9. Familial authority is specifically limited by the state in a variety of ways; the kinship unit is extremely permeable to external civil authority.

10. Court decisions seem in many instances to reflect certain customary norms that are not a formal part of the statutory or common-law systems—for instance, the "unwritten law" that exculpates a husband who kills his wife's paramour.

[6] Reprinted from Chester G. Vernier and Fred A. Weller: *American Family Laws*, Vol. I (Stanford, Calif.: 1931), pp. 102–03, with the permission of the authors and of the publishers, Stanford University Press.

The marriage contract is the first tangible evidence of the *institutional* character of the family. Most civil contracts may be broken by mutual agreement of the contracting parties. But in the case of a marriage "contract," American law generally regards mutual agreement not only as an inadequate ground for divorce, but as a specific bar to divorce. Mutual agreement to contrive a divorce is "collusion," which the law at least nominally regards as fraud and as a sufficient basis for denying a divorce. Evidently marriage is not an ordinary civil contract. American family law treats marriage and kinship relations in terms of status rather than contract. When one contracts to have a house built, the agreement affects only specified rights and obligations, but marriage involves blanket obligations (to "love, honor, and obey"), not a specific limited sector of life. By marriage a person not merely "enters a contract" —he becomes a different legal person; there is a change in status that cannot lawfully be changed simply by a change in will or by mutual agreement.

Furthermore, the tests of capacity to make marriage contracts differ from those of ordinary civil contracts. The courts have often held, for example, that a marriage illegally entered upon by minors is valid if there is a child or if the wife is pregnant. There is thus a general tendency to recognize as legal and binding those marriages that are marriages in social fact, even if the parties were originally not technically competent to contract marriage.

The divorce laws are especially instructive as to the peculiar nature of marriage. Though with much variation from state to state, the majority of jurisdictions, even those with "liberal" divorce laws, give marriage a status radically different from other contracts.[7] Usually the "rule of recrimination" applies in divorce proceedings: divorce is denied when *both* parties are guilty of behavior that would justify it if only one partner were guilty. Mutual violation may thus result in the court's refusal to grant a decree. This situation is just the opposite of the rule in ordinary contracts, where mutual breach of contract rescinds the agreement. Furthermore, most jurisdictions deny absolute divorce where con-

[7] See Chester G. Vernier and Benjamin C. Duniway: *American Family Laws: Divorce and Separation*, Vol. II (Stanford, Calif.: 1932).

nivance is proved—that is, when one spouse consents to, accepts, or aids in acts that would otherwise be valid grounds for the decree. Divorce is usually denied for collusion—agreement of husband and wife to "impose upon the court." More striking is the denial of a decree because the plaintiff has condoned offenses that would otherwise entitle him to divorce.[8] So far does the legal system go in trying to preserve marriages that thirty-two states explicitly provide that a divorce may not be granted solely on the basis of the uncorroborated testimony, admission, or confession of the parties.[9]

Such examples could be multiplied, but these perhaps illustrate that marriage—and kinship relations generally—is in law relatively durable, difficult to dissolve, and productive of a far-reaching change in the status of the person.[10] The law seems to regard these statuses and relationships as valid unless proved otherwise—the burden of proof is upon him who would terminate a relationship or avoid a responsibility. These norms are detailed, relatively permanent, and of basic structural importance. The legal structure thus reflects the moral consensus of the society that fulfillment of marriage and kinship obligations are considered crucially important.

The legal order thus both reflects and helps to create a given family system. Much of family law—including statuses enactments, common law, and judicial precedents—simply summarizes or codifies current social practice. Much law, however, tangibly influences marriage and kinship relations, even where it does not unequivocally reflect public opinion. (At the time of enactment the requirement of medical certificates, waiting periods, and the like for couples wishing to be married must have been considerably "ahead" of popular thinking.) On the other hand, marriage and family law that runs counter to popular beliefs and well-established behavior tends in the long run to be modified, formally abolished, or tacitly ignored. Nevertheless, such adjustments are usually slow,

[8] Ibid., p. 79.
[9] Ibid., p. 141.
[10] Obviously, actual social practice may not be in accord with the official norms; for the moment, however, let us consider only the nominally dominant rules.

and many divergencies between law and practice typically exist at any given time.

Of course law seldom perfectly embodies the current social practice, still less the current wishes, aspirations, and dissatisfactions of the people. There are invariably "maladjustments" or areas of tension and confusion at the "growing points" of the law, partly because the main formal function of law is to provide security by ensuring a general predictability in recurring situations. The major basis for predictability is the fact that previous cases have been decided in a certain way. Thus there is great judicial emphasis upon precedent, general rejection of retroactive legislation, and a pervasive "conservative" tendency in the legal system. Therefore in periods of rapid social change, problems arise that the law cannot cope with except in a way that no longer accords with the beliefs and desires of most members of the society. Thus legal norms can never be safely taken as adequately descriptive of actual social relations.

In addition, a rule is of course *general* and hence cannot fit exactly all the manifold details of blurred and endlessly changing human affairs. Not even the most astute legislator or judge can foresee all the varied situations that will eventually complicate the application of a particular statute or decision.

Moreover, laws, being formal and generalized, cannot allow for "exceptions," "peculiar cases," and unusual circumstances—especially numerous in kinship relations and therefore never completely covered by the explicit provisions of the law.[11] In general, *the more detailed regulation of the kinship system is left for diffuse cultural standardization, not enforced by a formal social organization.* The legal net is too wide-meshed to catch the smaller variations.[12]

---

[11] Indeed, the legal structure is itself forced to set up an elaborate series of social mechanisms for "fitting" the law to the "unusual" situation. Equity proceedings provide the clearest explicit instance but much the same purpose is served by jury trial, by wide statutory leeway for administrative or judicial discretion, by the right of appeal, by advisedly vague legal language, and by many other means.

[12] "In the great interstitial areas of life where institutional controls cannot easily reach, particularly in the primary group, control will be determined by the interplay of personality." Jessie Bernard: *American Family Behavior* (New York: 1942), p. 428.

As we have said, the inflexibility and generality of legal rules prevents their completely describing the whole kinship structure. Equally important, the family is hard to regulate from outside. If it is to have any real existence it must have some autonomy. Otherwise it becomes a merely nominal group or an appendage of some other organization. In America, the privacy, inviolability, and independence of the family household still have deep cultural roots —although it is no longer quite true that "every man's home is his castle." Family behavior is hard to reduce to rule, for diffuse symbolisms and personal motives influence the social meaning of acts. Often more important than a specific overt act, easy to identify objectively, are the imputed motives and meanings from a long series of subtly interrelated actions. Apparently identical acts may have exactly opposite meanings to the members of the family.

Therefore evidence about American kinship structure must include more than "law." The following synthesis draws upon law, statistical records, literature, and the enormous corpus of sociological and psychological research.

3. Main Defining Structural Features

IN THE American kinship system, (1) the incest taboo everywhere forbids a person to marry father, mother, and children, grandparents, uncle, aunt, niece, nephew.[13] In twenty-nine states intermarriage of first cousins is forbidden; intermarriage of blood relatives is seldom otherwise limited. (2) Marriage is monogamous and there is no prescriptive pattern for kinship marriages. (3) No discrimination is made between paternal and maternal relatives for marriage purposes. (4) Although the "family name" descends through the male line, there is little other emphasis upon the male line of descent. The descent system tends to be bilineal or, more strictly, multilineal.

These characteristics indicate a highly dispersed system of inter-

[13] See Vernier and Weller: *American Family Laws: Introductory Survey and Marriage*, Vol. I, pp. 173 ff.

marriage and kinship.[14] From any given individual X the ancestral lines can theoretically fan out indefinitely into the past, so that any of many lines of heredity may be emphasized for some purposes. Similarly the lines of descent disperse among a large number of kin-name groupings.

Thus, (5) there is an extreme emphasis on the immediate conjugal family.[15] In a highly developed consanguine kinship system, by contrast the tightest unit is the descent-group of siblings,[16] a group of brothers and sisters whose spouses enter as strangers and remain always somewhat so. In America the solidarity of spouses is stressed, to the exclusion of in-laws.

The extraordinary emphasis in modern, urban, middle-class America upon the marriage pair is bound to result, in so far as it is actually carried out, in a greatly simplified kinship structure of isolated families.[17] This has profound socio-psychological implications, to be examined later.

(6) The immediate father-mother-children family tends to be the effective residence, consumption, and social unit. No extended kin-groupings are of more than negligible importance in these respects, except among a few relatively small, deviant population elements.

[14] The best structural description is: Talcott Parsons: "The Kinship System of the Contemporary United States," *American Anthropologist*, Vol. XLV, no. 1 (January–March, 1943), pp. 22–38.

[15] Margaret Park Redfield: "The American Family: Consensus and Freedom," *American Journal of Sociology*, Vol. LII, no. 3 (November, 1946), p. 175: "The American family—parents and children—appears on the surface as a simple conjugal type with no important or formal connections with remoter kin, no rituals of ancestor worship (except, perhaps, in the case of the D.A.R.'s), and no intricate economic ties. It is a small compact group of two generations, bound together by ties of affection and functioning to care for the young until they reach years of maturity and can repeat for themselves the process of family rearing."

[16] Cf. Ralph Linton: "The Natural History of the Family," in Ruth Anshen (ed.): *The Family*, p. 25.

[17] Cf. Margaret Mead's statement: "A primary stress upon the husband-wife relationship results in a bilateral kinship system and a very simple kinship structure which lacks the continuity of descent groups . . . the family founded upon the husband-wife relationship is too unstable and discontinuous a form of organization to provide the type of firm structure which is given by social groups based on blood relationship." *Encyclopaedia of the Social Sciences*, Vol. VI, p. 67.

The doubling-up of families in the same household ordinarily occurs only under economic depression, housing shortage, or extraordinary family circumstances. Even grandparents in the home, once more or less taken for granted, has become unusual.

The isolated conjugal unit is regarded as desirable, right, and proper by social consensus. It is felt that each "family" (typically this is simply *assumed* to mean "immediate family") *should* be an autonomous group. It is considered unfortunate if for any reason other relatives have to reside in the household. Except in extraordinary crises parents are specifically expected not to "interfere" with the families of their children.

(7) In urban communities, which are increasingly representative of the country as a whole, the family group is typically a consuming rather than a producing unit. Kinship units as work groups and productive organizations have largely disappeared except in farming and certain types of small retail businesses. The family producing unit characterizes societies with relatively little industry and economic specialization. The family farms and the small shops and stores of earlier America combined functions that have been separated in an age of giant corporations, mass industry, and highly specialized occupations. The co-operation of all family members in a common economic enterprise made for a kinship grouping quite different from that of the modern urban family.

(8) Because the conjugal family is the unit and the kinship system is multilineal, American society little emphasizes family tradition and family continuity.[18] Of course the "old society" families of Charleston, South Carolina, and the Beacon Hill families of Boston, for example, put considerable stress upon lineage and collateral kinship. Significantly, however, such groups are commonly regarded as so exceptional as to be ready subjects for comment. Among many wealthy, "upper-upper" groups there has developed a marked concern with family continuity and tradition, but they are neither types nor "models" for the society as a whole.

[18] The following statement is a reasonably accurate description of the modal pattern: "The family is thought of not as an organic structure to be handed on from generation to generation but rather as the individual creation of each generation and enduring rather less than a lifetime." Redfield: "The American Family: Consensus and Freedom," p. 176.

Significantly also, families wishing to emphasize continuity and tradition often have a very difficult time doing so. A thriving business is done in ferreting out genealogies, tracing descent from notable persons, discovering (or inventing) coats of arms, and so on. This desire for family history is specific evidence of the lack of continuity. One does not need a specialized search for traditions, genealogies, and symbols where these things are a solid part of actual family life.

(9) There is comparatively free choice of mates. In fact, American mate selection is an application of "free competition" in the institution of marriage. The whole detailed system of "dating" is a unique American arrangement.[19] Within certain legal barriers,[20] the choice of spouses is purely personal; the kin of the prospective mates have no right to interfere. Parents are usually asked to sanction the marriage choice but this convention is residual. The free choice of mates is made possible by the autonomy of the marriage unit. The married pair do not have to fit into an established kinship unit with consequent important and complex repercussions upon many other individuals. This autonomy in turn rests upon geographic and occupational mobility. "Arranged" marriages typify social systems where the new couple will reside near one or both of the in-law families, maintaining intimate association with a continuous and extended kinship group; a marriage is a sort of "treaty" between groups, as well as a personal contract between individuals. The individualistic mate-choice in America is thus partly accounted for by the isolated conjugal unit, the discontinuity of generations, the devaluation of kinship, and the extensive social mobility found in our society.

Social systems in which a considerable number of individuals are in a complex and delicate state of mutual interdependence tend greatly to limit the scope for "personal" emotional feeling or, at least, its direct expression in action. Any considerable range of affective spontaneity would tend to impinge on the

[19] See the discussion by Willard Waller: "The Rating and Dating Complex," *American Sociological Review*, Vol. II, no. 5 (October, 1937), pp. 727–37.
[20] The most important legal barriers concern "race," degree of consanguinity, age, and physical or mental health.

statuses and interests of too many others, with disequilibrating consequences for the system as a whole. This need to limit affective spontaneity is fundamentally why arranged marriages tend to be found in kinship systems where the newly married couple is incorporated into a larger kin group. . . .[21]

Either a matrilocal or a patrilocal rule of residence concentrates a solidary kin group into which new nuclear families must be incorporated. As the wider kin group preponderates, marriages tend to become arranged unions serving group interests rather than personal affinity alone.[22] Our own "neolocal" system of residence in which a new household is located independently of either family, frees mate choice from many restraints of the locality-kin grouping, and at the same time works toward bilateral descent.[23]

(10) Linked to the father-mother-children unit and free marriage-choice is the tendency for adult children to disperse from the parental household. This geographic dispersion of children has reached extraordinary breadth in America.[24] As we shall see later, it is directly tied up with vertical mobility between social classes.

Briefly, then, these are the main structural features of the dominant kinship system in the United States. The interrelations of these features warrent further examination.

As an obvious consequence of the prohibition of intermarriage among members of the nuclear family there is created a division between what Warner has usefully termed the *family of orientation* and the *family of procreation*. The family of orientation is the family of father, mother, brothers, and sisters into which a given individual Ego is born; the family of procreation is established by Ego's

[21] Parsons: "The Kinship System of the Contemporary United States," p. 30.

[22] Cf. Mandelbaum: "The Family in India," in Ruth Anshen (ed.): *The Family*.

[23] Murdock: *Social Structure*, p. 209: "The final result of neolocal residence is thus always bilateral descent."

[24] Cf. Linton: "The Natural History of the Family," in Ruth Anshen (ed.): *The Family*, p. 31: "The outstanding feature of this [the current family] situation is the almost complete breakdown of the consanguine family as a functional unit. . . . This breakdown seems to be directly correlated with the increased opportunities for both spatial and social mobility which have been created by the current technological revolution."

marriage and consists of his spouse, sons, and daughters. Ego is the only common member of the two families, and in the American case each member of the two families is typically linked by marriage to one other previously unrelated nuclear family. Thus the two families typically link outward to as many previously unrelated families as there are individuals who marry, and this widening web extends backward and forward indefinitely. The end result is a kinship system structured on an "onion" principle, with successive "layers" arranged symetrically around the two nuclear families at the center.

Thus, the core of the kinship system from any given individual's point of view consists of the seven kinship positions of father, mother, brother, sister, spouse, son, daughter. Each of these positions is specifically distinguished from any relatives outside the two nuclear families—a situation radically different from any kind of clan system. As one looks backward in time, the first ascendant layer beyond this central core consists of the families of orientation of Ego's parents, his grandfathers, grandmothers, uncles, and aunts. Except for the patrilineal inheritance of the family name, no further terminological distinctions are made within this group of kinsmen. Looking "forward" the same principles apply: in the first descendant families (those established by Ego's children) children's spouses are assimilated to the status of son or daughter, as the case may be, and the offspring are simply grandchildren. The same undifferentiated symmetry holds for the first collateral families established by Ego's brothers and sisters; both terminologically and in social fact they are not differentiated by the sex of the sibling or of Ego, and the children of these families are impartially nephews and nieces.

In the fully developed case, therefore, the main nexus of the American system is found in these six types of interrelated nuclear units: Ego's family of orientation, his family of procreation, his "in-law" family, and the first ascendant, descendant, and collateral units. Within this nexus, the three major bases of classification utilized are sex, generation, and affinity. Beyond this inner circle of relations, there is only the undifferentiated collateral category of "cousins," without distinction by sex or line of descent, and the successive ascendant and descendant relatives distinguished only as "greatgrandfather," "great-greatgrandfather," and so on. In both the ascendant and the collateral directions the socially effective relations tend to fade out rather quickly.

Thus the system places special importance upon the nuclear family unit, and isolates it from an extended kinship grouping, and therefore makes the marriage bond the keystone of kinship structure. A series of further implications follows from the interrelated structural characteristics already outlined.

4. Patterns of "Equality"

THE INDEPENDENCE of the nuclear family in our system is connected with certain equalities in kinship and marriage relations.

IN-LAW FAMILIES

First, the autonomy of the nuclear family not only makes loyalty to that unit more important than loyalty to in-laws, but it also puts both in-law families in an equal relation to the married couple.

The strong emphasis for *ego* as an adult on the marriage relationship at the expense of those to parents and siblings is directly correlative with the symmetrical multilineality of the system. From the point of view of the marriage pair, that is, neither family of orientation, particularly neither parental couple, has structurally sanctioned priority of status. It is thus in a sense a balance of power situation in which independence of the family of procreation is favored by the necessity of maintaining impartiality as between the two families of orientation.[25]

The husband's family has no superiority—of authority, for instance, over the conjugal unit—nor does either line have a clearly

[25] Parsons: "The Kinship System of the Contemporary United States," p. 30.

preferred claim to distribution of gifts, favors, visiting time and other evidences of concern, respect, or affection. Just as parents are not supposed to show favoritism to any particular one of their children, and are supposed to show the same regard for the latter's spouses as for the children themselves—so the married children in their turn are not expected to "discriminate" in favor of either the husband's or wife's family. When a husband or wife insists upon ignoring the wife's (husband's) family, there will probably be tangible social repercussions.

SIBLING EQUALITIES

A second equality is that of siblings in inheriting property and enjoying parental favor.[26] American law generally makes siblings equal heirs to intestate property.[27] A parent may favor one child

[26] One may be allowed to suspect that in many kin-groups in all cultures there is a strong pressure in actual personal-social relations toward equality of parental affection and concern for the children. Sibling jealousy, protests against "favoritism," and demands for equality of placement in the immediate family group are by no means confined to the United States. The point here, however, is that this may or may not be institutionalized, in the sense of general social sanction of equality or of birth-order preference, and that the fact of institutional sanction or the lack of it makes an important difference in what does happen in fact.

[27] A good example is supplied by the inheritance law of New York State, which contains the following provisions. "The real property of a deceased person, male or female, not devised, shall descend, and the surplus of his or her personal property, after payment of debts and legacies, and if not bequeathed, shall be distributed to the surviving spouse, children, or next of kin or other persons, in manner following:

1) One-third part to the surviving spouse, and the residue in equal portions to the children, *and such persons as legally represent the children if any of them have died before the deceased.* (Italics added)

8) Where the distributees of the deceased, entitled to share in his estate, are all in equal degree to the deceased, their *shares shall be equal.* (Italics added)

11) *Relatives of the half-blood shall take equally with those of the whole blood in the same degree.* (Italics added)

14) The right of an adopted child to take a share of the estate and the right of succession to the estate of an adopted child shall continue as provided in the domestic relations law." *New York, Decedent Estate Law, Sec 83.*

Note that the equality principle is specifically extended to descendants by affinity.

rather than another, but if the parent actually makes a very unequal bequest, except under very special circumstances, the action is likely to seem "arbitrary." This fact alone tells us that there is no generally approved principle of inequality.

In spite of considerable divergence among subgroups, in American society as a whole parents are expected to treat their children "impartially" in other ways. Neither sex nor age sanctions unequal affection. Of course, duties and privileges differ with sex and age, but only as "formal" requirements for adapting the child to the general age-sex patterns of the larger society, and are not considered to represent "favoritism." The very fact that favoritism is disapproved shows the acceptance of impartiality as a norm.

Furthermore, parents are expected to accept their children's spouses without discrimination. Thus children-in-law are assimilated to the family pattern of symmetrical equality.

HUSBAND-WIFE EQUALITIES

Both of the features just described relate to the statuses of the husband and wife. The impartial treatment of in-law families is favored by the equality of husband and wife, which rests partly on the isolation of the nuclear family; both of these facts foster equality of status between respective in-law families. This equality leaves the ties of the nuclear families to be determined by situations. The pattern of in-law equality is the favored resolution of the "bargaining" possibilities.

Of course, equality is only relative or comparative. There is not exact equality and certainly not identity of rights and duties. Many current discussions of the "democratic" American family almost imply that all family members are completely equal in capacities, rights, and duties. But obviously an infant is not "equal" in these respects to the parent who cares for and disciplines him. Family statuses differ and have different values. Family organization must have an elaborate division of labor and differentiation of authority among the various members so long as any coherent group exists at all. Nevertheless, institutionalized rights and obligations are dif-

ferently distributed among the pivotal family statuses in different
societies and are differently valued. For instance, the formal authority of the father is certainly less in contemporary American
society than in the European tradition. The wife and mother has
correspondingly greater rights in certain respects.[28] These are not
"accidental" variations, but rather derive from the basic kinship
pattern we have been examining.

5. Family Roles

THE ROLES OF WOMEN

As THE marriage pair, rather than a more extended family
unit, becomes the crucial link in the kinship system, the roles of
husband and wife become correspondingly separated from wider
kinship rights and obligations. Neither partner has immediate
recourse to a solidary group of kinsmen. Their relative isolation,
especially in a mobile and competitive society, tends to concentrate
into the marriage relationship the partners' emotional needs for
security and affection. This situation in itself tends toward husband-wife equality, for these needs are not easily met except on a
basis of intimate congeniality that in our culture is difficult to
achieve in formally inequalitarian relationships. The equality of
spouses is clearly encouraged also by the lack of strong priority of
either line of descent.

Since husband and wife constitute the most basic solidary group
in the kinship order, they must, partly because of peculiar features
of the social stratification system,[29] be treated by the wider
community as a unit and thus as social equals in important respects.
Were this not the institutional pattern, ordinary social intercourse
between the individual family and outside groups would certainly

[28] For the legal situation see for example: Chester G. Vernier and John B.
Hurlburt: *American Family Laws: Husband and Wife*, Vol. III (Stanford,
Calif.: 1935).

[29] See chap. 5.

put such serious strain upon the marriage bond as to threaten it. It is not a trivial matter of "mere convention" or "manners" that in the typical middle-class, urban community, if either spouse is invited to a mixed "social" gathering, the other spouse must be likewise invited. For any aggregate of persons becomes a real social group only by being identified as a unit, by sharing a common set of experiences, and hence by sharing a common universe of meanings and symbols. This kind of solidarity is, of course, quite compatible with marked differentiation of sex roles and with inequalitarian husband-wife relationships; but once we are given a kinship system of dispersed, multilineal nature built around the marriage bond, the pressures to treat the nuclear family as the primary unit are bound to work toward equalities between husband and wife.

The so-called emancipation of women has been greatly exaggerated and misinterpreted in much contemporary discussion. Yet there is no doubt that women in the United States have a relatively great amount of freedom. The disappearance of formalized chaperonage is in itself an important indication of emancipation. Our statutory laws have greatly modified the older common-law conceptions in the direction of equalizing the formal rights of husband and wife. Married women may make contracts, own property, make wills, and sue or be sued in their own right. Some court decisions now even affirm that the husband and wife may sue each other. The legal status of such husband-wife suits is still confused and ambiguous, but they mark a radical move not only toward equality of rights in law but also toward an individualization ("atomization") of the legal structure of the family.

Besides legal rights, American wives hold a remarkable set of customary or conventional intrafamilial rights that, although perhaps less rigid and explicit, are hardly less common or less important. Not even in theory is the wife expected to render unquestioning obedience to her husband, much less in actual practice. The marriage relationship most commonly held up as a model is one in which joint decisions are reached. It remains true that general consensus still holds that in the last resort the husband should be "head of the house," but it is felt that only in rare circumstances will "patriarchal" rather than "democratic" processes be desirable.

Many discussions of the position of women in our social order have failed to make certain essential distinctions. Probably the most frequent and important source of confusion is failure to distinguish among the *evaluation of women*, the *formal rights of women*, and the *roles expected of women*. It is possible to have a society in which women are highly valued, yet do not share many of the formal rights exercised by men or play masculine roles. In early America, for example, women did not lack a place of high honor and esteem, although they were confined to distinctly feminine roles and were without many legal rights that have been since acquired. Similarly, formal "equality of legal rights" turns out to be a question-begging term unless distinguished from the broader patterns of sex roles. Thus the failure of the husband to provide economic support for the wife is a criminal or quasi-criminal offense in every jurisdiction except Mississippi. Under a principle of strict equality, the wife would bear a corresponding obligation, and seventeen jurisdictions have specified that the wife is required to support the husband under certain circumstances. Nevertheless, that the law presupposes differential sex roles is clearly demonstrated by the legal status of alimony, which generally is still considered to be a continuation of the husband's obligation to support the wife—an assumption that obviously does not correspond to the facts in a great many contemporary divorce cases.[30]

Probably the most obvious change in the general social position of women has been a blurring of the feminine sex role in the masculine direction. Some specific evidences may be briefly enumerated:

1. *Legal rights:* women vote, hold public office, practice professions, hold and dispose of property, etc.
2. *Occupational role:* women participate in paid work outside the home on a large scale; they have entered traditionally male occupations.
3. *Educational participation:* there are coeducational school

[30] Chester G. Vernier and Benjamin C. Duniway: *American Family Laws: Divorce and Separation*, Vol. II (Stanford, Calif.: 1932), pp. 259 ff.

systems, colleges, and universities; graduate studies are sometimes open to women.

4. *Recreational patterns:* women participate in active sports, patronize drinking places, etc.

5. *Courtship behavior:* women have a kind and degree of freedom and initiative in courtship not before sanctioned.

6. *"Symbolic" evidences:* women emulate men's clothes in their slacks, tailored suits, etc.

Nevertheless, women's roles remain clearly distinguished in a number of ways.[31] Housekeeping and the care of children is still the primary role of adult women. In 1940, only 16 per cent of all married women were reported by the United States Census to be "in the labor force," that is, working for pay or seeking work.[32] The percentage of married women in the labor force is highest among younger women, urban women, those with no children under ten years of age, and those whose husband's income is in the lowest brackets. In the higher income levels, the working wife seldom has a job equal to that of her husband in status or pay. In spite of long agitation for the principle of equal pay for equal work, it is difficult to find evidence of husbands and wives competing on an equal basis and in large numbers in precisely the same occupations;[33] where women work in wage-earning occupations it is usually out of the presumed necessity of supplementing the husband's income, and the "career jobs" (white-collar, professional, and business) of married women will typically not be in *direct* competition with men in their husbands' occupation.

Married women are now generally entitled by law to their earn-

[31] Cf. Parsons: "The Kinship System of the Contemporary United States" pp. 33–6.

[32] See the valuable article by John D. Durand: "Married Women in the Labor Force," *American Journal of Sociology*, Vol. LII, no. 3 (November, 1946), pp. 217–23.

[33] The practice of equal pay for women and men in the same jobs has undoubtedly gained ground in recent years, partly under the influence of the industrial labor unions. However, as late as 1933 the comprehensive survey of the President's Research Committee on Social Trends complained that "it is almost impossible to secure wage data for both men and women doing precisely the same tasks, even within the limits of a single occupation." *Recent Social Trends*, Vol. I, (New York: 1933), p. 736.

ings for services rendered to third parties outside the household. Nevertheless, "In the main the courts have jealously guarded the right of the husband to the wife's services in the household. Even in jurisdictions in which the spouses may freely contract *inter se*, the wife cannot contract for services to which the husband is entitled as implied in the marital relation." [34] Furthermore, women working in paid jobs outside the home are typically concentrated in occupations most closely allied to traditional homemaking roles: in domestic service, teaching, nursing, laundry service, needle trades, as waitresses, hairdressers, dieticians, social workers, and so on. Because women are employed in the less well-paid jobs and because there is a widespread tendency to pay women less than men even within what is essentially the same occupation,[35] the average income of working women is considerably below that of men. Clearly women are not employed on the same basis as men, and in times of economic depression there is a strong tendency to discharge women workers first; in any severe economic crisis there is vigorous agitation to send women "back to the home."

In short, even in our "emancipated" society there remain persistent and important pressures tending to preserve the roles of women as mothers and homemakers. These pressures are neither wholly arbitrary nor a simple matter of social inertia and the survival of traditional prejudice. If women were to compete for jobs on an equal basis with men, drastic changes would be necessary in the family system, or in the occupational structure, or in both. So long as women bear children, who must be cared for and trained during the extended period of dependency, there must be *some* social arrangement to ensure that the necessary functions are performed. We can imagine a situation in which men, children, and retired elders might take over the major part of child rearing; or, we can conceive of homemaking and child rearing functions being performed by professional workers operating through new forms of

[34] Vernier and Hurlburt: *American Family Laws: Husband and Wife*, Vol. III, p. 195. Incidentally, this passage is a tribute to the individuation of the modern family as well as to the persistence of traditional family rights. It is significant that this legal question can ever arise on a scale worthy of comment.

[35] A not uncommon practice is to give women and men slightly different specific job-designations even when the actual work is practically identical.

social organization. *Complete* freedom of occupational competition for women would certainly involve one or both of these paths— or the disappearance of stable family units as we know them. At present, the family system is made partly compatible with the employment of many married women by: (1) low birth rates and small families; (2) extrafamily service agencies providing certain household aids and child care; (3) the tendency not to employ women in jobs that compete with those of men in the same socio-economic class. The last factor, whatever psychological problems it creates for women, tends to reduce the possibilities of a husband-wife competition for status that can be quite disruptive of marriage solidarity.

At the same time, however, the family structure does help establish equality of the sexes and removes many elements of psychological dependency in the feminine role.[36] Feminine roles are therefore often poorly defined, and the fundamental choices that women make are frequently complicated by insecurity, vacillation, and cross-purposes.[37] Parsons has pointed out three broad patterns of adjustment: (1) the "glamour girl" role, which emphasizes personal attractiveness; (2) the "domestic" role, which maintains the older pattern of the wife and mother; (3) the "good companion" role, in which the wife tries to balance the obligations of home and family against her desire to accept wider social responsibilities and participate equally with her husband in many activities.[38] The first pattern is inherently unstable and nonfamilistic. The forces tending towards equality and the cult of individual per-

[36] The new economic bases of family life are of particular importance, especially "the progressive diminution of the economic dependence of spouses upon each other." Ralph Linton: "The Natural History of the Family," in Ruth Anshen (ed.): *The Family*, chap. 2, p. 33.

[37] Compare the statement by Margaret Redfield: "The American Family: Consensus and Freedom," p. 182: "Although American women are freer than most other women, they have often not known what to do with their freedom. This seems to come from the fact that beyond the roles of glamour girl and nursemaid, the part to be played by women is but vaguely defined in our society."

[38] "Age and Sex in the Social Structure of the United States," *American Sociological Review*, Vol. VII, no. 5 (October, 1942), pp. 610–13. There are certainly other patterns, e.g., the unmarried "career woman."

sonality (which is itself reciprocally related to the small-family pattern) militate against the second; so does the great emphasis upon romantic love, even after marriage. Thus the multilineal kinship system, the small family, and the patterns of free mate-choice and romantic love all favor a role for the married woman as an "equal partner."

At the same time, as we have seen, there are many restrictions on women's careers outside the home. Since it is largely through success in such careers that an individual's prestige rank is established in our society, many modern women suffer major internal conflicts. Their search for an equivalent for the male's occupational role has led to a striking participation in "culture" (art, literature, etc.), in philanthropic and community service work, and in many other broadly humane activities. The extraordinary development of women's clubs—a development that has latterly become the subject of considerable attention by foreign observers [39]—provides a good illustration of this attempt at "deflected achievement."

THE ROLES OF CHILDREN

European observers of the American scene seem to be almost universally impressed by the freedom of children in their relations to parents and other adults. They note that at an early age children begin to be treated as individuals who are entitled to be consulted, to state their wishes, to ask the "reason why" for orders or requests.[40] They are struck by the lack of severe authoritarian relations between parents (or teachers) and children and by the way in which children enter into adult conversations and "talk back" to adults. To many observers from other cultures of Europe and Asia, the urban middle-class child appears to be overly assertive, undisciplined, lacking in respect for his elders—in short, a "spoiled

[39] E.g., Goeffrey Gorer: *The American People* (New York: 1948).
[40] E.g., Kurt Lewin: "Some Social-Psychological Differences between the United States and Germany," *Character and Personality*, Vol. IV (1936), pp. 265–93.

brat." The pervasive emphasis upon "freedom of expression" for the child is often noted as a further indication of "lax discipline."

Do these appraisals point to anything real in patterns of child-adult relations? There seems to be little doubt that on the whole American children have extraordinary freedom in certain respects and develop, at any early age, patterns of "independence" in marked contrast to the roles of children in corresponding social and economic classes in nearly all the major cultures of Europe, Asia, and Latin America. It is certain that in the past the ideal patterns for children's roles were more nearly indexed by such maxims as "spare the rod and spoil the child" and "children should be seen and not heard." [41] There are conspicuous tendencies toward the indulgence of children in their wishes—so much so that American sociologists and psychologists can speak seriously of the filiocentric, or child-centered family. Unquestioned obedience is usually not required of children.

This summary appraisal is necessarily vastly oversimplified and couched in advisedly general and qualified terms. There are enormous variations in child-rearing patterns among various classes and subcultures within the United States; [42] there is nothing like complete uniformity in the use of corporal punishment, nor in the kinds of demands made upon the child as to toilet training, punctuality, cleanliness, aggression control, nor in the extent to which

[41] It is impracticable here to detail the mass of diverse evidence bearing on the above statements. Some of the pertinent facts and interpretations may be found in the following references: Anshen (ed.): *The Family;* Bernard: *American Family Behavior;* Arthur W. Calhoun: *A Social History of the American Family* (New York: 1945); Willystine Goodsell: *A History of Marriage and the Family* (New York: 1935); Bernhard J. Stern: *The Family: Past and Present* (New York: 1938).

[42] See for example: Allison Davis: "American Status Systems and the Socialization of the Child," *American Sociological Review,* Vol. VI, no. 3 (June, 1941); Kingsley Davis: "The Child and the Social Structure," *Journal of Educational Sociology,* Vol. XIV, no. 4 (December, 1940); Allison Davis, Burleigh B. Gardner and Mary R. Gardner: *Deep South* (Chicago: 1941); Arnold W. Green: "The Middle Class Male Child and Neurosis," *American Sociological Review,* Vol. XI, no. 1 (February, 1946); Martha C. Ericson: "Child-Rearing and Social Status," *American Journal of Sociology,* Vol. LII, no. 3 (November, 1946); Allison Davis and Robert J. Havighurst: "Social Class and Color Differences in Child-Rearing," *American Sociological Review,* Vol. XI, no. 6 (December, 1946).

parents require affection rather than simple obedience or respect from the child. Nevertheless, there seem to be broad tendencies toward permissive discipline in certain respects [43] and toward an idealization of childhood. The sources of these tendencies are very complex indeed and cannot be treated adequately in a work of the present character. In part they stem from the high evaluation of individual personality and from the cultural emphasis upon the future. The confusion of standards of conduct in a complex, heterogeneous, rapidly changing culture and the effect upon the child of subjection to multiple and divergent social authorities in the persons of parents, teachers, social workers, play groups, and so on, both play a part. Furthermore, the urban child cannot easily be directly initiated into the standards of the adult culture, because the occupational and residential patterns do not permit, for example, the social apprenticeship of sons to fathers that occurs so easily in stable agricultural societies.[44]

The segregation of the immediate conjugal family from a wider kinship group has highly significant effects upon the child. Instead of developing diffused emotional ties to a large group of adults, the child must manage his needs for dependence and growth in relation to a few persons—chiefly his father and mother. Parents thus necessarily play a two-sided role in relation to the child, ministering to his wants and gratifying his demands for care, security, and affection, but also thwarting him in various ways. In so far as the nuclear family is the prime socializing group during the early years of life, the inevitable ambivalences of the child towards the agents of socialization are focused upon the parents. This tendency is to some degree offset by play groups, nursery schools, kindergartens, adult neighbors and friends who play a part in the child's emotional world. At the same time, however, in the American school or play

[43] This in spite of the rigor with which middle-class white children are early required to control impulse (cleanliness, certain overt forms of aggression, sex, toilet training). The "permissiveness" applies, not to these areas, but to the degree of control by parent figures over social assertiveness and demands for attention or care from adults. Incidentally, it is curious how lacking we are in precise descriptive "maps" of the limits and rigidities in different areas of the child's behavior in the various classes and groups of our own society.

[44] Cf. Parsons: "Age and Sex in the Social Structure of the United States," p. 605.

group the child must compete for place and is thus thrown back upon his one ascribed group—the tiny circle of the family—for reassurance and security.[45] Thus we have the curious fact that as the effective kinship unit has become smaller, the importance of the immediate family has in some respects become enhanced.

As in many other societies, the early socialization of children is largely carried out by the mother, but in urban America, especially in the middle and upper classes, her role tends to bulk larger and to extend to later years of childhood and youth. The father's role in the home is residual and tends to be heavily encroached upon by the demands of his job.[46] Thus he often appears to the children as a somewhat harassed man who passes briefly through the home at evening and on weekends and holidays. Since the segregated nuclear family is the emotional center of the child's life, the mother plays a role unlike that of any other adult member of the child's social circle. Her importance to the child is the greater because in our culture the child is expected to love, as well as to obey and respect, his parents.

The precise consequences of this dependence on the mother are as yet imperfectly understood. Certain obvious hypotheses have been widely discussed. Philip Wylie has made much of an alleged "Mom complex." [47] Geoffrey Gorer has attempted to analyze the implications of the "encapsulated mother." [48] They contend that because American women are the prime socializing agents for boys as well as girls, the male identifies women with "morality," with far-reaching consequences in sexual adjustments, standards of masculinity, and attitudes toward many moral standards. The

---

[45] This is one of the ways in which parents "capture" the child. Cf. the concept of "personality absorption" suggested by Arnold W. Green: "The Middle Class Male Child and Neurosis," *American Sociological Review*, Vol. XI, no. 1 (February, 1946), pp. 31–41.

[46] The central role of the mother appears to be most marked in the "commuter family," in business and professional families, and in certain unstable family groupings of working-class populations, e.g., the "mother-centered" urban Negro family. The father still plays a more positive role in much of rural society, in some ethnic groups having a "patriarchical" tradition, and in established upper-class lineages.

[47] *Generation of Vipers* (New York: 1942).

[48] *The American People: A Study in National Character* (New York: 1948).

overweening role of the mother, they suggest, lays the basis for many of the difficulties that plague the male adolescent in his attempt to establish an adult masculine role. These problems obviously demand a great deal more penetrating research; now we can only point out plausible hypotheses.

In America there appears also to be relatively great stress upon "rational" methods of rearing the young. Though most marked in urban and well-educated groups, there is a very general disinclination throughout the society to advocate child-training methods merely on grounds of tradition. Furthermore, American parents seem avidly to seek scientific information and the advice of experts or pseudo-experts; they very often are preoccupied with "problems" of child rearing; [49] they often show definite signs of uncertainty and insecurity as to how to bring up their offspring. There are a multitude of magazines, bulletins, pamphlets, newspaper articles, "columns," and so forth, dealing with how to treat the child, and there is considerable instability in the popularly accepted recommendations in these matters. At one period, all babies must be fed on rigid schedule; they must be handled as little as possible; they are allowed to "cry it out"; "overprotection" and "spoiling" is avoided with something approaching moral horror. Within a few years, the tenor changes—the despised rocking-chair is back in psychiatric favor, mothers are told to indulge their propensities to hold and cuddle the child, rigid schedules for feeding and sleeping are modified in the interest of "fitting the regime to the needs of the child." In short, fads and fashions characterize popularly accepted dictums on child care and training.

Can such variable and subtle patterns be dependent in any way upon the rather gross structural features with which we have just been concerned? We contend that these socio-psychological conditions are *in part* direct consequences of the structural emphasis upon the marriage bond, and thus, upon the isolated conjugal family unit. Of basic importance is the lack of intergeneration continuity resulting from the isolation of the conjugal unit. This isolation is, in turn, largely, although by no means entirely, con-

[49] Witness the incessant discussion of this topic so typical in middle and lower-upper class urban groups.

ditioned by the geographic dispersion of adult children. An extreme case might be that of an urban middle-class family unit of husband, wife, and one child living two thousand miles away from the rest of their kin. Under circumstances like these, which are certainly more or less approximated by millions of American families, the immediate family is almost entirely cut off from authoritative guidance by the older generation. The young mother faces child-training problems *as an individual,* without that stabilizing continuity of contact with elders and the wider kinship group that has been typical of the historical experience of the human race. She is equipped with whatever memories she may have of her own childhood and with her observations of the socialization of other children, but this experience is often inadequate as a guide to the highly specific and pressing problems she confronts in rearing her own children. The father is in a similar, although perhaps usually even worse, position. Both have absorbed something of the general ethos of respect for rationality, practicality, scientific methods, and thus they tend to seize upon the latest pronouncements of the presumed experts in order to gain some sense of dependability and security.

THE ROLES OF ELDERS

Reverence for the old was a phase of a society that placed strong emphasis upon family life. . . . A society that has shaped its ideals about progress can never place its affairs in the hands of the old and give them the reverence that a society does that lives in the past. . . . The decline of ancestor-worship, the competitive character of modern economic life, democratic government, individualism, and the cult of progress, have thus all conspired to reduce to a marked degree the functions and rank possessed by the aged in earlier society.[50]

As this quotation suggests, American society has little place for the aged person. We must therefore ask: What is the status of the

[50] Cecil C. North: *Social Differentiation* (Chapel Hill, N. C.: The University of North Carolina Press, 1926), p. 84.

aged person in the family system? What features of the family system make his role insignificant?

In comparison with past periods of our own society and with the traditionalized rural societies of present times (old Ireland, China, India, or central Europe), the elders in America have little functional place in the kinship system and occupy a position of relatively low prestige or esteem. The basic pattern of the modern urban family is incompatible with the traditional roles of the elders. There is strong resistance to sharing the household with aged parents or other relatives; physical facilities tend to be designed for the small family. Urban life on the whole favors the active adult; industry on the whole has favored the younger worker. Our large urban centers have made little provision for offsetting the problems of the aged.[51] The obligation of children to aged and needy parents is still recognized by the legal system but often does not have social acceptance.[52] The 1940 United States Census showed that only 36 per cent of households with both husband and wife present contained any relatives 18 years of age or older. Sixty per cent of these relatives were single children, 12 per cent were other children or their spouses, and only 10 per cent were parents of the husband or wife of the household.[53] In popular literature, songs, movies, and the like, youth is represented as the ideal time of life. A culture that glorifies youth, action, strength, and competitive success, a culture that prides itself upon being modern, up-to-date—this kind of culture is not likely to accord age the immediate respect that it can command in more highly traditionalized social structures. Where social change is slow, the elders are the great repository of knowledge and lore; but in rapidly changing societies like modern America derogatory terms like "old fogy" can become common. The intergeneration cultural gap

[51] Cf. Helen H. Brunot: *Old Age in New York City* (New York: 1943). "The community has almost no resources for recreational or social activities for elderly people."

[52] Few systematic studies have been reported. One bit of supporting evidence is supplied by Robert M. Dinkel: "Attitudes of Children Toward Supporting Aged Parents," *American Sociological Review*, Vol. IX, no. 4 (August, 1944), pp. 370–9.

[53] Paul C. Glick: "The Family Cycle," *American Sociological Review*, Vol. XII, no. 2 (April, 1947), p. 171.

resulting from rapid social change, which is to be discussed below as a factor in problems of adolescence, thus turns out to have as its reverse side a certain social isolation and loss of firm, institutionalized status and esteem for aged parents.

Working in the same direction are at least two other major extrafamilial influences. First, for several generations many millions of American children have learned to deprecate in some measure the culture of their immigrant or second-generation parents. In the attempt to become "American" they have rejected much of the culture with which their elders have still been identified—thus they have tended to ignore, scoff at, or openly rebel against the ways of the elderly family members and the authority and social esteem of the elders has been diminished.

Secondly, vertical social mobility has inevitably been corrosive of the status of parents of adult children. The small farmer or worker whose son has become a highly successful businessman or professional worker will typically not have the same position in the family structure as he would had his son been his apprentice in a stable occupational system. Rapid upward social mobility thus appears to deprive elderly parents of an important social function and prevent a high development of institutionalized esteem for the aged.[54]

The specific impact of these and other influences is reinforced by the position of the nuclear family unit in the kinship system. The emphasis upon the marriage pair inevitably means less stress upon the parent-child bonds. The independence of the households of married children is in part simply another way of stating the minimal role of parents. Census data for 1940 showed that four fifths of married couples establish separate households upon marriage. With wide geographic dispersion of children and with relatively high mobility—in 1940 only 41 per cent of the heads of families were living in the same house as in 1935—one can almost say that the elders often have little authority in the kinship structure

---

[54] The American case is best seen in contrast with kinship structures in which old age is highly esteemed and the authority of elders is great. See Francis L. K. Hsu: "The Family in China," Ruth Anshen (ed.); *The Family*, pp. 73–92.

simply by virtue of having no family group in which authority can be exercised.[55]

There are, of course, variations in subcultures of the United States. Highly stable rural landowning families, certain families with long-established wealth, some closely-knit ethnic and religious groups give greater place to the aged. As a general principle, however, it can be predicted that a "vestigial" role for the elders will be most conspicuous in those population segments in which the nuclear-family pattern is most strongly developed.

Indirect evidence is considerable. The increasingly widespread concern over old age as a "social problem," and agitations concerning old-age pensions and retirement plans provide some. As Parsons has suggested in discussing the Townsend program and the widespread attention it aroused, more than mere "economic security" is involved in the agitation for old-age pensions. The most fantastic schemes receive a wide hearing, partly because the whole old-age problem becomes psychologically overdetermined, on the one hand, by reason of the social isolation, insecurity, and sense of futility that beset functionless elders, and on the other, by reason of the reluctance of young adults to accept the support of aged relatives, coupled with their residual guilt-feelings.[56]

A somewhat more specific piece of indirect evidence is the existence in our society of "pools" of elderly persons living in certain urban centers. In some resorts, such as Long Beach, California and St. Petersburg, Florida, there are great numbers of retired individuals or elderly couples living apart from other relatives and associating chiefly with others in a like situation.

Indeed, of the population in these two cities 15 and 24 per cent, respectively, are over sixty. By contrast, in centers of industry such as the steel town of Gary only 4 per cent are aged sixty or

[55] Cf. Glick: "The Family Cycle," p. 171.

[56] From their origins in commercial promotion schemes, Mother's Day and Father's Day have proceeded to rapid institutionalization largely because we have a society in which grown children are typically separated from their parents. The enormous vogue of various kinds of family greeting cards is another evidence of attempts to maintain symbolic, "long-distance" solidarity in a social structure that tends to render a more tangible solidarity impossible. Probably there are important elements of "overcompensation" in these efforts.

more, and in the metropolis of Chicago only 5 per cent. Although the situation is less striking for villages and small towns, both census statistics and monographic studies show that village populations tend to include disproportionately large numbers of elders, and it is possible to identify a fairly distinct social type of village that has as one of its main characteristics a concentration of "retired" persons, especially widows and widowers from farm areas.

Some of the important social and psychological implications of an extreme development of the isolated nuclear family for the position of aged persons thus seem to be identifiable and subject to at least a broad structural analysis. One other extrafamilial factor of great significance remains to be mentioned: the prevalence of abrupt retirement in our occupational system. In most past societies, the active adult only gradually relinquished his occupational responsibilities as he approached the end of his life.[57] Even in the United States this pattern remains important for landowning farmers and some business proprietors and professional persons. However, the dominant patterns for urban occupations have come to be either retirement at a fixed age (common with government workers, white-collar business jobs, hired professionals, and so forth) or simply discharge and inability to get another job (frequent among wage earners). Where these practices prevail, the elderly person is left doubly bereft of social function and life rationale; he has no occupation and little place in the families of his children or in any other kinship grouping.

THE ROLES OF YOUTH [58]

It seems clear that there is in American culture a strikingly high evaluation of "youth" as a time of life. Yet in this same culture, adolescence tends to be a period of relatively great stress and strain,

[57] This pattern is certainly typical of contemporary agricultural societies. In some hunting and military societies, the active adult role was terminated rather abruptly, but usually with provision for respected substitute functions.

[58] The sociological study of adolescence has been advanced in recent years by such analyses as the following: Kingsley Davis: "Adolescence and Social Structure," *The Annals of the Academy of Political and Social Science*, Vol. 236 (November, 1944), pp. 8–15 and "The Sociology of Parent-Youth Conflict,"

and the "problems of youth" are the objects of widespread discussion and concern. Certain features of the kinship system can be shown to be directly related to this seeming paradox.

The "problems" of adolescence arise in the transition from one social status to another—from the dependent status of "child" to the responsibility and autonomy attributed to the mature adult. In a great many societies this transition is clearly defined by public rites or ceremonies and by a variety of other means that have in common the definite signalizing of a well-understood transition from one status to another. In American society, there are only a few rudimentary equivalents of such *rites de passage*, the "coming-out party" of upper class girls being probably the closest. For the vast majority of the population, the transition from child to adult is institutionally recognized only by disparate events (high school graduation, getting a full-time job, marriage, and so on) that are not closely integrated into a pattern. The relative lack of *rites de passage* for adolescence both reflects and contributes to the uncertainty and instability faced by the adolescent. The lack of clear structuring varies, of course, with region, social class, ethnic group, and rural or urban residence as well as with sex; probably it is at a maximum among the culturally marginal and mobile elements of the urban middle classes. Boys and girls face qualitatively different ambiguities and uncertainties, but both often find it difficult to tell when and how "adult" behavior is expected. This indeterminancy in social expectations is a phenomenon almost unknown to the youth of simpler and more stable societies.

Under these circumstances, furthermore, the adolescent reaches biological maturity considerably in advance of social maturity. The extended period of formal education and the compulsions to be economically self-supporting before marriage tend to defer marriage well beyond the age of full biological maturity. Yet the society emphasizes premarital chastity while at the same time it permits and encourages young people of opposite sexes to associate closely. The resulting strains and difficulties are themselves en-

---

American Sociological Review, Vol. V (August, 1940), pp. 523–35; Parsons: "The Kinship System of the Contemporary United States." The following discussion obviously relies heavily upon the analyses of Dr. Davis.

hanced by an appreciable lack of clarity in *de facto* social codes. The adolescent has to deal with these bio-social problems for several years while he or she anticipates full emancipation from parents, mate selection in a relatively competitive marriage market, and the eventual establishment of a separate and independent household.

We have seen that the family system is organized in such a way as to "require" the emancipation of young people from the family. In general, the children of the parental household are expected, and thus feel obligated, to leave home, get a job, and establish their own families, especially in the socially mobile groups in which the children are expected to move up in the social and economic scale. Because our occupational structure is still one of rapid change, competitive placement, and high specialization, the tendency is to defer final occupational choice until after childhood. Yet, if the young person is to enter a "good" occupation, he is likely to need an extended period of specialized training. Thus among the middle-class groups, at least, he must choose his occupation as an adolescent, but without clear and institutionally stable guiding definitions and prescriptions. The lack of arranged marriage and of hereditary occupational placement gives him great freedom at the very time that the parental family is in the process of relinquishing its control over him; but because the emancipation process is not clearly structured, this release from parental control often is halting, erratic, and ambiguous. The exact nature and timing of his assumption of adult privileges and responsibilities are left to be settled by a "bargaining struggle."

This struggle is often emotionally intense; for the adolescent deals with a small family, not with an extended group of kinsmen; instead of diffused emotions and the unanimity of authority, there is a focus upon the parents—who may or may not be supported by the larger consensus of the community. Furthermore, even while the youth is casting off parental guidance and control, he is likely (for reasons already suggested above) to be in special need of security and emotional support; for the tiny island of the immediate family is frequently his only dependable support in the surrounding sea of competition and instability. Out of this changing balance of dependence and independence, needs and claims, comes much of the adolescent behavior described by exasperated or concerned adults as vacillating, erratic, chaotic, or queer.

A certain amount of conflict between parents and youth is to be expected in any society because of intergeneration differences in interests and perspectives and the correlative differences in social rights and responsibilities. In our society these differences are greatly intensified by the relatively low degree of family continuity in conjunction with the rapid rate of social change—change that is assimilated more rapidly by youths than by their elders. So extreme is this gap between generations in some instances that parents and their adolescent children literally represent subcultures. In a complex society, the authority of the parents in this type of situation is continually challenged by other vested authorities as well as by youth. This clash of authorities is a specific manifestation of the broader problem of cultural conflicts and lack of integration.

Thus it is partly the institutional characteristics of the American family, not particular personalities, nor a generalized "human nature," that give rise to certain typical "problems" of adolescence.

6. Romantic Love

THE GREAT emphasis in American culture upon idealizing romantic love depends closely upon certain features of the basic family system. With the diminution of the extended family and the correlated loss of many previous functions of the nuclear unit, the family's chief "function" has come to be that of providing affection and security. When choice of mates is relatively free, personal attraction bulks larger in marriage than it could under any system of arranged marriages; it is a commonplace hypothesis in the sociological literature that our emphasis upon romantic love is in part an equivalent for the group support and regulation of marriage in the less diffuse and mobile systems of many other societies. At the usual age of first marriage, the young person is still acquiring emotional independence from the parental family, under the multiple stresses just discussed. The "need" for dependence is strong, and the institutional demand for independence is strong. Under these circumstances, it is necessary to break through complex and deep-seated resistances to marriage and its responsibility and emotional independence without the help of a clearly defined system of mate choice based upon status and wider kinship regulation. An almost compulsive emphasis upon romantic love emerges in part from this situation.

Furthermore, young people who have been brought up in the relatively isolated and autonomous small-family unit probably bring to marriage a tendency to depend emotionally upon one or a very few persons, and, in the extreme cases, after marriage are almost completely thrown back upon one another for full emotional response and basic psychological securities. In a mobile, competitive world, so largely dominated by relatively impersonal and segmented social relationships, the courtship process and the marriage relation can thus come to carry a kind of intensity and importance not typical of other types of societies. The ideals of premarital chastity and lifelong fidelity in marriage, in so far as they are socially effective, increase this intensity.

All these indirect influences or "secondary institutions" operate in a family system that has already freed the spontaneous affective inclinations of the young couple from elaborate restrictions. In proportion as marriages are not arranged, they are left to the choice of the potential partners, and, as institutionalized status (such as social class or caste) is less important, the choice rests more on individual qualities and achievements. Because American society has come to permit considerable personal choice, the pattern of romantic love is encouraged both by the family structure and by a series of indirect consequences of that structure. Of course, the extreme stereotype of romantic love is largely a "cultural fiction." Marriage partners available to any given individual are severely limited in practice by race, religion, social class, propinquity, and so on.[59] Nevertheless, our culture continues to idealize romantic love.

[59] For some of the evidence see Davis, Bredemeier, and Levy: *Modern American Society*, chap. 22, pp. 585–614.

7. Family Instability

IN SPITE of many cultural prescriptions nominally supporting the permanence of the marriage tie and the solidity of the nuclear family, American society is characterized by high rates of divorce and other forms of family dissolution. The legal atomization of the family into separate legal personalities is far advanced; the family is extremely permeable to external agencies and influences, from nursery schools to radio and from the social worker to the truant officer, the military draft, and even the political party. Many marriages are childless. Kinship obligations are not strongly upheld, and many of these have been taken over by the State. The surviving family unit is, therefore, a small permeable group. It is emotionally intense, but is weakly supported by the surrounding society. Unwillingness to assume "full-scale" family obligations is common. In sum, "familism" has been reduced to secondary importance in the social fabric.[60]

Although statistical evidence on family stability is far from adequate, we can roughly estimate the divorce rate. The ratio of divorces in a given year to the average number of marriages in each year of the preceding decade is a good index of marriage instability, since most divorces occur within ten years after marriage. This ratio has risen from six per cent in 1890 to about forty per cent in 1947.[61] From 1867 to 1932, divorce has occurred in increasingly earlier years of marriage: during 1867–86 a marriage was most likely to break up in its seventh year but by 1922–32, in its third and fourth year, and today probably in the third year. Although divorce rates are higher in urban than in rural areas, divorce is invading the open country; for example, a recent study

[60] Some modern students of the family are sufficiently impressed with the signs of family instability to argue that our society will soon face a major "family crisis." The most prominent exponent of this is Carle C. Zimmerman: *Family and Civilization* (New York: 1947); and *The Family of Tomorrow* (New York: 1949).

[61] See the estimates cited in the article by Kingsley Davis: "Children of Divorced Parents: A Sociological and Statistical Analysis," *Law and Contemporary Problems* (1944), reprinted in Davis, Bredemeier, and Levy: *Modern American Society*, pp. 680–1.

showed about one divorce for every four marriages even in the most rural counties of Ohio (1939–47).[62]

Most divorces dissolve *marriages* rather than *families;* apparently about two thirds of all divorces are childless. In desertions and informal separations, on the other hand, it appears that there is a smaller proportion of childless couples than in the total population.[63] Through a lack of data concerning desertion and nonsupport, however, we must rely chiefly upon divorce as an index of family instability. Judged by divorce alone, the United States certainly has one of the highest rates of family dissolution in the world. Differences among national divorce laws and customs make strict comparison very dubious, but without doubt family break-up is very frequent in our society, by any standard of comparison.

How is this family instability to be explained? Full causal analysis is impossible here, since a full "historical" treatment would deal with all of American civilization. However, the preceding discussion has provided important clues.

Popular explanations of "the divorce problem" commonly stress the alleged personal incompatibility of the spouses. Yet plainly personal incompatibility explains very little, for why does the incompatibility ever arise, why does it lead to divorce, and why do families often endure even in the face of severe interpersonal tensions? There are structural factors far more basic than the "reasons" commonly advanced for family breakdown. Marriages dissolve because: (1) divorce or separation is *permitted*, and (2) there are few strong internal bonds holding the marriage together, and (3) the marriage pair or family unit is not well-supported by the surrounding social structure. Modern America combines all these features. It permits divorce far more readily than formerly. At the same time the American family has lost many of its former functions—the multiple activities that once centered in and around the home. The family as an almost purely consuming and affectional unit contrasts sharply with the old-style "trustee family"—prac-

[62] A. R. Mangus: "Marriage and Divorce in Ohio," *Rural Sociology*, Vol. XIV, no. 2 (June, 1949), p. 132.

[63] Davis, Bredemeier, and Levy: *Modern American Society*, p. 682; Ernest R. Mowrer: *Family Disorganization* (Chicago: 1939), pp. 99–100.

tically a self-contained social system, combining economic production, education, "government," religious functions, "social security," including several generations and comprehending nearly
all phases of the individual's life. The sharing of common tasks in a
collective enterprise in such families was one manifestation of the
close economic and social interdependence of family members.

Modern family instability is often blamed directly upon the loss
of multiple functions. It is better to say that the remaining family
"bonds" bear too heavy a load and break under it. As the family
has become less important, it has also become more important; as
the scope of family activities has narrowed, the emotional significance of the surviving relationships has, in one sense, increased.
High expectations are imposed upon a relatively fragile structure.
For instance, the dream of perfect husband-wife compatibility in
the more extreme versions of romantic love conflicts with the fact
that families have few common activities and institutional supports.

The American family is not a dying institution. It is even possible that it will be strengthened by new forces in the future. At
the present, however, in addition to stresses within the kinship
structure, it is subject to multiple strains from other institutions,
e.g., occupational structure which seems incompatible in many
ways with stable family life.[64] Further attention will be given to
these problems in several later chapters.[65]

[64] One student of the family has gone so far as to say: "The family as an
institution is basically . . . opposed to the tenets of free competition upon
which our economic order rests." Jessie Bernard: *American Family Behavior*,
p. 542.

[65] See esp. chap. 13.

5. Social Stratification in the United States

1. Introduction

As OUR brief survey of kinship and the family has suggested the isolation of different "institutional areas" for purposes of analysis is somewhat artificial; in concrete social life there is no sharp line separating one institution from others and actual social situations represent a most complex crisscrossing of numerous normative systems. Thus the full extent of institutional interdependence cannot be seen until all the major institutional complexes have been described. It follows that no one institution can be adequately analyzed until we have some understanding of all the others; yet one must have some information about each institution in order to comprehend the actual functional interconnections of all of them. Therefore we will first present a provisional and incomplete analysis of each institution, reserving to a later chapter the more complicated problems of interrelation of institutions and other structures in the total society.

The consideration of kinship structures leads us quite easily into an analysis of social stratification. For example, it has already been observed that the emphasis in American society on "moving up in the world" is of great importance in explaining the diminished importance of extended family ties and that social stratification is related to problems of solidarity of the nuclear family itself. As a matter of fact some of the crucial questions we have to ask in diagnosing any society concern the extent to which, and the specific ways in which, kinship plays a part in the systems of stratification of that society. Is the family or kinship a main criterion of "ranking"? Is the unit of ranking an individual person, or a kinship group, or something else? To what extent is family membership an advantage in maintaining or attaining a given position in the stratification order? To move toward answers to questions of this character we have first to consider what we mean by words such as "social stratification," "class," "caste," "rank," "prestige," and the like. There are great variations in the meanings commonly attached to such terms, and the formal definitions that have been set forth often do not fit the available facts. We must therefore be explicit about our own concepts in the present analysis.

2. Major Concepts and Problems

"STRATIFICATION" of society, whatever else it may mean, certainly denotes *some* way whereby some kinds of units are arranged in *some* kinds of strata. Conceivably the units might be nations, religious organizations, castes, military groups, "races," or any other socially real categories into which human individuals are placed. We are interested here in two kinds of units: (1) the individual person, (2) the kinship group.

What is "stratification"? Every classification of human beings is also a potential ranking, and the number of possible classifications is indefinitely large. We might stratify people according to their emotional stability, their ability to play badminton, their knowledge of medieval Latin, the color of their hair, the number of friends they have, the reputation of their ancestors. Actually, only a few of the qualities of individuals or groups are seized upon as either criteria or symbols of station. Nevertheless, all known societies have some system of ranking their constituent members or groups along some kind of superiority-inferiority scale. Theoretically, all individuals might be valued *equally* but in no large-scale or long-continued social grouping have they been so; the differential valuation of men is a universal formal property of social systems.[1]

For present purposes we shall consider social stratification to mean the *ranking of individuals on a scale of superiority-inferiority-equality, according to some commonly accepted basis of valuation.*[2]

We are interested, not in any and all varieties of stratification, but rather in *institutionalized* stratification, that is, a system of ranking that is generally accepted as right and proper, as morally justified, by the groups within which it operates. By no means all superiority-inferiority relations are of this nature. Many of them are based very largely on power alone. A small-scale instance is provided by the ranking according to physical strength and fighting prowess found in boys' gangs, a ranking somewhat analogous to the pecking order observable among animals. In society at large an individual or a group may use coercion to gain or maintain station, even though the methods may run counter to many of the major institutionalized values nominally accepted in the society. Furthermore, in a large and complex social aggregate there are wide variations in the degree to which the legitimacy of a given system of stratification (or of the positions occupied by various individuals within it) is accepted by various groups or subsystems of the collectivity.

The term "ranking" seems at first glance to carry a fairly clear meaning, perhaps because of our common-sense knowledge of military hierarchies. Actually, several specifications are necessary to make the term analytically useful. In the first place, *the accurate ranking of individuals is possible only within a given scale of valuation.* The accepted scales of valuation of different societies, or even of subgroups in the same society, often have little in common. How, for instance, does one judge accurately the relative standing of a Spanish bishop of the Roman Catholic Church, a Brahmin, a French general, an American millionnaire, a Russian commissar, a

[1] Of course, the extent and *kind* of inequality varies tremendously from one culture to another.

[2] This conception has been developed by Talcott Parsons: "An Analytical Approach to the Theory of Social Stratification," *American Journal of Sociology*, Vol. XLV, no. 6 (May, 1940), pp. 841–62.

Swedish scientist, a member of the English nobility? Individuals occupying these positions have "high" rank in their respective social systems, but what common denominator would permit precise ranking of each position relative to the others? [3] In less marked degree the same difficulty characterizes a complex and dispersed collectivity such as the United States. The Nob Hill "society" of San Francisco may be in some ways similar to the Beacon Hill "society" of Boston, but it is difficult to compare the rankings of the two local systems. Furthermore, the stratification that prevails within specific social organizations such as churches, armies, factories, governments, families, criminal gangs, schools, and so on (segmental stratification) must be distinguished from caste and class arrangements, which crosscut communities and the more inclusive society.[4] Segmental stratification is most conveniently studied as a part of actual *social organization*, class or caste stratification as a part of the broader *institutional systems* of a society. Our present interest is thus in the second type, by which persons are summarily given a station [5] in a scale of objective privilege and responsibility and in a correlative scale of invidious prestige and deference. An individual's position in this scale is in part, however, a weighted sum of his positions in the various segmental orders to which he belongs. In American society, these orders include specific religious groups, families, cliques, formal associations, residential groupings, ethnic or racial categories, and, especially important, occupation; a person's occupation and his rank within it are pri-

[3] As Speier has correctly emphasized, no single objective basis for stratification is determining for all societies; institutionalized stratification is a matter of reciprocal evaluations, and the privileges or disadvantages of different social positions are to be understood as "the objective manifestation of social evaluations which are implied in the way the individual and his external qualities are typically treated by men of different positions, and in the way that men of different positions are typically treated by him." Hans Speier: "Social Stratification in the Urban Community," *American Sociological Review*, Vol. I, no. 2 (April, 1936), pp. 194–5.

[4] W. Lloyd Warner and Allison Davis: "A Comparative Study of American Caste," in Edgar T. Thompson (ed.): *Race Relations and the Race Problem* (Durham, N. C.: 1939), chap. 8, p. 220.

[5] Kingsley Davis: "A Conceptual Analysis of Stratification," *American Sociological Review*, Vol. VII, no. 3 (June, 1942).

mary influences upon his rank on the scale that stratifies the whole society.[6]

In the second place, rank may carry with it many and diverse kinds of permitted, forbidden, and enjoined behaviors, various degrees of privilege and power. Thus, the "elite" groups are in part defined as elite by the deference that they receive from others. "Deference" may take an almost indefinite number of forms: acquiescence in material advantages or other objective privileges, tones of voice, ritualized salutations and leave takings, use of honorific titles, order of precedence, and so on. Whatever the specific behaviors and symbols, their common element is their generally recognized social meaning as deferential. The elite groups may be further defined by their share of various kinds of tangible privileges and immunities—for example, high income, possession of valued material goods, exemption from burdensome tasks, special immunities (from taxes, for instance, or from jury service, military service, prosecution for various misdemeanors, crimes), access to the person and goods of others, specific power and authority. Thus prestige is the "subjective" aspect, *wealth* (command over purchasable goods and services) and *power* (ability to control the acts of others) important "objective" aspects of station.

Much confusion in the consideration of stratification can be avoided by holding fast to the following elementary distinctions.

1. Stratification refers to the existence of a rank order. Such an order *can have a specific meaning only within a given social system.*

2. Any given ranking system can be analyzed in terms of:

(a) the *distribution of objective privileges*, e.g., income, wealth, safety (health, crime rates), authority, etc.;

(b) *subjective rankings* by members of the society (prestige and esteem);

[6] Always, of course, a given individual's summary rank is influenced by the age and sex categories to which he belongs. Thus in certain situations, a lower-class adult may have age prerogatives that override class distinctions in dealing with an upper-class child or youth. Similarly, occupation may be a primary stratification mark only within racial or ethnic categories.

(c) the *criteria of rank*, whether personal qualities or achievements, family membership, possessions, authority, or power;

(d) the *symbols of rank*, e.g., style of life, clothing, housing, organizational membership, etc.;

(e) the *ease or difficulty* and *frequency of changes in rank-position;*

(f) the *solidarity among individuals or groups sharing a similar position* in the system:

(1) *interaction patterns* (clique structures, common organizational memberships, intermarriage, etc.);

(2) *similarity or dissimilarity of beliefs, attitudes, values;*

(3) *consciousness of stratification position shared with others;*

(4) *concerted action as a collectivity*—for instance, "class warfare."

The nature of many controversies current in the literature on social stratification can be clarified by reference to these basic elements of the problem. For instance, the Marx-Engels theses distinguish classes according to relations of individuals to the means of economic production—in our terms, according to the objective distribution of one special privilege. The possession of rights over the means of production is regarded as carrying with it intrinsic social power, including that of legalized coercion. Eventually class solidarity develops out of similar objective position (f–2), leading to class consciousness (f–3), and finally to concerted action (f–4). These different aspects of Marxian theory are often commented upon as if they constituted a single, unitary conception.[7]

In part because of the availability of the data, a great many investigations have utilized occupation as the defining mark of class. The usefulness of this approach is apparent; in our modern society a person's occupation is one of the most important determinants of his whole way of living. Occupation alone, however, will not identify social class position. Unfortunately, data corresponding

[7] For a quite different kind of analysis, see: W. Lloyd Warner and Paul S. Lunt: *The Social Life of a Modern Community* (New Haven, Conn.: 1941); W. Lloyd Warner, *et al.: Social Class in America* (Chicago: 1949).

to the elements affecting stratification outlined in points a–f(4) above are as yet extremely scanty, and accordingly we shall be forced to rely heavily upon occupation as a rough index of social rank. Interpreted with care, however, the available information about occupational groupings throws a great deal of light on the stratification systems of our society. For example, it can be used to indicate, crudely at least, the relation of individuals to the means of production ("who controls the means of livelihood") and the way this relation affects their social and political attitudes.

The ranking of individuals according to occupational activity is affected by two main considerations: the prestige of the occupation and the rank of the individual within it. In American society broad occupational groups are evaluated according to a definite pattern that places at the bottom of the prestige scale manual labor [8] and unskilled personal service involving direct personal dependence upon superiors. Above this level the prestige of occupations seems to follow roughly the degree of skill presumed to be entailed and the size of the income derived. The authority over persons inherent in a given occupation further modifies the rank-order; for example, factory foremen or policemen or judges seem to receive an added increment of prestige on this ground.

Popular evaluations of occupations, at least at the level of abstract stereotypes, seem to be highly crystallized and have remained stable over a considerable period of time. In some twenty serious studies of the social prestige ranking of occupations which have been made during the last twenty-five years in the United States, there is remarkable consistency in the rankings reported.[9] The pioneer study by Counts in 1925 reported a scale found to be practically unchanged in 1946 when Deeg and Paterson repeated the same ranking procedure. Furthermore, the findings of the scattered special studies agree quite closely with the 1947 nation-wide survey analyzed by North and Hatt. This study seems to invali-

[8] See the evidence in Cecil C. North and Paul K. Hatt: "Jobs and Occupations: A Popular Evaluation," *Opinion News* (September 1, 1947).

[9] See the summary and bibliography in Maryon K. Welch: "The Ranking of Occupations on the Basis of Social Status," *Occupations*, Vol. XXVII, no. 4 (January, 1949), pp. 237–41. Cf. also the two articles by Raymond B. Cattell in *Journal of Social Psychology*, Vol. XXI (February, 1945), pp. 3–55.

date the objection raised that most studies have dealt with samples of students lacking realistic occupational experience.[10]

Individuals are also judged according to their prominence, ability, or "reputation" *within* a specific occupation. The individual's rank (his "standing") is dependent not only upon his occupation but upon his success in it; he is "the best doctor in town," "a leading lawyer," "the crack salesman in the Eastern District," and so on. These evaluations play a complex role in establishing an individual's class position. Within a specialized occupational field, the social evaluations especially important to him are those of his peers—of other people who are technically competent to judge his performance. These informed valuations, however, are only loosely correlated with broader "reputation" in the total community. In a highly specialized occupational structure, competence in occupations requiring complex technical knowledges and skills can be accurately judged only by other experts in the special field. General community reputation is only in part established on the basis of strict technical competence; it is also affected by a wide range of irrelevant factors. For instance, most people are necessarily *not* competent to judge the skill of a medical doctor; yet their ignorance is no bar to the establishment of his definite reputation. The "best doctor in town" might owe his ranking in large measure to a good bedside manner, the "right social connections," and a variety of other extramedical factors. There is, indeed, an observable tendency in such instances for reputation to become cumulative, in part just because there is both a strong need to get the best doctor and a lack of the technical knowledge for making a selection.

We must consider also the definiteness of the stratification structure. On the one hand, we have the sharp delineation of specific positions within a definite formal organization; within a modern army, for example, there are clear-cut ranks, each of which carries defined rights and duties along with a specific "package" of claims to prestige and deference. The army has a hierarchy of institutional office. The positions are explicit and the stratification is to an important degree "objective"—a matter of directly observable

---

[10] W. H. Form: "Toward an Occupational Social Psychology," *Journal of Social Psychology*, Vol. XXIV, First Half (August, 1946), p. 87.

privileges and responsibilities. At the other pole of organization, we have the local community, where the individual's station is determined by the judgments of a loosely defined aggregate of associates, acquaintances, and other local residents. Although the position of citizen "No. 1" may be unmistakably clear, he holds it by a diffuse cultural consensus; it is not explicit and carries no definite body of duties and privileges. One has to know the community attitudes to define the individual's position; whereas in the organized hierarchy, such knowledge is not necessary—a commanding general is a commanding general so long as he holds this position within the going organization, regardless of the diffuse valuations of soldiers and other citizens.

Thus the station of any individual may always be in part described by pointing to his *objective privileges*, or his *general prestige* in the total relevant community, or his *specific position within an organized group*. What, then, are the *criteria* by which individuals or groups are placed in any given position in a stratification system?

To begin with, we know that different cultures emphasize different criteria. In some societies at some periods we find a rigid inequalitarian system in which an individual's position is determined for life by *birth into a family of a particular category or grade*. The theoretical ideal type of such a caste society would exclude every consideration for placement save birth alone. Other cultures emphasize *possessions:* not birth, but the fact of wealth becomes primary in invidious social evaluation. Still other cultures may attribute high position to individuals on the basis of certain *personal qualities:* beauty, wit, physical strength, religious piety, possession by spirits, or whatnot. This kind of evaluation merges into that based on the criterion of achievement: if personal qualities designate what the person is considered to be, achievements identify what he does. The acts that are valued highly are very different in various cultures—the known range includes ascetic achievements (of monks, hermits, saints, etc.), military prowess, scientific work, commercial success, artistic accomplishments, and so on. Finally, there is considerable intercultural variation in the use of *authority* as a criterion of rank. Authority exists in all societies; that is, there is some form of recognized ("legitimate") right by which some individuals control the acts of others, even when the control may conflict with the immediate wishes of those subject to it. Again, however, the social evaluation of authority has a wide range, some societies make the exercise of authority the main criterion of general social rank, whereas others deprecate it. Authority shades off into the sheer exercise of nonlegitimized *power*, that is, the purely coercive control of others, without support by social consensus. Of course, authority often emerges from illegitimate seizure of power, and sheer power sometimes commands a grudging admiration and ambivalent prestige even in our own society.

Six classes of criteria of evaluation have now been outlined: [11]

1. Birth (or more broadly, membership in kinship unit)
2. Possessions (wealth and income)
3. Personal qualities
4. Personal achievement
5. Authority
6. Power

The nature of the differential valuation of individuals is clarified by the distinction drawn by Hiller between "intrinsic" and "extrinsic" valuations.[12] Perhaps this distinction comes out most clearly when authority is vested in formal organizational status. Here, the valuation of the *office* may diverge rather widely from the valuation of a *specific person occupying the office*. If the office carries great authority within a social complex itself receiving high social valuation, it must by that fact receive a measure of respect and prestige. This prestige tends to be transferred to the person occupying the status. The minister receives deference because of his institutional function; only gross failure or misconduct can prevent any individual in such a position from receiving at least a minimum of institutionalized deference. Similarly, respect is required for the symbols of legitimized authority, irrespective of the intrinsic

[11] This classification is taken from Parsons: "An Analytical Approach to the Theory of Social Stratification," pp. 848–9.

[12] E. T. Hiller: *Social Relations and Structures* (New York: 1947), pp. 191–215.

qualities of a particular officer. It may be said that there are "good" leader-follower relations when the followers respect both the office and the person occupying it. There is then an integration of the two types of valuation. Of the several bases of valuation outlined above, only personal qualities and achievements are intrinsic—and the latter only in so far as achievements are taken as indices of the "quality," "nature," or "character" of the person. The other main criteria of ranking—possessions, group membership, power, and authority—are extrinsic.

Social stratification typically focuses upon extrinsic criteria; for it is these that largely permit an extended scale of ranking. The intrinsic valuations appear more often as *prerequisites for consideration of the individual on the legitimate rank-order scale;* for instance, only individuals who are "persons" fall into the major ranking system. Others are in some sense "outside" the structure—slaves, foreigners, heathen, excommunicated, lumpenproletariat and the like. They are considered to belong to another social system, to be "outside the pale" or even in an entirely different category of being.[13] The distinction between intrinsic and extrinsic valuations is closely related to the distinction between esteem and prestige.[14] A good servant may be held in high esteem but be invested with very little prestige. The first is a valuation of his personal qualities or his performance of an accepted role; the second is a valuation of his functional position in the social system.

Intrinsic valuations tend to be equalitarian. For instance, the religious concept of the person as having an inviolable soul accountable only to God, a concept current in our culture, gives *everyone* *some* positive value. It establishes a floor below which invidious devaluation of the human individual cannot go. In contrast, by the criteria of extrinsic valuation there are persons and groups that are valueless, or of negative value.

We can show, in principle, with great precision the distribution of scarce values, the allocation of privileges, among the individuals or other social units within any given social system. It can be ex-

<hr>

[13] Cf. James West: *Plainville, U. S. A.* (New York: 1945), pp. 125–6, on the "people who live like animals."
[14] Davis: "A Conceptual Analysis of Stratification," p. 312.

pressed in objective, statistical terms once we know what the relevant privileges are. Groupings or strata derived from such measurements are not necessarily real social groups, however, but may represent simply the more or less arbitrary classification of the investigator. The distribution of privileges (the criterion of extrinsic evaluation) begins to take on full sociological meaning only when it is related to *prestige rankings, social-interaction groupings,* and *beliefs and values held in common.* We shall use the term "social class" to refer to an aggregate of individuals who occupy a broadly similar position in the scale of prestige. These rankings can then be analyzed according to their sources and supports in economic position and political power, and in terms of their relations to attitudes and social organization.

In approaching American society, we will have to locate its particular system of social classes with reference to three ideal types of stratification structures. The first, that of *caste,* is a system in which an individual's rank and its accompanying rights and obligations is *ascribed* [15] on the basis of birth into a particular group. In the theoretical, fully-developed system, birth alone determines the person's class; no change is possible because of personal qualities or achievements. In the second type, that of estates—a form approximated in some parts of Europe during feudal times—classes (nobles, clergy, and commoners, for instance) are rigid and transmission of position is largely hereditary. However, some limited upward mobility is permitted: the exceptionally gifted and energetic peasant lad can on occasion enter the priesthood or the military services and advance to high rank. There is likewise some restricted opportunity for interestate marriages, the prototype being the marriage of the commoner girl to a man of a higher estate. Finally, the third ideal type of stratification is the open-class system. Here the various strata are highly permeable; there is a great deal of rising and falling in the scale. At the theoretically conceivable extreme, "classes" would be merely those temporary and

[15] See Ralph Linton: *The Study of Man* (New York: 1936), pp. 115 ff., for the distinction between ascribed and achieved status. Hiller: *Social Relations and Structures,* has added a category of assumed status for those positions that are not "achieved" but are entered on a basis other than that of birth.

nominal aggregates of individuals who happened at any particular time to receive about the same evaluation. Birth into a particular family of a particular group would be formally irrelevant to the later class position of the individual. Obviously such a society is highly competitive. Individuals must compete for status on the basis of personal qualities and achievements.

3. The American Case

IN A caste or castelike society, the "upper" groups control the criteria for ranking and successfully impose their standards upon the whole society. To take an American example, in plantation areas of the Old South the dominant white upper classes defined not only their own position but that of "lower-class" whites and of the Negro population as well.[16] In a long-established castelike order, at least under the conditions of a stable agricultural society, a justifying ideology can come to be so widely accepted that even in the lower castes the standards of the dominant orders become the criteria of ranking. In an open-class society, on the other hand, there is no single accepted standard; each group or stratum tends to have its own perspective. Presumably those who in their own eyes are "upper-class" will always attempt to set the scale for the entire population, but in a highly mobile, competitive system there may be considerable and effective disagreement. Differently located strata will emphasize different criteria of ranking. Thus, in our own society the upwardly mobile "middle classes" tend to stress competitive occupational achievement and "respectability," whereas the newly arrived members of the upper strata emphasize wealth, and the established upper-upper groups give disproportionate weight to lineage ("purity") and to certain

---

[16] Wilbert E. Moore and Robin M. Williams: "Stratification in the Ante-Bellum South," *American Sociological Review*, Vol. VII, no. 3 (June, 1942). For evidence on the importance of the middle classes in that society, see Frank L. Owsley: *Plain Folk of the Old South* (Baton Rouge, La.: 1949).

symbols of secure status.[17] If a society is to function, of course, there must be some minimal consensus as to the criteria for the social distribution of rewards and for the assignation of prestige rankings. However, as the United States demonstrates, there is room for much variability and inconsistency in the criteria for determining class membership in a complex open-class society. By "American" ideals, *position should be based upon personal qualities and achievements*. With one important exception to be discussed later—that of discrimination against minority groups—it is held that our society is and *should be* one in which the individual is free to move into those positions in the society that he has earned by ability, skill, effort, and moral worth. He is supposed to rise or fall according to his own merits; his position is determined by what he is and does or can do *as an individual*. In its logically developed form this conception of the stratification process becomes an internally consistent scheme that satisfactorily explains and justifies the entire system. It runs as follows:

1. This is a society of equality of opportunity and free, competitive placement. ("Anyone who has it in him can get ahead.")
2. Hence, success is solely a matter of individual merit.
3. Hence, those who are at the top deserve to be there, and those at the bottom are there because of lack of talent or effort: it is "their own fault."
4. Thus the placement of individuals could not be otherwise without violating the value of individual achievement.

It takes no great acumen to see that actual equality of opportunity does not exist for a very great many individuals; nor is it difficult to show that inherited position, social "connections," and a variety of circumstances essentially irrelevant to strictly personal qualities and achievements help place individuals in the stratifica-

[17] These different perspectives and evaluations are more than "mere rationalization." Undoubtedly each grouping tries to establish a moral claim to esteem and prestige on the basis of the attributes it has in largest measure. Nevertheless, these variant perspectives prevent upper-class standards from dominating the system, that is, from "closing" it.

tion order. The more difficult and significant task is to go behind these rather obvious "discrepancies" and analyze the specific interplay of *different* institutional principles that operate in the stratification system.

OBJECTIVE STRATIFICATION

We may begin by briefly documenting the facts about stratification in the United States. We know that there are marked differentials in the distribution of scarce values. Forty-two per cent of the families in this country had an income of less than $1000 in 1935 and a select 3 per cent received $5000 or more; the great differences in total life-situation between the two groups can be readily visualized in terms of food, shelter, clothing, health, education, recreation, and general access to the comforts and amenities of life in our culture.[18]

This income stratification reflects an occupational structure in which roughly 47 per cent of workers are in unskilled and semi-skilled occupations, 12 per cent in skilled jobs, 17 per cent in clerical occupations, 7 per cent in professions, with the remainder of only 17 per cent made up of independent enterprisers, managers, owners, and officials.[19] The old middle classes of small businessmen, farmers, and free professionals are of decreasing importance in comparison with the new middle classes of salaried white-collar workers.

The role of differentials in wealth and income in our stratifica-

[18] And through these differentials, income is a primary determinant of generalized status; cf. Wilbert E. Moore: *Industrial Relations and the Social Order* (New York: 1947), pp. 483–4: "To a large degree the primary criterion of social status in our society is the economic worth of the individual. This is most clearly seen, of course, in the idea that the impersonal market rewards the efficiency and industry of the individual enterpriser. It is to be observed in unconscious caricature in the not uncommon remark that 'Businessman X must be worth close to $100,000.'" Reprinted by permission of The Macmillan Company.

[19] 1940 census data. Taken from the analysis of Alba M. Edwards: *Population: Comparative Occupation Statistics, 1870 to 1940* (Washington, D. C.: 1943), p. 187.

tion system is complex and varies greatly in different occupations
and communities. Wealth serves as the base for supporting a style
of life considered to symbolize class position, and people with
money attempt to buy the *symbols* thought to index high status.
The proverbial conspicuous consumption of the newly rich is
merely a salient instance of the purchased badges of rank.[20]
Wealth, furthermore, gives its possessor greater educational, occupational, and general cultural opportunity. In the race for
achievement, those who start without wealth have difficult hurdles
to clear before they can reach competitive equality with their more
favored rivals. In addition, wealth is very frequently interpreted
in our society as an index of achievement: he has money, therefore
he must be successful, and to be successful he must have achieved
something. For the primary status-giving positions throughout
most of our history have been in business, where the orientation to
profits has made achievement subject to the common measure of
money; and in our complex society, in which judgments of achievement have to span very diverse and specialized occupations, the
difficulty of finding a basis for comparisons leads to concentration
on some obvious and universal signs of status. Wealth, as the most
universal and easily recognized mark of occupational success, has
thus been a convenient symbol of achievement.

However, attempts to use wealth as the sole criterion of stratification set up powerful counterstrains. Much wealth is known to
have been acquired by morally disapproved means; much wealth is
inherited or acquired in other ways that can hardly be regarded as
"achievement." In a dynamic and violently oscillating economy,
there are such rapid changes in the income and wealth of large
numbers of individuals that widespread doubt is created as to the
correlation of wealth with achievement or personal qualities.
Finally, the occupational structure is so complex that income or
wealth clearly does not form a single scale for evaluation of movie
stars, business executives, ministers, athletes, university scientists,

[20] Thus Warner found that the highest proportionate expenditures for
automobiles and household maintenance occurred in the lower-upper class
among those families just on the margin of acceptance into the upper-upper
elite. *The Social Life of a Modern Community*, p. 299.

and so on indefinitely.[21] In some occupations, especially the salaried professions, it is not even supposed that income is a measure of the "worth" of a man's contributions; salary is supposed to be only token recognition and of a magnitude adequate to the style of life expected of a certain occupational status.

Nevertheless, both income or wealth and occupation are important criteria of status, and there is a very wide range in the distribution of objective privileges offered by both in the American population. Differences in these respects are closely related to a series of specific behavior-patterns that all together make up recognizably different, class-typed ways of living. To take only one example, the correlation of economic and occupational levels with participation in formally organized associations has been demonstrated in a large number of studies. For instance, Komarovsky found that in a sample of 2,223 adult residents of New York City, the percentage of persons belonging to formal associations was invariably larger the higher the occupational status.[22] Warner and associates reported that in "Yankee City" the percentage of persons who were members of some formal associations increased from only 22 in the lower-lower class to 64 in the upper-middle and 72 in the upper-upper class.[23] Even in the small town and rural areas, research has consistently shown different patterns of social participation among persons on different economic levels. The pattern is that participation in the family and in informal neighborhood relations makes up a larger part of all social participation for the poorer groups than it does for the wealthier. The upper economic groups are more likely to belong to segmental, special-interest associations.

There are other social effects of economic stratification in our society. In spite of the remarkable public-school system and provisions for economic assistance in securing college training, eco-

[21] For all these reasons, the notion that wealth and virtue are synonymous probably has lost some of its force in American culture. Nevertheless, there is still vitality in the older system of belief. See Moore: *Industrial Relations*, p. 487.

[22] Mirra Komarovsky: "The Voluntary Associations of Urban Dwellers," *American Sociological Review*, Vol. XI, no. 6 (December, 1946), pp. 686–98.

[23] *The Social Life of a Modern Community*, p. 329.

nomically "upper-class" persons can most easily secure an education. So far as the evidence goes, furthermore, it consistently shows that mortality and morbidity rates vary inversely with income. Sickness and health, death and life, are thus to an appreciable degree functions of economic position.

Objective evidence of stratification in the United States is to be found not only in the differences in occupation and income but also in the great differentials of authority and power. The growth of large centralized economic and political associations has meant the emergence of hierarchical organizations of sweeping power; in these structures it is possible for a few individuals to exercise quite comprehensive authority over large numbers of employees, union members, or citizens of the state. The military services, of course, provide the outstanding examples.

Finally, although the data are scanty and unsystematic, there are many converging indications that immunities and disabilities in the face of the law and penal system are correlated with caste and class position. Sutherland's studies of "white-collar crime" have shown that many business practices that are legally punishable offenses are either not detected or not severely dealt with when committed by middle- and upper-class persons.[24] Useem in his study of a small South Dakota town reports a tendency in the same direction.[25] Hollingshead shows how in a Midwestern town the system of discipline in the school is adjusted to favor the upper-class child.[26] Class discriminations in the administration of justice sometimes take the form of greater leniency in dealing with intra-group offenses of the lower classes or caste. As Myrdal has so well shown, this leniency results in lack of legal protection for the law-

---

[24] Edwin H. Sutherland: "White Collar Criminality," *American Sociological Review*, Vol. V, no. 1 (1940); "Crime and Business," *The Annals of the Academy of Political and Social Science*, Vol. 217 (1941); "Is 'White Collar Crime' Crime?", *American Sociological Review*, Vol. X, no. 2 (1945). See also, James S. Wallerstein and Clement J. Wyle: "Our Law-Abiding Law-Breakers," *Probation* (April, 1947).

[25] John Useem, Pierre Tangent, and Ruth Useem: "Stratification in a Prairie Town," *American Sociological Review*, Vol. VII, no. 3 (June, 1942), p. 341.

[26] August B. Hollingshead: *Elmtown's Youth* (New York: 1949), esp. chaps. 6 and 8.

abiding members of the lower stratum. On the other hand the lower-stratum individual who commits an offense against a member of the upper groups may be treated with unusual severity.[27]

In short, detailed study of stratification considered as a *distribution of objective privileges* clearly demonstrates the presence in American society of marked differentials in wealth and income and in social participation, authority and power, education, health, safety and legal protection. *This* kind of stratification, then, is a reality. Our next question is: To what extent do persons sharing similar objective positions have common attitudes and ideas and to what extent do those in dissimilar positions differ in their interests, beliefs, and values?

INTERSTRATA DIFFERENCES IN ATTITUDES

The broad answer to this question is that on a wide variety of political and economic issues and topics the culture orientations of individuals are closely associated with their occupational position and/or their income level, although the latter are not adequate to predict an exact pattern of ideology.[28] Whether or not one wishes to consider objectively defined income and occupational strata as "classes," it remains true that different aggregates of persons classified in these terms do show large differences in beliefs or attitudes.[29] The findings of one of the most comprehensive studies

[27] Gunnar Myrdal, with the assistance of Richard Sterner and Arnold Rose: *An American Dilemma* (New York: 1944), Vol. I, chaps. 24–7.

[28] Cf. this statement: "Occupation provides income, influences the location of residence, develops working habits, and makes associations and companionships."—Dewey Anderson and Percy E. Davidson: *Ballots and the Democratic Class Struggle* (Stanford, Calif.: 1943), p. 106. It is through the *similarity of circumstance* and through the *interaction* this occasions that both occupation and income level tend to evoke, and index similar cultural characteristics among persons of similar objective condition.

[29] Arthur Kornhauser has concluded that "Large and consistent differences do exist between income and occupational groups in their attitudes on a variety of broad social-political issues. . . ." See "Analysis of 'Class' Structure in Contemporary American Society—Psychological Bases of Class Divisions," in George W. Hartmann and Theodore Newcomb (eds.): *Industrial Conflict* (New York: 1939), p. 260.

of opinion data, analyzed by Centers, may be summarized in support of this contention. The main conclusions of this study included the following: [30]

1. *Characteristics of various strata:* Persons who identify themselves as "upper class" make up 3–4 per cent of the population; they think of the "upper stratum" as being composed largely of big business owners and executives and certain "higher" professional groups. Those persons who claim to be middle-class (some 40 per cent of the population) think of the middle class as made up principally of business and managerial occupations. The occupational groups most frequently identifying themselves as middle class were business owners and managers, professional persons, white collar workers, and farm owners and managers; however, substantial numbers of urban manual workers and farm tenants and laborers also claim to be middle class (rather than "working class"). Persons identifying with the middle class tended to say that the most important criterion of class membership, after occupation, is a person's attitudes—how he "believes and feels about certain things." Individuals who said that they themselves belonged to the working class defined the stratum mainly in terms of factory workers, laborers, farmers, service workers, and servants. Somewhat less than one half of those claiming working-class affiliation were office workers. The most important criterion for the working-class designation was the fact of "working for a living"—either at manual work or as an employee rather than a proprietor or free professional. Finally, the small proportion of the population identifying itself as lower class did so largely by the criterion of poverty.

2. *Socio-political attitudes:* In general, the more "conservative" opinions were held by persons from occupations popularly judged to be in the upper levels of an occupational hierarchy. The "higher" occupational groups were less likely than working-class people to approve strong labor unions and an exten-

[30] Summarized from Richard Centers: *The Psychology of Social Classes* (Princeton, N. J.: 1949), chap. 12, pp. 206–19.

sion of the role of government in economic affairs. Both "objective" occupational position and expressed class-affiliation worked in the same direction.

The general findings of this study have been supported and qualified by several other important investigations.

Kornhauser's summary of data from opinion surveys correctly points out that sharp cleavages between occupational groupings and income strata are evident on questions dealing with the distribution of wealth, the role of government in economic affairs, the place of labor unions, and with political affiliations and inclinations. At the same time, persons in the lower income levels "cling devotedly to the American belief in individual opportunity. They expect either themselves or their children to 'get ahead.' Thus important contrasts in class attitudes on deep-cutting questions of public policy exist side by side with rather general rejection by individuals of any feeling that they are permanent members of a 'class.' " [31] On questions presumed to index personal feelings of satisfaction or adjustment ("opportunity," "fairness," "liking your work," and the like), the proportion of "well-satisfied" responses is rather closely correlated with occupation and income. Expressions of discontent and frustration are increasingly frequent the lower the income and the occupational status; and persons at the higher-income levels who express personal dissatisfaction are far more likely than others of the same income to express political and economic views of a "liberal" or "radical" nature.

The data assembled in Kornhauser's work indicate that between the ideological extremes represented by the small group of wealthy and powerful individuals on the one hand and the disaffected among manual workers on the other, there is a large and inchoate aggregate of diverse groupings characterized by "moderate" attitudes.[32] The entire range of "classes" (that is, income and occupational levels) represents a continuous gradation of attitudes, with no sharply defined cleavages at any one point, and with great overlapping of opinions as between any two adjacent income

[31] Kornhauser: "Analysis of 'class' structure," p. 241.
[32] Ibid., pp. 260–2.

levels.[33] Middle-income groupings are heterogeneous in occupational composition and in attitudes; ideologically they constitute no definite class, but stand rather as a diffuse "cushion" between the wealthy top strata and the more militant sections of the wage-earning worker populations. The closest approach to a definable gap in political and economic attitudes occurs between the small segment of high-income people (roughly, the top 10 per cent) and the remainder of the population. At every income level, however, the connection between attitudes and objective economic position is attenuated and complicated by the influence of ethnic background, "racial" category, regional culture, religion, education, and a variety of other cultural and "personal" factors.

We may infer from the information reviewed thus far that:

1. There are large and consistent differences in "attitude" or "ideology" between persons differently circumstanced in income and occupation;
2. The attitudes of these various groupings nevertheless overlap, and a common value-system seems to extend quite widely through disparate economic levels.

These tentative conclusions are further supported by a study that analyzes a situation approaching the "crucial experiment" for the analysis of the relation between economic homogeneity and "class" attitudes. In 1938–9 Alfred Winslow Jones investigated attitudes toward corporate property rights among various occupational groups in Akron, Ohio.[34] One might expect class conflict in a one-industry city where there had been intense industrial conflict during the depression; but in fact there were important and pervasive middle-of-the-road attitudes towards corporate property that softened the differences in outlook between owners and workers. What Jones terms the "central morality" [35] of the com-

[33] Cf. Ibid., p. 261: "The class differences form a gradient rather than a series of steps."

[34] *Life, Liberty and Property* (Philadelphia: 1941), esp. pp. 318 ff.

[35] "The central morality is humanitarian and approves of acts in the interest of human welfare and alleviation of suffering even if they entail the infringement of corporate property. It approves of trade unions, and would like to see a well-led, unified, strong labor movement, but one that refrained from violence." Ibid., p. 339.

munity permeates the attitudes of workers and helps to shape the actions of their unions; a compromise ideology acknowledging humanitarian values and also admitting the legitimacy of many claims made for "property rights" is widely shared by persons of diverse occupations and economic levels.

VARIATIONS IN STRATIFICATION WITHIN THE SOCIETY

Although available studies of "class ideology" are subject to important criticisms because of theoretical and methodological gaps or deficiencies, there can be little doubt that there is a substantial correlation between *occupation* and *expressed class affiliation*, and between each of these and a pattern of *opinions on social, economic, and political issues.*

Although the existence of these differences in outlook among various occupational groupings is thus confirmed by a considerable body of consistent data, it must be stressed at the same time that the strata in question are in large measure statistical aggregates rather than *crystallized social groups.* Occupational "classes" constitute a rather irregular continuum rather than a series of clearly separate categories of stratification. Both the complexity of the income and occupational distributions and the relatively great amount of interstrata mobility, together with other factors to be examined later, work in the direction of blurring rigid distinctions. Although there are definite and remarkably stable stereotypes concerning the social ranking of occupations and groups of occupations,[36] the net result is that the precise rank of any particular individual is frequently ambiguous and that the entire stratification system is differently perceived by persons located at various positions within it.[37]

[36] Cf. North and Hatt: "Jobs and Occupations"; Maethel E. Deeg and Donald G. Paterson: "Changes in Social Status of Occupations," *Occupations*, Vol. XXV, no. 4 (January, 1947). The latter study repeated a test used by Counts in 1925; ratings assigned to broad occupational groups by a sample of 475 students in 1946 were not very different from those reported twenty years earlier.

[37] Cf. the suggestive diagrams and discussion in West: *Plainville, U. S. A.*, pp. 116–33.

As Sorokin has shown in a trenchant criticism of existing definitions of "social class," it is necessary to remind ourselves continually that a nominal aggregate of persons occupying similar occupational positions, or receiving similar incomes, or enjoying
equivalent prestige is not necessarily a unitary group, nor a self-
conscious stratum.[38] Recognizing this reservation, however, it is
still possible to show that occupational position carries with it a
characteristic economic position: for example, all unskilled wage
workers face the problems presented by relatively low income, lack
of capital, and the necessity of earning a living from the sale of
their labor in an uncertain market. Over a period of time, such
similar objective conditions tend to create—slowly or rapidly—
certain broad similarities in culture.[39]

This generalization needs to be translated into specific facts
concerning the American scene. Fortunately, the findings of several
intensive community studies are available as a check against the
data from extensive surveys. Monograph after monograph has
shown that in American communities: (1) income and occupational
strata consistently differ in behavior and attitudes; (2) different
occupational positions are given definite social evaluations; (3) consciousness of stratification is highly variable, but is universally
important.

It would be fruitless to review all the specific studies of named
and anonymous communities that have contributed to this portrait, but even a token roll-call will suggest the richness of the data:
"Middletown," [40] "Yankee City," [41] "Plainville," [42] "Elmtown," [43]

[38] Pitirim A. Sorokin: *Society, Culture, and Personality* (New York: 1947),
chap. 14, pp. 256–75.

[39] Cf. Pitirim A. Sorokin: *Social Mobility* (New York: 1927); Cecil C.
North: *Social Differentiation* (Chapel Hill, N. C.: 1926); H. C. Lehmann and
P. A. Witty: "Further Study of the Social Status of Occupations," *Journal of
Educational Sociology*, Vol. V (1931).

[40] Robert S. and Helen M. Lynd: *Middletown, A Study in Contemporary
American Culture* (New York: 1929); *Middletown in Transition* (New York:
1937).

[41] W. Lloyd Warner and Leo Srole: *The Social Systems of American Ethnic
Groups* (New Haven, Conn.: 1946); Warner and Lunt: *The Social Life of a
Modern Community*.

[42] West: *Plainville, U. S. A.*

[43] Hollingshead: *Elmtown's Youth.*

Akron,[44] Burlington (Vermont) [45] "Southerntown," [46] "Prairie-
town," [47] "Jonesville," [48] the monographs of the Division of Farm
Population and Rural Welfare,[49] the "middle-sized city" studied by
Mills,[50] Old and Rural counties in the Deep South,[51] Greenbelt
(Maryland).[52]

As such studies have cumulated, their findings have supported
and given concrete content to the further judgment that the nature
of the stratification system varies greatly from one part of the
United States to another and takes on special colorations in different
types of communities. The range of "objective" stratification
(income, power etc.) is certainly very much greater in the large
urban centers than in the smaller towns and rural areas; [53] it is
probable that cleavages in belief and values are likewise greater in
the larger centers, although precise comparisons on this point
cannot be made from the available research evidence. In the smaller
communities and in areas of static or declining economic opportunity, especially in the older settled regions of the Northeast and
South, highly developed local systems of ranking have become
established; and under these conditions relatively heavy weight is
given to lineal principles—to membership in the "right family," to
inherited wealth and position, to long residence in the community

[44] Jones: *Life, Liberty, and Property.*

[45] Elin L. Anderson: *We Americans: A Study of Cleavage in an American
City* (Cambridge, Mass.: 1937).

[46] John Dollard: *Caste and Class in a Southern Town* (New York: 1937)
(2nd ed., 1949).

[47] Useem, Tangent, and Useem: "Stratification in a Prairie Town."

[48] W. Lloyd Warner and Associates: *Democracy in Jonesville* (New York:
1949).

[49] Published as Rural Life Studies Nos. 1–6. The communities analyzed
were: El Cerrito, N. M.; Sublette, Kansas; Irwin, Iowa; the Old Order Amish
of Lancaster County, Pa.; Landaff, N. H.; and Harmony, Ga.

[50] C. Wright Mills: "The Middle Classes in Middle-Sized Cities," *American Sociological Review*, Vol. XI, no. 5 (October, 1946), pp. 520–9.

[51] Allison Davis, B. B. Gardner, and M. R. Gardner: *Deep South* (Chicago,
1941).

[52] W. H. Form: "Status Stratification in a Planned Community," *American Sociological Review*, Vol. X, no. 5 (October, 1945), pp. 605–13.

[53] See for example, the compilation and interpretation of data in Pitirim
A. Sorokin, Carle C. Zimmerman, and Charles J. Galpin: *A Systematic Source
Book in Rural Sociology* (Minneapolis: 1930), Vol. I, pp. 213–30, 362–96.

and to such symbols of status as manners, education, and place of residence.[54] These economically static areas are typically areas of heavy emigration in a society characterized by long-run expansion and movement. In so far as they are, the local stratification system tends to be stabilized by the departure of youths who are ambitious beyond the scope of their opportunities in the area, or who for various reasons do not find it easy to accept the rigidity of the local system. To the degree that local business and job opportunities become "appropriated" by specific families and cliques there develops a continuing structure of control by which the dominant strata, utilizing economic and political mechanisms (including local government and education), are able to perpetuate existing stratification differentials. With the passage of time, distinctive behavior patterns and social perspectives come to characterize different strata, and the more privileged portions of the community build ideologies buttressing this quasi-estate system.[55]

Thus Useem and associates found in a Midwestern town of 3500 population that the "elite" was marked off from the "Bottoms" by clear-cut differences in the total manner of living. Persons in the locally recognized upper strata, as compared with the persons from the levels of least prestige were: (1) more mobile, and engaged in a wider range of social interaction; (2) more "secularized," in a variety of ways; (3) less likely to exchange aid and advice among families; (4) less likely to make the family the center of their attention and social participation; (5) more likely to attribute high rank to personal excellence and to give quasi-biological explanations for the existence of low-status groupings. The detailed articulation of such a rigid local stratification structure is likely to be most marked in long-settled communities or regions that combine a static economy and emigration with considerable objective differentials in wealth and power. Other conditions being the same, the sharpness of divisions between strata or classes tends to be

[54] Florence Rockwood Kluckhohn: "Dominant and Substitute Profiles of Cultural Orientations: Their Significance for the Analysis of Social Stratification," *Social Forces*, Vol. XXVIII, no. 4 (May, 1950), pp. 376–93.

[55] All of these developments are illustrated in the descriptions of "Yankee City," "Prairietown," "Elmtown," "Jonesville," "Plainville," and Burlington in the studies cited above.

the greater the longer individuals remain in a given position and the less interstratum mobility there is.[56]

In the large centers of industry and commerce, finely-meshed stabilization of a ranking system is difficult to maintain, especially when economic opportunities are increasing and thereby attracting an influx of persons from other areas. Industrial or commercial expansion opens up the possibility of rapid occupational shifts, and geographic mobility tends to cut through the rigidifying factors of kinship affiliations and other established group memberships and identifications. The very fact that economic relations in the larger centers tend to become impersonal and narrowly specific in nature frees the individual from the lineal transmission of established status and permits him to compete for placement. At the same time, the urban center in our culture fosters great inequalities of wealth and power. Thus conditions are created favorable to lay stress upon individual achievement [57] and upon relatively impersonal indices such as wealth, conspicuous consumption, power, and office (especially offices of authority). In so far as there is rapid social change and marked oscillations in economic conditions, the tendency to freeze clear-cut lines of stratification is continually being countered; and to the degree that economic positions of individuals change rapidly, the ranking system exhibits a vague and shifting character. Rank tends to be conceived of in more abstract and categorical terms than it is in the smaller communities: persons become "working class" or "business class" rather than members of the "Smith family" or "the Tops." Among the studies already cited, those reported by the Lynds and A. W. Jones have depicted in particular the categorical cleavages that grow out of the occupational structure of industrial cities.

In the past the high vertical mobility of American society has prevented the formation of well-defined social classes. We have

[56] Cf. Sorokin: *Society, Culture, and Personality*, p. 274. A good example of how criteria of stratification may shift as a community becomes stabilized is supplied in Form: "Status Stratification in a Planned Community."

[57] Cf. Kluckhohn: "Dominant and Substitute Profiles of Cultural Orientations," p. 29: "The dominant cultural profile of the United States . . . can be actualized in concrete behavior only where there is expansion and movement of both people and economic production."

now seen that the society is nevertheless stratified in terms of the objective distribution of privileges and have reviewed some data suggesting that attitudes, values, and other cultural characteristics are appreciably related to objective position. We may now raise three additional questions for more systematic attention:

1. To what extent is there continuity in the objective positions of individuals—to what extend is there intergeneration transmission of position?
2. To what extent does "class consciousness" exist? What awareness is there of social stratification?
3. To what extent do various strata in our society constitute solidary social classes?

STABILITY OF OCCUPATIONAL POSITION: TRANSMISSION OF POSITION

In seeking an answer to the first question, we must once again resort to data on occupations as primary evidence. Analysis of intergeneration transmission of occupation in the United States has to reckon first of all with the change from an agrarian and trading society to a mass-production industrial economy, especially since about 1870. The proportion of the gainfully employed male workers who were working in agriculture and allied extractive occupations declined from slightly over 50 per cent in 1870 to less than 20 per cent in 1940.[58] The proportion of workers employed in manufacturing and mechanical industries remained practically constant over this interval, whereas the proportions employed in trade, public service, clerical, and professional pursuits increased greatly; for instance, of the total population gainfully employed in 1870 approximately 4 per cent were in trade, but by 1940 the figure had risen to 17 per cent. These drastic shifts from the primary extractive and processing occupations to employment in secondary and tertiary industries signify that a high degree of precise occupational continuity from father to sons is not to be expected. Of macroscopic

[58] See H. Dewey Anderson and Percy E. Davidson: *Occupational Trends in the United States* (Stanford, Calif.: 1940).

proportions, furthermore, has been the attrition of the "old middle classes" of independent farmers and small manufacturers and the emergence of an as yet amorphous congeries of "new middle classes" composed of clerical, technical, managerial, and professional groups. These new middle classes are diverse in social origins, in specific economic interests, in political inclinations, and in general style of life. Since the occupations represented in the new middle classes *are* new, the personnel has necessarily been drawn in large part from other, older employments.

For the past three centuries or so, the long-run trend in Western countries undergoing industrialization and urbanization has been apparently toward a decrease in hereditary transmission of occupation,[59] at least up until very recent years. The increase in urban at the expense of rural employments, the incessant subdivision and specialization of jobs, rapid technological changes, and the rise and decline of industries have all contributed. The entire economic system of our own society has been continually reshaped in quite drastic ways over the comparatively brief period of national existence. In consequence, every major occupational category contains recruits from a variety of other occupational backgrounds. The United States is thus very far indeed from the model of a pure caste system in which the occupations of the fathers are, for good or ill, visited upon the sons for generation after generation. Nevertheless, our society is at the same time far from the opposite pole of zero occupational transmission. We must locate it between these two extremes.

A comprehensive review of those studies of occupational transmission that were available in the late 1920's, indicated that "in the majority of cases the sons enter the occupation of the father in a greater proportion than any other one; . . . each of the occupations is recruited principally from the sons of the fathers who have such an occupation." [60] This same review showed, furthermore, that occupational shifts typically do not represent sudden jumps from occupations very low to those very high in income or

---

[59] See the summary and evaluation of evidence in Sorokin: *Social Mobility*, pp. 421–4.
[60] Ibid., p. 438.

prestige, or vice versa; shifts are rather to roughly adjacent occupations. Except for periods of mass social upheaval, vertical occupational movement largely occurs step by step—unskilled to skilled laborer, clerk to manager and so forth—rather than by the spectacular ascent of the Horatio Alger myth or of the latter-day Hollywood success story.[61]

Some examples from monographic studies will help us to visualize in concrete terms the stability of occupational placement.[62] In the study of "Central City," [63] it was found that nearly three fourths of the small businessmen came from the upper half of the occupational-income scale, and no free professionals or big businessmen were derived from backgrounds of low-income white-collar or wage-worker occupations. Of the higher white-collar category 61 per cent derived from the upper half of the income hierarchy; of the lower white-collar grouping, 49 percent were of upper-half extraction. In terms of job histories, both the stratum of small businessmen and of lower white-collar workers show extensive upward mobility: only 1 in 5 of the small businessmen were in an occupational-income level so high at the time of marriage; two thirds of foremen were wage-workers at marriage. On the other hand, professional workers were overwhelming in that category by the time they married. The same is true at the bottom of the income-occupation scale; about 90 per cent of all categories of labor were wage-workers at marriage. In Mills' words: "There is rigidity at the

[61] Cf. Leo C. Rosten: *Hollywood* (New York: 1941): "One reason for Hollywood's stars becoming national idols is that they represent a new type of hero in American experience. Hollywood's children of fortune are not the thrifty newsboys of the Horatio Alger stereotype—honest, diligent, pure of heart; here, instead, are mortals known to be spendthrift and Bohemian. . . . They represent a new type of folk-hero in a society whose ethos rests upon hard work and virtuous deportment" (pp. 12–13). And again: "Hollywood means Luck" (p. 15). Reprinted by permission of Harcourt, Brace and Company, Inc.

[62] These studies are few, scattered, and difficult to compare, but their findings can be checked to some degree against census data and against the cumulative picture derived from more general historical and sociological studies. The net result may seem in some respects to resemble an incomplete jig-saw puzzle, but we can only hope that early research will fill in the most serious gaps in available information. Cf. Sorokin's remarks (in 1927) in *Social Mobility*, p. 414.

[63] Mills: "The Middle Classes in Middle-Sized Cities."

bottom and at the top—except among small businessmen who, relative to comparable income groups, have done a great deal of moving up the line." [64] Findings consistent with Mills' conclusions have been reported by several other local studies. In a study of Greenbelt, Maryland, for example, it was found that 71 per cent of manual workers had been engaged in manual labor as their first job and 82 per cent of persons in white-collar occupations had started as white-collar workers.[65]

Among the recent studies a significant fragment of data comes from the research carried out by Anderson and Davidson in San Jose, California during 1933–4.[66] These investigators studied 1,242 male workers constituting a sample of 7 per cent of the city's gainfully employed. Their findings suggest that, for the particular population studied, *specific* changes of occupation by an individual worker and specific shifts in occupation as between father and son, may actually have increased during the last generation, as a result of increased occupational specialization, technical innovation, and rapid shifts in job and business opportunities. On the other hand, the general socio-economic level of the person's occupation may have remained constant or have decreased. The most striking change in occupational distribution as between fathers and their sons is a drastic decrease in the proportion of "proprietors," matched by increases especially in professional, clerical, and semi-skilled categories. Census data reveal a similar situation for the nation as a whole, although the information available is not precise enough to permit the isolation of anything like completely homogeneous occupational groupings.[67]

The stability of strata in modern society is profoundly affected by the educational opportunities available to youth. Our society has succeeded to an extraordinary degree in approaching formal equality of opportunity for elementary and high school training, but the higher reaches of the educational ladder are less equally ac-

[64] Ibid., p. 523.

[65] Form: "Status Stratification in a Planned Community."

[66] Percy E. Davidson and H. Dewey Anderson: *Occupational Mobility in an American Community* (Stanford, Calif.: 1937).

[67] See the comparison of data for 1910 and 1940 in Edwards: *Population: Comparative Occupation Statistics, 1870 to 1940.*

cessible. There is evidence, gathered, however, before the great postwar expansion in college enrollment, that *even among boys of the same high I. Q. level,* fathers' occupational position is highly correlated with college attendance.[68] Since a college education is probably increasingly a prerequisite for entrance into middle or upper strata occupations, it is a key influence upon the fixity or mobility possible in the stratification system. For, as Sibley has aptly noted: "Not universal equality of status but a high rate of vertical mobility has been the most important demographic basis of this nation's tradition of classlessness." [69]

To what extent are the upper occupational strata self-perpetuating and closed groupings tending toward a real social class of "aristocratic" inclination? Clearly aristocracy of the European pattern was very early destroyed by the conditions of American life, and no important hereditary upper "estate" survived the fluidity of eighteenth and nineteenth century society in the United States. Out of the reshuffling and turmoil of our dynamic economy, however, there have emerged new strata possessing concentrated control of wealth and power.[70] The social origins of the top occupational strata obviously are a matter of prime significance to an appraisal of the extent of "closure" of the stratification system.

Taussig and Joslyn showed from a sampling of business leaders just prior to the depression of the 1930's that higher business positions are occupied by persons drawn mainly from business and professional strata rather than from the ranks of farmers and laborers. Of the 8,749 persons responding to a questionnaire sent to 15,101 directors, officers, partners, or owners of business organizations judged to be of major importance in the national economy, 50 per cent were sons of major executives or owners of businesses. Yet businessmen constituted only 7.4 per cent of the married males in 1880.[71] Furthermore, almost one half of the sons of large

[68] Elbridge Sibley: "Some Demographic Clues to Stratification," *American Sociological Review,* Vol. VII, no. 3 (June, 1942), pp. 322–30.

[69] Ibid., p. 322.

[70] See Anderson and Davidson: *Ballots and the Democratic Class Struggle,* p. 230.

[71] F. W. Taussig and C. S. Joslyn: *American Business Leaders* (New York: 1932), p. 88.

owners and major executives were connected with the father's business, and of those probably three fourths possessed substantial control of the business.[72] They also found that many of the fathers had engaged in the same occupation as the paternal grandfather. The greatest continuity was found among major executives and large owners; fathers of important businessmen were less likely to have followed their own fathers into farming, clerking or selling, or positions as minor executives.[73] These findings for a loosely defined top stratum of businessmen are consistent with Sorokin's results from a study of American millionaires and multimillionaires.[74] Sorokin showed an even greater closure of occupational origins among the very wealthy than was found in the less affluent business leaders.

STRATUM SOLIDARITY: PATTERNS OF INTERACTION

The materials so far reviewed certainly show that American society is marked by a wide range of objective stratification and of prestige rankings. Stratification is not a clear, unitary system, however, but is rather a loosely articulated series of ranking systems, varying from one sector of the society to another and changing through time. Vertical mobility is still great, blurring rigid class distinctions and diversifying and shifting the patterns of ranking. Nevertheless, pervasive forces are working in the direction of stabilizing objective privileges, creating ascribed statuses and hereditary positions, stabilizing class-typed values and beliefs, and separating various strata from one another by differences of culture and by closure of social interaction. We must therefore appraise the extent to which objective strata and prestige categories constitute real social groups rather than arbitrary statistical ag-

[72] See Ibid., pp. 112 ff.

[73] Ibid., p. 139. It is to be noted that since these data concern the ancestors of present business leaders, a high degree of occupational transmission of the lower positions could not occur—only continuity or upward mobility is to be expected in the nature of the data.

[74] Pitirim A. Sorokin: "American Millionaires and Multi-Millionaires," *Social Forces* (May, 1925), pp. 627–40.

gregates or points on a continuous scale. Are there any clearly
discernible "breaks" in the structure of stratification that mark
off one "class" from another?

The social separateness or solidarity of groups can be provision-
ally tested by discovering the extent to which their members
associate intimately or intermarry. Visiting together and eating
together are universal symbols of solidarity and usually imply
approximate equality of status, at least in the immediate social
context. Some American students of stratification have even used
intimate social interaction as a criterion for identifying social
classes; although this procedure is inadequate, such interaction
still serves as one important index of stratum solidarity. If persons
of like economic circumstances associate among themselves, interact frequently, intermarry—and do not interact frequently on an
intimate basis with persons of a different economic level or occupational grouping—everything we know about human behavior
tells us that over a period of time these persons will become increasingly bound together by cultural consensus, by awareness of
common interests, by interpersonal attachments and understandings, and by an increasingly shared total pattern or style of living.
The development of a web of social relations within a stratum of
like-circumstanced people is accordingly one of the most significant
signs of the emergence of true status groupings from what may
formerly have been diffuse prestige strata, occupational categories,
or simple aggregates of separate individuals and groups possessing
the same share of the scarce values of the society.

The formal associations of American communities, of course,
often cross-cut a wide range of strata—as Warner, for example,
has shown in "Yankee City." Formal organizations of a community-wide nature serve to link together in the prosecution of common purposes very diverse segments of the community and to this
extent militate against the separation of strata and the cleavage
of the community into disparate status groupings. On the other
hand, less impersonal, less segmental, and less functionally specific
social relations are likely to reveal the presence of prestige distinctions and segregated social interaction.

For the time being we will leave aside the very sharp insulation of ethnic and "racial" groupings that characterizes American social structure. Although ethnic, racial, and religious distinctions are obviously related closely to stratification and social class, the two phenomena are different.[75] The former are of importance to us here only in so far as they blur potential class solidarity. The diversity of racial stocks, ethnic categories, and religious affiliations in the United States quite obviously hinders the development of unitary class groupings: every separation or distinction on these grounds throws together persons of dissimilar objective position and/or prestige and divides groups having similar economic and political interests and characteristics. The result is a *segmentation* of potentially solidary classes, simultaneously favored by other factors such as the relative weakness of kinship structures, the complexity of the occupational system, the geographic dispersion of the society, and the varying incidence of social privileges (for instance, legal equality versus great economic inequalities). In short, the role of religion and nationality provides a specific illustration of the general fact that a pluralistic society does not favor the crystallization of clear-cut, unitary classes. Thus, as Sorokin has indicated, "at the end of the nineteenth century and the beginning of the twentieth, there was no American 'aristocracy of the aristocracies.' . . . Its [America's] aristocracy was a composite, mosaic aristocracy. . . ." [76]

In the very top ranks, however, a small segment of very wealthy, powerful, or otherwise important individuals and families do form "an informal but real multibonded upper stratum. . . ." [77] With the consolidation of wealth and power into certain hereditary "dynasties," common association, intermarriage, and awareness of class interests tend to consolidate a true upper estate.[78] Even in relatively small cities and local communities, this interweaving of

[75] Ethnic and racial factors help fix the ranking of individuals; class distinctions stratify ethnic groupings internally. But individuals may belong to the same stratum and be divided by ethnic or racial lines, and stratification occurs where no ethnic or racial distinctions exist. The two systems thus crisscross while remaining analytically separate.

[76] Sorokin: *Society, Culture, and Personality*, pp. 302–3.

[77] Ibid., p. 293.

[78] Cf. Ferdinand Lundberg: *America's 60 Families* (New York: 1937).

multiple ties among upper economic strata has been well-documented.[79]

In Kaufman's study of a small rural community, the heads of the 455 family units were ranked by local raters into prestige classes on the basis of the "standing," "respect," or "reputation" of these families in the community, and the extent of intimate association among these families was then ascertained. When each mutual visiting relationship was defined as a bond between families, over three fourths of the bonds had a range of one half a prestige class or less.[80] The summary finding was that "prestige class was related to informal association in two ways. First, the number of associates that an individual had was correlated with his prestige rank. Second, the intimate associates of a community member were very likely to have a prestige rank the same as, or similar to, his own. This latter finding lends support to the hypothesis that the smallest class unit is the friendship group or clique." [81] Membership and leadership in formal organizations was also closely related to prestige class, which was, in turn, more closely correlated with informal and formal social participation than was either ethnic membership or place of residence.[82]

West's study of "Plainville" observed that stratification could be most clearly discerned in intimate visiting and "social" activities. In the more impersonal and restricted interactions outside the context of family and clique, the associations of male groups freely crossed lines of stratification.[83] On the other hand, churches, clubs, and visiting cliques were definitely status-bounded units, composed of persons of the same prestige class.[84]

[79] Cf. the community studies previously cited.

[80] Harold F. Kaufman: "Prestige Classes in a New York Rural Community," *Memoir 260*, Cornell University Agricultural Experiment Station (March; 1944), p. 14.

[81] Ibid., p. 15.

[82] Ibid., p. 42.

[83] *Plainville, U. S. A.*, p. 198.

[84] Ibid., p. 134. It should be kept in mind that the locale of this study is a village (275 population) and its rural hinterland, and that out-migration of young people is heavy. (Cf. p. 24: "The outside world absorbs about half of all who are born in and around Plainville.") See also Hollingshead: *Elmtown's Youth.*

In both of the studies just reviewed, the identification of prestige classes on the basis of ratings assigned by local informants probably results in accenting the amount of class-bounded interaction. Nevertheless, the data still show that relatively intimate types of social interaction tend to be closely bounded by the lines of local prestige classes.

Studies of the marriage patterns in a number of American communities indicate similar class boundaries.[85] Mills in his study of a medium-sized city shows that it is most usual that marriages are made between stratum equals, but that enough cross-stratum marriages occur to prevent "social closure" of income-occupation strata, at least at the broad intermediate levels of the hierarchy. Among small businessmen slightly more than one half had married women whose fathers were in the upper half of the income-occupation distribution, and 40 per cent had married the daughters of wage workers. In the higher white-collar occupations, about one half of the men studied had married into families in the upper half of the hierarchy. Among clerks about the same situation prevailed; among foremen ("lower white collar") there was more intermarriage with daughters of wage earners, but 27 per cent had married daughters of small businessmen—about the same percentage as among clerks, minor managerial, and salaried professions. Other studies have made similar findings.[86]

Kingsley Davis, in summarizing evidence on class endogamy in the United States, has concluded that "social background and the social limits to competition mean that most Americans marry

[85] Mills: "The Middle Classes in Middle-Sized Cities," pp. 523, 526.
[86] M. R. Davie and Ruby Jo Reeves: "Propinquity of Residence Before Marriage," *American Journal of Sociology*, Vol. XLIV, no. 4 (January, 1939), pp. 510–25; J. H. S. Bossard: "Residential Propinquity as a Factor in Marriage Selection," *American Journal of Sociology*, Vol. XXXVIII, no. 2 (September, 1932), pp. 219–24; D. M. Marvin: "Occupational Propinquity as a Factor in Marriage Selection," *Publications of American Statistical Association* (1918); T. C. Hunt: "Occupational Status and Marriage Selection," *American Sociological Review*, Vol. V, no. 4 (August, 1940), pp. 495–504; R. M. Williams: "Rural Youth in North Carolina," *Bulletin No. 324*, North Carolina Agricultural Experiment Station (June, 1939); Milton Barron: *People Who Intermarry* (Syracuse, N. Y.: 1946), pp. 292–3.

within their own social class." [87] The exact proportion of marriages
that are class-bounded depends, of course, upon how one defines the
limits of "class"; however, the general tendency for like to marry
like—economically, occupationally, and culturally—is well established. Since marriages create families and children initially absorb
the culture of their parents, and since the *initial* status of the child
must be that of his parents, class endogamy necessarily generates
forces tending toward the emergence of recognizable status groupings from aggregates of objectively like-circumstanced persons.
It is in this way that the apparently discrete facts of occupation,
income, residence, visiting, intermarriage, and child training are
woven into the pattern from which definite status groupings can
emerge. That the crystallization of such social "estates" in the
United States is far from complete is simply testimony to the dynamic nature of an open-class structure that still, to some extent,
does not follow the line of least resistance.

"CLASS CONSCIOUSNESS" AND AWARENESS OF STRATI-
FICATION

To what extent is there awareness of classes and class membership in contemporary American society? To what extent has this
awareness developed into "class consciousness" in the Marxian
sense? How does consciousness of stratification vary among the
various classes, strata, and other segments of the society? What are
the more important factors that accentuate or de-emphasize
awareness of class? Questions of this order are of prime significance
for understanding the possible implications of objective social
differentiation. There is no warrant for assuming in advance that
objective stratification automatically and inevitably leads to a
particular state of class consciousness. Possibly the fairly widespread reluctance in American society to recognize or admit that
there are social classes checks the crystallization of invidious
distinctions. For lack of awareness of class, or resistance to such

[87] Kingsley Davis, Harry C. Bredemeier, and Marion J. Levy, Jr. (eds.):
Modern American Society (New York: 1948), p. 611.

awareness, means that in ordinary person-to-person social inter-action the symbols of prestige are not given maximum stress; there is instead a certain pressure toward informality and "democratic manners." The minimal use of honorific titles, for example, con-trasts with the meticulous use of them in certain European cultures; the German use of the husband's title in addressing a married woman ("Frau *Doktor* Schmidt") typically impresses Americans as being pretentious or absurd. Great men are expected to be simple and "folksy" in their personal dealings. In relations be-tween persons of unequal position, ritual signs of deference are often resisted by those of "lower" position, who tend to take pride in rejecting others' claims to symbols of superiority. In particular, there is special resistance to privileges and demands for deference based solely upon formal position or rank rather than upon dem-onstrated personal qualities and achievements.

One of the most comprehensive compilations of systematic evidence on these points has come to us from studies of American soldiers in World War II. Extensive research demonstrated that soldiers wanted privileges to be "earned" rather than be categorical, and that the rigidity of military deference-requirements was probably a major cause of the resentments of enlisted personnel toward officers and toward the system of military rank.[88]

Civilian society in America is not a classless system. . . . But, at least within white civilian American society, there is no such yawning social chasm as that separating enlisted men and officers in the Army. Civilians might complain that they can-not afford the Waldorf-Astoria or abstain from going there because they would feel uncomfortable about their table man-ners, but they have the *right* to go there, whereas enlisted men did not have the right to venture into relatively commodious establishments reserved for officers only. And the officers' superior status was openly asserted and had to be continuously acknowledged by a host of acts symbolic of deference—such as saluting and the use of "Sir." The nearest analogy in civilian life would be that of the social relations of whites and Negroes,

[88] For the detailed findings see Samuel A. Stouffer et al.: *The American Soldier* (Princeton, N. J.: 1949), Vol. I, chaps. 2 and 8; Vol. II, chaps. 3 and 6.

especially in the South—witness the often used phrase "caste system" to describe the Army.[89]

The military service in wartime elicited a very marked and widespread consciousness of differential ranking; the change from civilian position was usually abrupt, ranks were conspicuously symbolized, differences in privilege were explicit and universally known, frequent promotions emphasized tantalizing rewards for the able or fortunate. Military doctrines often clashed with ideologies of democracy and equality. There was—officially—little flexibility in the patterns of authority and deference, but in practice the influence of the wider culture softened the inequalities of the hierarchical system. Indeed, the strength of the modifying tradition was dramatically symbolized when an official War Department board (headed by General James Doolittle) made this statement: "Americans look with disfavor upon any system which grants unearned privileges to a particular class of individuals and find distasteful any tendency to make arbitrary social distinctions between two parts of the Army." [90]

In the wider civilian society of the United States, consciousness of class differences is minimized by: (1) the tendency in our culture not to give clear recognition to invidious distinctions; (2) the rather marked diffusion of equalitarian social manners through a wide range of occupations, income levels, and positions of authority; (3) the wide accessibility of such commonplace symbols of "respectable" position as automobiles, the less costly versions of fashionable clothing, or even the occasional opportunity to attend commercial amusements carrying prestige; (4) the many legal or political rights that are nominally universal: the franchise, the right to hold public office, the equal responsibility for military service and jury duty, the right to a public school education and the accessibility of college training, the availability of a wide variety of public services open to all citizens.[91] Finally (5), there is per-

[89] Samuel A. Stouffer et al.: *The American Soldier* (Princeton, N. J.: Princeton University Press, 1949), Vol. I, p. 56.

[90] Cited in Ibid., Vol. I, p. 379.

[91] As always, subject to the exceptions still manifested in racial or ethnic discrimination.

sistent dissemination of the ideology of equal opportunity and a classless society.

Active consciousness of a definitely stratified order is further checked by: (6) relatively high social mobility—both horizontal and vertical—and the consequent fluidity of strata; (7) the complexity of the occupational structure; (8) the crisscrossing of diverse criteria and symbols of position, such as income, residence, religion, ethnic background, education, family prestige, organizational affiliations, manners, and so on.

Even a brief consideration of the causes contributing to awareness or lack of awareness of stratification shows that several quite different problems arise in considering the psychological reactions to the objective structure of stratification. First of all to what extent do Americans *recognize differences* of income, wealth, safety, authority and power? Secondly, what is the extent and kind of *awareness of classes as status groups:* do people recognize definite groupings of persons having a similar prestige rating, style of life, and ingroup restrictions on social interaction? Third, is there real psychological *identification* with "one's class"—a sense of belonging to a solidary group of people having the same interests and values? Finally, what is the character and extent of *militant class ideologies* that define classes as struggle groups? The fact that these four questions, which concern four clearly different facets of "class consciousness," are often not distinguished in discussions of American stratification has led to unnecessary confusion.

Certain public opinion polls have been widely cited in an attempt to show that Americans predominantly think of themselves as "middle class." The *Fortune* Survey reported in 1940 that 79 per cent of the population designated themselves as middle class.[92] This proportion was derived from two sets of responses. First, in answer to the question "What word would you use to name the class in America you belong to?", 47 per cent volunteered "middle class" or a similar term. Since many people (56.5 per cent) did not volunteer the words "upper," "middle," or "lower," a second question asked the respondent to choose one of these three terms. Confronted with this choice, enough people selected the middle-

[92] *Fortune* (February, 1940).

class designation to bring the total to 79 per cent. The American Institute of Public Opinion found a higher figure by asking people to place themselves as middle class, the upper, or the lower.[93] The distribution of replies was:

> Upper class.............. 5%
> Middle class............87
> Lower class............. 8

In both of these surveys the distribution of replies did not vary greatly among the different income and occupational levels of the population. Such unanimity fits so little with the objective and attitudinal *differences* consistently shown in studies already reviewed in this chapter that doubts are raised as to whether these results actually index class awareness or identification. The findings certainly show that Americans typically do not describe themselves as either "upper" or "lower" class *when explicitly asked to choose between these terms and "middle class."* This reaction is not especially difficult to understand. To openly characterize oneself as upper class is widely felt in our society to be an offensive arrogation of privilege. On the other hand, the term "lower class" has acquired a connotation of moral opprobrium that describes far more than the bare fact of low economic level. Many Americans will readily admit to "being poor" but will consider it an insult and moral outrage to be called lower class.

So tenacious and deeply ingrained are the axioms of the equalitarian ethic that, as we have previously noted, there is considerable reluctance to discuss social stratification except in oblique and indirect fashion. Something real is being defended when wage workers refuse to accept the label "lower class": deference is real, and self-abnegation is real, and the workers' insistence upon social respect is a tangible influence in blunting and controlling the prestige claims of economically well-to-do groups. It is broadly correct to say of American workers that they "do not want to be set off as a class apart [i.e., as a prestige class], and if the agencies

[93] George Gallup and Saul F. Rae: *The Pulse of Democracy* (New York: 1940), p. 169.

of public opinion were to attempt to set them off, the result would be nothing but resentment."[94]

The finding that three fourths or more of national cross sections of the adult population label themselves as middle class may thus be partly an artifact of the specific questions asked. Indeed, when "working class" is added to the list of choices, a rather different picture emerges. In the survey analyzed by Centers, a national sample of 1100 white adult males were asked: [95] "If you were asked to use one of these four names for your social class, which would you say you belonged in: the middle class, lower class, working class, or upper class?" The replies were:

	Percentage
Upper class	3
Middle class	43
Working class	51
Lower class	1
Don't know	1
Don't believe in classes	1
TOTAL	100

Thus, the term "working class" is selected by fully half of those responding—a larger proportion than accept the characterization of middle class—and there is a much closer correspondence between objective economic position and self-designation of class than in the *Fortune* and Gallup surveys cited above; in other words, the label "working class" is acceptable to what is objectively the working-class population, whereas "lower class" is not.

Unquestionably an overwhelming majority of American adults recognize that great differences of wealth, power, and prestige are to be found in our society. It would be incredible if they did not in a society that has so long and fervently followed the lure of success and that subjects its members to incessant reminders, through all the major agents of communication, of the rewards and comforts to which they may aspire. A culture that makes a fetish

[94] Jones: *Life, Liberty, and Property*, p. 349.

[95] Richard Centers: "The American Class Structure: A Psychological Analysis," in Newcomb and Hartley (eds.): *Readings in Social Psychology*, p. 483.

of the six-figure incomes of movie stars, baseball players, and captains of industry cannot very easily make a complete secret of the magnitude of objective differences in the distribution of social rewards. The striking fact, however, is that these differentials are so infrequently perceived as *class* differences; the tendency rather is to see them as *individual* differences, as the fortune of particular persons who happened to have the ability or luck to attain them. Our evidence seems to indicate that only a minority of the wage earners consider upper strata to have a systematic and continuing ascendancy.

The awareness of classes as status groupings (prestige classes) may be similarly characterized. *Individual differences in prestige* are typically recognized, often with remarkable precision and fidelity, but again, stubborn resistance to the notion that there are fixed prestige groups is quite widespread. Prestige groupings almost seem to be thought of as simple ratings of individuals or families on a scale of temporary competitive placement, rather than as established ranks or definite layers in the social structure.[96] However, both the sensitivity to prestige ranking and the awareness of a *system* of prestige classes are highly variable as between different portions of the population. It seems to be true, for example, that in relatively small communities, those groups considering themselves to be upper class see the whole community as systematically arranged into definite prestige strata, whereas at the lowest economic levels there is only a vague conception of a ranking system.[97] Warner indicates, for instance, that the lower-class person perceives class as a matter of wealth and power.[98]

Perception and awareness of prestige arrangements are affected not only by location in the class structure but also by mobility. In a local ranking system, the most definite and precise discriminations will typically be found either among the stable upper strata, where persons have had opportunity to become thoroughly familiar with the entire structure and have had many occasions

[96] For vivid illustrations of this orientation among workers see Katherine Archibald: *Wartime Shipyard* (Berkeley, Calif.: 1947).

[97] Cf. the studies of Warner, A. Davis, Useem, West, Hollingshead and others.

[98] Warner, Meeker, and Eells: *Social Class in America*, p. 57.

to develop awareness of class differences, or among those mobile persons who have in their own lives traversed a considerable portion of the prestige scale.[99] In general it seems that the finest distinctions are made in "looking down" upon the rank just below one's own or up to a position that is the object of immediate aspiration.

The large amount of vagueness and indeterminancy, especially in the great "middle-class" sector, is of great significance. In general the very top and bottom strata are clearly recognized, but the intermediate gradations tend to be only loosely defined, and subdivisions of the large middle stratum have low social visibility.[100]

Because of the very nature of prestige classes, precise and stable discriminations can be maintained in a detailed way only within the confines of a community small enough to be comprehended as a whole, and nearly all of the research evidence on prestige classes has come from relatively small communities and groups—from a Plainville or Elmtown rather than from Detroit, Chicago, or Los Angeles. The large city is too complex, too mobile, too subject to change to permit the precise elaboration of ratings that can place every family in a village in an exactly defined niche. Prestige stratification, in other words, is a different kind of system in different types of social structures within the United States. In the larger urban areas, the recognition of prestige differences becomes closely tied to the symbols of wealth and power, and only within the limited circles of more or less intimate association are more complex criteria employed and the finer distinctions drawn. The *total character* of the stratification system therefore varies according to the nature of the more inclusive social structure of which it is a part.

[99] Cf. the hypothesis advanced by Warner and Lunt: *The Status System of a Modern Community*, p. 44.

[100] Cf. the penetrating comment of Pfautz and Duncan: "The concept of 'closure,' which is crucial for the structure of status groups, would seem to have little meaning relative to the 'middle' classes; whereas the estate-tendencies at the extremes of the social class configuration as well as the 'communal' character of the upper-uppers and lower-lowers are obvious from the data at hand." Harold W. Pfautz and Otis D. Duncan: "A Critical Evaluation of Warner's Work in Community Stratification," *American Sociological Review*, Vol. XV, no. 2 (April, 1950), p. 212.

It follows from the preceding discussion that one type of class consciousness consists of an awareness of prestige rankings and/or the recognition of at least partly closed status-groupings sharing similar social ratings. This is *not* the same as a class consciousness in the politico-economic sense. The latter does not rest to anything like the same degree as the former upon intimate association, common culture, or homogeneity of social origins and current outlook. It consists of an awareness of similar economic and political interests; in its most fully developed form it is a belief in the identity of interest of all in one's own "class" and a conception of the class as a struggle group fighting for power against an opposing class or classes.[101] Similarity or identity of objective economic and political interests does not in itself necessarily lead to class consciousness, class identification, or class action. Full awareness of class interests, in this sense, is a highly sophisticated response, greatly dependent upon the perpetuation of a particular situation over such a period of time that an "explanatory" ideology can be developed, communicated, and widely accepted among people in similar political and economic circumstances. If there is to be collective class action oriented to class interests, it is of decisive importance, furthermore, that class be perceived as part of a *definite system of power*. Otherwise, similarity of condition may lead to amorphous "movements," made up of many isolated and limited struggles between classes, but not to a unitary class consciousness, nor to the Marxian class struggle.

It seems plain that a high development of militant political and economic class consciousness does not as yet exist in the United States. This conclusion is warranted in spite of several important indications of increased class awareness, notably the tendency of workers to gravitate towards political affiliations that partly express class interests, and the emergence of mass industrial

[101] It is this type of class consciousness that is referred to in the following statement: "Highly competent leadership therefore seems to be required to *make a potential class aware of its existence*, by analyzing the totality of conditions which explain its self-identity." (Italics added.) Reprinted from D. Anderson and P. E. Davidson: *Ballots and the Democratic Class Struggle* (Stanford, Calif.: 1943), p. 252, with the permission of the authors and of the publishers, Stanford University Press.

unionization. Modern developments of this kind certainly represent mass action that is partly determined by recognition on the part of large numbers of individuals that they have economic and political interests in common. But there is as yet no real evidence that the middle and working classes contain a high proportion of persons who have developed a *systematic* conception of belonging to a definite class set against an opposing class.[102] The failure of communism to win any appreciable following in the American labor movement is by itself impressive testimony to the lack of militant class orientation. Unfortunately, we do not have the data necessary to say just *how much* of *what kind* of class consciousness is to be found among the various economic strata. It is quite possible that the small business elite of wealth and power is marked by a self-consciousness of class and of the broad power implications of its position. The same may well be true of some relatively small, well-disciplined groups of industrial workers. On the other hand, the diverse, mobile and unorganized middle strata show a notable unawareness of class [103] and certainly are very far from homogeneity of social perspectives. Not only awareness of class, but the very criteria and symbols of ranking are, as we have said, differently perceived from various locations in the structure. When a stratum has possessed wealth and its attendant advantages over a long period of time, especially in relatively stable communities, it tends to minimize the economic base of prestige-class distinctions and to lay stress upon manners, morality, ethnic or religious background, family history, and long residence in the community. It tends to look down upon the *nouveau riche* and, as Anderson aptly puts it, to be "conspicuously unostentatious in its manner and possessions." [104] On the other hand, people in the

[102] Archibald has observed that in a transient and uneducated group of wartime shipyard workers, resentment against wealthy, powerful, and educated groups did not "evolve into resentment against a distinct class of exploiters or expropriators. . . ." *Wartime Shipyard*, pp. 183–4.

[103] For example, see the suggestion: "Most class-conscious persons, it would seem, confine their thought of class to common modes of consumption, especially of the 'conspicuous' variety, paying little attention indeed to the economic base." Reprinted from D. Anderson and P. E. Davidson: *Ballots and the Democratic Class Struggle* (Stanford, Calif.: 1943), p. 251, with the permission of the authors and of the publishers, Stanford University Press.

[104] Anderson: *We Americans*, p. 128.

least privileged strata tend to see the upper portions of the structure largely in terms of wealth and power; and toward the possessors of economic power the less advantaged working groups hold complex and ambivalent attitudes. Disapproval of great wealth mingles with admiration of success and envy over its rewards. The degree to which differential reward is felt to form a *legitimate* order is always a crucial datum for diagnosing the stability of any social system. Accordingly, this consideration of differing class-perspectives raises the final question of this chapter: To what extent is American social stratification an integrated system, and how, short of perfect integration, can it exist as a working reality?

STRAINS, TENSIONS, AND COMPENSATIONS

We have seen that there are great differences in the objective rewards received by various strata in our society. We know that elsewhere in the world, violent class struggle has driven societies and communities into sharply polarized camps, has led to civil war, has become the base and doctrine of vast political movements affecting most of the world in this generation. How is it possible that in the complex fabric of American society very different income-occupation strata and prestige classes can exist without severely disabling conflicts? In the United States itself, clashes of interest between *economic* groupings have been frequent, and some of these struggles—especially between industrial workers and their employers—have borne a definite "class" quality. Certainly one cannot assume that our modern society is inevitably immune to class conflict. The stability of the stratification order cannot be taken for granted; rather, a primary problem is to explain specifically how the *relatively* low degree of tension and conflict in the American case has been possible and to appraise the probability of a continuing peaceable order.

Let us first ask what important foci of strain can be identified in the contemporary stratification order, and then seek to discover what alleviating factors or "compensations" there may be. In the first place, awareness of actual inequalities in wealth and related objective advantages tends to be sharpened by the large and frequent fluctuations in economic conditions, especially since the society possesses no long-established aristocracy whose position could appear to be historically validated by usage and venerable tradition. Furthermore, American life has a public character, and wide publicity is given to luxury and conspicuous consumption of the wealthy. The conjunction of these factors with the equalitarian ideals of the culture gives power and wealth high social visibility and renders it difficult to establish differential privilege as an unquestioned prerogative of any special group or class. The main historic justifications for great wealth have seen wealth as the reward of effort, achievement, and the related virtues so familiar in the secular derivatives of Protestant ethics. But the old cultural axioms equating wealth and virtue were never completely immune to criticism and have become increasingly subject to skepticism and attack in the twentieth century. Among wage workers there is a fairly widespread conviction that wealth is largely the result of inherited position, "pull" and "connections," or luck. In so far as the basis of economic affluence is thought to be blind chance or the consequence of the principle "first come, first served," differentials of wealth may be tolerated and envied, but they are not likely to be admired as morally excellent. We have already noted that wealth or income does not correlate very precisely with socially valued accomplishments in the diverse fields of the occupational structure. Tensions arising from this source constitute another index of the value conflict engendered by the presence of imperfectly institutionalized economic power.

To some degree, of course, these are perennial problems of all complex societies. The problems seem significant in the United States precisely because economic activity is so dominant a part of the society and because personal achievement is a central justification for differences in social rewards among men who have been encouraged by their culture to claim equality of opportunity.

Probably the most obvious focus of conflict in the American system is the clash between the principles of achieved status and status gained by birth or group membership. Belief in equality of opportunity, in free competitive placement, and in rewards somehow proportioned to the individual excellence of personal qualities and achievements conflicts with the tenacity of family and clique in perpetuating established position and differential opportunity; and patterns of discrimination and preference restrict the opportunities of persons in "minority groups," which altogether probably include one third of the total population. On many fronts and in many guises this widely ramified conflict of normative standards and actual power groupings permeates the American scene. In its multiple extensions throughout the culture, it can also be said to be one of the main problems in integrating the values of the whole society.[105]

A third primary area of strain, closely related to the two already mentioned, consists in the tendency to establish relatively high levels of aspiration at nearly all levels of the income-power hierarchies. The concentration of attention and effort upon secular success, the high evaluation of power, the belief in unlimited opportunity—these and similar influences tend to create a continuous upward pressure in the system and discourage resignation, withdrawal, and apathy. The model American "has enough to hope for more," and his culture on the whole continually reinforces his ambition without at the same time setting clear, customary limits to it. Obviously these pressures do not affect all segments of the population equally, but do constitute one of the features of American society that differentiates it from the major societies of Europe and Asia. And in so far as there is this optimistic aspiration (whatever its precise empirical importance may be), the smooth working of the system is dependent upon very considerable opportunities for actual success among the highly motivated portions of middle and working strata. A sudden and severe blocking of mass ambitions in a society such as this would certainly have a very important effect upon the stability of the entire structure. By giving full weight to these features of American society we may diagnose quite important strains in the system. Objective stratification is great and is

[105] Cf. chap. 11.

subject to high social visibility. Value conflicts center upon the role of inherited or "unearned" wealth and of wealth obtained by non-institutionalized means; and somewhat less obvious but still significant tensions are aroused by sensed discrepancies between reward and merit—as "merit" is culturally defined by the nominally dominant consensus. Notions of social justice are to an appreciable degree polarized into the camps of the "haves" and the "have-nots." And cleavage in the moral framework of the system is especially marked where the criteria of equal opportunity and personal achievement meet head-on with systems of ascribed status and preferential opportunity—most conspicuously in the case of ethnic, religious, or racial minorities.

All these elements exist in the broader context of a relatively secularized, unhistorical, and dynamic culture. To an impartial and detached observer the combination must appear to make a highly volatile social situation. That against such a background, and in an industrialized society, so little class conflict and so little political organization of workers has occurred is a fact so astonishing as to call for a far more comprehensive analysis than can be touched upon here. Certain influences, however, appear even in a preliminary inspection, to help stabilize the existing stratification order. In briefest summary, these compensatory factors include at least the following:

1. The high level of real income and the relatively wide distribution of a "comfort" level of living.
2. The actual incidence of upward mobility and the attendant hope of "getting ahead."
3. The existence of a large middle-income, middle-prestige aggregate.
4. Widespread legal and political rights, nominally equalitarian.
5. The accessibility of public facilities and services.
6. The prevalence of equalitarian symbols and behavior patterns.
7. Intrastratum heterogeneity in culture.
8. Mutual insulation of prestige classes.

9. Participation in common organizations and activities.

10. Persistence of a complex body of beliefs and values that lends legitimacy to the going system.

Others can undoubtedly be found, and the actual dynamic role of those listed is at present a matter of hypothesis rather than of rigorous demonstration. Nevertheless, our preceding analysis has suggested credible theoretical and factual grounds for thinking that these elements do play important parts in the real working equilibrium of stratification in America. At this point we can make only brief comments on each factor.

The high level of real income in the United States has been copiously documented: if America has not been the Eldorado it was thought to be by countless immigrants to its shores, it has, at any rate, produced a high level of material comfort for the great majority of the population. It is true that the material rewards of the system have often proved to be insecure and that great enclaves of the population still do not share greatly in "the American standard of living," but the tangible rewards are great enough, seen against any standards of comparison accessible to the population, to be a strong force supporting the *status quo*. At the same time the real possibilities of acquiring greater income and prestige have reinforced efforts to strive within the system rather than to challenge it. These real possibilities—combined with the persistence of the attitudes of an earlier era—have lead to the transfer of hope and ambition to the next generation. Belief in the American Dream of upward mobility is resilient and thus far has been sufficiently reinforced by actual rises to stand as a prime support of adjustment to the existing situation.

In both of these respects, the amorphous middle classes play a crucial part. Diverse in occupation and ambiguous in political orientation, various segments of the middle-income strata are linked by social origin, association, and intermarriage to both the wage-worker and the employer-executive strata. Permeated with the "central morality" analyzed by A. W. Jones, some parts of the middle groups lean now to one side and now to the other on issues of governmental policy and industrial organization. It is this middle aggregation that is often the solid core of reality behind the figment of "the Public" to which both labor unions and management or employer groups sometimes appeal in times of industrial strife. Typically disliking extreme solutions, the middle strata tend to advocate compromising, middle-of-the-road policies. The old platitude that a strong middle class is a primary bulwark of social stability is not any the less valid for being commonplace, and any serious study of the American case is surely forced to impute a major role to these groups as a stabilizing "third party" between capitalist and proletariat.[106] It must be conceded also that the very vagueness of prestige-class distinctions within the middle-income levels, and between them and other portions of the hierarchy, is significant in blurring potential lines of identification and conflict. Furthermore, the middle strata exhibit enough examples of upward mobility to stand as a concrete symbol and embodiment of the reality of opportunity.

Turning now to the possible role of equal legal and political rights, one is confronted with complexities that defy brief analysis. On the one hand, although nominally equal rights and obligations exist with respect to the franchise, political officeholding, military service, jury trial, and so forth, and conceivably encourage hope of more effective guarantees of equal opportunity, yet any "favoritism" shown the upper strata—less severe punishment for misdemeanors, less liability to the more dangerous and arduous military duties—we would expect to increase frustration and disillusionment. On the other hand, equalitarian political rights undoubtedly are apprehended by a high percentage of the American people as a real bar to status-justice and the arbitrary exercise of economic and political power. Even as sheer creeds these equalitarian rights have tremendous appeal.

A major consequence of the extremely complex situation thus far described is a vagueness of class discriminations and a notable flexibility in certain types of interpersonal relations in which the

---

[106] This is definitely *not* to say that American middle classes would play this role under any circumstances. Experience elsewhere would suggest that a suddenly impoverished and socially disorganized middle stratum may be a fertile source for aggressive political movements.

exact determination of relative rank is a problem that does not
need to be raised. Not only is this indeterminancy characteristic
of many commercial facilities and services, but it is increasingly
reinforced by public, governmental, and civic services and facilities
that are either free or accessible at a nominal charge: libraries,
parks, playgrounds, resorts and reserves, health services, educational facilities, and so on. In a society where so much of life is
lived outside the home, the relative "openness" of so many areas
of activity to a wide range of classes must be taken seriously as a
mitigating factor in the impact of differential privilege and prestige
distinctions.

The vagueness and flexibility of status discriminations in the
special cases just mentioned points to a more fundamental basis
for a low friction component in the American system. Our society
is characterized by a high ratio of "secondary" to "primary" social
contacts; a very great deal of social interaction is casual and segmental—whether it be functionally specific economic transactions,
or the casual interaction of the audience or recreational crowd.
And where social relations are highly segmental, or compartmentalized, they concern a limited area of activities and interests
and very often can be insulated from any integral ranking of the
person. There is accordingly considerable leeway in ordinary life to
avoid distinctions of station that engender hostility.

One striking and insufficiently analyzed fact about the nature of
stratification in the modern urban setting is that interstrata relations tend to be *impersonal* and *categorical* rather than relations of
personalized superordination and *subordination*. Under the feudal
system of medieval Europe, the relation of individuals in lower
strata to those above them were relations of personal dependence
and obligation; one owed fealty to a *particular* lord, and one owed
him the services and deferences in perpetuity, at least in theory.
Furthermore, the bonds between superior and subordinate positions were *multiple* and *cumulative:* in one person were combined
certain aspects of our modern taxcollector, judge, policeman, land-
lord, employer, military chief, and on occasion, religious leader.
In a relatively static agrarian economy, with local production for
local use and with low geographic mobility, the relations of social

classes became rigidly stylized person-to-person relations; stratification became an all-enveloping mode of actual social relations,
affecting practically all of the individual's interests and values, and
hence was most closely related to his self-esteem. In contemporary
America, on the contrary, many interstrata relations are either not
sharply defined as invidious, or else are peripheral to the individual's total activity and personality. The weight of authority
and the exactions of deference tend to be diffused among a variety
of specific statuses; the worker who has a subordinate role in the
factory may still have in many instances opportunities for superordinate status in off-job activities. The impersonality of authority,
together with geographic and job mobility, tends to reduce the
possibility of total personality involvement in particular hierarchical arrangements.

We have already noted the prevalence of "democratic" manners in interstrata relations and have suggested that symbolic
behavior of this sort must be given real weight as a factor of flexibility in the stratification scale. It may be, and probably is, of
minor influence in comparison with the complex of opposite forces
that create class-bounded interests, opportunities, and values, but
it minimizes demands for deference and thereby makes it possible
to an important degree for less privileged members of the society to
avoid continual reminders of status differences in contexts where
intense emotions might otherwise be aroused. It is our hypothesis,
therefore, that equalitarian symbols and behavior patterns are not
inconsequential "illusions" that simply "mask the real class struggle," but rather that they have a tangible cushioning effect upon
interpersonal relations between persons of different station in the
stratification scale.

Intrastratum heterogeneity in culture is of importance here because it reduces the potentiality of *class-structured collective action*,
especially in labor organization and political action. Every main
income or occupational category in American society is partially
segmented by social categories attributed to real or assumed
ethnic, religious, and racial differences. Industrial unionization has
been retarded by such cleavages and distinctions among workers.
As ethnic differences are gradually decreasing, they become less

divisive, but for several generations they have worked against the
development of a unitary labor union movement or a continuing
political organization of workers. Cleavages centering around religious affiliations, ethnic backgrounds, and "racial" categories
have been, in this sense, interchangeable with class cleavages.
Whether the results may have been desirable or undesirable from
other points of view is irrelevant to the effects in segmenting
economically similar strata. Not only ethnic divisions but other
types of diversity—those of region, skill level, social origin—
have contributed to the lack of a common culture among aggregates of persons having the same "relation to the means of production."

The actual sociological character of a stratification system, it is
now apparent, includes far more than either the objective distribution of scarce values or the institutionalized scale of social ranking.
This situation is clearly illustrated by the next factors to be considered: the mutual "insulation" of prestige classes on the one
hand, and the participation of differently evaluated individuals in
common organizations and activities, on the other. Both must be
discussed together because seemingly opposite tendencies here can
in some respects have similar consequences. As a preceding discussion of intrastratum solidarity has shown, there are definite
tendencies for intimate ("primary") social interactions to be restricted to relations between persons of about the same economic
level and/or prestige station. Cliques, friendships, visiting circles,
and marriages all show this pattern. In so far as they do, the most
intimate and comprehensive social relations do not involve direct
and continuing personal contacts with persons of widely dissimilar
rank. Such insulation of social segments does, indeed, reduce opportunities for communication and value consensus in society as a
whole. At the same time, at least in the short run, it establishes
buffers and barriers to relationships that contain the possibility of
serious conflict. To the extent that this insulation is a matter of
mutual preference rather than categorical exclusion that is felt as
stigmatic, it appears that the pattern helps stabilize the prestige-
ranking system, in local communities, at least. Opposed to this
insulation of strata is the crosscutting of class lines in organiza-

tions and activities of an impersonal and functionally specific nature, representing either *common* interests of the whole community or special interests that can be defined in such a way that class distinctions are largely irrelevant. Such activities and organizations are typically found in great variety in American urban communities; although research into their actual functions is largely lacking and greatly needed, it is probable that they contribute appreciably to the integration of the system.

Finally, we must return to the point suggested at the very beginning of this chapter: social stratification so far as it is widely accepted is part of the system of common values without which a society becomes a mere aggregate instead of a real system. No matter how unequal the distribution of social rights, no matter how differentiated the modes of living of various classes or status groupings, the *system* of stratification can be maintained on a largely voluntary basis so long as there is no widespread feeling that it violates grossly the *scale* of stratification (the morally justified criteria), and so long as there is a certain minimal belief in the legitimacy, or social validity, of the scale itself.[107] Thus there are two crucial questions to be asked in accounting for the stability or instability of any stratification order: (1) What consensus exists as to a scale of stratification; is there substantial agreement *at all levels of the actual system* upon the criteria of position that should be acknowledged, accepted, and applied? (2) How closely does the actual stratification order follow the institutional standards, in so far as the latter exist? To ask these questions is to focus our attention upon the role of values and beliefs in supporting and perpetuating the institutional system or in corroding its ultimate basis. In contemporary America, a large body of systematic beliefs and values serves to explain and justify both the going *system* and the nominally dominant *scale*. The research evidence prerequisite to an adequate appraisal of the importance of this "Middletown Spirit" [108] does not yet exist. But preliminary analyses, such as that

[107] In this connection compare the analysis of Melvin Tumin: "Reciprocity and Stability of Caste in Guatemala," *American Sociological Review*, Vol. XIV, no. 1 (February, 1949), pp. 17–25.

[108] Robert S. Lynd and Helen M. Lynd: *Middletown in Transition* (New York: 1937), esp. pp. 408 ff.

by Merton,[109] seem sufficient to establish the presence of a pervasive, meaningfully interconnected set of "folk doctrines," that explain and justify the existing order. Into this category seem to fall —to take only a limited sample of items—belief in equality of opportunity and the correlated beliefs that tend to equate ability and reward, the popular prestige of economic success, and the whole complex that we call "individual responsibility." The total relevant belief-value system in its most fully developed form emerged out of the middle-class society of nineteenth-century America. In our culture, no institution can long outlive *some* cultural rationale that can make its consequences seem "just," or at the very least, inevitable. If, as seems to be the case, this "creed" has lost some of its power to monopolize attention and to motivate optimistic striving, it still commands the allegiance of enough middle- and upper-income people to make it a stout support of the system. At the same time, another very different orientation appears to be replacing in appreciable measure the old work-virtue-reward complex among the wage-earner population. One central component— which, except quantitatively, is perhaps not so new as it appears— is an emphasis upon fortuitous success: the "lucky break," the "$64 question," the unexpected opportunity, the inspired idea, the winning number. The great cultural significance of a belief in Luck as the avenue of Success is that it decisively sunders reward from achievement and personal excellence. Chance is blind to moral worth and indifferent to striving; and if success and failure are thought to depend upon essentially accidental factors, neither the individual nor the social system itself can be perceived as the source of deprivation and malaise.[110]

The questions suggested by these latter observations reach beyond the available data and challenge the analytic capacities of present-day social science. They must remain as questions for the time. It will be enough if this exploration has suggested some of the major factors in the complex and changing balance of social stratification in the United States.

[109] Robert K. Merton: "Social Structure and Anomie," in Ruth N. Anshen (ed.): *The Family: Its Function and Destiny* (New York: 1949), chap. 12, 226–57.

[110] Cf. Ibid., pp. 243–5.

6. American Economic Institutions

1. The Nature of Economic Institutions

AMERICAN economic institutions often seem the most conspicuous feature of the social structure; America is said to be above all a "business civilization," impressive in its productivity, sometimes appalling in the violence of its economic fluctuations. The United States is the land of mass production; the Assembly Line is its symbol to the world. In an age of economic collectivism, it is widely regarded as the last major stronghold of "liberal capitalism." The economic system has acquired such independence from other areas of life that it often gives the appearance of being self-generating and self-perpetuating. Economic activity has become so sharply differentiated from the containing social structure that it is deceptively easy to think of "purely economic" activity and to identify economic institutions with the common-sense category "making a living." Yet from the accumulation of historical and anthropological knowledge about economic systems in widely different cultures we know that a sharp separation of "economy" from "society" is the exception rather than the rule. In nonliterate societies, production is typically for use rather than sale, and it is difficult to identify economic activity as something apart from family life, religion, magic, politics, ceremonial, and social relations generally; economic activity is embedded in and controlled by the society, even in a complex communal society such as existed in medieval Europe. In American society, on the other hand, the price-market system seemingly has been sundered from its social matrix, and, as Polanyi expresses it, has become an "autonomous zone" that tends to create "the delusion of economic determinism as a general law for all human society." [1]

What then do we mean by "economic"? What is an "economic institution"?

In all societies men have wants that must be satisfied if life is to continue; and they have farther wants, the satisfaction of which is an integral part of a meaningful way of life. The facts of "need" and "preference" are intrinsic to man in society. Men "want" or "need" [2] some things more than others, but many of the things they want are not available in unlimited amount. Hence, scales of preference arise—value priorities and value hierarchies. This problem of choice-in-scarcity is the heart of the matter. *Some* values, such as those of religious devotion, group pride, community recreation, are inherently nondistributive; they are participated in rather than divided up. One person's enjoyment does not diminish another's participation in the same value complex—indeed, the value may *require* that others share it. But other values are distributive: they are divisible, and what one person appropriates diminishes what otherwise would be available to others.

Thus human wants cannot all be satisfied. "Goods" are scarce. Even in a society of unlimited abundance of material goods, *time* would still be limited—so much time expended in securing one utility means that much less available to be spent in alternate ways. Every satisfaction of a want "costs something." The cost of a given resource in the production of a given utility is the sacrifice of its potential productivity in other possible applications. The basic economic problem, formally considered, is thus the allocation of scarce means to alternative ends. [3] Since no society has unlimited

---

[1] Karl Polanyi: "Our Obsolete Market Mentality," *Commentary* (February, 1947), pp. 109–17; reprinted in Logan Wilson and William L. Kolb: *Sociological Analysis* (New York: 1949), pp. 557–67.

[2] The frequent use of quotation marks here is necessary: they are warning signals that all these words are full of ambiguities. In the socialized human being, "needs" are typically very far from being simple biological cravings.

[3] "An economic element enters in only insofar as the comparative scarcity of alternative means to a given end becomes relevant to the choice between them. This is always a consideration in addition to the technological, not in place of it. It means that the costs of use of a given means for a given end are considered.

resources there will always be this central problem, whether the economy is capitalistic, socialistic, communistic.

Economics as an analytic science deals systematically with the principles of rational allocation of scarce means for maximizing the satisfaction of wants, under various sets of formal assumptions about the social order. There are economic principles that apply to the isolated human individual apart from society ("Crusoe economics"), but it is the analysis of economic activity of functioning societies that is of use to the sociologist. The usual types of formal economic analysis—whether classical, neoclassical, or Keynesian—presuppose the existence of a going social system that supplies the framework for economic activity.

The great tradition of economic thought, beginning with Adam Smith and Ricardo, postulated an abstract economic system in which the rational activity of men in the market generated a mechanism that could be visualized as completely self-contained and self-adjusting. This theory rested upon stringent, but often implicit and unrecognized, assumptions. It was forced to suppose that men are economically rational—that they try to put resources to the most productive use (that is, to the most profitable use) under changing costs and prices. A system of free competition—the "perfect system of natural liberty"—presupposes a price-market system in which each producing, selling, and buying unit is so small that in acting alone it cannot have an appreciable effect upon the market, and in which the number of these units is indefinitely large. If the units of the system are to have independence, decisions of any one unit must be without effect upon the decisions occurring in other units. Under perfect competition, consumers have free choice of goods, and no producer controls more than a minute fraction of the output. Production responds to open-market demand rather than to direct order, and the interaction of an indefinite plurality of individuals each seeking to sell as dearly and buy as cheaply as possible has as its unintended by-product the

---

This, in turn, means that their comparative urgency for this and alternative ends becomes involved. Thus the fundamental economic facts are scarcity, adaptation of means to alternative ends and cost." Talcott Parsons: *The Structure of Social Action* (Glencoe, Ill.: 1949), p. 655.

maximization of utility of the whole aggregate. Assuming perfect mobility of the "factors of production"—capital, labor, managerial capacities, and so on—resources will shift out of any line of production less profitable than alternative uses of resources. Through the sensitive mechanism of prices competitively determined in the open market, every change in supply and demand is immediately transformed into decisions that continually "correct" the allocation of resources.

If this ideal system is to work, men must have knowledge adequate for economically rational action, and freedom and incentive to carry the action out. Even more important, the role of force and fraud in the allocation of goods must be minimal. There must be substantial equality of bargaining power, since any very great measure of inequality invites coercion. One may *trade*, or one may *take;* much of human history has been a story of the appropriation and use of goods through force rather than exchange—a long story of plunder, theft, piracy, extortion, tribute, brigandage, and the varied exactions of military conquest and rule. An orderly system of peaceable economic exchange can never safely be taken for granted as a universal human desire. On the contrary, economic activity by its very nature generates strong centrifugal tendencies toward breaking through social regulation. For economic relations always involve a measure of social distance and easily lead to acts of violence. When there is a well-established system of social norms regulating economic activity, these tendencies are inhibited, suppressed, or channelized within the framework of the larger value system of the society. But even in the most firmly established economic systems conflict easily emerges from economic dealings.[4] In the trivial case the outraged customer complains to or attacks the dealer who has "overcharged" or "cheated" him; in the wider arena, employers and employees resort to force and fraud, or nations fight rather than compete in the market. There is no guaran-

[4] Cf. Florian Znaniecki: *Social Actions* (New York: 1936), p. 593: "For trading arrangements to be safe, it is not enough for them to be objectively profitable to the parties: they must be subjected to specific positive norms which isolate them from extraneous sources of conflict, and prevent all conflicts that occur in the very process of bargaining from spreading beyond the trading situation." Reprinted by permission of Rinehart & Company, Inc.

tee in the nature of economic activity itself that it will fit into a larger system of values or of orderly social relations. Hence, institutional or normative regulation is just as "normal" and inevitable as in any other sectors of conduct.

The whole economic order, looked at sociologically, is a network of norms and expectancies—a web of "promises" as to the course that economic action will take, or is supposed to take. Thus in the United States, retail trade is typically carried on under a one-price system: the seller offers an item at a standard price, and the customer either buys or does not buy at that one price. There is little of the bargaining and haggling so characteristic historically of the market; the one-price system is a notable step toward impersonality in trade and stabilizes definite expectancies of behavior.[5] How strongly this whole pattern is invested with a socially normative quality may be seen in the "moral indignation" of the naïve American tourist in dealings with Italian taxicab drivers, Eastern traders, or their counterparts in his own culture. Even ordinary economic transactions deal constantly with promises for the future. Currency consists of promises and is accepted in exchange as a matter of "faith" in its future redeemability in goods and services. When belief in redeemability disappears, as in periods of severe inflation or of serious social disorganization, the currency may become mere paper. Stocks and bonds are promises, as are checks, insurance policies, deeds, bills of sale, contracts. As Durkheim so cogently showed over fifty years ago, there is a noncontractual element in contract; the dependability of economic promises, the fulfillment of contracts, cannot be explained adequately on the basis of the immediate interests of the contracting parties. A system of free contract could hardly function if every contract had to be enforced by private sanctions whenever the immediate interests of the contracting parties did not completely coincide.

The effect of social norms upon economic activity is further illustrated by the fact that in our free society no one is free to sell

[5] The importance of the one-price system for our entire economy has been well stated in the report of the National Resources Committee, *The Structure of the American Economy*, Part I (Washington, D. C.: 1939), p. 98.

himself into slavery.[6] Economic pressures have often led to slavery, peonage, indenture systems, imprisonment for debt, and the like. There is certainly no immediate *economic* reason why the individual who has no values to offer in exchange except his own person should not sell himself as a slave.[7] In so far as our culture values personal freedom, it must erect institutional barriers that limit the encroachment of economic pressures. For instance, although the enforceability of private contracts is essential to the American economic system, contractual obligations are regularly set aside in bankruptcy proceedings. The laws and customs of bankruptcy provide for "wiping the slate clean," for the discharge of indebtedness through distribution of assets, even though the bankrupt individual or firm is able to meet far less than the full amount of indebtedness owed. Without this "abrogation of contract," the businessman could easily fall into life-long personal servitude to his creditors.

There is, then, no such thing as the "pure play of economic forces." Freedom of contract has basic institutional limitations. Freedom of consumer choice is confined to a culturally approved or tolerated range. The technically efficient means of securing goods through force and fraud are subject to continual normative regulation. And, indeed, the very character of men's so-called economic interests is not a constant feature of an invariant human nature, but takes distinctive forms in different cultural settings. Not even "economic rationality" can be taken for granted as a fixed characteristic; rather, the kind and extent of economic rationality is dependent upon very complex conditions of the total social structure. For instance, American patterns of "business careers" would be impossible under such conditions of internal warfare and political instability as have prevailed in large portions of Asia during the past twenty years.

A market-price economy is a *cultural* fact. Goods might be

---

[6] This way of putting the situation was suggested to the writer by lectures of Talcott Parsons at Harvard University.

[7] Nor are there immediate technical or economic reasons why opium should not be dispensed over the soda fountains of American drug stores or hand grenades freely sold at the "Five and Ten." On purely economic grounds, any taste whatsoever may become the basis of production and trade.

distributed on the basis of power rather than exchange. Production might be carried on with forced labor, or with labor bound to a particular social authority, or with the "contributed" effort of the family or other communal group. Not only compulsion but every form of traditionalized personal dependence and social immobility is a barrier to the operation of a true market economy.[8] As Weber has correctly insisted, economic activity is the "profane" activity par excellence and is universally felt to be inappropriate in primary "sacred" social relations. The commercialization of property and of labor, which was absolutely essential to the development of modern capitalism, is, historically speaking, a recent and extreme development.

2. Types of Social Mechanisms Controlling Economic Activity

IN SOME of the most abstract models of a *laissez faire* economy, economic activity is considered to be primarily self-regulating—that is, noneconomic factors are considered formally irrelevant to the determination of the course of economic action. It is assumed that wants can be taken as constant or at least that economic activity does not itself change the character of wants. That the individual will pursue "self-interest" is taken as axiomatic. The role of social control is seen almost entirely as the limited intervention of the state to enforce contracts and to exercise police controls over force, fraud, and gross social disorder. In the main, any other ways in which social controls and noneconomic values might affect strictly economic behavior are not systematically taken into account and hence, by implication, are seen as irrelevant or of negligible importance.

So long as economic analysis is clearly seen as a *partial* analysis of economic action and so long as its analytic assumptions are

[8] Znaniecki has analyzed some of the basic social reasons for the fact that "trading is known to be slow in appearing within collectivities whose participants are used to primary patterns of accommodation." *Social Actions*, p. 589.

recognized as simplifying abstractions, it can be utilized as a profitable source of sociological knowledge. For example, one can make predictions as to what action would follow in particular situations *if* men were to follow the dictates of rational economic interest, *if* resources were perfectly mobile, *if* competition were completely free, and so on. Armed with these predictions, one can then compare them with the actual course of action, and the agreement or lack of agreement of the two will offer clues as to other important factors affecting behavior.[9] In many stock market transactions, for instance, or in the disappearance of an overvalued money according to Gresham's Law, or in the substitutability of competing commodities, actual behavior may correspond rather closely to the predictions of the abstract economic analysis. But there will often be wide divergences between economic model and actual behavior, and it is precisely such divergences that frequently offer us fruitful insights.

Although all these qualifications are perfectly plain to the sophisticated student of economics, many of what are for economic science *methodological devices* (such as the useful analytic fiction of perfect mobility, or economic rationality) can become actual working assumptions of the larger culture. As implicit or explicit assumptions they can then make a real difference in the very character of the operating economic system. Such assumptions frequently become so explicit, systematic, repetitive and widespread as to constitute a large part of the explanatory and "justifying" creeds or ideologies of the system. It is roughly correct to say that the ideology of the early twentieth-century American business civilization included as basic tenets: belief that the greatest economic good of the society would be achieved through the unrestrained play of individual self-interest; faith in the sanctity of "private property"; belief in freedom of contract; the assumption that that economic order is best in which there is a minimum of state regulation; belief in the ability of a competitive market to maintain itself and to allocate the society's resources in the optimum manner. In their most clearly and fully developed forms,

---

[9] Cf. Max Weber: *The Theory of Social and Economic Organization*, trans. by A. M. Henderson and Talcott Parsons (New York: 1947), pp. 107 ff.

these conceptions, together with others congruent with them, were resolved into the picture of an automatically self-adjusting economy, composed of rational economic atoms, continually maximizing economic welfare through free competition. Only two types of mechanisms controlling economic activity were fully explicit: (1) *the changing prices established in the open market;* (2) the very limited *"policing" functions of the political order.*

Actually the social controls of the economy are numerous and often far from self-evident. First of all, the *market mechanism* itself is a control. Given a money economy and an organized market structure, the interdependent actions of numerous individuals and groups as they buy and sell changes and readjusts specific prices continually. And since every price is interdependent with other prices and is at the same time a cost to someone, the market mechanism constitutes in fact a vastly ramified impersonal system of controls over economic behavior. When the numbers of participating individuals and groups are large and when they are widely dispersed, this control is in the nature of an invisible "field structure": [10] entirely impersonal forces seem to shape the ebb and flow of economic fluctuations, and it is difficult to identify, or assign responsibility to, any tangible agent or focus.

It is through the institutional arrangements of the "free market" that the external control of production is effected in *laissez faire* economy. There is an established, impersonal system of property and of exchange relations, not enforced *as a whole* by any one specific social authority, in terms of which decisions regarding economic production and exchange must take place. Yet, if the market mechanism is to be really free, there must be rules limiting compulsion, fraud, and collusion; prices must be determined by a "willing buyer and a willing seller." Competition without rules is inconceivable; nevertheless, the controls of the market system, once institutionalized, are relatively nonlocalized, impersonal, and nonspecific. The market-price mechanism is a "constraint" that may require drastic personal discipline and great modifications of individual behavior, yet these controls have long been regarded

[10] This convenient term has been used by Karl Mannheim. See his *Man and Society in an Age of Reconstruction* (New York: 1940).

either as inevitable ("natural," an unchanging condition to which adjustment must be made), or as moral imperatives, or as both. So long and in so far as the undesired consequences of the system were regarded as outside the sphere of purposive social control, the constraints tended to be accepted with relatively little protest.

The "market" does not constitute an autonomous, inevitable, self-caused system, but is in its turn dependent on quite specific institutional structures. Thus an enormous number of *specific cultural norms* that have binding and directing influence upon economic action constitute a second type of control. These norms are varied in object, content, and mode of influence or enforcement; they include statutory laws, common law, court decisions and interpretations, governmental regulations and policies, business codes, union rules, diffuse "customs," "trade practices," and many other varieties of normative standards that taken together make up a regulative framework without which a complex economic system is simply unthinkable.[11] Third, there is the directive influence of *common cultural goals*, which may be collective aims such as military victory, or distributive goals such as profit making. At one time the economy may concentrate upon refrigerators and fashionable clothing; then, within a few months, the national resources are turned toward production of tanks and guns. Furthermore, the very constitution of economic "interests" and economic wants varies greatly not only from one culture to another but also in important ways from one historical period to another within what is broadly the same culture. The productive "surplus" remaining after subsistence needs have been met may be invested in tools and factories—but it may be, and has been, used to construct magnificent cathedrals, or used up in conspicuous consumption as part of a culturally stylized game of prestige. The ends for which wealth

[11] For some purposes it would be important to make precise distinctions among a number of these specific types of norms. At this point, however, it is sufficient to establish only the broadest outlines of institutional patterning. The discussion of the above paragraph is concerned with "the canalizing action of laws, rules, and customs whereby the community shapes and moulds and canalizes the actions of many separate individuals into coordinated form without the exercise of direct administrative control." *Structure of the American Economy*, p. 97.

is sought vary greatly among known cultures: wealth may be a symbol of achievement, a means to power, a validation of social-virtue—or it may be avoided on magical or religious grounds. Evidently a significant part of the "controls" of economic action in every society lies in the dominant goals and interests; and consumer wants, saving and investment patterns, work incentives, and the whole pattern of allocation of resources are in part cultural variables not deducible from intrinsic economic considerations alone.

A fourth type of controlling mechanism consists of *administrative* or *organizational co-ordination*, enforced by a definite and identifiable social organization, whether it be a factory, a corporation, a trade association, a labor union, a government bureau, or any other organized grouping. The dramatic expansion of controls of this kind during the past half century is one of the outstanding social trends of the present era.[12] In contrast to the constraints of the market, administrative controls tend to be localized, specific, and susceptible to a greater degree of interpretation in terms of personal or group "responsibility." It is one thing to see prosperity or economic disaster in terms of "the market" or "the business cycle"; quite another to see it in terms of the C.I.O., U. S. Steel, the Department of Commerce, or "that man in the White House." The nature of these controls can be made to stand out in sharp relief if one contrasts the organization of agricultural production with that of large-scale industry in the period immediately prior to the advent of the New Deal in 1933. There were some six million essentially independent farm units reacting to the changing structure of prices and costs—typically small family enterprises, operating without any important *organizational* integration. With only minor exceptions, such as the chain farming carried on by certain commercial organizations, there were no administrative controls extending from one center to a number of producing units. Whereas much of large-scale industry in this period could be described as

[12] "A century ago when business enterprises were small and government activity was relatively less important, the market played a major coordinating role. But during the past hundred years great segments in the organization of economic activity have gradually but steadily been shifted from the market place to administrative coordination." *Structure of the American Economy*, p. 97.

large systems of centralized control, with relative "anarchy" be-tween systems,[13] agriculture presented a picture of many very much smaller control systems unconnected with one another save by diffuse cultural structures, including both the family system and the mechanism of the free market. Volume of production, time and place of production and sale, type and quality of com-modity, allocation of productive resources—under the "liberal" system all were decided upon by large numbers of small producers acting independently. In modern large-scale industry, on the other hand, a single corporate organization will control a large number of subsidiary units through an elaborate administrative network. Although the corporation as a whole is subject to the final test of profit and loss in the market, the allocation of resources within the organization itself is not necessarily dictated by "free market" principles. Control of behavior, and thus of economic decisions, within the large industrial enterprise or grouping of enterprises is *social* in nature: it is effected through established patterns of au-thority in an elaborate quasi-bureaucratic hierarchy, not through the impersonal pressures of the market. Furthermore, elaborate systems of *inter*corporate co-ordination have grown up, in the form of interlocking participation, common sources of financing, trade associations, "interest groupings," cartels, and so forth. Thus there is a formal organization of, and concentration of eco-nomic control in, large-scale industry that contrasts sharply with the family-farm system of agriculture, and perhaps even more sharply with the quasi-mythical portrait of an economy of in-dividualistic competitive production.

The degree of what we have called "administrative" (or organi-zational) control is only *one* sign that the present American economy differs from that of "capitalistic" legend. Such scholars as Max Weber, Sombart, Veblen, Commons, Briefs, and Durkheim have repeatedly shown that the high development of certain capitalistic features in modern Western societies is a unique histori-cal phenomenon due to an unusual combination of technical, political, and social conditions. Following Weber it can be said that

[13] P. Sargant Florence: *The Logic of Industrial Organization* (London: 1933), p. 8.

a fully rationalized, capitalistic, free-market economy requires at least the following: [14]

1. Relatively complete separation of the *economic* uses of goods, services, human beings, and other means of production from all their other uses. For example, ownership of land as a transferable, alienable commodity is utterly different from feudal "ownership," which is inseparable from political authority (juridical, military, and so on). A house as a market good is separated from the social values and obligations attached to a "family homestead." Above all, the treatment of labor as a commodity necessitates separating economic considerations from traditional social obligations and ethical sentiments.

2. Maximum concentration of rights over the nonhuman means of production in the hands of "owners."

3. The existence of formally free labor, which has no fixed right to a particular job. Workers are not bound by obligations of dependence to particular employers; conversely employers do not have inalienable duties to particular workers. Ideally, the workers cannot gain a livelihood from fixed property, for it would tend both to reduce mobility and to weaken the control of the employer.

4. Freedom of contract—the absence of a high degree of regulation of consumption, production, and prices. Within very wide institutional limits the market mechanism is free to operate with a minimum of noneconomic "interferences."

5. A reasonably stable, or at least *predictable* political order, including a calculable legal system and governmental administration. Authority for the enforcement of contracts is indispensable. The ideal political order is one that operates according to fixed, explicit rules, with a minimum of arbitrary authority, unpredictable change, and retroactive regulation.

6. A "formally rational" monetary system.

7. Some relatively high degree of control over the technical

[14] For a more complete discussion see Parsons's introduction to *Theory of Social and Economic Organization*, especially pp. 43–51. The present section is heavily indebted to this source.

bases of production. Thus, it is a great advantage of the factory over the farm that it is not so subject to the vagaries of weather and other natural conditions. Similarly, a disciplined—that is, calculable—labor force is necessary for the maximum rationality of a capitalistic market economy.

Other conditions could be listed as significant bases for the type of economy under consideration—for instance, the separation of "household" from "business"—but those already mentioned are sufficient to underscore: *first*, the complexity of the institutional elements involved in economic activity; *second*, the interdependence of "economic" institutions with other parts of the social order; *third*, the frequently unrecognized existence of multiple control systems that are inevitable under *any* economic system.

3. Major Structural Characteristics of the Present American Economy

OUR primary question now is: What are the *main* features of the institutional framework that surrounds economic activity in the United States? To answer this question we shall have to cut through the infinite detail of concrete facts to single out *dominant* features: for example, we shall devote little attention to agriculture and very small businesses, not because these are not important, but because they are structurally less crucial than large industrial and financial organizations. Secondly, we shall have to distinguish between the cultural "theory" or ideology of the institutional system and the realistically effective goals and regulations.

In this context the sociologically significant features of the economic system can be summarized.

1. It is an economy of mass production, operating under a factory system utilizing a highly developed technology.
2. Industrial production is characterized by a minute specialization and division of labor.[15]

[15] It is worth noting that the 1940 United States Census of Manufactures found it necessary to recognize 446 separate *industry* classifications, consolidated into 20 broad industrial groupings.

3. Industrial processes, tasks, and products are highly standardized.

4. That portentous social invention, the corporation, is the dominant form of organization of business enterprise.

5. Corporate ownership is widely *diffused;* production and control are highly *concentrated.*[16] Ownership and management of corporations have become separated, with far-reaching consequences.

6. There are very important systems of intercorporate co-ordination and control.

7. Large-scale units and administrative co-ordination lead to quasi-monopoly, "imperfect competition," and price rigidities.

8. Large-scale industrial labor unions play an increasingly weighty role.

9. Because of specialization of production, a highly developed monetary and credit system, and other factors, the various segments of the economy are closely interdependent, and changes in any one major portion of the system have immediate and complex repercussions elsewhere.

10. Central governments, both Federal and state, intervene in economic activity on a wide scale through direct regulation and facilitation and through the indirect consequences of their other operations.

11. "Property rights" are in a state of rapid change, and the facts are radically different from those envisaged in popular ideologies and in certain important legal fictions.

12. The entire economy is subject to incessant development and innovation, through factors ranging from the impact of revolutionary inventions to the influence of international politics and war.

Such an economy is very different from nineteenth-century *laissez faire* conceptions of the American system and cannot be described adequately by summary labels, such as "capitalism" or

[16] "The corporation has become more than a method of doing business; it has assumed the aspect of an institution of social organization comparable to the state itself." A. A. Berle, Jr. and Gardiner C. Means: "Corporation," *Encyclopaedia of the Social Sciences*, Vol. IV, p. 422.

"corporacy." We must make a careful examination of the facts bearing on such outstanding characteristics as have just been outlined.

THE DOMINANCE OF THE CORPORATION

Although sole proprietorships and partnerships are still numerous and vital in the economy, by far the most important form of business organization is the corporation. Corporations today account for over 80 per cent of the total production of goods, workers employed, and wages paid.[17] In agriculture, service trades, certain branches of construction, certain types of retail trade, and a few other, relatively minor, industries (such as manufacturing of women's clothing) corporations still do not predominate in production. But in the crucial heavy industries, such as steel, the corporation almost completely rules the field, and in the key sector of economic control represented by finance, corporations do more than 80 per cent of the business. The corporation is thus the dominant institutional form of economic organization, and the modern period can be well characterized as an age of corporacy.[18]

Manufacturing in the United States is almost completely carried on under the corporate form of enterprise; even prior to World War II, corporations accounted for 92 per cent of the total output in manufacturing.[19] Furthermore, although one half of the employers in the United States employ three workers or less and 90 per cent employ 30 or fewer workers, this 90 per cent employ less than one fifth of the employees. On the other hand, the top 5 per cent of employers employ 70 per cent of all workers.[20] In fact, small producing units employing five or less workers account for only one third of the nation's economic activity; at the other extreme, another third is represented by only a few hundred very large

[17] William H. Husband and James C. Dockeray: *Modern Corporation Finance* (Chicago: 1947), p. 20.

[18] David Lynch: *The Concentration of Economic Power* (New York: 1946), p. 9. This is a summary and analysis of materials produced by the investigations of the Temporary National Economic Committee.

[19] Lynch: *The Concentration of Economic Power*, p. 94.

[20] Ibid., p. 114.

organizations.[21] Not only is this a corporate economy, but its center of gravity lies in the *large* corporation. With the concentration of economic activity in extremely large administrative structures, the corporation increasingly assumes powers and responsibilities that go beyond the merely "economic." For example, a great "private" agency of communication, the American Telephone and Telegraph Company, employed about 270,000 persons (in 1935), more than the entire staff of the United States Post Office Department (about 260,000).[22] In number of employees, at least, our leading corporations rival sovereign political states.

Industrial wealth and production are highly concentrated in a relatively few large corporations. The apparent degree of concentration varies somewhat, depending upon which of various possible indices are used to estimate it, but the central fact is quite clear. In the year 1935, for example, just 100 companies accounted for 32 per cent of the total value of all products manufactured in the United States. The amount of concentration differs, of course, in different industries.[23] Among the 200 largest nonfinancial corporations, there were only 10 in the fields of mail-order businesses, retail chains, and department stores, and these 10 accounted for only about 8 per cent of all retail sales. But 90 per cent of railroad mileage was operated by companies on the list of the 200 giants; 80 per cent of electric power was produced by corporations on the list. The 40 largest public utility corporations in 1933 controlled 80 per cent of total assets in the industry. In that same year the *200 largest nonfinancial corporations held about half of the total industrial wealth or about one fifth of the national wealth.*[24] In finance, the 30 largest banks held about one third of all banking assets outside the Federal Reserve System; among life insurance companies, the 17

[21] *Structure of the American Economy*, p. 104.

[22] Cf. Wilson and Kolb: *Sociological Analysis*, pp. 553–4: "The large-scale industrial corporation is the fundamental power structure of those modern economic systems which still function under free-market economic institutions."

[23] Lynch: *The Concentration of Economic Power*, pp. 248–50.

[24] See Marshall E. Dimock and Howard K. Hyde: "Bureaucracy and Trusteeship in Large Corporations," *Monograph No. 11*, Temporary National Economic Committee (Washington, D. C.: 1940), pp. 4–5. (Hereafter cited as T.N.E.C. *Monograph No. 11*.)

largest controlled over 80 per cent of total assets of all life insurance companies.[25] In 1937, the Metropolitan Life Insurance Company alone held 18 per cent of total assets reported by all companies; it had nearly 5 billion dollars in assets, or a wealth greater than any one of 38 states in the country.[26]

In certain industries a very few large producers practically monopolize production. Thus 3 concerns manufacture 86 per cent of automobiles, 2 companies produce 95 per cent of plate glass, 3 firms account for 90 per cent of cans; in 1937, one company produced all the virgin aluminum in the United States.[27] In two industries perhaps most expressive of modern industrialism—steel and petroleum—the great concerns overshadow the scene. In the petroleum industry, 20 companies account for two thirds of the investment and for 80 per cent of domestic sales of gasoline. In steel, the ten largest companies hold 88 per cent of the assets, and the United States Steel Corporation alone accounts for 40 per cent of the capital invested in the entire industry. Large size does *not* necessarily mean monopoly; it does not tell us directly how much concentrated control, economic or social, may exist. It does, however, mean that the social structure of very large economic organizations becomes a primary problem in the analysis of the total economic system.

Although the corporation is of prime importance as a source of production and as a large-scale unit of social power, small economic enterprises predominate numerically. Most of the approximately 6 million farms in the United States are small family enterprises. In the nonagricultural industries, individuals and partnerships far outnumber corporations; they number about 2 million in manufacturing, mining, trade, and service, whereas there are only about a half million corporations in the whole economy. Politically and socially these entrepreneurial units of the system are of great strategic significance, as the previous discussion of social stratification has illustrated. But they are not the most important producers nor do they wield central economic influence and control.

[25] *Structure of the American Economy*, p. 103.
[26] Lynch: *The Concentration of Economic Power*, pp. 118–20.
[27] Ibid., p. 117.

Corporations are not new. And there are fields in which they are not yet the dominant form of enterprise. But what is distinctive of the modern period is, first, the enormous extension and consolidation of the corporate system; second, its emergence (since the Civil War) in fields previously thought unadapted to its extensive development—manufacturing and, increasingly though slowly, retail trade; [28] third, the increasingly clear and marked development of certain internal corporate structures, above all the separation of ownership and management and the elaboration of hierarchical social structures.

It was clear to Berle and Means over two decades ago that a few huge corporate units rather than many small private enterprises form the core structure of American industry.[29] It is even clearer today that any really serious attempt to understand the industrial system, the larger economic system, and indeed, the total social structure must grapple firmly with the nature of the corporation and its place in the network of economic institutions.

INTERCORPORATE CO-ORDINATION

The extent of economic concentration is not adequately shown by data on the part played by individual corporations. In some fields the number of important companies is so small as to indicate at once monopolistic competition, but in most instances the extent of centralized co-ordination will be understated unless we examine some of the numerous and intricate mechanisms whereby corporations are linked together into control systems of varying extent and unity. Among the more important are:

1. interlocking directorates;
2. intercorporate stockholding;
3. concentrated stock ownership by individuals or groups in several corporations;

[28] See A. A. Berle and G. C. Means: *The Modern Corporation and Private Property* (New York: 1934), pp. 10–17.

[29] Ibid., pp. 45–6.

4. common servicing by large financial organizations; investment blocs;
5. trade and business associations;
6. legal and contractual controls (utilized to co-ordinate sudcontractors, retail outlets; patent controls, etc.);
7. informal or tacit agreements and "understandings."

The establishment of *interlocking directorships* is an old method of achieving corporate integration. It does not necessarily lead to co-ordination: the directors in question may be inactive, or in a weak position on the boards of directors, or unable to exert a primary influence upon the managerial officers of the corporation.[30] Also, interlocking directorships among competing companies are subject to legal discouragement under Section 8 of the Clayton Act (1914), although this provision has proved to be considerably less than fully effective.[31] Certainly, however, the device is very common among noncompeting companies, and where extensive interlocks do exist, they unquestionably help to form at least a certain "community of interest" that often may be expected to lead to substantial co-ordination and harmony of action. In 1935, there were 3,544 directorships on the boards of the 200 largest nonfinancial and the 50 largest financial corporations; one third of all these directorships were held by 400 men. Although there were 25 firms among these giant companies that did not share directors with any others on the list, 151 companies interlocked with 3 or more others, and 10 interlocked with 26 or more.[32] Among life insurance companies, the five largest interlock with 780 corporations, of which 100 are other insurance companies and 145 are banks.[33]

[30] T.N.E.C. *Monograph No. 11*, p. 6.

[31] A Brookings Institution study called it "singularly ineffective." Leverett S. Lyon, Myron W. Watkins, and Victor Abramson: *Government and Economic Life* (Washington, D. C.: 1939), Vol. I, p. 289. On the other hand, Lynch (*The Concentration of Economic Power*, pp. 232–3) holds that the legislation has been effective, broadly speaking. Of course, enforcement of the Clayton Act has varied greatly at different times; one's judgment of its effectiveness in the present connection depends also in part upon an appraisal of the frequency of "dummy" directors and other informal means of circumventing the intent of the act.

[32] T.N.E.C. *Monograph No. 11*, p. 7.

[33] Lynch: *The Concentration of Economic Power*, p. 232.

Intercorporate stockholding is another type of link in the integration of clusters of corporate interests. Among the 250 large corporations cited above, at least 30 were shown by the studies of the National Resources Committee to be tied to other corporations on the list by important stockholdings.[34] The control potential of intercorporate stockholding is greatly increased when a number of corporations with similar interests converge upon a crucial "gateway" in an industry or group of industries. One of the clearest instances is the ownership of indispensable pipe-line systems by a few of the large corporations in the petroleum industry.[35] Sometimes very wealthy *individuals or groups of individuals* can achieve substantial concentration of control through minority stockholdings in groups of companies—for example, the role of the Rockefeller family in several major oil-producing companies. *Financing organizations*, especially the large investment banks, play a strategic role in intercorporate co-ordination. During 1934-9, the six leading investment houses managed 57 per cent of the nearly 10 billion dollars worth of securities registered with the Securities and Exchange Commission. The 38 leading firms accounted for 91 per cent of all securities handled,[36] and, although their "influence" or "control" is hard to measure exactly, they cannot fail to carry an important degree of interest in and influence over the companies they serve. Furthermore, the financial companies themselves invest heavily in nonfinancial corporations: in 1935, about one quarter of all corporate bonds were owned by financial houses, and a large volume of short-term loans and credits are advanced by them to other corporations.[37] Concentrated gateways of finance inevitably mean intercorporate linkage of the large industrial organizations.

Financial control of one kind or another is only one means, though an extremely important means, of intercorporate co-ordination. The *trade association* is another. In the United States, it seems to be the latter-day equivalent of the older trusts. The

[34] *Structure of the American Economy*, pp. 158–9.
[35] Cf. Lynch: *The Concentration of Economic Power*, pp. 221–3 and 233.
[36] Ibid., p. 128.
[37] *Structure of the American Economy*, p. 160.

trade and business associations differ greatly among themselves in organization, aims, methods, and power, but they constitute in sum total a controlling system of real significance in various branches of industry and trade.[38] As of 1937, it was estimated that there were 2,400 national or interstate associations.[39] The business associations in banking, railroads, and electric power cover nine tenths or more of the respective industries. The National Association of Manufacturers includes enterprises employing about one third of the workers in manufacturing, and the officers and directors are drawn in considerable part from the largest corporations.

Among the varied activities of business and trade associations are gathering and disseminating information, developing and promulgating standards and policies, focusing attention, upon, and encouraging common action with regard to, governmental policies, influencing public opinion, establishing agreement on price and production levels. Some specialized associations in the past have supplied services of a very tangible nature to their members—for example, the strike-breaking activity of the National Metal Trades Association.[40] Probably of more long-run significance, however, are activities of a more diffuse and indirect character: for example, price reporting systems can be effective indirect controls upon pricing policies. It is not possible to make any general appraisal of the importance of trade associations in price determination, but in some specific industries they appear to contribute heavily to price leadership, collusion, resale price maintenance, and other patterns of unified action; in other industries, however, these consequences are lacking or minimal.

Certain other intercorporate linkages are maintained through *direct use of controls established by law*. Probably the most striking example is furnished by the so-called fair trade laws, which provide for price maintenance contracts between manufacturers and retailers. Under the provisions of these laws—which by 1939 had been enacted in 43 states—the manufacturer enters into a contract

[38] See the careful review by Lyon, Watkins, and Abramson: *Government and Economic Life*, pp. 274–84.

[39] There were well over twice as many local associations: 4,100 state and local trade associations and 5,400 local chambers of commerce.

[40] *Structure of the American Economy*, p. 165.

with a retailer stipulating the minimum resale price of a trade-marked product; when any *one* such contract has been established, all other retailers in the state who have knowledge of the contract are bound by statute to hold to the minimum resale price established in the contract. Prices are thus fixed "vertically," rather than horizontally through agreement among the retailers.[41] If a particular retailer sells below the stipulated minimum, he is subject to a damage suit by other retailers or by the manufacturer.

This type of price agreement was at one time held to be illegal, but was later made possible by the Miller-Tydings Act of 1937 and by a Supreme Court decision of 1936 holding that the California and Illinois laws were not price-fixing acts. The actual effect of the legislation, of course, is to permit manufacturers and dealers to fix prices at will. Unquestionably such legal controls set into motion pressures toward further controls. Thus, as the editors of *Fortune* have cogently argued, the tendency in the "fair-trade" pricing of drugs is to set minimum prices that give a relatively high margin of profit in order to "protect" all retailers. The high profits then induce other types of retail outlets to stock drugs, and demands arise to restrict drug sales to druggists; the next step would be a system of restrictions on the number of druggists.[42] Although the resale price maintenance laws have not yet led to quota systems for entrance into the affected occupations, the "protectionist" principle embodied in such legislation is widespread in the present-day business community.

Practically any legal measure may become a part of the institutional framework of economic activity. Taxation, for instance, is not simply a neutral means of raising revenue; it is an instrument of public policy. The power to tax is the power to create or destroy, economically speaking. Tariffs, monetary policies, subventions have similar potential effects. In many instances, regulations and laws established and enforced for nominally noneconomic reasons have important indirect economic consequences. A few illustrations will stand muster for a very numerous universe.

The manifest goal of building codes is to protect public health,

[41] Lynch: *The Concentration of Economic Power*, p. 146.
[42] "The 'Fair' Trade Controversy," *Fortune* (April, 1949), p. 76.

safety, and convenience. In actual operation, some state and municipal codes minimize competition and protect favored positions among contractors and craft unions.[43] Likewise, sanitary regulations, inspection requirements, and safety provisions turn out with noteworthy frequency to be means of co-ordinating economic action or centralizing control. For example, the requirement that milk be pasteurized led quite directly to the growth of giant milk distributing firms, primarily because large capital is required for effective operation of pasteurizing plants. Or a given city may require that all milk sold there be from herds certified by municipal inspectors as free from tuberculosis. Suppose that the milk shed immediately surrounding the city is under severe competition from an out-of-state area with lower production costs, located a hundred miles away. If the municipal inspectors find it possible to inspect all dairy herds in the hinterland, but never get around to the inspection of herds in the outside region, the local milk shed receives a noneconomic protection against the competition of the outer area. Many such trade barriers are established at the behest of, or with the acquiescence of, labor groups, farmers, and individual businessmen. They illustrate well how public regulatory action can become part of the interlocking structure of economic interests and organizations, corporate or otherwise.

A variety of control patterns have grown up around *patent rights*. A sufficiently powerful and adept concern may "fence in" competitors by securing patents on all foreseeable improvements in machinery or techniques. The competing owner of a given patent can thus be prevented from improving his technical position and may even be completely immobilized from exploiting his primary patent by suits or the threat of suits for infringement of patent rights. When a new improvement is patented, the inventor or patent holder will find it difficult to sell his improvement except to the holder of the central complex of rights in the same field; the original patent controls can thus be further bulwarked by purchase of improvements made by others. In the entire process, the large-

---

[43] Cf. Thurman Arnold's comment that certain of these measures "are not building regulations but protective tariffs against other parts of the nation." *The Bottlenecks of Business* (New York: 1940), pp. 36–7.

scale, well-financed research and development arms of corporations obviously have great advantages.[44] Buying and suppressing an improved patent in order to protect the investment already made on the basis of an older patent; making applications for patents in order to delay a competitive improvement; continuing and ingenious litigation against inventions seen as threats, litigation that may be so time consuming and expensive as to block effectively new competitive techniques or processes—all these devices enable dominant concerns or groups of concerns to maintain favorable positions.

Single inventions are often of maximum usefulness only when combined with other inventions. Often the patent rights to such complementary inventions will be in different hands; often also, patents may overlap in their claims. To meet these problems, systems have developed for crosslicensing and for pooling of patents. In the automobile industry, there are provisions for interchange of patents on a royalty-free basis, and in many other instances pooling and crosslicensing are common. It is difficult to weigh the effects of these arrangements: on the one hand, they undoubtedly facilitate technically useful combinations of patent rights; on the other, they are always potential sources of monopolistic control. At any rate, no matter what social evaluation may be assigned to them, these systems constitute still another example of specific institutionalized controls that extend between the organized enterprises of the business world.

IMPERFECT COMPETITION

A perfectly competitive economy is never found in any actual society, although it has been approximated in some portions of Western societies during the past three centuries. In general, it has been most closely approached during those periods in which

[44] Cf. Lyon, Watkins, and Abramson: *Government and Economic Life*, pp. 138–9. The classic case of fencing-in is usually thought to be that of the Hartford-Empire Company in the glass container industry (cited on p. 138). See also the description in Lynch: *The Concentration of Economic Power*, pp. 273–9.

agricultural societies have been becoming rapidly industrialized—
when the basic character of the social structure has been changing,
traditional barriers and restraints have been dissolving. Then an
economy subject to principles different from those guiding the environing social structure has temporarily arisen, and economic
units, still small, have not yet become consolidated into new systems of *social* organization.

During the second half of the nineteenth century in the United
States conditions favored an approximation to a system of free
competition. Both extractive and manufacturing industries were
carried on by units small enough and independent enough to prevent any single one from dominating the market. Fixed capital
and overhead costs were small, so that direct costs took a determining role and entry into production was relatively easy for
the small entrepreneur.

The facts we have just reviewed, however, show that today
competition in a free market has been partly, if not largely, re-
placed by a highly tangible web of financial and organizational
controls. There are nodes or foci of concentrated production and
centers of control in many crucial parts of the economic web, from
which lines of control gradually fade out into areas of relatively
free markets and independent production. Where there is consolidated control, there is what economists call imperfect competition,
whether monopoly, duopoly, oligopoly, or some intermediate shading of these.[45] In addition to the restrictions upon competition already discussed there are others arising from the "intrinsic" character of the present economic structure. The enormous capital
investment now necessary in many industries eliminates or drastically limits the opportunities for new firms to enter the established
field. Strategic control by existing large concerns over critical supplies of materials, techniques, or personnel has the same effect.
Modern mass advertising tends to create extreme differentiation of
products (even among those of essentially the same technical merits

[45] Economic theories of imperfect competition are illustrated by such well-
known analyses as: Edward G. Chamberlain: *Theory of Monopolistic Competition* (Cambridge, Mass.: 1933); Joan Robinson: *Economics of Imperfect Competition* (London: 1933).

and cost) and thereby creates dealer and consumer preferences that militate against free entry of new competitors. When such "manufactured" patterns of preference are bolstered by resale price maintenance systems, exclusive-dealer contracts, and similar devices, they take on added solidity as barriers.

We must not overlook the increased possibilities of various kinds of informal agreements or "collusion" where a few great firms dominate a given field. Closely related, in effects upon the competitive system, are the widespread phenomena of price leadership, basing-point systems, and other versions of administered prices.[46] Outside of some form of collusion or of governmental action, imperfect competition in general, and administered prices in particular, arise only when a few large producers supply a major portion of a given market; but as we have already seen, in a number of very important industries a few firms do so, and the decisions as to production and price made by any one producer cannot then be assumed to be independent of other producers.[47] It is not easy to detect imperfect competition, and its incidence varies greatly from one portion of the economy to another. Sheer size of the leading concerns tells us very little, for giant companies may make a wide range of products and have little control of the market for any one of them. What is crucial is size *in relation to a particular market for a particular product*.

If prices are administered, they are administered *by* someone. A degree of market dominance sufficient to permit price administration on a national level is possible only when economic enterprises are very large or held together into tight systems of control or agreement. And it can surely be expected that the norms and goals guiding the "control" groups in the large corporation in a position of monopoly, oligopoly, or price leadership will take into account more than short run profit. The impersonality and anonymity of

[46] On the general notion of administered prices vs. market prices, see *Structure of the American Economy*, pp. 108–10.

[47] Ibid., p. 116: "In summary, it can be said that there is such a degree of concentration in relation to the market for the bulk of goods in the American economy that to a major extent the prices of goods are formed on an administered basis rather than on the basis of a free market."

the open market will diminish as tangible groups have to be considered, whether as opponents or "colleagues." Managers and directors will be increasingly moved by considerations of power, of institutional stability, and of the perpetuation of a given organizational pattern.

Free markets do not automatically maintain themselves. Economic combination is frequently at least as advantageous as individualistic competition. When, as in the present-day American business community, the term "price chiseller" becomes a popular epithet, business associations advocate a "live and let live" policy, and the word competition is coupled with "cutthroat," and when big business, small business, and labor groups are busy building a finer network of organization—then we begin to see a new cultural atmosphere surround the structure of economic life.

OTHER "BARRIERS" TO A PERFECT MARKET SYSTEM

The ghost of the "economic man" has been repeatedly laid in recent years. Our previous discussion has perhaps suggested some of the specific reasons why he cannot exist. But there are others.

For economic man to function perfectly in a perfect market, resources, including labor, must be freely mobile. Labor is not freely mobile. Not only does it fail to shift from nation to nation as wage levels would dictate, but it is significantly immobile even within the borders of proverbially rootless America. For short-run periods each locality is a quasi-independent labor market.[48] Marked *regional* differences in wages persist over long periods. Agriculture tends to be chronically over-blessed by available labor.[49] Again, "free entry" into business is supposedly essential for a self-adjusting competitive system. New enterprises challenge the old in high-

---

[48] *Structure of the American Economy*, p. 117.

[49] Robin M. Williams: "Concepts of Marginality in Rural Population Studies," *Rural Sociology*, Vol. V, no. 3, September, 1940; Wilbert E. Moore: "Migration and Social Opportunity," *Rural Sociology*, Vol. VII, no. 1, (March, 1942). A comprehensive work which throws much light on "noneconomic" factors in migration is Julius Isaac: *Economics of Migration* (New York: 1947).

profit business, thus putting resources to most profitable use and preventing monopoly. Actually, of course, entry into occupations and economic enterprises, although free in form, is never unimpeded. First of all, and of prime importance, sufficient initial capital is difficult to raise. Small firms are in fact financed chiefly from personal savings and by loans from friends and relatives, and the larger new firms rely mainly upon savings of wealthy individuals. Very few new concerns are able to secure adequate bank loans or to sell sufficient securities on the public market.[50] Because the small firm does not have easy access to capital from the open capital markets, it is highly vulnerable to taxation or other measures that limit its capacity to secure such access.[51] Besides potent controls previously discussed, exclusive-dealer contracts, price-decline guarantees, and long-term staggered contracts provide other barriers to free entry.[52] Also, certain types of labor contracts and agreements operate to bar new firms from certain industries or localities. When a particular area or field is dominated by a few concerns, the aspiring newcomer may be met by a wide range of deterring actions, ranging from simple persuasion to threats, litigation, or violence. Financial controls are potentially important in checking very large new enterprises. A number of legal obstacles play a part —for instance, licensing provisions and franchises.[53]

Finally, the organization of a national economy for military and other political ends is not compatible with *laissez faire*, nor with any sort of "free" economic system. War, preparation for war, the international commitments incurred in preparing for wars or striving to prevent them—these inevitably lead to drastic modifications of the system. Consumer wants are affected, and goods may be distributed by rationing rather than pricing. Resources, in men and capital, are allocated to ends quite different from those that would otherwise prevail. Explicit regulation grows.

[50] Data for these conclusions are analyzed by Alfred E. Oxenfelt: *New Firms and Free Enterprise* (Washington, D. C.: 1943), pp. 146–60.

[51] Cf. Lewis H. Kimmel: *Taxes and Economic Incentives* (Washington, D. C.; 1950), pp. 35–6.

[52] Oxenfelt: *New Firms and Free Enterprise*, pp. 162–3.

[53] Ibid., pp. 166–70.

Thus we see that our present economy is a congeries of control systems and that its capitalism is very different from that of earlier ideology. Nowhere is this fact more apparent than in the newer modes of corporate organization. If there can be said to be a "characteristic" unit in the system, it is the corporation, which accordingly deserves further attention.

4. Nature of the Corporation and Its Organization

So FAR we have talked about the corporation as if its nature could be taken for granted. Yet the deeper consequences of corporate organization are certainly not self-evident. The present-day corporation is more than a socially neutral mechanism for doing business: as Berle and Means have said, it "has attained a degree of prominence entitling it to be dealt with as a major social institution." [54]

Corporations in the modern sense first arose in trading enterprises subject to great risks and requiring large amounts of capital. In America a corporate charter was originally regarded as a contract between the state and the corporation for carrying on certain activities and was minutely scrutinized and rigidly protected. It was regarded as a special privilege, not as a "right," and until well into the nineteenth century each charter usually required a special act of the state legislature.[55] Later, however, incorporation became simple and easy, and this loosening of the early rigid legal controls was of notable importance in the development of the modern structure.

[54] *The Modern Corporation and Private Property*, p. 1.

[55] Ibid., pp. 129–30. The gradual loosening of the early detailed regulation is an illuminating chapter in the history of economic and social change in the United States.

It is often said that the most important feature of the corporation is the principle of limited liability. This feature is itself derived,
in our legal system, from the more basic *right of the corporation to
exist as an entity* apart from the individuals who are associated in
the organization. The partnership is a cumbersome form of organization, especially for large businesses, because the partners retain
their separate legal personalities and are individually held responsible for the entire enterprise. The corporate device at one
stroke decisively cuts through the identification of concrete persons with the enterprise; thus an abstract legal fiction can for many
purposes operate with the unity of a private person.

The corporation is, then, a recognized legal entity having the
rights of an individual to hold property, sue and be sued, enter into
contracts, and otherwise conduct business in its own name. Although the corporation as such is fully liable for its financial obligations, the shareholders have only a liability limited to the
amount of stock they hold. Through the right of the stockholder to
transfer his shares, the total enterprise acquires continuity of
existence. In actual practice it thus possesses institutional immortality; investors may change and personnel may come and go,
but the corporation exists indefinitely, subject only to the necessities of the balance sheet and to charter renewals, which are
usually granted. Unity, combined with limited liability, greatly facilitates the accumulation of large capital sums, increases the flexibility of financing, and allows diffusion of ownership; thousands of
investors can contribute capital to a corporation that operates as a
single unit.

Just as the factory system brought large numbers of *workers*
under unified direction and control, so the corporate system
brought numerous bits of *wealth* together under a single management. The tremendous economic and social power of the large industrial corporation of our time represents the combination of
these two features. It is difficult to realize what a basic change in
the organization of society is thereby effected.[56]

[56] Ibid., p. vii: "It is the essence of revolutions of the more silent sort that
they are unrecognized until they are far advanced."

PATTERNS OF CONTROL

If one could consider the corporation as if it were a political state, its citizens would be shares of stock rather than persons.[57] The share of stock is certainly one of the great social inventions of all time. By means of it great aggregates of concretely indivisible industrial goods can be divided into small, uniform packages of rights to income and control, easily transferable, and hedged in against liability. The consequent dispersion of ownership, however, most definitely does not lead to a corresponding dispersion of direction and control of the corporation itself. On the contrary, the seeming paradox is that the more widely stock ownership is diffused, the more likely it is that effective control of business wealth will be concentrated.[58] In a small or moderate-sized corporation, where there are only a few stockholders, ownership and management tend to be closely identified; not so in the very large corporations, which account for about one half of the nation's industrial wealth.

The best one-sentence characterization of the ownership of corporations is that *investment ownership* is widely diffused whereas *control ownership* is highly concentrated. The following salient facts summarize the pattern:

1. *Corporate shares are held by large numbers of individuals.* As of the end of 1937 it was estimated that about 8 to 9 million persons owned stock in corporations. At the same date, there were roughly 26 million shareholdings, of which 22 million were in common stock, and the great bulk of these were held by domestic individuals.[59]

[57] Wilbert E. Moore: *Industrial Relations and the Social Order* (New York: 1946), p. 75: "Put in terms which are only slightly oversimplified, the corporation in legal theory is a fictional person whose behavior is determined by its elements, which are pieces of paper."

[58] Moore: *Industrial Relations*, p. 77: "The concentration of economic *power* is in fact chiefly made possible by dispersion of capital ownership."

[59] Raymond W. Goldsmith, Rexford C. Parmelee, and others: "The Distribution of Ownership in the 200 Largest Nonfinancial Corporations," *Monograph No. 29*, Temporary National Economic Committee (Washington, D. C.: 1940), pp. 11–12.

2. *Most shareholders own only a small number of shares*. Over 90 per cent of the stockholders had net incomes of less than $5,000 a year in 1937; [60] about one half of all stockholders received less than $100 in dividends in that same year, and their aggregate dividends accounted for less than 5 per cent of the total dividend income of individuals.[61]

3. In spite of the dispersion of ownership indicated by the large number of shareholders, *stockholdings are actually highly concentrated among a relatively few persons*. For 1,710 companies with stock listed on a national securities exchange, stockholdings of $10,000 or more were only 4 per cent of all shareholdings, but accounted for 60 per cent of the total value of stocks outstanding.[62]

4. Among the 200 largest nonfinancial corporations, *the top 1 per cent of shareholdings include approximately 60 per cent of the common stock of these corporations*. The 20 largest holdings of common stock accounted for 50 per cent or more of all common shares in one fourth of the corporations; in only one fifth of the cases did the 20 largest holdings amount to less than 10 per cent of the common stock outstanding. This concentration of ownership in the very large corporation implies that a comparatively few shareholders have power over the investments of large numbers of small stockholders, who are typically passive and inarticulate in the direction of the corporation's affairs.

In only a few of our large corporations is absolute control wielded by individuals or family groups who own a majority of the shares. Ordinarily shareholding is so widely diffused that a minority bloc or "management" can achieve substantial control; [63] occasionally no one may have control—there may not be any one unitary locus of control that by itself dominates decisions.

Berle and Means showed for the 200 largest nonfinancial corporations in the United States at the beginning of 1930 that five

[60] Ibid., p. 10.
[61] Ibid., p. 13.
[62] Ibid., p. 15.
[63] Berle and Means: *The Modern Corporation and Private Property*, pp. 30 ff. Cf. the more recent data and analysis cited by Moore: *Industrial Relations*, pp. 76–85.

major patterns of control could be distinguished, distributed as follows: [64]

	Percentage of 200 Large Corporations
Apparent Locus of Control	
1. Management group..............	44
2. Legal device (e.g., holding company, voting trust, etc.)...............	21
3. Minority stockholding bloc........	23
4. Majority ownership..............	5
5. Private Owner...................	6
6. Receivership....................	1
	100

The companies in which control rested in the hands of persons or groups having a majority of the voting stock thus amounted to only 11 per cent of all the giant corporations. More recent studies have substantiated these general conclusions.[65]

For most of the corporate economy, the bulk of the stockholders have shifted to the status of mere investors. Control has moved into the hands of management and minority blocs; although the small stockholders are the great majority of all stockholders, they hold a rather insignificant proportion of the shares. A recent compilation showed that in corporations listed on a national securities exchange 2.6 per cent of the stockholders owned 67.7 per cent of the shares, and on the other hand, that the 56.6 of the shareholders owning 25 or less shares each accounted for only 4.2 per cent of the stock owned.[66]

[64] A. A. Berle and G. C. Means: *The Modern Corporation and Private Property* (New York: 1934), p. 94. Reprinted by permission of The Macmillan Company.

[65] See Robert A. Gordon: "Ownership by Management and Control Groups in the Large Corporation," *Quarterly Journal of Economics*, Vol. LII (May, 1938), pp. 367–400.

[66] Helene Granby, with R. W. Goldsmith and R. C. Parmelee: "Survey of Shareholdings in 1,710 Corporations with Securities Listed on a National Securities Exchange," *Monograph No. 30*, Temporary National Economic Committee. (Hereafter cited as T.N.E.C. *Monograph No. 30*.) (Washington, D. C.: 1940), pp. 118–19.

Two crucial points emerge from the above facts: (1) to a large degree ownership of stock has been divorced from control over the specific uses to which capital resources are to be put and from power over business policy; (2) the dispersion of ownership is so far advanced that a further splintering of rights occurs in the form of management control.

Thus the governments of large corporations fall into three main types, representing successively greater separation of ownership from directing power. At one extreme is the comparatively rare "complete" ownership (the close corporation) or majority control. At an intermediate point along the scale, there is "financial control"—a complex balance of power in which compact minority blocs of stockholdings or outside financial interests are the major influences in the central direction of the company. Finally, when ownership is so dispersed that no real financial control centers exist, the stockholders become pure investors and control devolves upon the officers and directors, who can then within very broad limits become self-directing and self-perpetuating. In nearly one third of the largest corporations no visible center of control through stock ownership can be found.[67]

Corporate control structure is often incredibly complex, shifting, and blurred, but we can see that at the very least it is now possible for persons to control a large business enterprise without having *any* appreciable ownership rights in the traditional sense. A new social type has been created: instead of the old Captain of Industry, we have the professional salaried executive, nominally the employee of the stockholders, but actually the general of an industrial army. The directors are elected by "the stockholders"—that is, by such groups as are able to mobilize effectively concentrated aggregates of voting power—and with the senior officers of the corporation they make up the main "management" group. This group is legally held in a "fiduciary" relationship to the body of stockholders; their position is one of trust and accountability; they are

[67] Granby, Goldsmith, Parmelee: T.N.E.C. *Monograph No. 30*, pp. 103–04. However, "the largest blocks of stock are in most cases in the hands of a rather small group having a community of interest based either on family relationship, on corporate ties, or on long-standing business connections." (p. 113).

in theory bound to exercise "fidelity to the interest of the corporation" and to carry out their functions with "reasonable care and reasonable prudence." [68] The exact legal meaning of this fiduciary status is extremely unclear at many points. An officer or director is not at liberty to use his position for personal gain at the expense of the corporation as a whole, but whether he is equally responsible to the *individual shareholders* is a question upon which legal precedents are divided. In recent years, however, statutes and court decisions have tended to impose increasingly rigorous fiduciary standards upon management. Much of the talk of trusteeship, social responsibility and the like is, of course, as yet largely sentimental rather than realistic, but it reflects the underlying structural changes that have separated financial "ownership" from controlling power and have catapulted management to a position of such autonomy as it now tends to hold.

THE NATURE OF CORPORATE PROPERTY

There has resulted the dissolution of the old atom of ownership into its component parts, control and beneficial ownership. This dissolution of the atom of property destroys the very foundation on which the economic order of the past three centuries has rested. [69]

The great development of the corporation signifies an entirely new system of property rights. Under the prior system of private and *individual* property, the entrepreneur was a clearly recognizable and dominant social type. An individual or group of partners both *owned* and *managed* the business; they advanced the capital, took the risks, made the managerial decisions—and incurred the penalties or reaped the rewards of the whole venture. In the closely held corporation, especially during its early development when the typical corporation was a pygmy by modern standards of compari-

---

[68] Husband and Dockeray: *Modern Corporation Finance*, p. 308. See Berle and Means: *The Modern Corporation and Private Property*, chaps. 5 and 6, and pp. 220 ff.

[69] A. A. Berle and G. C. Means: *The Modern Corporation and Private Property* (New York: 1934), p. 8. Reprinted by permission of The Macmillan Company.

son, the stockholders really "owned the business." But in the large corporation of our time, "ownership" has become fragmented: it is simply one bundle of rights standing alongside other rights—the prerogatives of management, the intervention of government, the emerging status claims of labor. To understand the present economic system it becomes essential to look more closely into the meaning of property.

Property consists, first, not of *things,* but of *rights;* it is not a concrete object of reference, but a socially recognized claim. The essence of property is *an institutionalized right of persons or other social units to scarce values.*[70] In our complex economy, many very important property rights concern such "intangibles" as trade marks, patents, franchises, insurance, company good will, even the right to a job. Second, property rights are always institutionally limited and regulated; for they establish schedules of *priority* for the use, transfer, or control of scarce values. In some property systems, various kinds of rights to the same concrete object (or "locus of value" as Moore terms it), [71] are diffused among several different parties. In America, however, the older conception of "private property" emphasized *concentration* of rights in the hands of an individual owner,[72] reserving to the society only such residual powers as the right of eminent domain and various particular uses of "police power." Ownership can refer thus either to (relatively) *unlimited rights* or to *unitary control.* Third, property may be held by individuals or by *other* social units—by governments, kinship units, churches, or other organized social entities. Property may be "private" in the sense of maximizing the bundle of rights assigned to a particular social unit, yet *nonindividual* in the locus of those rights. Finally, there is a broad distinction between rights of control and rights of beneficial ownership of property; for instance, one may control the uses of a good without enjoying the other

[70] Wilbert E. Moore: "The Emergence of New Property Conceptions in America," *Journal of Legal and Political Sociology,* Vol. I, nos. 3–4 (April, 1943), pp. 34–5. Our whole discussion draws heavily upon the ideas advanced in this penetrating essay.

[71] Ibid., p. 37.

[72] It is partly because of this conception that "property" and "things" are so easily confused in our usual thinking.

values attached to it, or one may enjoy the fruits of a scarce value without having the right to determine the use to which it is put.[73]

What then are we to make of corporate property? We cannot here untangle the law of corporate property, but the main features have a certain sharp simplicity. If instead of asking "who owns the corporation" we ask "what *rights* are represented in corporate property," it is apparent that ownership of corporate property diverges in several important ways from unlimited ownership of individual private property. There are, first of all, *investment rights* of bondholders, creditors, and shareholders. In varying degrees, all of these owners are entitled under specified conditions to a return from funds they have placed at the disposal of the corporation. But they are not necessarily individual persons—they may be other corporate entities, or the corporation itself. It is therefore possible for ownership of a "private" corporation to be as non-individualistic as government ownership. Secondly, the—by now proverbial—separation of investment rights from managerial control means, of course, that the stockholders do not have unlimited rights nor unitary control. Except for powerful minority-bloc stockholders, the owner of a voting share turns over to the managerial group or other "control center" the actual disposition of his funds; and stockholders who *do* control the corporation have their powers by virtue, not of their stock, but of their position in the corporation power structure. The property represented by shares of stock is further limited by governmental regulation channelizing the uses of capital. It is potentially, and to some degree factually, limited by rights or quasi-rights of labor.

Thus we have the "dissolution of the atom of property" referred to in the quotation at the head of this section. The label "private property" is a legal fiction of little help in determining what constitutes effective control of the productive apparatus of the society. Property is always a social fact and the real issues of public policy concern *what* control, by *whom*, for *what*, not whether or not property is to be regulated. For "property" means in part precisely the

[73] Cf. the related distinction between active property and passive property made by Berle and Means: *The Modern Corporation and Private Property*, pp. 346–7.

exclusion of individuals from the use or enjoyment of certain scarce values except under specific conditions subject to the control of the property holder. Rights belong to someone or some social entity, and they are only rights so long and to the extent that they are respected by others. Every property right therefore implies the duty of someone to respect that right, and every legitimized right of access to scarce values is at least potentially a form of property.[74] Corporate property is no exception and exists only so far as the dominant social consensus gives value and legitimacy to it.

INTERNAL ORGANIZATION OF THE CORPORATION [75]

At this point it will be useful to review what has been discussed thus far. Beginning with a consideration of economic activity and economic institutions in general terms, we saw that normative regulation is a universal and indispensable property of economic systems just as it is of every other sector of social systems. We outlined certain dominant features of the American economy that seemed to be of special sociological interest, in particular, the dominance of corporate organization and the importance of large corporations. We then touched upon various types of intercorporate co-ordination and influence and arrived at the conception of a corporative *system* permeating the economy, especially in financial and industrial fields. Some of the many ways in which economic activity is controlled other than by the free market system were briefly reviewed. With this broad picture in mind we have returned

[74] In the concise analysis by Max Weber, "property" was restricted to those appropriated rights that extend beyond the individual's lifetime and that are heritable. See the discussion by Parsons in *Theory of Social and Economic Organization*, pp. 40–1 and ff.

[75] In addition to sources already cited, useful references on this topic include: James Burnham: *The Managerial Revolution* (New York: 1941); Chester I. Barnard: *The Functions of the Executive* (Cambridge, Mass.: 1938); Ralph C. Davis: *Industrial Organization and Management* (New York: 1940); Harvey Pinney: "Administocracy, Inc." *Social Forces*, Vol. 19, No. 3 (March, 1941); F. J. Roethlisberger and William J. Dickson: *Management and the Worker* (Cambridge, Mass.: 1939).

to a closer inspection of control and ownership of the corporate unit itself.

We must now give brief attention to two other main aspects of corporate organization: (1) the internal differentiation of authority and function; (2) labor relations. We may think of the corporate unit as a single plant or as a series of plants, offices, stations, etc. under central management.

The corporation is a social organization—a system of human relations. The business corporation has profit making as its goal: it must meet the test of rational capital accounting or go out of business. Its means for attaining that end are its technical apparatus and materials, human labor, and "organization." We are interested in the social arrangements whereby the efforts of large numbers of persons are integrated toward corporate objectives.

At the center (or, if you will, at the top) of the corporate organization is a small group of persons who by virtue of their formal office are given continuing responsibility and authority for forming and carrying out policies. They have great authority and overlook a wide range of general organizational problems. Frequently they are salaried managers to whom has been delegated a large part of the powers nominally held by stockholders and directors. Usually, as we have seen, they also include representatives of financial control who are not employees of the corporation. The latter act as the mediating link between "outside" ownership, investment and creditor interests, and the internal body of the corporation as an operating unit.[76]

From the central control group the organization extends downward and outward through the progressive subdivision and delegation of *authority* and of *specialized functions*. What is commonly known as *"line"* organization is a hierarchy of positions that defines who will give and receive what orders, commands, requests, and suggestions—invariably creating a hierarchy of prestige or rank. In principle the subdelegation of authority can go on indefinitely,

[76] For simplicity we are concentrating upon the industrial corporation, since it illustrates all the essential features of fully developed corporate organization.

but there are always practical limitations.[77] In very large organizations, the hierarchy tends to become cumbersome—the line of communication has a large number of transmission points, and a mass of detailed decisions converge upon the top positions; but this problem is partly avoided if each successively lower position in practice deals with questions of detail within the framework set by more general orders received from superordinate positions. A more difficult problem is presented by the many quite different areas of technical specialization that must be co-ordinated, and various "functional" schemes of organization in addition to, or in combination with, the line organization have developed in answer to it. Departmentalization represents only a slight departure—several functional areas may be mapped out and placed under subexecutives while otherwise straight-line authority delegation is practiced. Somewhat greater modification of the line structure leads to a line-staff scheme, in which technical specialists act as advisors at various levels, but do not themselves hold authority. At the theoretical extreme, every office of authority would also be an office of specialized technical competence: the *technical hierarchy* and the *authority hierarchy* would coincide. However, this splintering of direction and control creates such numerous problems in organization that it is rarely approached in the industrial corporation.[78] Instead there typically emerges a basic line organization, which is then broken into functional branches and combined with a staff (technical) organization.

The internal differentiation of authority and of areas of competence in the large industrial corporation is highly developed. It is possible to identify six fairly distinct groups: (1) executives or top managers; (2) technical specialists; (3) junior line-supervisors ("middle management"); (4) secretarial and clerical workers; (5) first line-supervisors (foremen, etc.); (6) shop and bench workers.[79] The whole structure exhibits regularities of belief and behavior that bear a remarkable resemblance to those of nonindustrial or-

[77] See Moore: *Industrial Relations*, pp. 96 ff. for a good brief discussion of industrial organization.

[78] Ibid., pp. 101–3.

[79] This is Moore's adaptation of the categories used by F. J. Roethlisberger. Ibid., p. 120.

ganizations of large size. In fact, students of industry now recognize that what we have here is a particular subtype of bureaucratic social organization.[80]

The notion of bureaucracy is an ideal type, which by definition never exactly fits any particular organizations. Organizations are not bureaucratic *or* nonbureaucratic; there are differing kinds and degrees of bureaucracy. It is an interesting commentary upon the importance of culturally standardized "blind spots" that so many people still think of bureaucracy as confined to political government; but viewed as a descriptive label rather than as a curse word, it simply refers to the archetype of formal, functionally rational organizations that may be as diverse in other respects as schools, churches, universities, armies and business enterprises. As an ideal type, bureaucracy is a formal order that co-ordinates the diverse but interdependent activities of persons into a definite organizational pattern. As described in detail by Max Weber and others,[81] bureaucratic organization is defined by the following main characteristics:

1. There is, typically, an explicit definition of official activities considered to inhere in specific statuses; areas of authority and competence tend to be formally specified.

2. There is a high degree of specialization of functions and duties.

3. Authority inheres in the *office* rather than in the person.

4. There is a clear separation between "private" or personal activities and the activities carried out within the organization

[80] "Bureaucratic" is being used descriptively, not polemically.

[81] All roads here start from Max Weber's *Wirtschaft und Gesellschaft* (Tübingen: 1922), pp. 650–78. See also: Karl Mannheim: *Man and Society in an Age of Reconstruction* (New York: 1940), esp. pp. 46–9, 53–60, 319–25; Everett C. Hughes: "Institutional Office and the Person," *American Journal of Sociology*, Vol. XLIII (1937); Robert K. Merton: "Bureaucratic Structure and Personality," *Social Forces*, Vol. 18 (1940); E. T. Hiller: "Social Structure in Relation to the Person," *Social Forces*, Vol. 16 (1937); Carl J. Friedrich and Taylor Cole: *Responsible Bureaucracy: A Study of the Swiss Civil Service* (Cambridge, Mass.: 1932). Much of the literature in this field is predominantly evaluative rather than analytical. Cf. for example: Carleton K. Allen: *Bureaucracy Triumphant* (London: 1931); James M. Beck: *Our Wonderland of Bureaucracy* (New York: 1932).

or in its name. For instance, the officeholder must spend his entire working time in the service of the organization. There is, furthermore, a sharp distinction between his personal possessions and the goods of the organization; private budget and organizational budget are two different worlds.

5. The functioning of various offices within the organization is governed by generalized, abstract, but definite rules, which involve the categorizing of problems.

6. Procedure tends to be formal and impersonal, especially in dealings between superordinate and subordinate offices. Communications are recorded; forms of communication are stereotyped and ritualized; the intrusion of "personal" elements into organizational activities tends to be discouraged.

7. In an ideal bureaucracy, the selection of all except the highest policy-determining officials is by appointment (rather than election, inheritance, and so on) on the basis of technical competence.

8. Organization is hierarchical. Every office is a link in a chain of authority, and as a general rule communications (orders, requests, information, etc.) pass through all the offices intermediate to the positions of the communicants.

9. The structure of offices is maintained by a relatively explicit and rigid discipline, as is shown by the imposition of various sanctions expected to encourage accuracy, caution, punctuality, methodical procedure, close co-ordination of activities.

10. A less essential but common characteristic of bureaucracy is provision for security of tenure among the officials—promotion by seniority, annual-wage plans, pensions, and fixed-tenure provisions that hold in the absense of quite gross negligence or misconduct.

11. There is a frequently noted tendency to maintain a body of "secrets of the office"; many organizational details are closely guarded against observation by outsiders.

These features have, of course, both "negative" and "positive" consequences. The alleged advantages include precision, reliability, functional rationality, accurate co-ordination of large systems of activity, minimization of personal elements irrelevant to purposes of the organization; the disadvantages include tendencies toward ritualism, multiplication of procedures beyond the point of maximum efficiency, lack of adaptability to new situations, excessive power striving.

A widespread development of bureaucratic structures has been a conspicuous feature of industrial societies during the past century. Since Weber's analysis it has been recognized that bureaucracy is by no means limited to the state but is a prominent characteristic of the highly developed capitalistic systems of western Europe and America. The "discovery" of bureaucracy has even led to claims that a revolutionary shift in power is occurring—not from the capitalists to the proletariat, but from the capitalists to the bureaucrats. This thesis contains unacceptable elements of exaggeration and oversimplification, but the tremendous growth in the social importance of bureaucracy cannot be doubted.

Our attention will be focused upon the *formal* organization. Recent research, it is true, has conclusively demonstrated the pervasiveness of *informal* organization that invariably accompanies the formal structure. It is simply not possible to predict behavior in any organization from its "blue print" formal structure, and a major part of the management of an enterprise is necessarily devoted to understanding and dealing with groupings, relationships, sentiments, and practices that are not formalized or even explicit.[82] Nevertheless, our present interest is primarily in the formal structure, partly because informal organization will be discussed in Chapter 12, and partly because the formal order is the indispensable framework that canalizes even the informal patterns.

Some of the most important features of bureaucracy appear to be inseparable from any large-scale organization. "Organization" means co-ordination and predictability. Where, as in the large industrial corporation, large numbers of people are simultaneously engaged in highly specialized activities focused upon a single objective, the "need for co-ordination" is enhanced while its at-

[82] "Over and beyond the officially expected rights and duties, lines of authority, and rigidly defined relationships, any managerial system is characterized by a great variety of informal, unofficial activities, attitudes, sentiments, and symbols." Wilbert E. Moore: *Industrial Relations and the Social Order* (New York: 1946) p. 121. Reprinted by permission of The Macmillan Company.

tainment is rendered more difficult. With increasing size of organization the diffuse and informal methods of communication and control that work well in small groups become increasingly hazardous and ineffective: co-ordination is hampered by overlapping authorities, gaps in communication, contradictory orders, and vague and shifting loci of responsibility. Sheer size of organization is enough to create *indirect* communication: face-to-face contact of all the communicating parties is impossible. As indirect lines of communication are set up, the formality of the organization is increased; for instance, communications must be authenticated when they pass between persons who have no direct contacts.[83] *Size* plus *specialization*, therefore, tend to produce bureaucracy. Specialization of function complicates the problem of co-ordination by necessitating both indirect communication and special co-ordinating centers.

The modern industrial corporation tends to be bureaucratic not only because it is large and highly specialized but also because the workers are "separated from the means of production," and are dependent upon paid employment. Such is the case in American industry, and it is reinforced by the absentee ownership discussed above—ownership that necessitates delegation of authority from stockholders to directors and executives and from these to still other subordinate officers, with subsequent subdivision of authority and need for co-ordination. The existence of a "final control group" (whether "ownership" or "management") is thus crucial to hierarchical organization. If the organization were not responsible *as a whole* to some control group, there would not be the same pressure for unitary policy and control, and such co-ordination as remained could operate through the interaction of *functionally* specialized offices rather than through a chain of command. We could imagine, for instance, that a corporation holding all its own stock and manufacturing a single standardized product for an absolutely stable market might attain such equilibrium that there would hardly be a sharply graded hierarchy. But actually the industrial corporation

---

[83] "The extensive use of more or less rigid and precise rules and working procedures is well-nigh universal among the giant corporations." T.N.E.C. *Monograph No. 11*, p. 33.

is responsible to control groups and typically produces several products for changing markets and with changing costs. The need for co-ordinated *changes* to meet new conditions pushes the organization toward hierarchy. Thus the wider the extent of functional specialization, the more likely it is that authority will be vertically subdelegated.[84]

Bureaucratic formality arises partly from hierarchy itself. Hierarchy as involving differentiated functions, formal rules, and routines has already been discussed. But hierarchy further involves giving and receiving orders, with all the attendant possibilities of friction and conflict. By formality of procedure, "arbitrary" action can be limited, responsibility located and fixed, and *personal* involvement minimized. Furthermore, formality maintains vertical "social distance" between statuses, so that very diverse and perhaps sharply incompatible persons can nevertheless interact sufficiently to fulfill their organizational functions. Formality, thus, not only "protects" the subordinates from arbitrariness but also supports the impersonal authority and prestige of the superiors and so helps maintain hierarchical control.

In its procedures and in its statuses, the large industrial corporation fits the theoretical model of bureaucracy quite closely. However, it differs from governmental bureaucracy in not being likely to hire and promote on the basis of systematic, impersonal tests of technical competence, such as Civil Service examinations.[85] Also, in all except the very large and long-established quasi-public corporations, it is taken for granted that family connections and other nontechnical factors will be important in determining status and rewards within the organization; thus, what would be condemned as nepotism in the government corporation is "normal" in the business corporation. Again, the business corporation has to show return on investment rather than simply stay within an appropriation. Finally, relations with employees, especially rank-and-file workers, obviously differ. (Corporate labor relations will be discussed in the next section.) Even with all these differences there

---

[84] Cf. Moore: *Industrial Relations*, p. 110.

[85] It is not necessary to elaborate the fact that factors other than scores on official examinations are also important in government service.

is still an impressive similarity between the business corporation and governmental organizations of similar size. This similarity is significant, for it means that much of "free enterprise" ideology is simply not applicable to most employees of large industrial corporations.

In the cultural theory of economic individualism, a person's rewards were earned by free competition in the market; effort and shrewdness were indexed by economic gain derived from a relatively impersonal process; personal success was not directly dependent upon a particular person's opinion of one's ability. Thus if John Jones, merchant, was able to buy cheap and sell dear, he was an economic success, no matter how intensely he might be disliked by competitor Sam Smith. But if Sam Smith is a higher official in a corporate hierarchy, Jones' chances for promotion may not be unaffected by Smith's opinion of him on other than technical grounds. The banal example takes on significance when related to the dominance of the corporation: in established industries, the primary career-pattern is promotion in the *bureaucratic scale*, not competitive success as an individual entrepreneur. Therefore, every step up (or down) the ladder is dependent upon the decision of a particular superior office.[86] And positions may be assigned partly on the basis of class or ethnic background and family or clique affiliations. The corporation may develop informal groupings which act like "political machines" in rewarding members and excluding outsiders. At the logical extreme, membership in a particular informal group becomes a prerequisite for advancement. Though this extreme may not be reached in the large corporation —indeed, it is probably less important there then in small or medium-sized businesses—its institutional importance is difficult to overemphasize. Impersonal competitive placement in the open market employs universalistic norms, applying to individuals regardless of their particular group affiliations; *particularistic* norms, on the contrary, make group memberships and personal relations determine social position and economic reward. When businesses were small, outside regulation minimal, and the market competi-

[86] Except, of course, as rights of promotion are limited by seniority provisions or other impersonal and automatic criteria.

tive, the universal norms were continually reinforced by the character of day-to-day economic activity. In the large economic enterprise of today, however, universalistic standards depend upon deliberate policy. It is no longer even seemingly "automatic." Wherever the large corporation extends in American economic life, purposive control replaces the diffuse mechanisms of the market. *Cultural* structure becomes *social* organization, and this change is perhaps one of the deepest meanings of an age of corporateness.

The vertical organization of the large business concern always manifests a fairly clear "breaking point" between the office and the shop—between the executive, clerical, staff, and supervisory force on the one hand, and the rank-and-file workers on the other. Yet within both these broad divisions there is a continuous gradation of income, authority, and prestige. The many persons in intermediate ranks constitute a significant portion of the new middle classes discussed in Chapter 5. Obviously these are "middle class" in a very different sense from the self-employed owners of small business that political rhetoric praises as the "backbone of the country." To place the white-collar employees of the new business bureaucracies in the same category as the old entrepreneurial groups obscures at least as much as it reveals. The salaried employee differs from the stereotyped "businessman" in life situation, avenue of success, discipline and self-direction, specific goals and motivations. These are some results of the new modes of American economic organization.

THE "PROFIT MOTIVE"

Under the strict theory of private property and free competition, business takes all the profits it can get and bears all losses, even to the extent of complete failure. But in the present economy of huge interlocking units it is very doubtful if any large sector of the economy will be allowed to collapse. The tremendous interdependence of the existing system is such that unchecked deflation quickly spreads cumulatively from one sector to another. Thus, in the depression of the 1930's the threatened collapse of American agriculture immediately had severe impacts upon life insurance companies and other large holders of farm mortgages, upon the agricultural implement industry, and upon many other strategic industries. Total bankruptcy of the nation's railroads would drag along with it a host of indispensable financial organizations. Whatever the economic advantages of thoroughgoing depression in "purging" the economy, the political and social interests are not likely to permit unrestrained losses so long as there is a going social order at all.

Thus the risk-taking functions of private business are being shifted to the larger society through governmental intervention, with corresponding controls and limitations upon business, and the "profit motive" ceases to that extent to regulate economic activity.

Otherwise, too, the profit motive has been radically transformed. Although business is expected to produce profit, it is no longer universally true that "profits are the reward of enterprise." The wage workers and salaried officialdom of a corporation are motivated by profits only indirectly, in that their jobs require continued solvency in the total enterprise. In so far as the direct recipients of profits, the stockholders, do not manage the business, profits can not directly inspire effort and efficiency. Profit making is a second-order control, so to speak, and may very little "motivate" those actually operating the business. The separation of ownership from control shows that the "profit motive" is not a *motive* at all but an institutional goal; it is not a psychological state but a social condition. The fully developed corporate form today is likely to be manned by people with goals and incentives not so different from those of the personnel of nonprofit organizations. This fact is not envisaged in the traditional theories of property and economic incentives, and neither the law nor popular thought has yet come to terms with its implications.[87]

[87] Cf. W. E. Moore's comment: "The ideology of 'free enterprise' is still widely expressed by corporation executives who are not in fact engaged in anything approaching free enterprise in the traditional sense, and is facilitated by judicial interpretation of corporate ownership of private property." "The Emergence of new Property Conceptions in America," p. 49.

5. Labor Relations and Labor Organizations

ANYTHING like a complete picture of American labor relations is too broad and complex to be given here. We merely outline the basic institutional elements without descriptive detail, concentrating upon *industrial* labor, ignoring the migratory agricultural worker, the domestic service worker, the employee of the small shop, the remnants of independent crafts, and many others, important as they are. For most wage earners are employed in industry; there the crucial problems of power and conflict lie; and there the pattern is increasingly set for labor in other fields—for example, even the service and clerical occupations are being increasingly mechanized and industrialized.

American labor relations have developed in an economy with rich resources and scanty population, and these in combination with an open class-structure and a democratic political order have given a number of distinctive features to the American case. The absence of feudal or other traditionalized social ties facilitated an early and thoroughgoing commercialization of labor. Labor became a market commodity in an individualistic economy. Unionism developed late, and against strong opposition. The extraordinary amount of violence accompanying the efforts of workers to organize has stamped labor-employer relations with a peculiarly American conflict psychology. Yet the underlying dynamics of the labor movement are broadly similar to those of Western Europe, reflecting similar institutional conditions.

As American industry developed and the wage earner became a factory "hand," labor relations became capitalistic market relations. Though ideology and law assumed equality of bargaining power, the individual worker was obviously not equal in bargaining power to his employer. The worker, personally free but propertyless,[88] was fully exposed to the insecurities of a fluctuating job mar-

---

[88] As Briefs has put it, his status became permanent but his job was not. Goetz A. Briefs: *The Proletariat* (New York: 1937), chap. 3.

ket. As new large-scale industries built factories, the workers were recruited from European immigrants and American hinterlands. While industrialization was transforming American society from about 1880 [89] to 1919, most workers were first generation factory workers; their fathers had been farm people, and they entered industry as raw recruits for whom factory discipline was a sharp break with previous modes of life. Ethnic cleavages hampered coherent, united, and disciplined labor organization. Outside the skilled crafts and some occupations dominated by skilled European workers—for instance, brewing and some portions of the coal mining industry—the labor force was constituted mainly of heterogeneous, unorganized, relatively unskilled workers without factory experience, who hoped soon to escape from wage work. They were spread over a vast territory, often disunited in creed and language, subject to incessant shifts in the labor market and rapid technological innovations. Their thinking was individualistic, stressing equality of opportunity, individual responsibility, and advancement through personal efforts. Small wonder that unionism, especially industrial unionism, developed slowly and with great difficulty.

These workers confronted a system in which employers were institutionally committed to treating labor as a commodity and were bound to accept no other obligations to the employee than paying wages.[90] Capitalistic labor relations are segmental, not inclusive; only the cash nexus, the money wage, controls; the employee is free to quit his job and the employer is free to turn the worker out upon the streets; not personalized ties nor *noblesse oblige*, but the market bargain is the bond.

Now economic relations as defined in Western culture are *contractual*—that is, segmental, limited, explicit, and formally voluntary. A contract is supposedly to the "interest" of all parties concerned, benefiting each; the obligations and rights are stated,

[89] After the first large craft union (the Knights of Labor, organized in 1869) had foundered on the rocks of a disastrous political effort, the American Federation of Labor dominated the labor movement from the late 1880's until the emergence of the C.I.O. in the 1930's.

[90] Znaniecki: *Social Actions*, p. 615: "A perfect worker in a capitalistic enterprise is one who does exactly anything he is told to do, and does it for no other reason than because he is paid to do it."

and limitations placed upon any attempt to broaden the stipulated terms. In all these particulars, contractual relations contrast sharply with kinship relations, friendships, and other "particularistic" relationships.

Labor-employer relations in our society are contractual, and thus arise many "labor problems." Being contractual, industrial employment establishes no nexus of common loyalties, interests, or obligations beyond the segmental, impersonal exchange of wages for services, impersonal in that no account is taken of values of individuals *qua* individuals. One is not interested in the other person's life except in particular, defined, and limited aspects. Impersonal relations thus depend upon limited "interests" such as economic exchange, and in so far as these interests are instable, the relations based upon them will be transitory. In strict capitalistic theory the employer has no more right to expect "loyalty" from his employees than the latter have to expect security from him. This is an *institutional* fact, not a matter of the motives of particular individuals.

In a dynamic economy, with technological change and short-term economic fluctuations, the contractual system of labor produces insecurity for the isolated individual worker. Just as any form of personal dependence is alien to contractual money-wage employment, so security of status has no institutional basis in the relations of workers to *particular* employers. In addition, the individual worker's bargaining power is strikingly unequal to his employer's. Without a mythical "natural identity of interests" between employer and employees, this weakness of bargaining power further contributes to the economic insecurity of the unorganized workers.

These basic characteristics of capitalistic labor systems are certainly not peculiar to the United States. However, other features of American labor relations do not have the same cross-cultural generality: the slow unionization, the prevalence of violence, the persistence of craft unionism and the lateness of industrial unionization, the lack of "class consciousness" and political emphasis among labor. All these are interrelated. Thus, the open resources, expanding economy, and fluid class structure during the nineteenth century delayed the formation of a permanent wage-worker stratum. Ethnic and racial heterogeneity split labor. The lack of traditional solidarities and traditional ties to employers favored an individualistic, competitive outlook among workers as well as employers. In turn, the lack of labor solidarity minimized its political effectiveness and left the government—including the important judiciary—in the hands of business groups, with consequent further barriers to the organized articulation of labor's interests. Employers held what Laski calls "the atomic view of industrial power" [91]—the conception of a business as the unitary, private possession of its owners and managers and of the workers as "tools" having no claim or voice in determining the conditions of their work. Workers believed in (or at least hoped for) individual advancement, and held a strongly equalitarian creed. Both parties had a firm sense of their "rights," and these rights were often incompatible. In this sense, labor relations were, and are, *moral* relations, and the bitterness and violence so common in American industrial history stem from conflicting values. To the clash of pecuniary interest has often been added a sense of moral outrage, for what is frequently thought to be at stake is an institutional principle—the "right of a man to run his own business as he sees fit," the "right of the worker to a decent wage," the claim of labor to have a voice in the internal affairs of the enterprise.

Yet there has never been any really "radical" large-scale labor movement in the United States. The older craft unions have been thoroughly capitalistic. They fought to win members the right to bargain collectively and then, the best pay and working conditions possible within the system—all this against formidable opposition. The labor-union movement developed by continual battle rather than peaceful expansion, yet the craft-type union has typically acted on "business principles"; it became another business enterprise, with labor as its product. Even the newer industrial unions have concentrated upon immediate tangible benefits rather than upon reshaping the system.

Industrial unionism, however, does mark a change in some very

[91] Harold J. Laski: *The American Democracy: A Commentary and Interpretation* (New York: 1948), p. 203.

important industries. Covering entire industries instead of specialized trades, the large industrial unions match the giant corporations.[92] Mass unionism is a reaction to mass industry and to the
concentration of economic power in the large corporations and their
interwoven communities-of-interest. It reflects the rise of a popu-
lous stratum of "permanent" industrial workers—fathers and sons
of workers. Individually powerless, the industrial workers are
massively powerful when welded into United Steelworkers of
America, or United Automobile Workers, or United Mine Workers.
When Big Business and Big Labor collide—as they must, for the
sources of conflict are built into their institutions—the struggle
tests our society's capacity to maintain a tightly articulated economy within the bounds of democracy.

The industrial worker and his unions cannot be understood in
strictly economic terms, nor in terms of a society of farmers,
small businesses, and independent craftsmen. He does not own
the materials or machines he works with, nor control the conditions of his work. He is subject to the rigid and detailed discipline
of mechanized, repetitive operations. Although the alleged loss of
skills and "sentiments of workmanship" is probably overempha-
sized in our time, machine tending is the archetype of industrial
work. The skills of the factory operative often become obsolete
through further mechanization. If he dreams of individual achievement, the corporate hierarchy is, to say the least, not easily climb-
able. His stake in the job is in wages not rewards of achievement
"cumulative, unique, tangible and recognized." [93] Significantly, out
of insecurity, the recognition of collective fate of limited opportunity, the unions have developed automatic standardized criteria for
job holding and wage levels. Seniority, for example, is a security device that sacrifices nominal opportunities for competitive advancement in favor of an impersonal safeguard against chance and favoritism in promotion, pay, discharge, and lay-offs. Likewise "equal

[92] Wilson and Kolb put the situation neatly in their statement that the
unions become "rivals of the corporation for control of the labor market within
the old institutional framework." *Sociological Analysis*, p. 554.

[93] The quoted phrase is from a stimulating unpublished paper, The Social
Situations of Farmer and Factory Worker, by Mr. Nelson Foote of Cornell
University.

pay for equal work," so firmly embedded in industrial unionism, rules out not only age and sex but also ability, character, and "need" as criteria for rates of pay. The striving of industrial workers for stability and certainty is further shown by more sophisticated schemes, such as pensions, annual-wage plans, union contracts that tie wage levels to a cost-of-living index.

The worker's economic situation is most fully significant in its effects on *social* status. Unionism, and efforts toward quasi-professional status for industrial work, are largely a reaction to the low social esteem of factory work both by the "general public" and by the workers themselves. One of our widest valid generalizations from experience is that human beings dislike not leading a meaningful and respected life. The total life-situation of the factory worker as previously described deprives him of many of the supports for a sense of personal integrity—for instance, the impersonality of "being treated as a number," the degrading of skills, the opprobrium directed toward "labor," the insecurity of employment, the lack of personal involvement in the task, or of participation in decision making. These are not *all* the relevant conditions, nor do all apply to all workers. Deprivation of status and self-esteem have been, beyond question, prominent in industrial history in this and other countries. Unionism is one reaction to the threat not only to the worker's economic security but to his total social security. Labor-management strife is only partly "dividing the spoils"— important as that is. Workers are social beings (even as executives are), and threats to their wages, tenure, or control of their own destiny are not just segmental and peripheral threats but endanger the only life open to them. In response, they form not only unions, but many other defenses, such as elaborate informal organizations and group solidarities within the plant.[94] Unions are mainly signifi-

[94] This aspect of the sociology of industrial relations has been much investigated in recent years. Its substantial importance can be recognized without allowing it to overshadow either the bed-rock problem of power or the encompassing institutional framework. Representative works dealing with this field include: F. J. Roethlisberger: *Management and Morale* (Cambridge, Mass.: 1941); Elton Mayo: *The Human Problems of an Industrial Civilization* (New York: 1933); Thomas North Whitehead: *Leadership in a Free Society* (Cambridge, Mass.: 1936); William F. Whyte (ed.): *Industry and Society* (New York: 1946).

cant in the larger structure of industry as foci of bargaining power and as potential sources of political power.

As struggle groups, unions have used various modes of organization and strategic devices. Craft unions of highly skilled workers can restrict the production of new workers by apprentice, training, and licensing provisions. Another, less rigorous, method for fencing in a labor market is the closed shop, which makes union membership a condition of employment. Such protective devices as insurance, relief, and retirement funds, both strengthen the worker and improve the union's support and striking power. Above all, of course, the unions must rely as a last resort upon direct action—the strike, the sympathetic strike, the boycott, or whatever other concerted pressure may be expedient, legally or otherwise, at a particular period. Against these methods employers use devices similarly diverse in form but alike in intent and consequence: employer's associations, lock-outs, armed force, strike-breakers, company unions, legal action, propaganda. Where compromise and conciliation end, industrial conflict begins; this conflict is an only somewhat muted version of war, and all the devices of war are familiar to the American industrial scene.

It is never safe to ignore the role of power in economic action. The modern labor-union movement makes increasing use of its political power to reach its objectives.[95] The destruction of independent labor organizations in totalitarian countries shows how all the effective weapons of the workers can be swept from their hands through political action. The newer industrial unions take a far more vigorous and broad interest in legislation and politics than did the older "business unionism," partly because their relations with the corporations are so important for social order and social integration that the power of government is bound to be invoked in cases of prolonged conflict.[96]

The confrontation of large corporation and organized workers is a central fact of our economic system that is utterly alien to the ideology of an atomistic, free enterprise system. The traditional

[95] Cf. Moore: *Industrial Relations*, p. 357.
[96] Cf. Benjamin M. Selekman: *Labor Relations and Human Relations* (New York: 1947), pp. vii, 211–12.

culture of capitalism at least provided a moral structure for the compromising of rivalries and for the bargaining process in a world of small enterprise; but the violent economic struggles of the present period are sufficient evidence that it can do so no longer. None of the traditional concepts—"private property," capital, labor, enterprise, individualism—has its old meaning. A corporation is not an "individual," a corporate executive is typically not "running his own business," an assembly-line workman is not an independent craftsman. Yet for the foreseeable future the corporation and the union will occupy the center of the stage—unless the third member of the cast, government, takes over the full play. The potential directions in which the economic order can move deserve close inspection, since a reconstitution of the criteria of economic morality and legitimacy is already well under way.

This problem is usually posed as a choice between "liberal capitalism," "communism," or "fascism," but our present analysis indicates that this way of seeing the problem is not analytically productive. Nineteenth-century-model capitalism met an unrecognized demise some time ago, and not even artificial respiration seems to hold much promise of success at this late date. On the other hand, authentically totalitarian concepts are so alien to the American needs and traditions that one must rationally doubt that they necessarily represent the "wave of the future."

One important native brand of thinking blends the old economic individualism with the acceptance of bigness. It sees the importance of power, accepts the corporation as the locus of economic control, and envisages a society of large business units organized as hierarchies headed by a benevolent ("socially responsible") elite of managers. This nascent corporativism is as yet only vaguely formulated, but it probably represents the closest approximation to a native ideology contra the newly based claims and aspirations of unionized labor.

At the other extreme, there are various versions of "proletarian" ideologies, among which Communism, however, is a minor item. But of more interest to us here are other solutions, between hierarchism of left and right, which do not envisage the destruction of democratic institutions. The professional business managers are beginning to accept notions of responsibility that allow labor an important measure of self-government. Similarly the professional labor union administrator is increasingly willing to think of industrial and societal as well as labor problems. Many unions now press for efficiency in work, actively interest themselves in production problems, and find substantial areas of common interest with managerial groups. The professionalization of the industrial workers themselves is of major importance to both developments. As workers advance in educational level, in security of employment and wage, in measure of respect, self-direction, and accountability accorded them in the general community, they become increasingly "professional" and not merely "workers." [97] It is true that the degrading of skills through technological change is an obstacle to the development of an integral quasi-professional status for industrial labor; but the new technologies also require skilled workers to service the complex machines and processes. At the same time, the unions are becoming far more than fighting organizations or bargaining agencies. They increasingly provide educational programs, recreation, health services, aid in unemployment, illness, death. The new labor statesmen (Walter Reuther of United Automobile Workers is one of the clearest examples) recognize that continuing organizations must satisfy multiple interests.

It must be noted also that new procedures for resolving tension and conflict in industrial relations are contributing in a significant way to the formation of new institutional norms. Procedural devices have no magical properties and cannot create the illusion of harmony when real conflicts of interest are present. They can, however, ease communication, clarify expectations, and gradually contribute to a common set of codes and understandings. Much of the rawness, violence, bitterness of industrial relations is traceable to the lack of just these codes.

The possibility remains, of course, that the industrial union will gradually harden into a self-perpetuating bureaucracy, so that the worker will be subject to two rigid hierarchies instead of one. But

[97] The writer is indebted to Mr. Nelson Foote for the idea of professionalization as a basic process in American labor relations. Foote is testing his hypotheses in a forthcoming study of industrial Detroit.

both the corporation and the union have open to them the techniques and arts of group consultation and decision, of conference and discussion, of on-job training and upgrading by merit. To what extent such "democratic" flexibilities will actually prevail against the many forces tending toward hierarchy only the seer could say.

6. Security, Rigidity, and Possible New Directions

THIS brief analysis of economic institutions necessarily has to leave out far more than it can even suggest. It would not be wise to end, however, without mentioning certain implicit problems raised by the presence of a "security psychology" in an age of corporacy. The following relevant facts seem well-established:

1. Workers fear job scarcity. They are sharply conscious of insecurity. They frequently strive for monopoly controls.

2. Managers and investors frequently, if not typically, act as nearly like monopolists as their control of a favored business situation permits.

3. Both labor and business interests are importantly *organized*. The economy is to a large extent an administered, organized system of massive units.

4. The corporation and the union are in rivalry for the allegiance of the workers. Workers *qua* workers are not union-inclined without question; more typically they see themselves as being "bid for" by the union and the company; they constitute one corner of a triangle.

5. The basic framework of labor relations is confused and changing—a "crisis-conditioned, unformed institution" [98]—and the unsteadiness and ambiguity of the legal and moral order opens the door to the relatively free play of power, and to all the suspicions, tensions, and recriminations that always arise from the exertion of power without consent.

[98] Selekman: *Labor Relations and Human Relations*, p. v.

Deep-seated forces are driving large groups of men into highly organized power units focused upon the advancement of partly disparate economic interests. Out of the clashes of these groups grow political pressures and State regulation. Unless the corporations and the unions can develop mutually acceptable relationships that prevent paralyzing conflict, increased government intervention is perfectly predictable. And in the American scene this intervention poses a deep conflict of values. The individualism of enterprise is disappearing into the corporation, the individualism of work into the discipline of the factory and the union. More and more, industrial relations concern masses, organizations, groups and the differentiated statuses within these group entities—not the relations of a homogeneous aggregate of separate and equal individuals. The very real human beings who make up these social bodies have interests and values—desires for security, status, recognition—that they can attain only through participation in collective action. Already workers in many instances have established something definitely resembling a "property right" in their jobs. The crucial question would seem to be whether and in what manner "security" can be attained—through relations to *particular employers*, to *unions*, or to *government*, or to some particular combination of these.

Already we have a widespread development of *status laws* in our economy: special legislation for farmers, industrialists, workers and so on; special codes of rights and duties for different statuses and for differently situated groups.[99] One conceivable course of development would be toward what might be termed a neofeudal restrictionism. This will be favored by every circumstance that either establishes fixed status prerogatives in the industrial system, or develops legal and customary supports of monopoly, or increases the dependence of the worker upon a particular employer. The last is especially important, for it offers the possibility of a true "road to serfdom."[100] If workers in their search for protection against

[99] Moore: *Industrial Relations*, pp. 394–5.

[100] Friedrich A. von Hayek in *The Road to Serfdom* (Chicago: 1945) has argued that increased governmental intervention represents a new serfdom. It is definitely worth emphasizing that quasi-feudal structures would more easily be developed through paternal industrialism.

economic vicissitudes were to succeed in "appropriating" their jobs from a particular employer, there would be two enormously significant side effects: first, every job opportunity thus appropriated would be withdrawn from the job market—it would truly become "private property"; secondly, the worker would be increasingly dependent upon a specific employer. Since all the advantages of security and advancement would be bound up with this employer, the mobility of the worker would be diminished; nor is it to be supposed that employers would indefinitely accept duties toward a particular worker without demanding and getting rights of their own. The general tendency would be therefore toward establishing employer-employee relations marked by something close to "fealty" of the worker to the employer; faint analogues are presently found in the "loyalty to the firm" demanded in certain paternalistic companies. There would be a number of other rigidifying effects—stronger resistances to technological innovation, emphasis upon hierarchical and hereditary principles of industrial organization, freezing of existing geographic patterns of industry.[101]

Against the possibility of this sort of development in the American economy is ranged an impressive set of institutional and technical barriers. Only a few of the most important can be mentioned. In the first place, the total economy is subject to considerable instability and to powerful continued pressures for change (for example, international competition, the disruptions of war, the periodic imbalances of "trade cycles"). A rigid job-status regime requires a rather high degree of stability in techniques and in the total economy; thus feudal economies are likely to be agrarian and localized. Second, the dual influences of government and the unions are already widespread and important; as they become firmly established, they limit the ability of particular employers and particular workers to form personalized and localized relationships.

[101] Lest these suggestions seem merely hypothetical, we may remind ourselves that many of the effects suggested are foreshadowed by the familiar one-industry town in which an employer attaches workers to the firm by benevolent "nepotism," seniority systems, health and welfare plans, home ownership, company unions, and other devices, "respectable" or not from the standpoint of union philosophies.

Third, the cultural values characteristic of workers, as of much of the whole society, induce a strong aversion to relations of personal dependence and paternal authority; this resistance has deep roots and a long historical background and is typically given up only under severe pressure. Thus there are quite tangible legal barriers against many of the more extreme forms of personal dependence, "peonage," for instance. The highly developed money economy and the extreme commercialization of goods and services is a fourth inhibiting influence. Finally, the basic character of the business enterprise itself—the impersonal, deracinated corporate structure with its numerous nondirecting "owners" and its nonowning specialized managers and functionaries—does not offer any firm basis for particularized loyalty or dependence. Besides, so long as labor is a cost to be minimized in an instable economy the possibility of wholesale de-grading, shifting, and lay-offs will not be easily given up by business management.

What other lines of possible structural development are indicated by analysis? There is the pattern before us of "socialism" in Great Britain, and of varying forms and degrees of Stalinist communism compassing many vast areas both industrial and agrarian, and of Italian, German, Spanish, and South American versions of fascistic or corporative states. In several of these latter instances we have seen how the way for totalitarian control was prepared by industrial bureaucracy and cartels, so that a political coalition of disaffected social groupings—ranging from big industrialists and landed proprietors to peasants, conservative white-collar clerks, and workers—could simply take over a centralized, hierarchical administrative apparatus for new purposes, or for old purposes in new guises. In America, one might say, indeed, that to have "government take over business" would be equivalent in large part to having business take over the government—so powerful, organized, and interdependent are business structures and business interests, and so inescapably intertwined are they with government. Given the present institutions of property and authority, what could we expect from the formula "less government in business, more business in government"? Along this road would probably be met further restrictions of labor organizations, further development of bigness and centralization in business, and pervasive merging of economic and political power.

Alternatively, should further extensions of governmental activity in economic life be accompanied by a really strong political labor movement, the existing structure of industry is capable of being turned in "socialistic" directions. For the immediate future, however, anything like real "nationalization" of industry is not to be expected from this source; it is not indicated by the intent of labor organizations, nor by their power to secure united political action, nor by the actual balance of powers that constitutes the American government-in-being.

The actual nature of the American economy and of the forces shaping the directions of its change cannot be neatly summarized by ideological labels. There is no easy escape from the laborious task of tracing concretely and in detail the norms and values and the real operating relationships of an economic structure that must seem excessively untidy to those who have become enamoured of simple and rigid formulas for complex and detailed problems. To repeat: This is an economy of giant corporations and giant unions. It is also an economy containing a diverse agricultural industry, organized in family enterprises, with an overlay of co-operative organizations and governmental regulation and assistance. It is also an economy containing many small business. There is a very considerable measure of public ownership, municipal, state, and federal. Over this heterogeneous complex spreads an increasingly pervasive web of visible social controls and explicit regulation. It is no longer even a slightly daring prophecy to say that no long-run diminution of the social control of economic affairs is in prospect. The hegemony of the market is past, the administered economy is here. The questions that remain can be squeezed into issues-in-principle and pressed to a conclusion in conflict and repression, but they can be subjected to reason, discussion, research, negotiation, and disciplined interplay of power within a morality that cuts across class-bounded moralities. We cannot say which roads will be taken, nor impose further value judgments upon the attention of the reader. But we can see how thin is the line between "economic" and "political" activities and how questions of power unavoidably confront us at every turn. It is for this reason appropriate to turn now to consideration of political institutions in the United States.

7. Political Institutions of the United States

1. The Nature of Political Institutions

IN ANY very complex society certain systems of cultural norms and social organization become sufficiently explicit and differentiated to be labelled as political. We then speak of government, the state, political parties, sovereignty. The apparent ease with which one can observe governmental organizations and political parties tends to give us an unwarranted assurance about these common-sense distinctions. What is ordinarily labelled political is by no means identical with the political elements in our society analytically considered. We must therefore make a brief analysis of the general problem of political power before turning to the specific American case.

Inherent in the association of human beings in society is the problem of regulating the power of some individuals or groups over others. The basic political process is precisely the acquisition and exercise of power by certain individuals or groups over others; an abstract economics for the isolated individual is conceivable, if unimportant, but a similar political science is not.

Power, however, takes many specific forms. Fundamentally there are two broad ways in which some men control others. First, they may control the situation within which people must act, either directly or by changing the way in which people perceive it. Thus, by supplying information they may force recognition of new aspects of the situation, leading to a change in behavior. Or, they may be able to use the *offer of advantage* or the *threat of dis-*

advantage to bring about desired action from others. Secondly, under certain circumstances, one may control others by directly appealing to, or changing, their attitudes (values, sentiments) by persuasion and propaganda.

Politics is sometimes called the "engineering of consent." People are given information to affect their decisions; they are appealed to on the level of values and ethical norms; governments use a variety of rituals and ceremonies to symbolize and dramatize authority. There is also the persuasion of political reward, ranging from the ward leader's patronage or bribe to the offer of national economic advantage in world trade. And there is everywhere, after all, the use of coercive power—whether its role be large or small, overt or concealed.

It is of little use to characterize the political process so broadly as to cover all conceivable modes of influencing behavior—to obscure by synthesis what must be separated by analysis. Our first central question thus becomes: What, in analytical terms, is essential to politics and the political? A formulation of considerable scientific usefulness regards the regulation of *coercive power* as the essential element. We may approach this formulation through a series of propositions:

(1) *Social power* is the probability of the effective control of an individual or other social unit by another, irrespective of the former's wishes. The actual *fact* of power can be taken quite apart from the various *bases* on which it may rest.

(2) A particular variety of power is *coercive advantage*. Coercion is an effective threat of disadvantage to another unless he conforms, follows, obeys. "Illegitimate" coercion takes such forms as extortion, blackmail, armed robbery and the like. "Legitimate" coercion, by organized governments, takes the form of fines, imprisonment, loss of civil rights, death, or other fates of greater or lesser punitiveness. Its "legitimacy" depends solely upon how the effective community under observation regards it.

(3) Unregulated coercive power is always potentially disruptive of a social system. There is no assurance that it will be used in accordance with the major value systems of the society. Sheer naked force or the threat of such force is an inherently instable

phenomenon in social life, and every continuing human group works out elaborate ways of controlling it.

(4) *Political institutions* are the complexes of norms regulating the acquisition and exercise of power by some individuals over others within a given territory, through social structures claiming a monopoly of ultimate authority.

(5) The most prominent political institution within our society is the *state*. It seems impossible to gain any clear notion of what the state might usefully mean by considering only the ends to which it is devoted. There is hardly any human interest that some political association that we would be forced to recognize as a state has not undertaken to further; hardly a collective activity for which some state at some time has not taken responsibility. Nor is the state satisfactorily defined as the expression of concentrated force; for power and force are ubiquitous in associations and groups that are clearly not states. We might say that the state is an association to which a society attributes legitimate authority—but authority is also held by churches, families, clans, tribes, and many other diverse groupings. We are forced to define the state in terms both of the means most peculiar to it and of the (imputed) legitimacy of these means and the structure using them. Tentatively, then, we shall consider the state to be the structure that successfully claims a monopoly over the legitimate use of coercion and physical force within a territory.[1] The American state in this sense consists of all normative structures of this kind in our society. It is to be specifically distinguished from the *government*, which is the particular group of persons that at any given time mans the apparatus of the state. Government is the legitimate power-holding *group*; the state is the *structure* by which the group's activity is defined and regulated. A state may exist while particular governments rise and fall within it. The state is the form of which the government at any particular time is the operating embodiment.

Indeed, there is in the exercise of power and authority a "web of government," in MacIver's suggestive phrase, that spreads

---

[1] In this as in most of the foregoing we are following Weber's formulations. Cf. H. H. Gerth and C. Wright Mills (trans. and eds.): *From Max Weber* (New York: 1946), pp. 77–8.

throughout the entire society.[2] There is governing—the exercise of
socially validated authority—in the family, in the school, in the
economic enterprise, and in the religious group just as there is in
the state itself. The state is but one of the relatively distinct institutionalized sectors of social life that becomes differentiated from
the total community as a society becomes complex. Neither state
nor government is, or can be, coextensive with the total society.

The basic political problem arises from the fact that in any aggregate of human beings seeking to attain goals there is always the
possibility of conflict. Persons want scarce values, and their efforts
to acquire them may not leave "enough and as good" for others.
As Thomas Hobbes clearly saw, if men are enough alike to have approximately equal capacities for desiring scarce values and if no
bonds except the pursuit of immediate interests unite individuals,
society becomes a normless jungle in which every man's hand is
against his neighbors.[3] Obviously, this portrait of society is not
realistic, but shows vividly that in the immediate interests of discrete individuals there is no guarantee against conflict. Even if the
goals or ends of individuals are compatible, there is still the possibility of conflict over the means used. Above all, other human individuals are always potential means for the attainment of any
one person's goals, and control of others is always a technically
effective way of advancing interests that may be contrary to the
interests of those controlled. Thus there is always a "demand"
for power. Like money, power is a "universal" means—it may be
used in the service of a great variety of goals—and like money it is
avidly sought. Its exercise can easily disrupt normative controls.

There is, furthermore, a premium upon control of territory as
well as people in political processes. For social aggregates necessarily occupy geographic territories, and the most destructive kind
of conflict—physical violence—must occur within a definite place.
Sheer contiguity is of prime importance in the problems of power
and conflict.

Conflicts disruptive of social order can be minimized in three

---

[2] R. M. MacIver: *The Web of Government* (New York: 1947).
[3] See the discussion of the Hobbesian dilemma in Talcott Parsons: *The
Structure of Social Action* (Glencoe, Ill.: 1949), pp. 89–102.

ways: (1) by agreement upon common values that the members of the society can share; (2) by agreement upon the norms that will govern the means used to attain ends; (3) by the authorization of power to coerce, expel, or eliminate dissident and alienated elements of the social aggregate. Government rests upon all of these. Political authority, based upon a value consensus in the relevant social group, never lasts indefinitely without the backing of coercive power; but, on the other hand, political power without authority cannot maintain itself for long. Even the governing elite of a dictatorship that rules by terror must be held together by something other than coercion; and often sheer force is defeated by those apparently helpless against it.[4]

Indeed, "there is authority beyond the authority of government. There is a greater consensus without which the fundamental order of the community would fall apart." [5] Thus political authority cannot be understood exclusively as a matter of forms, procedures, constitutions, laws. All these may be full of effective social meanings; but they may be ritualistic pretensions, shadowy fictions. For a primary task of a modern government is the regulation of the conflicting and divergent loyalties and interests that a nation as a *territorial* unit almost universally embraces. Indeed, it has even been held that the state is simply a neutral reflection of an ever-shifting balance of power among diverse interests.

To this conception belongs a doctrine that sees a system of checks and balances as a necessary base of the political order—a theory that has been particularly congenial to the pluralistic American society. The actual cultural heterogeneity of the society has made it extremely difficult to secure consensus upon *common* ends. At the same time, the political dominance of landed proprietors and commercial and business groupings through so much of national history easily combined with a philosophy of natural rights and *laissez faire* to produce effective agreement on broad *procedural* questions. If the positive common ends of the state could not be agreed upon, except within a highly limited scope, it was

[4] Cf. Charles E. Merriam on the "Poverty of Power," chap. 6 in *Political Power* (New York: 1934).

[5] MacIver: *The Web of Government*, p. 85.

nevertheless possible to establish a framework of political *method* within which disagreements and conflicts could be resolved.

Agreement upon the procedures for acquiring and using power and for settling conflicts is not, however, necessarily an agreement upon form only. In democratic political orders, the procedures of governing and being governed acquire in marked degree the status of ends in their own right. For the essence of political democracy, one of its few dogmas, is that the policies of the government are continually subject to criticism and revision; the rulers are accountable to the electorate. Power can be acquired and exercised only within definite limitations.

The amoral Leviathan—the rule of untrammeled might—may be glorified by modern apostles of totalitarianism, but it is not a sociologically defensible description of states as they are; only under the most extreme conditions of social dislocation is it approximated. It is no accident that international politics is the area of governance where "rules of the game" are least honored and where coercion plays its most massive role: the absence of common values and norms that alone can keep conflicts of interests between nations within bounds contrasts strongly with the degree of normative order within national boundaries.

On the other hand, there is a common tendency, perhaps especially in American thought, to slur over or minimize the great historical significance of coercive power. The facts of how the strong tend to behave toward the weak are bitter medicine for a people who believe in the "consent of the governed." Undoubtedly the widespread use of force indicates that a society lacks integration of its value systems; the most stable order has least need for show of force. But equally certainly political institutions are not the result of a "social contract" of the individuals who make up the society, or who did so at any time in the past: we must reject Locke along with Hobbes.

The decisive points already suggested can be put briefly:

1. The political is the realm of power.
2. Power alone is not enough.
3. Regulated power, based on value consensus, is the core of

working politics. The legitimized coercive potential of the state is its most systematic expression.

4. The norms and values that constitute political institutions are not contractual in origin, nor do they simply represent domination by force.

5. The state can never be coextensive with the society; the political is always only one aspect of social control and social consensus.

6. Back of the formal structure of the state is always an informal pattern of operating practices and relationships, which may or may not correspond to the official pattern. Back of the operating government are the groups and interests that supply the dynamic element in politics.

In a period when states claim monolithic power, encompassing whole societies, it is necessary to emphasize that there are always definite limits to the obedience that political authority can elicit. One of the first practical axioms of command is never to give an order that cannot or will not be obeyed, and even the most dictatorial authority discovers points beyond which it cannot go. Even a legally all-powerful state is always hedged in and restricted to some degree by competing social authorities and the values they represent.[6]

The coercion exerted by the state in our society falls in three main areas. First is the broad category of "police power," the power to regulate without taking possession of property, believed necessary for maintaining internal peace and order and controlling aggression. Many other associations or other social units exercise legitimate coercion of various kinds;[7] but the state attempts to reserve to itself the peculiarly important sanctions of organized physical force, including the death penalty. Formerly its monopoly

[6] Charles E. Merriam: *The Role of Politics in Social Change* (New York: 1936), pp. 83–7.

[7] "The state can throw a man into prison. But an employer can take away his job. As the state can deprive a man of his life, the church can threaten his happiness for the future and make him extremely uneasy and unhappy while he lives. The state may tax, but the monopoly may raise prices and lower standards." Charles E. Merriam: *Public and Private Government* (New Haven, Conn.: Yale University Press, 1944), p. 9.

of physical force was far less complete—the state shared this sanction with the church and the family.

Second is the taxing power. Although the citizen who pays taxes receives some public services supported from tax funds, he does not thus buy these services, for he is not free to decide not to pay because he does not want them. Furthermore, taxation readily lends itself to punitive ends. Indeed, the problems of taxation well illustrate both the power of the state and its limitations, and the dynamic forces and competing values back of policy determination. For taxes represent a mixture of voluntary contribution, payment for services, and legalized confiscation; of the three elements, the last bulks large, partly because behind the impersonal authority of the taxcollector are the differentiated interests that try to put the burden of taxation upon some other sector of the population. What is to be the incidence of property taxes, income taxes, corporate profits taxes, sales taxes? Because each type tends to bear most heavily upon particular groupings and because the most powerful blocs politically are not necessarily the largest numerically, it is highly probable that in our own society most citizens pay a large part of their taxes under some measure of compulsion.

Third is the monopoly of armed warfare; the state raises huge military forces that quite clearly could not be assembled on a voluntary basis, and it alone has the power to make war and agree to treaties. Furthermore, it dictates what persons may enter or leave its territory under what conditions. It also controls foreign trade through export and import regulations, financing, and tariffs. In the American case there are several additional types of state coercion, including the right of eminent domain (the confiscation of certain kinds of property), jury duty, and others.

Obviously, the use of force has not been successfully confined to the government; force and threat of force are potential in human relations of any kind and are by no means rare in actuality. Wherever cleavages of values run deep enough, the only arbiter may become violence. In the United States we have had one revolution, one giant rebellion, a long series of smaller insurrections and riots (Whiskey Rebellion, Dorr War, Black Patch War, the Great Riots, etc.), violent employer-labor relations. Consensus, compromise, consent—these are words for an integration of interests and values that does not come easily and cannot always be maintained.[8]

The root of politics is the problem of order in society. In a small group in a stable environment, with a highly integrated value system, the problems of order may be so slight that the diffuse interaction of the whole grouping is sufficient to enforce norms and to contain whatever power striving might emerge under these conditions. Political *organization* is lacking; and political institutions exist only in germ, diffused throughout the society and only indistinctly defined or recognized. Nevertheless, the political is always present, even if latent or covert; and with the development of any marked social differentiation or individualistic striving or cultural heterogeneity, definite and systematic institutional forms appear for the channeling and control of power. A definite state emerges with the establishment of a governing association having its own norms, especially those of the law.

The problem of social order is perhaps especially prominent in modern industrial societies, where several conditions weaken social consensus of the total society regarding the values, ends, and rules of associational living. Among these conditions, four seem especially important. (1) The sharp internal differentiation of occupations and economic positions gives each special economic group and economic "class" its own social perspective and its own specific economic interests, both of which are often in deep opposition to those of other groups. (2) Because of international mobility, the political collectivity contains peoples of diverse cultures. Consensus is correspondingly difficult to achieve except in such highly abstract terms that apparent agreement may often fail in practice to avert serious tensions and cleavages. (3) The indirect and quasi-anonymous nature of many important activities, especially economic, removes them from direct community-wide surveillance and control. Adulterated food processed in one locality may be purchased by a buyer three thousand miles away. (4) Rapid changes in social structures tend to unsettle convictions, to bring norms into question, and it is correspondingly difficult for the in-

[8] On the above points see the excellent brief analysis by V. O. Key, Jr. in *Politics, Parties and Pressure Groups* (New York: 1942), chap. 22.

dividual to discern clear expectations that can guide his own behavior.

The main kind of agreement upon values that remains possible is
a consensus, not upon specific ends and particular actions, but
upon relatively generalized principles, or upon inclusive and relatively unexplicit symbols.[9]

Political democracy, as understood in the United States, has
not been thought to require centrally enforced unanimity on
specific values and beliefs. Its great problem today is to reconcile
the valued flexibilities and freedoms of its governing institutions
with the pressures for consensus upon action in meeting crises.
Thus we must examine next the institutional framework with
which American society confronts both the continuing and the
newly emerging dilemmas of power in society.

2. The Structure of the American State

ANY summary description of a political system so complex
as ours must be overly simple and incomplete. By listing, however,
a few salient features of the nominally dominant cultural structure,
we can find convenient points of anchorage for observing the system as a whole. At the level of *manifest* cultural norms, then, the
American state is marked by these characteristics:

1. It is a limited constitutional democracy, republican in
form.

2. It is a federal system; certain rights are reserved to the constituent states.

3. It is supposed to be a "government of laws rather than
men"; there is great emphasis upon the written Constitution,
which is interpreted by a judiciary of extraordinary powers.

4. The Constitution separates the governing powers and provides a complicated system of checks and balances.

---

[9] The significance of this "attentuation of common values" was acutely
seen by Emile Durkheim. Cf. Parsons: *Structure of Social Action*, pp. 323 ff.

5. The authority of power holders tends to be functionally specific and explicitly defined.

6. In theory, there is universal adult suffrage and the universal right to hold public office.

7. An extraordinary number of public offices are filled by popular election. The principal policy-forming officers are elected at regular and fairly frequent intervals.

8. The legal system explicitly lays down an elaborate system of civil rights for individuals.

9. Legislative bodies are typically bicameral; representation is based upon territory.

10. Certain of the above features lead to patterns of political behavior not provided for in the ideal patterns of the state— political parties and interest-group representation, for instance.

11. The formal structure of the state is derived in part from strictly *cultural* influences; ideas, ideologies, and values supply the axiomatic "definitions of the situation" through which new or problematic political action is perceived at any given time—for example, ideas of natural law and the value and inviolability of the individual personality, the negative valuation of centralized authority, or the instrumental conception of government. On the other hand, political action, like all other social action, is not an automatic emanation of cultural values, ideas, or creeds; it is the action of concrete personalities motivated by goals and standards not deducible from laws, constitutions, and other formal elements of the state. Thus our political institutions cannot be adequately understood without analyzing specific connections between them and other parts of the social structure.

12. In particular, the roles of economic interests, class structure, and ethnic or racial groupings are crucial to the concrete political processes of our society.

In the following sections the cited references will suggest the enormous amount of painstaking work in political science and sociology that we should not and cannot attempt to summarize. Our aim must be confined to gaining perspective and seeing interrelationships; we cannot attempt comprehensive analysis.

THE FEDERAL SYSTEM

The American political structure is federal rather than unitary in form; that is, subunits of the state have powers such that no level of authority has the ultimate right to pass upon all governmental acts. The system is multicentered, and the subordinate centers retain a marked degree of autonomy. It is the United States, not the United State. The structure of the central government is approximated on a smaller scale in each of the federated states, and each reserves some rights not subject to review by the central authority.[10] The federated system is marked by dual citizenship—a person is at the same time a citizen of the United States and of Nevada or Maine.[11] There is even a complete dual system of courts.

In theory, the central government can exercise only those powers given to it by the written constitution, whereas all other powers are reserved to the states; the nominal powers of the central government are thus strictly limited, leaving the states broad residual rights.[12] The central government cannot confer upon subordinate governments, or take away from them, functions and procedures. It cannot prescribe the official conduct of state or local officials. It cannot at will change the powers of state or local governing bodies. It cannot abolish states, counties, or other local units. No state may without its own consent be deprived of equal representation in the Senate. The Bill of Rights as it has been interpreted by the courts applies only to the *national* state. Limitations upon the invasion of individual rights by local and state governments and by private persons or organizations have to be sought mainly in the laws of the several states. Inherent in a system providing such an impressive amount of legal autonomy for the parts are con-

[10] E.g., the regulation of the suffrage; criminal law as applied by the state courts. See MacIver: *The Web of Government*, pp. 160–1.

[11] The Constitution left many ambiguities and difficulties in the concept of citizenship. See John P. Roche: *The Early Development of United States Citizenship* (Ithaca, N. Y.: 1949).

[12] Just the opposite principle is sometimes followed in federal unions, e.g., the Dominion of Canada.

flicts of authority and consequent pressures to establish a priority order for the laws and regulations established at the various levels of the structure.[13]

The federal system, like the separation of powers and checks and balances to be discussed below, is a mark of the *pluralistic* nature of American society as a whole. In its origins, it reflected both the compromises with local vested interests and state autonomy and the distrust of strong centralized government that had been a characteristic of the national culture from colonial times. It seems curious to foreign observers that in certain sections or localities are permitted practices offensive to national majorities and damaging to the international relations and world position of the nation as a whole. In a federated nation with "regions as unlike as Norway and Andalusia" [14] what is "American" takes on rather different forms under the elastic formula of *e pluribus unum.* The institutions intended to limit governmental power, to diffuse authority, to control popular demands, to leave maximum power to private individuals and associations now struggle with the massive strains of industrial society and world power. The cultural heritage of political forms and creeds is molded and transmuted into new and often unrecognized directions as shifting but powerful interests contend within a changing moral framework. It is in this perspective that the normative patterns now to be examined take on their limited but important causal role in the dynamics of the American social order.

A "GOVERNMENT OF LAWS RATHER THAN MEN"

This phrase represents a creed of the American political tradition. It suggests a state ordered by impersonal and universal rules, detached from the persons who govern and from the passions and foibles to which they may be heir. Back of the phrase is the

[13] See William Anderson: *American Government* (New York: 1942), p. 61, for a useful classification of the main parts of this system.

[14] Dennis W. Brogan: *U. S. A.: An Outline of the Country, Its People and Institutions* (London: 1941), p. 9.

Western legal and philosophic tradition of natural law, inherent rights, universalistic ethics, impersonal justice. Notwithstanding the extent to which the creed has not been practiced, the notion that laws bind those who make and execute them has been of first-rank importance in the shaping of our political institutions. But the sociologist must subject the notion to two major qualifications: first: it remains a mere creed unless there exist social bodies with the interest and the power to implement it. The entire conception of the rule of law has been elaborated as an ethical system in periods when nothing approximating an embodiment of it could be found in operating political associations. Second, laws are of different kinds; they differ as to source. There is the law of custom: the sanctioned, enforced rules that are never enacted or promulgated but that may form a regulative network more widespread and effective than edict or statute. There is common law, consisting of the accumulated decisions and opinions of the courts as they have interpreted custom and preceding court actions. There is administrative law, ground out as power holders devise rules to direct their own activities. What laws "stand above the state"?

We have seen that many of the important governmental norms are not matters of constitutional nor enacted law. The extent to which custom rather than law "is the king of men," even with emphasis on a written constitution and a penchant for law making, can be easily documented. Congress ordinarily holds public sessions, but nothing in the Constitution says that it must. The Constitution implies that presidential electors are free agents, but the Electoral College simply registers the popular vote and it would be thought outrageous for it to do otherwise. The Constitution specifies that representatives in the House must reside in the *state* they represent, but custom requires that they reside in the *district* they represent. The president's cabinet rests upon custom; so do political parties.

It appears that there are at least four main ways in which a government may rule by law. First, the power holders who make up the executive arm may be closely limited by rules not of their own making. The discretion, the "arbitrary" personalized power, the "unending audacity" of the official may be checked. Second, it may be out of the power of the legislature to remove certain rights; a fundamental law may be reserved as inviolate. Third, there may be an emphasis upon *cultural* structure rather than *social* organization—upon the "rules of the game," rather than upon detailed supervision within a definite politically controlled organization. Specific actions may not be positively enjoined; rather the limits of permissive action may be set.[15] Fourth and finally, government by law may mean that the interpretation of law is monopolized by a group relatively independent of the legislature or executive. The existence of a separate legal tradition interpreted and enforced by such an independent body has been in fact a conspicuous and crucial feature of Anglo-American history. A judiciary not dependent upon any other *one* political authority is in a position to insist upon legal continuities and legal limits that would otherwise be subject to much greater pressure from the holders of legislative and executive authority.

"Government by law" in America has tended to *limit and define the areas of authority and competence of officials of the state*. The individual is ruled by a number of different, and to some extent, competing authorities; the military officer can give orders legitimately only to his subordinates in the service, the policeman's reach is explicitly limited and circumscribed, the judge is not empowered to detect and prosecute as well as render judgment. Of course, as we shall see, the actual behavior of officials rarely follows with exactness the formal categories laid down by law and other explicit regulations. Nevertheless there is a great difference between latitude in interpretation or *sub rosa* evasion or violation of the institutional norms, and a change in the formal institutional principles themselves. That authority is conceived in our culture as *limited, functionally specific*, and *subject to law* is of central importance.

Nevertheless, general "principles" and explicit legal provisions are almost never detailed enough to cover the problems raised in real situations. The "impersonal majesty of the law" must be filtered through lawyers, juries, judges, administrators. The practical meaning of a constitutional precept, statutory enactment, or

---

[15] Examples: rules of contract; import duties; taxes; law of torts.

common-law doctrine is never simply given, but is always determined by interpretation. A crucial example is provided by the "due process" provisions of the Constitution (the Fifth and Fourteenth amendments), which forbid Congress or the states to "deprive any person of life, liberty, or property without due process of law." Clearly these clauses were intended to protect individuals or groups from unrestrained governmental action, but who is to decide what constitutes due process of law? As Professor Corwin has shown in a notable analysis,[16] judicial interpretations, for most of the nineteenth century and the first three decades of the twentieth, turned "due process" into an elaborate bulwark of established property rights and used it as a means of blocking governmental action that might have curtailed the liberty of property in the interest of protecting or extending other liberties such as civil rights.

Realistically then, our legal system provides a government of laws only in the sense of a general framework, not in the sense of a fixed and determinate regulation of action in all its details. This framework remains a crucial factor in shaping political institutions, and nothing said above is in detraction of that fact. But the determination of what "the Law" is, is just as much a "political" act as any other process in which social power is at stake. The importance of law is that it provides a relatively *explicit* and relatively *systematic* constellation of rules, and that these rules are maintained by definite bodies of men who have an institutionalized interest in enforcing them.

THE SEPARATION OF POWERS [17]

The separation of powers in the American system is an example of a political device whose significance and functions are by no means identical with those commonly imputed to it. It is usually supposed that its prime *intent* as well as its actual *function* is simply

[16] Edward S. Corwin: *Liberty Against Government* (Baton Rouge, La.: 1948).

[17] A clear and brief analysis of this problem is given in W. F. Willoughby: *The Government of Modern States* (New York: 1936), pp. 241 ff.

to *limit* the power of the state by dispersing authority among legislative, executive, and judicial branches of the governing apparatus. Unquestionably, the Constitution was drafted with a vivid sense of the dangers of strong government. The popular will exerted through the legislature was perhaps as much feared, however, as was executive autocracy. The limitation of the state through the separation of its powers enabled centers of private power, especially in business, to act with a minimum of state intervention; at the same time basic changes in the political structure were rendered difficult from lack of focus for authority sufficient to deal with the broader social and economic issues.[18] Thus, in so far as the separation of powers was actually instituted, the state was not only limited but also made relatively unresponsive to mass demands.

The separation of powers is real, as one can see by looking at the repeated struggles between the president and Congress, the Congress and the courts, the courts and the president. But it has never been so complete or clearly defined as the standard phrase might seem to indicate. In fact, from the very beginning of the Republic, the principle was squarely contradicted by the doctrine of checks and balances. Since each major branch of the state is given the authority to check certain actions of another branch, each necessarily has some real power over the area of authority officially allocated to another. The Constitution itself, therefore, did not establish anything like a complete separation of powers.

First of all the president has important constitutional controls over Congress. He has the power to veto legislation, and a veto can be overridden only by a two-thirds majority. He thus has not only the power to check legislative action but also a means of influencing the character of legislation before its passage. For the threat of veto can sometimes force the alteration of whole measures, or specific portions of them. The responsibility of the president to report to Congress on the state of the union and to recommend legislative action has provided the executive branch with an important legis-

[18] The most important economic and social forces of modern society extend far beyond regional and local bounds. Thus the incorporation laws of the single small state of Delaware have had an enormous impact upon the *national* economic and political structure.

lative role. Successive presidents—especially in periods of crisis—
have taken the original vague authorization as the basis for sub-
mitting whole legislative programs to Congress, and as leaders of
political parties and dispensers of patronage they have been able to
put strong pressure upon legislators to vote in accordance with
their recommendations. Equally important, the president possesses through legislative delegation a most impressive set of
powers for "administrative action" that in intent and in consequence amounts to authority to legislate.

In addition to these highly important controls exerted directly
through the office of president, the executive branch increasingly
engages in an enormous amount of *de facto* legislation in the form
of administrative orders, regulations, and rulings laid down by
various departments, bureaus, commissions, and so on. Statutory
law, like the provisions of the Constitution itself, is necessarily
couched in terms too abstract and general to cover all the concrete
problems raised by the attempt to apply it, and administrative
rulings are forever modifying, extending, contracting, reinterpret-
ing the intent of enactments. As the scope and complexity of executive action have expanded, the role of administrative discretion has
inevitably had a corresponding development, and the rule making
of the executive branch has become a substantial part of the legal
order.[19] This function may be regarded as judicial if we remember
that it is essentially what the courts do in rendering decisions upon
problematic situations that have arisen under the law; it may be regarded as legislative if we remember that the rules laid down by the
administrative body usually have the force of law, subject to the
possibility of judicial review if challenged, and of course, to possible
legislative retraction of statutory powers.

The growth of widely extended and highly complex administrative activities creates tendencies toward: (1) the delegation of legislative powers to executive agencies; (2) an increased proportion of
legislation initiated and influenced by executive agencies; (3) the

---

[19] "The theory that all legislative power must be exercised by the legislature is increasingly belied by the facts and reduced to the status of a legal
fiction." J. Roland Pennock: *Administration and the Rule of Law* (New York:
1941), p. 60.

increased role of governmental administrative agencies and their employees as "pressure groups"; (4) a diminished influence and prestige of legislative bodies. The separation of powers is, more and more clearly, a creed rather than a specific operating principle.

By virtue of a long series of "unplanned" changes, then, the executive bodies of the state have acquired vastly increased importance. In Chapter 6 we saw how the growth and internal differentiation of the business corporation can lead to the separation of ownership from control, and to the growth of managerial power. In governmental bodies the growth in volume, scope, and complexity of activities creates a similar transformation in which *residual power* gravitates to the *active* and *continuing* control centers of the executive agencies.

Thus the executive legislates. On the other hand, legislative branch shares the powers of the executive. The most conspicuous constitutional provision in this connection is the requirement that treaties be made with the advice and consent of the Senate. Furthermore, Congress has a clearly important control over executive performance through its control of appropriations: by withholding funds it can exert decisive influence upon specific executive actions. In recent years, congressional investigating committees have become another potent and spectacular legislative control upon the executive. Other informal types of legislative intervention in "executive" matters have developed. As many observers have pointed out, the main standing committees of Congress form a quasi-executive body.[20] They do so much of the decisive work of Congress that they acquire a focal power not only in shaping legislation and in determining what measures will or will not be brought to a vote but also in influencing executive action. For the key officials of governmental agencies affected by a particular committee—military affairs, for instance—will be in frequent liaison with that body and will inevitably both influence and be influenced by it.

Of the three major branches of the state, the most nearly autonomous is the judiciary. Yet it is also the branch that most

---

[20] Cf. Harold J. Laski: *The American Democracy* (New York: 1948), pp. 75-6.

clearly intervenes to control actions in the areas of authority nominally reserved for the executive and the legislature. Through the process of judicial review, the courts are able to negate legislation and to disallow executive action at numerous crucial points. No act of the legislative branch is final until it has been passed upon by the courts, and in practice the anticipated reaction of the judiciary is bound to become an important factor in the shaping of legislation in the first place. Above all, any sharp departure from traditional conceptions is almost certain to raise the issue of constitutionality, as the series of Supreme Court decisions in the wake of the early New Deal so well demonstrated.

In the federal system of courts, the independence of the judiciary is supported in a very specific way by two provisions: (1) judges are not removable from office "during good behavior"—that is, short of the rare and difficult procedure of impeachment, they hold indefinite tenure; (2) salaries are not to be reduced during an incumbent's continuance in the office. Once appointed by the president and confirmed by the Senate, a federal judge therefore commands a considerable immunity to immediate extraneous pressures. The autonomy of judges in some state courts, however, is reduced by their popular election for short terms of office. Judges in these states are directly subject to most of the informal obligations, party considerations, and interest-group pressures that affect the elected legislator.

But purely formal considerations are enough to show that the independence even of the judiciary is also interdependence. The jurisdiction of the courts is always limited by the action of the legislative bodies, and the pronouncements of the courts are ineffectual except as they are supported and enforced by executive agencies. Judges themselves are either appointed or elected; the appointing authority is unlikely to ignore completely such considerations as the political affiliations and views on social issues of potential judges; specific party ties and interest-group obligations are likely to influence the judicial behavior of elected judges. Finally, long practice sanctions the power of legislative bodies to establish rules of procedure for judicial processes.[21]

[21] Anderson: *American Government*, p. 590.

Because the major branches of the government are partly separated and yet highly interdependent, its structure is necessarily complex; there are many areas of overlapping authority, of ambiguous jurisdiction, of cross-purposes. The necessities of consultation and compromise produce large numbers of "tangent organizations" for liaison and mediation.

Since large-scale government actions only rarely fall completely within the authority of one branch of the state, and several centers of power must agree before the most important policies can be determined or carried out, policy is established after extensive deliberation and explicit consideration of a wide range of interests. On the other side of the coin, however, the separation of powers tends to make it difficult to arrive at clear decisions or to arrive at them quickly. Thus there is a tendency to concentrate power in a single source when there is urgent pressure for rapid and consistent large-scale decisions,[22] illustrated in the United States by the increased power of the executive branch in periods of national crisis, especially war.[23]

THE PRESIDENCY

The presidential system in the American government gives the chief executive a position very different from that of a prime minister in a cabinet system.[24] In Great Britain, for example, a cabinet composed of the heads of executive departments holds undivided party leadership and guides the legislative program as well. The prime minister as party leader must maintain his hold upon the party and upon the House of Commons in order to continue in office. The government may fall at any time if majority support of the cabinet fails. Through the close liaison of cabinet and com-

[22] See Max Weber's analysis of collegiality and the separation of powers: *The Theory of Social and Economic Organization*, trans. by Henderson and Parsons, pp. 392–406.

[23] See the extensive evidence in: Clinton L. Rossiter: *Constitutional Dictatorship: Crisis Government in the Modern Democracies* (Princeton, N. J.: 1948).

[24] Cf. Key: *Politics, Parties and Pressure Groups*, pp. 492–4.

mons, a unified legislative-executive program is facilitated. Legislation is not subject to nullification by an independent judicial branch. In the American system, the basic separation of powers militates against common action by the president and Congress.[25]

The relations between the president and Congress are only to a small extent specified by law. Beyond some highly general assignments of authority, the Constitution itself gives little guidance.[26] The office of the president is therefore left relatively open to the influence of noninstitutionalized forces: the personality of the incumbent, the shifting balance of party power, the presence and character of domestic and international crises. In the presidency more clearly than elsewhere in the federal structure, we can see the impact of great forces focused through the personalities who have filled the office in crucial periods: Washington, Lincoln, Wilson, F. D. Roosevelt. Since no clearly defined institutional role has been provided for the extraordinary demands forced upon the president in emergencies by the structure of the state, the chief executive has been granted special powers in crisis that in the long run have increased the authority and prestige of the office. Powers invoked in war, revolution, and disaster have broadened from precedent to precedent, particularly since the revocation of legislatively delegated authority would require a systematic planning that Congress has not often exercised. The delegation of powers has then frequently been left on the statute books.[27]

Because of these characteristics, the presidency provides a particularly clear case study of the dynamics of political processes. The written Constitution together with the traditions and vested interests that have accumulated around it seem to impose quite rigid barriers against the assumption of emergency powers by the president. The whole weight of the legal forms is toward the continuation of established patterns, short of the most drastic emergencies such as actual military invasion or widespread rebellion, and the United States has experienced relatively few and relatively

[25] Although, as already noted, the separation of the two is by no means complete.

[26] If the Constitution is a model of brevity, it is also a document that is silent on many central problems of government-in-operation.

[27] Rossiter: *Constitutional Dictatorship*, pp. 219–20.

slight deviations from constitutional forms in the presidency.[28] Of course, until the last twenty years, there have not been crises so frequent and so severe as those of most European countries. On the other hand, each major crisis has been accompanied by a drastic increase in the powers of the president,[29] thus illustrating the principle that groups or social systems that *are* going concerns typically react to grave external threat by an intensification and concentration of authority.[30] In America emergency conditions typically enhance executive powers at the expense of other branches.

Limited though its authority unquestionably is, the presidency is far and above the most potent single focus of power in the federal system. Precedents have already been established [31] that indicate potentialities for even more sweeping presidential power, given combinations of such other factors as national crisis, strong party support, and a skillful and aggressive president. To the present time, however, the presidency is an *office*, not a position solely of personal leadership, nor of authority not bounded by constitutional rules. In Weber's terminology, it is more nearly legal bureaucratic leadership than charismatic or traditional leadership. Some of the actions of F. D. Roosevelt may have stamped him in some quarters as a "dictator," but any analytical comparison will quickly show how very far the New Deal presidency was from the rule of a Hitler or a Peron, especially in its responsibility to a prior body of laws, and the fact that it was limited by the judiciary and legislative branches.

CONSTITUTIONAL GOVERNMENT

American political institutions grew out of deep aversions to *strong* government and to government of *undefined powers*, aversions that led to emphasis upon a written constitution, established

[28] Ibid., pp. 209–15.

[29] Rossiter documents this point in detail in *Constitutional Dictatorship*, esp. pp. 215–20.

[30] Cf. Robin M. Williams, Jr.: *The Reduction of Intergroup Tensions*, Bulletin No. 57, Social Science Research Council (New York: 1947), p. 58.

[31] E.g., Lincoln's abrogation of the civil rights of citizens outside the zones of actual military operations.

as superior to the ordinary law-making process and subject to
direct change only by special methods. But the written constitution is a special device rather than a defining criterion of the constitutional state. Constitutional states do not require written constitutions (nor do such states have to be democracies), but they
must have *a body of fundamental rules by which those who govern are
themselves governed.* The rulers must be bound to a "legitimate
order"—an established body of law, precedent, and custom—that
they are considered to have no right to violate. They must derive
their authority in the eyes of the governed from their position in
this cultural structure and be restricted to acts this position authorizes. Constitutionalism implies government based on rules,
precedent, principles. Its opposite is the rule of the charismatic
leader to whom is imputed (by his followers) an authority that is
absolute, or at least indefinite, and that resides solely in the
"magic" of the *person* who rules. Whether the personal ruler be
"hero" or "opportunistic tyrant," he rules in himself and not as a
constitutional officer.

It is decisive for a social order whether its political structure is
one of *persons* or of *offices*. Constitutional government, when fully
developed, achieves the separation of *government* from the *state;*
of the person from the office he occupies. The separation is often
less than complete, but in large measure authority can be detached
from specific persons and lodged in the impersonal structure of the
state association. We can then see the phenomenon of the citizen
who loathes and hates a particular president but reveres the
presidency, the many people who scorn the incumbent government
but value the system under which it operates. The worth of political institutions is partly dissociated from the worth of individuals
who represent them.

Constitutional government requires that the state not be
identified with the total society, but be firmly subjected to *control
by* it. For if state and government are subject to laws not of "their
own devising" nor under their control, those laws must be derived
from elsewhere in the larger community. There must be groups
among the ruled that can resist effectively any pressure of government upon the normative boundaries.

THE CONSTITUTION

The powers of the government of the United States are set by the somewhat elastic but definitely constricting bounds of a written constitution. Around that document has gradually accumulated a tremendous number of interpretations and commentaries, of court decisions, of beliefs and myths.[32] The Constitution enjoys a veneration that makes it a substantial barrier against sudden or far-reaching changes in the structure of the state. There is a "psychology of constitutionalism," [33] a widespread conviction that the Constitution is sufficient to cover all emergencies, that deviations from its provisions are unnecessary and dangerous, that a breach of the Constitution would bring down the whole structure of ordered and lawful government.

When it was written, the Constitution was a drastic innovation, not only in its content but in its basic idea that the form of government could be purposively determined.[34] It was radical in the root sense of that word. Yet, in a similar root sense, it has had conservative consequences. During the period of consolidation of authority and partial return to prerevolutionary conditions that always follows the instituting of a new state, the Constitution was one of the few symbols of national scope available to the loose federation of weak and disunited provinces. Furthermore, it has been a rallying point for conserving (maintaining) the political and civil liberties of individuals.[35] But it has been conservative in a

[32] D. W. Brogan is not greatly overstating the case when he says: "In most matters an irreverent people, the Americans are the most reverent people in the world in political matters. They regard the Constitution as sacred, as a national talisman . . ." *U. S. A.: An Outline of the Country, Its People and Institutions* (London: Oxford University Press, 1941), p. 30.

[33] Rossiter: *Constitutional Dictatorship*, p. 211.

[34] Merriam: *The Role of Politics in Social Change*, p. 124: "It was the most monumental heresy of the eighteenth century and denounced by all but the revolutionaries of that day."

[35] Konvitz has distinguished *political rights*, such as the right to vote and hold office; *civil liberties*, such as those enumerated in the Bill of Rights; and *civil rights*, such as the right to employment and public access and accommodation without discrimination. Milton R. Konvitz: *The Constitution and Civil Rights* (New York: 1947), p. vii.

more conventional sense, also, for it was actually adopted in a period of what was close to counterrevolution, and a major force in its drafting and adoption was the desire to insure internal stability and the protection of property and trade.[36] Undoubtedly the Constitution can be interpreted to conform to the interests of the more prosperous and propertied groups, and a stable legal order and venerated symbol of that order is advantageous to those interests.

This dual conservatism partly explains how it is that the Constitution can be defended with equal fervor by individuals whose motivations and interests are in most respects sharply opposed. The document has become almost a symbolic "sponge" that can absorb the allegiances of persons having amazingly diverse interests, values, ideas, political philosophies. Although the process by which this absorption occurs is not well understood (and is a research problem of first interest), its existence is probably of real importance to social stability. As with many other symbols of government, the very indefiniteness of the popularly imputed meanings facilitates a sense of order and integration not derivable from the specific applications of political doctrine.[37]

If, however, the Constitution is to provide guiding principles for the working legal order of the state, it must be specifically interpreted in order to resolve problems. And it is here that the document becomes a reality in substance rather than in symbol only. The Constitution-in-being is to a very large extent the aggregate of numerous definitions and interpretations by generations of legislators, lawyers, judges—and above all, by the Supreme Court.

THE SUPREME COURT

In the British system, from which the American state drew many of its own patterns, the courts do not have the power to declare

---

[36] The classical reference is Charles A. Beard: *An Economic Interpretation of the Constitution of the United States* (New York: 1913).

[37] It has been suggested that the American Constitution had certain similarities to the British Crown as a point of anchorage for loyalties.

any act of Parliament "unconstitutional"; fundamental constitutional law and ordinary or derivative law originate from the same source; there is no unitary written constitution. The constitution is what Parliament makes it.

In the American system, the courts have assumed and regularly exercise the power to declare constitutional or unconstitutional the acts of Congress, state legislatures, local governments, executives at all levels. The final test of legal validity is the ruling of the Supreme Court. The Constitution is what the Court says it is.

The present extraordinary role of the Supreme Court was not envisioned in the formation of the Republic. The powers now exercised are the outcome of a long development in which the authority of the Court was greatly extended, largely on its own initiative.[38] There were three crucial turning points in the process.[39] The first is usually considered to be the action of the Court under Justice John Marshall in *Marbury v. Madison*. It refused to accept a scope of jurisdiction and declared its constitutional incapacity to take certain actions. The case did not establish the Court's power to declare legislative acts unconstitutional, but only the Court's right to determine *its own* limits of jurisdiction under the Constitution. In the Dred Scott case (1857) the Court took the second decisive step in the extension of its own powers: it ruled upon the constitutionality of *congressional* action and thereby staked its claim to final review of legislative action.[40] Finally, its interpretation and use of the doctrine of "due process of law" in the 1880's gave the Court the power to pass upon the *methods* by which governmental powers were used, as well as upon the substantive content of laws and regulations.

The power assumed by the Court to declare acts of the national

[38] Robert E. Cushman: "The Role of the Supreme Court in a Democratic Nation," reprinted in A. N. Christensen and E. M. Kirkpatrick (eds.): *The People, Politics, and the Politician* (New York: 1941), pp. 562–76.

[39] A similar observation applies to the presidency. In both cases a basic question is suggested: What exactly is the *process* by which *new* authority is established? At the "growing points" of political authority we might look for clues for a more adequate theory of social change.

[40] These two cases were the only instances prior to 1883 in which the Court had declared acts of Congress unconstitutional.

legislature unconstitutional strikes many foreign observers as the most notable characteristic of the American state. Yet, as Anderson has said, these decisions "are also only the most striking and dramatic examples of a regular judicial activity that runs from the very lowest courts up through the ranks to the highest court in the land." [41] In all these courts the judges regularly pass upon complicated situations, full of gaps and apparent inconsistencies and ambiguities, and their decisions—quite apart from "integrity" or conscious bias—are necessarily affected by ideas and interests in no meaningful sense a part of law. That variation and instability in judicial decisions are very considerable is shown by differing opinions within the same court on a given case, different decisions by different courts on the same point of law, reversals of a court by itself at a later time. Any careful study of what the courts, including the Supreme Court, actually do shows that the process is not merely one of "discovering what the law is" but also of making and changing it.

In view of these facts, it is impressive that the courts, and especially the Supreme Court, are widely regarded as endowed with detachment and infallibility. And to the extent that this belief prevails [42] the stability of the state is supported through faith in the continuing judiciary.

LEGISLATIVE BODIES AND REPRESENTATION

There sometimes appears in our culture cynicism and disaffection concerning American political institutions because they do not provide for direct democracy in the details of governing. But the direct rule of all the people is never found in any social groups save the smallest and most homogeneous and could not be the ex-

[41] The author adds: "Sundays and holidays excepted, there is probably no day in any year when some court somewhere in the land is not holding some government to have acted unconstitutionally, or at least beyond its powers." William Anderson: *American Government* (New York: Henry Holt & Company, Inc., 1942), p. 70.

[42] Note that in the national survey analyzed by North and Hatt the occupation of Supreme Court judge was popularly rated as the highest rank in a list of 90 occupations. Logan Wilson and William L. Kolb: *Sociological Analysis* (New York: 1949), pp. 465–6.

clusive governing system of a large and complex modern nation. Political action through delegated authority is the only functionally feasible form of democracy in our present type of society.[43] Actually, of course, the legislative bodies of the nation in several respects more nearly represent "popular will" today than at earlier periods in our history, owing to such devices as the direct election of senators, the recall, referendum, and initiative systems in various states.

However, popular control of legislative bodies has been limited at both national and state levels by long terms of office and staggered terms for the upper house, preventing quick responses to popular will. The veto powers of the state and national executive and judiciary further weaken popular expression. Within the legislative, a similar effect is also secured by the large majorities required for constitutional amendments. Other arrangements have the consequence of removing the members of legislative bodies themselves from direct popular control—the use of voice rather than roll-call voting, the disposal of legislation in the closed deliberations of legislative committees, control of nominations by a relatively small group of party leaders.[44] This representation is subject to popular control only intermittently and often only quite indirectly. Nevertheless, legislative bodies in the United States are composed of popularly elected and formally free representatives, sharing power with partly autonomous executive and judicial agencies.

It is of great importance that representation in our legislative bodies, from the Congress on down, is on a *territorial* basis, and that the territorial units (states, districts, counties, wards, etc.) do not necessarily, nor even typically, correspond to real social groupings nor homogeneous interests. As a result (1) the repre-

[43] This is not to say that direct democracy could not conceivably be instituted, but only that it would require drastic sacrifices of other values.

[44] However, the modern party convention and the direct primaries are probably more open to mass influence than were the earlier procedures of the legislative caucus, which prevailed until the 1820's. (See Key: *Politics, Parties and Pressure Groups*, pp. 361–73.) Incidentally, the history of the various nominating arrangements well illustrates how essentially the same processes can continue to operate through superficially very different political forms.

sentative does not represent a unified group, and (2) groups and interests are not given official representation by anyone entitled to act in their name, but must find their own channels for influencing legislation.

We all know that the national Congress and nearly all of the state legislatures are divided into upper and lower houses, but it is not self-evident how this system came to be or what consequences it may have. Bicameralism, like the separation of powers, was a device to limit governmental powers. Historically, it was the result of a compromise in the Constitutional Convention. There the representatives of the larger and more wealthy former colonies favored a national legislature made up of representatives apportioned to the states on the basis of population or taxable wealth. The smaller states favored a single chamber composed of representatives in equal number from each state. After bitter dispute an upper house was established with fixed and equal representation by states, and a lower house with representation by states in proportion to population. Since the Senate shared treaty making and appointive powers with the president, the smaller states were insured an authoritative voice in major national policies. Since the House was charged with the initiation of financial measures the larger and wealthier states were given special weight in legislation affecting their economic interests. The familiar precedent of the British Parliament provided the broad outlines of the bicameral form, and the compromise concerning the basis of representation adapted it to the American situation. Once the national system had been established it served in turn as a model for the individual states.

In the national legislature, the power and prestige of the Senate as against the House rests upon definite and sociologically instructive grounds. The Senate is endowed by the Constitution with the treaty-making power, which it shares with the president, and therefore plays a central role in international relations; it likewise has the power to confirm or reject major appointments made by the president, and it is not slow to exercise this prerogative. Its small size as compared with the House makes possible greater freedom of debate and greater ease of interpersonal contact. The senators serve for long terms, and the security they gain upon election is conducive to independence of action. Because of long tenure and control of appointments and other patronage [45] Senators are often able to build powerful state party organizations with which they can oppose the president or national party leadership. The Senate is often at variance with the president and with the House, partly because of overlapping terms of office: senators serve for six years and one third of them are elected every two years, whereas the president serves for four years and the representatives for two years. This device obviously contributes to the separation of powers, but by the same token it creates conflict within Congress itself.

In Congress, as in the state legislatures, the legal forms of procedure are not definitive of the law-making process. Above all, the party machinery plays a primary role in shaping legislation and enforcing discipline. In each legislative body, an inner circle of leaders from each party attempts to give direction to party members; nearly all of the elaborate organization entailed is extralegal. Furthermore, legislative bodies are subdivided into numerous committees that act as sublegislatures—rules committee, steering committee, and a number of important standing committees. In these small groups much of national policy is made. One of the most interesting "unplanned" extralegal groups is the congressional committee of inquiry, a direct outgrowth of the separation of executive and legislative branches under a presidential form of government. Congress makes laws and appropriates funds for agencies over the specific operating practices of which it has little formal control. Unable to exercise the continuing surveillance of administrative action possible under a parliamentary government by reason of the presence of executives before the legislative body, Congress has developed this alternative method of overseeing administrative action.

The prevalence of the committee form of organization in legislatures reflects both the need for small working groups in delibera-

[45] Through the extralegal custom of "senatorial courtesy" the Senate insures that appointments in any particular state that are objectionable to a senator from that state will not be confirmed.

tive bodies and the collegial nature of the larger organizations. Although there is a measure of hierarchy in the legislative branch —committee chairmen, speakers and presiding officers, party whips, and so on—a popularly elected body is always a "college" of approximate equals who must reach their decisions by discussion, negotiation, "pressure," and various informal arrangements, rather than by a strict chain of command.[46]

The extraordinary number of informal arrangements, committees, liaison agents, and so forth, in our legislative bodies is favored by the large numbers of individuals involved, the deliberative nature of their tasks, and the lack of detailed legal definition adequate to specify necessary operating procedures; but it also derives from the separation of the legislative from the executive agencies. Congress has only indirect contact with the administrative departments, bureaus, commissions, and the like. Its members are subject to the pressures of groups in the specific districts or states that they represent, whereas the president is more nearly the focus of *national* problems and interests.[47] The various particular executive agencies have their own organizational commitments, their vested interests, their special constituency pressing upon them to advance particular interests. Thus the legislative and executive branches have different perspectives and interests; and there is no clear-cut constitutional channel for relating the two. Therefore informal methods are largely used for executive-legislative communication and influence, and considerable tension between the two branches is frequent.

EXECUTIVE AGENCIES

Previous discussions of the separation of powers and of the presidency have already indicated some of the characteristics

[46] The relatively loose and slow-moving collegial organization tends to change under conditions of crisis. In emergencies legislatures tend to limit debate, to intensify and concentrate internal leadership, to delegate powers to executive agencies. The nominal form of Congress was about the same in 1933 as in 1925; yet the Hundred Days of the first New Deal Congress manifested a very different *de facto* organization and procedure.

[47] Key: *Politics, Parties and Pressure Groups*, pp. 505–06.

of the executive branches of the state. The over-all character of governmental administration in this country has been strongly influenced by the popular distrust of executive agencies,[48] which are perennially seen as threats to "representative government"; the word "bureaucracy" is a prime political epithet. This attitude, founded in the early revolt against the executive authority of the British Crown, has been maintained in part by legislative and judicial attacks upon the executive arm as a competitor for power and prestige.

Yet generalized resistance to expansion of executive functions has not checked *specific* demands upon the state, having the cumulative effect of enormously increasing the amount and scope of administrative action, especially during the past half-century. Along with the sheer expansion—whether measured by personnel or by expenditures—have gone tendencies toward: (1) greater specialization of functions, both of agencies and of specific positions; (2) greater organizational complexity, both within particular agencies and among interdependent agencies; (3) greater professionalization of officials, through training, permanence of office, standardized technical qualifications; (4) elaboration of administrative rules, and other bureaucratic characteristics; (5) political neutralization of the public employee; (6) growth of administrative discretion and the rule-making powers.

We now have an enormous maze of interdependent and crisscrossing agencies, and the problems of co-ordination and control are correspondingly difficult. Inevitably, there is much overlapping of authority, with resulting interagency competition and defensiveness.[49] That these patterns are rooted in deep and persistent forces is indicated by the long history of successive administrative

---

[48] In these pages, the term "executive" is used to refer to the broader organization with a maximum of policy-determining authority; "administrative," to refer to the more nearly routine execution of policy. The distinction is one of degree, and exact demarcation is not essential for most purposes of the present discussion.

[49] Contemporary illustrations are abundant—the struggle over the establishment of a unified military department, the recurrent differences between the State Department and the military agencies over foreign policy.

reorganizations at both Federal and state levels that recurrently face the same essential problems.

The multiplicity of Federal agencies reporting directly to the president, as well as the existence of practically independent commissions and boards, makes presidential supervision and control almost impossible except on a sporadic and tenuous basis.[50] Executive control at the state level is also difficult.

These problems are primarily the outcomes of institutional structure, not of particular personalities or political party affiliations of the officials. Much criticism has been leveled at the waste or inefficiency entailed by a structure in which authority is so dispersed and central co-ordination is so tenuous. But Americans do not seem to think efficiency the highest value to be sought in government. The practice of rotating short-term elective offices, still common at state and local levels, is not efficient wherever either continuity of policy or specialized technical competence is of importance. The establishment of overlapping or conflicting executive agencies has been dictated, not by considerations of over-all efficiency, but by the desire to satisfy separate interests concerned with particular problems.

The separation of the chief executive positions from the legislative branch leads executive agencies to act very much like private pressure groups.[51] They seek to influence public opinion generally, to build up favorable attitudes in special publics, and to influence directly the legislature. They frequently propose, try to alter, or try to defeat legislation. They "lobby." They often act to an important degree as the "functional representatives" of special segments of the population—agriculture, labor, business interests. It is becoming increasingly clear that administration is never clearly nor wholly separated from legislation and hence always involves questions of politics, and that government itself, in the form of these agencies, is thus becoming an increasing important influence upon legislation and national policy.

[50] For discussion and evaluation see The President's Committee on Administrative Management: *Administrative Management in the Government of the United States* (Washington, D. C.: 1937).

[51] Key: *Politics, Parties and Pressure Groups*, pp. 175–89, 194–97.

Furthermore, there are political problems within both Federal and state bureaucracies. Where some reasonably effective merit system is in operation, the lower ranks of the hierarchy are filled by persons selected on the basis of examinations aimed at specific vocational qualifications, but the upper policy-forming positions are usually filled either by "political" appointees who do not make a career of government service [52] or by men who have demonstrated special competence outside of the system of qualifying examinations. Department and bureau chiefs are thus not infrequently opposed or circumvented by the permanent staff. Rarely are the directing officials pure administrators who simply carry out delegated policies; they are more nearly political strategists who for the time being initiate and promote policies of the government in power. The presidential cabinet is far from a perfect co-ordinating mechanism for such officials, who tend to serve only so long as they agree with higher policies. Such a structure is one source of difficulty in attempting to secure unified policy on foreign and domestic problems.

We have now seen many instances of how artificial and misleading are the labels "legislative" and "executive" if taken as literally descriptive. An essential lesson, indeed, for the serious study of political institutions is that the label does not necessarily describe the fact and that the only remedy is attention to the details of actual behavior. Many contemporary organizations and activities of the state defy conventional classification. The quasi-public corporation, such as the Tennessee Valley Authority, is neither wholly "government" nor wholly "business," [53] and its administrative problems could be comprehended equally as well by either a business executive or a Washington bureau chief. Eighteenth century labels cannot give us the key to current social structures.

In the immediate future, the pressure of international situations

---

[52] Laski: (*The American Democracy*, pp. 99–108) notes the contrast with the British system.

[53] See Merriam's discussion on pp. 47–54 of *The Role of Politics in Social Change*. See also the list of "border line" actions on p. 114.

alone will doubtless tend to tighten and unify administrative machinery and enhance the authority of the chief executive posts. Such developments represent modifications of the doctrines of federalism and separation of powers. Quite clearly also, the position of military agencies deserves attention, in view of the long period of turbulence that probably lies ahead.

THE CIVIL AND THE MILITARY POWERS

Under the Constitution, Congress may not infringe "the right of the people to keep and bear arms" (Second Amendment). This provision has never been interpreted as a right of citizens to take up arms against the state; indeed, it succeeds the phrase "A well-regulated militia being necessary to the security of a free State . . . ." It was the view of the early American leaders that the maintenance and regulation of military forces is a crucial problem of all states, and that the status of military agencies has peculiar significance to a political democracy; their concern is reflected in several major constitutional provisions.

In the formal structure of the American system, the military agencies are subdivisions of the executive branch, subject to certain checks by Congress. A civilian—the president—is commander in chief of the armed services, in war and peace, and in the past each main division of the military arm has been headed by a civilian. The official line of authority thus runs to a popularly elected chief executive. Congress is given control of appropriations, and the Constitution specifically limits any military appropriation to a term of two years. All military officers are nominally commissioned directly by the president; Congress is invested with the power to make "Rules for the Government and Regulation of the land and naval Forces" (Article I, Section 8). Finally, the power to declare war is assigned to the elected Congress, and the control of foreign policy is mainly vested in the president and the Senate.

Clearly the Constitution was intended to insure the supremacy of elective, civilian control over the armed forces of the national government.[54] Similarly, in the various state constitutions there is usually some explicit statement that the military powers are subordinate to civil authority.[55]

The one major exception to civil supremacy provided for by the Federal Constitution authorizes Congress to suspend the privilege of *habeas corpus* only during invasion or rebellion, when presumably the civil courts are unable to operate in normal fashion. Until recently the most dramatic instance of the suspending of *habeas corpus* was Lincoln's authorization of military arrests and trials of civilians outside the zone of military operations and in areas in which the civil courts were in operation. Although the Supreme Court ruled in *Ex parte Milligan* against the validity of the judgment of the military courts under these conditions, the possibility of military rule without the protections of civil procedures has remained. Indeed, World War II brought the forced removal of Japanese American citizens from the West Coast; and the military rule of Hawaii again raised the constitutional question in a form similar to *Ex parte Milligan*. The Supreme Court held (in 1946) that the military courts have no jurisdiction over civilians in areas where the usual civil courts are able to carry out their duties and where no immediate military danger exists,[56] thus once more affirming the principle of civil supremacy. But despite constitutions and statutes, military powers vastly increase during war, and the longer and more severe the conflict the greater the increase.

The relatively small and subordinate part played by military authority during most of national history is, of course, not explicable merely by the existence of constitutional provisions and

[54] "The founders of the American republic knew that again and again in the course of human affairs liberty had been destroyed by military dictatorships and in framing the Constitution they sought to establish firmly the supremacy of the President and Congress over the military arm of the Government." Charles A. Beard: *American Government and Politics*, p. 285.

[55] All the foregoing are official norms that do not completely correspond to the facts. For example, the civil heads of military departments have not been able always to control the military personnel. See Lindsay Rogers: "Civilian Control of Military Policy," *Foreign Affairs*, Vol. XVIII (1940).

[56] In *Duncan v. Kahanamoku*. See Rossiter: *Constitutional Dictatorship*, pp. 284–5.

paper barriers. For long periods no large standing military forces were necessary. Until now, although the forms of large-scale military organization have been fully developed, the standing army has been small enough [57] to make military influence upon political forms slight except in periods of large-scale warfare.[58]

Modern military organization is not only hierarchical but in many respects is practically the archetype of bureaucratic structure. The continued existence of large military forces over a long period of time produces a segment of the population likely to be appreciably alienated from civil standards. The American tradition has always favored the temporary citizen-soldier. Clearly this tradition is strained by sustained large-scale warfare or by long periods of mobilization just short of war.

3. The Rights and Duties of Citizens

THE RELATION of the individual to the state demonstrates the distinctive nature of the political monopoly of power. For the individual's allegiance to the state, unlike his membership in a labor union or a church, cannot easily be transferred, and he can resign from citizenship only at the cost of resigning from the whole society at the same time. That the status of citizen is a primary base for a series of other statuses is shown by the contemporary plight of large numbers of stateless persons who exist by sufferance within alien and often hostile nations or in international enclaves. The state's monopoly of authority renders the rights and duties of citizens a matter of special interest to each individual—and to the sociology of political behavior.[59]

[57] The entire Regular Army of the United States consisted of about 165,000 men in 1940, on the brink of World War II.

[58] Yet it must not be forgotten that Federal troops have been used to put down "domestic disturbances" in well over a hundred instances in our national history. Cf. U. S. Army Service Schools: *Military Aid to the Civil Power* (Fort Leavenworth, Kansas: 1925), pp. 185–200; Bennet M. Rich: *The Presidents and Civil Disorder* (Washington, D. C.: 1941).

[59] For a compact but detailed description of legal aspects of citizenship and civil rights see Anderson: *American Government*, chaps. 16 and 17.

In America, popular tradition has emphasized the *rights* of individual citizens against the state. Yet there must always be a duty wherever there is a right, for a right is meaningless unless someone has the duty to respect it. Our present concern is to discover the salient features of the normative reciprocities that define the statuses of citizens in relation to the American state.

Democracy cannot be identified with majority rule; the twentieth century has certainly furnished enough examples of dictatorial governments representing, or claiming to represent, substantial majorities of the population. Democracy is often thought to be a system in which minority elements are expected to acquiesce in any majority decision, but if so, the American system differs from it in two basic respects: (1) many of our political institutions check and limit direct majority rule; [60] (2) a long list of rights are reserved to individuals, or more narrowly to citizens, as inviolable by ordinary legislative or executive action.

Such rights imply, of course, definite limits to majority rule and popular sovereignty. Unlimited popular sovereignty permits individuals no rights that the state is bound to recognize; the state is supposed to embody the people, and the representatives of the state are bound only by the expressed will of the electorate. The doctrine of unlimited popular sovereignty, at first glance so preeminently democratic, can thus quite easily justify absolutistic government. For majority rule is no guarantee of individual freedom; majorities can be as intolerant of dissent as any minority. The basic conception that the individual has rights the state must respect presupposes that the state is not coextensive with society, but is only an institution within it.

In American constitutional law there are the well-known formal provisions of the Bill of Rights and subsequent amendments.[61] In addition, a multitude of specific rights has been held to inhere either in citizenship in the United States or in citizenship in the separate states, or simply in residence within United States juris-

[60] Many of these "buffers" have been mentioned already, e.g., the role of the judiciary as a nonelective group with great power over acts of elected representatives.

[61] Cf. the listings cited by Konvitz: *The Constitution and Civil Rights*, pp. 33–4.

diction.[62] Yet none of these rights are absolute. Slavery and involuntary servitude are forbidden, but military service, jury duty, imprisonment for law violation, and various civil duties are compulsory. Compulsory sterilization and vaccination have been held by judicial decision as not violating personal liberty under the Fourteenth Amendment. Freedom of religion is guaranteed, but some laws are upheld that impose disadvantages or disabilities upon particular religious groups. Freedom of speech is a basic tenet of civil rights, but its specific interpretation always draws limits to permitted communication. All rights are subject to complex variations in judicial interpretation and executive action; all have at some time been subjected to powerful demands for abrogation.

A narrow interpretation of the Constitution limits only the *national legislature* from abridging or interfering with the basic liberties set forth in the Bill of Rights, and the Federal government has only limited power to check state and local governments or private groups or individuals who may seek to deny these rights, except when such action falls within its express jurisdiction. The widespread denial of the suffrage and other rights of citizenship to Negroes is an example of how state and private action may nullify the seeming guarantees of the Constitution.

There is a sense in which the rights of free communication and free assembly are not privileges granted by the state, but are conditions prerequisite for the existence of the state in the form of a constitutional democracy.[63] Unrestrained freedom is, of course, impossible, for the freedom of one group or individual beyond certain limits infringes the freedom of others. Yet a very broad latitude for expression of opinion and for private action is a defining condition of a democratic system.[64] These freedoms are difficult to establish and precarious to maintain. Success seems to depend upon: (a) the absence of large groupings having basically incompatible values that could create fundamental cleavage of the social

[62] A long series of court interpretations have had to deal with questions as to whether a given right applies to *citizens* only or to *individuals*, including aliens.

[63] This view has been stated by Archibald MacLeish in his "Freedom to End Freedom," *Survey Graphic*, Vol. XXVIII (February, 1939) pp. 117–19.

[64] MacIver: *The Web of Government*, pp. 198–9, 202–06.

order; (2) relative absence of severe and long-continued external threats to the society; (3) division of social power among several different groups or strata, so that no united minority (or majority) can seize power and suppress dissent. The interests and values that have become attached to inherited doctrines and political forms may also play a part in the American case.[65]

These considerations suggest a broader hypothesis. The rights (immunities, privileges, liberties, etc.) of individuals within the political order depend, on the one hand, upon the widespread and ingrained value systems of the culture that live in individual personalities. Effective support of the principle that the governments, majorities, or private associations and individuals cannot violate certain rights of persons requires, at the least, conviction that value divergences are not so important as the worth attached to individual personality. The rights of individuals are never secure unless a large proportion of the population have real emotional reactions against violations of those rights. On the other hand, value consensus alone does not guarantee the preservation of rights. Those whose rights are violated must have the power to strike back; acquiescence in the violation of rights means that in the long run they will cease to exist.

An example of how essential is organized power in establishing social rights is provided by the history of the "elementary" rights of the citizens in the United States to vote and to hold public office. Only after lengthy struggles were property qualifications dropped, certain religious qualifications removed, minority races and women enfranchised. A study of the history of these changes is rewarding in showing how far from automatic they were, how intense and continued was the organized effort required to effect them, and how determined the opposition.

Thus individual rights in the United States have had their source both in abstract ideals and concrete "necessities." A creed of democracy was developed in America upon conceptions of ethical equality that can be traced back in part to the universalistic ethics

[65] For example, groups that may have an immediate desire to suppress other groups may be deterred to some extent by allegiance to legal symbols that they hesitate to violate for fear of other repercussions.

of the Judaic-Christian tradition, to Roman conceptions of universal law, and to the merging of the two in doctrines such as those of natural law and the social contract. It found a realistic social base in widespread economic and cultural opportunity, in the needs of a new state for mass support and armed service from the population at large, and in the lack of sharp class divisions. The absence of strong temporal powers of an established church favored doctrines of democracy and tolerance. These influences, although changed in some degree, continue and help to make it possible for many (not all) minorities to protect themselves and others from what they consider inequalitarian and arbitrary governmental actions.

4. Political Parties and the Voters

AT THE center of the web of government is the formal structure of the state, interlaced on the one side with idea and value systems and on the other with the informal organization of governing as a concrete social process. Operating through, and in relation to, this whole structure are the millions of individuals and thousands of specific associations and groups that constitute the society as a whole. Between these individuals and groups and the state are the organized political parties, which in some respects are an extension of the governing association itself. Political parties were not mentioned in the Constitution, and their later role was evidently not at all foreseen. The Constitution-makers established a system of indirect election for crucial elective offices—senators were elected by the state legislatures, and the president was to be chosen by the Electoral College, itself chosen by the state legislators. Not foreseen were the extension of suffrage, the growth of the party system, and the eventual change of the Electoral College to a ceremonial body that merely transmits the results of the popular vote in each state.

But a mass of voters can not elect representatives without some organization to propose candidates and focus political issues.

Parties began as purely "private" groupings, in response to the need for machinery to translate the popular will into the selection of governors. Gradually parties came to be regarded as public or quasi-public agencies and their activities to be defined and regulated by law.

It is notoriously difficult to define just what is meant by "party." Groupings called parties are organized in widely different ways, use a variety of methods, have different kinds of objectives. All parties have in common, however, the organized striving for control of the governing apparatus—they are continuing associations specifically organized to secure power over personnel and policies of the state. They represent an open rather than a closed type of social relationship, and their immediate end is always the capture of power. Americans are accustomed to parties that (mainly) seek power through nonviolent means and take it for granted that a party defeated at the polls will accept the result more or less gracefully, or at least peaceably, and will simply bide its time to win victory in its turn by conventional methods. Quite obviously, however, there are parties that do not operate in this way. Americans are accustomed, furthermore, to parties that maintain themselves by voluntary recruitment and are not an official part of the administrative structure of the state; but the incorporation of the party as a closed group into the personnel of government, as in Soviet Russia or Nazi Germany, reminds us that very different arrangements are common elsewhere.

The United States is remarkable among the major societies of the modern world for the continuity and stability of a two-party system. Much effort has been devoted to explaining why political parties are strong in the United States, and why the two-party system is maintained. The system of political democracy itself has been basic, but several more specific factors have been at work. The large number of elective offices running for relatively short terms makes it extremely difficult for the unorganized voters to select candidates, and the division of authority between Federal and state governments, which makes it necessary to control both in order to carry out an effective national program, further strengthens the system. Established parties also tend to be perpetuated by the vested interests their presence has created and by the traditional loyalties they have attracted. Furthermore, the separation of powers makes control of both the executive and the legislative branches especially important and thus impels those who wish power to consolidate their forces in a united organization.

In its historical origins the two-party system was "in the culture," having been already well developed in Britain out of social class divisions. It has been favored by the presidential form of government, including the parallel system of governorships in the individual states. The separate and unitary executive cannot be divided up among a coalition of minor parties, as is possible with the cabinet of a parliamentary state.[66] A broad division of economic interests between agriculture on the one hand and trade, finance, and industry on the other helped for a long time to give added stability to the system. Once established it created its own vested interests and cultural rationales. Furthermore, and of primary importance, the social order has been *relatively* free of the deep ethnic, religious, and class cleavages among politically effective portions of the population such as have produced a multitude of special-interest parties in Europe.

Many observers of American politics have criticized the party system because of the lack of clear party principles. From the Civil War until the New Deal the two major parties differed so little in policy and ideology as to constitute parties essentially organized around patronage. But this very lack of sharply defined principles is a source of stability in the system. Each party is a melange of diverse economic interests, religious groupings, ethnic stocks, and so forth, and thus must compromise and integrate numerous conflicts in order to gain national power. The struggle for power therefore concerns immediate problems; conflicts cannot be brought to the sharp definition of irreconcilable principle without destroying party unity. And this relatively easy going and flexible situation is expressive, in its turn, of the broad value consensus of the society.

[66] The presidential form is not necessary to a two-party system, as the British Empire shows.

Both major parties accept "political democracy" and a "capitalistic" economy, and their similarity is clearly shown by comparison with European parties of extreme Right and extreme Left. Since 1932 the Democratic party has had a special appeal to workers, and higher-income groups have been disproportionately in the Republican camp, but each party includes substantial numbers from every economic stratum.

Each party also includes diverse sectional interests; in Congress, Southern Democrats even work with Northern and Western Republicans. The organization of the parties on a local and state basis means that national organization and national issues tend to be considered in terms of their implications for state and local elections; in any particular geographic area, the party label may tell nothing as to the policies followed. No one would assume that "Democrat" in Mississippi means the same thing as "Democrat" in Michigan. This internal diversity is to some degree resolved or covered over during the actual campaign in national elections,[67] but in Congress and in state legislatures intraparty blocs of insurgents frequently function as loose subparties. National party control is often so weak that elected representatives vote along the lines of particular interests represented among their constituents with great disregard for party regularity.

Two features of our political institutions have worked against the development of class parties: first, territorial representation; second, the widening of the electorate to include nonpropertied sections of the population. The first creates the mechanical difficulty of finding, in a relatively fluid and heterogeneous society, districts in which one economic stratum is decisively and continually dominant.[68] The representatives may attempt to be the

[67] Not entirely or always—witness numerous third-party splits, e.g., Populism, Bull Moose, Dixiecrats.

[68] Such dominance *does* occur. It is favored where a considerable proportion of the electorate is disenfranchised and where the masses are uneducated, poor, inarticulate, and divided by factionalism or lines of racial and ethnic cleavage. As Key has shown, parts of the South are characterized by conditions that lead to the political dominance of a small, economically privileged minority. V. O. Key, Jr., with the assistance of Alexander Heard: *Southern Politics* (New York: 1949), pp. 8–9, 17–18, 307–08.

voice of particular classes, ethnic groupings, or other special interests within their district; but they may instead try to reconcile
divergent and conflicting interests into some conception of the
"general welfare" that guides their legislative activities. The
second alternative, of course, receives the highest nominal value
in our culture; it is also in many ways the most difficult course. The
"general welfare" is nebulous and finds few organized and politically potent groups to give it voice, whereas special and segmental
interests are likely to be highly articulate and politically conscious.
If parties corresponded closely to the interests of different economic
strata, each stratum might receive unequivocal representation or
be without any effective political influence, depending upon the
shifting power balance of the various groupings. It is doubtful,
however, whether parties organized strictly along the lines of economic class would be compatible with a true party system.[69]

The extension of the suffrage has inhibited narrowly class-
bounded parties by making it necessary for the privileged strata to
appeal to the masses of the voters. It has thereby helped to create
parties (formally) based on issues. How important these tendencies
are is a matter on which informed judgments differ, and there are
those who view American parties as essentially screens hiding the
underlying forces of narrow class interests; but it must be granted
that the combination of territorial representation and mass
electorate has muted the clash of organized class interests.

We have emphasized the two-party system, but other parties are
not unimportant. Minor parties have seldom polled more than 5 per
cent of the popular vote, and their strength has typically been
dispersed among a variety of small parties, but their total influence
has been much greater than the electoral returns would suggest.[70]
On several occasions a third party has seriously challenged the
dominant parties—the Populists in 1892, the Bull Moosers in 1912,
and the Progressives in 1924. The threat of strong third-party

[69] MacIver maintains that "any full identification of party and class is
perilous to the democratic structure." *The Web of Government*, p. 211; see his
whole discussion on pp. 208–24.

[70] Key: *Politics, Parties and Pressure Groups*, pp. 273–4.

movements has undoubtedly been of importance in the incorporation of their demands into later policies of the major parties.[71]
Minor parties rather clearly serve to crystallize and focus issues
and grievances not being expressed through the traditional parties.
When one of them establishes a territorial base by achieving control
of state governments, it sometimes gains a bargaining position by
holding a balance of power between the other parties. This situation is rare, however, and may not always be so effective as the
alternative procedures of working as a cohesive faction within a
major party, or of operating as a "pressure group." [72]

In the modern period of intense nationalism and heightened
social tension, public hostility toward the more extreme deviant
parties takes on a quasi-religious character. The Communist party
is, of course, the archheresy. Intolerance toward it, though bearing
no close relation to the size or influence of the party, may threaten
the tradition of toleration for other deviant parties.

PARTY ORGANIZATION

"Party membership" is an indefinite term because of the loose-
ness of organization and the varying degrees of participation characteristic of our main parties. Does a party consist of all persons
who vote its ticket in a particular election? Those who vote it
regularly? Those who are registered and entitled to vote in its primary elections? Or those who actually do vote in the primaries?
Or the "active workers" of the party? Or only the continuing
leadership? In national elections as much as 30 to 40 per cent of the
qualified electorate does not vote, in local elections as much as 80

[71] For example, an impressive proportion of Populist demands, regarded
as wholly radical at the time, have been incorporated into later national and
state legislation. See John D. Hicks: *The Populist Revolt* (Minneapolis: 1931),
esp. pp. 403 ff.

[72] On the above points see Key: *Politics, Parties and Pressure Groups*, pp.
287 ff. Also Arthur N. Holcombe: *The Political Parties of Today* (New York:
1924); John D. Hicks: "The Third Party Tradition in American Politics,"
Mississippi Valley Historical Review, Vol. XX (1933); Frederick E. Haynes:
Third Party Movements Since the Civil War, with Special Reference to Iowa (Iowa
City, Iowa: 1916).

per cent.[73] Probably not more than 10 per cent of those who vote a party's ticket should be classed as active workers. The core of a party is quite small—the more or less continuously active leaders and officials, whose security and status are most closely bound up with the party's fortunes.

The formal organization of the major parties is built upon the small local units headed by precinct leaders ultimately responsible for getting out the vote. Through the thousands of these workers at the bottom of the national party hierarchy, the party must make its bid for power. Above the precinct comes the ward or district, which includes several precincts, and above this is the city or county unit. In each of the last a party committee attempts to guide and co-ordinate the political activities of the ward and precinct leaders. Within each state there is a state committee, and at the top of the structure is the national committee, composed of one man and one woman from each of the forty-eight states plus representatives from certain territories and dependencies. Members of the state committee represent electoral units such as congressional districts, counties, and judicial or legislative districts. Both the unit of representation and the method of selecting members vary from state to state. In some states the members of the committee are elected by the voters in primary elections, in others by some form of party convention or by automatic representation of local leaders. Usually the state committee is defined and regulated by laws. Members of the national committee are selected by the state delegates to the national party convention. The chairman of the national committee is named by the presidential nominee and has the responsibility of managing the national campaign. Around the chairman is built a small continuing staff that is greatly augmented during the course of the campaign itself.

In practice, however, this formal hierarchy does not accurately indicate the real pattern of organization and control. Great power may rest with leaders who occupy no official party position. Cliques

[73] Key: *Politics, Parties and Pressure Groups*, p. 609. Other valuable references on this topic are Harold F. Gosnell: *Machine Politics: Chicago Model* (Chicago: 1937); Edward M. Sait: *American Parties and Elections* (revised edition, New York: 1939); John T. Salter: *Boss Rule* (New York: 1935).

and factions form at all levels of the organization and contend with one another for power within the party. The nominally dominant national committee is often controlled by leaders at the lower levels of the hierarchy.

The functioning party machine is thus a loose alliance of state and local organizations. The national chairman is able to exert unitary influence to any marked degree only during the crisis of a national campaign. His control rests upon the common hope of victory, upon funds and services that can be made available to local organizations, and—when the party holds national power— upon patronage. But control is shared in an extremely complicated way by the president or presidential nominee, the national committee, members of the party in the national legislature, state and local "machines," and even extraparty groups and organizations.

Patronage is in large part the foundation of party discipline, although its role has been diminished by the growth of civil service systems, the increasing importance of Federal jobs, the growth of professional social work and of insurance and pension plans, and the general shift toward more impersonal and centralized administration. Since control of patronage is distributed among many different officials (such as the president, senators, state and local leaders), party organization cannot be a clear hierarchy, but rather tends to take the form of a series of suborganizations centered around these various leaders.[74]

At the local level, informal personal ties and reciprocities of various kinds become important in the maintenance of party organizations.[75] Kinship ties, personal friendships, the dispensing of small favors, local group identifications—these are the primary ingredients out of which the precinct leader builds a reliable bloc of votes that he can "deliver" as the basis of his power in the party. These blocs of votes are the unit cells that are massed into the solid

[74] Again, a general principle: rigidly hierarchical organization finds its most reliable base in *appointment of personnel from above*. Where officials are elected, there is always the possibility that they will defy their "superiors" and appeal (sometimes successfully) to the electorate.

[75] Vivid documentation of local political organization is provided by William F. Whyte: *Street Corner Society* (Chicago: 1943).

core of party strength. Except in periods of great social disturbance, the party leadership built upon such units is self-selecting and self-perpetuating.[76]

In periods of social and economic stability this type of organization gives the appearance of complete permanence and invulnerability; it survives numerous internal splits and changes in leadership, and numerous "reform" attacks from the outside. Nevertheless, the system continues only under definite social conditions. It is at its strongest when political issues are few and trivial; any deep or revolutionary cleavage would go far to shatter the smooth operation of the established machines.

THE VOTERS AND VOTING BEHAVIOR [77]

American democracy is marked by a wide extension of the franchise, and a high value has been placed upon the privilege— at least until it has been won. The franchise is limited, of course, by voting qualifications that in various jurisdictions include age, residence requirements, citizenship, literacy, tax payments, registration, and various special provisions such as the disenfranchisement of certain kinds of offenders against the law and of those "mentally incompetent." [78] Property qualifications for voting were common in the early Republic—ten states required land ownership as a prerequisite for voting—and the right to hold public office was even more carefully restricted. Both voting and eligibility for public office seem to have been widely regarded as privileges granted by the state, not as rights automatically conferred by citizenship. For several decades after the Revolution, there was determined opposition to the removal of these qualifications,[79] and their absence in the national Constitution was not so

[76] Key: *Politics, Parties and Pressure Groups*, pp. 324–31.

[77] Valuable references are: Paul Lazarsfeld, Bernard Berelson, and Hazel Gaudet: *The Peoples's Choice* (2nd ed., New York: 1948); Key: *Politics, Parties and Pressure Groups*; E. H. Litchfield: *Voting Behavior in a Metropolitan Area* (Ann Arbor, Mich.: 1941).

[78] During the depression of the 1930's some interest groups even proposed to take away the voting rights from millions of persons receiving public relief.

[79] See the review by J. Allen Smith: *The Growth and Decadence of Constitutional Government* (New York: 1930), chap. 3.

much due to objections of political principle as to disagreements of the Founders over the kind of property requirement that might be established. In many instances the effect of property qualification has been re-secured in the states by alternative means such as stringent residence requirements that tend to exclude mobile workers from the ballot, and educational requirements (directed against Negroes in the South); and for long periods in many states, and even now in some, the lack of a really secret ballot placed many voters under the power of economically dominant individuals and groups. Formally free suffrage is, however, definitely the dominant ideal and obtains widely in actual practice.

The use of the ballot varies greatly from one election to another. The vote is heaviest in presidential elections,[80] and grows lighter in the successively more local contests. In purely local elections as few as one fifth of the voters may make the effective political decisions. Key has suggested that the low participation in state and local elections probably increases the chances of control by a tight party organization.[81] At any rate, the extent of nonvoting documents the tendency for parties to be mainly constituted by a minority of active persons.

The following rough generalizations about voting behavior are supported by considerable evidence:

a. *Use of the franchise*

1. Institutionalized disenfranchisement prevents the voting of most Negroes and many of the poorer whites in several Southern states (poll taxes, literacy tests, and so forth).

2. Although aliens were permitted to vote rather generally until the 1920's, all noncitizens are now barred from the polls.

3. The general tendency is for older voters to exercise the franchise proportionately more often than younger voters.

4. Women are generally less likely than men to vote.

5. Persons in higher economic positions are more likely to vote than poorer people. Business and professional groups are especially likely to vote.

[80] Since 1910, between 55 and 65 per cent of the qualified electorate.
[81] *Politics, Parties, and Pressure Groups*, pp. 608–09.

6. Well-educated persons are more likely to vote than are persons with fewer years of school or college training.

7. A large proportion of nonvoters are characterized by political apathy—a kind of generalized indifference—rather than by restraints from specific barriers. Expressed interest in national elections is more frequent among men than women, urban than rural persons, among persons of high social and economic status and education, and among the middle-aged rather than the young. According to the data of one study, three fourths of the nonvoters were so by deliberate decision; they intended in advance not to vote.[82] There is some evidence that political apathy tends to be most frequent among elements of the population that have been repeatedly blocked in their social and economic aspirations,[83] and those who in general constitute the least articulate and less advantaged portions of the community.

8. Nonvoting would seem to be maximized, aside from barriers mentioned in points 1 and 2 above, when elections are frequent, ballots long and complex, registration procedures time-consuming and difficult. Given constant conditions in these respects, however, nonvoting is a significant index of the degree to which elections involve meaningful issues.

b. *Party voting*

1. A high proportion of voters regularly vote for the same party. The exact proportion varies from period to period and from one area to another, but certainly has not dropped below one half in any recent national election, and probably has hovered around 70–80 per cent for long periods.[84]

2. "Traditional" voting is most marked in periods of relative

---

[82] Lazarsfeld, Berelson, and Gaudet: *The People's Choice*, pp. 46–7.

[83] Some data on this point will be contained in a forthcoming report, the 1948 Voting Study, an analysis of the campaign and voting behavior in Elmira, N. Y.

[84] Lazarsfeld and associates found in their study of the 1940 election in Sandusky, Ohio, that 77 per cent of the voters voted as their parents and grandparents habitually had—*The Peoples Choice*. See also the data cited in Key: *Politics, Parties and Pressure Groups.*

stability and prosperity, and we cannot assume that it will necessarily continue to be of primary importance.

3. The independent or shifting votes are numerous enough to make the margin of victory in many, if not most, elections. Hence, decisions on the basis of issues are potentially decisive, even when the majority of votes are "regular."

c. *Factors associated with vote*

1. Voting against the party in power tends to increase in periods of economic adversity, but there are many possible offsetting factors.

2. Although economic status alone is far from determining party affiliation or inclination, there has been for many years a marked tendency for the wealthier groups to vote Republican, the poorer groups, Democratic. (There is an exception—much of the South, in which the Democratic party is eminently conservative.)

3. In northern and western states, the highest percentage of Republican affiliation is found among persons who are high in socio-economic status, Protestant, rural rather than urban, identified with "business" rather than "labor." [85]

d. *The process of vote determination* [86]

1. Changes in voting intentions during the course of a campaign lead to greater *homogeneity* within subgroups and consequently to a *polarization* of attitudes in the total community.

2. Stability of voting intentions appears to be a source of personal security in group contacts and is reinforced by interaction within politically homogeneous social circles.

3. Persons who change their voting intentions during the course of a campaign, and they are small in number, tend to be those who are either relatively little concerned with the outcome of the election or subject to contradictory group affiliations.

[85] Lazarsfeld, Berelson, and Gaudet: *The People's Choice*, chap. 3. For example, of the wealthy Protestant farmers 75 per cent were Republicans, whereas of the urban Catholic workers 90 per cent were Democrats.

[86] The whole field of the social psychology of voting has received astonishingly little research attention. Most of the tentative generalizations stated here have been drawn from ibid.

4. Face-to-face contacts in small groups are of primary importance both in reinforcing attitudes and in stimulating change.

5. Attention to political propaganda is selective; persons attend to those items toward which they are already favorably disposed, and a large proportion of those who are initially "undecided" emerge at the end of a campaign with a predictable stand. This process has been called activation.[87]

6. Voters of definite early intention need *reinforcement* of existing attitudes through arousal of interest and monopoly of attention.[88]

7. The role of local party organization is, or may be, significant in all these processes but seems especially important in getting the nonvoter to vote and in activating the last-minute "waverer." The proportion of conversions as a result of machine activity seems to be quite small.

Incomplete and tentative as these findings are, they do point to several conclusions anticipated in our previous analysis. (1) The immediate economic position of the voter *cannot* entirely explain the direction of his vote. (2) Degree of interest in political affairs varies greatly among individuals and among different social strata and groupings. (3) Degree of interest and direction of voting are closely related to the group identifications and affiliations of individuals. (4) Since group affiliations represent the microscopic level of institutional structures, election behavior is partly predictable in terms of basic social and cultural organization. It is not whimsical or reflexive, and future research may be expected to fill out a picture of its regularities through the analysis of personal motivation in concrete social situations.

5. Interest Groupings

OUR analysis of political behavior has moved through three main levels: first, the explicit cultural structure of the state—the

---

[87] Ibid.

[88] Again the reader is warned that these findings are based largely upon a single study of a particular campaign.

relatively stable norms that guide the recurrent activities of governing; second, the less explicit norms of political practice or government-in-being; third, the structure of parties and the characteristics of voting behavior. Back of all this structure, or underlying it, are the strata, associations, groups and other social units or categories of the total society, identifiable because they carry on activities that reflect various interests and values and express them in various symbols. It is then in these numerous crisscrossing groupings and their changing systems of values, beliefs, and interests that we have to look for the bases of politics and governing, for the sources of the demands for power and of the acquiescence to authority. The structure of political institutions, it must be remembered, consists solely in relatively repetitive behavior directed by relatively enduring norms. Behavior is repetitive and norms are norms only as there is maintained a relatively continuing set of beliefs, values, and interests among the individual members of the society. It is in this area, therefore, that we have also to look for the dynamics of the political institutions, remembering always that, although social structure *is* structure, it is nevertheless always changing.

Detailed analysis of so-called interest groupings (or "pressure groups") in our society is available elsewhere,[89] and we can present here only a highly general overview of their nature and significance.

1. There is a prevalent interest-group conception of politics, as the "great game" [90] of who gets what, when, and why.[91] Politics is seen as maneuver for advantage, and the state as a mediator among pressure groups.[92]

---

[89] Representative examples include: Donald C. Blaisdell: "Economic Power and Political Pressures," *Monograph No. 26*, Temporary National Economic Committee (Washington, D. C.: 1941); Key: *Politics, Parties and Pressure Groups* (here as well as at several other points in this chapter we have relied heavily upon this discerning work); Peter Odegard: *Pressure Politics, The Story of the Anti-Saloon League* (New York: 1928); John T. Salter: *Boss Rule: Portraits in City Politics* (New York: 1935); Belle Zeller: *Pressure Politics in New York* (New York: 1937).

[90] Frank R. Kent: *The Great Game of Politics* (New York: 1923).

[91] Harold D. Lasswell: *Politics, Who Gets What, When, How* (New York: 1936).

[92] Cf. MacIver: *The Web of Government*, pp. 219–20.

2. Great economic specialization creates numerous specific interest groups in agriculture, industry, trade, finance, labor, professions.

3. Cultural diversity creates special groups working for the interests of (a) particular religious organizations, (b) ethnic or racial categories, (c) sectional or regional areas, (d) a great variety of special causes, movements, tastes, from antivivisectionists or vice crusaders to proponents of world government.

4. In short, the society is characterized by a large number of powerful interests, many of which are highly organized and highly skilled in the political arena.

5. Organized interests apparently propose most of the statutes passed by state legislatures, and originate much legislation in Congress.

6. Organized interests maintain continuing relations with administrative agencies whose activities affect them.

7. Not all pressure groups work for the immediate self-interests of those they represent. There are disinterested interest groups whose objectives are not narrowly bound up with the wealth, power, prestige, or other distributive interests of their members.

8. Many interest groups are not only highly organized but represent vast numbers of individuals or great aggregates of economic power.

9. Governmental action tends to pass over the least well-organized segments of the public in favor of the aggressive group with a *specific* program.

10. Possibly, although not certainly, the marked articulation of pressure groups is a rigidifying influence upon the social order. It is so, by definition, to the extent that such groups are successful in gaining political privilege.

What main categories of interests are important in the American political scene? The major groupings are unquestionably "economic," although not by any means always economic classes. First and foremost are the highly organized and economically powerful business groups, from which have developed many effective pressure groups. Among *general* organizations, the two outstanding instances, of course, are the National Association of Manufacturers and the Chamber of Commerce, with its more than seventeen hundred local units. Both organizations actively seek to influence governmental policy. Some of the most active business pressure groups, however, are specialized—for instance, the Committee of Utility Executives that fought the 1935 Public Utility Holding Company Act, or the numerous permanent trade associations. Business groups both favor and oppose particular items on programs of legislation, but in recent years their major emphasis has been upon blocking undesired action—opposing increased taxation, social security, extension of public regulation, and so on. As a general rule they have favored state regulation rather than Federal, apparently on the dual assumption that forty-eight states permit many delaying battles and that state regulation, when established, is easier than Federal to deal with.

As a counterweight to business pressures stand the labor unions and their political-action adjuncts. Like business groups the unions have contributed, although not so heavily, to campaign funds; they actively favor or oppose legislation; they propose laws; they exercise wide surveillance upon legislative action. As noted in Chapter 6, there are considerable differences in the orientation and tactics of the major unions. For a long time the American Federation of Labor opposed government interference in labor-management problems and has only slowly modified this stand. Since it is in the main a loose federation of diverse craft-type unions, it is not always highly cohesive or united in policy. The C.I.O. is characterized by a more systematic political consciousness and a greater willingness to enter directly into political campaigns. But both organizations attempt to influence Congress and various state legislatures and interest themselves in an imposing array of proposed legislation, ranging through specifically "labor" or "anti-labor" bills to measures dealing with insurance, health, civil rights, immigration, and many others.

Agriculture provides a third great aggregate of organized interests. Farm blocs have demonstrated themselves to be highly effective pressure organizations during the last two decades, in a period when agriculture was becoming a less important part of the economy.[93] There are a number of major organizations: the American Farm Bureau Federation, the National Grange, and the Farmers Union, plus such compact and specialized agencies as the National Co-operative Milk Producers Federation.

The organized professions are in part economic pressure groups, sufficiently distinct from labor, business, and agriculture to justify separate mention. Outstanding examples are the tightly organized and powerful American Medical Association, and the American Bar Association.

Fifth, we find a variety of pressure groups organized around problems of ethnic, religious, or "racial" interests. There are the numerous neofascist and antiminority organizations, such as the Ku Klux Klan.[94] There are the "prominority" organizations such as the National Association for the Advancement of Colored People and the various hyphen-American organizations. Although not all of these act directly as pressure groups, they are seldom politically irrelevant. The same can be said for many organized religious bodies, especially of the lay auxiliaries of the Catholic churches.

Sixth, but not necessarily of that rank in importance, are the organizations of military veterans, especially the American Legion. Commanding the presumption of a strong moral claim upon the society, veterans' organizations are typically able to work without concentrated opposition from other powerful pressure groups.

In addition to these there are a great many miscellaneous groups, varying greatly in importance, and concerned with nearly every imaginable issue.

Beyond the organized associations are broader and more diffuse

[93] This curious fact suggests a necessity for further intensive study as to why agriculture is so seldom denounced as a "selfish interest." The pathos built up around farming and rural life in our national history apparently has much to do with the contrast between the reception of the demands of agricultural and of labor groups. See John Gauss and Leon Wolcott: *Public Administration and the United States Department of Agriculture* (Chicago: 1940), pp. 17 ff.

[94] See, for example, John M. Mecklin: *The Ku Klux Klan* (New York: 1924); Donald S. Strong: *Organized Anti-Semitism in America* (Washington D. C.: 1941).

alignments of interests such as represented in rural-urban conflicts,[95] sectional or regional constellations,[96] interstate or inter-
district opposition.[97] These territorial alignments appear to be decreasing in importance, however, with the spread of urbanism and
economic specialization and the increased ease of national communication and interregional mobility.

It is in the form of organized associations or groups that interests
directly contend for power. Interest groups become pressure groups
by exerting their influence at any level or in any branch or division
of government. Their points of pressure are directed at whatever
centers of power may be present.[98] This activity constitutes "lobbying." The older techniques of lobbying by outright or thinly
concealed bribery and intimidation have tended to give way to
other methods less vulnerable to public condemnation. The representatives of interest groups try to influence legislation both
directly, by immediate contacts with legislative committees at
formal hearings and in personal conferences, and indirectly, by
mobilizing support "back home," either by inciting petitions, let-
ters, and so forth on a mass basis or by activating strategic individuals presumed to have influence with legislators. Practically
every organized interest of any considerable importance has its
representatives on duty at the key points of political authority.
Lobbying is a continuing and "normal" part of the governing
process in America.

Attempts to regulate lobbying have not usually been directed at
the *sources* of lobbying in powerful but not officially represented
interests; rather they have sought to make lobbying public and in
some measure accountable. Thus, many states require some registration of paid lobbyists and attempt to regulate the methods used
in influencing legislation. The effectiveness of this regulation is
doubtful both because of the vagueness of the legislation and the
lack of rigorous enforcement. Indeed, lobbying seems to be an un-

[95] Prohibition, taxation, daylight-saving time, governmental subsidies.
[96] The Cotton South *vs.* the dairying North, the agricultural-debtor West
vs. the industrial-financial East.
[97] "Backcountry" *vs.* seaboard, upstate *vs.* downstate.
[98] Key: *Politics, Parties, and Pressure Groups*, p. 227: "Where power rests,
there influence will be brought to bear."

official provision for functional representation of interests.[99] Lobbying could be abolished in the American system—by providing official interest-group representation, or by organizing parties strictly along lines of special interests, or by other equally drastic action; but now pressure groups, operating as lobbys, make up a "third house" of our legislative bodies and are an inseparable part of the administrative process.

The low repute of lobbying—like that of "politics" more generally [100]—is the result, in part, of "misplaced" norms; activities considered legitimate or even virtuous in business, for instance, are condemned in politics. But wherever strong interests are organized, they will be represented in government in one form or another—officially or unofficially, openly or covertly. The alternative is a system of functional (proportional) representation, but this on a national scale in the United States seems more nearly calculated to intensify rather than diminish the clash of interest groups. Another is the pulverization of private groups, leaving only isolated individuals outside of the organization of the state itself.[101]

Pressure groups are not unique to America, nor to democracies. Even in the most rigid dictatorships, there are conflicts of interests, factions, pressures; and these may be all the more powerful for being concealed. What is characteristic of the United States is the

[99] See the statement of E. Pendleton Herring: "Lobby," *Encyclopaedia of the Social Sciences*, Vol. IX, pp. 565–8. Herring calls the lobby a "political institution."

[100] The generally acknowledged low repute of "politics" and the "politician" is documented by more systematic evidence. A nation-wide survey reported in 1946 that 65 per cent of American adults said they would not want a son to go into politics as a life career, but 63 per cent said they would want him to be a lawyer. The expressed aversion to politics as a vocation was general in all parts of the country, rural and urban, and was found in all age groups, occupation classes, and educational groupings. The National Opinion Research Center comments: "That a certain stigma should be attached to politics in the eyes of the public, while the law is regarded as an upright and honorable calling, may seem paradoxical in view of the fact that the legal profession perhaps oftener than any other serves as a stepping-stone to a political career." Opinion News, N.O.R.C. (August 6, 1946), Vol. VII, no. 3.

[101] A condition approached in Germany and the Soviet Union in recent years. For valuable evidence on the latter case see Alex Inkeles: *Public Opinion in Soviet Russia* (Cambridge, Mass.: 1950).

relative openness of the whole process and the large number and variety of highly organized groupings.

None of the main classes of interests roughly distinguished above are homogeneous or without sharp internal conflicts. In agriculture we have Western farmers, who may want Federal reclamation of lands, versus their Eastern competitors, who either may not care or may oppose it; in industry there are the makers of steel and the users of steel; in labor there are diversities among the A.F.L., the C.I.O., the railway brotherhoods, independent unions. *Any* group may become a pressure group—governmental agencies themselves can and do function as such.

The relation of interest groups to the state extends the pluralism and separation of powers into the institutions of the state itself. Theoretically, at least, the state is not identified with any particular segmental interest. As examples we have the separation of church and state, the ultimate political authority officially favoring no religious group; the limitation of direct governmental control of economic affairs; the lack of official representation of interest groups in legislatures; the absence of parties avowedly representing ethnic, racial, religious, or class groupings. The state is supposed to be the mediator and integrating focus for the numerous discrete interests of a differentiated society. Although this function is increasingly strained today, thus far the system has been elastic enough to survive quite revolutionary transformations of social structure.

In early America, property owners generally held the political power, and the main road to power was through the control of property. Many political thinkers wanted to restrict suffrage and eligibility for public office to those who had "a stake in the community." In our day, property and power are increasingly divorced. Ownership of business does not necessarily mean economic power; and the politically powerful are not necessarily propertied. The power of management in the corporation and of the leaders of labor unions, farm organizations, business associations, and so on, comes, like political authority, from position in a functioning organization. The structure of power in the large economic organization is already somewhat similar to that of a "socialistic" order.

The historic association of property with power has now been shattered in country after country, most dramatically in the totalitarian regimes that have shown that *control* is what counts, not the form of property rights.[102] The National Socialists in Germany could leave the outward pattern of property largely intact while drastically amassing power—in the end practically depriving the nominal property owners of power. The lesson thus taught is reinforced by the experience of capitalistic countries, including the United States, in progressively divorcing control rights from ownership rights. The corporation has shown as decisively as the total dictatorship that individual ownership rights are no longer either a necessary or a sufficient condition for social power. Modern developments have made it increasingly plain that control is the central problem for economics as well as for politics, and that the distinction between economic power and political power can become hazy indeed.[103]

Conversely one must agree with Weber that the political organization of national states already resembles what some forms of socialism advocate for economic organization. For, with nationalism, the local rulers and feudal estates "had been expropriated of their political means and had been displaced by the salaried officialdom of the modern bureaucratic state. The state had 'nationalized' the possession of arms and of administrative means." [104] In feudalism, economic power and political power were *merged*, but both were territorially and organizationally *diffused* rather than centralized. In a completely collectivistic society, however, the *anschluss* of economics and politics is not only complete but it is centralized: state and economy become one, and under unitary direction—in contrast to democratic political orders, in which there are *separate* economic and political elites, supported by multiple and *different* interests.

Even with all the enormous consolidation of economic power in organized business and labor, the American economy still has com-

---

[102] Cf. Peter F. Drucker: *The Future of Industrial Man* (New York: 1942), esp. pp. 75 ff.

[103] As Merriam, along with many others, has pointed out. *Public and Private Government*, p. 10.

[104] Gerth and Mills (trans. and eds.): *From Max Weber*, p. 49.

peting, divergent, and conflicting interests; consequently there is far from complete unity or centralization of economic power, and particular economic interests do not completely determine political policy. A similar granulation of political power is still characteristic. Of course, the "separation of powers" and "a system of checks and balances" cannot mean in the twentieth century what they did in the small agrarian republic of 1789; the great extension of the powers of the presidency, for example, is an expectable consequence of the demands that wars and economic crises have made upon a governmental machine originally designed to disperse and limit both the power of officials and the voice of the people.

6. The System as a Whole

REPEATEDLY in different aspects of American political institutions and political behavior a common pattern emerges: *the balancing of interests and compromising of conflicts through multiple power-centers, numerous separate channels of influence, and the subdivision of political authorities.* We might call this "political pluralism." It is manifest in the federal system, with its complex division of authority among various levels of government; in the separation of powers, and in the further subdivision of functionally specific authority within the major branches; in the loose "federal" organization of political parties, and in the system of territorial representation.[105] It reaches extreme development, with important side-effects, in the politics of factionalism. In the "invisible government" it is manifest in the cross-pressures of numerous interest-groupings: diverse agricultural interests, manufacturing interests, separate business groupings, governmental officialdom, veterans, racial and ethnic minorities, religious groupings, geographic sections, professional associations, and so on.

To those who favor a unitary and centralized system of Left or

[105] Cf. Key: *Politics, Parties and Pressure Groups*, p. 27: "The division of sectional interests into separate states probably contributes to national unity by splintering and weakening the potential strength of sectional drives."

Right the present structure of American political institutions is an
anachronism. On the other hand, those who accept not only the
fact but the legitimacy of a plurality of value systems and specialized interests in modern political society, may accept American
politics as a process of cross-pressures, compromises, and the slow,
uncertain, and uneven growth of consensus, which has to be rewon
from time to time. In the latter case there is little of the logical
symmetry of systematic political creeds. The system is actually a
congeries of continually changing subsystems; it is a multifaceted
process rather than a unitary and fixed political mold.

On the other hand, the limited and fragmented state of our
eighteenth century simply could not survive today. The eighteenth
and nineteenth century philosophy of "boycotting government" [106]
paralleled the conception of society as an aggregate of discrete individuals bound together in a system ruled by natural laws; within
a framework of "natural justice" each individual acting in his own
interests would contribute to the public good; it followed that the
best government was that which governed the least. In fact, of
course, the American state after 1791 was never so weak or limited
as this political philosophy required but it did leave extraordinary
scope to private and decentralized power and to local autonomy.
The "negative state" was functionally suited to a society of self-
sufficient local areas and small-scale economic enterprises. Limited
government was favored also by the infrequency of foreign wars,
and by economic opportunity coupled with a belief in self-reliance
and self-confidence.

There has been much concern in American culture with whatever is called "democracy" and "freedom." The present analysis
concludes that the individual freedoms that apparently matter
most in our culture depend not so much on political forms as on the
basic social structure. Americans must have discovered that constitutions and bills of rights are not easily exportable to societies
with radically different values. "Freedom," in one of its important
meanings, is an attribute of social structure.[107] Requisite for maxi-

---

[106] The phrase is Merriman's. *Politics in Social Change*, chap. 10.

[107] See the stimulating analysis by Gerard De Gré: "Freedom may be defined in terms of the probability that specific groups or individuals can formu-

mal personal freedom are (1) dispersion of power, *and* (2) limitation of both public and private power by rules that take their departure from a high evaluation of individual personality and consent. The political institutions dominant in our society require a tolerance of value diversities and conflicts of interests.

We conclude at the point where we began this chapter. Where there is power, there is always the possible abuse of power; hence political problems are inescapable in human society. This chapter has tried to analyze only a few specific examples of these problems for one culture.

---

late their ends of conduct and initiate a course of action with a minimum degree of constraint from other persons, and with a high degree of predictability of the consequences of their acts within the institutional and associational structure of the community." "Freedom and Social Structure," *American Sociological Review*, Vol. XI, no. 6 (October, 1946), p. 530.

8. American Education

1. Education as an Institution

THE STUDENT of social systems must grasp many inter-related processes simultaneously. What is called "the state of the system as a whole," difficult as it is to grasp or describe, is one determinant in the behavior of the distinguishable parts of the system. We have examined the family, the system of stratification, and the economic and political institutions. We turn now to an-other major and permanent institution—education.

Educational institutions derive from these two irreducible facts:[1] (1) human culture is learned, not biologically inherited; (2) very young human beings are both plastic and incapable of sur-vival, much less of developing social personalities, without adult care and teaching. The cultural heritage must be renewed for each generation; society is daily invaded by new "barbarians" [2] who have to learn thousands of specific skills, beliefs, knowledges, val-ues, and norms if the culture is to have any continuity. A complex, technologically advanced society, greatly dependent upon science and rapidly changing, requires an elaborate system of instruction and indoctrination if it is not to regress to simpler levels.

In a broad sense "education" is the totality of human teaching and learning. Even in the narrower sense of direct and intended in-struction, it is an important aspect of many social actions not ordinarily thought of as "educational." Through most of history,

[1] Cf. Joyce O. Hertzler: *Social Institutions* (New York: 1929), chap. 9, pp. 153–64.

[2] Cf. the striking statement by R. Pinot quoted in Pitirim A. Sorokin: *Contemporary Sociological Theories* (New York: 1928), p. 85.

and for the vast majority of the world's peoples today, education has not been provided by specialized personnel functioning in a separate organization, but has been part of the ordinary routine of the society. Parents, elders, craftsmen, priests, warriors, and others have instructed the young in the knowledges, skills, traditions, beliefs, and values of the particular social group. Indeed in all societies the ordinary day-to-day interaction of an individual with other individuals, from birth onward, continually "instructs" and reshapes his behavior.[3] Everywhere, the child absorbs an enormous and complex range of cultural materials as a more or less unplanned, informal by-product of growing up in a family and community.

Nevertheless, some formalized education is found in even the "simplest" cultures; if not schools in our sense, there are definitely institutionalized and systematic patterns of indoctrination and instructions—for instance, secret societies or initiation rites. In societies that like ours have highly developed occupational specialization and considerable general cultural heterogeneity, specialized agencies of education develop and elaborate their own norms and goals, their own forms of organization, their own systems of statuses, and their own specially trained and disciplined personnel. Education comes to be thought of as something one "gets," not the total experience of the whole personality.

It is one of the distinguishing marks of modern secularized societies that education has been so removed from kinship and religious groupings. Although even in the United States organized religious bodies still conduct much educational activity and families do not always turn over their children to the school completely, or without reservations and emotional ambivalence, the degree of separation of formal education from family and church is extraordinarily extensive and sharp.

Educational influences operating directly upon the child include, of course, not only the socialization of family and playgroup and

[3] "In the main, we get more training in the standardized ways of living and interacting that constitute the institutional life through the informal contacts with our fellows and our environment than from formal education." Hertzler: *Social Institutions*, p. 156.

the formal instruction of the schools, but also the enormously expanding impact of the mass media of communication—radio, television, books, magazines, the omnipresent flood of "comic books," and motion pictures. The social effect of these media is still obscure, but unquestionably they reach incredibly large audiences and carry ideas and values often different from, and in conflict with, those that the schools attempt to inculcate. We must restrict our present analysis largely to the influence of schools and colleges, but we must not overestimate their power and significance. For much of the most vivid and lasting learning occurs outside of the schools, and a sharp contradiction between academic instruction and other personal experience is often, if not typically, resolved in favor of the latter. Beginnings have been made in the accumulation of evidence.[4]

Education is no more emotionally neutral than any other institution, and one must always remain aware of its dynamic elements and its "psychological" dimension. Of every educational situation it is important to ask:

1. *What* is being taught or learned? What content, intended and unintended, is being transferred?
2. *Who* is teaching? What are his or her position, derivation, and characteristics?
3. *How* is teaching being done? What are the organizing norms, the techniques, methods, interpersonal relations, and their consequences?
4. *To whom* is the teaching directed?

The answers vary tremendously from one culture to another, and we shall soon inspect some of the ways in which our own culture contrasts with others.

---

[4] Examples include: Herbert Blumer: *Movies and Conduct* (New York: 1933); Henry J. Forman: *Our Movie Made Children* (New York: 1934); Charles A. Siepmann: *Radio, Television, and Society* (New York: 1950); Paul F. Lazarsfeld: *Radio and the Printed Page* (New York: 1940); Paul F. Lazarsfeld and Frank Stanton: *Radio Research, 1941, 1942* and *Radio Research, 1942, 1943* (New York: 1943); Paul F. Lazarsfeld and Frank Stanton: *Communications Research, 1948, 1949.* (New York: 1949); Robert K. Merton: *Mass Persuasion* (New York: 1946).

The school is a definitely segregated social system, with its own patterns of authority and control, its distinctive groups and forms of organization, its special ceremonies and rituals, its peculiar language, its special norms and values.[5] To a large extent it is both a distinct social unit and a separate culture, depending upon the type of school. The homogeneity of the school culture and its unity and intensity of ingroup identification are usually greatest in schools that are simultaneously small, long established, maximally separated from the larger community, and relatively homogeneous as to the class, religious, and ethnic backgrounds of staff and students. These conditions are met in high degree in many wealthy private boarding schools, in certain established "prestige" colleges, and in some small rural schools. In the cities, on the other hand, many of the large public schools draw upon a heterogeneous student population and are unable to develop more than a highly formal unity.

The school as a social organization is split internally into many subgroups and subcategories. In the larger schools the student population is divided into numerous cliques, gangs, and other informal and diffuse groupings; it is sharply age-graded; it has many formal organizations and special extracurricular activities. The teaching staff is likewise organized into cliques and factions, and is graded into prestige ranks and placed in a hierarchy of authority; it may have its professional organizations or even its teachers' union. Over teachers and students in the public schools is the authority of a principal, superintendent, or other executive officer. Behind the administrative authorities are the school boards. Operating at all these points, and at others, are the influences of parents and their organizations and of numerous special interests and groups from the larger society. The school is thus, like every other important social organization, both subject to forces arising outside it and self-directing and self-activated.

The school comprises a complex system of reciprocal statuses and roles. The positions of teacher, student, parent, school administrator, board member, and so on are definitely institutionalized,

[5] Willard Waller: *The Sociology of Teaching* (New York: 1932), chaps. 2 and 9.

but not without tension and conflict. Parents and teachers seldom agree upon the standards by which the child is to be judged.[6] Parents tend to see their children as members of the most intimate primary group, as projections of their own hopes and fears, as beings for whom they are accountable in the eyes of the community. Teachers tend to see the same children more impersonally and more nearly in terms of the school's requirements for discipline, control, scholastic achievements, or other special standards. Obviously the schools could not exist at all were these divergencies complete, but because school and family thus differ, an important degree of latent or overt conflict is built into the institutional situation itself.[7]

In our society much teaching is "ideational"—the teaching of ideas *about* activities rather than the demonstration of activities— and the young may be trained for future roles in which the teacher has himself had no direct experience. By contrast, in societies with a slight division of labor, "teaching" is carried on by persons who are themselves actively performing the roles into which they are inducting others.[8] Such is the primeval teacher—the craftsman, soldier, priest, farmer, hunter, ruler—who trains others out of his own accumulated lore and experience. With the development of a more highly dynamic and differentiated society, however, the teacher who explains rather than demonstrates appears, at first usually in the priesthood, which has developed in all major societies with a written history. To transmit the sacred lore to new members of the priesthood there emerges the religious scholar and the sacred school.[9] With any advanced secularization of the culture, "schools" in the modern sense arise in two main ways: first, special branches of study become gradually separated from the sacred tradition; second, separate secular schools with their own lay teachers are established *de novo*.[10] As the society becomes more complex, the teacher becomes more specialized and less likely to *practice* his specialty; he becomes an expert or adviser.

---

[6] Ibid., esp. pp. 68, 69.

[7] The proliferation of Parent-Teacher organizations is partly a symptom of the tensions generated at the point of tangency between family and school.

[8] Florian Znaniecki: *The Social Role of the Man of Knowledge* (New York: 1940).

[9] Ibid., chap. 3.   [10] Ibid., p. 115.

Thus, the teacher emerges—and the secular school. What are the main outlines of the "separate culture" of a secular school system?[11] In the first place the primary teacher-student relationship is a relation between those who wield institutional authority and those who are supposed to accept it. It is *also* mainly a relation between older and younger persons. Between teachers and students there will typically be differences in interests and values, in standards of conduct, and in the complexity of organization of perceptions and behavior. Schools in different cultures differ greatly in the kind and degree of teacher-student conflict and rigidity of discipline. Fragmentary evidence indicates that school discipline is less severe and the teacher's role less authoritarian in the United States than in European countries generally, even prior to the 1930's.

The public, secular school of modern nations does not merely copy the culture of the local community in which it is located; it acts as a center for the diffusion of a much wider national and international culture. It often passes on new techniques, ideas, goals, and standards of conduct that differ appreciably from those current in the local area; and thus on occasion it comes into conflict with parents and with locally powerful individuals and groups. What it does in fact teach will typically represent a compromise between these out-of-school influences and the professional and personal inclinations of the teachers. On the other hand, the school's tendency to diffuse a wider culture can be highly significant in producing cultural homogeneity in complex societies. The United States provides one of the great examples—its public schools played an enormous role in the "Americanization" of many millions of children of European immigrants.[12]

Perhaps the most crucial point about the separate culture of the school is precisely its separateness; for the fact that educational organizations are specialized and segmented parts of the society is

[11] Here we borrow ideas freely from Waller: *The Sociology of Teaching*, which contains insights concerning the sociology of education that have seldom been equaled.

[12] Cf. Denis W. Brogan: *The American Character* (New York: 1944), pp. 135, 141.

both product and further cause of separateness and difference. Consider how remarkable is the central fact of a modern school system: from the age of six or less until late adolescence or early adulthood, children and youths are removed for a large part of most days of every year from the tutelage of family or church and from active participation in the ordinary activities of the wider society. Despite vocational training, "community-centered schools," "activity projects," and the like, the typical school is decisively separate from wider community activities.[13]

The school creates special attitudes in its teachers. Upon them impinge, not just the needs and demands of the pupils, but the expectations and evaluations of other teachers, of administrative superiors, of parents, of other individuals and groupings in the wider community. The resulting "teacher morality" has much in common with the norms of other professions but shows understandably unique features. The teacher is expected to show "impartiality," to treat students with formal equality, and to maintain a certain impersonality or social distance in dealing with them.[14] He is not supposed to court popularity among the students. There are conventions of formality in teacher-teacher relations, especially in the presence of pupils. There is a code of workmanship—standards of proficiency and conscientiousness in doing one's job. Quite frequently the demands and expectations to which the teacher is exposed result in an emphasis upon punctuality, caution, and personal conformity beyond that found in the free professions or among business groups in the same communities.

The students also inherit and develop a special culture. One of its

[13] This is a descriptive, not an evaluative statement. Some "separateness" is inevitable if there are to be schools at all.

[14] The significance of these patterns has been analyzed only generally. One consequence is certainly to minimize personal attractions and antipathies that might be disruptive to learning; formality also insulates the teacher from direct personal vulnerability on matters outside his or her special institutional authority and competence. There are, quite certainly, other "functions." (Cf. Waller: *The Sociology of Teaching*, chaps 9, 10, and 14.) The norms of impartiality and formality are not, of course, invariant and are not always controlling. For further examples, see August B. Hollingshead: *Elmtown's Youth* (New York: 1949), chap. 8.

prime components, in our public schools at least,[15] is group solidarity: the pupils are for certain purposes a group united against the school authorities. There is an injunction against "tattling" or "squealing" and disdain for the "teacher's pet." Students tend to establish with teachers the social distance that the teachers themselves feel an obligation to maintain. In their informal activities, students emphasize the hierarchy of age and make distinctions that seem incredibly fine to many adults. They demand exact conformity to the standards commonly shared at a particular age-grade level. They emphasize extracurricular activities and tend to deprecate "excessive" scholastic achievement.

The above generalizations merely indicate a few of the relatively distinctive normative patterns of the school. The concrete norms vary, of course, through time and from one type of school to another, but we must pass over these variations at present.

We must not forget that educational institutions in *any* society are always affecting and being affected by other institutions. They are, for example, never really politically neutral, for seeming neutrality inescapably involves acceptance of the existing situation. It does not follow that education is not more "free" in some societies than in others, but educational systems cannot be fully understood without analyzing their specific interdependence with other components of the culture and the social system.

2. General Characteristics of American Education

IN THE United States there is no nation-wide system of schools under a central authority, nor is there any organized national enforcement of standard curricula, organization or methods. Yet there is an "American system" clearly different from the educational institutions of many other cultures. Its unity is one of

[15] The pattern probably has fairly wide cross-cultural application, but the differences commonly noted, between Germany and the United States for instance, are enough to warn against too ready generalization.

cultural themes and cultural structure rather than of centralized social organization. For we have one-room rural schools and giant urban schools; "progressive" schools and those that cling to the three R's; we have "colleges" that are trade schools, and "colleges" in the tradition of the European universities. Standards vary, textbooks vary, controls vary, aims and methods vary. How can there be a "system" or "institution" in all this flux and variation? [16]

The unifying characteristics of American education are to be found in common normative standards—conceptions of what education should be, its aims and functions. Yet even these show much diversity, as we shall see. Nevertheless, cultural themes, or the generalized assumptions and values [17] that can be inferred from the institutionalized norms, provide the best point of departure. Despite diversity, there is substantial evidence of institutional consistency and regularity, provided that we are willing to cut through the surface details.

FAITH IN EDUCATION

The common cultural framework consists, first of all, in the widespread "faith in education," noted by foreign observers as characteristic of the American scene for well over a century. Yet there is also a strong tendency to deprecate the value of formal education. Education in general receives tremendous acclaim; education in particular is the object of widespread disaffection, criticism, and low esteem. To some Americans, however, education is a magic

[16] "As one looks at the public school system of America, the first generalization one is tempted to make is that it is not a system at all and that no generalizations about it are true." Harold J. Laski: *The American Democracy* (New York: 1948), p. 328.

[17] Counts speaks of "controlling ideas" and contrasts the systematic and consistent content of educational theories with the rough-hewn principles that have to be dug out from actual educational practice. He correctly points out that the cultural themes established in the second way are often rather different from those set forth in the thought of educational "theorists." George S. Counts: *The American Road to Culture, A Social Interpretation of Education in the United States* (New York: 1930), chap. 1, esp. pp. 3 and 7.

panacea,[18] the prime agency of progress; and America's faith in universal public education is its greatest asset. This faith is typically supported on two main grounds: first, that a democratic society requires an educated citizenry so that individuals may participate in the decisions of public policy; second, that education brings economic rewards and social advancement to the individual and strength and security to the national society.

Evidence of faith in education and the identification of education with the schools is not hard to find.[19] American expenditures for education are impressive. There is the universality of compulsory attendance at elementary and secondary school, and the very high attendance rates. There is the widespread "testimony," not just of professional educators but of broad sectors of the population.[20] There are, comparatively, richly endowed colleges and universities. The observant traveler finds that in the small American town the public school building dominates the scene much as the cathedral dominates the towns of Latin America and much of Europe. On the other hand, a very large, although not exactly ascertainable, proportion of those Americans who profess enthusiasm for education are giving their support to a symbol or an ideal creed, not to the realities presented by schools. Organized education raises problems—about the pay of teachers, the degree of equality of opportunity for students, the freedom of the teacher to pursue inquiry. Education-in-practice is frequently attacked as "too impractical," or as too expensive, or as corrosive of established beliefs and values, or as an incitement to discontent, or as too much concerned with irrelevancies or frills. Faith in education is not universally shared, nor is it all of one piece. Its components deserve closer examination.

Much of this ambivalence reflects two contrasting attitudes: the practical interest in formal training as a means to occupational success; and the interest in the training of "the whole man"—the

[18] For a remarkable example see Raymond M. Hughes and William H. Lancelot: *Education, America's Magic* (Ames, Iowa: 1946).

[19] Cf. Counts: *The American Road to Culture*, p. 17.

[20] One bit of survey evidence on attitudes toward college education may be found in "Higher Education, the Fortune Survey," *Fortune Supplement* (September, 1949).

liberal-humanistic tradition with its stress upon the "social value of the mind disciplined by instruction to understand the world about it" [21] and upon intrinsic values in the cultural legacy. Education has been accepted by many not as an end in itself, but as a means to specific goals. The influence of older religious and classical education aiming to inculcate certain beliefs and values for their own sake never disappeared so completely from the American public school as some of the critics of education have believed—at the least the schools are expected, as Waller has said, to be "museums of virtue." [22] But the practical and the liberal curricula have contended in the public school and the struggle has been intense, partly because different social groups have had different interests in the outcome.

Liberal education has seemed a suitable mark of "culture" and prestige to an economically secure elite (and to many who have aspired to join them), but it has seemed immensely "impractical" to most farmers, self-made businessmen, and workers. They may have given it a certain deference as an esoteric, quasi-magical body of learning, but it has not been in the main what they wanted for their own children. Thus education receives mass support, but the alleged faith in it is the resultant of complex and partly conflicting evaluations.

MASS EDUCATION

In the United States we have *mass* education. Attendance in a tax-supported public-school system is compulsory.[23] Probably nowhere else has a society devoted so much of its time and resources to formal schooling.[24] In 1945–46 there were nearly 28,000,000

[21] Laski: *The American Democracy*, p. 324.

[22] This happy phrase occurs on p. 34 of *The Sociology of Teaching*.

[23] The first compulsory school attendance law was established by Massachusetts in 1852; by 1918 all states had some legislation of this type. Newton Edwards and Herman G. Richey: *The School in the American Social Order* (Boston: 1947), p. 672.

[24] "In the United States over one-fifth of the people spend most of their waking hours as pupils in educational institutions. This situation is unique in human experience and, in fact, is without historical precedent in the nation." Paul H. Landis: *Population Problems* (New York: 1943), pp. 336, 337.

students taught by 1,078,379 teachers.[25] From generation to generation since the middle of the nineteenth century, schools have multiplied, enrollment has grown, curricula have broadened and diversified, higher education has vastly expanded. Our educational system has not just grown; it has exploded into a giant nation-wide enterprise. It tends furthermore, to have "mass" organization and practices. In the large urban schools, in the increasingly dominant consolidated school of the small town or rural area, and in the great metropolitan universities (though not in many experimental schools nor the many small schools and colleges), much of the organization and procedure is basically affected by the presumed necessity of "processing" great numbers of students through standardized stages.

The most important influences in the rise of universal public education include at least five that continue into the present. First, the early dominance of sectarian Protestantism in America, with its reliance upon individual access to religious truth as revealed in the Bible, was a real spur to elementary education. Most sects required that their members learn to read; many established schools and colleges. In more subtle ways, also, neo-Calvinistic movements created a predisposition toward formal education. The churches, at war among themselves, could well utilize literate defenders and argumentative skills; the school provided an agency for the total discipline so important to the sterner branches of ascetic Protestantism; and the intellectual schematization of knowledge fitted the concept of an ordered, (and for many sects) predestined, world. A second major influence was the establishment of political democracy and the gradual widening of suffrage, which seemed to call for extension of educational opportunity to at least the politically responsible elements of the nation. Third, an awakening political consciousness, combined with extremely widespread and intense desires for upward social mobility, led the "common man," under upper-class leadership, to support the establishment of the great public-school systems. Fourth, after the emergence of

[25] Biennial Survey of Education in the United States, 1944 and 1946, Federal Security Agency, Office of Education: (Washington, D. C. 1949).

complex, large-scale industry the needs of business for technicians and for literate, skilled workers gave further impetus to mass education. Finally, after the turn of the century, with the immigration of large numbers of non-English speaking people, the already established public schools were seized upon to "Americanize" foreigners and their children, to replace their Old World culture with some version of a new common culture. Thus the United States, like modern dictatorships, though to far less degree and for different purposes, has relied upon state-supported, compulsory education to establish national unity.

There are other influences; but those mentioned indicate what different forces have produced and now support the public schools.[26] In fact this very capacity to mobilize the support of such multiple interests and values goes far to explain the wide popular base and continuing vitality of organized education.

Let us summarize certain other important characteristics of American educational institutions:

1. *Organization and control:*

a. The schools are predominantly state-controlled, although many are private (both secular and religious). A uniform education is formally available to all social and economic classes.

b. Local and state governments control the school system. In the past, an extreme degree of local control has existed; at the present, some faint beginnings of national control are discernible.

c. The nominally supreme authority over the public schools is usually vested in officials either elected directly, or appointed or elected by governors, legislatures, or boards that are themselves elected by popular vote.

d. At the local level, there is typically a marked, although decreasing, degree of autonomy for "lay" boards of control that represent influential segments of the community.

---

[26] Many of them can be subsumed under widespread and long-enduring cultural themes—the high evaluation of children and youth, for instance, depending in part upon a belief in the future and in "progress."

e. In the larger and more centralized school systems authority seems to be centered in the chief executive officer at each level of a firmly established hierarchy. Procedures are standardized.

f. Students pass through a continuous series of stages from nursery school or kindergarten to the university, the stages usually unbroken by special selective examinations at any step until entrance into graduate or professional schools and often not then—in marked contrast to European systems generally.

g. There is on the whole one single system of elementary education, uniform for all who attend the public schools, in contrast to the older European pattern in which pupils destined for secondary and higher education have been given separate and different treatment.[27]

h. There is an omnipresent "grading" system, which typically assigns quantitative scores for standardized competitive achievement.

i. Teacher-student relations are highly conventionalized but are on the whole more "informal" and equalitarian than in European systems.

2. *Financial bases* (their sociological significance):

a. The public school system is supported by general taxation and is open—with few exceptions—to all pupils without payment.

b. Because the major incidence of taxation for the support of public schools falls upon real property, support of the schools typically arouses sporadic conflicts between large property-holding groups and other elements of the community.

c. Because all are required to submit to taxes, yet members of some religious groups wish to maintain their own schools, questions of taxation easily become conflicts over general social policy and have, perhaps increasingly, taken on a political character.

[27] However, the European and American systems were rapidly converging toward a common pattern in the period between the World Wars I and II.

3. *Cultural "themes":* [28]

a. Emphasis is put upon the practical usefulness of formal education. Contemplative or speculative thought, art, highly abstract theoretic work are relatively little valued.

b. Emphasis is put upon competitive success.

c. Continuous and widespread stress is put upon conformity to group standards, largely those of broadly middle-class strata.

d. Great attention is paid to the creed of democratic values, and teacher-student relations are supposed to be "democratic."

e. In practice public schools attempt to develop patriotic values and beliefs (the theme that Counts called "national solidarity").

These themes (or patterns of values) are summary descriptions of extremely complex tendencies in the whole culture. No one theme stands alone as clearly dominant; not only does each have its counter-theme, but each is at some limit checked and redefined by a constellation of other values. Furthermore, the identification and description of such generalized patterns of values requires, because of serious gaps in the evidence, a considerable measure of judgment based on a wide range of credible information rather than upon rigorously systematic data. Nevertheless, an examination of these themes, even if brief and oversimplified, may be helpful not only in understanding educational institutions but also in preparing the ground for a more intensive study of value systems at a later point. [29]

PUBLIC CONTROL AND "SECULAR" INSTRUCTION

The elementary and secondary schools are overwhelmingly public rather than private: in 1945–6, private-school enrollment

[28] The term "theme" has been advanced by Morris E. Opler to describe "a postulate or position, declared or implied, and usually controlling behavior or stimulating activity, which is tacitly approved or openly promoted in a society." "Some Recently Developed Concepts Relating to Culture," *Southwestern Journal of Anthropology,* Vol. II, no. 2 (1948), p. 120.

[29] Chap. 11.

was only 11 per cent of elementary and 9 per cent of secondary enrollment. A little over one half of the colleges and university enrollment is in privately controlled organizations, but the long-run change has been toward state-supported centers. The principle of governmental responsibility for education has been firmly embedded in our contemporary culture, although only after a long struggle.

Since our political institutions separate church and state, government-controlled schools cannot in theory give "sectarian" instruction; although in practice, they are far from being completely secular. When the state school systems were established, most states contained several religious groupings, each intensely serious about its differences from the others but rarely dominant enough to get its own views adopted as school policy. The resulting compromise tended to make the public school a religiously neutral meeting-ground for the community. Nevertheless, in the more rural areas, especially where a single Protestant denomination or aggregate of denominations monopolizes the allegiance of the community, religious rites and religious instruction in the schools are still common; and in many states, organized religious bodies attempt to influence the content of instruction and, in some instances, try to remove the barriers to religious teaching in publicly supported schools.[30] Furthermore, although secular control is very clearly supported in the legal systems of most states, the exact line at which instruction or observances become "religious" or "sectarian" is the subject of widely differing legal interpretation. In few parts of the nation can the schools be described as neutral towards religion.

EQUALITY OF OPPORTUNITY

We saw in Chapter 5 that the educational system is one of the most important channels of vertical social mobility. Not only do

[30] See National Education Association of the United States, Research Division: "The State and Sectarian Education," *Research Bulletin*, Vol. XXIV, no. 1 (February, 1946); J. Paul Williams: *The New Education and Religion* (New York: 1945).

the schools transmit the culture; they also winnow and sift the individuals who pass through them. As the day of the self-educated, self-made man passes in the United States, education becomes the ladder or escalator to white-collar, technical, managerial, and professional occupations. If there is to be even nominally free access to the better-paid and prestige-carrying occupations, the necessary education must be open to all who have the capacities and motivation to acquire it. The American system has gone very far in this direction.

Through high school, the public-school system is open to all students of defined ages, although many individuals leave school before reaching the legal age limit, and in a number of states the age of effective compulsory attendance is passed before high school graduation by a considerable proportion of the students. After high school, the economic status of the young person's family becomes more important than his academic abilities in determining whether or not he will secure a college education,[31] owing not only to the heavy expenses but also to the more subtle but perhaps equally tangible influences of class-typed goals and the expectations of teachers and others in the wider community. In so far as the society maintains anything like its present family structure and systems of social stratification, some barriers of the latter type will remain, but economic barriers are being broken down by loan funds, scholarships, assistantships, other forms of employment while in college, public aid to veterans, reduced tuition charges and fees in colleges supported by state and federal appropriations. Certainly the college is highly accessible and relatively inexpensive by comparison with the old continental universities. Though equality of opportunity for all who are equally gifted is not complete, it is greater than in any other nation, unless the mass training in the Soviet Union be considered comparable.

There is, however, one great exception. The dual educational system of most Southern states quite clearly does not provide Negroes with educational opportunities equal to those of whites,

[31] Reference may be made again to Elbridge Sibley: "Some Demographic Clues to Stratification," *American Sociological Review*, Vol. VII, no. 3 (June, 1942). Cf. also Waller: *The Sociology of Teaching*, pp. 20–1.

although the disparities are decreasing in some areas and breaches have been made in the system of educational segregation. In lesser degree opportunity is limited in other regions of the country by more-or-less informal and subtle discrimination against minority groups.

Nevertheless, giving full weight to these discriminations, it remains true for the United States as a whole that education is formally open to nearly everyone.

An educational system may follow the "Jeffersonian" model— it may open the race to everyone but eliminate all but the best from the final heats; or it may adopt the "Jacksonian" system and provide education at all levels for anyone. Recent trends in American education apparently have been mainly "Jacksonian," despite the fact that the schools and colleges are probably more important as selective agencies now than ever before. Universal public education has decreased the role of the family in training the child; changes in occupational and technological requirements have emphasized formal training; changes in the economic structure have increased the importance of education as a means of social mobility. Consequently, we find increased pressure to graduate all students from high school, to admit all high school graduates into college,[32] and to permit college students to continue in college as long as they wish.

The desire for education and the insistent demand for freely accessible schools and colleges owe much to the demand for equality of opportunity and to resistance to the development of a separate educated class. Americans generally use any term comparable to "intelligentsia" chiefly in irony or derogation, partly because of distrust of a class isolated from the larger whole by a different and "superior" mode of training. This attitude has been one of the foundations for the uniform system of public schools and helps to explain why that system has been so slow to give up college-preparatory curricula for the great majority of high school students who do not go on to college. This insistence upon the same kind of education for everyone has continually conflicted with the

[32] Some state universities are forbidden by law to refuse any applicant who can present evidence of graduation from an accepted high school in the state.

Jeffersonian competitive-selection orientation. Both are authentically "American" and often are simultaneously held by the same people. In recent times, the movement for general education [33] has taken much of its strength from the former tradition.

However, in the development of vocational curricula, of junior high schools, of "community colleges" and junior colleges are tendencies toward the elaboration of different kinds of education for different types of students. The crucial questions of social policy are becoming: (1) whether the student will be able to transfer from one type of curriculum to another,[34] (2) whether, and in what wise, *all* pupils are allowed to participate in a common educational culture.[35]

STATE AND LOCAL CONTROL

Until well into the twentieth century the financial support and the organization of the schools were overwhelmingly local, and there still is very little centralized direction typical of secular school systems in continental Europe; for public education fell among the powers reserved to the several states, since it was not specifically delegated to the Federal government by the Constitution, and the states have in general left much control to the local communities. Nevertheless, free communication and a common culture have led the various formally separate systems to move in similar directions, and the contemporary result certainly merits the name of a national system.

Most state school-systems are highly decentralized, with consequences too complex to be traced in detail here. Clearly local autonomy has favored experiment with nearly every conceivable variation of organization, methods, goals, curricula, but it has also led to the uneven development of public-school systems and the very great disparities among states, among localities within states,

[33] See the Report of the Harvard Committee: *General Education in a Free Society* (Cambridge, Mass.: 1945).

[34] Malcolm S. Maclean: *Scholars, Workers, and Gentlemen* (Cambridge, Mass.: 1938), in its entirety.

[35] Report of the Harvard Committee: *General Education in a Free Society.*

and between rural and urban areas, in financial support, length of school year, teacher training, and range and quality of the curriculum. Furthermore, it has favored an extraordinary responsiveness of the school to local demands. The school is supposed to be directly responsible to the people and the servant of their wishes, not the extension of the centralized authority of an inclusive church or state.[36]

Decentralization has several other consequences. For example, each area must compete for skilled teachers and administrators, who tend to flow to the wealthier systems—to the North and East, and, within the states, to the cities and to the well-supported, centralized rural systems. In so far as this process gives "better" education to certain areas, it creates for them a competitive advantage; to him that has, more is given.

The details of the organizational structure of the various state systems vary, but a basic pattern has become typical. A state board or commission, nominally headed by a superintendent (or commissioner), may be vested in office either by direct popular election (most common), or by election by the legislature or the state board of education, or by appointment of the governor. Formerly the state superstructure had very little real authority over the local systems, but today there are tendencies toward state centralization. The state agency influences local systems mainly through its power to allocate funds and set and enforce minimum standards. For example, the role of state as opposed to local or county financing has increased markedly in recent decades; the states' share of the total appropriations from tax receipts for public-school use increased from only 19.5 per cent in 1931-2 to 35.5 per cent in 1945-6.

At the grass-root level of city, county, or independent rural systems, the schools are governed by lay school-boards or equivalent bodies, composed mainly of persons from business and the professions and typically representative of relatively conservative

[36] Unlike European systems that were established by central governments, largely with explicit national ends in view. Paul Monroe has suggested that American schools were initially more nearly an outgrowth of "democracy" than of "nationalism." See *Essays in Comparative Education* (New York: 1927).

attitudes toward education.[37] Usually elected by the voters, their members may or may not represent the choice of a majority of the electorate.[38] In either case, however, the elected members keep the school program close to at least that segment of the community from which they come. In this sense the public schools are in high degree the product of the communities in which they are located.

The supervising agency in most states still has only a tenuous control of the local schools. Any major change has to diffuse through a multitude of discrete systems. Great variations in educational procedures and standards result, as is known by many battered college freshmen from inadequate schools. In our increasingly interdependent society centralization and standardization will doubtless grow.

THE PUBLIC SCHOOL AND THE COMMUNITY

The concrete focus of the system of elementary and secondary education is the school in the local community. The school is a surrogate family, a center of cultural diffusion, a storage place for ideals. In the school, all other institutions converge. Through specific interpersonal relations there comes into the school the influences of family, class, church, business, government; the school is a knot in the web of community life. It is common, therefore, that American communities expect the school to play a part that will not modify the local culture greatly. Yet the teachers' training is presumed to make them different from the community. Hence a problem arises: the teacher must be different, yet not change anything in the culture; she (for over four fifths of public-school teachers are female) must be a stranger, yet an ingroup member. It almost seems that the schools are therefore destined to be staffed by people institutionally committed to perpetual dissatisfaction.

[37] George S. Counts: "The Social Composition of Boards of Education," *School Review and Elementary School Journal: Supplementary Education Monographs No. 53* (1927); Jesse H. Newlon: *Educational Administration as Social Policy* (New York: 1934); Hollingshead: *Elmtown's Youth*, pp. 123–42.

[38] Cf. the reported situation in a small Midwestern town where popular apathy and technical maneuver combined to make the elections of the school board a ritual endorsement of a self-perpetuating group. Hollingshead: *Elmtown's Youth*, pp. 123–4.

Teachers are often held to standards of conformity and pro-
priety not expected of other professions; for there has been a close
historic association between school and church in this country,
and the latent social functions of the school are, in fact, similar
in several respects to those of religious organizations. Willy-nilly
the educator deals with values; he has exceptional opportunity to
examine the unexamined axioms of the culture and interpret its
crucial but vulnerable symbols. Since society is so largely equivalent to consensus, those who deal with values and beliefs as part
of their occupational role—ministers, judges, writers, some artists,
social scientists, teachers—touch upon the sensitive fringes of the
bases of social order. In part for this reason, persons who deal with
the beliefs and values that the community feels basic to its existence are the object of special surveillance and concern.

The roles of teachers are influenced by several rather more
specific factors. Public school teachers are predominantly young,
unmarried women.[39] Over most of the United States, they are
"of native white stock, of rural or small-town origin, and from
lower-middle-class homes." [40] Recruited in large numbers to meet
the demands of a rapidly expanding school population, they have
never had in any large proportion either the bargaining power of
effective unions nor the quasi-monopoly controls over entrance
into the occupation so consistently exercised by certain other
professions. Wage or salary levels have been low in comparison
with other professional or semiprofessional occupations requiring
equivalent amounts of training. In spite of the verbal acclaim
bestowed upon education, the teacher has not received a particularly high prestige rating. North and Hatt found that a national
sample of adults ranked "public-school teacher" thirty-sixth in a
list of ninety occupations.[41]

[39] Percentage of men teachers, in 1945–6 was 17. In 1870–1 it was 41; in
1909–10, 21.

[40] Lloyd A. Cook: *Community Backgrounds of Education* (New York: 1938),
p. 300. Data on which these findings are based have been drawn from the
studies of Evenden, Coffman, Moffett and Kiely (cited by Cook, pp. 300–2).

[41] Wilson and Kolb: *Sociological Analysis*, p. 466. This finding is, of course,
based upon "stereotype" reactions to direct questioning in a brief interview and
is not to be taken as a precise index. It seems safe to interpret it as a roughly
valid indication of the approximate rank of the occupational stereotype.

The teacher touches the community at its most sensitive spots.[42] She transmits beliefs and values to the relatively unformed and plastic child, thus not only engaging in the very heart of the process of cultural continuity but putting herself in a "triangular" relation between parent and child. So long as the family is to any degree a solidary unit, it will not be a matter of indifference to parents how teachers influence their children, and cultural continuity exists only to the extent that fathers and mothers can still communicate with their sons and daughters. Where the community is homogeneous in culture and the teacher is drawn from that same culture and thoroughly imbued with it, no particular acute problem arises. The teacher will be a fairly exact parent-surrogate, faithfully transmitting both the overt and covert content of the culture with a minimum of conflict. As the teacher, by training and background, diverges further from the local norms, friction grows. Cultural heterogeneity of the community also creates problems; the teacher may then face divergent and often contradictory demands from different elements of the population. The most severe tension probably arises, however, when the local community possesses a tightly unified culture and the teacher diverges greatly from it— as when urban, college-trained, professional-minded teachers are employed in stable, rural or small-town school systems. In these situations the teacher is a "stranger," not initially identified with any local ingroup, and by definition initially alienated, in the strict sense, from local groups and their standards.[43]

INTERNAL ADMINISTRATION OF THE SCHOOL

The administration of the public schools has been often and well described, and we will focus only briefly upon the most generic

---

[42] See Cook: *Community Backgrounds of Education*; Howard K. Beale: *Are American Teachers Free?* (New York: 1936); K. H. McGill: "The School Teacher Stereotype," *Journal of Educational Sociology*, Vol. IV (1931), pp. 642–50; S. R. Ellis: "Social Status of the American Teacher," *School and Society*, Vol. XXXI (1930).

[43] Cf. Cook: *Community Backgrounds of Education*, pp. 308–09.

outlines.[44] The principal or superintendent holds office under the scrutiny of a lay group and maintains his position only by balancing local power-groups. Under the shadow of the cost-conscious board of education, he must mediate between school and community. He is head of a formal structure, but confronts the informal operating codes and subgroupings—among teachers—that have become so familiar to us in observing other institutionalized organizations. The formal aspects of the school are generally most emphasized where its real social structure is least secure; there is then reliance on detailed textbooks rather than teachers,[45] much protocol among the staff, much stereotyped conformity, elaboration of distance-stiffening social procedures in all interpersonal relations. There are strong tendencies to move all children along a defined path by uniform stages and with the same educational procedures. As the size of school units and systems increases, the centers of policy making move farther from the child, and considerations of administrative ease and of economy of money and effort then bulk large. On the whole, it appears that at all levels American education has increasingly adopted systems of administration similar to those of business and government.

FEDERAL INVOLVEMENT IN EDUCATION

State and local responsibility for education is still primary, but we must note the new place of Federal agencies.[46] A summary of Federal education activities requires thirty-four finely printed pages.[47] Land grants for education began in 1785, and the Morrill Act of 1862 gave specific support to state agricultural and mechanical colleges. Federal sources have subsidized vocational education,

[44] For detailed background see Waller: *The Sociology of Teaching;* Cook: *Community Backgrounds of Education*, chap. 17.

[45] Noted by Monroe: *Essays in Comparative Education*, p. 244, as a salient trait of our schools.

[46] Remarks to follow are based largely on Hollis P. Allen: *The Federal Government and Education* (New York: 1950). This is the study of education written for the Hoover Commission Task Force on Public Welfare.

[47] Ibid., pp. 23–56.

agricultural experiment stations, agricultural extension, veterans' education, and many other special types. Federal agencies have extensive in-service training programs and have connections with colleges and universities for both pre- and in-service personnel training. Military and civil agencies operate colleges and universities, or graduate schools. Federal educational expenditures probably total several billion dollars.[48] There is no integrated Federal program; diverse arrangements are made with states, with other governments, with colleges and universities. Many agencies participate, with varied aims, organizations, fiscal bases, and legal positions. At least two hundred recognizably separate programs are in operation, slanting into the state and local systems at various angles.

Past Federal programs have encouraged and indirectly guided education, with little direct and detailed control.[49] The strong fear of a centralized education program has been partly responsible for scattered and un-co-ordinated Federal effort. Most national funds go to specialized education, and not to a coherent general program. This arrangement seems to be what American society "desires," at least by default, although the resulting "imbalances" receive unfavorable comment.[50]

THE GRADING SYSTEM

In part a symptom of standardized administration is the practice of assigning quantitative and presumably interchangeable grades. Although there are signs of increasing dissatisfaction with these devices, they remain characteristic of American education generally. The grading system is convenient and economical. By reducing qualitative variation to differences that can be marked on a single quantitative scale, it provides impersonalized data for sorting

[48] Ibid., p. 6; on p. 290, the total is estimated at over 3.4 billion.

[49] The Smith-Hughes Act (1917) first gave a Federal agency the right to accept or reject state programs (vocational education) through control of funds. Adolph E. Meyer: *The Development of Education in the Twentieth Century* (New York: 1939), p. 386.

[50] Allen: *The Federal Government and Education*, pp 289–91.

individuals into the different educational channels. Once the examining and grading systems have solidified, any major change is rendered difficult by the inconvenience and confusion it is presumed to entail. Thus we have an elaborate educational accounting system in which the units are courses and marks instead of dollars and cents. There is rather frequent criticism of it—for instance, that the grade tends to be confused with the learning it purports to mark.

ORGANIZED INTERESTS AND EDUCATION

The educational system is subject, of course, to attempted influence by organized associations of laymen, whose activities testify to a belief in its importance. The number of these organizations is uncalculated but extremely large and includes all major types of organized interests of our society. The larger and more effective include business, labor, patriotic, religious, benevolent, youth, citizen-training, military, peace, fraternal, and political associations. There are prominority and antiminority groupings, associations of reactionary, conservative, liberal and radical inclination. Each is devoted to its own version of the American Way of Life, and few leave the schools to train youth without outside guidance. In general these interests give full loyalty to the present social order. The larger and more powerful of them are, of course, the more influential in the educational system, and they generally operate with slogans and programs couched in terms of patriotism, religion, free enterprise and other reinforcing acknowledgments of faith.[51]

"PRAGMATISM"; PRACTICALITY

Having reviewed some characteristics of the organization of education, we turn now to treat briefly certain cultural themes and values.

[51] Among the many studies that attest this estimate see Bessie L. Pierce: *Citizens' Organizations and the Civic Training of Youth* (New York: 1933). Cf. Denis W. Brogan: *U. S. A.* (London: 1941), pp. 135–41.

The epithets of a people always hint at their basic value patterns. Among the favored terms of derogation applied by Americans to education we find "impracticality, "frills and fads," "long-haired professors," "theorizing," and so on through a long lexicon. The public supporting organized secular education has not greatly tolerated learning for learning's sake, nor "education for gentlemen;" historical erudition, Greek, Latin, and classic-humanistic learning have fared rather poorly in comparison with vocational and scientific training—from physics and chemistry to typing, cooking, or bee keeping. Modern American education is permeated with a very strong utilitarian and pragmatic emphasis. Its purpose is not thought to be the training of dilettantes, nor well-rounded gentlemen of the aristocratic tradition. Education is not diversion or amusement; it is serious business, and the prime questions are: "What use is it?" "What can you *do* with it?"

INDIVIDUAL COMPETITION AND SUCCESS

In the modern school or college teamwork is highly lauded, but probably football rather than classroom examinations is in mind. Stress on individual competitive success still typifies most of our higher educational system and is widespread in secondary schools.[52] The schools must be open to talent; all pupils must be motivated to succeed; the individual child or youth must sink or swim on his (alleged) own merits. Evidence of these attitudes includes: indoctrination in the goals of success and in codes of competition, competitive grading, "selling" education on its presumed money-value. Of course, group endeavor and social rewards for co-operation are not lacking in American education, but they have probably not rivaled the emphasis on competition. World events and the consequent domestic changes may, however, radically affect this particular value complex in our time.

[52] Counts, again, presents a lucid account of this aspect. See *The American Road to Culture*, chap. 5.

CONFORMITY

Much of what the school teaches is incidental to its explicit aims and goals. Perhaps few schools explicitly "indoctrinate for conformity," although "character development" and "education for citizenship" frequently are pseudonyms for instruction that in fact, if not in intent, produces generalized acquiescence to established authority and convention. But any education must educate for conformity to *something*—a point that certain educational theorists in the United States seem never to have admitted.

Much of the conformity learned in American education seems overt and bare, and educators themselves often wonder to what extent it indexes a firm adherence to shared values. Whatever their psychological quality, however, *common* patterns of behavior and beliefs are greatly increased by the training offered by the schools.

DEMOCRATIC CREEDS AND BEHAVIOR

Early American education was strongly class-limited, and the later public schools temporized between radically democratic notions and the rather different views of portions of the influential classes.[53] (The creedal democracy of the textbooks took on new colorations during that long half-century from 1875 to the 1920's when business power and prestige encouraged "business management" in the schools. Strict chain of command and unquestioning obedience of pupils pleased writers who admired business hierarchy.) [54] The ideals taught in the public schools have been largely "democratic," the teacher-pupil relation relatively informal, the peer-groups equalitarian; but the authority structure of the school has been, broadly speaking, less democratic than the creeds.

Some of the meanings of democracy as value will be examined in Chapter 11. In education, evidences of democracy appear in the demand that everyone have the same access to education, in the

[53] Merle Curti: *The Social Ideas of American Educators* (New York: 1935), pp. 194–9.

[54] Ibid., pp. 230 ff.

creed of individual worth, in the pooling of diverse social classes in the school room. A teacher is not supposed to comment on the humble or condemned origins of any student. If racial and other minority-group discrimination, or the limited communions of fraternity and sorority, or the aristocracy of got-here-first—if any of these prevail, as they often do, they do not constitute the standard of educational direction.

EDUCATION IN NATIONAL BELIEFS AND VALUES

Education at all times and places seeks to induct the young into membership in the society—whether community, tribe, nation, or something else. Whatever the effective intrasociety group that controls the educative agency, it will seek to give the students a common language, and a common set of ideas, beliefs, and values, although in modern times some educational programs have also sought to encourage students to learn about, and to appreciate positively, other cultures.

European educational systems generally have been national not only in organization but also in direction and content, and American education, though lacking central organization, also achieved substantial unity around a core of national values. Up to the most advanced university instruction, the history and culture of the United States dominates the curriculum. Theories of education that would encourage a world rather than national view have been much discussed, but have not been the base of equally substantial action. In all periods of national crisis, educators have swung quickly behind national unity.[55] Whether in peace or war, the public schools have constituted an enormous instrument of national solidarity.

UNCERTAINTY OF AIMS

However, there is, finally, uncertainty. In American education— as throughout the main societies of the world—old faiths and old

[55] Curti: *The Social Ideas of American Educators*, pp. 542–4.

cultural patterns have been shaken or dissolved. American education is stamped by variety, experiment, improvisation, eclecticism, and aversion to total planning.

Critics of American education have commented on the outstanding lack of agreement concerning the ends that the schools should serve.[56] Such agreement, however, requires a unified and stable society, and such a society we do not have. Short of forced unanimity, educational aims here are likely to retain much diversity, with only the gradual convergence produced by increased homogeneity in the whole culture.

3. Colleges and Universities

A CENTER of "higher learning" in America may be anything from a trade school to a university group occupied in the most highly developed research and scholarship. Here again we encounter enormous diversity and change. Like the secondary schools, colleges and universities are characterized by mass enrollments, a relatively open entrance basis, a multiplication of specialized courses of instruction, an emphasis upon practicality and conformity, a relative devaluation of intellectual and contemplative interests (in far lesser measure, of course, than in the high schools), a growing prominence of administrative standardization. The American universities are not purely "centers of higher learning"; they are also, in varying degrees and in varying ways, secondary schools, "social clubs," vocational preparatory schools, purveyors of mass athletics, and military-training stations.

The early colleges in America were mainly schools for the training of clergymen; ecclesiastical controls and theological emphasis characterized nearly all centers of higher learning until well into the nineteenth century. Secular instruction grew out of the gradual separation of special subjects from the older disciplines and was encouraged by the substitution of business men and other lay persons for clergymen on the governing boards of the colleges and uni-

[56] See especially Counts: *The American Road to Culture*, chap. 11, and Laski: *The American Democracy*, pp. 331 ff.

versities. Later on, wholly secular colleges and universities began to
emerge in great numbers, especially with the mushroom growth of
state universities after 1870. Now, religiously controlled colleges
with very few exceptions are relatively small and their total influence is quite secondary to the large state and privately endowed
universities. The earlier theological tradition has left its stamp in
many subtle ways upon the universities, in organization, methods
of instruction, curriculum, and definition of the teacher's role; but
the system of higher education like the public school system is
dominately secular in its control and in its curriculum.

Also like the public schools, the colleges and universities tend to
be controlled by a combination of business groups, political officials, and professional administrators. The governing boards of the
larger private universities are heavily weighted with business men,
and the objective dependence of the university upon endowments
undoubtedly has an influence upon the policies it follows.[57] Just as
the privately endowed university seeks support from the wealthy,
the state university has to deal with the politically powerful. In
both instances, the American university seems highly responsive
to social forces that impinge upon it from outside.

Nevertheless, the universities are the great repositories of
science, so crucial to both peaceful and military technology, and
they are one of the main custodians of universalism in ethics, and
the symbol and source of the professionalism that is increasingly influencing the social order. The disappearance of the universities
from America for a few years would certainly lead to vast changes
in all other institutional systems.

Public reactions to higher education follow the general pattern
found in the attitudes toward the public schools, but certain items
have a different intensity and the total configuration is somewhat
differently arranged. Main public attitudes include the following:

1. There is overwhelming generalized approval of college or
   university education, especially for boys. It is felt that the colleges generally do their work well.

   [57] Although not always to the extent suggested by its caustic and perceptive critic, Thorstein Veblen in *The Higher Learning in America* (New York:
1918).

2. College education is valued chiefly as a means to occupational success. Higher education is generally thought of as a weapon or tool in individual competition.

3. Correspondingly, relatively low (but increasing) value is attached to training in the arts, citizenship, "character development," and other indoctrinating, liberal, general, or humanistic studies. A liberal arts, or "cultural," education is more often approved for women than men.

4. Substantial minorities of the population have several important criticisms and fears, viz.:

a) A conception of higher education as impractical, or as detached, isolated, or alienated from the viable values and concerns of the society;

b) a fear of academic freedom; a hesitancy to indorse the full discussion of man and his problems—of religion, or communism, for instance;

c) ambivalence towards, or outright rejection of, the specialist and the scholar (frequently, an attitude of half-reluctant respect mingled with apprehension and hostility—shown, for instance, in the projective stereotype of the "diabolical scientist").

In several respects, then, the society cannot seem to agree with the universities, yet cannot do without them.

UNIVERSITY ADMINISTRATION—AND THE FACULTY

Uniformities in administrative structures and methods cannot be expected to extend to details among all the diverse types of colleges, research institutes, state universities, private universities, technical schools, and denominational colleges found in the United States. Yet a broadly common pattern can be discerned. It consists of the superimposition of a centralized quasi-bureaucratic organization upon the old "college" as a community of scholars and teachers. In the older tradition the collegial organization was a

loose association of individuals; departmental chairmen and deans
tended to serve briefly and to hold a rather tenuous and uneasy authority. In the minds of the professors, the Faculty and the University were synonymous. The internal hierarchy of the faculty
tended to be one of academic prestige rather than administrative
authority. The concept of individual and departmental autonomy
was strong. As universities have become great centers of undergraduate teaching, however, the nonfaculty administrative organization has expanded rapidly, and authority has tended to move toward the president and the officials responsible directly to him.
The administrative bureaucracy mediates between the university
and the board of trustees (and through them to centers of power in
the larger society) and tends to be acutely aware of the demands
and criticisms of influential segments of the outside community.
It is concerned with placating ruffled parents, raising funds, attracting students, increasing the renown of the organization. Because of the nature of its responsibilities, the pressures to which it is
subject, and possibly because of some selectivity in its personnel,
the administrative group differs in its interests, goals, and standards from the scientists, scholars, and teachers who make up the
faculty. Tensions and misunderstandings are therefore common,
and in some instances both severe and chronic.[58]

Unless a university faculty is made up of a mass of purely routine
teachers, it has characteristics that militate against its organization into a strictly hierarchical body along the lines of an army or a
business corporation. Although the American university professor
is typically dependent upon a fixed salary within a definite organization, and hence does not operate with the autonomy of the free
professional, he is still very far from being a strict "employee." [59]
For the professor is a professional specialist doing work of a high
order of complexity, and within his special field it is unlikely that
persons "above" him in an administrative hierarchy will be
competent to judge or supervise his work in any detail. The *techni-*

[58] For the bitter flavor of the attitudes held by an iconoclastic scholar toward the administrative group, see Veblen: *The Higher Learning in America,*
especially pp. 220–4.

[59] Logan Wilson: *The Academic Man* (New York: 1942), pp. 72–93.

cal and the *administrative* hierarchies do not coincide.[60] This functional basis for individual autonomy is reinforced by the long tradition of academic organization, extending back into medieval Europe, which emphasizes the governing of the university by collective action of a body of professional equals.

Modern university organization in the United States thus embodies a continuous struggle between the centralized-bureaucratic system and the diffused-collegial system. Often the model of the business corporation has been so faithfully followed that the faculties have no real voice in the determination of policies or major administrative procedures; but many other universities, among them some of the most eminent, still provide for a considerable measure of faculty participation and control. Even so, however, faculties typically have no institutional channel for direct communication with the governing boards and little direct voice in the selection of the president; [61] and as universities have increased in size and complexity (the two traits are correlated but not identical), a large number of problems of finance, public relations, internal co-ordination, university-wide planning, and the like create strong pressures for delegation of responsibility to a nonfaculty administrative group.[62] Informal and equalitarian relationships then tend to disappear in favor of hierarchy, formality, standardization. External political and financial pressures work even more unreservedly in the same direction. As a result the American university has moved far from the conception of a community of scholars.[63] It is not yet a rigidly hierarchical or centralized struc-

[60] This situation is also common in certain kinds of business and governmental organization. Cf. Robin M. Williams, Jr.: "Some Observations on Sociological Research in Government During World War II," *American Sociological Review*, Vol. XI, no. 5 (October, 1946), pp. 573–7.

[61] Wilson: *The Academic Man*, pp. 76–9.

[62] It was Veblen's wry conclusion that most of these problems had been created by unnecessary expansion of administrative apparatus in the first place. His solution was simple and drastic: abolish the university presidency and the governing board. One does not have to accept his rather mordant evaluations to appreciate his sharp discernment of university structure. See *The Higher Learning in America*, chap. 8.

[63] For a vivid picture of the older ideal-pattern see Carl Becker: *Cornell University: The Founders and Founding* (Ithaca, N. Y.: 1943), pp. 193–204.

ture, and, indeed, it cannot be if it is to *create* as well as *disseminate* knowledge.

American colleges and universities, like the secondary schools, are not tightly integrated into a common organization. The large numbers of individual units are marked by diversity, change, and experimentation. The interuniversity organizations provide some common direction, but in a loose and uneven way, and these organizations are themselves of widely different types. Some are organizations of professors, some of administrators, some of specific professions. Much flexibility and creativeness is thereby engendered, as well as much work at cross-purposes.

Relations among universities are often competitive. The prestige of a particular university is widely felt to be enhanced by every increase in the size of its student body and the magnitude of its financial resources—and by the victories of its athletic teams.[64] This competitiveness, however, may make some contribution to the universities' manifest aim—the transmission and creation of knowledge—even when the actual goals of university administrators are to increase the wealth, size, and public renown of their institutions.[65] Budget increases do not automatically lead to better academic work, but they make it possible for *professional* opinion to exert pressure for better faculty and better facilities for research and teaching; and as students are better trained, there is created a more sophisticated body of alumni who make high academic standards a test of university prestige.

THE UNDERGRADUATE CULTURE

The more or less segregated life of the undergraduate develops, of course, a special culture. Patterns change—the 1950's are not

[64] There is evidence that a large minority rather than a majority of the population assumes that athletic prowess indexes the total educational quality of a college or university. See *Fortune Supplement* (September, 1949).

[65] A general principle is here illustrated: participants in systems of social action can contribute to achievement of the goals of the system without necessarily or even typically consciously working towards those goals. Indeed, the accomplishment of such goals appears to depend upon the mobilization of a variety of particularized goals that are seldom identical with the manifest ends of the total system.

like the flapper and coonskin-coat era—but some uniformities do persist. In the coeducational university, for instance the student body is typically composed of young adults (mainly aged eighteen to twenty-three) of both sexes, unmarried, separated from family and community of origin, culturally heterogeneous, living in a transitory world.

There is a formal regulative university culture of rules and established traditions. There is an informal student culture with controlling norms on studying, dating, stratification, drinking, and so on indefinitely. Students' standards are often contrary to official norms.[66] Their special culture has continuity in spite of rapid turn-over of personnel; each individual in going through college spans seven academic classes—his own, the three preceding, and the three following. The manifest aim of the students is to learn from formal instruction; what actually happens is a notably more complex matter.

Colleges are custodial as well as educational; college administrators spend much time dealing with or preventing breaches of mores. The supervision, isolation, and control of masses of students to whom parents and others are not ready to give adult liberties and responsibilities is a task of real difficulty. It is in the intense group life of the campus that undergraduates take on the codes and acquire the ideas about conduct that are most powerful in regulating their college life. They form themselves into fraternities and sororities, segmented units of the campus society that develop great ingroup solidarity, serve as a mark of prestige, and train their members in orientations appropriate to their later roles in business and professions. Students not belonging to these organizations form their own; a considerable minority, however, become isolated or participate only in fleeting and chaotic social configurations.

[66] A classic on the topic is E. Y. Hartshorne: "Undergraduate Society and College Culture," *American Sociological Review*, Vol. VIII, no. 3 (June, 1943).

4. Cultural Goals and Educational Creeds

WHAT goals can an educational system have? It can be directed toward: (1) the absolute preservation of a static culture; (2) the production of a special ruling class, with virtues appropriate to the kind of authority exercised (Sparta, Rome, China); (3) the shaping of a "liberal" elite (Athens, England); (4) religious indoctrination (in part, medieval Europe, early New England, the nations and tribes of Islam); (5) the production of technologists—specialized workers, "useful" scholars, engineers, scientific technicians; (6) an inclusive humanistic training, intended to develop vocational competence, broad knowledge of culture, and motives for participating fully in the society.

No society ever focuses entirely on any one of these constructs. When we look closely at the special American case, however, it is possible to be more prosaic and more exact.

American education as a total configuration has aimed at the shared but competitive goals of individuals and groups, rather than at unitary collective ends. The crosscurrents of different educational orientations are many, but some main directions are summed up in the perceptive title of Malcom S. MacLean's *Scholars, Workers, and Gentlemen.* The earliest American schools at the elementary level aimed at the three R's and "moral instruction," and at the college level at the production either of clergymen and theologians or of "gentlemen" in the classic tradition.[67] The scholar of the older tradition was the highly selected and highly trained repository of the classic learning. His modern opposite number is the research scientist, for the old-style scholar has receded from the apex of the academic world. The scholar's education has never found a favorable context in American society, except when tied to the training of religious leaders. Neither a frontier society nor a business civilization values contemplation and detached intel-

---

[67] For a wonderful, not to say incredible, picture of the latter, see Daniel Defoe: *The Compleat English Gentleman* (London: 1890).

lectual activity above utilitarian activity. In the dominant cultural stereotype the scholar is an "impractical" misfit.

The educational ideal of the gentleman, so strong in the English background, was cultivated for a time in the upper-class reaches of our society, especially in New England and the ante-bellum South. Many of the early political leaders of the nation were so educated. But as the whole culture became more and more preoccupied with technology and business, the rounded education originally developed for a social elite was increasingly overshadowed by vocational, professional, and scientific training. Furthermore, for a long time in our society there were very few gentlemen owing to the relative lack of an established aristocracy, the fluidity of social stratification, the preoccupation with business success, and the strong pressure of Jacksonian principles rooted in the political strength of an expanded electorate. In recent times some of the old ideas of the gentleman's education have been revived. It even reappears in strangely streamlined fashion in new doctrines of "training for leadership." The newer versions of education for gentlemen are most characteristic of private preparatory schools and of the endowed "prestige" universities.

Formal education in our society often seems to the advocates of social changes of various kinds to be primarily a stabilizing and conservative force, transmitting and reinforcing the *status quo ante*. Clearly pressures are sometimes brought to bear upon educators to discourage criticism, or even analysis, of a very wide range of topics. Nevertheless, in America education as a whole is much more dynamic than in many if not most societies about which we have any accurate knowledge on this point.

We have already seen enough of the cultural diversity and conflicting interests in the total society to show us that organized education is not likely to show unity of objectives. Indeed, there have been times when many educators strove for something they thought to be complete value neutrality. During and immediately after World War II, however, a growing movement away from ethical neutrality and from a kind of eclectic factualism began to reach the proportions of a dominant trend among the theorists of education.[68] The challenge of totalitarian systems provoked resurgence of emphasis upon education aimed at the development of particular values. Many educators have been questioning the exclusive stress upon "activity" and skills found in some schools. Educational philosophers have again begun to use freely words and phrases that had for a time seemed outmoded—"character," "moral values," and "the development of ethical judgment."

[68] Examples are many. See: John L. Childs: *Education and Morals* (New York: 1950); Robert B. Raup, G. E. Axtelle, K. D. Benne, and B. O. Smith: *The Improvement of Practical Intelligence* (New York: 1950).

9. Religion in America

1. Introduction

ALL societies have some system of beliefs and practices that may be termed religious. No society stops with the modes of meeting the recurrent and structurally important problems discussed previously—kinship, social stratification, economic activities, political processes, and education. It is within the residual area that we must seek to identify religious phenomena, and, as in the case of institutions already discussed, we must locate the generic elements of the institution before describing the particular forms it assumes in America.

The first problem is to formulate criteria that will make it possible to identify and describe meaningfully the patterns of religious institutions. Our immediate task is to understand what we mean precisely when we say that individuals accept or reject certain ideas or beliefs about the meaning of life, practice or fail to practice certain religious rituals, follow or do not follow certain rules of conduct sanctioned by religious authorities.

American social scientists have apparently neglected religion for understandable if complex reasons, but the neglect is serious because no society can be understood without also understanding its religion. We are not bound to give full credence to the assertion that we live in a secular world. Probably in no other modern industrial state does organized religion play a greater role. An attempt to analyze American society without attention to religion would result therefore in a queerly inaccurate reading of the system.

It is so difficult to reduce religion to a general formal definition
that the attempt may not be worth the effort, but we can at least
circumscribe its area within the realm of the attitudes men take
toward those entities and events that they interpret as being beyond the range of ordinary human understanding and control.
Religious attitudes are narrower than moral attitudes, which may
refer to the secular or profane world. Men classify entities and
events as sacred and profane, with many complicated intershadings
between the two; the sacred is not necessarily a separate class of
phenomena, but is part of a continuum ranging from the purely
technological, through the conventional, aesthetic, and moral over
to those orientations of high seriousness in which religion is to be
found. Religion deals with "sacred things" that are objects of nonempirical ideas and of intense moral respect. As Durkheim insisted,
the quality of sacredness is superimposed, not intrinsic to the objects, events, and entities to which sacredness is imputed.[1] There is
nothing sacred about a wooden image; but an image of Christ is in
another realm. A crucial instance of the independence of sacredness
from physical objects is the rural schoolhouse taken over for church
services: local dances, once held in the same building are now
taboo.[2] Sacredness, like salvation, is not directly observable.
Nevertheless, both make a *difference* in what people do and say:
a man says he is "saved," and we can observe alterations in his
conduct.

Men have beliefs that are nonempirical and cannot be tested
by scientific methods. *Some* beliefs and ideas are scientifically false,
but everything that is not scientifically valid is not ignorance and
error. If a man claims to have x-ray vision, we can test him and
send him to a psychiatrist, but if he claims to have found salvation,
we cannot in the same sense check his statement. Nor can we test
the claim to the superiority of Buddhism over Christianity or the
reverse as we can a claim regarding the relative candle power of
two types of artillery flares.

[1] See the discussion of Durkheim in Talcott Parsons: *The Structure of
Social Action* (Glencoe, Ill.: 1949), chap. 11.
[2] From an unpublished report by William G. Klein on a Kentucky mountain community.

Many religious beliefs and ideas fall in the vast heterogeneous category of the *non*scientific. They are not *un*scientific, because science cannot help in judging their validity. This obvious point is sometimes overlooked, with serious consequences to science itself. The present analysis attempts to be a scientific, sociological treatment, raising questions to which facts derived from observation can provide answers. It is therefore not connected with the ultimate value or validity of religions. When we analyze religious norms and values in terms of their functions for other aspects of the society, we are not concerned with the truth or validity of those norms and values. If we say that certain religious beliefs divert attention from social problems and thus facilitate acceptance of the social order, we should also remember that we can apply the same analysis to demonstrated scientific theories.

We will give some attention to a functional approach—the causes and effects of a given social phenomenon in relation to the other social phenomena. For example, we will find evidence suggesting that particular religious orientations reduce anxiety in situations of stress. However, we do not wish to imply that religious functions could not be carried out in other ways, or that the functions we will discuss are all there are, or that certain values could not be achieved more readily by institutional changes.

This study regards institutions as complexes of obligatory norms for conduct and has mainly emphasized those norms that define specific status in terms of expected and approved patterns of behavior. Every concrete religious system enjoins some norms of this nature. Thus, the *ethical norms* of Christianity and Judaism constitute a set of widely acknowledged standards supported by moral indignation against violations. Many religious norms, however, specify the relation of the believer to nonhuman or suprahuman entities. In a religion with a definite supernatural referent, the norms derived from relation to the supernatural tend to extend into every area of behavior. Purely religious principles dealing with man's relation to religious entities comprise only a small part of the total religion. Religions also have normative *systems of ideas and beliefs* regarding, for example, the nature of man, the cosmos, supernatural entities. Religion is distinguished from other institutions by its central orientation to problems of meaning and its emphasis upon ultimate ends of conduct. The body of cognitive ideas merges with myth on one side and with theology and philosophy on the other. Organized religions are characterized also by a *system of rituals* such as communion or baptism that are given their meaning at one level by the beliefs and orientations. Another component is the *organized religious community*—which need not be a "church" in our sense; the religious community assumes many diverse forms and has many different types of leaders, such as priests, rabbis, or prophets. Religion is characterized by a large symbolic component arising from the "arbitrary" nature of religious referents, the complex relation of abstract beliefs to action, and from other important factors. Religious symbols have a wide range of referents—to external nature, to aspects of the social structure (father, king, lord, mother, etc.), to subjective conditions, to supernatural entities. There also is a proliferation of cross-symbol referents. Logical inconsistencies between beliefs can coexist without apparent difficulty—for instance, a Protestant may believe that souls go directly to heaven, yet that ghosts are abroad on the earth.

Around the periphery of religion are numerous more or less closely related systems of art, literature, etiquette, and magic. The latter, for example, is ritual directed to empirical ends and is often marginal to religion—for instance, the use of prayer as a means of bringing rain to New York City in 1950.

Actual religious behavior represents a variety of fulfillments, escapes, aspirations, fears, and so on. The specific value and motive components can be discovered only through an intensive analysis that will not be attempted here, since our concern is with general features of the human situation out of which religious institutions arise. In most general terms, religion provides men with a way of facing the problems of ultimate and unavoidable frustration, of "evil," and the generalized problem of meaning in some nonempirical sense, of finding some ultimate why.

First, there is death. Of every ten persons born, ten die. For man, mortality represents a fundamental and unavoidable frustration of deep desires and wishes. In the course of a normal life-span, every person loses by death persons of crucial emotional significance to him. People ask for a meaning that goes beyond medical or physiological explanations.

Unavoidable frustration arises also from imperfect or limited control of physical nature and of society. In our time, men ask whether the universe is basically safe for human manipulation. Every society raises such questions of meaning and develops some answers to them.

Then there is the problem of evil.[3] Men everywhere have standards of conduct, the mark of being human. Yet everywhere standards are violated; everywhere, at some time, evil seems to prosper and flourish. And the old questions stand: Why does evil exist, why is there moral obligation, why must the good be destroyed? Religious institutions develop as *one* answer to the deepest human questionings; any persons who have believed it possible to "abolish religion" have succeeded only in renaming it.

In one sense the whole of Western civilization has the same religious orientation—it is transcendental and monotheistic with a universal ethic having supernatural sanction. One has to go to Asia or to nonliterate societies to find a really radically different orientation. American religion has other features in common with the religions of other Western societies; it is as American as the Hebrew writs or the Roman Church. Our discussion will deal with a few central elements common to Western religions and then touch on points distinctive to America.

The influence of Judaic-Christian doctrines upon our culture has been profound. For example, the religious doctrine of the soul is so crucial and pervasive in Western conceptions of man that its full cultural significance is not always recognized and has never received the analysis it deserves. The idea that man has a soul and that all souls are "equal before God" has been basic to the ethical evaluation of individual personality. The idea of the worth, dignity, and inviolability of the individual unquestionably owes much to

[3] Not all religions contain a radical sense of evil. The "wrong" in some systems is just the inappropriate. Sin is apparently more culturally localized than guilt and shame. Whatever the case, there are norms and values, and there are violations of them.

this belief, as do humanitarian ideals and various philosophies of human equality. The original notion of equality here was not equality of rights but a common humility before the Deity that proved historically to be compatible with rigid social hierarchy; a more radical concept of equality was always latent in the system.

We can be sure that social action is never simply an emanation of religious ideas. Given a religious interest, however, the ideas *define* the situation—for example, whether there is salvation, and if so, salvation for what and from what. Religion is always an interest, reciprocally related to an idea, that partly derives from and reacts back upon the "realistic" social situation. For example, the Christian doctrine of the soul does not by itself lead to ethical equality, but it makes a *difference*, and the difference it makes is, in part, in the direction of high evaluation of the human individual *qua* individual.

The basic religious orientations of all Western societies are similar in their *unitary focus* and their *future-orientation*. There is a single deity, and the universe is seen as moving toward a definite ultimate end. Western religion has been chiefly monotheistic and eschatological and, although opposing tendencies—for example, impersonal pantheism and ideas of indefinitely recurring cycles—have arisen and remained in the Western tradition, they have never captured the culture.

Judaism and its Christian offspring have been dynamic, rather than passively receptive of the social order. Ascetic Protestantism and its "social gospel" offshoots have been particularly prone to social and political concerns, but even Lutheran and Roman Catholic branches have always been somewhat unwilling to make unqualified submission to secular authorities.[4]

What has just been said may seem to constitute a problem in the scientific understanding of religion, since both religion and magic receive greatest emphasis in situations of extreme stress.[5] However, while intense interest in religion seems clearly associated

---

[4] E.g. the well known case of the Catholics in Nazi Germany.

[5] Note the significant, although limited, data from the experiences of American Soldiers in World War II in Samuel A. Stouffer and others: *The American Soldier*, Vol. II (Princeton, N. J.: 1949), pp. 172–91.

with stress, it should be noted that not all such situations are re-solved by religious formulations. Interest in religion is one of several responses to crisis, especially when nothing can be done to alter the threatening or depriving external situation. The fires of religion glow most intensely in the blast of collective terror, deprivation, and social disorganization. New religions, or at least new sects, commonly arise in such periods of social turmoil. The fervor of the martyrs, the passionate devotion of that "inner proletariat" that created a new world within the collapsing frame-work of Rome—these are not the characteristics of the sober, safe, respectable, careful, ritualistic heirs of the tradition.

The answer to the implied question can be stated simply, al-though its full ramifications constitute another matter entirely. The answer is in part semantic: there is religion$_1$, religion$_2$, . . . religion$_n$. Established religions can tolerate considerable indif-ference. An organized religious body, dependent upon and inte-grated within the social structure can deal more easily with passive conformity than with extreme piety. The militant advocate of the strictest interpretation of religious norms tends under such circum-stances to be regarded as a fanatic and as disturbing the true sense of the established religion—no matter how necessary he may be to the continuation of the fundamental tension from which the re-ligion draws its most compelling motives and values. For example, the Roman Catholic Church devised various monastic orders in which the drastically spiritual elements could be insulated from the steady operation of the ordinary religious community.

The *newly created religion* is specifically alienated from, and usually opposed to, the social order within which it emerges. It is, in fact, always a danger to the established interests of the society, unless it can be used, as it often can, to divert disaffection away from direct attack upon the controlling centers of the secular order —observe how opposed to the whole existing society are the Je-hovah's Witnesses and how easily their political potential is taken into camp. The newly created sect most usually seeks to *withdraw* from the society rather than to attack it absolutely, but every deliberate alienation of this sort is a break in the social fabric that secular authorities are understandably reluctant to approve.

The *specific* content of religious systems does, of course, vary enormously. There are tangibly different social implications as among these possible concepts of the world: (1) as an illusory, magic garden in which personalities consist of temporary and accidental aggregates of an eternal, impersonal world-stuff; (2) as planned by a single, rational, omnipotent Deity and populated by minor replicas of Him; (3) as a nurturing realm of numerous vague and benevolent spirits; (4) as a battleground of fierce and evil powers, warring eternally for glory and domination. Religious orientations toward the secular world range from uncompromising rejection to a kind of acceptance in which the sacred-secular distinction is hardly made. Similarly the nature and extent of ritual and concrete symbolism vary widely, as do the ethics sanctioned by the religion proper, the attitude toward traditionalism, and the organization of the religious community. Conceptions of deity extend from highly anthropomorphic ideas, richly decorated by myth, to a transcendental orientation with very little intermediate symbolism.

Such radical variation is so well known that we can here dispense with documentation. It is enough for the moment to accept two basic points; one, *religion is a variable in human societies;* two, *differences in religion make a difference in social conduct.* Variations and changes in religious ideas and values are, by hypothesis, systematically related to variations and changes in other aspects of culture and society. It follows that religion can be treated as a real variable and can be brought within the framework of causal-functional analysis. It is not necessary to seek a universal definition of religion, since interest will be directed toward the influence upon behavior of *specific*, analytically different religions. For purposes of understanding American society we do not have to deal with a religion undifferentiated from the intertwined matrix of communal life. Long ago in all Western societies, religion became a definite cultural precipitate, embodied in separate organizational forms and institutionally segregated. This fact offers a considerable convenience in analysis, if we do not let it blind us to the more diffuse but very tangible operation of religious ideas and values.

In so far as religion represents a complex of ultimate value-orientations, it can never be a neutral factor in social integration. Every functioning society has to an important degree a *common* religion. The possession of a common set of ideas, rituals, and symbols can supply an overarching sense of unity even in a society riddled with realistic conflicts, for example, Europe in the late medieval period. The intense solidarity that is faciliated by religious unity, under certain objective conditions can be reversed and the possibilities of intense conflict heightened when two interacting social systems possess radically different religious orientations and are sharply opposed in such secular interests as wealth and power. Holy wars are not the gentlest of wars.

The realistic social consequences of variations in religion can be briefly illustrated by the well-analyzed case provided by ascetic Protestantism[6] in its relation to economic institutions. The hard core of the ascetic varieties of Protestantism was Calvinism, and from the latter developed a religious system that combined a transcendental interest with an attempt at active mastery of the secular world. The system emphasized an *active*, not a contemplative or ritualistic attitude and contained a prominent element of rationality, both in its deep aversion to traditionalism (especially toward anything suggesting idolatry, magic, ritual or mysticism), and in its attempt to make a rational system of ethics as a whole. The idea of a Divine plan in nature helped prepare the way for the development of physical science.

Broadly speaking, ascetic Protestantism attempted to make every man God's agent (a spiritually superior individual) and a laborer for the literal establishment of the kingdom of God on earth—in short, an ascetic living in the world rather than in the cloister. The organized church tended to be a disciplinary agent rather than a sacramental order; the individual was thought to have direct access to God, and his ethical responsibility was total; he was saved or damned as a whole; there was no avenue for relaxation of discipline. Prior Christian doctrines holding that

---

[6] The standard starting point: Max Weber: *The Protestant Ethic and the Spirit of Capitalism*, trans. by Talcott Parsons (London: 1930); Cf. Parsons: *The Structure of Social Action*, pp. 500-33.

specific good works, confession, etc. could absolve particular sins "atomized" the religious personality in contrast to the neo-Calvinist insistence that one's works were signs of eternal grace or damnation.

Originally the doctrines of predestination in Protestantism postulated an elite who were saved and others who were from the beginning condemned—there was no external signal to show the individual in which category he fell. This hard doctrine apparently did not lead to passivity—if one took it seriously, one also took one's religious responsibilities seriously. But the inner loneliness and insecurity occasioned by taking literally so bleak and inscrutable a theological position made it likely that the individual would look hard for some external sign that he could interpret as a sign of religious grace. As a result various doctrines developed in which good works were held to be a sign of religious salvation.

This doctrine easily led to the justification of worldly prosperity on religious grounds, encouraging systematic and intensive economic activity. It was a duty to be active in the calling God gave one in the secular world. All the virtues of sobriety, rationality, activity, frugality, impersonal devotion to a specific calling, and so on, so prominent in the total system, were congenial to successful business endeavor. Given the *objective possibility* of capitalistic enterprise, such a doctrine could actually motivate men to accumulate wealth on the basis of religious imperatives.

It is difficult to imagine a more appropriate example of how a religious position can support dynamic secular activity than that just sketched. Weber's thesis on the relation of the Protestant ethic to the development of modern capitalism may be critized on other counts, but four points seem incontestable: 1) the religious ideas and values of ascetic Protestantism tally point for point with the ideas and motives "required" for disciplined, rationalized, persistent capitalistic effort; 2) Protestantism preceded the rise of capitalism in many areas; 3) religious attitudes were only *one* of several primary causes for the development of capitalism, but were equally indispensable for the specific structure of the latter; 4) the specifically religious ideas evolved in a complex mutual

interrelation between an environing social structure, a complex
of religious *interests* (for instance, a sense of sin and a need for
salvation), and other specifiable social elements.

The above case, presented in compressed and highly simplified
form, is one important example of how religious ideas can influence
action. It is a hint rather than an analysis and, as Weber himself
stated, tends to emphasize only one side of the causal chain. If
we say the role of Protestantism in capitalism illustrates the influence of religion on society, it may be advisable to consider
briefly the opposite type of problem. For example, it is commonly
observed that "emotional" sects in our society are usually found
in socially marginal or disorganized populations, whereas the most
prosperous, stable, and secure groupings tend to be characterized
by formalistic religious practices and lack of overt fervor. Seriously
deprived, frustrated, or oppressed groups, having no major realistic
control of their situation, tend to produce sects and cults with a
proliferation of emotional religious observances, especially if there
is a free religious structure. The formal patterns of a universal
established church can strongly inhibit and channelize such religious activity, born of desperation and alienation. (In these circumstances, however, functional equivalents are likely to be discovered upon close inspection.) Here, then, is an instance of the
influence of society upon religion. Closer analysis will verify this
supposition, but will also show once again that the relation is
reciprocal. Without some prior cultural definition of the situation
in religious rather than in political or some other terms, the evangelical sect could not appear in the same way.

Enough has perhaps been said to indicate the possibility that
analysis of religious institutions will be an extremely valuable
approach to a diagnosis of the social system as a whole. The sociology of religion is not obsolete in this age of technology and science.
There is no dialectic that makes it impossible to understand
electronics without being an atheist; and the indications are that
religious phenomena have more causal significance in social process
than is commonly believed.

2. Relatively Distinctive Features of American Religious Institutions

RELIGIOUS differences within Western cultures overlay a massive structure of common values and beliefs; Protestants, Catholics, and Jews can communicate within a shared cultural universe. As we have said, it is only in a detailed and relative sense that American religious institutions differ from their European counterparts; however, it is possible to outline certain characteristics that are relatively distinctive of religion in America. Most briefly:

General institutional system

1. The principle of separation of church and state is dominant; there is no established church.

2. Large numbers of diverse religious groupings coexist— ecclesia, denominations, sects, and many forms of cults, embodying various specific beliefs.

3. A relatively great degree of religious freedom exists; religious toleration is emphasized.

4. There are pervasive tendencies to emphasize the perfectibility of man and the possibility of human progress—in relative contrast to much of the nominally accepted theology and to the dominant themes of the European tradition.

5. There has been a comparatively far-reaching secularization of beliefs, especially in Protestant groupings; an alienation from literal dogmas that predominated earlier; acceptance of religion on grounds of expediency; withdrawal from intense involvement in strictly religious problems, and an associated interest in practical, secular activities carried on under church auspices.

6. There is a general doctrinal cleavage between the orthodox (fundamentalist) and "liberal" Christian beliefs, paralleled to some extent by a similar division in Judaism. This cleavage not only separates different denominations but is often an active problem *within* each of them.

7. Nonparticipation in organized religion is due mainly to indifference rather than to militant opposition.

Religious organizations

8. Religious bodies tend strongly toward local or congregational autonomy; even within relatively unified denominations there are powerful centrifugal or secessionistic pressures. Protestant groups accent these features more than do Catholic groupings, but even the latter stand out in contrast to the European tradition.

9. Partly as a corollary of this trait, religious organizations tend to allow a relatively great role to lay leadership and to democratic control. Again, Protestantism gives the freest rein to these tendencies, but American Catholicism inclines more notably in this direction than does Catholicism in Europe or Latin America.

10. Evangelical activity, proselyting, missionary effort, and revivalism are strongly emphasized, partly as a consequence of religious freedom and the multitude of sectarian groupings.

11. Specific organizational forms vary greatly as do the activities of local congregations within a given denomination. The bare, sparse "services" of the small rural church stand in contrast to the multiple activities of the large, wealthy, secularized, urban establishment with its youth groups, dances, movies, athletic organizations, lectures, home services, bazaars, and so forth.

12. Since there is no established church, religious organizations must depend for financial support upon formally voluntary contributions. An extensive *overt* commercialism has thus emerged—for example, businesslike advertising, provision of what were formerly secular services and activities, and formally organized fund-raising activities.

Orientation to the secular world

13. Worldly success is widely and overtly approved—not condemned, ignored, or covertly sanctioned. This pat-

tern is riddled with permanent ambivalence, and it is difficult to speak of it without being misunderstood, but we will indicate more exactly later how ethical approval of secular success operates in its cultural setting.

14. Religious bodies tend generally to remain markedly aloof from those specific political struggles not impinging immediately upon their particular interests. Here again Catholicism on the whole differs from Protestantism, but American religious culture has mainly tended to eschew the age-old intimate relation between religion and state, church and rulers.

15. No really important and militant anticlerical movement exists here as yet, partly because as we shall see, organized religion is relatively uninvolved in active politics, organized religious forces are dispersed, and there is an effective tradition of toleration.

16. As in all major civilizations, religion in America is characterized by a deep and enduring struggle among the main attitudes toward the secular world: active mastery, extreme devaluation and withdrawal, passive adaptation, or approval.

17. With some conspicuous exceptions, organized religion in the contemporary United States takes a conforming or conserving attitude toward the main features of the social order.

18. Modern American religion inclines generally toward a remarkable perfectionism and optimism in spite of nominal allegiance to a dominantly sombre and pessimistic theology committed to doctrines of the evil nature of man, the corruption of the world, the tragedy of sin and ultimate damnation.[7]

19. No unequivocal cultural meaning can be attached to words such as "religious nonconformity" or "dissent" in America, for reasons given above. There simply is no Church, in the integral absolute sense familiar to Europeans

[7] This tendency has been authentically discerned by William L. Sperry: *Religion in America* (New York: 1946), p. 15.

from the Thames to the Danube, and hence there is not a unitary religious attitude toward the world of men and affairs.

Quite clearly, the above points touch only a few elementary characteristics of American religion. The following consideration of the major features just outlined will also note briefly certain other patterns.

LACK OF AN ESTABLISHED CHURCH

The first clause of the Bill of Rights, prohibiting the establishment of a state church, simply legalized the social condition already existing in America. From the colonial beginnings, the immigrating population had a variegated religious composition—a sizeable Catholic minority, a few Jewish people, and an enormously varied aggregate of dissenting Protestant sects. Perhaps much more significant, no single one, nor any practicable combination of these groups, was powerful enough to dominate the national government or to wield completely authoritative power in any one of the newly formed states. It was accordingly impossible to secure political consensus as to which *one* church should enjoy state establishment, and the strongly sectarian groups were certainly unwilling to see any rival receive such privileges.

Out of this heterogeneity, therefore, emerged the separation of church and state, which tended to produce further religious diversity. The taxgatherer was separated from the tithecollector, and the religious aspects of the total social structure barred both unitary church organization and any major state support of a particular religious body. The culture remained dominantly Protestant and overwhelmingly Christian, but politically supported religious monopoly was gone—a decisive departure from the European tradition. The single fact of the absence of an established church was therefore centrally important for the total character of religious institutions in this country.[8] It was both the product and

[8] Cf. Henry K. Rowe: *The History of Religion in the United States* (New York: 1924), pp. 52 ff.; Thomas C. Hall: *The Religious Background of American Culture* (Boston: 1930); William W. Sweet: *The Story of Religions in America* (New York: 1930); Sperry: *Religion in America.*

cause of denominationalism, with its attendant evangelism, and imposed on the churches the necessity of competitive financing through voluntary contributions. It also encouraged lay representation and control in church organization, as opposed to control by an ecclesiastical hierarchy, and facilitated local independence and secession tendencies in the individual denominations. It tended to reduce the symbolic reinforcement of mutually supportive political and religious authority by largely insulating religious from political organization. This eventually strongly encouraged jealous defensiveness among Protestant sects against the state. Although the Catholic churches (and to a lesser degree, the Lutheran denominations) have not held this attitude strongly, they also have been profoundly affected by lack of establishment.

No one church in American communities can speak for the entire people; as private associations all religious bodies are legally equal to each other. Although religious groupings throughout this society are stamped by recognizably "American" qualities, they are diverse, pluralistic, and incessantly changing; the principle of nonestablishment in religion operates somewhat like *laissez faire* in the economy.

As Sperry indicates, the United States as a total culture does not understand the idea of a universal church; [9] it comprehends only the environing facts of numerous types of churches, cults, sects, denominations. Whatever unity there is in American religion is cultural rather than organizational, diffuse convergence rather than an authoritative and centrally controlled system of beliefs and symbols.

RELIGIOUS FREEDOM AND TOLERATION [10]

Each dissenting group that came to colonial America wanted religious freedom for itself, but was by no means prepared to

[9] *Supra*, pp. 9–10.

[10] Convenient background sources: Hall: *The Religious Background of American Culture*, pp. 127–46; Laski: *The American Democracy* (New York: 1948), pp. 264–6; Sperry: *Religion in America*, pp. 6 ff.; M. Searle Bates: *Religious Liberty: An Inquiry* (New York: 1945).

grant religious liberty, or even toleration (a different thing), to all other sectarian movements. Freedom and toleration were only very gradually established in the face of the rival imperialism of sectarian groups, each holding staunchly to its own cherished version of the true faith, and in most cases utterly impatient of dissent. Intolerance pervaded the early period of intense religious interest [11] and internecine religious competition. Orthodoxy was intense, group contrasts great. Aside from the early efforts of Roger Williams and the Calverts to establish toleration, there was no initial commitment to a religious freedom.

Major factors in the rise of religious freedom and toleration include the following: (1) there was no cleavage between two or only a few opposing religious groupings, but rather a fragmented diversity of numerous small sects; ingroup solidarity was diffused, and conflict could not be massive or unitary; (2) no one religious grouping had the opportunity to seize a dominant political position; (3) due to the circumstances of settlement, there was no prior established church common to all the colonies [12] and therefore no vested ecclesiastical interests in property, office, and institutional prestige; (4) outside the solid centers of intense religious orthodoxy there was much public indifference to organized religion in the late eighteenth century; expanding economic and social opportunities tended to distract men from religion; many important political and intellectual leaders were thoroughly secular; (5) the dissenting varieties of Protestantism had the incipient principle of toleration: since the individual believer had direct access to Divine truth through the Bible, valid religious experience could be approached by divergent paths; (7) settlers were needed to provide labor, to aid in military security, and to increase capital gains, and the colonies accepting immigrants of various faiths could foresee tangible economic advantages. The factors named [13] are

[11] Men are always likely to be intolerant of opposition to their central ultimate values. In the formative period of the American political community, differences in formal religious beliefs and practices were widely interpreted as *ultimate* value-differences.

[12] Although most of the colonies did have some form of establishment, and some states persisted in it until the 1830's.

[13] Other factors were the loose contacts with the parent organizations in

enough to indicate how power considerations, economic interest, religious organization, and creeds converged to produce religious freedom—even though in a broad sense, "nobody intended it." [14]

Religious liberty, once established as an official national doctrine, reinforced the continuing forces of a pluralistic society until the broad principle had worked deeply into the whole cultural fabric. Intolerance and conflict still occur in very substantial proportions, but they are opposed to, and not supported by, the dominant institutions.

DIVERSITY OF RELIGIOUS GROUPINGS

The 1936 census of religious bodies listed over 250 denominations and cults, not including many special groups such as Jehovah's Witnesses and the Father Divine movement. This great diversity has been encouraged by a cultural setting that has given free play to the dispersive tendencies of Protestantism and to leaders with new revelations—for example, Joseph Smith, (Mormonism) and Mary Baker Eddy (Christian Science). Often the appearance of a new grouping, whether by schism or by separate genesis, has had only a secondary relation to strictly religious differences, and has reflected instead secular differences such as national, racial, or class distinctions. One finds, for example, Swedish Lutherans and Norwegian Lutherans, southern and northern branches of several denominations—a residue of the Civil War—separate Negro denominations, class-typed fundamentalistic denominations and cults such as the "Holy Roller" groups.

Most of the 256 denominations are quite small. Religious bodies having 50,000 or more members account for 97 per cent of church memberships, whereas the remaining 3 per cent is scattered through more than 200 groupings. The largest single organized church,

---

Britain and on the Continent; the pressure of British proprietors to increase settlements; the fact that at the time of the Revolution there were only a few thousand Catholics and a negligible number of Jews in the whole country.

[14] A specific example of the fact that unforeseen and even unwanted consequences are common in collective social processes.

the Roman Catholic, reported about 20 million members of a total reported church membership of 56 million,[15] while the six largest Protestant groupings accounted for another 25 million; [16] and the number of Jewish persons in communities having synagogues was roughly estimated at 4.6 million.[17] However, the social importance of the smaller bodies is not adequately represented by their numerical standing, since the presence of so much diversity unquestionably strongly influences the total religious scene.

The formation of cults and sects constitutes a fascinating and important sociological problem; however, only a few points can be mentioned here. Cults and sects like other new religious movements are most likely to arise out of rapid social change, the disturbance of value-systems,[18] and conditions of religious liberty produced by religious heterogeneity. The genesis and continued survival of small schismatic sects [19] is facilitated by the separation of church and state and the fact that congregational forms of church are well-adapted to schism. The tightly-knit sect is most likely to survive where there is sharp cultural isolation, frequently the result of a rural mode of life but also of systematic cultural barriers. Cults and sects are developed by strata and groups that are culturally marginal by reason of poverty, low social status, political domination by an alien culture, or, in some instances, ethnic and racial discrimination.[20] Where there is marked social cleavage as between

[15] The total number of church members is underreported by the United States Census. All these data are highly approximate, and it is especially difficult to determine the number of persons actually active in the Jewish religious organizations. (Probably close to half of the persons reporting the Jewish faith are not active in a synagogue or temple.)

[16] According to the *Yearbook of American Churches*, on the basis of data for varying dates between 1936 and 1943, total church membership was approximately 67 million.

[17] Sperry: *Religion in America*, appendix compiled by Ralph Lazzaro, p. 287.

[18] Cf. Laski: *The American Democracy*, p. 292. Many observers have noted this tendency.

[19] Sperry: *Religion in America*, p. 77.

[20] For particular analyses of the various factors suggested above see: Liston Pope: *Millhands and Preachers* (New Haven, Conn.: 1942); Elmer T. Clark: *The Small Sects in America* (Nashville, Tenn.: 1937); Reinhold Niebuhr: *The Social Sources of Denominationalism* (New York: 1929); Sweet: *The Story*

classes, nationalities, races, etc., sects expressing the separate aspirations of contending groups or strata tend to solidify the existing cleavages, although they may not enhance the power of the weaker groups.

For over a century, the main denominational cleavages in the United States have not been based primarily upon doctrinal religious differences, but upon political and economic bases. Lesser denominationalism appears to be the outcome of (1) major changes in religious value-belief systems (for example, a shift from theological to ethical interests; increased secularization); (2) the gradual blurring of ethnic and sectional divisions that have contributed so much to denominationalism; and (3) the convergence of common interests among Protestant bodies—in reaction to growing Catholic strength, to the felt dangers of secularization and of certain political movements, and to certain trends in ecclesiastical thought.[21]

What Sperry has called the "religious fecundity" of our society is one of the dominant aspects of its religious history. The resulting mosaic of diverse religious bodies is an important and integral part of the loose, experimental, pluralistic motif running through the total pattern of American culture. Denominationalism and the multiplication of sects is an intrinsic potentiality of a religious system emphasizing individual spiritual independence.[22] How much sectarianism actually occurs, however, depends upon the broader social context, and there are convincing indications that the environing structure of American society no longer supports the proliferation of denominations. There is now a movement for a consolidation and federation among Protestant denominations.[23] There are inclusive national bodies such as the Federal Council

---

of Religions in America; Sperry: *Religion in America;* John B. Holt: "Holiness Religion: Cultural Shock and Social Reorganization," *American Sociological Review,* Vol. V, no. 5 (October, 1940), pp. 740–7.

[21] Among such trends: a sophisticated effort to state the central ethical contentions of Christianity and Judaism. In addition to the factors listed above, there are a number of less obvious causal conditions that could be given adequate treatment only in a monographic work.

[22] Rowe: *The History of Religion in the United States,* pp. 52 ff.

[23] A convenient summary of this situation is provided by Sperry: *Religion in America,* chap. 2.

of the Churches of Christ in America, a loose but influential organization, and the still more inclusive National Conference of Christians and Jews. Several important denominational mergers have been achieved in recent years, for example the union of northern and southern Methodists, of Congregational and Christian denominations. The drift toward union is shown also by the appearance and vitality of "conference" forms of organization and the growth of "community churches." These tendencies appear to be consistent with the dominant trends toward centralization in other institutions.

ORGANIZATIONAL FORMS

The variety of systems of beliefs and values in American religious culture is paralleled by diversity in organizational norms. Three main ideal-types of church organization can be distinguished: the episcopal, the presbyterian, and the congregational. The essential differences can be suggested in an oversimplified way by saying that the center of gravity of the episcopal type is the ecclesiastical hierarchy; of the presbyterian, the constituent church bodies; of the congregational, the individual believer. The episcopal pattern is characterized by a definite ecclesiastical hierarchy having centralized control of appointments; church authority flows from the highest office down to the members. The prime example is the Roman Catholic Church, but about 78 other religious bodies, claiming about 38 million members in 1943 [24] are similarly organized. In a presbyterian structure, the church hierarchy is modified by lay representation in governing bodies, priestly rank is not strictly graded, and the individual *churches* are the units making up synods and finally the denomination as a whole. Religious bodies of this type number 52, having about 6 million members. The congregational denominations are rather loosely organized and go much further toward local autonomy and lay control; in the most extreme cases they have no formal priesthood or ministry and permit all members to act in this capacity—for

[24] Ibid., p. 284.

example, the Society of Friends. Bodies organized in this way number 99, having about 21 million members.

Falling somewhat outside of these three ideal types are religious bodies such as the Salvation Army with its quasi-military structure, as well as many groups that are simply amorphous and shifting clusters of adherents who follow some charismatic leader like Father Divine. Scattered through certain urban areas (for example, Los Angeles) and culturally marginal rural localities, one finds a variety of small "congregations" led by lay preachers who claim authority by revelation rather than by investment from an established denomination or sect.

INDIFFERENCE AND OPPOSITION TOWARD ORGANIZED RELIGION

In America there is no sharp division between those within the religious fold and those outside it, as there tends to be in Europe.[25] It is extremely difficult, in fact, to determine just how many members the churches have, since no clear boundary marks off members from those who participate without formal membership. Militant secular opposition rarely occurs in America. Anticlericalism is typically mild or individualized, and many persons not adhering to churches take an active positive interest in religious ideas and values: the fringe of sympathetic bystanders is very large.

Disaffection with religion in this country generally takes the form of indifference rather than opposition.[26] Churches die of gradual social anemia rather than of violent illness. Perhaps the nearest approach to an anticlerical movement consists of nativist movements directed against Catholicism, but even here no recent movement has acquired a definite focus or established a real united front. The numerous cross-cleavages in American religion tend to diffuse conflict at the same time that they partially prevent the churches from having a concentrated social or political impact.

[25] Sperry: *Religion in America*, pp. 19–21.
[26] Cf. Laski: *The American Democracy*, p. 295.

SECULARIZATION

Much has been said about the secularizing tendencies in our culture. Although adequate research is badly needed on this matter, the following observations seem well supported in a general way. It is variously noted that much of religion has become a matter of private ethical convictions; that the churches are active in secular affairs; [27] that religious observances have been losing their supernatural or other-worldly character.[28] It is said that religion in America tends to be religion at a very low temperature. Men of religious convictions note with concern the fraying of the Christian (and Judaic) tradition as a new generation emerges, having little training in, or attachment to, religious doctrine, and wonder if the "moral capital" of the past is being dissipated.[29] Many observers comment critically upon the "fragmentation" of religious organization and upon the allegedly corrosive effects of the multiplicity of belief systems.

On the other hand, the already reviewed evidence shows that militant anticlericalism is lacking, that church membership is large, and that, in some areas, fervent sects are continually arising. We know further that religion is given continued public and political approval, that "Godless" is a powerful epithet, that the non-adherents of the churches nevertheless tend to regard religion as vaguely "a good thing," [30] and that recent and continuing world crises appear to have been associated with increased interest in religion.

How, then, can we appraise secularization in American culture? These propositions are ventured: 1) Interest in religion is a drastically changing variable, linked with such factors as social stress, attacks upon religion, degree of mass involvement in other types

[27] "Activism" is often applied to American religion as a term of reproach by European churchmen.

[28] For example, see Denis W. Brogan: *The American Character* (New York: 1944), p. 66.

[29] Cf. Sperry: *Religion in America*, pp. 255–8.

[30] In Sperry's delightful phrase, these are the people who are "imperfectly irreligious." *Religion in America*, p. 256.

of values. 2) No permanent trend in secularization has been conclusively established. 3) Present tendencies include: continued vitality of sect-making elements, slow erosion of religious beliefs in sophisticated strata, pressures towards revived concern among the bulk of the population. Neither intense mass religiosity nor complete secularism appear to be permanent historical possibilities. America is not irreligious, but a whole configuration of forces has pressed in the direction of a slow but pervasive withdrawal of attention and affect from the organized traditional religions. It is frequently suggested that modern nationalistic values and practices are in some way a secular counterpart of traditional religion. Much of the personality identification and involvement once centered in the churches appears now to flow into various types of private, personal relations, or into nationalistic or other secular "religions."

A broad hypothesis, worthy of intensive study, is that the main result of modern secularization of organized religion is the destruction of the belief in a transcendental being, which removes both the supernatural sanctions for our ethical system and a central value focus for the established beliefs. In any event, it might be said that ethics tends to replace a transcendental deity. We have no systematic empirical evidence as to whether, to any degree, an intense belief in a deity to whom the individual is in some sense personally accountable provides both an active tension and a unifying symbolic focus for values and beliefs; nor do we know how such a religious conviction affects tangible social relations.[31] Nevertheless, the widespread loss of a belief in a transcendental God would be the most far-reaching aspect of secularization— deeper in its long-range implications than disaffection from any particular organized religion.

Religious groups tend to vary in their attitude toward the social order in accordance with the forms of their organizations.

[31] For example, there has been some disciplined speculation to the effect that a certain ethical universalism, combined with "impersonalism" in social relations, results from neo-Calvinistic religious beliefs in which duty to God takes the central place and other human beings become means to the glory of the Deity.

(1) The established church—the *ecclesia*—[32] claims authority over all or nearly all members of a given society, often extending across national political boundaries; it is typically accommodated to the existing social order, sometimes holding political authority itself or, at least, actively supporting secular authority. (2) The *sect* is a religious protest group that tries to insulate itself from the larger society or, failing that, attacks the secular order. (3) The *denomination* is a tamed sect, that has made its peace with other religious groupings and either supports or tolerates the mundane society. (4) *Cults* are loose, personalized groupings, tending mainly, although not universally, to withdraw from and deprecate secular activities.

The ecclesia is characteristic of societies having a relatively stable and unified ruling group, and has its greatest strength in societies of an isolated-sacred type. Sects and denominations emerge as societies develop a complex associational structure. Cults occur most frequently in highly differentiated and fragmented societies, especially in urban civilizations marked by a high degree of anomie (normlessness). America has been prolific of cults and sects, some of which have been militantly reformist, others quietistic; some have voiced an eschatological pessimism about man and society.

OPTIMISTIC BELIEFS

The reciprocal relation between specifically religious beliefs and other elements of the culture is exemplified by the changing nature of basic concepts of man and society held in American religious groups. A peculiar sort of secularization has occurred: despite a theology, inherited from Europe, that stressed original sin, the innate depravity of man, and the evils of the world and the flesh, our religious culture rapidly became permeated with an optimistic view of the perfectibility of man and his institutions. For three

[32] Cf. Leopold von Weise and Howard Becker: *Systematic Sociology* (New York: 1932), pp. 621–28, reprinted in Wilson and Kolb: *Sociological Analysis*, pp. 655–8.

centuries there has been a seemingly increasing tendency to give lip service to pessimistic religious doctrines while avoiding their (apparent) behavioral implications. The resolute self-confidence and optimism so often noted in American history derived partly from religious ideas and values, but its main roots were apparently in other portions of the culture and in the objective situation of a wealthy, strong, and expanding society.

EVANGELICAL ACTIVITY AND "COMMERCIALISM"

Critical observers of the American scene have sometimes commented unfavorably upon tendencies toward highly competitive proselyting and toward aggressive fund-raising activities. These tendencies are of importance, but we are not required here to evaluate them, only to understand them. Both derive, at bottom, from the lack of an established church and from the multitude of denominations. The dependence of the churches upon voluntary contributions for financial support supplies a strong pressure toward commercialism, reinforced by many other influences arising in a business culture. And in so far as each religion believes it has the one true faith, there is always a latent missionary drive in its belief system, and its officials and members are committed to some measure of "competitive" activity.

POLITICAL NEUTRALITY

Separation of church and state has had subtle consequences, notably some complex effects upon the political attitudes of the churches. The Roman Catholic Church has not disclaimed its original desire for political establishment, but has temporarily accommodated itself to being the largest and most powerful single denomination. Protestant groups vary greatly in their attitudes toward the state and toward political issues, but in general they give strong support to the separation of church and state, and vigorously resist even the slightest action that can be interpreted as "state interference." Although the individual churches, denominations, or even interdenominational organizations often take a public stand on social issues, no church body is able to exert direct influence upon government through publicly recognized channels, and no one corporate voice can speak for organized religion as a whole—such a development would require a radical transformation in the whole institutional framework of religion in America. Organized religion does have, through informal channels, however, a real power in a number of state legislatures, and on occasion, in Congress.

Judaic-Christian ethical standards could hardly be promulgated by the churches without reference to political issues and events, and the churches, as a whole, have always insisted upon the right, at least, to make moral judgments about the social order. In making these judgments, the churches, because of the principle of separatism, become outside critics or proponents—"friends of the court"—rather than integral components of the system of secular authority. Nearly every variant group and stratum in the society has had the support of some church or sect that interpreted Christian doctrine in the light of that group's needs and interests. The political position of the churches, especially perhaps of the Protestant denominations, has varied accordingly and has changed drastically over the course of time. The separatist tradition has encouraged political neutrality—for example, "preachers should not meddle in politics," and the divided political allegiances of the members of most large denominations has worked against any partisan (party) indorsement by the organized religious bodies. In general, the churches tend to refrain from corporate political action on partisan issues, but by serving as public forums and informal pressure groups they have a political weight important enough to be a tangible factor in the calculations of practicing politicians.

The political thought of the churches has been strongly shaped by the class affiliations of the membership, by economic and political pressures, by the changing dominant interests and values of the wider secular culture.[33] There was a long period, lasting into

[33] For an excellent detailed account of this, see Henry F. May: *Protestant Churches and Industrial America* (New York: 1949).

the fourth quarter of the nineteenth century when the main, although not the only, pattern of organized religion was to support doctrines of *laissez faire* and sanctity of property. Wealth was regarded as a reward of moral virtue; social rewards and deprivations were believed part of a divine plan. This relatively unified outlook began to crumble in the 1880's and 1890's. The evangelical equalitarian element, always germinal in Western religions, then came increasingly to the fore, notably in the "Social Gospel." Although not a direct political movement, the "liberal" formulations of the Social Gospel prepared the way for new concepts of the social responsibilities of the state in the twentieth century.

Thus, religious beliefs and values, although molded by nonreligious forces, have their own inner dynamics. It seems to be impossible to predict the political thought of the churches from a knowledge of the most immediate economic and political interests of their constituents.

A FURTHER NOTE ON CATHOLIC AND PROTESTANT ORIENTATIONS

We have emphasized the fact that, from a wide comparative perspective, the main branches of the Judaic-Christian tradition have many important beliefs and values in common. There are, however, perceptible disagreements in American culture, constituting the immediate source or symbol of appreciable tension between different religious groups. Tension over real differences in values and beliefs is usually compounded with other sources of cleavage: class and ethnic affiliations, economic competition, "projective" antipathies, and others.[34] We are not concerned here with intergroup relations, but with certain salient differences in *institutional* beliefs and practices.

One can speak here of *tendencies* only; not all members or officials

[34] For certain analytic hypotheses on these problems see Williams: *The Reduction of Intergroup Tensions*, pp. 51 ff. Cf. also, Talcott Parsons: "Racial and Religious Differences as Factors in Group Tensions," in Lyman Bryson, Louis Finkelstein, and Robert M. MacIver (eds.): *Approaches to National Unity* (New York: 1945), pp. 182–99.

even of the relatively unified Roman Catholic Church are in complete unanimity on all the matters mentioned below.[35] Still, certain differences in beliefs, implied values, ritual practices, and form of organization are clearly present as social tendencies, rather than either-or contrasts. We have already noted the contrast between the hierarchical Catholic organization and the presbyterian and congregational forms within which most Protestants participate. The norms of organization are closely tied to differences in the basic cultural definition of the church: in the one case, it is regarded as Divinely instituted; in the other, as a human device for collaboration in religious affairs. On the one hand, Church officials are conceived to be vice-regents of the Deity; on the other, respect for ministers tends to be more strongly tempered with a view of them as fallible humans, imperfectly seeking religious truth. Although some important Protestant denominations are liturgical, most of them tend to minimize rituals and church symbolisms.

Catholic and Protestant groups also differ broadly in the emphasis laid on the individual person as over against the corporate body. Under medieval Catholicism the individualistic implications of the Christian emphasis on the salvation of the individual were largely neutralized by the role of the Church as the supreme earthly repository of divine authority and salvation. The individual had access to the Deity only through the church hierarchy, a disciplined religious group controlling dogma, creed, and ritual, and suppressing dissenters or incorporating them into various special religious orders.

In Protestantism, on the other hand, the Scriptures became the touchstone of orthodoxy, and, since there was no universal church to decide between differing interpretations, the individual had to judge for himself. "In the last analysis . . . the emphasis was not on the preservation of a tradition of values *common* to the members

[35] The common Protestant stereotype of the Catholic organization as a completely rigid hierarchy, with detailed control over the beliefs and actions of every parishioner, is highly exaggerated. The Church claims ultimate authority and stands absolutely on certain dogmas, but is highly elastic in many matters falling outside of the inner core of doctrine and ritual.

of the community, even to all Christians, but on the safeguarding of the freedom of conscience of the individual in his *differences* from others. . . ." [36] The doctrine of free access of the individual to religious salvation thus contained an inherent centrifugal element. One consequence was the multiplication of denominations and sects as diverse doctrinal interpretations emerged.

On the side of the cultural definition of personality, many early Protestant groups stressed a doctrine of total, integral religious responsibility of the individual. Sin was no longer regarded as an isolated act that could be wiped out by specific amends, confession, or ritual absolution. The doctrine of specific forgiveness for specific faults allows for a certain flexibility of the religious personality, and, especially when the universal church is regarded as the mediator between God and man, it *permits*, at least, a distinctive kind of "conscience"; one's conscience can be clear if one accepts the authority of the church and deals properly with each specific transgression as it occurs. On the other hand, if one takes seriously the most rigorous Protestant conceptions, then the soul is saved or damned as a whole, and specific repentances alone are no guarantee of salvation. If taken seriously, this concept of religious personality requires a rigorous discipline of all activities and the total life-span of the person. Rousseau had this necessity in mind when he said that Protestantism, in attempting to escape from the monastery, had instead made every man a monk; that is, that the "heroic" discipline formerly reserved for the religious elect was now doctrinally obligatory for everyone.

The Reformation was individualistic in still another sense. When religious salvation was *a strongly desired goal*, the emphasis on the direct relation between the individual and God tended to de-emphasize the personal relations of individuals to others, either singly or corporatively. In the ideal-typical case, the relation to the Deity was thus literally all-important; other individuals were important only in so far as they affected in turn one's own relation to the Deity. Thus, to the degree that the doctrine was accepted in actual fact, social relations became indirect and instrumental

[36] Parsons: *Structure of Social Action*, p. 54.

in a unique way. They were relations *through* the common object of religious attention and devotion; they were instrumental in the measure that other persons were means or hindrances to one's own salvation.[37]

Undoubtedly the rigor of this ideal-typical position has been greatly relaxed in modern times; and it is entirely possible that the mass of Protestants never fully accepted the sterner theological formulations of it. However, the Protestant does differ from the Catholic position in the respects just suggested. Broad analyses of historical and statistical data—such as the works of Weber and Troeltsch—have supplied some highly illuminating clues as to the significance of these differences in religious value-orientations for social conduct. More precise analysis now awaits upon further research and theoretical development.[38]

FUNDAMENTALIST-MODERNIST CLEAVAGES

For purposes of comparison in the preceding sections we formulated a historic ideal-type of one major Protestant orientation. It has been abundantly shown, however, that "Protestant" is a label covering a heterogeneous assemblage of organizations and of systems of belief and practice that would require volumes for any detailed analysis. Here we shall be content with the convenient example provided by Fundamentalism versus Modernism (or, liberalism), a division that cuts its way across the total pattern of religion in America. In broadest outline, the Fundamentalist position stresses belief sanctioned by authority, interprets sacred writings literally, stresses otherworldly concerns rather than social issues.[39] Fundamentalism has the greatest strength in rural areas,

[37] Ibid., pp. 54–5.

[38] The above sketch of certain aspects of Protestant and Catholic orientation is, of course, highly selective and is formulated in ideal-typical terms, having no pretension to completeness. It simply suggests once more how certain connections between religious phenomena and the social structure can be posed for empirical research.

[39] Cf. Laski: *The American Democracy*, pp. 286–9; Sperry: *Religion in America*, pp. 104, 110, 136–9.

especially in the South. It represents past Protestant orthodoxy, often most strongly supported by groups that have been increasingly assaulted by rapid social change and by insecurity-engendering cultural influences.[40]

The modernist or "liberal" movements deviate from the position just suggested in their attempts to reconcile their beliefs with the findings of science and of history, and to apply Christian doctrines to modern social problems. The broad inclination of modernism toward ethics rather than salvation and toward rationalism rather than traditional beliefs has apparently appealed to the relatively secularized elements of Protestantism, especially to socially and economically secure urban groups.

These doctrinal cleavages represent different transformations of religious ideas and beliefs as these have interacted with secular thought and have been remolded by theological analysis of prior positions; at the same time, the objective social situations of believers have encouraged modifications in the typical religious positions of different classes, ethnic groups, and the like. At the present time, Protestant Fundamentalism is largely carried by encysted sects, or portions of denominations, that hold the allegiance of groups that are defensive against secularism, urbanization, and industrialism.

In these compressed pages we have neglected (or left with only passing mention) a great many important aspects of our religious institutions—notably, the special features of Judaism, the processes of development from sect to denomination, the major doctrinal positions within Protestantism (for example, the marginal case of Lutheranism), and the more exact evidence on the social correlates of different religious systems. We have only attempted an elementary sketch of the most central and distinctive norms and values in the major religious traditions of our society and will now turn to a broader consideration of the interrelations of religion with certain other institutions.

---

[40] Catholic fundamentalism is of a different order, especially with regard to the rule of the Church as the guardian of orthodoxy.

3. Relations of Religion to Other Institutions

BECAUSE of its crucial position in the total value-integration of a society, religion has widely ramified relations with other institutions. For example, a religious system may strongly support the family—sanction marriages, supervise child care, ritualize bereavements; or, require celibacy or the severance of family ties; either way, however, the two institutions are not mutually indifferent. It has been indicated that the attitudes of religious bodies toward the state range from the ready acceptance of certain ecclesialike organizations to the radical antipathy of a sect such as the Jehovah's Witnesses.[41] Generalizations here are subject to considerable hazard; it is only by specifying *different* religious orientations that precision can be introduced into the analysis. Most of the assertions to be made in this section refer, explicitly or implicitly, to particular types of religious orientations or organizations. The following propositions are representative of descriptive generalizations that are current in discussions of the social role of religion in America.

Social Stratification:

Local religious groupings in the United States tend to be sharply segregated along lines of social stratification; this applies also, to a less extreme degree, to larger groupings (sects and even whole denominations).

Political Activity:

At least nominal public acceptance of religion tends to be a prerequisite to political success, and to a lesser degree to business success in the smaller communities.

Multiplicity of religious affiliations of the political electorate, under the two-party system, encourages sectarian neu-

[41] Herbert H. Stroup: *The Jehovah's Witnesses* (New York: 1945), especially pp. 147–68.

trality of the parties. This is expressed in selection of candidates of various numerically important faiths, in avoidance of controversial statements on religious issues, and in many other ways.

Education:

Organized religious groups are generally concerned over the presumed secularizing influences of public education and strive with widely varying intensity and success to promote or supply religious instruction.

Family:

Even though civil marriages are everywhere legal, the great majority of American marriages are performed by religious officials; the church is still felt necessary to give ceremonial sanction to the family.

Economic Activity:

In most of the important religious groupings, the churches have advanced doctrines approving of business activity and established economic structure. These ideas, however, have involved considerable ethical tension, and there is a persistent tendency to demand that economic actions conform to religiously sanctioned norms.

General:

The intense pragmatism of American culture is exemplified in religious themes stressing the value of religion as a means to morality, peace and order, and worldly success. There is a marked tendency to regard religion as good because it is useful in furthering other major values—in other words, to reverse the ends-means relation implied in the conception of religion as an ultimate value in experience.

These are rough preliminary generalizations. Before continuing we must distinguish between religion *as a system of ideas and value orientations* and organized religion, i.e., the *formal structure of the community* of participants. We should not confuse intrinsic religion as a cultural fact with the churches that partly express it socially. For example, there are religious ideas and values in our culture that are socially far more dynamic than those typically advanced by the well-established churches.[42] Furthermore, the relation of religious ideas and value orientations to specific social action is always complex, and at least in our culture is typically loose and unstable for several reasons: 1) strict interpretation of Judaic-Christian ideas imposes very stringent requirements upon conduct that conflict with many other values and interests; 2) because of the nonempirical reference of religious systems, their social implications are peculiarly subject to arbitrary variation, and widely different definitions of a situation can be and are drawn from the same basic beliefs; 3) religious idea-value systems often influence conduct, not as exact definitions of expected behavior, but as diffuse symbolic configurations having a tendency to spread and thereby lend sanctity or legitimacy to a range of diverse social practices and structures.[43] Thus, we can take it as a postulate that no major institution is completely unaffected by religion. For instance, religious ideas and motivations played an important part in the rise of modern science, currently regarded by some people as the archenemy of religion.

As we noted earlier, every concrete religious grouping makes a tacit or avowed choice among these radically different possible orientations to the secular world: 1) militant attack upon it, 2) withdrawal or escape from it, 3) tolerance towards it, 4) active support of it. Within each of these four modes of approach there exist numerous qualitative variations; for example, withdrawal may mean escape from evil, or it may mean a positive and confident movement into experiences felt as superior to the ephemeral events of secular life. In this respect, as in many others, there are *varieties* of religious experience. There is always a certain tension between religious values—those concerned with "sacred things"— and considerations involving secular power of the religious organiza-

[42] Proof of this rests not only on logical or semantic considerations but also on the clear tendency for new sects to periodically draw the more radical implications.

[43] This fact is undoubtedly one of the reasons why religion is so important to social integration.

tion. A religious organization never represents only a purely religious set of values and ideas—the latter appear to be phenomena of personal experience that are not fully compatible with the inevitable compromises of a continuing organization. We can make the imprecise but valuable generalization that, where religious liberty prevails, the orientation of an organized religious body can be predicted by looking at the realistic social positions of its constituency—for example, secure groups that are well satisfied with the distribution of social rewards generally support religious organizations that approve of and reinforce the secular order; deprived and disaffected populations without effective political power tend toward sectarian withdrawal from an evil world; similar populations that see a realistic hope of social power tend to develop sects or movements aimed at attack upon or reform of the society.[44] We can leave aside here the situation under an inclusive established church.

One of the most important findings that can be drawn from the analysis thus far is this: *American religious organizations are extraordinarily segregated from other institutionalized structures.* It is perfectly true that *norms* having religious referents and sanctions run through a wide variety of activities outside of organized religious bodies. But the very fact that religion in our culture is so frequently equated with the churches is a telling indication of the compartmentalization of religious norms. Religious ideas, symbols, beliefs, values have become firmly solidified in definite social organizations having their own specialized personnel, symbols of separate identity, special channels of communications, and segregated group affiliations. In addition, the separation of church and state has tended to isolate the churches from political power and from educational influence. These factors and the fragmentation of religious organization have made it possible for secular powers to force the churches quite generally into neutrality, isolation, or "bystander" support with reference to other institutions. The

---

[44] It must be stressed that religious movements constitute only one of several possible kinds of collective action in response to the indicated conditions.

churches have often been told to "stay out of politics" (or, business affairs, etc.) and have sometimes heeded the admonition. The public generally assigns organized religion a special, circumscribed place as the repository of values that are inherently of the highest good, but that should be safely insulated and restricted to ceremonial occasions ("Sunday religion") so that they cannot interfere too much with the ordinary business of the society. This tendency may be given radically different evaluations: it may be called "religiosity" rather than religion, with Laski,[45] or "traditional" rather than "intrinsic" religion, with Yinger,[46] or it may be highly approved. We are not concerned here with these questions of value, but wish only to point out the relatively circumscribed and separate position of organized religion. Although there now seems to be some movement toward a closer involvement of religious organizations in the wider life of the society, it is still generally true, as Christian Gauss has said, that religion does not "permeate and inform" the other phases of our culture to the extent characteristic of earlier centuries.[47]

Although only a judgment, the opinion may be ventured that in the late nineteenth century the ascetic Protestantism that gave moral and symbolic reinforcement to economic pursuits and nationalistic aspirations lost a large part of its dynamic quality. With the rise of social protest movements in the early twentieth century, a number of religious groups reasserted their role as ethical critics of the society; but because most of the activities associated with the Social Gospel were utopian and unorganized, their social influence was diffused and indirect,[48] although in the long run substantial. Although there is a prophetic and radically ethical strain in the basic religious tradition, the corporate actions of the major churches appear to have been mainly shaped by external

[45] *The American Democracy*, pp. 320–1.

[46] *Religion in the Struggle for Power*, pp. 6–11.

[47] Cf. the pertinent remarks of Constantine Panunzio: *Major Social Institutions* (New York: 1939), chap. 19 and pp. 498–9.

[48] Yinger: *Religion in the Struggle for Power*, pp. 135–8. Chapter 5 of this work is a valuable treatment of the relation of the churches to economic issues.

forces rather than by the immanent development of religious value-orientations. This fact has led to the continual emergence of lower-class sects, alienated from the established denominations; it has meant that the churches have usually followed rather than led social change. As Yinger has well emphasized, religion is one among many of the interests of men and organized religion is one among many of the groupings sharing social power. Organized religions, once firmly established, typically resist change in their own doctrines and polity, as well as in secular affairs having religious relevance. This tendency, of course, is not confined to America or the West. Indeed, Judaic-Christian systems have inclined far more to innovation than other major world religions.

In the above paragraph we explicitly restricted the generalizations to the major churches that include the majority of church members and in any short-term perspective represent the preponderant social power of organized religion. However, a minority in most denominations does not sanction the *status quo*, and in the sects there is still more frequent expression of radically ethical positions. If the sects are often otherworldly and to that extent direct men's interests away from social issues and problems, it remains true that sects and sectarians represent the modern analogues to the ancient movements of ethical prophecy; they perpetuate the "explosive element" [49] in the tradition. Some organized churches so stress faith, ritual, and worldly unconcern or obedience to constituted secular authority that their main social effect probably is to help stabilize existing secular arrangements. It would be a gratuitous error, however, to accept this relatively simple relationship as definitive of the social place of institutional religion. There are limits defined by religious idea-value systems beyond which even the most conservative churches will not readily acquiesce to secular powers, and the small ethical sects (and analogous subgroupings within larger bodies) serve both as stimulus to less innovative churches and as curators of uncompromising religious ethics.

[49] Ibid., p. 226.

4. Religion and the Structure of American Society

WITH its mosaic of organizations and beliefs, American religion is at one with the inveterate cultural pluralism that, at least up to now, has been one of the most outstanding traits of this society. The weakened place of the church as the intermediary to the Deity has contributed to sectarian divisions, and the very form of organization of many Protestant churches has reinforced pluralistic tendencies. Nearly one third of all church members belong to congregational bodies whose loose organization and strong local autonomy seem to represent sheer anarchy to Europeans steeped in the tradition of the universal church. The organizational structure of the churches, therefore, resembles the diffuse and decentralized institutions of kinship, stratification, and education more than it does the economic and political systems. American religion for all its diversity demonstrates, with regard to cultural themes, the tendencies toward individualism, pragmatic emphasis, and ethical and humanitarian concerns [50] encountered in several other phases of the culture.

A society's common-value system—its "moral solidarity"—is always correlated with and to a degree dependent upon a shared religious orientation; more precisely, among the common values of a society are those of "intrinsic" religion, characterized by nonempirical referents and moral respect. This particular class of values is reciprocally related to other values current in the society. Now, social tension and struggle arise from two broad types of dividing factors. First, there are the differences in "interests" centered around scarce and divisible values: mainly power, prestige, and wealth—corresponding to the institutions of government and politics, social stratification, and economics. So far as a society focuses attention and effort upon the divisive "intermediate

---

[50] As contrasted with transcendental problems, on the one hand, or ritualistic concentration on the other.

values," other things remaining the same, it will decrease its internal cohesion or solidarity.[51] But there is another type of social cleavage based upon incompatibility of ultimate values—say, between a devout Quaker and a storm trooper—in which differences go far beyond any question of immediate instrumental values. Where the members of a social aggregate hold ultimate convictions in common, there is a cohesion capable of overriding otherwise disruptive conflicts over scarce means-values. On the other hand, it equally follows that when such a solidary grouping is faced with another grouping similarly committed to a different common-value system there is increased likelihood of severe conflict. Our society places great emphasis upon the competitive institutions; the past devaluation of shared collective aims and the stress upon interests that set group against group and individual against individual has produced obvious strains on consensus. In addition, there are many ethnic and other cultural differences. The mere fact of such internal diversity does not necessarily diminish social stability—many societies have been both stable and integrated over long periods while maintaining great intrasocietal differentiation. What appears to be especially crucial in the American situation is the fact that so few cultural differences are stable, rationalized, and taken for granted.

At the most abstract level of values and symbols, there is enough commonality in America for religion to be on the whole a unifying factor, especially when there is awareness of radically different orientations elsewhere. Nevertheless, the great variation in specific religious beliefs and practices has very important divisive implications. Even the most general and universally acknowledged religious principles have variant results in practice. For instance, all our major religious bodies officially sanction a universalistic ethic and doctrines of religious equality; in so far as these principles are believed in, it would seem *a priori* that they should mitigate tensions concerning social stratification, both by softening the asperities of invidious comparison and by providing religious

[51] Our statement here has to be carefully guarded because the concrete results are highly variable in different cultural contexts.

"compensations" for lower strata. It is equally plausible *a priori* to suppose that such doctrines could lead to increased resentment by making social inequalities harder to endure. The potential consequences are not always the actual consequences. The present survey indicates that the strictly religious interests of the churches, although they have an independent role in society, are in America subordinated to other institutionalized interests.[52] The integrative role of religion is in this wise minimized.

The questions raised by religious diversity concern the future development of American social structure as a total system. The consequences of religious liberty are here fully at hand, regardless of one's evaluation of them. It can be said on strictly empirical grounds that religious toleration, in a broad sense, is essential for the continuation of the most distinctive aspects of the institutional structure. The suppression of any important existing religious group, for example, would unquestionably deal a serious symbolic blow to the whole system, with extremely deep, complex, and far-reaching repercussions. The religious conflicts moving partly beneath the surface are to an important extent checked and blunted by diversity and freedom. It is commonplace to say that no one is tolerant of ultimate values differing radically from his own, and there is truth in this statement even though its essential terms are all ambiguous. Religious toleration in this society can be interpreted, at least in part, as a sign that the crucial values of the system are no longer couched in a religious framework. However, more basically, "free" institutions and groups can arise only under conditions of considerable social heterogeneity in interests and values. Critical social thought, invention and innovative behavior, "secularization," a limited government founded on impersonal universal law—all these are fundamentally dependent upon the existence of varied groups within the area of interaction of a given society. Once secularization has gained momentum—after arising in the interstices of a complex structure—it in turn con-

[52] "Subordinated" here obviously represents a very complicated estimate. The above statement may be taken as the author's considered judgment rather than as an attempt at scientific generalization.

stitutes a dynamic tendency toward further secularization, up to a point determined by complex functional limitations, whose specification cannot be taken up here.

A homogeneous society will be a "sacred" society, marked by an absolute value-system and intolerance of deviant behavior. In a situation marked by many contending groups (classes, religious groups, ethnic groups, and so on), there are strong pressures toward secularization. These can be clearly seen in the interplay of multiple attacks and counterattacks and in the emergence of defenses, rationalizations, accommodations, philosophies of compromise and toleration that are found in such situations.[53] The breach of monopolistic control of thought and valuation that occurred with the disintegration of the medieval church opened the way to these developments in religion. The contact of varying and conflicting social perspectives and belief systems of differently situated groups and strata worked toward both relativism of values and toward a certain kind of intellectual objectivity. In the culture of the United States we find a massive laboratory in which to observe these developments.

In an age of localism, internal cleavages among religious groupings in the United States could be partly neutralized by geographic insulation. Now that no important group is really isolated from others, a different basis of relationship is inevitable. For all the specific religious differences found in the culture, the total scene is still one of relative peace.[54] This result depends upon an implicit value-consensus in which religious differences are subsidiary to the values of religious liberty. This consensus, in turn, is not a mystical emanation, but is maintained by a number of quite specific conditions and mechanisms—for example, the pluralistic

[53] These processes have been sketched by students of sociology of knowledge. Cf. Karl Mannheim: *Ideology and Utopia* (New York: 1936), pp. 5–20, 250–6; *Man and Society in an Age of Reconstruction* (London: 1940), trans. by Edward Shils, pp. 79–107.

[54] The importance of anti-Protestant, anti-Catholic and anti-Judaic currents is recognized. Still, these have not recently led to overt conflict on anything approaching the scale often recorded in other societies, and it is not to be assumed that *religious* differences alone account for that conflict which does exist.

power-balance, the vested interests of established religious organization, particular features of the political structure (such as two-party system, Constitutionalism as mediated through the judiciary). In the last analysis, however, none of these conditions, singly or in combination, are sufficient to explain the place of religious institutions, and we come back once more to the existence of a residual common-value element that provides the indispensable meanings and rationales for the complex and unusual structure.

10. Institutional Variation and the Evasion of Normative Patterns

1. Introduction

WITH the provisional description of religion, we complete our selective outline of major institutional structures. In the interests of brevity we have omitted many normative systems, for example, those involved in recreation, art, law, and science.[1] However, a minimum sample of functionally crucial norms has revealed certain clues as to the dynamic interrelations of institutions in the society as a whole. We have also observed ambiguities in norms, conflicts of institutions, variations in nominally accepted standards, but the preceding discussions probably have made institutional systems seem more rigid and clear than is justified by the concrete facts.

First of all, the institutionalized norms of social conduct never fully define concrete action. A norm is a statement (not necessarily explicit) of the course that action *should* follow, not a description of the action that actually occurs. Social action, on the other hand, is always specific and situation-bound: it is action here and now—under particular circumstances of time and place, of particular

---

[1] No reader of these pages will need to be reminded of the enormous significance of science in modern society. This significance is far from being solely a matter of contributions to physical technology, as world-shaking as that is. Advances in medicine and in the social or behavioral sciences have already worked silent revolutions of dimensions not yet widely realized. Above all, *the general culture of scientific work* has permeated vast areas of the social structure.

configurations of values, interests, knowledges, and powers. It is affected by a variety of *non*normative conditions that limit or facilitate the actions prescribed. As was shown in Chapter 3, many norms are so highly generalized that their specific implications for action can be drawn only imperfectly by a long process of cultural accretion; and many others seem to make demands upon conduct that are extremely difficult to meet in practice.

If we compare institutions to a skeleton, or to the girders of a building, or to a "grid" across the social fabric, we do not intend that such statements be taken literally. An institutional norm is not a point or a line, but a *zone:* typically a norm is subject to appreciable variations in perception and application, even under highly favorable circumstances. There is usually a "permissive" zone of variation around even the most specific and strongly supported norms; certain kinds and degrees of overconformity and of underconformity are expected and tolerated. The ambiguities and variability of norms are important but difficult to recognize because of our persistent tendency to think of institutions as solid and well-articulated entities. Even in a highly unified culture, different portions of the normative structure always manifest a wide range of obligatoriness, explicitness, and specificity. Shading off from the level of the most obligatory norms are norms of lesser definiteness held with lesser firmness, as shown for instance by vagueness of definition and by lesser severity of penalties for violations—for example, the conventional or preferred patterns of etiquette and fashion. All these are still parts of the manifest—"public," "official" —cultural structure; they are real prescriptions as to the course action is supposed to follow, but the extent of consensus and the severity of sanctions is lower than for institutions—for example, "there is no disputing with tastes." As MacIver has said: "Society does not need common rules for everything." Our own society has many areas of relative indifference or quite vague definition. Any widely applicable norm necessarily covers a variety of concrete situations, where it engages in action along with other norms. Hence, there is a certain variability that is intrinsic to institutions as well as to other normative patterns.

We have seen that one of the important defining characteristics of culture is that it contains systems of normative regulation of conduct. Inherent in the social interaction of people everywhere is the formal necessity for regularized expectations of others' conduct; and stable expectations can be built up only on the basis of some actual regularity. As any given aggregate of human individuals continues to interact under relatively constant external conditions over a period of time, most of the major life-situations become structured in terms of mutual expectancies for conforming patterns of behavior, some of which become morally obligatory because of their functional importance *in terms of the society's value system*. The norms having this quality are linked together into the clusters or complexes we have termed "institutions."

Now it is conceivable that a culture could be so well integrated that (1) its basic normative patterns would remain stable over very long periods of time, and (2) that at any given time deviations from conformity to the norms would be slight and rare. Among the gross conditions conducive to this stability and conformity are such elements as a small population, with stable birth and death rates, adjusted to a stable physical milieu, and isolated from other cultures. It is possible that the members of such a society would eventually work out behavior regularities and normative structures so well adjusted to individual needs and to the exigencies of social organization that violations of institutional norms would be exceedingly rare and there would be a high degree of consistency of behavior with its ideal patterns and neat interlocking of norm with norm throughout the culture.

In actual fact we do not know of any large-scale societies in which such perfect integration has been achieved. Every modern society that is at all complex carries a culture in which there are very many important strains and "inconsistencies." With increasing size and complexity of the society, subcultures appear, carried by relatively autonomous groups or strata within the larger society. Within a given political entity such as a nation the differentiation of groups may proceed to such a degree that we have to be quite cautious in speaking of *a* culture at all; we may find only a tenuous linking together of a congeries of groups each with its own comparatively distinct value-system, its special problems, its distinctive social perspectives. Often, territorially adjacent groups living under the same larger political structure subscribe to opposing values and follow antithetical norms in important areas of life. A morally obligatory norm in one group may be merely tolerated in another and thoroughly disapproved in still another. For purposes of sociological analysis there then arises the very tangible question as to what is a "deviation from the norms" as over against "a tolerated pattern of evasion," or a distinct "subculture."

Much of the apparent inconsistency in American culture is nothing more or less than the hallmark of a society with marked internal social differentiation. It is not difficult to see that a Mexican American village in Arizona is different from a town in the backcountry of New Hampshire. The two communities differ appreciably in language, in religion, in many other of the major institutional frameworks. They have in common an allegiance to the same national authority with respect to certain impersonal rights and obligations (voting, taxes, military service, etc.), and they share certain very broad cultural values. The fact that the two communities represent subcultures is, however, unmistakable. But it is equally clear that this situation does not necessarily constitute any particular problem for the society as a whole so long as the two groups are not in direct interaction and do not directly confront one another's differing orientations. The same holds for other types of groups or social categories—racial divisions, social classes, specific occupational groups, and so on—so long as there is mutual insulation. Each separate grouping remains separate, at least to the extent of restricting its contacts with other groupings to impersonal, functionally specific relations. Thus, although the total larger society may be very diverse internally and may form only a loosely integrated system, within each subculture there may be high integration of institutions and close conformity of individuals to the patterns sanctioned by their own group.

The possibilities for the smooth functioning of such a "mosaic" society are not, to say the least, very great in the modern world. Diverse subcultures have been linked together through the extraordinary development of transportation and communication, occasioning widespread mutual awareness of other groups and their cultures, as well as much direct personal contact. This awareness of differing or similar values and specific patterns of conduct is rarely a matter of emotional neutrality; the presence of conflicting normative standards is typically not taken in a purely "factual" way, but on the contrary produces some degree of social tension. When originally segmental groups interact with others and begin to lose their closed, quasi-autonomous character, what were at first *conflicts between the standards of different groups* tend to become *intrapersonality conflicts* for the individual. It is in part through this specific dynamic mechanism that a "strain for consistency" is set up in the total culture.

Problems of interinstitutional conflict, therefore, become very real and concrete when seen in terms of the typical *personal* dilemmas involved. The "relation of Church and State" is an abstract formula that may embrace the problems of a conscientious objector—or of a group confronted with secular school requirements contrary to their religious beliefs. The tensions between family institutions and the economic order are observable in such specific cases as the disruption of family groups through unemployment. Thus, the collision of semiautonomous institutional systems is a major area in which the student of society must look for sources of deviant behavior patterns, and for change in the normative patterns themselves.

The most general conditions for a high degree of conformity among institutional norms have already been suggested—basically, conditions that make it possible for conformity to produce conformity. When in any group or social system there is high consensus on the *standards* of conduct, ordinary social interaction continually reinforces conformity by precept, example, approval (respect, affection, etc.), and a great variety of complex and often unconscious mechanisms. Behavior is incessantly and subtly corrected by the responses of others; firmly interdependent expectations are integrated into mutually supporting self-other patterns.[2]

---

[2] This sentence is built upon a large body of modern sociopsychological research and theory. Cf. George Herbert Mead: *Mind, Self, and Society* (Chicago: 1934); Leonard S. Cottrell, Jr.: "The Analysis of Situational Fields in

Incipient nonconformity is subject to immediate and unanimous attempts at control, and overt nonconformity occasions reaffirmation of the threatened norm through disapproval and the imposition of sanctions.

To summarize the points thus far discussed:

1. Even within a relatively unified and stable culture there is some normative variability because of the *generalized nature of norms* vis-a-vis the specific situations of action, because of the *causal role of nonnormative conditions* and because of *individual differences in perception and interpretation*.[3] It is a fact that in many instances nominally accepted norms are too difficult or stringent for full conformity.

2. Many societies contain appreciably different subcultures. American society is a conspicuous case. Much deviation from allegedly universal norms represents a clash of subcultures. As subcultures interpenetrate, some of these conflicts become intrapersonality conflicts.

3. In a society possessing high normative consensus, interactive processes control and reinforce conforming behavior in such a way as to redirect incipient violations.

In the United States nonconformity to nominally accepted norms partakes, of course, of the intrinsic sources of ambiguity and deviation found in all cultures, as well as of the differing standards of relatively separate subcultures. Also, a relatively high rate of certain types of nonconformity is expectable because of rapid social change. Another specific set of factors working in the same direction is found in the often-noted tendency in our culture to establish legal or other official regulation that is manifestly contrary to widely accepted practice. This is in part traceable to a moral-ritual attitude toward law—that law should set up ideal norms "to educate the people," even though strict enforcement is impracticable. Laws often more nearly represent expressions of

---

Social Psychology," *American Sociological Review*, Vol. VII, no. 3 (June, 1942); Parsons: "Propaganda and Social Control." Highly relevant is the work of Harry Stack Sullivan, Jean Piaget, Karen Horney.

[3] These differences are accepted here as given facts; to explain them is a major task for psychology and social psychology.

sentiment than realistic means for direct regulation of behavior: by "passing a law" certain values or ideals can be affirmed without seriously affecting social practice. Furthermore, as we saw in Chapter 7, much legislation is the work of small but powerful pressure-groups whose wishes may diverge quite widely from those of the majority.

Furthermore, there is no doubt that American culture as a whole is strongly task-centered and success-centered. Emphasis on the goals of wealth, power, and prestige creates a "bombardment of interests" that tends to break down the restraining power of the institutionalized definitions of appropriate means to reach the cultural goals. As the extreme, the emphasis upon "getting yours" in terms of individual success becomes so great that "anything goes"—action escapes from all normative regulation except the tests of technical efficiency in reaching the prized goals. In so far as social rewards come solely or chiefly from the achievement of goals rather than from conformity to the rules of the game, there is a long-run pressure toward high rates of individual deviation and nonconformity.

Any individual relates himself to whatever norms he takes to be generally accepted in his society in one of the following ways: (1) He accepts them as morally binding upon his own conduct as well as upon that of others—for example, he conforms in the absence of external sanctions; he feels guilt or shame if he deviates; he actively advocates, defends, or enforces the norms. (2) He accepts the norms only as *conditions* that he takes into account because of the extraneous rewards or penalties attached; conformity and nonconformity are appraised in utilitarian terms. (3) He decisively rejects the norms *per se*, either by withdrawal or active attack.

Full conformity throughout a society or group is dependent upon the actors' having adequate *knowledge of the norms*, an *identification with them*, and *support and reinforcement* from other persons. Both normative consensus and individual conformity can be maintained only by incessant effort and active social evaluation. Even under the most stable conditions of high cultural integration, the smooth flow of conduct along group-sanctioned channels is only seemingly automatic, and modern societies have shown the possibilities for virtually complete dissolution of entire institutional systems. Such dissolution seems generally to involve both a gradual loss of motivation (the spread of apathy) and a high rate of contranormative behavior. Open violation of a norm, strongly supported by most of the community, is simply "crime" or "misbehavior"; but if a large number of individuals commit such violations, the norm itself becomes problematical—the situation either is approaching a split into subcultures, with different standards, or the norm is losing its controlling authority generally. The fact that norms are often vague and are not all felt as equally obligatory or real must be re-emphasized when we use terms such as "evasion," "deviation," or "violation." All cultures have numerous alternatives and flexibilities in their effective norms; in the small and allegedly "simple" societies in which many theorists have professed to see the ironclad mold of clear and unbending custom, modern anthropology is demonstrating a degree of flux and variability not so different from our own society.[4] There are "ideal" norms, and then there are "latent" (covert or unrecognized) norms, shading over into *sub rosa* practices and countermores patterns. In addition there is differentiation of norms by age, sex, class, and so on. It is important not to mistake differentiation or permissible variation for evasion or violation.

We are interested in a still more complicated situation, namely, one where a publicly accepted norm is covertly violated on a large scale, with the tacit acceptance or even approval of the same society or group, at least so long as violation is concealed. *Public* violation, on the other hand, is often felt to require punishment, even when private evasion and violation is prevalent and widely recognized. It is not always simple to determine whether one is observing *evasion* of a norm actually expected to guide real behavior or simply an *alternative norm*, widely accepted or acquiesced in, although of lower cultural value than the ideal but nominal standards.[5] Frequently a manifest institutional pattern seems

[4] Morris E. Opler: "Cultural Alternatives and Educational Theory," *Harvard Educational Review*, Vol. XVII, no. 1 (Winter, 1947), pp. 28–44.

[5] Again, these types of situations are not confined to our own society. A recent text in anthropology speaks of "a customary way of not conforming to

symbiotically related to an opposing pattern that is also accepted. Thus, a strong patriarchal family system, giving women a markedly subordinate status and enforcing rigorous feminine chastity, frequently occurs along with a highly developed system of prostitution. Or again, bureaucratic organizations require that requests or orders must be recorded in writing and passed along all steps in an administrative hierarchy; but this rule typically is accompanied by an informal system of off-the-record communication and action, operating without official sanction. Such patterns may be as normative as the manifest rules and may even be essential to the attainment of the major values being sought in the system.

Perhaps the most interesting example of apparently counter-institutional patterns is found in those not infrequent instances in which individuals are punished precisely because they *fully* carry out the prescriptions of a moral code—even when the code is nominally and publicly placed at the apex of culturally approved values. Sometimes these heroic individuals are regarded as "saints"; but they are also regarded, in certain circumstances, as "fanatics," "trouble-makers," "subversive"—the person who takes literally religious injunctions against killing and refuses military service, for instance, or the zealous proponent of absolute truth who refuses to tell conventional "white lies," or the minister who insists upon a literal implementation of brotherly love in intercultural and interracial relations. Thus, established institutions may thrive upon a relatively large amount of passive conformity and discreet deviation, but are often allergic to full and energetic conformity to their more "utopian" norms.

In summary, within any given social aggregate, variations in

---

custom . . ." and cites specific examples—James S. Slotkin: *Social Anthropology* (New York: 1950), pp. 81 ff. Firth documents established modes of circumventing mourning taboos in Polynesian society—Raymond Firth: *Primitive Polynesian Economy* (London: 1939). Similarly, Malinowski shows patterned evasions of exogamy rules in the Trobriands—Bronislaw Malinowski: *Crime and Custom in Savage Society* (New York: 1926), pp. 71–84. See also Morris E. Opler: "Rule and Practice in the Behavior between Jicarilla Apache Affinal Relatives," *American Anthropologist*, Vol. XLIX, no. 3 (July–September, 1947), pp. 453–62. This article shows that even the "basic" rules of kin avoidance are waived or permissively violated under certain circumstances.

normatively orientated behavior may represent: (1) rebellion against the norms; (2) anomic withdrawal of support; (3) personal or idiosyncratic interpretations; (4) subcultural differences; (5) alternative patterns within the same subculture; (6) regularized evasion (or violation) of utopian and "heroic" standards or of norms expected to control actual behavior. Analysis of each of these variations is necessary for a full picture of the state of a social system. For the time being it seems most illuminating to concentrate upon patterns of regularized evasion.

The typical situation producing large-scale patterned evasion of nominally dominant norms appears as follows:

1. For "reasons" functionally important to the social structure and the main value-systems, a certain activity, thing, belief, etc., is prohibited and widely condemned.

2. But a large proportion of the socially powerful, and otherwise functionally essential, members of the relevant adult population demand the prohibited element.

3. Normative consensus is insufficient to prevent this demand from arising or to deter considerable numbers of individuals from catering to it.

4. But consensus is great enough to prevent a public repudiation of the norm itself. (This fact derives from 1 above.)

5. Many of those who violate or evade the norm hold "essential" [6] status in the social system; there is accordingly a strong resistance to wholesale punishment. [See (2) above.]

6. Hence, the situation is handled by: a) public affirmation of the norm; b) covert acceptance of widespread violation and evasion; c) periodic token or "ritualistic" punishment, and/or punishment of those whose arrears unavoidably become public.

No comprehensive analysis or systematic comparison of data along these lines is available for American society as a whole. Some rather important evidence can be assembled, however, by examination of a few strategically chosen situations.

[6] The quotation marks here signalize a question-begging adjective.

2. Specific Examples of Patterned Evasion

THE FOLLOWING more-or-less random listing of a few well-known examples of established modes of contravening norms usually thought of as "dominant" in our society will serve as preliminary orientation to our present problem:

1. Prohibition *vs.* the bootlegging and speakeasy industry, prior to repeal of the Eighteenth Amendment.
2. Impersonal, disinterested governmental services *vs.* political graft, "fixing," "status justice."
3. Family mores *vs.* prostitution.
4. Classroom honesty *vs.* accepted patterns of "cribbing."
5. Promotion by technical competence *vs.* nepotism, racial discrimination, etc.
   a) Systematic evasion of civil-service laws.
6. Universalistic legal justice *vs.* white collar crime, the public defender system, bias in jury selection.
7. Prescribed patterns of sexual behavior *vs.* the patterns revealed by the Kinsey reports.
8. Legal rules regarding divorce *vs.* actual court practice ("void" divorces, the "alimony racket").
9. Professional codes *vs.* such practices as fee-splitting among doctors, ambulance-chasing among lawyers.
10. Ethical concepts of truth *vs.* some advertising, financial transactions, etc. ("business is business").

The items named are diverse enough to illustrate how very different concrete problems contain common factors. We will now describe some of these cases briefly.

Civil-service laws or merit systems are widespread in American governments. These systems were established after long effort and many struggles, often against the overt or covert opposition of legislators and political leaders. Merit provisions manifest the high value placed upon universalistic standards of achievement and reward in the occupational structure, and have been widely acclaimed as major reforms. However, numerous evasions of the manifest intent of civil-service laws exist.[7] The basic legislation itself is sometimes very limited in applicability. For example, it may exempt all important officials (department heads, etc.) from civil-service regulation, together with their immediate staffs; it may exempt the great mass of unskilled and semiskilled workers—often the majority of the governmental employees. Similar effects are secured by the device of noncompetitive examinations. Biased grading of examinations sometimes occurs. An important evasion is the large-scale use of "temporary" (exempt) appointments that are repeatedly renewed. A still more involved device is that of appointing employees under exempt job-classifications, but utilizing them for duties nominally attached to nonexempt positions, leaving the latter jobs unfilled. There is also the practice of contracting for services from private business rather than directly employing the necessary personnel. This practice has been extended to using vouchers for materials to pay for contracted services. It is sometimes possible to control the merit commissions, which are appointed to administer the law, by control of their membership, for example, by appointment of "right guys" who operate behind the respectable façade provided by "honest but ineffective" members. The entire merit system may be sabotaged by deliberately inadequate appropriations for enforcement and administration. This is not quite so obvious, perhaps, as the outright abolition of classified jobs and the reassignment of these tasks to "politically" appointed personnel under different labels, but it appears to be of comparable effectiveness.

Turning to a somewhat different example, we find that divorce law and its practice is instructive. In most states a divorce cannot be based legally upon mutual agreement: this would be collusion, a specific bar to absolute divorce. Actually, however, it has been estimated that over 90 per cent of divorces in the United States are in fact divorces by mutual agreement; most proceedings are not contested, and decrees are very rarely challenged. Further, divorces

[7] V. O. Key, Jr.: "Methods of Evasion of Civil Service Laws," *The Southwestern Social Science Quarterly*, Vol. XV, no. 4 (March, 1935), pp. 337–47.

are regularly granted by states lacking legal jurisdiction to issue the decree.[8] The ordinary Reno divorce is usually treated as valid, even though it is "void" in the dominant legal theory that requires *bona fide* residence in the state granting the divorce. Although the courts are able to find legal doctrines to justify their refusal to treat these divorces as void, the law as written doctrine differs obviously from the law as practiced by the courts—an instance of dead-letter law, systematically circumvented by the courts themselves in response to social pressures. There is also the well-known and widespread evasion of laws concerning the "grounds" for divorce. New York State requires unilateral proof of adultery, and for those willing to accept a judicial record of this offense divorce is relatively easy and quite binding. There is little doubt that a thriving "industry" has emerged for fabricating evidence of adultery; the legions of professional correspondents, private detectives, cameramen, informers, etc., are the overt symptoms of a *system* for evading the legal norms.

"Political corruption" is so widespread and persistent as to be a "normal" process in many communities. Political parties want votes and the funds necessary to get votes; business groups want protection and privilege; quasi-criminal and criminal elements of the community want immunity.[9] These highly specific wants represent strong interests and tangible advantages. Organized vice, gambling, crime are big industries, supplying products for which there is a heavy demand but which are publicly disapproved; the underworld is thereby vulnerable and at the same time able to pay well for the privilege of systematically violating the law. On the other hand, the mass of those voters who disapprove of political corruption is often apathetic about the (largely unnoticed) day-by-day alliance of business, government, and crime. Politics is a relatively minor and episodic interest with them—whereas to the practicing politician it is a full-time way of life, to the businessman it is a

[8] Fowler V. Harper: "The Myth of the Void Divorce," *Law and Contemporary Problems*, (Durham, N. C.: 1935), pp. 337–41, 344, 346–7; reprinted in Davis, *et al.*: *Modern American Society*, pp. 691–4.

[9] Cf. F. Stuart Chapin: *Contemporary American Institutions* (New York: 1935), pp. 36–40. Chapters 3 and 4 are valuable reading in their entirety.

crucial factor in operations, and to the gang leader or captain of organized illicit business it is a matter of survival.

Commodore Vanderbilt is credited with the vehement rhetorical question as to whether anyone supposed that a railroad could be operated in accordance with the laws. He referred to a legitimate industry. In the highly organized illicit business built up under the direction of Al Capone, there was order and conformity, but only because of the latent structure of legally forbidden but widely accepted practices. Capone is said to have protested, almost plaintively, after his conviction for income-tax evasion [10] that all he had ever done was to supply beer and whiskey to "our best people." Back of organized crime is an elaborate network of connections with the police, the courts, and legitimate business.[11] Especially interesting are the situations in which, externally, the law takes its course and the larger community sees a ceremonial reaffirmation of its institutional rules—as, during prohibition, when, on periodic "round-up days," mass arrests were made, the offenders given nominal fines or sentences, and permitted to return to business.[12] The objective effect upon the liquor industry was about that of a license-fee system. However, public reaction to this system differs sharply from the reaction to "bribes" paid to policemen or judges in order to attain the same end. In both cases the law violator stays in business at a price; but the latter practice is culturally registered as a law violation, the first is a ceremonial affirmation tending to assimilate or obscure the covert pattern of evasion. The same pattern of ritualistic law "enforcement" is often found in commercialized vice, where recurrent raids are widely dramatized and have some real effect in dispersing and concealing organized prostitution and even reducing its prevalence, but do not succeed in suppressing continuous evasion.[13] Here also the covert

[10] *Not* for bootlegging, destruction of property, extortion, purveying of commercialized vice, etc.

[11] See the authoritative study, *The Illinois Crime Survey* (Chicago: 1929), esp. pp. 815–21, 1001–21.

[12] The theoretical significance of this case was first called to the writer's attention by Dr. Robert K. Merton.

[13] Compare the conclusions of the following: Walter C. Reckless: *Vice in Chicago* (Chicago: 1933); Kingsley Davis: "The Sociology of Prostitution,"

pattern has extensions into the political system (elected officials, party leaders, police, the courts) and into legitimate business— real estate, for instance.

Any serious study of these matters shows why the waves of reform so often break upon the reefs of those established evasions which often seem to be "secondary institutions." The existence of a continuing relationship between organized crime and the governmental structure depends not only upon subcultural differentiation [14] and the convergent interests of personnel in the two structures, but also upon the supporting portions of the overtly legal business system and upon the fact that many of the end products of crime are in great demand by considerable numbers of the outwardly law-abiding population.

Reform that attempts simply to suppress these patterns, or to deal only with the "supply" side of the equation, is not likely to be successful. Realistic social action will have to take into account: (1) the pervasive vested interests in institutionalized evasion and violation; (2) the existence of a "demand"—not confined to the *declassé* portions of society—for illicit activities and products; (3) the partial dependence of patterned evasion upon the particular nature of the dominant institutions. Thus, we might postulate a situation in which persons lacking in technical competence and administrative integrity are elected to offices of great community responsibility at salaries considerably below the going rate in private business. Let us suppose also that the majority of the population tend to deprecate "politics" and is apathetic about the government; at the same time, the government requires many services and products from private business and the latter is subject to inspection and regulation. If, furthermore, the norms of business-government relations are ill-defined and a case of "graft" is exposed, a frequent public reaction is to "kick the rascals out,"

American Sociological Review, Vol. II, no. 5 (October, 1937); *The Illinois Crime Survey*, pp. 845–63.

[14] It is certainly no surprise that criminal groups have their own codes and loyalties, nor that crime and delinquency are "normal" in many sectors of the society. The gangster is often no less a hero in his own subculture than the successful political leader or businessman, and it is not always simple to discover the differences among the three categories.

without altering the basic structural situation.[15] When considering reform it is always relevant to appraise the total consequences—what will the proposed alterations cost, in the broadest sense.

The cases examined so far have been instances in which the manifest, official norms apparently enjoy strong popular support—that is, the norms are really expected to control behavior. In certain other instances there seems to be a larger utopian component in the norms that are circumvented. As we have observed, a norm is, by definition, not always perfectly actualized.[16] If the publicly avowed standards are highly generalized and conflict simultaneously with strong interests and tacitly accepted values and operating rules, what then emerges is typically not considered an "evasion"; rather, there is an abstract creed, given great symbolic importance but culturally insulated from operating practice. For example, a policeman is supposedly an impartial instrument for law-enforcement. However, quite aside from criminal connivance, the policeman usually has a wide range of discretion in when, how, and upon whom he will visit sanctions. He may show "favoritism"—or he may show kindness, take intentions and extenuating circumstances into account. The prosecuting attorney is perhaps even more clearly involved in extralegal considerations. In both instances, however, the official is expected to give public and ceremonial expression to the impartiality of the law.

The American jury system is a venerated institution: not only is the right to trial by jury written into the Constitution, but its importance in a democratic system of values is generally taken for granted. Nevertheless, the jury system often becomes a means whereby skillful or powerful law violators escape punishment, and the system of selection and trial procedure goes far to prevent

[15] Few have surpassed Lincoln Steffens in grasping the intertwined causative factors in this type of situation. His insights are still fresh, although some of the patterns have changed somewhat by now. Cf. *The Autobiography of Lincoln Steffens* (New York: 1931), esp. pp. 215–38, 407–15, 464–9. See also John T. Salter: *Boss Rule: Portraits in City Politics* (New York: 1935).

[16] In the case of a society committed to extremely "high" standards, i.e., those that for any reason are difficult of attainment, much of the dynamism of the social system seems attributable to a continuing tension between ideal norms and situational realities.

jurors from playing the ideal role culturally attributed to them.[17]
It has been shown (for example by the Ruth Commission in Penn-
sylvania) that jurors are frequently ignorant of essential facts and
of legal terminology, that cases are sometimes decided without an
understanding of the charges or even without knowledge of which
case is being passed upon. The important point here is that the
jury may absorb a large part of the "blame" for seeming mis-
carriages of justice while the abstract symbols and the creedal
norms of The Law remain unscathed. The full functional significance of this pattern has yet to be adequately analyzed, but its
possible role must not be overlooked.[18]

Circumvention of norms is not confined to crime and "disrep-
utable" behavior; it is common to find within a particular ingroup
regularized systems of conduct that are contrary to publicly
voiced standards that have the position of "mores." In the field of
education, the importance of "connections" in academic place-
ments has been pointed out by Wilson, who shows that much
favoritism is due to technical and institutional barriers to free,
impersonal competition; [19] also the norms of "impartial appointment on the basis of merit" are sometimes violated because of
personal ties, internal university politics, and so on. Here some
interesting data are provided by Hollingshead's study of appointments in a Midwestern university for the period 1885–1937. He
indicates that membership in the ingroups of alumni, friendship,
and family effects four fifths of all appointments, leaving one
fifth in which relatively impersonal criteria of professional competence were alone the deciding factors.

A final illustration may indicate how this type of analysis applies
to large-scale social problems. Intergroup relations oriented to
"racial" distinctions constitute a chronic and serious problem in

---

[17] E. H. Sutherland: *Principles of Criminology* (Philadelphia: 1934).

[18] Some unsystematic but highly suggestive leads have been formulated in
Thurman W. Arnold: *The Symbols of Government* (New Haven, Conn.: 1935),
chaps. 6–7.

[19] Logan Wilson: *The Academic Man*, pp. 50–1, 54–6. See also A. B. Hollingshead: "Ingroup Membership and Academic Selection," *American Sociological Review*, Vol. III, no. 6 (December, 1938), pp. 826–33.

the United States. The problem, however, exists in different forms in different groups and localities, and the normative regulation of interracial behavior falls into a number of different levels. In some areas, especially in rural portions of the deep South, tension and conflict arise largely from the efforts of the white population to maintain castelike controls and privileges. The problem there can be analyzed as a clash of subcultures, each relatively unified as to the rightness of its standards. Myrdal's thesis of an "American dilemma" [20] in which the white person is torn between his creeds and his specific operating practices would not apply to the case in which the dominant whites feel little value-conflict in supporting inequalitarian, discriminatory patterns. For example, the legal doctrine of "equal but separate" public services for whites and Negroes is largely a cultural fiction: national law requires equality, some localities insist upon segregation, and castelike prerogatives, and the unequal and separate facilities result. The specific evidence of normative conflict is that there is at least an *awareness* of different standards and an attempt to justify the local system. One can move through many intermediate types of such situations to something very close to "institutionalized" evasion in some Northern cities. In New York State, for example, it is illegal to refuse service to Negroes in commercial establishments. There is enough social consensus to support the passage of such legislation; there is considerable public disapproval of discrimination; many white people feel uneasy or guilty when they act in ways defined as "discriminatory" or "prejudiced." Yet there are well-marked patterns of informal segregation, and the legal barriers against discrimination are often evaded. For example, restaurants have developed very elaborate devices of evasion such as the "freeze-out," in which service is delayed on various pretexts for an intolerable length of time, or the "friendly brush-off"—an appeal to the Negro patron to leave "because the other customers will object"—or the "rough house" pattern of cold food, overcharges, spilled soup, brusque service, etc.[21] These acts are often performed by persons professing

[20] Gunnar Myrdal, with the assistance of Richard Sterner and Arnold Rose: *An American Dilemma*, 2 vols. (New York: 1944).

[21] A large body of unpublished data on such patterns has been gathered in

belief in equal rights. Patterned evasions are, probably typically, the products of specific, recurring *situations* in which immediate interests, group stereotypes, and interpersonal ties and expectations take precedence over the more abstract ideal norms.[22] Quite clearly, many of the specific situations that emerge are so delicately balanced that an apparently trivial factor can move the pattern decisively over to either the discriminatory or the nondiscriminatory mode.

The consequences of the widespread and dramatic exposure of such covert systems of institutional evasion deserve analysis on a scale far beyond what has been done. It seems to be generally assumed that public exposure of violations of norms strengthens consensus and the commitment to the dominant institutions. This assumption is sometimes true, but in other cases the disclosure may actually weaken support of the nominal institutional regulation by changing expectations (the realization that many others share the practice) and by activating interests and values previously defined as forbidden.

The considerations just reviewed indicate why a sociological analysis cannot stop with treatment of the manifest institutional structure. The manifest norms must be known but an understanding of violation, variation, and evasion is equally necessary, both for science and for social action. Culture and society are always changing, and the first tiny breaches of normative structure are to be carefully watched in any attempt to comprehend the sources of social change.

---

studies by the Cornell Social Science Research Center under a grant from the Rockefeller Foundation. Publication of the findings is planned for the near future.

[22] " 'The American Dilemma,' referred to in the title of this book, is the . . . conflict between, on the one hand, the valuations preserved on the general plane which we shall call the 'American Creed,' where the American thinks, talks, and acts under the influence of high national and Christian precepts, and on the other hand, the valuations on specific planes of individual and group living, where personal and local interests; economic, social, and sexual jealousies; considerations of community prestige and conformity; group prejudice against particular persons or types of people; and all sorts of miscellaneous wants, impulses, and habits dominate his outlook." Myrdal: *An American Dilemma*, 2 vols. (New York: Harper & Brothers, 1944), p. xliii. Our analysis would add to this the considerations outlined on pp. 354–6 above.

Because previous chapters have so closely focused upon the main institutions of the society, it is especially necessary here to stress the relation of individuals to their institutions. No one lives in a culture as a whole. We live in particular segments of the total culture—in a particular family, class, school, church, and so on. What we directly experience is always a variant of the patterns discernible by external scientific abstraction, and each of us has countless occasions for idiosyncratic interpretation of norms. The most complete description of institutional norms would still not tell us exactly how to act in specific situations. It is therefore not a source of wonder that there is variation, evasion and complex change in institutions; it is at least equally remarkable how much regularity, conformity, and predictability do exist.

3. Cultural Fictions

IMPLICIT in the foregoing discussion are distinctions among various levels of "reality" in the normative definition and regulation of conduct. In some cases, cultural blueprint and typical behavior are so congruent that either one can be predicted from the other with a low margin of error; however, we have seen instances in which stated norms and observed behavior differ widely. Regularized evasions sometimes are a means to fill a gap between norm and action; in other cases, they resolve the clash of two or more norms, having conflicting behavioral requirements.

We come now to a still different phenomenon, that of "cultural fictions." [23] A cultural fiction exists whenever there is a cultural description, explanation, or normative prescription that is both *generally accepted as a norm* and is *typically followed* in conduct but is at the same time markedly at variance with the subjective conceptions or inclinations of participants in the pattern, or with certain objective scientific knowledges. Many so-called fictions are simply "arbitrary" from the standpoint of any particular individual

[23] "Fiction" here has no ontological significance; it is used only as a convenient descriptive term, to be understood in the sense indicated by the discussion to follow.

—although *not* necessarily so from the perspective of the functional needs within a society having a particular set of value orientations,[24] for example, language, methods of measuring space and time, numerous minor social usages, the elaboration of etiquette. Many, if not most, cultural norms are not rigidly anchored in the nature of man as a biological organism nor in the nature of the physical environment. To take one of Woodward's deliberately commonplace examples, there would not seem to be any biological or physical factors that would indicate a fork as the suitable instrument for eating peas—a spoon would seem to be more efficient and possibly more adaptive biologically. The prescribed usage is in this sense arbitrary, although agreement upon any one procedure does provide predictability and to this extent facilitates social interaction.[25] Clearly identifiable cultural fictions occur when private affective and perceptual responses do not correspond to the overt pattern; for example, the chief executive expresses deep regret over the resignation of a subordinate when it is clearly understood that everyone was elated to see the event accomplished. Such conventional forms of expression and interaction are pervasive even in a society so loosely organized and informal as the United States.

When conventional forms are consistently practiced by all members of a social group, they typically evoke sentiments felt to be consistent with the outward pattern of conduct. They are not then "mere forms" but actually define the individual's conception of proper and desirable behavior; the individual "really feels" and "wants to act" as the convention dictates he should. Conventions supported by such psychological involvement are not fictional except in the sense that all social norms and values are fictional because they are validated by consensus and practice rather than by realities independent of the social system.

[24] These remarks will depend heavily on the stimulating paper by James W. Woodward, "The Role of Fictions in Cultural Organization," *Transactions of the New York Academy of Sciences*, Series II, Vol. VI, no. 8 (June, 1944), pp. 311–44. Our treatment, however, does not intend to treat as "fiction" all social practices which cannot be given a "scientific" rationale.

[25] Woodward says that in this example there is an implicit fiction. We prefer here to say that it is an "arbitrary" usage, and to reserve the term "fiction" for instances of divergence between cultural norm and the actors' private perceptions and evaluations of the situation.

To the degree that the "as if" conventions serve to limit and define spontaneous personal responses, they facilitate social interaction of various kinds. Even when unguided private sentiments are such as would disrupt interaction, a common orientation to conventional froms provides the minimal predictability necessary to continued participation. Stereotyped behavior (including statements of sentiment, feeling, value, etc.) becomes "fictional" only when the *culturally ascribed meaning* of the behavior is in opposition to the *privately held meanings actually operative* in the situation. In extreme instances it is possible to identify a very complex structure of "fictions": individual A and individual B may each be aware they are using fictional forms and that the other individual is also aware that they are and yet continue to act conventionally. As Woodward suggests, formality (conventionalization, protocol, etc.) tends to be at a maximum when *it is important that interaction occur*, there are *few and weak positive ties* between the participants, and the interaction involves relatively *severe conflicts of interests or values*.[26] Examples include diplomatic convention, military courtesy, much of etiquette, academic decorum, judicial procedures. In our own society, as in others, it continually happens that certain beliefs are expressed, values stated, assumptions accepted, actions performed when the participants in the pattern themselves recognize fictional ("pretend") elements in what they are saying or doing. In a great many of these patterns, not "hypocrisy," but functional deviousness [27] is perhaps the most meaningful characterization of the situation.

If cultural definitions are to be socially effective, however, they must be invested with some kind of reality by the society's members, and the pressure to accept fully the definitions and prescriptions become the more intense the greater the stress and the higher the ranking of the values involved in any particular case. One can arrange cultural items in continuous gradients, from usages and

[26] "The Role of Fictions in Cultural Organization," pp. 326–32.

[27] Ibid., p. 329. See also, Wilbert E. Moore and Melvin M. Tumin: "Some Social Functions of Ignorance," *American Sociological Review*, Vol. XIV, no. 6 (December, 1949), pp. 787–95, esp. p. 791.

conventions practiced by individuals who accept them as necessary or expedient fictions over to the abiding beliefs and values not regarded as in any sense fictional. Hence, the determination of just what is a cultural fiction (and in what sense) is rarely even so apparently easy as in the case of the peas-and-fork example. When the culture bearers themselves are *not* aware of any "as if" element in their practices or beliefs, is there ever any basis for imputing such an element to their behavior? To many people in America the large corporation represents "private property"—they attach to corporate organizations the values and symbols historically associated with the control of property by individual entrepreneurs. Is this belief-value complex a cultural fiction or not? The answer appears to be yes and no: it is not a fiction to those Americans who hold the view, but it is a fiction if one compares the modern corporation to private property as defined in earlier periods. It is only in this limited sense that scientific analysis is justified in describing this cultural orientation as partly fictional. And this example, perhaps, has already implied that cultural patterns are especially likely to be perceived as fictional—both by participants and by analytical observers—when: (1) beliefs or value orientations conflict,[28] e.g., one particular social perspective no longer holds a monopoly, or (2) "creeds" enjoin beliefs without modelling the conduct required for their effective operation, ("lip service"),[29] or (3) certain practices and beliefs have ceased to command personal commitment or involvement from large numbers of people. Examples under each of these categories can be described in our own society. Thus, when we find verbal assent to creeds of democracy and equality existing alongside racial discrimination, the sources of seeming contradiction include elements of direct value conflict—and the "fictional"

[28] Under definable conditions this produces what Kenneth Burke terms "perspective by incongruity"—*Permanence and Change* (New York: 1936), Part II, esp. pp. 118 ff. Note in our modern society (just prior to World War II) the vogue of semantics and psychoanalysis, the development of relativistic thought, the prevalence of "debunking." And note also the very different developments which have been associated with war and politico-ideological conflict.

[29] Really a special case of (1).

appearance of the creedal beliefs may not be apprehended by persons caught in the cross-pressure.[30] Out of such conflicts there emerge, under differing conditions, the victory of one set of values, a compromise, or a new synthesis or mutation. On the other hand, cultural fictions often represent the more subtle processes of "loss of conviction," [31] expressed in the language of psychology as withdrawal of affect, or loss of identification and involvement. In the latter case, change in the main institutions and systems of belief derives more immediately from slow attrition than from revolutionary attack. On this large and complex problem we have as yet very little disciplined evidence. It is relevant, nevertheless, to note that value orientations retain effective regulatory power in conduct only to the extent that they are actually practiced—that is, defended when attacked, used as referents for concrete action, affirmed in social interaction. Only those orientations that are strongly invested with attention and effort escape the museum of cultural fictions.

4. Conclusion and Implications

IT HAS been repeatedly stressed in this chapter that social norms vary considerably in the way individuals conceive of and conform to them. In addition, we suggested the crucial point, in connection with cultural fictions, that shared assumptions and expectations can play an essential part in behavior, even when regarded by the actors as fictional or when so described by external analysis.[32] Recent empirical studies investigating the variability

[30] Self-conscious and deliberate use of a normative facade to conceal radically antithetical values does occur, of course. But it is easy to overestimate its importance. As Machiavelli long ago understood, it is very difficult for men to be consistently and thoroughly "bad" and hypocritical at the same time.

[31] Cf. Archibald MacLeish: "The American State of Mind," *The American Scholar*, Vol. XIX, no. 4 (Autumn, 1950).

[32] Cf. Gustav Ichheiser: "Misunderstandings in Human Relations: A Study in False Social Perception," *American Journal of Sociology*, Vol. LV, no. 2, part 2 (September, 1949), pp. 1–70. See esp. p. 44: "For it is in the nature of human relations that their basic assumptions and expectations have to be

of norms and their modification under situational cross-pressures seem to support the lines of analysis followed here. Thus, Stouffer suggests: "It may be precisely the ranges of permissible behavior which most need examination if we are to make progress in this realm which is so central in social science. For it may be the very existence of some flexibility or social slippage—but not too much— which makes behavior in groups possible." [33] Institutional flexibility, within limits, appears to be a necessary condition for the functioning of social systems. Moreover, some evasions and violations of particular given cultural rules seem clearly "functional" for the maintenance of *other* cultural structures in the same society.[34] Thus in the end the subject matter of the present discussion resolves itself into questions of values and value priorities. All that social science, as science, can do is to analyze the imperfectly understood conditions which are causal in the appearance of deviant behavior, institutionalized evasion, cultural fictions—and normative change. We have not undertaken to judge—either to condone or to condemn—the observed patterns. Whatever the analysis may have left undone, it has quite forcibly confronted us with the basic question of the role of *values* in the functioning of social systems. To this question, the following chapter will be devoted.

---

accepted as valid even if at times these are much at variance with the facts which they allegedly represent. Otherwise, a predictable functioning of social relations would not be possible, and society, as we know it, could not exist."

[33] Samuel A. Stouffer: "An Analysis of Conflicting Social Norms," *American Sociological Review*, Vol. XIV, no. 6 (December, 1949), pp. 707–17.

[34] The *literal* enforcement of every norm subscribed to by the members of American communities would certainly produce tensions on a scale so enormous as to challenge imagination.

11. Value Orientations in American Society

1. Why Study Values?

IN SKETCHING the main outlines of the ordered institutional life of the United States our focus has been upon recurring ideal patterns—and those systematic deviations that are sufficiently persistent, uniform, and enduring to be thought of as *structure* in a large and heterogeneous society. The analysis began with the institutionalized and conventional prescriptions for approved conduct. These ideal patterns were shown to be inferences from observations of concrete behavior, but analytically different from the total behavior taken at a common-sense level of observation. Our second level of analysis therefore had to concern itself with factual regularities in behavior—not just with norms, standards, and orientations but with the interaction in which norms are imperfectly actualized.

This step-by-step analysis has traced a part of the most obvious structural framework of the American social order. Even this limited degree of analysis required a rather sharp focus upon certain portions of society and accordingly a systematic neglect of others. In short, to gain insight into the structural elements of norms and social organization we have deliberately put on "blinders" to shut out other observations. This process is legitimate, indeed unavoidable, in any systematic examination of a social system; but we must not stop with our first approximation.

Our next step is to describe the major patterns of values that can be identified in American society. Of course, "American values" are not values necessarily exclusive to, or even peculiar to, the United

States, nor do all Americans share them. We wish to discover the extent to which any particular value or value complex is in fact present in this society.

There are, however, important grounds for expecting American culture to be characterized by a value system appreciably different from other cultures. Most obvious perhaps is the different environment—different location, physical surroundings, climate, resources, and so on. Equally impressive are the many diverse cultural strains and the subsequent crosscultural contacts within the American aggregate. Aside from these, and from any possible genetic selectivity, we have the general theorem that a society separated from others by spatial and socio-political barriers will, over a period of time, develop a relatively distinctive culture.

The data cited in following pages indicate that in a broad comparative view, American culture does bear out this proposition. The real problem, however, is to identify and appraise the value patterns that are relatively most distinctive and important.

We cannot, however, proceed to identify these patterns without first seeing how the concept of social institutions involves the concept of value. For the individual facing his culture, institutions are a sort of map or "blueprint" of the main outlines and contours of expected and obligatory conduct. Institutionalized rules at any given time in a particular culture implicitly say: "These and these are the things that are expected, these and these are the probable consequences of conformity and nonconformity." In addition to this function of *orientation*, institutions often represent *internalized values* that are felt as binding for the personality—conscience, life goals, preferred subjective states of various kinds. In fact, the continued existence of any particular system of institutions depends upon the extent to which the pattern contains values actually invested with affect and meaning for the participants. Thus institutions typically are both "facts of the external world" that the individual must take into account and value patterns within the personality. Every act, or failure to act, in the interdependent web of socio-cultural life has consequences; institutions and the values they represent are continually being reinforced, maintained, changed, or destroyed by the shifting patterns of human thought and action. "Stability" of culture is, therefore, a dynamic process in which a delicately balanced system of values is maintained.

Americans currently face a period in which few institutions, beliefs, or values can any longer be taken for granted. All are under strain; all are challenged. Basic transformations of man and society are now underway, and many vital choices of values must be made.

2. What Is Meant by Value?

It is essential for *this* analysis that we secure a clear conception of what values are and of how we may recognize and analyze their role in a system of motivated social action. We are concerned with values as observable variables in human conduct, not with an appraisal of various values as being better or worse than others, nor with the meaning and ontological status of value as a concept, however important these problems may be. For our purposes, we must seek a conception of value that can be referred to definite evidence.

We will begin by regarding value as any aspect of a situation, event, or object that is invested with a *preferential interest* as being "good," "bad," "desirable," and the like. Any formal definition of value is likely to be too general to be of great use to a sociological analysis, and a general definition seems to involve an inevitable circularity—to define value as "interest" is only another way of saying value. It is enough here if we circumscribe the boundaries of value. What we can recognize as values have these qualities: (1) They have a conceptual element—they are more than pure sensations, emotions, reflexes, or so-called needs. Values are abstractions drawn from the flux of the individual's immediate experience. (2) They are affectively charged: they represent actual or potential emotional mobilization. (3) Values are not the concrete goals of action, but rather the *criteria* by which goals are chosen. (4) Values are important, not "trivial" or of slight concern. (Although this statement is circular, it suggests the possibility of studying values through the study of choices.)

For present purposes we may follow Linton in treating all shared values as *cultural* values by definition. *Social* values, however, not only are shared by a number of individuals but are regarded as matters of collective welfare by an effective consensus of the group.[1] Neither of these classes of value is necessarily identical with ethical or moral values; the latter involve relatively systematic ideas of the good as apart from sheer interest, desirability, or expediency.

Clearly there are often intense and widespread *interests* that are both ethically disapproved and held to be inimical to group welfare —murder or vice for example. On the other hand, we easily recognize values that are at the same time interests or desires of individuals, objects of ethical approval, and approved as conducive to group welfare: for example, personal honesty or a happy monogamous marriage. Furthermore, there are the dramatic and often tragic situations in which an ethical value is in conflict with a current social value—the situation, for instance, of the conscientious objector in time of war.

Values are thus "things" in which people are interested—things that they want, desire to be or become, feel as obligatory, worship, enjoy. Values are *modes of organizing conduct*—meaningful, affectively invested pattern principles that guide human action.

Empirically considered, value is not an all-or-none matter, but a continuum. At one pole, we find those intense and rigid moral values that are true matters of conscience—integral components of the superego. Values of this order are present when the individual who violates them shows a reaction of strong guilt or overwhelming shame and the group imposes strong censure upon the offender. Such moral values are the core of the individual's internalized conscience. They also define the central institutional structure of

[1] These distinctions can be maintained without confusion only by recognizing other possible usages of the terms "social" and "cultural" as applied to values. *Social* values have been considered variously as: (1) conducive or essential to the welfare of a collectivity taken as a whole; (2) constituting models or goals of personal behavior in social interaction; or (3) common to the members of a given social aggregate. The term "cultural value" is sometimes reserved for the value inherent in culture objects (systems of thought and belief, art, artifacts, and so on) as distinct from actual social relations. In the present analysis, values attached to timeless objects of culture are of interest only in so far as they play a role in social interaction.

the society—although the accepted mores do not necessarily coincide with the "highest" social ethics and the ethical position of any given individual may not be identical with either the mores or the highest ethics. From the point on the value continuum at which the moral quality is emphasized, values shade off into those evoking less intense guilts and less severe social sanctions—for example, aesthetic standards, conventional proprieties, and simple norms of expediency or technical efficiency. Only careful research testing can establish the position of any "alleged" value along this continuum in the actual functioning of a society.

Values concern the goals or ends of action and are, as well, components in the selection of adequate means. Even in so far as choice is not deliberate or conscious, all action nevertheless is of one kind rather than another. Some balancing of alternatives must occur whenever alternatives exist. Since acts, including failures to act, typically involve a renunciation of other possible courses of behavior, every act "costs something." In this sense, values and their arrangement into hierarchies are defined by choices.

When we say that a person "puts a high value" on something, what do we mean? We seem to mean that the person is willing to expend effort or make sacrifices to attain or maintain a certain identifiable state of affairs. To "put a high value on education," for example, may mean such behavior as long and arduous study, the sacrifice of money that could have been spent for other purposes, the acceptance of deprivation with regard to many attractive immediate gratifications. Since the human life-span is not infinite, all such expenditures of time involve the sacrifice of alternative uses. In this sense, the choice of values involves an "economy" of human energy.

At first glance, then, the criterion of *choice* seems to provide an adequate way of defining values empirically. We reason that any choice involves a renunciation of other values: the choice of A over B, B over C, and so on, would thus define a hierarchy of values. If we look for crucial situations of choice and systematically record typical modes of choosing, we can then characterize the dominant and subsidiary values in any given group or situation. Linton reports that among the Comanche Indians of the Plains, when the camp was raided by an enemy group, a man was supposed to save his mother-in-law before attempting to escape himself or save his property. In so far as this ideal pattern was actually carried out, it evidently represented some guiding principle as to the priority of values in that culture. To take a different illustration, a Chinese son in the old tradition would have been expected to save his father from danger before helping himself or his brother. There are many such examples of crucial choices, and, indeed, our unreflective sense of values is to an important extent compounded from observing, hearing about, and participating in exactly this way in the various kinds of choices within situations set for us by the surrounding culture.

Data on choices may be derived from direct observation of spontaneous behavior, from testimony of witnesses, from self-reporting, and from various indirect evidences. Thus, for example, in a society with a highly developed money economy, much can be learned about the patterns of general values from the patterns of money expenditure, since money is a particular measure of economic "value"—that is, of value in exchange. The study of family budgets, general patterns of consumer expenditure, public expenditures, the flow of the national income, and so on, is subject to interpretation in these terms. If we know that at a given level of income, rural families invest a larger proportion of their net income than do urban families, whereas urban families are more likely to put their funds into present consumption,[2] we can immediately begin to raise questions as to the respective values placed on, say, security or current enjoyment by the two groups.

An important difficulty in using choices as indices of values lies in the gross quality of concrete choices. The so-called simple choices of everyday life typically concern selection among *complexes* of values. To study for tomorrow's class rather than to attend a play in the company of friends—neither course taken purely as behavior in itself indicates a value. The motives may be

[2] Cf. Carle C. Zimmerman: *Consumption and Standards of Living* (New York: 1936), chap. 13.

positive intellectual interest, fear of disapproval, longing for sociability, aesthetic values, and so on indefinitely—not isolated values, but interconnected systems of values. Indeed, it is often difficult to determine exactly what values are at issue. This limitation is not hopeless, however, for we have evidence that cultural standardization so defines and limits choices that we can expect to find in any given group or social system a regularity of choices in recurrent situations that under systematic study reveal a pattern of values.

Another possible test for the existence of values is to observe *directions of interest*. To what do people "pay attention"? We may study a society in which literature and other arts are permeated with an otherworldly emphasis. We may find on every hand, in the conversation and daily activities of the people, a preoccupation with transcendental or supernatural formulations of life problems. A first approximation might justify the statement that such a society is marked by a strongly religious value-system, subject to further testing from other sources of evidence.

We may also secure evidence on values by focusing upon what people say their values are. We find, in fact, that a great deal of verbalization consists in the explicit avowal or disavowal of certain values. *This* is said to be good, *that* bad; this is desirable, that undesirable; this is worth working or fighting for, that is worthless. Thus the Westminster Assembly said: "Man's chief end is to glorify God and enjoy Him forever." This statement appears to represent a value system rather different from that indexed by: "Man is the measure of all things." The explicit statements of value positions are, of course, not completely reliable. They may represent "mere lip service," largely divorced from realistic conduct. No student of human conduct can accept uncritically, as final evidence, people's testimony as to their own values. Yet actions may deceive as well as words, and there seems no reason for always giving one precedence over the other.

Even when not explicitly stated, values can often be inferred directly from verbal materials. In argument, for instance, the statements arousing "heat," emotion, and so on, are clues to values. In assertion and counterassertion, there frequently emerges level after level of favorable or unfavorable reactions—a "regress".

that in certain cases can be followed back to certain irreducible or ultimate values.[3]

Verbal materials may also be analyzed by more complex methods going beyond the explicit, manifest, or apparent content. Systematic attention should be given to those implicit premises necessary for a meaningful account of (to "make sense of") explicit statements. It is commonly observed, for example, that what is *not* said is often more significant than what is said, reminding us again that the things in a culture that are most completely taken for granted typically turn out to be of fundamental importance in that culture.[4]

The material thus uncovered or reconstructed does not, of course, consist wholly of values, but includes "beliefs" and other cognitive elements. In its most simple and somewhat misleading formulation, a belief is a conviction that something is real, whereas a value is a preference. Thus, a man may *believe* (that is, say he believes) that there is life after death, but this statement tells us nothing directly as to whether immortality is for him a positive or a negative value, or a matter of indifference. Two people may believe that Mussolini "made the trains run on time," but for one this belief signifies approval of Italian Fascism, whereas for the other it indicates the "false efficiency" of a system violating basic human values in other respects. Although beliefs are often opportunistic in shaping themselves to interests, the relation is reciprocal and sometimes allows a considerable degree of independent variation. Otherwise stated, value relates closely to cognition, but the perception of what is supposed to exist is distinct from the subject's bias of favor or disfavor toward this supposed reality.

For purposes of social analysis, one great advantage of testimony,

[3] "Ultimate" or "irreducible" here refers only to the fact that a point may be reached at which a *basis for discussion no longer exists*, that is, there is an incompatibility of bias that cannot be resolved. We do not wish at this time to go into any broader questions as to what ultimate values may mean, except to point out that value positions that appear irrevocably incompatible are sometimes subject to redefinition that discloses a deeper agreement.

[4] In one respect, the residue-derivation technique of Vilfredo Pareto helps identify such implicit configurations. Much of the work of psychiatrists and clinical psychologists, and much of psychological testing (for example, the use of projective techniques) is directed to the discovery of meaning, beliefs, and values that are not readily made explicit by the person himself.

or of verbalization in general, is its capacity to reflect subtle shadings of values. This quality probably accounts for the common dissatisfaction with descriptions of behavior that neglect the reasons people give for their conduct. For it is in explanations and reasons that we often discover the significant value predicates that uncover the normative regularities behind seemingly varied actions.

Still another source of evidence is found by observing the reward-punishment system of a group or society, noting the incidence of *social sanctions*. What behavior is rewarded and praised? What is censured, disapproved, and punished? How great are the rewards and how severe the penalties? Under what circumstances is a given act, ordinarily disapproved, held excusable? What priority of values is involved in the "disapproved act" *versus* "extenuating circumstances"? What are the relatively stable and the relatively unstable elements in a series of related situations? When conduct must resolve two or more mutually incompatible value elements, how does the effective community react?

Chapter 3 suggested that observation of sanctions is a most useful way to detect the normative structure of a society. We can now re-examine the same data to track down more accurately the value elements in concrete norms. Recalling that a norm specifies what action should be carried out in a given situation and how the action should be performed, let us look for the implicit values. The parental dictum "You should wash your hands before meals" is a norm, and the "should" indicates "it is a good thing to do this." This statement may carry an implicit syllogism—for example, dirty hands carry germs, germs are a hazard to health, health is desirable, therefore the rule. Or, considerations of social conformity may be involved ("what would the guests think"), or aesthetic elements (dirty hands are ugly), and so on. On the conscious level, of course, such a normative statement may be largely unrationalized and taken as an unproblematic value in itself.

Suppose we assert that cleanliness is a major value in American society. We could establish or refute such a statement by recording the following types of observations: (1) In this society, people often choose between activities that promote cleanliness and other types of activity (for example, cleaning house *versus* going to church or enjoying leisure). A great deal of time and effort is lavished on washing hands, taking baths, preparing clean clothes, scrubbing and sweeping, collecting and disposing of trash, and so on. (2) Newspapers and magazines devote much space to news, articles, and advertising dealing with cleanliness and ways of promoting it in various areas of life. (3) Comments asserting or implying a bias in favor of cleanliness are extremely common, not only in response to direct questioning but in the form of unprompted statements. (4) Analysis of a wide sampling of spoken and written materials reveals an extraordinary number of instances that assume "cleanliness is desirable" as an implicit concept underlying the assertions. (Thus, in the frequent articles on new housekeeping methods there are many that never make the value statements directly.) (5) Children are approved and otherwise rewarded for cleanly behavior, but meet frowns, censorious speech, minor deprivations, and physical chastisement for certain violations of this pattern. Although the rewards and penalties may be less obvious in later life, adults, too, face sanctions for conduct disregarding this value.

Putting all these lines of evidence together and assuming for illustrative purposes that no important contrary facts are found, we can say that cleanliness is definitely a value in American society, or in whatever segment of that society we may have in view. However, in a sense it is arbitrary to formulate cleanliness as the complex that is to be termed a value. One might conveniently and legitimately go beyond this formulation to a concept of some more generalized value—for example, orderliness or personal self-discipline—provided only that other evidence and convenience in analysis warrant the more inclusive description. There may be many levels of generality that can be identified in this way, depending upon the nature of the data and upon the purposes of analysis.

This much detail concerning possible approaches to the empirical study of values in society seems essential in order to underline the nature of the present analysis. Starting with the initial location of value in a relation of a person to an object of interest, the sources of evidence mentioned above indicate just so many "operational definitions" of value: value as *overt choice or preference*, as *attention or emphasis*, as *statement* or *assertion*, as *implicit premise*, as a referent of *social sanctions*. These various evidences are "pointers" that say "this is what is meant." [5] Not all are of equal usefulness for every purpose, but all are useful. When used in combination, these several different approximations gain reliability in so far as they are mutually consistent.

3. What Are "Dominant Values"?

UPON leaving the United States after an extended visit, Sir William Beveridge observed that there were "six Americas in search of a faith." In a social order of the flux, variety, and groping suggested by this statement, can anything be said as to its hierarchy of values? Are there any focal values that can be held to be "dominant" in the American scene? Which values are *common* (shared), which are intense or less intense, which are persistent or transitory, which take precedence over others? To be at all specific about the structure of American value-systems, some concrete tests of value dominance are obviously needed.

Dominant and subordinate values *for a group or social system as a whole* can be roughly ordered to these criteria:

1. *Extensiveness* of the value in the total activity of the system. What proportion of a population and of its activities manifest the value?

2. *Duration* of the value. Has it been persistently important over a considerable period of time? [6]

[5] It should be noted at this point that "group value" is an ambiguous term that may refer either to (a) a *shared* value, as when "getting ahead" (as individuals) represents a value complex held in common throughout a group, or (b) a value *for* the group taken collectively (as military security may be so regarded). A "group goal" we may define as a future state of affairs intended to be reached by group (collective) action. ("Intended" means either explicitly stated, or inferred, by an observer.) Thus, a group goal is *not* necessarily identical, or even congruent, with the values, motives, or goals of individual members considered distributively.

[6] Or has it been thought important through time by the population in question? Not antiquity as objective fact, but antiquity as belief may be the

3. *Intensity* with which the value is sought or maintained, as shown by: effort, crucial choices, verbal affirmation, and by reactions to threats to the value—for example, promptness, certainty, and severity of sanctions.

4. *Prestige of value carriers*—that is, of persons, objects, or organizations considered to be bearers of the value. Culture heroes, for example, are significant indexes of values of high generality and esteem.

The application of these criteria may be illustrated by the value complex we call democracy. Let us, purely for purposes of convenient demonstration, define democracy as a combination of (a) high evaluation of individual persons apart from their extrinsic characteristics or positions, (b) elective rather than appointive or hereditary choice of leaders, (c) reliance upon discussion and group consensus in determination of collective policy, (d) reservation of certain minimal social rights on an equal basis to all group members. How would we, then, test the hypotheses (a) that democracy is or is not a value in America, and (b) that democracy does or does not occupy a dominant position in the value hierarchy?

The first step is to secure evidence as to the prevalence of democracy in the various institutions and subcultures of the society. To what extent is there democracy in family, education, religious group, stratification system, government, economic system? At once we are aware of great variation among and within the several institutional sectors. There are, for example, democratic and non-democratic family institutions. The criteria of democracy are met in full in some sectors of our political system, hardly at all in others. In the economic system, democratic organization is rare—hierarchy, subordination, and direction by authority are more usual.

As we take systematic inventory in this way, we find emerging from the mass of detail a pattern indicating that democracy is a widespread value in America. In comparative and historical perspective, the test of extensiveness shows a more pervasive emphasis on democracy in this society than in many other major systems,

---

more significant factor. This observation was suggested to the writer by R. Lauriston Sharp.

and examination of the historical record for the United States certainly shows a persistence through time of democratic values. However, there have been complex and often contradictory variations in this persistence in different periods and in different sectors of the society, and the specific meanings of democracy have changed in important ways. For instance, we have seen many manifestations of a tendency toward political democracy—such as the removal of property restrictions on voting and eligibility to office, and the abolition of slavery; we have noted, on the other hand, certain invasions of previously established rights—for example, the internment of Japanese American citizens during World War II. The more completely history is analyzed, the greater is our awareness both of the persistence of democratic values and of the inadequacy of summary characterizations of the culture as a whole. Attempts to estimate the *intensity* with which democratic values are affirmed, defended, sought, and maintained or the prestige accorded to democratic and nondemocratic culture bearers reveal similar complexity and variation.

Let us assume, however, that we have all the data specified earlier as requirements for determining the position of a value in a society. From these materials we can presumably say that value X is actually an operative value in the culture, and we can specify with some accuracy its place in the value hierarchy. We do not yet, however, have all the information needed for a definitive analysis of the part played by value X in the social system as a whole. For we have not yet faced the thorny problems posed by differing levels of valuation, differing degrees of ritualism or realism, and various types and degrees of value integration.

These levels of valuation of course represent analytic distinctions that overlap and crisscross in concrete experience. For example, the objects and events that are valued, typically are valued *both* as ends and as means to further ends. Likewise, the same value may have both ritualistic and nonritualistic modalities; or it may be the object of lip service, only, in one context and the focus of intense total behavioral involvement in another. Such complexities and variations, however, constitute questions of fact rather than of the scheme of analysis, which concerns us at the moment.

4. What Are Value Systems?

IT IS clear that in our society the range of interests, beliefs, values, knowledges, and so on is so great that *precise and detailed* characterizations can be done only for carefully delimited segments of the society. Any attempt to delineate a national character or typical American values or a national basic personality type is extremely hazardous not only because of serious gaps in the requisite data but also because of the enormous value-diversity of the nation. This diversity we know to be so marked that a common core of values that could be said to hold for even a plurality of the population would probably be quite thin and abstract. Furthermore, values change rapidly, especially in modern times, rendering any static cross-section inventory of only temporary validity.

These considerations explain why the present chapter speaks of American value-*systems*, rather than of American values. Certain common values and symbols may be of great importance in national integration, but we cannot be certain without further evidence. On the other hand, there are sound reasons for seeking value systems rather than discrete and isolated values. We might conceivably find that there are in fact no systems deserving the name; but looking for systems will keep us looking for relationships and interconnections, consistencies and inconsistencies, and hence help us to see form, order, and equilibrium where these actually appear.

"System" here refers to some determinate arrangement of parts or entities—that is, to a set of relationships that is more than a chance ordering of parts. To speak of value systems is, then, to imply that values are not simply distributed at random, but are instead interdependent, arranged in a pattern, and subject to reciprocal or mutual variation.[7]

In describing value systems in American society we are mainly concerned with the distinctive elements of these systems, and not

---

[7] James H. Tufts: *America's Social Morality* (New York: 1933), p. 24: "In studying the character of a group or of a people it is in point to look not only at this and that detail of conduct-business, politics, crime, philanthropy, vice— but also at the main end or ends, if there be such, which the group more or less consciously pursues."

with "universal" features shared by the human species as a whole. For example, we will give comparatively little attention to the unlearned biogenic "drives" or "needs" such as hunger, thirst, sex, activity, rest, and the like.[8] However important, this substratum of behavior is generic and subcultural; it does not specifically explain problems that are definitely sociogenic or cultural. All human beings know hunger, but hunger alone will not explain a Minnesota wheat farm, a culturally induced aversion to milk, or a social premium on dinner at the Waldorf Astoria. Of course, we shall deal with certain universal social values such as status and ethnocentrism; but our prime concern will be, not with the universality of these abstract patterns, but with their particular form and content in this particular culture.

5. The Problems of Consistency, Integration, and Levels of Valuation

EVEN the brief illustrative material so far considered suggests that American society does not have a completely consistent and integrated value-structure.[9] We do not seem to find a neatly unified "ethos" or an irresistible "strain toward consistency." Rather, the total society is characterized by diversity and change in values. Complex division of labor, regional variations, ethnic heterogeneity, and the proliferation of specialized institutions and

---

[8] For a brief summary of elementary social psychological theory regarding such "basic" needs see Muzafer Sherif: *An Outline of Social Psychology* (New York: 1948), chap. 2, especially pp. 19–31. Important recent work in the field of psychology is developing into a sharp challenge to the whole concept of "need." See, for example, the writings of A. H. Maslow, Dorothy D. Lee, Kurt Goldstein, Prescott Lecky, and Kurt Lewin.

[9] "A simple society with a culture all its own and with no disturbing contacts with the outside enjoys a success in conditioning its members no modern society can expect."—Ralph Linton: *The Study of Man* (New York: 1936), p. 110.

The theme of value diversity and change has been taken as the central thesis of a recent book with the revealing title *Problems of American Society: Values in Conflict* by John F. Cuber and Robert Harper (New York: 1948).

organizations all tend to insulate differing values from one another. Much potential conflict and strain—as well as much potential integration—is thereby avoided. Yet such insulation is itself peculiarly difficult to maintain in the American social order. For one of the most important features of that order is its delicate interdependence, especially in its economic and political structure. Because of this fundamental interdependence, individuals and groups holding different and often incompatible values not only become aware of one another but often interact directly. Millions of contact points involving problems of values are created in economic dealings, political activity, education, and other major areas of life. Simultaneously, mass communication creates gigantic magnetic fields of common and conflicting knowledges, judgments, beliefs, and values.

There are limits—although rather wide ones—to the degree of incompatibility of beliefs and values that can exist in cultures or in individuals short of the disappearance of a meaningful system. Clashes of value become crucial for social organization when they emerge in those areas of person-to-person interaction that are essential to the maintenance of the system—for example, in family life or in work relations. Persistent value-conflicts in these areas will lead, variously, to personality disorganization, to the emergence of insulating social mechanisms, or to the disruption of the system of interaction. Similarly, in mass behavior, persistent and widespread value-tension leads to political struggle, schismatic cleavages, or to the segregation of various groupings into a kind of mosaic society.

In America the whole problem presented by different levels of valuation has been newly emphasized by recent investigations such as Gunnar Myrdal's demonstration of the hiatus between the values of the American Creed and the operative values of the society.[10] The nominally dominant ideals of our society, for instance, would open opportunities for economic gain to all technically qualified persons irrespective of class, family membership, creed, ethnic or racial stock, religion, or other particularistic considera-

[10] Gunnar Myrdal, with the assistance of Richard Sterner and Arnold Rose: *An American Dilemma* (New York: 1944), Vol. I, p. xliii.

tions—and such has been the main tenor of the law, in spite of many exceptions. "Fair play" is often cited as a national virtue. Pronouncements of culture heroes, high officials, and other leaders have overwhelmingly emphasized a universal right to employment and other economic opportunities. Much of this ideal, however, has not become an integral part of daily life; there is a gap between culture and society marked by a lack of emotional commitment to this traditional value.

6. Major Value-Orientations in America

WE CAN now outline certain major value-configurations in American culture. For convenience, we will proceed by abstracting certain dominant themes from the many important regional, class, and other intracultural variations. The simplified picture that results will, of course, be inaccurate in every concrete detail— it will be a series of ideal types, subject to numerous exceptions. Nevertheless, these abstracted patterns will serve as working models against which variations and contradictions can be more clearly seen; the value configurations thus identified will represent *tendencies* only, but they will bring out certain regularities that would not otherwise be easily seen. As a first approximation we can use these tentative formulations in each instance as test cases.[11] For each alleged value-pattern let us ask: Is it actually an important value in American society? How do we know whether it is or not? Where does it stand in relation to other values? Within the total society, what groups or subcultures are the main bearers of the value, and what groups or subcultures are indifferent or opposed? How do the mutually supporting or antagonistic value-systems work toward or against the integration of the culture as a whole?

[11] Much of this chapter deals with matters on which we do not yet have clearly verified propositions or even an adequately organized body of facts. The author has tried to make plain where he deals with established facts and generalizations, and where not.

Such systematic questioning will help us avoid naive acceptance or rejection of the broad descriptive generalizations that follow. Reasonably adequate documentation is provided in the references cited, but limited space makes it impossible to present here anything like the full evidence *pro* and *con*. However, the entire preceding analysis should be considered in reaching conclusions. We will list a value or theme frequently observed in the American scene, cite a few illustrations, and comment briefly upon the nature and significance of the alleged value-pattern. That nearly every statement will bring up unsolved problems and gaps in existing knowledge represents, perhaps, the chief usefulness of the present compilation.

Many major themes in American culture have been identified. Thus, for example, Cuber and Harper maintain that it "would probably not be difficult to reach agreement, even among persons of diverse value orientation, that the following values are conspicuous parts of American culture." [12] The authors then list seven major patterns of value: monogamous marriage, freedom, acquisitiveness, democracy, education, monotheistic religion, freedom and science. This recent list agrees on several points with Coleman's compilation of "American traits," based on comprehensive sampling of the literature from early times down to 1940. Traits imputed to American society in all major historical periods included: associational activity; democracy, and belief and faith in it; belief in the equality of all as a fact and as a right; freedom of the individual in ideal and in fact; disregard of law—"direct action"; local government; practicality; prosperity and general material well-being; puritanism; emphasis on religion, and its great influence in national life; uniformity and conformity.[13] Coleman's analysis showed that nearly every conceivable value or trait had at one time or another been imputed to American culture by authoritative observers. At the same time, his "lexicographic analysis" did demonstrate a very substantial core of agreement that appears to reflect real and important value-constellations—different writers

[12] *Problems of American Society*, p. 368.
[13] Lee Coleman: "What Is American: A Study of Alleged American Traits," *Social Forces*, Vol. XIX, no. 4 (May, 1941), p. 498.

often formulate broadly the same values in different terms. Our own discussion of broad value-orientations now follows.

"ACHIEVEMENT" AND "SUCCESS"

First, American culture is marked by a central stress upon personal achievement, especially secular occupational achievement. The "success story" and the respect accorded to the self-made man are distinctly American, if anything is. Our society has been highly competitive—a society in which ascribed status in the form of fixed, hereditary social stratification has been minimized. It has endorsed Horatio Alger and has glorified the rail splitter who becomes president: "Periodic public opinion polls are not needed to justify the selection of Abe Lincoln as the culture hero who most fully embodies the cardinal American virtues. . . . Even the inevitable schoolboy knows that Lincoln was thrifty, hard-working, eager for knowledge, ambitious, devoted to the rights of the average man, and eminently successful in climbing the ladder of opportunity from the lowermost rung of laborer to the respectable heights of merchant and lawyer. . . ." [14]

Emphasis upon achievement must be distinguished from the broader valuation of personal excellence. All societies have standards of character and proficiency, and accord rewards to those best meeting whatever standards are most highly appraised, whether of military prowess, ritual knowledge, asceticism, piety, or what not. The comparatively striking feature of American culture is its tendency to identify standards of personal excellence with competitive occupational achievement. In the pure type, the value attached to achievement does not comprehend the person as a whole, but only his accomplishments, emphasizing the objective results of his activity. Because of the preoccupation with business, the most conspicuous achievements have been those centered in business enterprise. We can say, with Laski and many others, that

[14] Robert K. Merton: "The Self-Fulfilling Prophecy," *The Antioch Review* (Summer, 1948), p. 199.

the "values of the business man" dominate and permeate national life. Yet achievement has never been completely identified with sheer business success; for example, such an assumption does not account for the respect and prestige accorded to the professions. Seen in the context of other major value themes,[15] business success seems to be a dominant focus, but not the dominant value-pattern, in American society.

However, as already noted, economic success has been so heavily stressed in certain parts of our society as to impose a widespread and persistent strain upon institutional regulation of means used to attain this goal. At the extreme, only questions of technical effectiveness enter into the choice of means—thus the "Robber Barons," "business is business," and much organized crime, vice and racketeering. Perhaps the apogee of largely unrestrained economic acquisition was reached in the period of "business baroque" from about 1890 to 1912, when the leaders of business "exulted openly in power and riches, won by national centralization. . . ."[16]

Adequate research evidence is not as yet available to allow an accurate appraisal of the extent to which success rather than achievement has moved to the center of the values of our culture. Such evidence is greatly needed, for the question thus raised is fundamental to any real diagnosis of the current value-system. Whereas achievement refers to valued accomplishments, success lays the emphasis upon rewards. Amoral success-striving may not have gone to the lengths suggested by some observers,[17] but the

[15] The so-called success philosophy attains its full cultural meaning only along with a particular kind of moral individualism. See Cuber and Harper: *Problems of American Society*, p. 356: "The basic premise of this philosophy is that individuals, not classes, are the real competing units. A man is said to reap his reward by 'his own' efforts, skills, and perseverance."

[16] Miriam Beard: *A History of the Business Man* (New York: 1938), p. 641. For a similar period in the ancient world see Gilbert Murray: *Five Stages of Greek Religion* (London: 1935), p. 79. Compare also pp. 115 ff. for an analysis of the way in which the Good becomes assimilated to success (wealth and power) in a certain type of social order.

[17] Geoffrey Gorer: *The American People: A Study in National Character* (New York: 1948), pp. 169 and 172.

important point is that once success goals are divorced from the ultimate values of society, the way is opened for a corrosion of regulative norms.[18] If success alone becomes an overriding interest, the logical (although not inevitable) outcome is a nihilistic orientation in which power is deified—as in the "Fascist mentality." In the United States, the available evidence suggests that, even though success is often regarded as an end in itself and sometimes there is almost no positive relation between success and moral virtue, yet the success pattern is still linked to achievement, achievement is still associated with work, and work is still invested with an almost organic complex of ethical values. As Wecter has suggested, the American heroes are not merely successful—they must be successful within a certain ethical framework: they must be, or appear to be, "self-respecting, decent, honorable, with a sense of fair play; no Machiavelli nor Mussolini need apply." [19] The belief that virtue will be rewarded and that success attends upon effort dies hard; and in our culture failure is still more likely to be charged to defect of character than to blind fate, capricious accident, or impersonalized social and economic forces, and the wealthy and powerful still either desire or find it expedient to justify their position in the name of "service" and "stewardship."

The dimensions of success values may perhaps be clarified by an examination of the place of wealth and its attainment in the culture. Many foreign and native observers have viewed American society as grossly acquisitive and materialistic, as naively impressed by bigness, speed, wealth, and power. Such a view is too simple, as an examination of American attitudes toward money will illustrate.

We may begin by eliminating any interpretation such as "of course money is wanted because it is the universal agency for

[18] Some of the more important personality strains engendered by high levels of aspiration in a competitive order have been compactly analyzed by Karen Horney in several works; see, for example, *The Neurotic Personality of Our Time* (New York: 1937).

[19] Dixon Wecter: *The Hero in America* (New York: 1941), p. 482. (This comment has to be qualified to take into account a Huey Long and an Al Capone, as well as the hero worship of the movie stars who are presented as living in opulent success as the result of pure accident—unrelated to personal virtues.)

satisfying any desires that can be met by purchasable goods." [20]
For many profitable activities are socially condemned and not
widely carried on; and people strive intensely for wealth long
after their basic physical needs have been met or even after they
have achieved nearly every conceivable means for satisfying their
desires. Santayana's insight has more accurately indicated the
central function of money in the American value system: "It is the
symbol and measure he (the American) has at hand for success,
intelligence, and power; but as to money itself he makes, loses,
spends and gives it away with a very light heart." [21] In a society
of relatively high social mobility, in which position in the scale of
social stratification basically depends upon occupational achievement, wealth is one of the few obvious signs of one's place in the
hierarchy. Achievement is difficult to index, in a highly complex
society of diverse occupations, because of the great differences in
abilities and effort required for success in various fields. At the
same time, the central type of achievement is in business, manufacturing, commerce, finance; and since traditionalized social
hierarchies, fixed estates, and established symbols of hereditary
rank have had only a rudimentary development, there is a strong
tendency to use money as a symbol of success. Money comes to be
valued not only for itself and for the goods it will buy, but as
symbolic evidence of success and, thereby, of personal worth.

Much the same type of analysis applies to the so-called American
love of bigness. It is said that Americans are impressed by size
qua size; "bigger and better" is a childish love of quantity as such.
Actually the important thing is that "better" is presumed to be

[20] The American sociologist Charles Horton Cooley pointed out as long ago
as the turn of the century that "wealth as an object of ambition and a measure
of success owes its ascendency to its social implications, and the pursuit of it is
by no means a proof of materialism or sensuality. . . . The fact that a man
desires it, throws little or no light upon the real object of his ambition."—
Sociological Theory and Social Research (New York: 1930), pp. 222; the quotation is from the essay "Personal Competition," which first appeared as an
article in 1899.

[21] *Character and Opinion in the United States* (New York: 1920), p. 185. Cf.
Gorer: *The American People*, p. 177: "It can be said that, as a general rule, the
acquisition of money is very important to Americans, but its retention relatively unimportant."

implied by "bigger." Things are good not so much because they are big, but because goodness is assumed and bigness therefore means more of something already considered valuable. Again Santayana has well expressed the essential point: "Respect for quantity is accordingly more than the childish joy and wonder at bigness; it is the fisherman's joy in a big haul, the good uses of which he can take for granted." [22] Unquestionably, we are dealing here with a culture that values action and the mastery of the physical world,[23] and its whole history has been, in the main, an experience of expansionism and mastery: increasing population, increasing territory, increased levels of living, and so on indefinitely. Given the definition of such things as good, respect for quantity directly follows.

"ACTIVITY" AND "WORK"

In the United States is to be found what is almost the ideal type of a culture that stresses activity; it is no accident that the business so characteristic of the culture can also be spelled "busy-ness." Although one might quibble over Laski's flat statement that few Americans "find it easy to be happy unless they are doing something," [24] we know that a notable series of observers have overwhelmingly agreed that America is the land of haste and bustle, of strenuous competition, of "ceaseless activity and agitation." [25] In this culture the individual tends to "face outward"—to be interested in making things happen in the external world. In ideal type, he seeks to dominate the world of nature, to subdue and exploit the physical world around him. This pattern—which forms a *leit motif* in American history—may be explained historically, of course, as developing out of religious tradition, frontier

[22] *Character and Opinion in the United States*, p. 182.
[23] Cf. Laski: *The American Democracy*, p. 42: "No attempt to grasp the nature of the American spirit can be complete which does not emphasize the degree to which action is of its essence."
[24] Laski: *The American Democracy*, p. 15.
[25] See the summary in Lee Coleman, "What Is American?" pp. 492–9; also, Henry Steele Commager: *America in Perspective* (New York: 1947), p. xii.

experience,[26] ceaseless change, vast opportunity, and fluid social structure. Whatever its sources, the sheer fact of this emphasis on "action" is enough for present purposes.[27]

Directed and disciplined activity in a regular occupation is a particular form of this basic orientation. If Justice Holmes could say that the purpose of life "is to function," the resonance his words aroused in the culture applied particularly to *work* in a full time vocation. This high evaluation of work has been called typical of the culture by many students of the American scene.[28]

A strong cultural emphasis upon disciplined productive activity was to be expected in America during the first two centuries in which value systems were being generalized out of experience.[29] Work was required for *group* survival along the moving frontier from the first settlements until the continent had been won. The rule "he who does not work shall not eat" expressed the deadly struggles of the early settlement period. To this compulsion was added the dawning sense of the rich rewards to be had in a land of relatively unappropriated resources. Furthermore, the population was mainly recruited from the working classes of Britain and Europe;[30] except in a few areas of the South and New England, there was no aristocratic class to give prestige to leisure and to stigmatize manual labor and trade. Finally, there was the influence of the so-called Puritan tradition—that is, of all those varieties of

[26] Cf. Constance Rourke's characterization of the man of the frontier: "Strength was his obsession—size, scale, power: he seemed obliged to shout their symbols as if after all he were not wholly secure in their possession." *American Humor: A Study of the National Character* (New York: 1931), p. 36.

[27] For interpretations of this theme in literature see: Vernon L. Parrington: *Main Currents in American Thought* (New York: 1930); Henry A. Myers: *Are Men Equal?* (New York: 1945); Henry B. Parkes: *The American Experience* (New York: 1947).

[28] Lee Coleman: "What is American?" *Social Forces*, Vol. XIX, no. 4, (May, 1941), pp. 49–9; Tufts: *America's Social Morality*, pp. 38–43.

[29] Cf. E. T. Hiller: *Social Relations and Structures* (New York: 1947), p. 313.

[30] Max Savelle: *Seeds of Liberty* (New York: 1948), p. 219. "From the beginning, America was made up of what they call in England the middle and laboring classes, and it has aways remained so. This is, in fact, one of the important points about it."—James Truslow Adams: *The American: The Making of a New Man* (New York: 1943), p. 49.

Protestantism in which secular occupational activity was invested with religious sanction and in which successful works became a sign of grace. This "metaphysical drive to work" [31] permeated the older agrarian culture of this country [32] and exists even today in rural areas and among certain other subgroups that have not yet fully assimilated the more recent cult of success and conspicuous consumption.

In short, the emphasis upon work as an end in itself represented a convergence of factors all operating in one direction—a mutual reinforcement of self-interest, social recognition, and ethical and religious precepts; "work" therefore became a value incorporated into the ego ideal of the representative personality types of the culture and often approached the intensity of a true matter of conscience.

Although, as later discussion will show, work as an end in itself has lost a great deal of its earlier potency, it is still important to remember that it has formed one of the core elements in the historic culture. It was, however, closely linked to an agrarian social structure in which the independent farmer and the small business man were representative social types. In such a society, work was embedded in the wider meanings attached to these statuses. As the social structure has become more and more differentiated, as manual labor has lost its connection with the control of private property, and as differentials of wealth and power have become crystallized, work as such has been devalued. The focus of positive valuation is now shifting to certain patterns of achievement and success.

"MORAL ORIENTATION"

A third major value-configuration relates to a particular type of ethical quality in the total cultural orientation. Authoritative observers from De Tocqueville, through Bryce, Siegfried and others, down to such recent studies as those of Vernon L. Parring-

[31] The phrase used by Goetz Briefs: *The Proletariat* (New York: 1937).

[32] For a clear description see James M. Williams: *Our Rural Heritage* (New York: 1925).

ton, Margaret Mead, Gunnar Myrdal, and Harold Laski, have agreed on at least one point: Americans tend to "see the world in moral terms." They do not mean mere conformity to the detailed prescriptions of a particular moral code, but rather to a systematic moral orientation by which conduct is *judged*. It is asserted that the quasi-mythical figure, the "typical American," thinks in terms of right or wrong, good or bad, ethical or unethical. This attitude goes beyond questions of expediency or immediate utility —and beyond purely traditional or customary criteria of behavior —to test conduct against some systematic ethical principles. For example, Mead cites the query of a student who asked whether we *ought* to have a conscience.[33] And Myrdal says explicitly: "The conflict in the American concept of law and order is only one side of the 'moral overstrain' of the nation. America believes in and aspires to something much higher than its plane of actual life." [34] The presence of an element of moral overstrain in our culture seems to be established. It seems likely that this ethical tension is directly related to certain patterns of child-rearing in the society generally—however, this hypothesis remains to be proved. At least middle-class groups seem to teach children a moral code considerably more stringent than that practiced by adults in the same group. Parents hold themselves up as exemplary models— as "much better than they really are." [35] The emerging generation then becomes disillusioned about its parents and the contrast between nominal moral principles and actual practice; [36] yet the earlier ingrained ideals cannot be given up completely. This partial blocking in normative training has a wide range of consequences, including ritualism, "lip service," vacillating or compensatory behavior, "split between theory and practice," so-called "hypocrisy," and so on. Individuals facing severe tension between

[33] Margaret Mead: *And Keep Your Powder Dry* (New York: 1942), chap. 6.

[34] Myrdal *et al.*: *An American Dilemma*, Vol. I, p. 21. This phrase, however, is question-begging formulation, as we shall see in more detail later. "Overstrain" is itself a value-laden concept. However, it does suggest a strong tension between nominally dominant ethical principles and the pragmatic codes and exigencies of actual social life.

[35] Mead: *And Keep Your Powder Dry*, chap. 6.

[36] Cf. chap. 4 above.

their incorporated ethics and current social "realities" may resolve the conflict by developing a militant reform mentality [37] or becoming "cynical"—we often suspect that the self-styled cynic is a highly moral person who is reacting to loss of faith in the efficacy of his code. Often ideals are insulated from action or restricted to limited groups and narrowly circumscribed situations.

The central themes of morality in America have undoubtedly had a common base and unified direction, derived from Judaic-Christian ethics. Of special importance has been the so-called Puritan ethic. Beginning as a rigidly theocratic system, it has gone through drastic modifications. At first it was markedly averse to traditionalistic forms and uncompromising toward the profane world. At the extreme, there was literal determination to realize the kingdom of God on earth and a demand for a complete discipline of the total personality. When works came to be interpreted as a sign of grace assuring salvation, it was easy to arrive at a morality in which economic success became *prima facie* evidence of moral correctness.[38] In Laski's words: "What begins as a theocratic principle ends by becoming a tradition that it is not very easy to distinguish from utilitarianism. . . . To work hard, to lead an orderly life, to have a name for integrity and fair dealing, not to spend one's substance in reckless display, to have the resolution to carry out the purposes you undertake—it is, roughly, to an ethic such as this that the religion of America had been shaped when the basic tradition was formed." [39]

"HUMANITARIAN MORES"

We shall use the term "humanitarianism" to refer to another important value cluster in American society, meaning by it, em-

[37] Thus Harold D. Lasswell has suggested that anxiety from severe conscience assumed to be typical of much of middle-class America often leads to the attempt to enforce moralistic legislation upon others: "Emotional fixation upon the unqualified reaffirmation of 'principles' is one result of the anxieties generated by the threatened conscience." *World Politics and Personal Insecurity* (New York: 1935), p. 226.

[38] For interpretations of this aspect of our "moral orientation" see chap. 9 and its bibliography.

[39] Harold Laski: *The American Democracy* (New York: The Viking Press, Inc., 1948), p. 27.

phasis upon any type of disinterested concern and helpfulness, including personal kindliness, aid and comfort, spontaneous aid in mass disasters, as well as the more impersonal patterns of organized philanthropy. Do these things represent important values in America?

It would be easy to amass contrary evidence. We could cite the expulsion and extermination of the Indians, the harsher aspects of slavery, the sweatshop pattern in industry, and a long catalog of child labor, lynching, vigilantes, and social callousness in many forms. Probably few peoples have so copiously documented and analyzed what they themselves consider to be the "bad" aspects of their history—a revealing fact in itself, for it was broadly the same culture that produced the behavior, and then pronounced it undesirable or wrong. Even so, the evidences of humanitarian values meet all our tests for a major value. Certain patterns of mutual helpfulness and generosity were already apparent in colonial America—despite the stern theology and stringently disciplined individualism—and have persisted to an important extent down to the present time. Of course, it is only in a wide comparative perspective that the importance of the humanitarian mores can clearly be seen, making probable such hypotheses as "Americans are especially likely to identify with the 'underdog' rather than the 'bully.'" This identification is indicated in a quick, impulsive sympathy for people who are in distress "by no fault of their own"; in anger at the overbearing individual, group, or nation; in pride in America as a haven for the downtrodden and oppressed.[40] The proverbial generosity of American people toward other societies facing mass disaster—for example, earthquakes, floods, fire, famine—has elements of exaggeration and myth; but it does index a real and persistent theme broadly based on religious

[40] As in many other instances, the orientation has not been constant, and there are indications that the welcoming symbolism of the Statue of Liberty has lost much of its appeal in the mature economy of a world power in a time of international tension and crisis. Once again we must remind ourselves that values are subject to fluctuations and trends. Cf. Tufts: *America's Social Morality*, p. 35: "To speak of any single interest or end, as though the mind of the people were one and were settled upon the same objective throughout a period, is to assume too much unity and stability."

or quasi-religious ideas of brotherhood, even though it has often been overridden by dividing interests and competing values. The enormous range of relatively disinterested humanitarian activities in America—the commonplace Community Chest, the "service club" activities, the public welfare agencies, the numerous private philanthropies, and so on [41]—stands in striking contrast to the treatment meted out to "the poor" and the "sturdy beggars" in many other parts of Western society within the past two centuries.

As always, however, this value pattern does not stand alone but is reinforced and complemented, or checked and limited, by other values. Humanitarianism is closely related to the cluster of values implicit in the conception of a progressing equalitarian democracy. In the form of what might be called pseudo-humanitarian philanthropy, on the other hand, the pattern sometimes has lent itself to the justification of economic inequalities. Throughout American history, the humanitarian theme has clashed in a variety of ways with the conception of rugged individualism. Parrington has compactly summarized for an early period the conflict that still remains a prominent element in the shaping of the total value system:

> At the beginning of our national existence two rival philosophies contended for supremacy in America: the humanitarian philosophy of the French Enlightenment, based on the conception of human perfectibility and postulating as its objective an equalitarian democracy in which the political state should function as the servant to the common well-being; and the English philosophy of *laissez faire*, based on the assumed universality of the acquisitive instinct and postulating a social order answering the needs of an abstract "economic man," in which the state should function in the interest of trade.[42]

[41] The phenomenon of the "volunteer worker" is further evidence. There are reputed to be some thirty million persons in the United States who give unpaid help to various religious, social, political, civic, and service organizations. *Survey Graphic* (March, 1949), p. 137.

[42] Vernon L. Parrington: *Main Currents in American Thought* (New York: Harcourt, Brace and Company, Inc., 1930), Book III, p. xxiii.

EFFICIENCY AND PRACTICALITY

American emphasis upon *efficiency* has consistently impressed outside observers. The Germans even coined the term *Fordismus* to refer to the standardization, mass production, and "streamlined" efficiency of American industrialism personified on the Continent by the name of Ford. "Efficient" is a word of high praise in a society that has long emphasized adaptability, technological innovation, economic expansion, up-to-dateness, practicality, expediency, "getting things done." The mere listing of these words and phrases serves to bring out the multiple extensions of efficiency as a standard against which activity is judged. Such a standard is premised in the first place upon that active orientation to the world of the here and now, so characteristic of our culture. As we have emphasized, this crucially important canalization of interest at once sets this society apart from societies placing greater emphasis upon aesthetic, contemplative, ritualistic, mystical, or otherworldly concerns.

That being active is emphasized, however, tells us nothing about the kind of activity sanctioned. Even a culture centering its interest upon purposive technical mastery of its physical environment (and, to some degree, of its social problems also) might conceivably act in relatively traditionalistic ways. The Western world generally, however, has tended to unite activity and substantive rationality, focusing upon a choice of the most effective means for a given end. Since systematic wealth-getting, technological achievement, and productive organization of effort have been strongly sanctioned, pressure has been created to search for "better methods," with the result that America epitomizes high regard for efficiency in techniques. In this kind of social climate, there is high sensitivity to such epithets as "backward," "inefficient," "useless." "Technical values" are greatly appreciated; especially in skilled trades, technical, quasi-professional, and professional vocations there is systematic indoctrination in the standards of "doing a good job"—the difference between a skilled and an unskilled performance. Despite the continual pressure of pecuniary or profit-making considerations, the values of good technical performance certainly have a measure of independent influence.[43]

The elevation of sheer technique into something closely approaching a value in its own right involves the familiar tendency to turn means values into goal values through a gradual withdrawal of attention and affect from the original ends [44]—a development that is re-enforced in so far as immediate interests and short-run goals are stressed. A culture that in the first place tends toward an unhistorical and utilitarian orientation will be especially likely to encourage just those behavior patterns in which technical efficiency can become valued for its own sake.

Although efficiency can and has become in this way a true value, in certain areas of our culture it is a derivation rather than a basic theme. In economic activities and other fields that have acquired considerable autonomy apart from the ultimate-value systems of the society, the stress upon efficiency is a complex derivation from the values attached to action, to material comfort, and perhaps especially, to mastery over nature and disorder. For efficiency—like cleanliness, work, and systematic-universal ethics —is a *discipline*, and its meaning depends finally upon the broader meanings of the primary "orderliness" that underlies it.

Emphasis upon efficiency is obviously related to the high place accorded science (especially as translated into technology) and to the overweening importance attributed to practicality.[45] One of the blackest public curse-words we have is "impractical"—in the culture at large, the practical man is the good man, an embodiment of a major value. Although we could trace this interrelated set of attitudes back to the frontier tradition, there are more immediate influences in the contemporary culture contributing to its survival. "Practical" (pragmatic) orientation is basically short-range adjustment to immediate situations. The practical man concentrates upon goals attainable in the given situation and solves

[43] On the psychological side, closely related to Gordon W. Allport's "autonomy of motives."

[44] Robert K. Merton: "The Unanticipated Consequences of Purposive Social Action," *American Sociological Review*, vol. I, no. 6 (December, 1936), pp. 891–904.

[45] Laski: *The American Democracy*, p. 12.

immediate problems as they arise, leaving to others the more abstract and long-range problems. Thus it seems clear that practicality as a positive value involves very important presuppositions as to other values. For instance, it typically assumes the worth of the basic social order within which action occurs. It characteristically rests on a whole set of implicit premises, among which are the stress on *activity* and *rationality* already mentioned above.

Standards of pure efficiency can of course apply to any kind of human behavior; there is a technique for mysticism as well as a technique for producing automobiles. However, there is nothing practical, in the American meaning, in a dominant concern with purely aesthetic or intellectual interests, nor in veneration of the past; asceticism, philosophic withdrawal, pessimistic quietism have never very long or very greatly stamped the American ethos; such tendencies have been confined to depressed or oppressed cultural enclaves, to small sectarian movements, or to individuals alienated from the main currents of national life. In part this view of practicality lies back of the attitude caricatured in Henry Ford's dictum: "History is bunk." Americans have been called, though not with entire justification, a people without a sense of history, and it is significant that they generally have not been troubled in the least by such comments.[46]

The practicality theme represents at least three quite different although closely related dimensions: (1) the nature of the immediate ends for activity; (2) the guiding criteria for arranging ends into a hierarchy of value; (3) the implicit conceptual framework—the absolute social logics—within which values are perceived. With respect to the sanctioned immediate ends of conduct, we have already seen a convergence upon the goals of certain kinds of success, as defined by secularized Puritanism. Practicality as to concrete goals of actions correspondingly has meant the canalizing of action in the service of those specific life-models most highly approved in the general culture—broadly speaking, rational, strenuous, competitive striving for personal validation through occupa-

[46] The idea that America is a historyless civilization is, in fact, largely an illusion of observers who have not understood the basic world-view of the culture, especially its future orientation.

tional success. In so far as this definition of the situation has been accepted, only those things have been considered practical that contributed to this end. Second, as a guiding principle for arranging value priorities, practicality represents a particular form of what Max Weber called *Zweckrationalität* as over against *Wertrationalität*—the rational weighting of values in a pluralistic framework rather than overwhelming concern with a single value or end. In the latter case, all other considerations except the achievement of that end become irrelevant; in prototype this is the stand of the political or religious fanatic, the insatiable hedonist, the monomaniacal economic man. American standards of practicality seem to have led mainly in the direction of a multifaceted balancing of values. Finally, practicality affects the conceptual schemes (explicit and implicit) that broadly characterize the culture. Even American philosophy displays a practical and critical cast and has been in various ways pragmatic, instrumental, relativistic.[47]

Thus, the theme of practicality points us again to activistic, rational, and secular (but "ethical") emphases of the culture; at the same time, it hints of possible tendencies toward the dissipation of the content of "ultimate" values in favor of immediate adaptability to immediate interests and satisfactions. As a highly derivative pattern, practicality does not provide in itself any sure anchorage for continuing organization and integration of individual activity. In common with the emphasis on *procedure* in American concepts of freedom and democracy, the emphasis upon practicality indicates a society that has tended to take for granted the implicit value framework within which practical action acquires meaning and rationale.

"PROGRESS"

From the society's earliest formation there has been a diffuse constellation of beliefs and attitudes that may be called the cult of progress. This broad theme has no unitary value such as would tangibly regulate specific individual behavior, but is rather a

[47] Charles A. Beard and Mary R. Beard: *The American Spirit* (New York: 1942), pp. 661–70.

certain "set" toward life that has permeated a wide range of behavior patterns. Various aspects of this complex are those allegedly typical American traits discussed earlier—"optimism," an emphasis upon the future rather than the past or present, "boosterism," receptivity to change, faith in the perfectibility of the common man.[48] At least in the enterprising middle classes, progress has been a prime article of faith. Our rich vocabulary of epithets ("backward," "outmoded," "old-fashioned," "stagnant," and the like) can be understood *as epithets* only against the unquestioning assumption that the new is the better—that "forward" is better than "backward."

From De Tocqueville to Laski, inquiring foreign observers have been impressed with the faith in progress and the high evaluation of the future in the United States as contrasted with Europe. Americans have felt their present to be better than their past and have felt adequate to deal with a future that will be still better.

"Throughout their history Americans have insisted that the best was yet to be. . . . The American knew that nothing was impossible in his brave new world. . . . Progress was not, to him, a mere philosophical ideal but a commonplace of experience. . . ."[49]

The importance of the idea of progress is in part brought out by the examples of contrasting societies in which it has been, or is, absent. As John B. Bury has shown in a classic work,[50] the concept of progress has emerged only recently in history. For example, the ancient Greeks apparently believed in eternally recurring cycles, or else placed the Golden Age in the past. Medieval times tended to devalue radically the life of the present in favor of a static conception of society as far less significant than the supernatural world and the afterlife. Only with the breakdown of the feudal order and the emergence of a new society in western Europe did the idea become established that human nature is subject to continuous improvement and that society as a whole is inevitably moving toward a better order of life. This orientation, at first largely restricted to

[48] Coleman reports this general complex among the traits upon which writers on America have usually agreed.

[49] Henry Steele Commager (ed.): *America in Perspective* (New York: Random House, Inc., 1947), pp. xi and xiv.

[50] *The Idea of Progress* (New York: 1932).

small circles of intellectuals in Europe, was made to order for the formative years of the United States. In the beginning America was promise, rather than past; hope, rather than accomplishment. For a long period the promise was kept and the hope was fulfilled to a remarkable degree.[51] Belief in progress involves acceptance of changes, the idea that changes are tending in a definite direction, and the belief that the direction is good. To generations of Americans all three components seemed verified: things were changing, they were moving in a central direction, they were getting better.

In the form in which it had been molded by the Enlightenment, progress was conceived as the beneficent unfolding of man's capacities for reason and goodness. In the course of its later development, however, the idea picked up dominant overtones of Social Darwinism ("the survival of the fittest") at about the same time that its application was being more and more restricted to economic and technological realms. By the late nineteenth century, the concept had been largely assimilated to the values of a complex and expanding industrial order. Progress could now become a slogan to defend the course of technological innovation and economic rationalization and concentration. If small entrepreneurs, farmers, or urban workers felt economic distress, their condition could be considered a regretable but necessary and temporary by-product of the triumphant march of progress. Progress became identified with "free private enterprise," in fact, at a time when the individual entrepreneur was already clearly certain to be supplemented by vast economic organizations the development of which was to change the traditional *laissez faire* concepts of "private property" and "economic freedom."

MATERIAL COMFORT

In the 1920's during the triumph of the so-called New Era (of Permanent Prosperity), a highly critical French observer could say

[51] For the eighteenth century, Savelle comments: "The belief in self-help, and the faith in progress . . . sprang from the American's actual daily experience; they were true and valid because the individual and social achievements, repeated over and over again, had proved them so."—*Seeds of Liberty* (New York: Alfred A. Knopf, Inc., 1948), p. 220.

of Americans that they "consider it only natural that their slightest whim should be gratified." [52] Even during this period there were millions of Americans who would have considered themselves fortunate to secure basic necessities for nutrition and shelter; yet notwithstanding its exaggeration, Siegfried's comment points attention to the value placed upon a *high level of material comfort*. Even before World War II, the United States undoubtedly had one of the highest material levels of living in the world, as judged by such criteria as adequacy of nutrition, medical care, facilities for shelter, transportation and communication, and so on.

The fact that material comfort undoubtedly is highly approved and sought after in the culture [53] tells us very little in itself about what specific values are involved; the "American standard of living" has its undertones and overtones of meanings—from nationalistic identification, to symbol of success, competence, and power and from a token of moral excellence to something very close to a terminal "value" at the level of hedonistic gratification.

There is some criticism that passive gratification elements in American society have been receiving increased emphasis in recent decades. The most obvious although probably not the most important index of this trend is provided by commercial advertising that emphasizes comfort and effortless gratification: eat this, chew this, drink that; take a vacation; be catered to; and so on. The major focus is upon receiving, looking at, being catered to, in short, maximum pleasurable sensation with minimum effort or activity. It is estimated that every week in the year an average of more than eighty-five million Americans sit in the darkened confines of a motion picture theater to receive Hollywood's versions of life and history. "Spectator" sports fit the same pattern—huge audiences watch others perform.

The gratification motif appears in modern mass entertainment with all the clarity of a caricature. For motion pictures, Dorothy Jones's analysis of a hundred films appearing in 1941–2 showed a

[52] André Siegfried: *America Comes of Age* (New York: 1927).

[53] Cf. Laski: "No church which urged the desirability of asceticism had any hope of influence or much hope of survival." *The American Democracy*, p. 13.

predominance of the "happy ending"—at the end of the picture, about 60 per cent of all major characters were indulged with respect to all of their wants; about 10 per cent were deprived as to all of their wants; about 14 per cent were indulged as to some wants and deprived as to others.[54]

Lowenthal's study of biographies appearing in two mass circulation magazines from 1901–41 gives another illustration of the value stimuli to which Americans are exposed. He suggests that there has thus been a shift from the "idols of production" to the "idols of consumption"—from attention focused on substantial achievement in social organization and economic production to the people who embellish leisure time. "The first quarter of the century cherishes biography in terms of an open-minded liberal society which really wants to know something about its own leading figures on the decisive social, commercial, and cultural fronts." [55] But by 1940–1 the heroes are figures from the world of entertainment and sport—a "dream world" of leisure-time activities. Even within the general category of entertainment, the proportion from serious arts (fine arts, theater, music, etc.) declined from 77 per cent in 1901–14 to 9 per cent in 1940–1. Furthermore, in their content the more recent biographies emphasized the private lives and consumption of the subjects. "It is neither a world of 'doers' nor a world of 'doing' for which the biographical curiosity of a mass public is evoked. . . . Instead of the 'givers' we are faced with the 'takers.' " [56] Although the biographies approved in general of "doing things," success seems to be treated as something that merely happens—an accidental, lucky event—not a rational outcome of integrated effort.

The American experience gives some support to the hypothesis that in so far as a group or society is able to attain a high plane of material comfort, it will tend increasingly to emphasize the "hedonistic values," unless checked by internal social danger or

[54] Dorothy B. Jones: "Quantitative Analysis of Motion Picture Content," *Public Opinion Quarterly*, Vol. VI, no. 3 (Fall, 1942), pp. 411–28.

[55] Leo Lowenthal: "Biographies in Popular Magazines," in Paul F. Lazarsfeld and Frank N. Stanton (eds.): *Radio Research, 1942–1943* (New York: 1944), pp. 512–13.

[56] Ibid., p. 527.

outside threat. Apparently, at least in Western societies, the objective opportunity to secure material comforts elicits, in the long run, a desire for them. Once a high standard of living has been enjoyed, however, it is extremely difficult to reduce the level of sensation. As new wants emerge and are satisfied over a period of time, they become accepted, expected, "normal," and in this process they at the same time come to be felt as rights to which one has a moral claim. When the level of material comfort of a whole people has been rising over a considerable period of time, it will be reduced only reluctantly even under the duress of great social emergency.

EQUALITY

The avowal of "equality," and often its practice as well, has been a persistent theme through most of American history. Even modern economic organization, which in many ways epitomizes inequality,[57] has stressed "equality of opportunity." Yet few other value complexes are more subject to strain in modern times.

The United States began its independent political existence as a congeries of societies, which in the main had broken sharply with the traditions of social deference and with the hierarchical social structures that still characterized Britain and Europe. The generalization has its exceptions. New England had been ruled by an elite of the religiously elect. Remnants of feudal land customs had persisted for a time in various areas in such forms as quit-rents and primogeniture. Indentured servitude and imprisonment for debt had represented direct transmissions of neofeudal practices. But in general all individual arrangements embodying traditional social inequalities were dissolving.[58] In retrospect, as always, this result now seems to have been inevitable. Actually it was the conse-

[57] Note how far the ideology of Soviet Russia is from indicating the actual hierarchy of industrial organization there.

[58] "Feudalism never got a real footing in America. . . . The most striking feature of the land system of the colonists generally was the departure from the English system of primogeniture." W. Paschal Larkin: *Property in the Eighteenth Century* (London: 1930), pp. 140–1.

quence of a highly complex constellation of factors: laxity of political control by England partly as a result of the distance from Britain and Europe; only a small number of the colonists had been aristocrats, the majority was middle and lower class and many actively opposed some features of their parent society; mass accessibility to abundant resources, which made it possible for "anyone to become a king on his own" and thus helped to dissolve old hierarchies and social forms through movement, acquisition, independence, potential equality of all sorts and manners of men; the ideological forces; the deeply individualistic strain brought in through Protestantism, as well as philosophical and political ideas that worked in the same direction. (Locke and the French rationalists, for instance, affected not only the Founding Fathers but much wider circles of eighteenth century America.)

Other factors encouraging the emergence of equality as a value may be left aside for present purposes.[59] It will suffice here to see that this society in its formative periods was one that could, and wished to, break with its hierarchical tradition and that this result was favored by fundamental objective and ideological conditions. Thus, until the late nineteenth century America was able to develop without having to face widespread conflict between the principle of equality and the principles of achievement or freedom. In this remarkable historical experience, through generation after generation the values of equality were crystallized and elaborated. People saw the disappearance of primogeniture, the abolition of indentured servitude, of imprisonment for debt, of slavery, of property qualifications for voting and public office; there was provision for the common man to acquire a stake in the land and to secure a free public education; women gained one legal right after another; and even discriminations against minorities were sharply challenged time after time.

However, as De Tocqueville saw more than a century ago, America had to face sooner or later a conflict of values that he

[59] For example, the influence of geographic mobility, mutual dependence under frontier conditions, the lack of a complex division of labor and highly developed urban life, etc.

described as a contradiction between the principle of freedom and
the principle of equality. For instance, the cumulative effect of
freedom to pursue individual advantage, given the opportunities
and institutional framework of nineteenth century America, was
to destroy equality of condition. The liberty of which De Tocqueville spoke was a freedom from feudal or mercantilistic restraints
on the economic individualism so congenial to the early American
situation. But this freedom could only lead under the historical
circumstances to the emergence of what he called a manufacturing
aristocracy, an outcome far from the perfect commonwealth of
equal citizens that some idealizers of a yeoman republic desired.

Already it becomes plain that the meanings of equality are
various and that it does not help us very much to characterize a
society as simply equalitarian or the reverse. Modern America, of
course, shows inequalities of wealth, power, and prestige; and there
is far from being perfect equality of opportunity to acquire these
things. As Myers has eloquently indicated, men are not in fact
equal in any specific ability or capacity; [60] in a complex and
heterogeneous society they are likely to have very unequal access
to scarce goods. The extent of the so-called objective or material
inequalities, however, is itself in part a function of the basic value-
system.[61]

If equality is a basic value in our society, it must meet our
operational tests: (1) the individual must feel guilt, shame, or ego
deflation when he acts in inequalitarian ways; and (2) there must
be sanctions supported by the effective community for conformity
or nonconformity. The extensiveness of these reactions must be
weighed against parallel responses to any behavior manifesting
hierarchical principles of human relations. Although no such
quantitative assessment can be made from the available evidence,
it is nevertheless reasonably clear that inequalities, hierarchical

---

[60] Myers: *Are Men Equal?* The author, however, argues cogently for
intrinsic equality as a central element in the American ethos.

[61] When the modern proponents of "inevitable inequality" argue that
greatly unequal rewards are *necessary* in order to get the most *important* social
functions performed, it is seldom noticed that the question of necessity is
being begged along with the question of importance.

emphases, and various kinds of discriminations are common in American life. Taken as a whole America appears to present a highly confused situation in which conflicts and compromises are accompanied by myths, legends, and conventional fictions until the main value directions become excessively difficult to trace.

The problems can be grasped more readily if we differentiate among the several senses in which equality may be a value. It is useful, as we saw in Chapter 5, to distinguish between intrinsic and extrinsic valuations. Extrinsic valuations are those judgments of value that depend upon generalized social categories and external symbols of status such as sex, age, nationality, occupation, rank, income, wealth, medals, race, authority. Intrinsic valuation has to do with the immediately personal qualities of the individual apart from any categorical social attributes, and its presence is demonstrated wherever one person feels an obligation to treat another person as—in any degree—an end in himself rather than purely as a means. To put it negatively, the person is given an intrinsic value when we feel guilt or shame if we do not act with some regard for his presumed human sensibilities, regardless of his categorical social status or group membership. Whenever such intrinsic valuation is at work, it constitutes a "floor" below which the person cannot be devalued or degraded—a guarantee of minimal equality. Extrinsic valuations focus upon what a person *has*; intrinsic valuation concerns what the person is *qua* individual. It is obvious that the two imputations of value often do not coincide, as when we say that a man "doesn't deserve his rank," or "he may have a million dollars but he isn't worth two cents as a man."

At the level of explicit doctrine, intrinsic equality is widespread in American culture, both in the form of a specifically religious conception (the equality of souls before God, the divine nature within every person, and so on), and in the more secularized formulations that attribute an irreducible quantum of value to every person: "a man's a man for all that," "after all they are human beings," or the categorical imperative to "treat others as ends rather than means." At the level of overt interpersonal relations, adherence to a sense of intrinsic human value is discernible in a wide variety of specific behaviors—perhaps most obviously in "democratic manners." America has always impressed observers from more rigid and hierarchical societies as being marked by an extraordinary informality, directness, and lack of status consciousness in person-to-person contacts.[62] This general openness of social relations can only be maintained in a culture in which intrinsic personal value is a widespread and effective assumption.[63]

In more concrete terms, equality is exhibited in the way individuals actually *relate* to others in ordinary interpersonal activities. Are individuals in American culture typically related to others by superordination and subordination, or are interpersonal relations typically horizontal? The answer to so sweeping a question can be built up only by induction from the enormous variety of social rules actually existing in our society; a definitive analysis must wait upon a great amount of further systematic research. However, much of the evidence in the preceding chapters on the major institutions is relevant here: we have seen, for example, how the central family-type emphasizes equality of in-law families, and how the relations of husband-wife, parent-child, and sibling-sibling tend to be nonauthoritarian and nonhierarchical modes. In examining educational organization, it was suggested that, in spite of definite hierarchical emphases, the teacher-student relation in America is less rigid, formal, and authoritarian than in analogous European situations. On the other hand, we have seen much evidence of strongly hierarchical and authoritarian emphases, especially in large-scale economic and political organizations. And, running through the whole society, is the salient thread of non-equalitarian beliefs and practices concerning interpersonal relations with persons of a different racial or ethnic grouping. Nevertheless, in our provisional appraisal equality rather than hierarchy

[62] The references are numerous. See the works by Commager and by Parkes, already cited. Also Kurt Lewin: "Some Social-Psychological Differences Between the United States and Germany," *Character and Personality*, Vol. IV (1936), pp. 265–93.

[63] Cf. H. D. Lasswell: *World Politics and Personal Insecurity* (New York: 1935), p. 229: "The democratization of manners resulted in those 'man to man' forms of social intercourse which are so potent in reducing hostility against anybody who gets rich and stays a 'good fellow.' This relative universalization of deference claims has tended to nullify the consequences of a steep pyramid of wealth distribution."

seems on the whole characteristic of concrete social relations—although perhaps more clearly at the level of the *goals and standards* of conduct than in the uneven compromises of going practice. On this point, something approaching a crucial "experiment of nature" is available to us in the reactions of American soldiers to military life in World War II. Military organization is the example par excellence of hierarchy; in time of war its norms are supported by all the enormous social assent that war can generate. In World War II, the vast majority of American soldiers accepted the necessity of war and the legitimacy of military authority. Yet, as hundreds of specific studies showed, these same soldiers resented almost above all else the unequal privileges of officers and enlisted men and the insistence upon detailed observance of rituals of subordination and deference. It was clear also that one of the strongest forces that kept men working and fighting as organized groups was loyalty to their comrades and equals, that "team work" (the term is significant) rather than psychological dependence upon authority figures was the crux of the American version of military morale.[64]

A second major type of equality consists of specific formal rights and obligations. In the United States the strain toward equality of legal rights for all citizens or even residents has been strong and continuing. Formally equal civil rights—from military service to voting, from public education to taxation—represent not only freedom but also equality. In the sense of freedom these rights may be said to guarantee the individual a certain openness in his lifespace; in the sense of equality, they nominally establish a minimum life-space for every one. It is in this equality of specified rights that the second major theme of American equality has developed, rather than in doctrines of equal individual potentialities, achievements, or rewards.

The third type of equality is substantive equality of social and, above all, economic rewards. Here it seems quite clear that the

[64] See the findings presented in Samuel A. Stouffer *et al.: The American Soldier*, Vols. I and II (Princeton, N. J.: 1949), especially chaps. 6, 8, 9, and 10 of Vol. I, and chaps. 3, 6, and 7 of Vol. II.

principles of economic freedom and individual achievement have strongly dominated principles of equality.[65] The reigning conception has been that of *equality of opportunity* rather than *equality of condition*. Concessions toward substantive equality of condition—for example, the income tax in so far as it is graduated—have not leveled differences in wealth, and the upper and middle classes of the society continually have insisted upon a moral claim to the existing differentials. It is quite striking that one of the earliest and most widespread reactions to Marxism, as popularly understood, was to select precisely the idea of "equal distribution of wealth" as the target of censure and moral outrage.

Every principle of equality is subject to its sharpest violation in the case of minority groups, especially the American Negro. Few other aspects of our society are so well documented as this one.

In widest perspective it appears that the inequalities that are felt in American culture to contravene equality values most severely are of two kinds: first, the denial of nominally universal rights of citizenship and violations of nominally universal rules of impersonal justice; second, the denial of opportunities for achievement in the formally open competitive order. It is certainly true that American culture has never found it overly difficult to tolerate great differences in certain types of individual privileges or rewards. The tautology that inequality is not resented unless considered to be undeserved takes on an important meaning, however, as soon as we are able to specify what "undeserved" actually means. By and large in the United States, it has meant *categorical* privileges—rewards not earned by effort and achievement (including moral achievement) within the basic institutional rules for fair competition. Here is the core of "the American tradition" of equality. The dominant cultural value is not an undifferentiated and undiscriminating equalitarianism, but rather a two-sided emphasis upon basic social rights and upon equality of opportunity.

[65] Lewin: "Some Social-Psychological Differences Between the United States and Germany," p. 16: "In spite of the democratic idea of equality of men, proclaimed in the American Constitution as one of its basic principles, there are probably no other people as interested in *individual accomplishments* . . . as the Americans."

It is important to note the role of this value complex in the periodic resurgence of native, homespun "radicalism" in America. The historical record indicates that the demand for equality of traditional rights and equality of economic opportunity has not, in the main, grown out of imported ideologies, but has emerged from the received traditions. The long ground-swell of the Populist movement [66] in the late nineteenth century provides a good example of how American movements for economic reform, at least until the depression of the 1930's, have been essentially the attempt of the "little man," and especially of the farming population, to check the power of "big business." These movements never really challenged in any thoroughgoing way the concepts of private (individual) property and free enterprise; rather, they represented the counterattack of the old-style private (individual and familial) property and the free (small, independent, competitive) enterprise against the emerging forces of large-scale, corporate property and monopolistic industrial, financial and commercial combinations.[67]

It has been part of the fundamental pathos of American culture to believe that virtue should and will be rewarded—and more particularly that such economic virtues as hard work, frugality and prudence should receive a proportionate reward. The axiomatic value of this moral equation has been closely linked with the premise that everyone (at least, all in "one's own" group) has an equal right to fundamental opportunities. Without question, this whole principle is currently undergoing severe strain and extensive redefinition. Further discussion of these changes must be deferred to Chapter 14; the essential present point is that values of equality in the received American culture of the modern period have centered around the dual themes of civil rights and economic opportunity.

[66] An excellent source on this important phase of American history is John D. Hicks: *The Populist Revolt* (Minneapolis, Minn.: 1931).

[67] See the excellent discussion in Henry Bamford Parkes: *The American Experience* (New York: 1947), chap. 13. For example: "The antitrust laws were peculiarly American and were a product of the agrarian tradition; they had no parallel in Europe." (p. 292).

FREEDOM

We need no research to tell us that the verbal affirmation of the value of freedom is widespread and persistent.[68] The widespread positive reaction to the symbolic value of the word is illustrated in many ways. For example, a Gallup poll released in August, 1946, showed that freedom in general, or in some specific application, such as freedom of the press or of worship, is most often mentioned as the greatest advantage of the American form of government.[69]

That something real in actual social relations lies back of the word freedom cannot be doubted. Yet the reality is not in the unconditional listing of categorical freedoms, for it can quickly be shown that actual social life and "unconditional freedom" are contradictions in terms.[70] Furthermore, what are restraints from one point of view may be rights or "privileges" from another, as when a person wants "to do his duty" (and finds it to his advantage to do so).

American conceptions of freedom mainly stem from an orientation that characterized European thought for several centuries: freedom is compatible with causality and determinism; it does not mean uncaused behavior, but rather behavior that is not subject to restraints that are in some sense external and arbitrary. In this view, although behavior is always determined—that is, influenced, caused, or conditioned—it is nevertheless possible to give a definite meaning to the statement that it may also be "free." All life in society involves the limitation of behavior not only by the physical world, including the limitations of the human body and mind, but also by reciprocal rights and obligations among persons; every social group furthermore must cope with problems of authority and

[68] Savelle's conclusion from his study of the eighteenth century is: "Thus the great common denominator of American social thinking was the ideal of social freedom—freedom to rise, that is—individualism, and social fluidity. If the Americans still believed in aristocracy, it was now, in theory at least, predominantly . . . based upon the ideal of an aristocracy of merit, of individual worth." *Seeds of Liberty* (New York: Alfred A. Knopf, Inc., 1948), p. 280.

[69] See *Opinion News*, Vol. VIII, no. 6 (March 18, 1947).

[70] Cf. Linton: *The Study of Man*, chaps. 8 and 16.

power. What, then, is to be said of the American emphasis on freedom?

The historical context of freedom as a value pattern in our culture begins with the centuries-long process whereby area after area of life was removed from the web of interlocking controls of feudal Europe. With the rise of nation-states and of urban life and with the expansion of industry and trade, the settled, hierarchical society of Europe moved into an unprecedented colonizing phase. The American colonies were one result, and in them the trend toward emancipation was intensified. At one point it might be a struggle against quit-rents; at another, restiveness under mercantilistic restraints; still elsewhere, a revolt against an established religious hierarchy. Always the demand was for freedom *from* some existing restraint. That the major American freedoms were in this sense negative does not mean, of course, that they were not also positive: they were rights to *do*, by the same token that they were rights to be protected from restraint. Nevertheless, the historical process left its mark in a culturally standardized way of thought and evaluation—a tendency to think of rights rather than duties, a suspicion of established (especially personal) authority, a distrust of central government, a deep aversion to acceptance of obviously coercive restraint through visible social organization. At the time in which the primary political and economic structure of the new society was laid down, the great threat to freedom was perceived as coming from the centralized, absolutistic state, and the obvious course seemed to be to erect every possible barrier to centralized governmental control; the main import of the doctrine of checks and balances was to prevent the central state as much as possible from undertaking any positive action beyond a very few carefully defined areas of authority. Such a view of government reflected a society in which the politically effective elements of the community wanted above all to have "room" to make their own decisions, to develop their own spheres of social power, to escape from the surveillance of kings and ministers of state. This particular sort of freedom was premised on a sweeping faith: the confidence of the individual in his own competence and mastery.

It is thus in the peculiar features of the concept of freedom to which value is attached in America that our present interest centers. We know, for instance, that, when American leaders and the leaders of the Soviet Union say they value "freedom," the words do not carry identical value loadings. The differences cannot be wholly explained either as special pleading or as simple ignorance, and examination of the variation between the two orientations may help to clarify the American case. Broadly speaking, the Soviet conception of freedom emphasizes security in the sense of rights to employment, medical care, economic support, education, and cultural participation *within* an accepted framework set by the neo-Marxist state. In this system many of the liberties prized in Anglo-American culture are regarded as irrelevant if not meaningless. On the other hand, American spokesmen emphasize freedom of speech and assembly, a multiparty, representative political system, "private enterprise," freedom to change residence and employment.

The above contrasts, stated in oversimplified form, serve to pose more sharply the problem of what "freedom" it is that is valued in American society. In the historically developed orientation—which may no longer exist in the same form—the central principles seem reasonably clear. A major implicit cultural premise in the dominant valuation of freedom has been *the equating of "freedom" with control by diffuse cultural structure rather than by a definite social organization.* Thus, it has seemed to make a great difference whether the individual receives a certain income or has a certain type of occupation as a result of an apparently impersonal, anonymous, diffuse competitive process, as against "being forced" to accept that employment or remuneration by law or by the command of a visible social authority. A foreclosed mortgage has been culturally defined in a radically different way from governmental confiscation of the same property. To be tied to a given locality by diffuse cultural pressure and lack of economic opportunity is regarded as a quite different kind of constraint from such controls as a police order or a governmental regulation.

Upon this kind of axiomatic base, American culture has tended to identify a very great variety of forms of personal dependence as not freedom. To "work under a boss" was not so long ago regarded as a loss of freedom. The widespread reluctance to take employment as a domestic servant and the low evaluation attached to this type of occupation appear to reflect in part the same complex. One of the earliest and most persistent criticisms of American society by aristocratically minded foreign observers has concerned the absence of a docile serving-class and the impertinence of the lower orders.[71]

The underlying psychological constellation in traditional American attitudes toward freedom thus seems to be a posture of self-confidence and expansiveness, coupled with a tendency to reject all absolute claims to personal authority. This syndrome permeates relations of parents and children, men and women, employers and employees, the citizen and *Monsieur le Bureau*.

Viewed in these terms, the theme of freedom is far broader than any particular institutional sector of the society. It rests in the last analysis upon an even more basic conception of the individual as an integral agent, relatively autonomous and morally responsible. (See the section on "Individual Personality" that follows.) Above all, a sociological analysis must make explicit the difference between *freedom as a value* and the *particular historic definitions of freedom in terms of special institutional forms*. Liberty in America began as a release from certain political restraints; the economic liberty thus secured was eventually accompanied in its turn by discords and dislocations in the social structure. In our day the greatest threats to freedom, conceived in liberal democratic terms, appear in economic dislocation and class conflict. The reaction to this situation has given us a "welfare state" in which freedom is no longer so clearly tied to a social system of private property and inactive government. The necessary implications for freedom as value are by no means wholly clear; it is patent, however, that the dated and localized definition of freedom as practically synonymous with eighteenth century economic philosophies is no longer accepted by the great majority of people in our society.

The core meaning of this shift can perhaps be illustrated by a glance at the so-called *laissez faire* economics, which was so much more than either *laissez faire* or economics; it constituted, in fact, a

[71] Beard and Beard: *The American Spirit*, p. 488.

whole system of social philosophy, an elaborate and interconnected set of social values and beliefs. The conception of man around which the doctrine centered was that of the discrete human atom, calculating his economic self-interest and acting "rationally" in the unlimited pursuit of gain. The "perfect system of natural liberty," suitable to this concept, would guarantee the sanctity of contracts, the stability of media of exchange, and the rights of private property. In such a system, so its proponents believed, "when men are free from all governmental interference, virtue finds its tangible reward in wealth and vice its penalty in economic failure." [72] In this way religious axioms were assimilated to the theory of universal social good through economic competition. Support of such a system, under a political democracy, was sought through an additional doctrine, which in this case held that the economically successful are fittest because this very success attests to their moral superiority. Freedom then becomes the economic freedom of the entrepreneur, and democracy becomes a form of government giving maximum protection of property rights. Progress becomes technological advance and economic expansion. Individualism is equated with the right of the individual to use his property as he sees fit, within very broad limits, and to compete freely with others. Society is a neo-Darwinian jungle in which only the fittest *should* survive, and the fittest are those who can win out by intelligence, industry, or ruthlessness.

This "organic" cluster of doctrines has foundered against twentieth-century realities. Because the cultural definition of freedom has changed and because the threats to freedom are now apprehended in different quarters it is easy to assume that the emergence of the welfare state signalizes our departure on a "road to serfdom." We suggest that the status of freedom *as value* must not be prejudged because of changing social mechanisms. There probably is no such psychological entity as freedom; rather it inheres in the *logical implications* of certain types of behavior, of interpersonal relations, and of institutional control structures. So

[72] Myers: *Are Men Equal?*, p. 140. The passage cited is a paraphrase of the doctrines of Sumner, the Yale sociologist and economist, whose theories are a quintessence of social Darwinism.

long as American society safeguards the right of the individual to a wide range of moral autonomy in decision making, so long as the representative character structure of the culture retains a conscience that is more than simple group conformity—so long will freedom be a major value. Emphatically, institutional forms are not unimportant; but their significance must be found by specific analysis and not by uncritical prejudgment.

It remains to be said that freedom has not meant and does not now mean a wide latitude for idiosyncrasies of individual belief and behavior. Someone has said that "every Frenchman is different, and the more different he is the better he likes it." Regardless of the dubious accuracy of this formulation as applied to French culture (e.g. Norman peasants), it certainly could not be applied to describe the American situation. For an appraisal of the value of "external conformity" we turn to the next section.

EXTERNAL CONFORMITY

Even as early as the 1830's De Tocqueville commented on the necessity of safeguards against a possible "tyranny of the majority" in America and thought that public compulsion had already penetrated into private affairs in a censorious way not usual in the France of his day. Nearly a century later Siegfried, another and more critical Frenchman, visualized America as a land of vast uniformity in speech, manners, housing, dress, recreation, and politically expressed ideas. In 1948, Laski pointed to an "amazing uniformity" of values, thought that "business *mores*" had permeated the culture, and tried to show that "the American spirit required that the limits of uniformity be drawn with a certain tautness." [73] Many Europeans in the period prior to World War II had thought American conformity-behavior to have a certain harried, compulsive quality, and have referred to standardization, "flatness," and lack of individuality in comparison with the Continent. In the period between 1920 and World War II European observers seem to have been especially (and overly) impressed

[73] *The American Democracy*, pp. 49–51.

with conformity themes in America. Thus, Muller-Freienfels, in a book published in 1929: "Distance, uniqueness, and originality are European values, which are foreign to the American. His values are the very reverse of these: adherence to type, agreement, similarity." [74]

These appraisals—which in fact have often been biased and exaggerated—come as something of a shock to a people that has made much of individual initiative, the rights of the individual, personal independence, "rugged individualism." Yet it should be no surprise that an intensely active, democratic society should define tolerance of individual nonconformity largely in terms of sanctioning technological and economic innovation. In the field of so-called personal morals, the culture is one that still bears the impress of theology; there is a tendency to legislate conformity—a tendency acted out again and again from the early "blue laws" to Prohibition and the Hays Office. In the field of intellectual heterodoxy, although the United States has produced its Thoreau, its Henry George, its free thinkers and dissenters, a considered judgment would be that really radical nonconformity in speculative thought has not been outstanding, at least in comparison with other countries of Western culture. American "individualism," taken in broadest terms, has consisted mainly of a rejection of the state and impatience with restraints upon economic activity; it has not tended to set the autonomous individual up in rebellion against his social group. In a nation of joiners, individualism tends to be a matter of "group individualism," of the particularized behavior of subcultures.

Men universally seek the approval of *some* of their fellows and therefore try to be "successful" by some shared standards of achievement or conformity. This characteristic is the outcome of universal requirements of group life and of the basic nature of the socialization process; otherwise stated, conformity and the desire for social approval are formal qualities that are part of the very

[74] Richard Muller-Freienfels: *Mysteries of the Soul*, trans. by Bernard Miall (London: 1929). This view has been common among those who feel that if industry turns out standardized goods for a mass market it follows that the whole culture is "standardized."

definition of society. Our real interest is in knowing how rigid the conformity is and what specific content defines conformity or success in a particular group or culture. There are societies in which conformity may be a matter of proficiency in religious ritual, others in which it consists of exemplifying warrior virtues, others in which aesthetic activities are the measure.[75] Similarly, in all societies men tend to conform to the groups with which they are most deeply identified, but both the degree of conformity and its kind differ greatly in various cultures. In short, conformity can be treated as a value only in so far as *sheer adherence to group patterns* is actually divorced from the content and implications of those patterns. It is only among a people who have lost the capacity for autonomous value-decisions that the sheer conformity of a goose-step order can approach a terminal goal.

It is useful to examine American conformity emphases for the light they may throw upon other dimensions of the value system. Several general sociological hypotheses are relevant to this examination. We know that where a functioning group or society feels threatened from the outside, it tends to tighten social controls over behavior involving the group's solidarity and striking power. Wars supply the most dramatic examples, but the political "witch hunts" in periods of international tension are equally in point. We know further that a group ridden by internal insecurities and tensions will, under certain conditions that need not be specified here, tend to raise its threshold of toleration for nonconformity: "The looser the package, the tighter must be the string"— if the package is to hold together at all.[76]

---

[75] "A few hundred years ago it seemed the most natural thing in the world to the ambitious among our ancestors, to sell off their property, raise a company and set off to the Holy Land to rescue it from the infidels. This is incomprehensible to us, but we see nothing strange in a man of ambition and imagination devoting a lifetime of strenuous endeavor to the making of tubs or the organized slaughter of hogs." Charles Horton Cooley: *Sociological Theory and Social Research* (New York: Henry Holt & Company, Inc., 1930), p. 225.

[76] An alleged insecurity factor in American conformity has been often suggested. A representative statement is: "Today America shows perhaps more conformity in externals than any other country. . . . Americans had to establish a social tradition of their own to hold them together." H. M. Spitzer: "Presenting America in American Propaganda," *Public Opinion Quarterly*, Vol. IX (Summer, 1947), p. 219.

Some preoccupation with external conformity is to be expected in a society in which upward social mobility is highly prized and frequently achieved. The competitive striving of an upwardly mobile group in a society organized around the economic enterprise requires stringent discipline over the expression of sexual and aggressive impulses, over patterns of consumption, over the uses of time and resources. In this aspect, conformity is derivative from equality of opportunity in conjunction with success-striving. Furthermore, an emphasis upon external conformity easily develops out of the premise of basic human equality: if all are equal, then all have an equal right to judge their fellows and to regulate their conduct accordingly to commonly accepted standards; some such cultural equation has been widely accepted in the broad middle classes of American society. The exceptions to the pattern occur in those classes and groups in which special license follows from exclusion of the group from the application of principles of equality (for example, Negroes, the very rich, certain *declassé* strata, and so on).

Interestingly enough, the very heterogeneity of American culture tends to produce a stress upon external conformity. Given the varied cultural backgrounds of the population and the desire that the various groups should continue to live together in the same society, conformity in externals becomes a sort of "social currency" making it possible to continue the society in spite of many clashes of interests and basic values. If it is gradually learned that the exhibition of cultural differences—whether they be of dress, or language, or religious faith, or political philosophy—seems to lead to friction in interpersonal relationships or even to public disturbances, a whole series of complex adjustments are set in motion. Among the possible responses to such a situation is the practice of withdrawing tension-producing items from general social circulation: for example, one finds popular maxims such as "never argue about religion or politics." [77] The individual comes to reserve controversial matters to an intimate social circle of like-minded

[77] Obviously if people felt strongly enough about these difference-provoking symbols, this would not happen. The American situation implies that agreement on procedure has dominated over disagreement on other values.

persons; public discourse and behavior is correspondingly more highly standardized. An elaborate social currency develops; set conversation-pieces, clichés, and standardized public opinions that can be passed smoothly along the channels of social interaction almost as a counterpart to the flow of money in the exchange economy.

The economic system itself contributes to the conformity theme in two other main respects. First, the high degree of specialization of economic roles in a highly developed money economy means that much social interaction is functionally specific, impersonal, transitory, and frequently laden with clashes of immediate economic interests. These are precisely the kinds of conditions most likely to produce conventionalized or stereotyped behavior.[78] Secondly, the relations of individual economic dependence are often such as to permit stringent conformity demands: a pattern caricatured in the Hollywood "yes-man," or *The Hucksters*.

SCIENCE AND SECULAR RATIONALITY

It has become a commonplace observation that the application of science and related secular rational approaches have transformed the external conditions of American culture—along with many other major cultures of the world.[79] Applied science is highly esteemed as a tool for controlling nature. Significant here is the interest in order, control, and calculability—the passion of an engineering civilization. This interest is congruent with the externalized orientation that we have already met in several previous guises; historically it is linked also to the fundamental assumption of an

[78] Cf. James W. Woodward: "The Role of Fictions in Cultural Life," in *Transactions of the New York Academy of Sciences* (1944).

[79] Compare the statement of a prominent physicist: "Our culture has the outstanding property of striving to convert all experience into rational scientific knowledge."—Henry Margenau: "Western Culture and Scientific Method," in Lyman Bryson, Louis Finkelstein, and Robert M. MacIver (eds.): *Conflicts of Power in Modern Culture*, Seventh Symposium of the Conference on Science, Philosophy and Religion (New York: 1948), p. 16.

ordered universe in which rational human beings can continually improve their situation and themselves.[80]

But the prime quality of "science" is not in its applications but in its basic method of approaching problems—a way of thought and a set of procedures for interpreting experience. We need only mention the long history of the "warfare of science and theology" in order to suggest the conflicts of belief and value that have accompanied the rise of science. However, it may be well to remember that the antievolution trials occurred only a few years ago, and that popular attitudes toward science still contain strong ambivalences. The caricature of the "diabolical scientist" co-exists with the stereotype of the benevolent laboratory magician. Faith in science is a faith; its continued existence is dependent upon other convictions, and these other convictions are interdependent with the real social structure. Science is a particular manifestation of the rational-theoretic theme, which Northrop among others regards as a distinguishing feature of our entire culture.[81] It is this ordering and stabilizing component that links science to the broader tendency in our culture to translate experience into systematic abstract concepts—to transform the fleeting, confused flow of immediate experience into standardized categories that permit, and in part create, prediction and control. Thus, science, socially considered, is above all a *discipline*, as Max Weber has so eloquently shown.[82] Our main interest here is accordingly to ask: a discipline for what?

Very broadly, emphasis upon science in America has reflected the values of the rationalistic-individualistic tradition. Science is disciplined, rational, functional, active; it requires systematic diligence and honesty; it is congruent with the "means" emphasis of

[80] Clyde Kluckhohn and Florence R. Kluckhohn: "American Culture: Generalized Orientations and Class Patterns," in ibid., p. 111: "Our glorification of 'science' and our faith in what can be accomplished through 'education,' are two striking aspects of our generalized conviction that secular, humanistic effort will improve the world in a series of changes, all or mainly for the better."

[81] F. S. C. Northrop: *The Meeting of East and West* (New York: 1946).

[82] Especially in his *"Wissenschaft als Beruf,"* in H. H. Gerth and C. Wright Mills (trans. and eds.): *From Max Weber: Essays in Sociology* (New York: 1946).

the culture—the focus of interest upon pragmatism and efficiency and the tendency to minimize absolutes and ultimates. The applications of science profusely reward the strivings for self-externalizing mastery of the environment. We think it fair to say that science is at root fully compatible with a culture orientation that attempts to deny frustration and refuses to accept the idea of a fundamentally unreasonable and capricious world.

In recent years certain social scientists have held that science is "morally neutral." If they mean merely that science cannot allow its findings to be distorted by value presuppositions extraneous to its accepted methods and models of proof, then these statements are acceptable. But it must be quite obvious that the findings of science will often have important value implications. It must be clear that the problems chosen for study are, or may be, selected in part on the basis of nonscientific values. Finally, the existence of basic theoretic science and the free exercise of scientific method presuppose a definite social structure and system of values.[83] Honesty and clarity are not just luxury virtues in science; on the contrary, they are essential defining characteristics. The same can be said for the faith in the order of nature and the faith in human reason—these are elements of a definite credo, manifesting values that are widely assaulted in the contemporary world. Their preservation in America apparently depends upon the continued and adequate functioning of an orderly, pluralistic society.

NATIONALISM-PATRIOTISM

In every society we find men participating in certain groups to which they feel they owe loyalty and with which they identify themselves—and we find other groups identified as outgroups toward which the individual feels estrangement, sense of difference, or enmity. This distinction, in small, localistic nonliterate societies, is often so sharp that others are not considered "men." Analogous

[83] There are societies where biological theories must conform to political doctrines.

situations exist in the so-called complex civilizations, perhaps most strikingly in the denial of a common humanity to the enemy in time of war. Such intergroup cleavages involve that scaling of values called ethnocentrism, that is, the diffuse value-attitude making one's own group the point of reference for judging all others. All known societies are to some extent ethnocentric; individuals everywhere give a preferential value to their own culture. Strictly speaking, ethnocentrism applies to every distinctive group from the smallest clique to the largest civilization. Today, however, the sentiments attached to the nation-state have overwhelming importance, and nationalistic feelings seem the prime example of ethnocentric values. For this reason, it is particularly important to examine the place of nationalistic or patriotic values in the social system of America. We are dealing here with a diffuse and extremely complex phenomenon, and can do no more than to suggest a few very elementary points.

First, we distinguish between two polar types of nationalistic values that are inextricably mingled in concrete situations. The first type may be described as undifferentiated or totalistic nationalism, demanding total and unquestioning allegiance to national symbols and slogans and tending to make "Americanism" a rigid orthodoxy. Criticisms of any features of American life are close to treason, and "un-American" is the epithet for any deviation from a rigid, although vaguely defined, cult of conformity. The quasi-religious character of this complex is manifest in its creedal emphasis, its concern with ritual and symbolism, its elaboration of dogma and its correlative "inquisitions." The contrasting ideal type of national-patriotic orientation tends to place less emphasis upon undifferentiated loyalty, rather conceiving of patriotism as loyalty to national institutions and symbols because and in so far as they *represent* values that are the primary objects of allegiance. Thus, "America" may be felt as worthy of loyalty because it is considered to embody or to stand for political democracy, respect for individual personality, a high standard of living, freedom of worship, or any other important value. This pluralistic patriotism usually presupposes basic acceptance of the nation-state as a framework of allegiance, but it does not preclude critical appraisal of men, events or policies in value terms broader than those of in-group loyalty as such.

The possible tension between these contrasting orientations [84] is compactly summarized by the fact that a legislative group concerned with "un-American" activities can itself be condemned as un-American.

Nationalism in the modern sense is, of course, a relatively recent development in Western history. In the case of American nationalism, it is clear that the early colonists for a long time thought of themselves as Englishmen (or Germans, Swiss, etc.) rather than "Americans." Even after the establishment of the new nation it was not uncommon to find that "my country" might as well mean Dinwiddie county, Virginia, or the state of Vermont, as the nation taken as a whole.[85] It took the Civil War and a whole series of subsequent developments [86] to really displace provincial patriotism in favor of national feeling.

An important component of American nationalistic values is that a generalized sense of fulfilment and confident hope has been built into the culture for over two centuries, and even the shocks of recent depressions, wars, and other deep crises have not dissipated the widespread satisfaction of a people who feel that the country "has been good to them." Indeed, in some respects World War II and its aftermath seem to have reinforced the attitude by producing a vivid sense of the misery of other areas of the world. Bearing on this point, roughly comparable public opinion polls in a number of countries indicate that only in Australia (itself also a "colonial"

[84] Cf. Max Savelle: *Seeds of Liberty*, p. 568: "The split in nationalistic pride between those who glorify the melting-pot and those who fear the un-American activities of foreigners whose ideals do not exactly coincide with their own is no new thing; it has apparently been one of the dialectical strains within American nationalistic feeling almost from the beginning."

[85] Merle Curti: *The Roots of American Loyalty* (New York: 1946), chap. I.
Even in World War II, an appreciative chord was struck by the Secretary of the Navy when he told a Texas gathering that he had been assured that Texas would not make a separate peace.

[86] For example, modern methods of communication and transportation which break down the barriers between local communities. It may be added that the modern cult of nationalism has emerged concurrently with the dramatic weakening of family and other *gemeinschaftliche* structures, and there are apparently definite functional connections between these two developments.

nation) do so small a proportion of the people as in the United States express any desire to live in another nation.[87]

This sense of satisfaction incorporates supposedly *universal* values. A purely tribal patriotism conceives of its culture as having a unique destiny and does not think of extending its values to the rest of mankind. But American nationalism, like the religions that have contributed so heavily to the culture, involves the idea that the American way of life is so obviously morally superior that it should be widely adopted elsewhere.[88] This secular counterpart of the missionary spirit is both an index of the strength of nationalistic feeling and a potent source of understanding and resentment in international affairs. In peace as well as in war, the United States must appear to itself to have a mission as a crusader for righteousness.[89] Other peoples have not always regarded the matter in that light.

The universalistic elements in national feeling, however, have conflicted with certain kinds of expansionism, on the one hand, and tendencies toward isolationism and national autarchy on the other. American expansionism in its earliest phases was undertaken by the pioneer, the speculator, the trader, and the missionary, and aimed at the possession of the land, chiefly through purchase, rather than at the conquest and the rule of alien peoples. It was only toward the close of the nineteenth century when the economic exploration of our own backwoods was nearing completion that chauvinism of an expansionist turn became widespread.[90]

On the other hand, autarchic nationalism goes back to the very beginnings of the Republic. A sense of alienation from Europe, a "belief in the degradation of the Old World and the mounting fame of America . . ." (Curti), was common even before the Revolution.

[87] Surveys by International Gallup Polls, reported in *Opinion News* (June 15, 1948). (National Opinion Research Center, University of Chicago).

[88] Concerning the very tangible influence of a moralistic orientation, with its attendant "sense of mission," upon America's role in world affairs, see chap. 14 of Henry B. Parkes: *The American Experience.*

[89] This is abundantly documented in many studies. See for example Curti: *The Roots of American Loyalty*, pp. 48 ff.

[90] James Truslow Adams: *The American*, pp. 304 ff. and 346 ff.; Miriam Beard: *A Short History of the Business Man*, chaps. 24 and 25; Curti: *The Roots of American Loyalty*, p. 6.

The entire socio-economic situation of early America encouraged turning attention away from Europe and the past and toward the mastery of the new continent. Thanks in large part to geographic position—and the British Navy—nineteenth-century United States could with impunity make a slogan of the doctrine of no entangling alliances. The isolationism that began as a matter of necessity and historic accident became a positive virtue throughout a good part of the nineteenth century. Although the old-style isolationism has been rendered objectively impossible by World War II and its aftermath, some of the values it symbolized remain active in the current scene.

Perhaps the most important sociological generalization that can be invoked here is that intense nationalistic conflict will always have drastic consequences upon the value systems of a democratic society. In particular, it inevitably brings in its train a large military class—and a centralization of social power. The military state must by its own terms of existence have centralized control of production; it must regulate consumption—there is actually no more infallible prescription for the destruction of *laissez faire*, the free market and the individual entrepreneur.

DEMOCRACY

Like freedom or progress, democracy in American culture is a highly complex and derivative theme. The nation that fought a great war under the slogan of making the world safe for democracy lives under a Constitution that contains no direct reference to democracy; the democracy of the Founding Fathers is not that of twentieth century industrial society; the meaning of democracy is one thing to the American Negro and another to the Ku Klux Klan. Here again the cultural meanings of a value theme and its actual role in social structure are full of complex variations, conflicts, and shadings through time and from one part of the society to another at a given time. Furthermore, the content of democracy is in considerable part subsumed under other value complexes discussed elsewhere in this chapter: for example, freedom, equality, humanitarianism; and, in any case, a reference to democracy does not denote a clear, unitary value but a multiple nexus of more specific beliefs and primary values.[91] Nevertheless, no matter how elaborately qualified, the sheer prevalence of culturally sanctioned attention to something called democracy [92] forces us to include it in our listing of major value-themes.

Along with majority rule, representative institutions, and the rejection of the monarchical and aristocratic principles under which the society began, early American democracy stressed the reservation of certain "inalienable rights" as unalterable by majority rule. [93] Basically this sort of democracy rested upon the implicit belief in natural law as opposed to personal rule, and in the moral autonomy of the individual. The actual shape of the democratic credo was a synthesis of clashing ideologies; but it was the insistence of the average citizen upon equality of political rights that actually forced the Bill of Rights into the Constitution. Major themes in the gradual crystallization of the main democratic creed thus included equality of certain formal rights and formal equality of opportunity, a faith in the rule of impersonal law, optimistic rationalism, and ethical individualism. What the Kluckhohns have called the cult of the common man [94] was a major expression of the democratic ethos that developed out of these definitions of man and society. As already suggested in the discussion of freedom, the theme of democracy was, concretely, an agreement upon *procedure* in distributing power and in settling conflicts. Liberal democracy, American model, arose in reaction to an epoch in which the great threats to security and freedom were seen in strong, autocratic central government. The new system was devised in such a way as to limit and check centralized governmental

[91] Cf. Carl Becker's comment that democracy is a word "which has no 'referent'—there is no precise or palpable thing or object which we all think of when the word is pronounced." *Modern Democracy* (New Haven, Conn.: 1941), p. 4.

[92] It is sufficient to note that Coleman ("What is American?", p. 498) found that democracy is one of the few "national traits" mentioned by observers in all major historical periods.

[93] James Truslow Adams: *The American*, p. 258.

[94] Clyde Kluckhohn and Florence R. Kluckhohn: "American Culture: Generalized Orientations and Class Patterns," in Bryson, Finkelstein, and MacIver (eds.): *Conflicts of Power in Modern Culture*, pp. 106–28.

power and to establish an ordered pattern for agreeing to disagree. Such a pluralistic view of social power was clear and explicit on questions of procedure while it left the common ends of the society largely undefined.

As can be seen, the theme of democracy has converged with those of equality and freedom, and all three have been interpreted and reinterpreted along with the moralistic optimism of the doctrines of progress. Our previous surveys have shown some of the complicated deviations and conflicts within these orientations; the present section is briefly handled because of the overlapping of democracy with other themes. The cumulative review of major value-orientations seems more and more clearly to point to one central constellation that gives coherence to a wide range of others, including democracy. This nuclear or focal theme we shall call the value of individual personality. In one aspect, its relation to democracy has been given a classic statement by Carl Becker:

> Its [modern liberal democracy's] fundamental assumption is the worth and dignity and creative capacity of the individual, so that the chief aim of government is the maximum of individual self-direction, the chief means to that end the minimum of compulsion by the state. Ideally considered means and ends are conjoined in the concept of freedom: freedom of thought, so that the truth may prevail; freedom of occupation, so that careers may be open to talent; freedom of self-government, so that no one may be compelled against his will. [95]

Thus, in so far as majority rule and conditional and limited authority based upon uncoerced consensus are highly evaluated in the culture, the main American concepts of democracy are consistent with a particular set of value postulates concerning the nature and significance of the individual in society.

INDIVIDUAL PERSONALITY

Writing in 1897 Émile Durkheim incisively described a pattern of value in Western civilization that he called the cult of individual

[95] Carl Becker: *Modern Democracy* (New Haven, Conn.: Yale University Press, 1941), p. 27.

personality.[96] Basically this cult sets a high value on the development of individual personality and is correspondingly averse to invasion of individual integrity; to be a person is to be independent, responsible, and self-respecting, and thereby to be worthy of concern and respect in one's own right. To be a person, in this sense, is to be an autonomous and responsible agent, not merely a reflection of external pressures, and to have an internal center of gravity, a set of standards and a conviction of personal worth. Above all, the individual is not considered to be released from all socio-cultural controls. As Parsons has put it: "This is not a matter simply of freeing the individual from ethical restraints imposed by society, it is a matter of the imposition of a different *kind* of restraint. Individuality is a product of a certain social state. . . ." [97] Not the unrestrained biologic human being, but the ethical, decision-making, unitary social personality is the object of this cult of the individual. What is positively valued in the tradition now under examination, in other words, is not just any kind of personality whatsoever, but rather a certain kind of individual.

The personality that is the object of high value in this particular tradition is something of intrinsic worth, not valued simply as a member of a group nor as a means to some ulterior end. This orientation to the person, it must be repeated, is the product of a definite social situation. There is no real paradox in saying that individuality can be a social product and a common social value; the development of individual personality is a *shared value* rather than a *collective end* in a group or social system. The emergence and maintenance of this state, however, is intimately related to other aspects of the society. To maintain a high evaluation of individual personality in this peculiar sense is surely a difficult and precarious feat, for there are factors inherent in society that continually threaten the value. The crucial fact in this connection is that other persons are always potential tools or threats in relation to the attainment of any one individual's separate interests; control over others is always a potentially efficient means to securing one's individual desires. There is always some measure of this centrifugal

[96] *Le suicide* (Paris: 1897; new ed.: 1930), Book III, chap. I.
[97] Parsons: *The Structure of Social Action*, pp. 333–4.

bombardment of interest that creates pressures toward "using" other people in an essentially amoral utilitarian fashion. Under certain social conditions, the integrity of the individual *qua* personality may thus largely disappear. Slaves in the ancient world were not persons in the modern meaning. The fate of the laboring population during certain phases of the Industrial Revolution further illustrates how strong interests sometimes break through protective values centering around the person. A high valuation of the individual in the present sense, is difficult to maintain under conditions of great social stress, crisis, and privation—in war, famine, natural disaster, revolution, plague, and the like. In general, whenever great urgency is felt for the accomplishment of a collective task, requiring co-ordination, speed, and great differentials of sacrifice, there is a tendency to regard individuals as tools rather than values in themselves. Militaristic societies often tend to exalt the collectivity over the individual, and for functionally understandable reasons.[98] Similarly, an overwhelming stress upon profit making in organized economic enterprises quite obviously would tend toward an impatience with individual scruples, needs, and peculiarities and toward a calculating, impersonal use of others solely as a means toward the dominant end. In our own society the pressures and ambivalences involved in the valuation of individual personality are highlighted by the specific case of respect for freedom of conscience in religious matters.

We have said that the value of individual personality has been important in the received tradition of America, but that it is subject to very powerful contravening influences. What evidences are there as to its actual place in the total culture? In the first place, we note a large number of important legal provisions that appear to have as *part* of their function the protection of personal freedom or the physical or social integrity of the person; to mention a few— illegality of slavery and peonage (note that a person cannot even voluntarily sell himself as a slave); illegality of imprisonment for debt, and provision for bankruptcy proceedings (in this context, also, a limitation on economic rights in the interests of personal freedom); prohibitions against personal defamation (libel and

[98] Cf. Hiller, *Social Relations and Structures*, p. 321.

slander); prohibition of "improper search and seizure"; prohibition of "cruel and unusual punishment"; right of *habeas corpus*, and so on. Perhaps the most striking instance of the lengths to which the law has gone in the attempt to preserve the person from attack is found in the definition of suicide as a crime. The free individual in our society is not free to take his own life because of the axiomatic value which he is not presumed to have the right to destroy.[99] A number of facts, already cited in preceding pages also may be taken as evidence of the value attached to the integer-personality. So, for example, the presumed universal and impersonal system of legal justice not only reflects equality and democracy but also, at what is probably a still more basic level, the concept of an universal worth, a claim for consideration, simply because one is an individual. "Status-justice," graded according to external criteria of rank, birth, and so on, is in principle radically incompatible with this orientation. Similarly, humanitarian practices may be interpreted as partly expressive of concern for personality as a value—whatever *other* values and specific interests may be involved.[100] Still another, and crucially important, datum is found in the religious tradition of Western society, where the value of individual personality has stood in close relation to the religious doctrine of the soul—that every human being has an immortal soul and is by the same token invested with the value imputed to the soul.

The reality of the value of individualism in our culture is observed not only in derivative forms such as manifest ideology, law, and formalized behavior patterns but also at the level of implicit assumptions and unconscious practices. For example, it is typical of

[99] The contrast with Japanese *hara kari* or Hindu *sutee* is striking evidence of the basic nature of the value-belief complex we are examining.

[100] Again the general principle is illustrated that any concrete social behavior typically is multivalued; the referents of value can be disentangled only through painstaking analysis. Although the necessary research largely still remains to be done, sufficiently precise and comprehensive studies would probably show trace lines of this value in exceedingly diverse manifestations. To what extent is the practice of tipping resisted because of "degrading" implications? Is there repugnance to cremation of the dead because it is felt to be a symbolic dissolution of the concept of the individual? Is the value of individual personality an important factor in resistance to sterilization legislation—or to legalization of euthanasia?

the culture that the question as to whether there is actually such an entity as "the individual," "self," or "ego" is usually not even thought of, and, if raised, is greeted with surprise or shock. *Of course* individuals exist, of course they have separate individual needs and rights. As Dorothy Lee says:

> The value of individualism is axiomatically assumed. . . . A newborn infant must become individuated, must be taught physical and emotional self-dependence; we assume, in fact, that he has a separate identity which he must be helped to recognize. . . . The need for privacy is an imperative one in our society, recognized by official bodies such as state welfare groups and the Department of Labor. And it is part of a system which stems from and expresses our basic values.[101]

A society that draws up a Declaration of Rights for Children, that is revolted by self-immolation of the individual for the group, that perceives groups as aggregates of co-operating but separate individuals—such a society incorporates the value of the individual at the deepest levels of its unconscious presuppositions. As a matter of fact the sociologically alert student is likely to guess at once that so pervasive a theme is maintained by quite special modes of child training and basic socialization; the hypothesis would be that this value complex is embedded in the central affective-cognitive structure of the representative personalities of the culture.

RACISM AND RELATED GROUP-SUPERIORITY THEMES

The commitment of large segments of American society to doctrines stressing the value and dignity of the individual has been real, deep, and widespread. The same can be said of the principles of equality, of humanitarian values, of political freedoms—and so on through the list of "publicly dominant" value patterns already listed. Once full weight has been given to all these "rational-humane" values in the received traditions of the society, it must be

[101] Dorothy Lee: "Are Basic Needs Ultimate?" *Journal of Abnormal and Social Psychology*, Vol. XLIII, no. 3 (July: 1948), pp. 393–4.

recognized at the same time that the values of the Creed have continually struggled against pervasive and powerful counter-currents of valuation. One of the chief conflicts, and in many ways the most important conflict, has centered around those diverse patterns which have as their common element *the ascription of value and privilege to individuals on the basis of race or particularistic group membership* according to birth in a particular ethnic group, social class, or related social category.

Racialistic doctrines were first given widespread currency and intellectual elaboration in the slavery controversy during the decades immediately prior to the Civil War. The value anomalies into which the pro-slavery position led,[102] in a culture so strongly stressing an individualistic religion and a democratic political system, gradually produced an explicit system of thought which relied upon assumptions of biological superiority to buttress the existing system of power and privilege.[103]

Space forbids anything like full documentation of the pervasiveness of organic, or more narrowly racist, orientations in our society. Adequate evidence is to be found in works already cited. It is enough to say that categorical discriminations are widespread in established practice, and are often crystallized into whole systems of legislation. It is not necessary here to explore the fears, vested interests, and multiple sociopsychological sources of the superiority-exclusiveness theme indexed by these legal acts. We must agree with Opler,[104] however, that these facts—only a tiny sample of other similar manifestations—reflect a view of society that in its extreme forms implicitly rejects "freedom" and individual ethical responsibility, certain conceptions of progress, and rational mastery of culture. Thus, the organic-racist view of man—in so far as its logical implications are actually worked out in human relations—

[102] Wilbert E. Moore and Robin M. Williams, Jr., "Stratification in the Ante-Bellum South," *American Sociological Review*, Vol. VII, no. 3 (June: 1942), pp. 343–51.

[103] "The race dogma is nearly the only way out for a people so moralistically equalitarian, if it is not prepared to live up to its faith." Myrdal, *et al.*, *An American Dilemma*, Vol. I, p. 89.

[104] Morris E. Opler: "Cultural and Organic Conceptions in Contemporary World History," *American Anthropologist*, Vol. XLVI, no. 4 (October-December, 1944), pp. 448–9.

stands in sharp opposition to most of the value orientations already reviewed. If a society begins with the premise that the human nature of individuals is biologically fixed and that different physical types or "races" are innately superior or inferior, then the unlimited development of this theme will make meaningless, or positively evil, the values of equality, democracy, freedom, rationality, progress (in the sense of human improvement through learning), humanitarianism, individual achievement linked with moral autonomy, and the central values of personality. The ultimate logical outgrowth of complete organicism is an exclusionistic society, rigidly organized in a static hierarchy.

It becomes apparent that a very important part of the conflict of value systems in the United States can be economically summarized in terms of tension between *values centering around the concept of the responsible individual personality versus values organized around categorical organic conceptions.*

7. Conclusion

THIS rather lengthy and schematic review has not done justice to any one theme, but perhaps it has at least placed before us a range of important value-positions current in our society, and hinted at their complex interrelations. It must be always kept in mind that these themes, values, and systems of belief *do not operate as single and separate units* but *are in continually shifting and recombining configurations* marked by very complex interpenetration, conflict, and reformulation. Furthermore, our descriptive scheme that necessitated separate isolation and labeling of themes must not be allowed to leave the impression—to repeat an earlier caution—that values are disembodied elements which somehow function apart from concrete social relations and personalities. Everything described in this chapter must be capable of observation, in some sense, in the behavior of real personalities and in actual social structures, or else we have mistaken fancy for fact.

Perhaps the total picture may be clarified by a summary classification. In the first place, there are the quasi-values or *gratifications*, taken at a hedonic or physiological level, implicit in the entire analysis, and especially important in the section on "material comfort." Second, we may identify the *instrumental interests* or means-values, for example, wealth, power, work, efficiency. Although these interests may become values in themselves, it is convenient to consider them primarily as instrumental to the achievement of other values. Third, we have the *formal-universalistic values of Western tradition:* rationalism, impersonal justice and universalistic ethics, achievement, democracy, equality, freedom, certain religious values, value of individual personality. Fourth, there is a class of *particularistic, segmental, or localistic values* that are best exemplified in racist-ethnic superiority doctrines and in certain aspects of nationalism.

Running through these patterns of interests and values are certain still more general "dimensions" or "orientations" that are not typically explicit but must be identified by highly abstract inference. Because of this abstract quality, the inadequacy of the data, and the removal from observed phenomena by several stages of inference, the statement of such basic dimensions is hazardous and the following propositions must be taken as of only suggestive usefulness: [105]

1. American culture is organized around the attempt at *active mastery* rather than *passive acceptance*. Into this dimension falls the low tolerance of frustration; the refusal to accept ascetic renunciation; the positive encouragement of desire; the stress on power; the approval of ego-assertion, and so on.
2. It tends to be interested in the *external world* of things and events, of the palpable and immediate, rather than in the inner experience of meaning and affect. Its genius is manipulative rather than contemplative.
3. Its world-view tends to be *open* rather than closed: it em-

[105] In the nature of the case, anyone—including the author—can think of numerous exceptions to each of these generalized formulations, as well as widespread *alternative* themes.

phasizes change, flux, movement; its central personality types are adaptive, accessible, outgoing and assimilative.

4. In wide historical and comparative perspective, the culture places its primary faith in *rationalism* as opposed to *traditionalism;* it de-emphasizes the past, orients strongly to the future, does not accept things just because they have been done before.

5. Closely related to the above, is the dimension of *orderliness* rather than unsystematic *ad hoc* acceptance of transitory experience. (This emphasis is most marked in the urban middle classes.)

6. With conspicuous deviations, a main theme is a *universalistic* rather than a *particularistic* ethic.

7. In interpersonal relations, the weight of the value system is on the side of *"horizontal"* rather than *"vertical"* emphases: peer-relations, not superordinate-subordinate relations; equality rather than hierarchy.

8. Subject to increased strains and modifications, the received culture emphasizes *individual personality* rather than group identity and responsibility.

12. American Social Organization

1. The Nature of Social Organization

UP TO now we have spent most of our time looking at the *cultural* structure of American society—at its major institutional norms and salient value themes. Not much has been said about the actual social *interactions* and social *relations* that constitute the society as over against the culture. As Chapters 10 and 11 have suggested, however, social life is not a simple emanation or reflection of broad cultural norms; on the contrary, social organization may be analyzed in its own right as the other side of the culture-society coin. The present chapter will focus upon the web of recurring social interactions in which cultural norms and values are ceaselessly actualized, modified, evaded, or contravened—and in which new norms and values are created from time to time.

There are two main approaches for distinguishing cultural structure from social organization. The principal distinction has been implicit in the whole preceding discussion: cultural structure has been conceived as a series of norms or ideal patterns to which people are oriented. The cultural web of shared norms, goals, and values is *one* of the major determinants of social action. However, the interactions of persons in specific situations seldom perfectly follow the cultural blueprint and much patterning is not directly regulated by cultural norms.[1]

[1] For example, the regularity with which interracial marriages in the United States occur between a man of the subordinate group and a woman of the dominant group. This pattern is not directly prescribed by cultural norms; instead it is an indirect consequence of the system of race relations. Cf. Robert K. Merton: "Intermarriage and Social Structure: Fact and Theory," *Psychiatry*, Vol. IV (1941), pp. 361–72.

A second distinction, partly overlapping the first, is based upon the degree to which norms are enforced by explicitly designated cultural agents, whether these be individual positions or organized groups. Cultural regulation occurs where normative standards are maintained by the diffuse action of the whole social group—as in the mores of a small rural community. Sanctions are meted out through diffuse consensus; the mechanisms of enforcement of norms are nonnucleated; no particular individual or group is clearly responsible for maintaining the accepted patterns. On the other hand, a great many cultural values and norms are specifically allocated to particular functionaries for enforcement, fostering, and support. To the degree that regulation is thus focalized, cultural structure may be said to pass over into social organization.

In applying either of these distinguishing criteria we have to deal with continuous gradations rather than sharp dichotomies. Nevertheless, it is a great aid to clarity and ease of analysis if we hold continually in mind the primary division: on the one hand, a cultural structure (language, law, art, belief systems and ideas, various other symbols and symbol systems, norms of all kinds); on the other hand, ongoing interactions, regularized by mutual expectancies and concerns of the participants. It is in the immediate person-to-person relations that much of culture acquires meaning and affective value, and in them the individual anchors his perceptions and his personality organization.

Social organization refers to human action in so far as the actor takes into account the actions of others. As persons interact, mutual expectations and concerns arise, and as interaction continues over time, more-or-less definite *patterns* emerge. In the absence of structural expectancies, the simplest interactions become confusing: two people come face to face around a street corner and teeter back and forth erratically in the effort to structure the manner of passing. If there is a definite expectancy—that each will go to his right side of the sidewalk, or any other easily signaled rule—the actual course of action has a radically different quality. The *minimal* specification of social organization would thus run: it is that state of interaction in which the actions of any one participant are to an appreciable degree determined by his orientation to the behavior of other participants. Organization may be quite temporary—as in the patterned interaction of a street crowd—or relatively permanent, as in religious, political, or familial groupings. The patterning of action may be formal, rigid and explicit, or it may be flexible, vague, and implicit. In any case, the generic quality in which we are interested is the property of *recurrence:* the fact that interactions become predictable, that is, patterned, through participants' becoming aware of each other's behavior. Organization in this sense operates quite as clearly in a friendship as in an industrial corporation. Organization is a "special density of interaction," to use Chester I. Barnard's phrase, and its basic identifying mark is that participants come to act in regularized ways through meaningful apprehension of what others have done, are doing, and are likely to do.

Whenever a given interaction pattern is repeated often enough to give rise to relatively stable expectancies among the actors we call it a *social relation.*[2] There may be an appreciable degree of diffuse organization in a social aggregate, without the specificity and continuing structure of social relations. Like organization, however, a social relation is not an all-or-none matter: it always exists in some *degree*. At what level of structuring and permanence we decide to attach the label is largely a matter of convenience for various specific kinds of analysis.

We shall follow Wilson and Kolb [3] in designating as *social systems* all those social relations or complexes of relations that are clearly guided by culturally stylized rights and obligations shared by the participants. The most highly developed types are constellations of social relations in which conduct is defined and shaped by a definite system of institutional norms, for example, family relations or the social systems of organized religious bodies. From such definite and elaborated systems one can move along in a continuum over to the limiting cases in which interaction occurs without mutually shared codes of conduct. Strictly speaking, any fre-

[2] Cf. Max Weber: *The Theory of Social and Economic Organization*, trans. by A. M. Henderson and Talcott Parsons (New York: 1947).

[3] Logan Wilson and William L. Kolb: *Sociological Analysis* (New York: 1949), p. 263.

quently recurring social relation will be a social system—that is, we can predict that *some* concepts of rights and duties will come to be shared. The cultural regulation may be so rudimentary and superficial, however, that we find it more useful to speak of various kinds of *collective behavior* in which social relations are relatively unstructured by cultural norms. The extreme here is the transitory and amorphous *public* that momentarily crystallizes around a political issue, acts upon it, and then dissolves to re-form into a succession of other publics. Certain types of *crowds* also illustrate the situation of patterned interaction not closely canalized by norms of obligation and privilege linked to that interaction. Still a third variety of interaction falling outside the category "social system" as defined above, consists of the numerous *situational fields* in which people are thrown together in relatively unstructured, new or *ad hoc* situations that are not yet clearly defined or regulated culturally.

"Social group" is one of those treacherous terms with an apparently simple common-sense connotation that conceals multiple unclarities. As a crude first approximation, a group may be described as a given aggregate of persons playing interrelated roles, and recognized by themselves or others as a unit of interaction. The simplest operational index of a group is *the presence of relatively high interaction rates* among the members,[4] but this criterion is not sufficient to distinguish group from organization or relation. A social group is one form of organization and it *contains* social relations. It seems best, then, to reserve the term for those interacting aggregates of persons in which the participants regard themselves, for certain purposes, as a unit of solidarity possessing shared interests, values, or behavior patterns that set them off from other groups.

[4] A closely related index is the degree to which the aggregate is a closed system of interpersonal preferences or choices in the sociometric sense. Thus Lundberg and Lawsing have suggested that: "The surplus of choices received over the choices made (incoming over outgoing stimuli) may be regarded as a sort of index of the degree of cohesion or nucleation of any social segment,"— George A. Lundberg and Margaret Lawsing: "The Sociography of Some Community Relations," *American Sociological Review*, Vol. II, no. 3 (June, 1937), pp. 318–35.

The difference between a *social group*—as one form of social organization—and an *institutional structure* is vividly suggested by the case of a specific family group whose members disperse geographically when the children grow up. The institutions of kinship are still there—individuals know the generally expected and obligatory norms and could fairly readily be reactivated to practice them—but a real interacting group may almost, or completely, cease to exist.

A group differs from a mere aggregate of unrelated individuals just in so far as there is both *interaction* in terms of relatively stabilized roles *and* a sense of group identity. A company of raw recruits turns into a group as there emerges a recurrent network of role-patterned relations, together with an awareness of difference from other social aggregates.

Our observational tests for the presence of a group thus include (1) counting of interactions (2) testimony and other evidence of recognition of group identity. A third avenue of study is the observation of *social sanctions*. It may be taken as an identifying criterion that no organized group exists without a viable system of positive and negative sanctions that both index and help to maintain regularized patterns of behavior.

To understand *concretely* what occurs in the behavior of people in groups it it necessary to take into account a great deal more than the sheer *pattern* of interaction. The total behavior includes as formal and invariant aspects at least the following:

a) two or more persons playing interrelated roles in recurrent activities; to the degree that the group comprises a social system, the performance of these roles is directed and regulated by culturally sanctioned goals and means;

b) certain cultural goals emerging as group objectives; these need not be highly explicit nor identical with the goals and motives of individuals comprising the group's population;

c) culturally approved means—that is, normatively regulated ways of acting in relation to cultural goals;

d) sanctions—the patterned rewards and penalties already mentioned as a diagnostic sign marking the presence of a functioning social aggregate.

Knowing only these characteristics of a given group it will be possible to make many useful predictions about it. In fact, for numerous practical purposes of personal orientation or social management, accurate information on these four points may be sufficient. Where more specific and detailed description or prediction is desired, it is necessary to supplement the sociological first approximation by a study of the unique constellation of interacting personalities. The more specific our relation to the group becomes, the more important it is to know this peculiar configuration in its entirety. In this respect it is correct to support the common-sense hunch that intensive firsthand acquaintance with a group supplies knowledge not attainable in any other way. Furthermore, *dynamic* predictions about a group probably will always be greatly improved by intensive data on the specific personalities involved—over and above the stylized roles typically assigned in the group interactional process.

2. Main Types of Social Organization

EVEN on the basis of the very broad distinctions just made it is possible to begin developing descriptive hypotheses about American social organization. Remembering the great individual mobility and cultural heterogeneity, the student may guess that this is probably a society broadly characterized by: *relative instability of social relations*, *rapid emergence and dissolution of social groups*, and *relatively great importance of collective behavior in the total system*. As evidence presented below (pp. 462–72) shows, these particular statements are valid as descriptions of modal tendencies, of course, with proper detailed qualifications. However, to go much beyond such statements requires further analytical breakdown of the phenomena of social organization. In view of the form in which most of the available data are cast, it seems most useful to work with fairly concrete *types* of social organization, used as first approximations to the reality which we wish to understand. Whenever possible, the attempt will be made to show what meaningful variables can be isolated from these relatively crude classifications.

Sociological studies have developed a large number of typologies of social organization. Although diverse in content, in level or kind of abstraction, and in systematic quality, certain lines of distinction have recurred time and again under superficially different labels. One of the most persistent central themes has been the distinction between sacred and secular social structures. Certain aspects of this dichotomy run through the work of nearly every outstanding theory of society. Durkheim spoke of organic versus mechanical solidarity; Tönnies worked out the parallel distinction between *Gemeinschaft* (community) and *Gesellschaft* (association); Maine referred to a society of status versus a society of contract; Sorokin contrasts ideational and sensate systems; Cooley emphasized primary groups; MacIver developed the community-association contrast. In spite of various discrepancies and ambiguities, most of these attempts at classification draw a primary line of distinction between *societies* and *associations*. As Wilson and Kolb have stated it:

> A society is a social group within which the members share the basic elements and conditions of a common life. It is an inclusive group encompassing other social groups and relations. . . . An association, on the other hand, is much more limited in scope. It is organized around a limited set of interests or values which people believe they can enjoy through concerted action.[5]

Either societies or associations may be made up of few or many subgroupings, linked together in greater or lesser degree. In the case of total, inclusive societies the type concepts (*Gemeinschaft*, *Gesellschaft*, and so on) are necessarily quite general, serving however, the indispensable function of locating in the larger social framework the particular types of social relations, social systems, groups, associations, or communities that we may wish to study in detail. Such inclusive types must be employed with full awareness of their logical character: they are concrete types and therefore

[5] Logan Wilson and William L. Kolb: *Sociological Analysis* (New York: Harcourt, Brace and Company, Inc., 1949), p. 267.

will *never* fit exactly any particular society. Instead they represent logical extremes, against which the characteristics of any particular society can be brought out in sharp relief.

As we look at the known societies of the world, past and present, we find many approximating the model of folk or simple communal societies. These are usually relatively small and stable systems, economically self-sufficient, marked by absence of elaborate division of labor or highly differentiated associations; the whole unit is held together by rather rigid codes and value systems, enforced through diffuse pressure and mediated through a society-wide network of interpersonal relations.[6] Many other societies have retained the unity and rigidity or stability of the folk society to a high degree but have developed a fairly elaborate division of labor, complex social stratification and political systems, and differentiated and highly organized religious groupings. These complex communal societies have existed in the form of feudal orders, as in medieval Europe and in certain periods of Chinese history, in the caste society of India, and in many of the larger nonliterate societies studied in modern times. On the other hand, the Western history in which American society has had its being has been stamped for centuries by the unprecedented development of associational modes of organization. By briefly examining the polar types of communal and associational societies we will find paths into the analysis of other and more specific types of organization.

COMMUNAL AND ASSOCIATIONAL SOCIETIES: GEMEINSCHAFT AND GESELLSCHAFT

As already stated, the ideal types of communal and associational societies are only approximated in particular local communities or national societies. The prototype of the communal society is the isolated rural community (whether primitive or part of a modern nation); that of the associational society is the rapidly changing, specialized, segmented, and impersonalized urban center. Of course,

[6] Ibid., pp. 345–6.

New York or Chicago are associational aggregates only in part; and our El Cerritos, "Plainville," or Appalachian rural neighborhoods contain associational elements even within a broadly communal context.

Thus, what starts out as a broad classification of total communities or societies turns out, upon closer inspection, to imply a more specific classification of social relationships. The associational society has a large number and variety of specific associations, a loose articulation of the component units of the social structure, and few universally practiced behavioral codes; it gives an important place to law and administrative controls. The communal society, in pure type, would show relatively slow social change; few specialized, free-standing associations; rigid co-ordination or integration of subunits; many universally accepted values, goals, and norms of conduct; relative lack of specialized and impersonal mechanisms of social control.

Perhaps the central characteristic of associational relations is that they are instrumental in the service of further relatively definite interests. In so far as relations are associational they are precisely instruments, a means in the pursuit of ends, not the ends themselves. This instrumental character of associational relations is exemplified in various processes of political bargaining and maneuver, and in a wide range or relations primarily orientated to economic exchange and economic power. In communal relations, on the contrary, the main emphasis is upon the relation itself and the personalities and other values directly activated in it.

Communal relations are likely to stress diffuse attitudes (for example, respect, affection, loyalty, and so on) rather than rationally instrumental actions. Associational relations typically imply separateness of interacting persons, whereas in communal relations it is presupposed that the participants are linked together by many common activities and values. Closely related to this is the specificity of associational relations: typically they are narrowly and explicitly defined and restricted to a specific interest or life area. The prototype is the narrowly contractual relation of buyer and seller in an open market exchange transaction, in which everything is formally irrelevant to the relation except considerations of price, quantity, and quality of the goods being exchanged. The rights and obligations of the parties are specific and definite—neither more nor less than explicitly agreed upon for the specific occasion—and the establishment of any particular associational relation does not imply any *other* social relations between the participants. If the employee wishes to claim additional wages on the ground that he "needs it more" than the employer, there is nothing in the employer-employee relation itself that supports his claim. On the other hand, an identical claim by one's parents or other close relatives has an exactly opposite import; in this case, the burden of proof is shifted to the individual who wishes to deny a claim or refuse an obligation—one turns down his brother's request for a loan on grounds of some other and "higher" communal obligation. This indefiniteness of the common activities and ends is associated with the important part played by various kinds of symbolism in communal relations. The drudgery of household tasks has one meaning when the tasks are performed as employee and another when performed by a wife as part of her family role. In associational relations the major emphasis tends to center upon objective rights and overt performance; in communal relations, the stress moves toward questions of meaning, intent, motive, and feeling.

Implied in the schematic description given thus far is the tendency to define associational relations as emotionally neutral, or at least to consider the feelings of the participants as formally irrelevant. The proverbial impersonality of large-scale specialized associations reflects a task-centered or function-oriented mode of organization in which certain specific activities are supposed to go on irrespective of the subjective sentiments of the participants.

Now it is perfectly plain that concrete social relations will seldom if ever embody in pure form the whole complex of characteristics included in either of the two types. Each of the characteristics is a variable that will be found in greater or lesser degree and in combination with other variables. We regard concrete social relations, therefore, as the point of intersection of readings on all the variables in combination; in any one such cluster we will often find high development of certain associational elements along with high development of one or more communal features, or the reverse. For example, a doctor-patient relationship may turn out to be highly specific, limited, rational, and impersonal—however, we may find that the doctor, instead of pursuing his own immediate self interest, is treating the patient's welfare as an end in itself. But, again, if the ideal types are used cautiously as a means of analysis they will be highly useful in diagnosing any social structure. Their function in this respect is perhaps similar to the stain that a biologist applies to bring out features of a cell structure he wishes to observe. Such a classification can help us to formulate certain conditional—"if and when"—predictions or generalizations about contemporary social structures. In particular, our ideal types direct attention toward consequences and correlates of an extreme development of instrumental social relations.

We already know that the modern industrialized society of America is conspicuous for the development of highly specialized economic activities, of widespread commercialization of practices and activities, of large-scale political and economic structures, of high geographic mobility, of numerous special-interest groups. If, and to the degree that, the social relations emerging in such a context generally become instrumental in the service of specialized interests, we may expect the correlative conditions now to be sketched. Limiting our view for the moment to conditions prevailing in economic and political sectors of our large urban centers —that is, to those parts of American society in which highly developed associational relations are most frequent and in which they set the *dominant* pattern—we find many trace lines left by communal reactions to instrumental human relations.

We have seen that when social organization becomes solely a matter of association in the service of specific impersonal but individualized goals, then by definition the situation is one of a manipulative attitude toward persons. Now, an individual who thus manipulated all his human relations would be the logical extreme of what psychiatry calls the psychopathic personality—a person to whom all others appear simply as means to his private goals—and a social aggregate operating toward others solely in this way would be the pure distilled essence of the interest group. Obviously few individuals or groupings develop associational patterns to these extremes, and if they did, we should not have a society in any historical sense of the term. Nevertheless, it is not difficult to cite many examples in which a recognizable approximation to the pure type does exist. Certain kinds of advertising and propaganda and the attempted manipulation of legislation by pressure groups certainly qualify as cases in point. The impersonalized management of large bodies of men for military purposes sometimes is strongly marked by instrumental patterns: in the vernacular of the replacement depots (note the phrase) of World War II, one sometimes heard contingents of men spoken of in such phrases as "three hundred bodies for shipment today." Much seemingly communal behavior has come to be regarded widely as pseudo-*Gemeinschaft;* the favorite popular stereotype is that of the baby-kissing politician, but many other gestures supposedly symbolizing friendship or solidarity are met with the skeptical query, "What is he trying to sell?" (or, "put over"), "Wonder what he's after?"

In modern American society, a whole vocabulary has developed in tribute to the manipulative aspects of urban associational patterns. Indexing wariness and reciprocal distrust we have such idioms as: "to debunk," "What's in it for him," "Never give a sucker an even break." In reaction to sensed manipulation (real or imagined), there has developed a pervasive tendency to resist the acceptance of statements at their face value.

To meet a situation in which the areas of good faith in social relations are uncertain or importantly deficient, many individuals permanently reduce their expectations as to the sincerity of others, systematically discounting in advance the apparent motives and claims of other persons. So thoroughly has this skepticism permeated our urban society that large numbers of persons question their own statements. The classic phrase here is the well-known preface, "I may be rationalizing, but. . . ."[7]

[7] See Robert K. Merton: "The Sociology of Knowledge," chap. 13 in Georges Gurvitch and Wilbert E. Moore (eds.): *Twentieth Century Sociology* (New York: 1945).

The above observations suggest that in our complex social structure there will be many intrusions of *Gesellschaft* elements into relations traditionally defined as communal, and the reverse. For instance, the functioning of bureaucratic organizations typically shows some tension as a result of *Gemeinschaft* importations that run counter to the formal structure—in one direction, nepotism; in another, the expectation of or demand for *personalized* behavior when impersonal-categorical treatment is the organizational norm. Such misplaced relations and expectations are perennial sources of administrative problems.

The *Gemeinschaft-Gesellschaft* classification is a useful orientation device. It is not a theory of social organization and can become misleading if used indiscriminately. For purposes of the present chapter, this particular typology is a way of focusing upon very broad tendencies in the society as a whole, for example, the shift from rural modes of life, or the functional specificity of economic relations. For a more specific examination of the structure of associations and groups, we will find it convenient to utilize the notions of *formal* and *informal* organization, that follow next.

FORMAL VS. INFORMAL ORGANIZATION

Sociological analysis has continually to guard against the common tendency to think of organization solely in terms of *formal* organization. As has been reiterated already, the reality is that we have a continuum from extremely formalized and persisting structures over to transitory, informal, or even unrecognized clusters of interaction. To focus solely upon the more formal structures is to miss some of the most important things we need to orient ourselves in our society.

What, then, is formal organization and what is its relation to informal organization? The question can best be approached by examining a few simple but basic propositions about behavior in social aggregates. First, it is known that *the behavior of individuals in association with others exhibits a number of emergent properties, not predictable from knowledge of the participants taken separately.* Second, among the emergent properties of behavior in interaction is the *fact that an aggregate of persons that, for whatever causes, remains in meaningful interaction for any considerable period will develop regularized patterns of interpersonal conduct.* Leaving its genesis to one side, we simply can take this spontaneous tendency toward structuring as a fundamental empirical regularity, holding for hostile and discordant interactions (guards and prisoners, for example) just as for positive relations. Third, *every formal organization that continues for any considerable period develops an informal organization alongside the formal one.*[8] (For the moment let us defer asking what "formal" means.) The presence of informal organization is, in principle, easily demonstrable by fairly crude observation. In a certain college classroom, the teacher never assigns seats and roll call is never taken: there is no official or even explicit specification of seating arrangements. Yet within a few weeks the amorphous aggregate has become patterned; with high regularity the same individuals occupy the same seats day after day—an informal organization has emerged. Although at a rudimentary level, this sort of spontaneous structuring contains the basic elements upon which even the most elaborate organizational systems are built. Note also that this informal organization arose within and is added to the more generalized cultural patterning of appropriate classroom conduct.

One of the by-now classic illustrations of the emergence of informal organization within a formal structure is provided by the studies of Western Electric workers summarized by Roethlisberger and Dickson.[9] Investigations of factors affecting production had shown that output variations could not be accounted for by physical factors of lighting, rest periods, and the like, and had located the source of increased production in the social atmosphere of the work situation. It was quickly demonstrated that the formal organization

[8] Cf. Chester I. Barnard: *The Functions of the Executive* (Cambridge, Mass: 1938), chap. 9; Wilbert E. Moore: *Industrial Relations and the Social Order* (New York: 1946), chap. 15; Fritz J. Roethlisberger and William J. Dickson: *Management and the Worker* (Cambridge, Mass.: 1939).

[9] Ibid., pp. 522 ff.

of the factory was not predictive of workers' behavior. The official group leader was observed to act in many instances as a representative of the workers rather than management. Furthermore, output records showed an amazingly constant rate of production, quite incompatible with the assumed goals of maximum income. Individuals were punished by their associates for exceeding the production norm accepted by the group, and still more significantly, such imposition of sanctions was accepted by the recipients. All these clues clearly pointed to an informal organization, different from and even counter to the formal patterns. Through the network of interpersonal relations in the work group, it represented a powerful controlling force, but one that was largely unadmitted and unrecognized by the participants or their nominal supervisors. Thus, if we consider a formally organized group to be one in which the members interact as occupants of explicitly defined and interrelated roles, performing prescribed functions, we can predict that continuing formal groupings will quickly develop an informal organization, simply as a by-product of action directed toward the formal objectives of the organization. The explicit roles of the formal structure will be modified by the emergence of an informal sociometric pattern of interpersonal relations, attractions and repulsions. Lines of communication emerge outside the official structure. Subgroupings develop their particularized interests and loyalties, their partly divergent purposes.[10] The interpersonal and subgroup networks of informal character built up their own understandings, procedures, goals—sometimes emerging with relatively distinctive cultures different from the formal patterning.

Around this central fact of the inevitable emergence of informal organization within the formal structures, several other predictabilities emerge:

1. The major factors in the *immediate* causation of behavior must be present in the unit of interaction, which always has its informal aspects. This means that any larger organizational structure

---

[10] The importance of latent organization—as well as its inevitability—has been well stated by Philip Selznick: *TVA and the Grass Roots: A Study in the Sociology of Formal Organization* (Berkeley and Los Angeles, Calif.: 1949), p. 255.

determines behavior only as its forces are transmitted to individuals in the small units of immediate personal relations.

2. In all large-scale formal organizations: (a) *informal subunits* arise, and command their own segmental loyalties; (b) hence, the co-ordination of subunits becomes an important problem for the organization as a whole; (c) the segmentation of both formal and informal organizations creates special problems of communication.

3. All other things being the same, there is a high probability that as a formal organization continues to function the latent goal of *perpetuating the organization* will emerge as a major concern of organizational leaders.

4. All other things being equal, the larger the numbers of individuals and subgroups to be co-ordinated within a single organization, the more likely it is that the structure will become formalized; more specifically, that action will be increasingly oriented to explicit and impersonal rules.[11]

5. With increasing complexity of any given type of organization (especially those organizations oriented to action rather than to deliberation, consultation, and so on) there is a tendency for the structure to assume a hierarchical form.

These illustrative propositions already suggest that the concept of formality may involve a number of different dimensions. Formal organizations are characterized by a high *degree of repetitiveness* (stereotyping) in the behavior of the participants, but this is not a sufficient criterion, for many informal groups exhibit the same characteristics. Nor is it enough to point to the *rigidity of the regulative norms*, nor to the *severity of sanctions*, nor to the existence of *specialized roles*. All these phenomena are found in structures no one would consider formal. In combination with the above vari-

[11] Size is roughly correlated with structural complexity. Even in a structurally simple group, however, the addition of members rapidly produces changes in the internal organization. Cf. Margaret M. Wood: *The Stranger* (New York: 1934), p. 34. A considerable part of formal sociology is devoted to the analysis of group forms in relation to number of participants. See Leopold von Weise and Howard Becker: *Systematic Sociology* (New York: 1932). Analysis of small-group interaction is receiving increased emphasis in current American sociology. See, for example, George C. Homans: *The Human Group* (New York: 1950).

ables, however, three other items serve to define what we recognize as formal organization, namely: the *explicit* nature of organizational norms, a marked degree of *impersonality* (stress upon detachment rather than emotional involvement), and a relatively great emphasis upon well-defined patterns of *deference and social distance* between the occupants of hierarchically ordered positions.

These defining variables are intercorrelated—they tend to move together—but each has a considerable range of independent variation. In general we would hypothesize that formality, as the composite of the values of this cluster of variables, will be maximized when: (1) the activity of large numbers of individuals are being directed toward a common collective goal; (2) the organization includes many highly specialized roles; (3) the participants are culturally heterogeneous (in addition to their differentiated organizational positions); (4) the goals of the organization are considered highly important, tangible, and urgent ("required" co-ordination + speed = increased emphasis upon formal structure). The most important formal structures in our society are large-scale organizations, built upon minute specialization in the performance of tangible tasks and directed toward a common but complex goal that requires an elaborate co-ordination of activity. The extensive co-ordinative system depends upon a high order of predictability that is typically sought, in turn, by the standardization of artifacts, techniques, procedures—and social roles.[12] The greater the pressure for *precise* and *rapid* co-ordination, the greater the tendency toward explicit regulation, hierarchy, and impersonality. The greater the differentiation of interests, privileges, and functions among numerous specialized positions, the greater the possibility of attenuated value-consensus; and hence, within limits, the more tendency to stress explicit deference-patterns.[13]

The pure type of formal organization would be a de-personalized structure of explicitly defined and regulated statuses. We do not

---

[12] Compare this abstract formulation with the known characteristics of the U. S. automobile industry, or with those of a modern army. For the latter case: Samuel A. Stouffer, *et al.: The American Soldier*, Vol. II, pp. 76–149, and Vol. I, pp. 362–429.

[13] This correlate is not *inevitable*, but it is a frequent tendency.

find the ideal type, but we can observe fairly close approximations to it. The kind and degree of formality clearly depends in part upon the particular goals of the organization. Formality is also related to the external and internal stress to which the organization is exposed: the military protocol of the barracks is drastically modified in an active combat operation. And both goals and stress are interdependent with the degree and kind of value consensus existing within the organization: other conditions remaining the same, a highly unified group is not so likely to maximize formal structure as is a discordant aggregate.[14]

It is impossible here to go into a number of fundamental questions raised by this attempt at preliminary orientation. Under what specific circumstances, for example, may we expect centralization of control, or decentralization; explicitness of norms; rigidity or flexibility of organizational rules; impersonal or personalistic norms; hierarchy or democracy? Available data and theories lead us to suspect that *centralized control* will be maximal in formal organizations when rapid action is, for any reason, regarded as imperative and when the organization is thought (by its members) to be threatened as a whole by external groups. Organizational norms apparently are the more likely to be *explicit* the larger the number of individuals, the longer and more complex the channels of communication, the more varied the interests and values of the participating members. Norms tend to become explicit also in situations of change and crisis deliberation—for example, in newly formed associations. It seems to be a fact that the social groupings in which implicit-personalized norms are most prominent tend to be long established and nonspecialized.

Problems of this order as yet have not been given adequate research testing, although they are obviously open to such research.[15]

---

[14] In all the tentative generalizations suggested in this chapter we have to add the mental reservation, "within a broadly similar culture." For example, there is no guarantee that the formalities of Chinese or Japanese culture follow the same predictive principles.

[15] A praiseworthy attempt to state a series of basic propositions in this field has been made by E. T. Hiller: *Social Relations and Structures* (New York: 1947), chaps. 17–19.

The next section of this chapter will provide a few additional clues as to the incidence and sources of variation in the formal elements of social organization in the United States.

Aside from broad ideal-types (*Gemeinschaft,* formal organization, and so on) against which any particular social structures can be scanned and analyzed, a large number of more specific classifications are available. The latter have been constructed out of various combinations of diverse criteria; to illustrate by only a few, we have had typologies of groups and associations including one or more of the following variables:

1. *Duration:* "temporary" or "permanent."
2. *Size:* "large" or "small."
3. *Complexity:* inclusion of subunits and complexity of linkages among them.
4. *Criterion of membership:* voluntary or involuntary.
5. *Accessibility:* open or closed.
6. *Scope of interests, values, or goals:* "interest-group association" versus inclusive community.[16]
7. *Type of control structure:* hierarchical versus equalitarian.
8. *Centralization of authority:* focused or diffuse.

It is sufficient for present purposes if we recognize the large amount of taxonomic work which has been done on social organization, without going into details not essential for the immediate task at hand. Our major concern is with the most general characteristics of the organizational forms of point-to-point interaction,[17] with special attention to those features outlined in preceding pages.

[16] The sociological literature on community is very extensive. Among recent American works: Robert M. MacIver: *Community* (New York: 1920), and *Society: A Textbook of Sociology* (New York: 1937); Dwight Sanderson: *The Rural Community* (New York: 1932); Pitirim A. Sorokin, Carle C. Zimmerman, and Charles J. Galpin: *A Systematic Source Book in Rural Sociology* (Minneapolis, Minn.: 1930), Vol. I, esp. chap. 4.

[17] It is recognized that there is also organization resulting from the orientation of nominally separate individuals to similar diffuse influences—for example, what Mannheim calls unorganized masses, field structures (commerce, propaganda publics), situations, social mechanisms (division of labor, patterns of competition). Karl Mannheim: *Man and Society in an Age of Reconstruction* (New York: 1940).

3. General Characteristics of Social Organization in the United States

VIEWING American social structure from a highly general perspective, the following characteristics stand out as of special diagnostic importance:

1. There is a relatively slight development of stable groups and associations with marked *gemeinschaftliche* characteristics.

Items: divorce and family instability; comparative weakness of neighborhoods and other locality groups; permeability and instability of ethnic communities.

2. There is an enormous proliferation of formally organized special-interest associations of the most diverse kinds. Specialized associations have multiplied, whereas the parts played by traditionalized groupings based on proximity, diffuse common values, and direct and inclusive personal relations have all diminished.

3. Large-scale, centralized formal organizations occupy a very significant and increasingly strategic position in the total social structure.

4. Many groups and associations are highly transitory; both the birth rates and death rates of organizations are high; there is much shifting of individuals among organizations and sets of social relations.

5. Considerable portions of the social structure are marked by ephemeral, impersonal, segmental relations, corresponding to slight development of inclusive groups.[18]

Items: hobohemias, recreational patterns, migratory populations; in a different way, mobile and competitive occupational situations.

6. As an aspect of specialized *associations*, there is high specialization of social *roles;* individuals frequently play several

[18] "Casual fluidity is the 'American way' and by long habituation 'feels right.' " Robert S. Lynd: *Knowledge for What?* (Princeton, N. J.: 1939), p. 63.

different and segmental roles. Otherwise stated, there is marked compartmentalization of social activities—in particular, a radical separation of occupational activity from other life areas.

7. Local communities are highly open to chains of interaction initiated at far-removed centers of organization; they are also comparatively permeable to strangers.

8. Multiplication of specialized formal associations, especially of the centralized, hierarchical types, leads to development of numerous mediating, co-ordinating, or tangential organizations:

> *Items:* co-ordinating committees, clearing-house organizations; councils; multiplication of offices and associations charged with mediating and co-ordinating tasks; federated associations.

9. More generally, both the total social structure *and* the internal structures of large formal organizations are highly complex: in the latter, numerous specialized statuses are arranged in intricate systems within systems; in the former, varied groups, communities, and associations, are interrelated in extended networks, chains and subsidiary social systems.

1) THE ROLE OF PRIMARY GROUPS

It has first to be emphasized that great interstitial areas of the society lie on the margins of organization strictly conceived. In this twilight zone of semistructured interaction belong the casual crowds and audiences of metropolitan life—aggregates held together in highly transitory contacts by momentary polarization around a shared interest of some kind. Here also are many of the instable interactions of unattached persons living outside organized groups—the Bohemians, derelicts, and so on—who make up an appreciable part of the population of urban centers.

As has so often been pointed out, American society is marked by relative weakness of traditionalized groupings based on proximity, direct personal relations, and the intimate sharing of common values.[19] Small stable primary groups have been the building blocks of human societies over most of the world in all past history. The family, the neighborhood, the village or commune, the local band are the basic units upon which more elaborate and indirect social structures are erected. In the United States, these small units of intensive continuing personal interaction have been considerably attenuated by forces arising in the whole process of industrialization and urbanization. With high mobility, in a secularized, economically oriented culture, the local groups and family units take a less prominent place in the total social structure. Correlatively, increased importance attaches to organizations that are nonlocal and indirect. Nevertheless, it remains true that the various types of localistic primary groups are basic to the organization of American, as to any other, society. First are the millions of immediate-family units, each a cluster of intensive interaction. No one has counted the thousands of neighborhoods that still constitute vital social units for millions of people—even, contrary to some impressions, in the supposedly impersonal maelstrom of the great cities. Running through local social structures are numerous play groups, cliques, visiting circles, friendship constellations, and diffuse interpersonal attachments giving body and texture to the more formalized structures. Closely analogous groupings exist in the form of work groups, religious units, small groupings of interaction in schools—in short, within all large-scale formal organizations.

Thus we have, on the one hand, the diffuse relations and groupings of local neighborhoods and communities, of cliques and friendships, of work and play groups; on the other side, the more highly structured communal social systems of families, churches, social classes, minority groupings (in part), and various so-called fraternal or "social" organizations. So much at least is retained of *Gemeinschaft*-like structure.

Yet these groupings are increasingly overshadowed by other forms of interaction. We have been considering groups that are "organic": (1) *durable*, that is, persisting in the face of such factors

[19] Cf. Robert C. Angell: *The Integration of American Society* (New York: 1941), esp. chap. 2.

as external stress, shifting individual motives, segmental disadvantages, changes in membership; (2) manifesting high *continuity* of person-to-person relations—the same persons interact together over extended periods *and* with the expectation of continued interaction; (3) including an *extensive range* of activities, accounting for a high proportion of each member's total activities and interests; (4) tending toward diffuse, *nonspecific norms* of right and obligation.

We have suggested that these organic, or more broadly *Gemeinschaft*-like, groupings are relatively weak in American society. The basis for this diagnosis is not obvious, nor to be taken for granted. Let us attempt to appraise it. "Weakness" we can define to mean (sociologically) relatively slight development of the four characteristics just listed, for a high proportion of all social interactions; or (psychologically) slight involvement of individuals in such groupings. Types of these groupings include: stable locality groups, families, community churches or religious orders, highly developed and enduring occupational associations and work groups. Specific evidences of the attenuation of these groupings include:

1. high rates of population mobility, disruptive of locality groups; low development of traditional patterns of solidarity—for example, work exchange, community mutual-aid patterns.[20]
2. extremely high divorce rates; prevalence of migration from area of residence of parental family; discontinuity of generations; low interaction-rates in extended kinship circles; relatively great functional specificity in intrafamilial relations; high proportion of extrafamilial activities.
3. considerable secularization of organized religion; mobility of members; nonparticipation in churches.
4. high mortality of small business concerns; rapid shifts in industries and jobs; great geographic mobility of labor; functional specificity of occupations.

To these must be added, (5) the increased centralization of relatively impersonal large-scale political and economic associations, and (6) the presence of interstitial social zones in which many

[20] Partial functional equivalents in Community Chests and the like represent different group structures.

individuals are isolated from continuing interaction with a meaningful circle of close associates.

Every area of data just cited can be countered, of course, by contrary facts. The weighting of the opposing lines of evidence is a complex judgmental process and depends in part upon the standard of comparison, or base-line, chosen. It is the present thesis that in contrast to American society in previous generations there has been a definite over-all decrease in the proportion of social organization contained within organic groupings. This undoubtedly has profound social and psychological implications in many different ways,[21] for example, the great current emphasis on security can hardly be understood apart from the loss of stable group support for many individuals—it is certainly far more than a purely economic development.

2) PROLIFERATION OF FORMAL ASSOCIATIONS

The United States has long been characterized as "a nation of joiners," a happy hunting ground for "organizers," "promoters," and the like. It is said that American individualism is "group individualism." [22] As long ago as the 1830's, that extraordinary observer Alexis de Tocqueville remarked: "In no country in the world has the principle of association been more successfully used, or more unsparingly applied to a multitude of different objects, than in America." [23] A long line of perceptive foreign observers have also

[21] "From the psychological standpoint the key to the understanding of well integrated organic societies is to be found in the fact that in these societies the collective impulses and wishes are absorbed by the smaller groups of which they are composed. These smaller groups then canalize and direct their energies toward their own particular ends." Karl Mannheim: *Man and Society in an Age of Reconstruction* (New York: Harcourt, Brace and Company, Inc., 1940), p. 62.

[22] Angell: *The Integration of American Society*, p. 3: "So significant has become the role of free-standing groups in contemporary life that one is tempted to say that our society is characterized by group individualism." For a similar comment see Charles W. Ferguson: *Fifty Million Brothers* (New York: 1937), p. 12.

[23] Alexis de Tocqueville: *The Republic of the United States of America*, trans. by Henry Reeves (New York: 1877), Part I, p. 204.

commented on the extraordinary role of private associations organized around special interests. And the facts of the modern situation further document the enormous proliferation of formal organizations of the most diverse kinds.

As an exhibit in point, here is a brief list of organizations taken, partly at random and partly with malice aforethought, from the *World Almanac:*[24]

> Aaron Burr Association
> American Legion
> American Swedish Historical Foundation
> Anti-Profanity League
> Chinese Women's Association, Inc.
> Commercial Law League of America
> Cooperative League of the U.S.A.
> Daughters of Defenders of the Republic
> Elks, Benevolent and Protective Order of
> Horseshoe Pitchers Association of America
> National Resources Council of America
> Pulp and Paper Industry, Technical Association
> Speech Association of America
> Woman's Christian Temperance Union
> Woman's International Bowling Congress

The variety of voluntary special interest associations suggested by this sampling is documented by numerous community studies. Warner and Lunt were able to identify 899 associations in a city of approximately 17,000 people and to find for study 357 relatively permanent and important associations. The groupings studied were composed of 12,876 memberships held by 6,874 individuals.[25] Formally organized special-interest associations are most highly

---

[24] *The World Almanac and Book of Facts for 1950* (New York: 1950), pp. 575–94. The total list includes over 1000 organizations under the heading "Associations and Societies in the United States." Presumably this sample is highly selective, including only those considered important enough for listing in a very compact reference volume.

[25] W. Lloyd Warner and Paul S. Lunt: *The Social Life of a Modern Community* (New Haven: 1941), pp. 303 and 320. See the whole of chap. 16: "The Formal and Informal Associations of Yankee City."

developed in urban areas, but have increasingly pervaded the open country as well.[26] The range of interests represented by these associations is altogether impressive, and the variety of structures is correspondingly great. The private, voluntary, special-interest associations include benevolent and philanthropic groupings, fraternal orders, clubs, educational organizations, economic associations, special occupational groupings, and so on through numerous special categories. In preceding chapters we have already observed the multiplicity of religious denominations, of political pressure groups, of education-related associations. The pattern of multiple associations cuts across the major institutions and laces together the partly differentiated groups and strata of local communities.

Even a casual sampling of data on such associations will lend body to the above statements. Thus:

According to their own reports, the major fraternal orders in the United States claim a total membership of about 20 million persons.[27]

As of the late 1930's, there were over 1,500 chapters of national college fraternities and 600 sorority chapters.[28]

The distinctive "service clubs" (Rotary, Kiwanis, Lions, Civitans, Optimists, etc.) cover the nation, with some unit in practically every urban center.

Among special women's organizations, the National Federation

[26] A recent study of an upstate New York rural community covering an area with a population of 4000 revealed 129 formal organizations.—James E. White: "Theory and Method for Research in Community Leadership," *American Sociological Review*, Vol. XV, no. 1 (February, 1950), p. 55. Cf. F. A. Bushee: "Social Organizations in a Small City," *American Journal of Sociology*, Vol. LI, no. 3 (November, 1945); Mirra Komarovsky: "The Voluntary Associations of Urban Dwellers," *American Sociological Review*, Vol. XI, no. 6 (December, 1946).

[27] *The Encyclopedia Americana*, Vol. XII (1944 ed.). See also "Fraternal Orders," *Encyclopaedia of the Social Sciences*, Vol. VI, and "Masonry," ibid., Vol. X.

[28] Ferguson: *Fifty Million Brothers*, p. 35. "American secret and nonliturgical societies are in many respects singular. Whatever may be true of the rest of the world or of past history, we present an array of orders altogether baffling. . . ." Ibid., p. 5.

of Women's Clubs includes 14,000 member organizations claiming 3 million individual members.

There are giant veteran's organizations—the American Legion, Veterans of Foreign Wars, the American Veterans Committee.

In rural areas, there are about 11,000 agricultural co-operatives with well over 3 million members; the American Farm Bureau Federation (about 400,000 members) has state bureaus in 39 states; the National Grange lists approximately 800,000 dues-paying members; the 4-H clubs enrolled in 1935 about 2 million youth.

As of 1945, there were 123 *national* organizations devoted in whole or in part to work on problems of interracial and inter-cultural relations.[29]

As long ago as 1940, the C.I.O. was composed of 42 national and international unions and organizing committees, with 225 state, county and local union councils and 419 local industrial unions.

There are 1,500 national trade associations, 4,000 chambers of commerce, 70,000 labor unions—and 100,000 women's organizations.[30]

And so it goes. These, note, are in addition to the elaborate formal organization represented by business enterprises, foundations, and many other forms of private associations.

But what does this proliferation of associations mean? What are the sources and implications of such a conspicuous and pervasive patterning of social structure?

There is first of all the elementary and crucial fact of a *permissive power-situation*. The American political system not only tolerates but encourages private groupings. No totalitarian order can or will tolerate such widespread diversity of private associations relatively independent of the formal structure of the state. The situation in

[29] Charles S. Johnson: "National Organizations in the Field of Race Relations," *The Annals of the American Academy of Political and Social Science*, Vol. 244 (1946).

[30] See the amazing inventory in Jay Judkins: *National Associations of the United States*, United States Department of Commerce (Washington, D. C.: 1949).

the United States is obviously not one of complete freedom of association—the history of the labor movement is alone enough to disabuse us of that impression—but the main long-run tendency has been to permit very great latitude to quite diverse associations.[31]

A permissive governmental policy, based on a pluralistic power structure, makes *possible* the developments of interest here, but it is not enough. There must also be forces creating associations—"demands" for interaction not met by other forms of social structure. Why do we have so many formal associations when for most human beings in all past societies the full activities of life were sufficiently encompassed by the family, the work group, and the local community? The asking of this question itself suggests one element of an answer: the special-interest association and the formalized congeniality grouping partly replace the void left by the *dissolution of older patterns of group interaction.* As urbanization has advanced in a mobile, industrial order, the old social units have been shattered or reduced in importance. The proportion of people isolated from opportunities for stably recurring interaction in family, neighborhood, work group, and church has increased. But the demand or need for stable group support and intimate association has not diminished correspondingly. As enduring person-to-person relations become attenuated, isolation and insecurity increase. Group membership in a Rotary club may seem radically different from membership in the American rural neighborhood of a half-century ago, but the loss of the latter has been a tangible factor in the growth of the former.[32]

The incidence of different types of associations in various social strata suggests the sources from which they derive. In culturally

[31] "The phenomenal growth of fraternal orders throughout the English-speaking world since the middle of the last century has been associated with the development of democratic institutions and the consequent freedom to form voluntary associations for the promotion of common interests."—Frank H. Hankins: "Fraternal Orders," *Encyclopaedia of the Social Sciences,* Vol. VI, p. 423.

[32] Cf. Charles F. Marden: *Rotary and Its Brothers* (Princeton, N. J.: 1935). Marden implies that the service clubs represent, in part, reactions to the change from rural and village society to the urban situation of relatively great impersonality, competition, and psychosocial isolation.

marginal or uprooted populations in the lower income levels, it is the fraternal order, the religious cult or sect, or occasionally the union in which common support and defense is sought. In the top income levels, the prestige association is the form assumed by formalized congeniality groupings, although there is extensive participation in other voluntary private associations, based on considerations of civic duty, or prestige and economic advantage. It is in the broad middle classes that one finds the great development of private associations organized in the name of fraternal, civic, service, benevolent, educational, and recreational purposes. Many of these associations exhibit familistic and communal symbols and creeds that seem to contrast markedly with the competitive, functionally specific relations so highly emphasized in middle-class business and professional occupations.

More broadly, the multiplication of associations is an outgrowth of cultural diversity and occupational differentiation, as like-circumstanced individuals seek to interact with one another and to combine in the pursuit of specialized interests common to a particular segment of the population. The tendency to form associations around special interests represents also the dominantly activistic bent of American culture.

The voluntary fraternal or civic associations apparently serve a variety of functions for different individuals and groupings. These associations sometimes constitute an avenue for advancing the economic interests of individuals, through the opportunities provided for personal acquaintance, knowledge of business opportunities, and the like; and for the young professional or business man membership may be a *sine qua non* for success in some local communities. Certain organizations appeal to members as a badge of respectability or symbol of prestige. Many (overtly noneconomic) associations become means of economic and political control by particular groups and individuals over others. We have already suggested that such associations to some extent provide belongingness and a sense of community to many individuals having few stable and secure affectional or status bonds. The conspicuousness of benevolent and service motifs in these organizations further hints that they may provide ritual alleviation of anxieties and hostilities and guilts aroused in the area of competitive occupational life. But these are questions of social psychology that we must leave aside with this mention. We can be sure, however, that multiple motives are involved and that the nominal aims of these organizations do not fully describe their consequences.

Returning to structural matters, we are again reminded that associational proliferation is, up to a very high level, generative of further associations. Specifically, as the number of separate groups and associations increases within the same general community, the number of points at which two or more organizations impinge upon the same interest or simultaneously affect the same individuals will increase. Each point of intersection creates a need for regularizing the tangential interaction.[33] Thus, both the family and the school converge upon the child, and the Parent-Teacher Association mediates the triangular relation; or, the multiplication of benevolent, civic, and youth-training associations creates pressures that lead to community chests, councils, co-ordinating agencies, and so on. In some American communities, the large number of formally organized groups and associations appear to have reached practically the upper limit in their demands for participation—a limit imposed by sheer paucity of time, short of obliterating the basic institutions and informal groupings. This is the familiar picture of so-called overorganization in many local areas, a condition which would have been unthinkable in the old-fashioned rural community.

Voluntary associations in our society, then, are made possible by a permissive power-structure and are encouraged by diversity of interests and values, by the weakening of organic groupings, and by organizational complexity. Given these factors, impetus to the formation of voluntary private associations is also given by the shared values of equality and individualism. The absence of an established aristocracy in an equalitarian and activistic culture—to the degree that these conditions actually exist—facilitates private associations. A century ago the decentralized economic structure, the open stratification system, and the localistic-Federal political organization, all contributed bases for development of the private

[33] Cf. Eliot D. Chapple and Carleton S. Coon: *Principles of Anthropology* (New York: 1942), pp. 337–8, 418–25.

association as a basic social unit. Modern conditions of societal interdependence and centralization are now drastically altering the role of the small, local association.

3) SOME CHARACTERISTICS AND PROBLEMS OF LARGE-SCALE FORMAL ORGANIZATIONS [34]

While the total society shows a loose articulation of exceedingly diverse associations and groups, many of its component organizations have become very large, complex, and tightly structured. Although the over-all pattern is still pluralistic—with many relatively autonomous crisscrossing groupings—certain centers of organization have come to represent foci of centralized control over highly formalized structures. This centralization and bureaucratization of organized controls is not confined to the New Leviathan of modern government but is also characteristic of corporate business, of large labor unions and of many other associations. Thus, even at the level of the local community the ubiquitous Community Chest is one of the clearest homely examples of the degree to which the practices of large-scale formal organizations have permeated the voluntary private associations.

The prevalence of large-scale associations is so obvious, and has been so copiously documented in previous chapters (especially 6 and 7), that it is not necessary to present additional evidence here. The role played in the whole society by large formal organizations has enormously increased during the last fifty years. Massive administrative units and combinations of units constitute the order of the day in business, labor, government, and increasingly in education, religion, philanthropy, and other fields. These formal organizations constitute a giant superstructure upon the organic groupings of the old society. We seem to find that the disintegration of a localistic mode of social organization is accomplished by large-scale bureaucratization *and* by the growth of noninstitutional

[34] Available references on this subject are numerous and will not be cited at all the points at which they apply. For the general characteristics of bureaucracy see the references listed in chap. 6 above.

collective behavior. Americans may still talk in nostalgic terms of village and country life, but they are having to learn to somehow live with the large formal association. It becomes correspondingly important to understand the structure and functioning of the latter.

A large number of cumulated studies indicate that definite characteristics appear as a formal organization reaches a certain level of size and complexity. In so far as the organization is, for any reason, structured to act as a unit, there must be some central directing focus. Whether the officials at the directing center be elected or appointed, and regardless of how democratically derived may be the decisions they announce or execute, the unitary action of the organization must be taken through an extended chain of delegated authority and activity. The larger the organization and the more specialized its subunits and individual roles, the larger is the number of intermediaries between the center of authority and the mass of the members.[35] Organizational complexity on a large-scale is typically associated with "bureaucratic" characteristics, as previously noted in chapters 6 and 7 above.

To the degree that such organizations operate in terms of explicit, general rules and regulations, a complex set of consequences follow. Internally, the explicit definition of operating procedures maximizes the interchangeability of personnel and helps to insure certain gross predictabilities of behavior. Similarly, the formalization of office, including the definition of responsibilities, reduces the likelihood of interpersonal conflicts by furnishing unequivocal standards for determining jurisdiction. A system of rules often protects subordinates from arbitrary personal actions on the part of superior officials, in opposition to the development of segmental cliques and political machines within the organization.[36]

[35] Homans: *The Human Group*, p. 406 states this generalization in a somewhat different form.

[36] Any particular social structure is likely to have multiple functions rather than a single consequence. In the present case, it is likely that the same rules that protect subordinates and minimize cliques *also* operate to enhance the possibilities of *centralized* control, e.g., by making rewards contingent upon the rule-making authority rather than the subordinate official.

To release a large organization from the canalizing and restraining effects of a system of formal rules would be, in general, to open the door to widespread particularistic influences (favoritism, etc.) and to court the risk of internal schism and disintegration. On the other side, an impersonal system of generalized rules seems to have widely-noted negative consequences, for example, red tape. Categorical rules, in the nature of the case, do not allow for the full complexity of specific situations—it is precisely one of their main functions to reduce variation, flexibility, extenuating circumstances, and the like. This normative rigidity is a perennial problem in the relations of the organization to its public of customers, clients, or citizens. For to the individual facing the organization at its contact edge his own unique needs and circumstances are of paramount interest, whereas to the organizational official the situation is a case to be dealt with in terms of explicit general rules. The resentment of the citizen, client, or customer at "bureaucratic arrogance" is often the expectable consequence of these clashing perspectives, which in their turn are related to and in part derived from the basic structural situation.[37]

The impersonal-categorical structure of the large business or governmental organization thus continually produces the possibility of clashing norms and expectations at its outer edges. Internally, much the same type-problem arises. Many of the personnel (a significantly neutral word) enter the organization with values and expectations functionally appropriate to the intimate, diffuse, personalized relations of primary groups. If the organization emphasizes functionally specific, depersonalized behavior, such individuals tend initially to react in a personal, overtly affective manner to situations in which the norms of the organization call for specific, impersonal, disinterested action. Nominally institutionalized sanctions, for instance, are perceived as friendly gestures, favoritism,

[37] Problems of individual differences and individual motivation are not unimportant. It is a plausible hypothesis, for example, that individuals who are markedly insecure in their own personalities and group relations are especially prone as officials to rely upon the "letter of the law." For some suggestions on this point see Morris Rosenberg: "The Social Roots of Formalism," *Journal of Social Issues*, Vol. V, no. 1 (Winter, 1949).

dislike, insult.[38] The truly bureaucratic structure finds any high level of overtly affective personal relations disturbing. On the other hand, just to the degree that the organization *is* impersonal, it probably tends to produce anxiety and other tensions among its members—especially new personnel, and individuals at the subordinate levels of administrative hierarchies.

There are, of course, other problems—from the standpoint of the administrative center of the large organization—that arise from basic regularities of group process. Each subunit of interpersonal interaction tends to become a psychological reference group for its participants. It is accordingly not uncommon that loyalties to the subunit take precedence over the goals and norms officially dominant for the organization as a whole. Hence, a recurrent task of centralized administration is that of diagnosing and treating "excessive" segmentation of the organization.[39] It is quite possible that much of the administrative shifting of personnel and dissolution and regrouping of units, so common in large organizations, has as one effect the atomizing of solidary internal segments representing potential threats to unitary control.

Because of specialization, unit segmentation, and extended lines of indirect communication, every large organization encounters significant problems of communication. The difficulties are enhanced in some respects, in so far as the structure of offices is rigidly hierarchical, the opportunities for promotion are slight, and the personnel at various levels are recruited from different social origins. In passing through several intermediate links, communications are typically subject to reformulation and distortion; experienced administrators can almost always point to instances in which the original communication has arrived at its end destination in scarcely recognizable form.

In a very large organization that is marked at the same time by a high degree of functional specialization and great internal complex-

---

[38] And, of course, this meaning may on occasion actually be imputed to the act by all parties concerned.

[39] Again, there are multiple implications. Segmentation is often associated with power aggrandizement by officials, that is, empire building. Or the subgroup becomes a powerful source of resistance to technological and organizational changes initiated outside the group.

ity, the sheer problem of co-ordination of activity toward a common end becomes enormously difficult. The problem has recently appeared in perhaps its most obviously dramatic form in the organization of government for dealing with world problems, but the complexity of the co-ordinative problems of a large corporation, a large university, or a single governmental department are sufficient to tax, and sometimes overtax, the knowledge and ingenuity of those responsible for planning and administration.

We need not go on into the numerous specialized problems of the giant association: provision for the regularized handling of dissatisfactions; the phenomena of "telephone diplomacy," interstatus antagonisms, "buffer states," problems of recruitment, selection, training, promotion and demotion; and so on. Enough has been said to suggest one of our main points: that the large-scale formal structure by its very form creates a wide range of social problems and challenges not likely to be easily solved by automatic processes or common-sense notions. Even at a quasi-technical level ("social engineering") an understanding of these structures requires a range of complex social knowledge still not fully appreciated even among executives. And the problems of social organization are never merely technical, no matter how much the administrators seek to turn all questions of policy into questions of procedure. Instead, the questions of organizational structure and process are always value-laden; they always raise ethical issues. Thus there is meaning in the platitude that wisdom as well as knowledge is implicated in action in this field.

Two necessary comments remain to be added concerning the place of large-scale organizations in the society as a whole.

First, as the size and power of organizational units increase, *the consequences of decisions increasingly outrun the limits of the unit in which they originate.* As the chains of interaction and interdependence become longer and more intricate, actions taken at centralized decision-points have far-flung repercussions. As more and more of the social structure is aggregated or polarized into a relatively few giant associations, furthermore, each set of decisions elicits massive adjustments *en bloc* on the part of other large bodies affected by the act of any one of them. In an age of localism and small groups, the unforeseen consequences of organized actions had a limited impact on the wider society and often were in a sense self-corrective in the short-run because of the immediacy of the consequences. The policy decisions of a major corporation or labor union have consequences not only affecting vast numbers of individuals but also evoking secondary and tertiary adjustments over a long time-span.[40] Thus the collective action of the large organization is increasingly freighted with a public interest in the widest sense of the term.

A second implication seems of great importance in the whole problem of societal integration in the United States, as well as in other industrialized areas of the world. With the development of huge formal organizations, especially in economic and political fields, the dissatisfactions and frustrations incident to life in society become, at least potentially, subject to *generalized* imputations of responsibility. An American farmer faced by drought and Indian raids in 1790 was in no position to perceive his plight as the consequence of a definite social structure. A Detroit worker in 1950 knows the name of the company for which he works, can identify the union to which he belongs, is likely to have some opinion of labor legislation, and in some measure to be accustomed to praising or blaming highly visible social structures and their leadership. From the imputation of responsibility to a *specific* large-scale corporation, union, or political organization, it is not too difficult to define the situation in terms of an entire social system. It is noteworthy that political programs aimed at basic social change generally stress a systematic and total view of the sources of frustration. We are not saying that this stress necessarily occurs, but only that the modern social structure provides a screen highly receptive to such projections of responsibility—for good or ill. In short, the increased centralization and formalization of our social structure vastly increases the likelihood that any major change will become a *political* problem. There are currently many voices raised to ask that the large organization be "humanized"—given flexibility and brought into line with the values presumably basic for the individuals it affects. Other elements of the American population seem committed

---

[40] Cf. F. Stuart Chapin: *Contemporary American Institutions* (New York: 1935), p. 5; Angell: *The Integration of American Society*, chap. 11.

to maximum development of the formalized aspects of the large association. Whatever value position the student of these problems may take it is apparent that we have only begun to acquire the needed knowledge of the structures and processes implicated in these problems.

4) THE INDIVIDUAL AND SOCIAL ORGANIZATION IN AMERICAN SOCIETY

What does this provisional diagnosis of American social structure signify in terms of the individual persons whose repeated actions constitute that structure? Very briefly we will collate certain observations already implicit in preceding analysis.

The institutions of a society confront the individual in the form of *statuses*—established positions, culturally defined in terms of socially recognized and enforced rights and obligations, and subject to common evaluation by the group.[41] The social organization appears to the individual as a set of *roles*, partly corresponding to the statuses and partly a matter of incipient, latent, or noninstitutionalized regularities in individual conduct.

The most general function of social organization from the standpoint of the individual is that of providing predictability in interpersonal relations. Individual conduct can be organized only if there is some minimal regularity in the behavior of others. Otherwise, there can be no recurrent social referents for behavior and no such thing as adjustment, because the very social ground upon which the person stands provides no stability.[42] Some of the consequences of low predictability may be observed among "marginal men," adolescents, delinquents, divorced persons, expatriates and displaced peoples, organizational staffs subjected to drastic

[41] Here we follow Hiller: *Social Relations and Structures*, pp. 330–4.

[42] The solidity of social organization is a primary factor in the development of personality and in the determinations of specific behavior. This crucial point has been developed by numerous investigators, including Pavlov (by implication), Muzafer Sherif, Aleksandr R. Luria, Karen Horney, Harry Stack Sullivan, Howard Liddell, George H. Mead, and Kurt Lewin. Cf. Lewin's *Resolving Social Conflicts* (New York: 1948), Part 3.

changes in policy, and quite generally, in uprooted and socially mobile populations.[43] Rapid and important shifts in the social organization *to which the individual is oriented*—and especially in those specific groupings in which his basic role-involvements and sense of membership have previously been established—typically result in marked personal *dis*-orientations, manifest in erratic behavior and evidences of affective disturbance. These consequences are of varying duration, intensity and qualitative nature in different group contexts, but appear in some form and measure whenever individuals are repeatedly subjected to unpredicted variations in the structure of the social field that go beyond the zone of expectable instability established by past experience. At the extreme, one quite literally "does not know what to expect." If such dissolution of the social pattern involves values central to the person's self-identity, the shattering of stable social expectations seems catastrophic for personality integration. If these processes were to become general in a given population, *common* orientation would disappear, and with it society properly speaking.

Over against this protrait of *anomie*, we may contrast, first, the stable traditionalized social structures that in some respects provide high predictability and relatively rigid expectations. The price paid for this situation includes, among other things, lack of social mobility and of latitude for individual variation and spontaneity.

Then there are, second, the rigid centralized systems illustrated in the monolithic state or, on a lesser scale, in the giant economic organization. At the extreme, again, such structures assimilate into a pattern of discipline and hierarchy the major constituent groupings of the society. And this too has its costs.

In the present American case, the total social structure is, on the surface, paradoxical. On the one hand, the large numbers of industrial workers or employees of business or governmental organizations spend a major part of their lives in relatively rigid and explicitly regulated group contexts. This is the "disciple of the job"—a phenomenon so massive that only anthropological and historical contrasts enable us to become sensitive to its place as a central

[43] Not *all* the characteristics of these categories, of course, are attributable to instability or to changes in group membership.

radix of social organization in America. Likewise, the formalized control-systems of government interlace the society—from the local police to the F.B.I. and loyalty commissions, from the parking meter to the immigration station. On the other side, we are confronted with numerous evidences of instability and rapid change in the personal relations and group memberships of individuals—not only in the casual flux of urban recreation and in formalized special-interest associations and "social" groupings, but also in marriage and the family, in residence groups, and in class-typed social circles. It seems, therefore, that outside the sway of the relatively rigid and centralized association, very large areas of life are characterized by shifting and comparatively formless interaction.

We cannot here essay anything like a comprehensive appraisal of the character or incidence of "mass behavior" as over against formalized organization.[44] We shall have to be content with the unsupported observation that the consequences of apparent instability and rapid change in social structure do *not* seem to carry the disorganizing impact in American society that would be anticipated from the observed experience of *gemeinschaftliche* societies undergoing analogous instability. *If* this judgment is correct, and to the degree that it is, one clue to an explanation would seem to lie in the presence in this society of numerous well-elaborated patterns for coping with both social instability and changes in group memberships. To take only one prominent example, the whole system of vertical occupational mobility confronts the mobile individual with countless shifts in expectations and often with real and emotionally important changes in personality models, group memberships, and group identification. Withal, the *pattern* of mobility is expectable and expected. And—at least in the upward direction—there appear to be rather elaborate stylized mechanisms of withdrawal, alienation, entrance, and assimilation as the individual passes from one context to another. Analogous patterns seem to exist for the transitions of residential mobility. The very causal-

[44] This task can be successfully accomplished only upon the basis of much more extensive, strategic, and systematic research than is now in the storehouse. It is, however, at last a conceivable task—as is the future development of an analytical model of the social system as a whole.

ness, specificity, and impersonality of public contacts, we may suggest, tends to insulate individuals from many conceivably traumatic consequences of unpredictability and misplaced expectations.[45] Rigidity or flexibility, stability or change, predictability or its lack—these are, after all, *relative* notions. The most important fact, within quite wide limits, may not be the absolute amount of instability or change, but the *range of the expectable zone of variation*. In so far as individuals in our society have been prepared to discount a marked degree of change and variation, their reduced expectations of permanence and stability permit acceptance and support of a society of "becoming" rather than "being."

[45] One might think of many of the interactions of the type suggested as social relations at the periphery of personality.

13. Interrelations of Major Institutions and Social Groupings

1. Introduction

IN THE foregoing chapters, some attention has been given to the interrelations among various partially autonomous institutions, and it has been necessary from time to time to allude to social and cultural changes. But, in the interest of clarity, the preceding analysis concentrated on one thing at a time, and proceeded as if structure were a fixed state rather than a continually moving pattern, in order to arrive at a first approximation. We must now shift our attention to the massive problem of institutional interrelationships. Our questions must now be of this order: How do institution A and institution B interconnect? How does group X relate to group Y? How is norm 1 linked to norm 2, and this to still others? And what systems of interrelations exist, and how is it that the whole socio-cultural structure operates as a going concern?

We are in this way coming back to the primary question raised at the beginning of this book: how is it possible that the 150 million human beings living on a part of North America constitute a political entity and, in measure, a recognizable culture? Obviously we cannot hope here to answer such a question, but only to extend our understanding somewhat, by systematic consideration of the problems involved.

We will begin with a few propositions:

1. *Both institutions and groups can be treated as systems.* A system, it was said in chapter 3, is a definite arrangement of parts having boundaries, unity or cohesion, resistance to external forces, and enduring through time. In this sense, the concept is used as in the physical sciences, and the facts of human behavior are conceptualized as a series of systems: personalities, relationships, groups, associations, institutions, societies, cultures.[1] Using systems analysis, we can say that the family institution resists external forces (recognizing the elliptical nature of the statement, since concretely it is the individual *as a participant in* the institutional pattern who resists), or that an "economically rational" governmental policy is resisted because it "encroaches upon the rights of business," and so on. Such statements, of course, involve a very complex order of abstraction, and must be rigorously inspected; however, the emergent properties of groups and institutions are sufficiently well demonstrated to justify their analysis as real systems.

2. Institutions *are not completely separate or autonomous systems but show multiple interconnections and mutual dependencies.* Thus, the total society is constituted by various subsystems and their reciprocal linkages. Of course, not *all* structures or elements of any particular society are interrelated, and the existing interconnections vary tremendously in kind and importance; however, the search for interrelationships has already yielded enough knowledge to demonstrate the scientific value of treating a society, hypothetically, as a system composed of multiple subsystems.[2]

3. In any society, *the main institutions will not exhibit the qualities of a system in equal measure.* Where social patterning has developed

---

[1] The same holds for psychological problems. See: Robert B. MacLeod: "Perceptual Constancy and the Problem of Motivation," *Canadian Journal of Psychology*, Vol. III, no. 2 (1949), p. 61.

[2] Precedents for this approach are numerous. Compare the brief discussion of "integration" in Ralph Linton's *The Study of Man* (New York: 1936), chap. 20; It is pointed out by Eliot D. Chapple and Carleton S. Coon that functional interdependence can be demonstrated only from observation of systems undergoing *change*. *Principles of Anthropology* (New York: 1942), p. 462. Sorokin: *Society, Culture and Personality* (New York: 1947) continually emphasizes the idea of interconnected systems in both the social and cultural fields. From a radically different perspective, George C. Homans analyzes the small group as a system (*The Human Group*).

to the point at which subsystems of institutionalized behavior are identifiable at all—and we know of no continuing societies so "simple" that this is impossible—some institutions will be more segregated, self-contained, outwardly resistant, and so on, than others. This has been demonstrated, if crudely, in studies indicating that cultural diffusion and social change are initially absorbed by the least structured portions of institutional systems. Thus, when Western industrialism and constitutional forms of government came to Japan in the nineteenth century, the results broadly taken, were: (1) an assimilation of "capitalism" to the family system (rather than, as in the United States, an adaptation of the family *to* the economic institutions); (2) constitutional government took on strongly feudalistic features at the local level and a highly hierarchical centralized structure, organized on the principle of group responsibility, at the national level.[3] Speaking loosely but not incorrectly, we would regard this as a case in which the combined kinship-stratification systems proved to be more rigid than the indicated economic and political arrangements.

4. Contrary to all theoretical systems that posit the universal dominance of a particular institution, for example, the economic, *the central or leading institution(s) varies from society to society in a given period, and from one period to another in a given society.* Further, there may not in fact be any one clearly dominant institutional system. The easy literary labeling of whole epochs, itself in part a culture bound product of Western history, can create the impression that one era or society is wholly "religious," another overwhelmingly "economic," but this is an imposed, poetic unity, not a description of the actual multiplicity of institutional systems and group contexts.

It is as easy to state the logical and operational criteria for establishing the degree to which one institution predominates in a

<hr>

[3] Cf. John F. Embree: *The Japanese Nation* (New York: 1945), esp. chaps. 2–4; Hugh Borton: *Japan Since 1931*, Institute of Pacific Relations (New York: 1940); George B. Sansom: *Japan: A Short Cultural History*, 2nd ed. (New York: 1943); Charles B. Fahs: *Japanese Government: Recent Trends in Scope and Operation*, Institute of Pacific Relations (New York: 1940); G. C. Allen: *Japan: The Hungry Guest* (New York: 1938); Morris E. Opler: "Japan: The West of the East?" *Patterns for Modern Living* (Chicago: 1950).

society as it is difficult to find the required data. A first approach to the problem is the controlling observation of *change*. If we find that changes in institution A are invariably followed by important changes in institutions B . . . n, but that changes in institutions B . . . n are followed by few or insignificant changes in institution A—then A is presumably a "prime mover" or dominant vector in the social system. Such a clearcut situation not only does not exist empirically, but involves logical contradictions; however, *degrees of variation* in several interconnected institutions are, in principle, subject to observations testing such causal salience according to the model just outlined. A second and more specific procedure for appraising dominance consists of systematic observation of what occurs when *various sets* of *institutional norms conflict* in particular situations.[4] If particular norms, conceived as part of institution A, always or in some preponderant proportion take precedence over the *other* norms, this is a test of the extent to which one institutional complex is more predictive of behavior than others. This abstract statement is translatable into terms so specific as whether an American businessman renounces the purchase of a new car in order to give aid to a needy relative, a religious body, or to reinvest in his business. When value conflicts and value priorities entail definitely institutionalized norms of social relations, we are following the shorthand practice of speaking in terms of conflicts and compatibilities of institutions. The next section will confront some of the specific senses in which institutions are related; here it is enough to emphasize that accuracy on this subject requires that *specified* normative systems, not "institutions in general," be kept clearly in view. Even so, it is by no means simple to determine when certain norms are, or are not, "compatible." For one thing, the content accessible at a commonsense level quite often conceals and is at variance with less obvious functional patterns, for example, the way nepotism in government becomes loyalty in the family. Again, a particular norm or value does not have an absolute meaning in social action but depends upon *relations in a context*, for example, occupational duties that might seem *a priori* to be incompatible with stable family life can be transvalued as part of a total

---

[4] See chapters 10 and 11.

scheme of living, so that "job" and "home" do not compete but rather mutually reinforce a pattern of activity, which is valued *as a whole*. Furthermore, institutional patterns that seem logically in conflict are very often not involved in the same specific roles, groups, or situations, so that social action results in little or no conflict: for example, the same groups may hold simultaneously that government should stay out of business, protect the home market, force the "chiselers" to maintain prices, and regulate the labor unions.

From these considerations, another general rule can be derived: *institutional interrelations can be deduced only to a very limited and uncertain extent from the apparent content of cultural norms*. Therefore, before high-level generalizations can be derived in this area, specific norms and values must be empirically traced through specific social roles and social groups.[5]

2. How Institutions Are Related

IF THE assumptions stated in the preceding section are to be useful for the empirical study of society, we must be able to specify the modes of interrelation in a testable form. If institutions are systems, causally or functionally connected with other systems, we must specify the mechanisms of linkage.

To begin with, we may set up the model of a social system in which institutions are not embodied in clearly defined associations or groups, but are merely norm complexes to which the behavior of all members of the society is oriented. In such a case, institutions would be *cultural facts*, not *differentiated social structures* within the society; there would be definite norms and these would be institutional, in our sense, but they would neither be labeled as separate institutions nor carried in special organizations. No actual society is so little differentiated. Even in small nonliterate groups, subsisting by gathering and hunting, there is some organizational precipitate of institutional norms, e.g., a more or less autonomous

---

[5] For this reason, the title of the present chapter brackets together institutions and social groupings.

family structure, or a shaman, or a rudimentary chieftainship. In reference to such societies, however, it is initially difficult to think of institutional interrelations because the connections appear almost self-evident. The members of the society may not and usually do not think of separate religious, familial, economic, or political activities—they simply carry out their daily activities, that we, as outside observers see as a web of behavior controlled by norms that we would call institutional. In the course of a lifetime, any particular individual will participate in all these nonnucleated [6] institutions; for the most part there are no specialized personnel to maintain specific institutional subsystems. To the degree that this is the situation, *interinstitutional* relations are largely synonymous with *intrapersonality* adjustments: the integration of institutions is the integration of personalities. In his various statuses the individual functions in terms of ideas, beliefs, values, and norms defining his relations to other persons, and his total activity, therefore, requires the resolution of conflicting norms or beliefs that may occur in specific situations; any "strain for consistency," however, would be the adjustment of individual actors scattered through the system as a whole.

However, this model of a society with unspecialized institutions does not exist—even at a tribal level, societies exhibit considerable specialization of institutions. Certain activities are segregated, and responsibility for them assigned to chiefs, medicine men, and so on, and specialized norms develop to regulate these statuses. Each of these normative subsystems as they develop in a small society may be represented by only a few persons or a single person. In a larger society with more definite specialization, such status systems typically become the basis for definite organizations composed of specially designated personnel. Whenever specialization appears, relations between institutions become relations of groups, organizations, or social categories *mediated through the direct person-to-person interaction of individuals occupying differentiated statuses.* This is a mode of connection very familiar to us—the minister

[6] The term is from F. Stuart Chapin: *Contemporary American Institutions* (New York: 1935); see especially pp. 13 ff. We are here borrowing the term for a temporarily more restricted usage.

consults the mayor, the parent interacts with the teacher, the banker talks with the legislator. Back of the interacting principals are the respective "constituencies" (parishioners, or family members, or voters, and so on) who comprise reference groups for the institutional representatives. Of course, the intrapersonality adjustments continue also at this level of structural segregation. The new element here is the direct interrelation of specialized roles, representing partly autonomous normative systems.

An obvious secondary elaboration of this pattern is the development of chains of mediated interaction—from institution A to B, and thence to C and D—as when the minister intercedes with the judge on the behalf of a youthful offender to have the latter remanded to the school which in turn deals with the family. Various still more complicated structural variations arise out of such mediated or tangent relations. Thus, the Supreme Court in our political system is a complex mediating agency which deals with problems involving every major institution of the society.

What we are directly observing here is still the concrete behavior of individual persons, from which, we must remember, institutions are abstracted—just as personality systems or groups are inferred from similarly concrete behavior. These abstracted systems are not arbitrary; they are necessary to account for observed properties of conduct. Here, as always, we are interested in *differences:* what difference does it make if institutional norm complexes are, or are not, incorporated into separate systems of social organization; and, if there are relatively autonomous institutional systems, what relations subsist among them? For example, it can be noted quickly that an outstanding feature of modern American society is the extraordinarily sharp separation of institutions, at the *social* level. Each institutional cluster in our society *tends* to be segregated from others and to involve distinctive statuses occupied by specialized personnel. The common tendency to equate religion with the church, education with the school, politics with government is partly based on the recognition of such distinct systems of activities, beliefs, knowledges, values, and symbols.[7] *One* aspect

[7] Cf. Constantine Panunzio: *Major Social Institutions* (New York: 1939), chap. 24.

of this differentiation and segregation is that individuals are involved in multiple statuses and multiple group memberships; we are thus familiar with role segmentation, and also with the fairly common situations in which there is some type of conflict of roles or group memberships. Another feature of the situation is perhaps less often noted in its full significance, namely, the orientation of individuals in one status or group to *other* statuses or groups, as with the orientation of the teacher *as educator* to the parent *qua* parent. Even the most highly specialized statuses are not related only to similar statuses but to different statuses located in separate groups or associations. Under certain conditions, those occupying a similar status may form an organization that interacts *as a system* with a body whose members are persons holding a polar status in a two-sided relation: for example, workers who comprise a labor union which deals with employers. And in a highly complex structure, there will be still another organizational level comprised of mediating and coordinating systems, represented by role specialists in their own partly independent groups or associations.

As the cultural fact of institutionalization is translated into special areas of organized interaction, the *organization* (the church, capitalistic enterprise, and so on) may develop considerable autonomy in relation to the values and norms of other institutionalized organizations, and this, indeed, has happened on a vast scale in the United States.[8] In the present situation, although not in all situations, there are general tendencies for these organized structures to become larger, more complex, more centralized in control. As this occurs, in such a highly interdependent society, the numerous interactions of large and elaborately organized systems frequently lead to "institutional imperialism" as one system seems to "encroach" upon another.

It has been shown, then, that institutions may be interconnected through *intrapersonality responses* to different norms and values, through the *direct interaction of role specialists*, through *mediated*

---

[8] As chapter 6 indicated, a crucial instance was the partial "escape" of economic activity from the control-systems of local community, church and government.

relations involving several institutions.[9] American society has gone very far in the creating of definite organizations with specialized personnel to carry on activities culturally assigned to the institutional areas broadly distinguished in earlier chapters. The general significance of this is that *different individuals* and *different organizations* are the prime carriers of the various sets of norms which otherwise would be partial systems of the same personalities or overlapping roles in a relatively undifferentiated community. Perhaps it can be shown that kinship and social stratification are, in the present sense, the least specialized institutions, since they are relatively diffuse, nonnucleated systems, permeating a very wide range of actions; but even here there are many areas of relatively sharp separation and insulation.

"Strains" in the interrelations of institutions appear as: 1) personality conflicts and the resulting responses to these conflicts; 2) social conflict, either of *associations* or "communal" groups (for example, ethnic groupings). These conflicts, as a matter of fact, furnish some of the clearest indications that we actually are dealing with real systems.

Finally, institutions are related through processes not involving person-to-person interaction, either directly or through specialized representatives. These are the processes Karl Mannheim designates as "field structures": recurring mass influences transmitted through the society as segmental reactions of individuals to common stimuli: mass propaganda, changes in interest rates or wages, unemployment. These diffusely received influences are highly relevant to institutional stability *and* to institutional change. However, they represent the marginal area of collective behavior, and are not concerned in the present discussion.

These seem to be the most important forms of institutional linkage and reciprocal effect. We will now illustrate how the approach suggested here applies in studies of kinship and political and economic institutions from the contemporary American scene. The treatment is necessarily excursive since rigorous analysis

---

[9] In these terms, a "simple" society would be defined as one in which unmediated relations dominated.

would require a synthesis of current and future basic research that does not yet exist.

3. Selected "Case Studies" of Institutional Interrelations

CASE #1: KINSHIP IN THE WEB OF INSTITUTIONS

SEVERAL suggestions as to the place of kinship relations and family groups in the society have already been advanced (especially in chapters 4 and 5). For example, there is the proposition that our industrial and commercial order, with its great specialization and rapid change, favors the small, isolated, discontinuous, nuclear family of neolocal residence. By the same token, this type of family system is encouraged by high rates of vertical social mobility. The converse propositions also hold.

Thus, a system of strong extended kinship relations may be expected to be a partial barrier to the free mobility of labor and economic resources from one geographic area or line of production to another. And, the greater the role of kinship in the total social structure,[10] the more likely it is that social strata will be rigid and social mobility low. Also such a society will tend to be traditionalistic in other major respects, for example, in religion, education, government; and to de-emphasize and resist social change. At the same time, the larger the areas of social relations defined in terms of kinship, the more likely it is that the dominant norms in *other* institutions will be particularistic rather than universalistic: the stranger will tend to be outside the sphere of morality, unless he can be assimilated to a kinship status; law and justice will tend to be conceived in terms of *particular* statuses; an especially

---

[10] By "greater role" we mean: a higher proportion of individual interactions with persons who are "relatives," or otherwise stated, a higher percentage of all social relations which are culturally defined by the facts of marriage and descent. There are other useful operational indexes, e.g., inventories of choice-behavior, of expressed norms.

sharp distinction is likely between ingroups and outgroups.[11] It is also less likely that other types of relations, for example, economic, will be functionally specific—as it is sometimes said, kinship is fundamentally opposed to contract. Or, to turn to political structures, such societies appear especially likely to have hierarchical governing structures built upon local segmental groups. On the other side, the lack of a strong centralized government is often associated with marked development of family authority and with a salient role for kinship in the regulative order of the entire society.[12] Where kinship groups are strong, extended, and stable in dominantly rural societies, we seem to find that the organization of the state is a sort of film on the surface of the society, failing to penetrate directly to the mass of individuals. One notes also that modern revolutionary totalitarian movements seem initially to invade the family in many respects, for example, encouraging children to inform on their parents.

These illustrations indicate that the place of kinship in American social structure is actually a special case of interrelations requiring wider examination. The important question for the study of the total ramifications of kinship can be put specifically: how and to what extent is the fact of relation by birth or marriage socially utilized in defining and regulating activities outside the immediate system of the family itself? From this way of raising the problem there follow innumerable further and more specific questions. For example:

Who "owns" property? Who transmits it to whom, and how? Who or what cares for and supports dependent persons, the very young, the aged, the ill, the disabled? Where, how, and by whom are religious rites performed? (e.g., "family prayer," or only an outside official service.) What is the part of kinship units in economic production?

[11] A caution is necessary: for the moment we are stating hypothetical *correlations*; direct causal relations are not implied.

[12] Cf. Carle C. Zimmerman: *Family and Civilization* (New York: 1947), p. 14: "The abundance of law and order agencies and the multiplicity of external bonds holding societies together during the periods of statute law and strongly developed central governments made the internal cohesion of family groups less and less necessary as a unified social force."

To what extent and how is kinship a criterion for or advantage in securing political power?

To what extent is trade divorced from kinship ties and obligations?

How permeable, and in what respects, is the family unit to actions of persons outside the kinship status-system?

To continue with the last question, we have previously diagnosed the modal American family type as extremely permeable to external influences, both culturally and in actual interaction patterns. As will be recalled, the legal order penetrates into family solidarity by a vast number of provisions which assign *individual*, not family group, responsibilities and rights, as for example in limiting parents' rights to control and discipline children.

From similar indications we have concluded that the kinship system plays a *relatively* dependent part in the total institutional structure, especially as related to the economic and political areas. It is perhaps in these areas that we have the most convenient access to further clues as to dynamic interconnections.

Kinship plays into the economic structure, in the first place through *occupation*.[13] By definition, kinship is particularistic in its basic pattern; it is the basic area of status ascription and the primary orientation is to "*who* you are"—not what you are or can do. In contrast, the occupational structure in our society is much more universalistic—the central criteria concern abilities and capacities and achievements, rather than status tests (family membership; "who" needs the job, and so on). From these two propositions, it follows that since an emphasis upon occupation as a primary determinant of social station necessarily implies a lessened role for kinship, a reduction in the size and scope of the basic family unit becomes a meaningful consequence of our elaborately differentiated occupational structure. This has just been stated as a formal deduction from the definitions given. But much evidence supports the conclusion that the small-family system results in part from competitive occupational placement in a dynamic economy, as when economic changes force families to

[13] The relations to social stratification must be passed over at this point.

disperse. Competitive occupational placement seems to strain family solidarity, creating pressures both toward reduction in size and toward insulating certain family roles from the competitive matrix.[14] The absence of the worker from home and family during his occupational activity, has as one consequence for family structure, the mother-centered pattern of child training, and the lack of an occupational apprenticeship of sons to the father. Whatever degree of father-son discontinuity is thus introduced is reinforced by rapid changes in occupational opportunity (as well as by the pattern of upward social mobility). Still more generally, the removal of economic production from the home radically affects the total pattern of family relations. It would seem that the most important fact is not the loss of economic functions as such but the reduction in intrafamily interaction centered upon purposeful common goals and involving numerous shared understandings, expectations, disciplines, and affective patterns.[15] As has already been noted, another factor here is the functionless place of aged persons in the family system, due in part to the demand for relatively young workers. The aged tend, involuntarily, to become merely consumers rather than producers. Because the breadwinner role and male authority in the family are connected it seems likely that this occupational pattern has weakened the father's influence with his mature sons, and has affected family structure and function in many other complex ways.

The instability of the economic system has periodically subjected family solidarity to severe strains. But here we note that the same mass impact, for example, unemployment, is *not* followed by a simple and undifferentiated change in family units. The limited available evidence indicates that unemployment intensifies the previously established latent structure of the family unit, that is, strongly solidary families tend to retain their unity best, disunited families become more disunited.[16] In any case, a

[14] See the more detailed discussion in chapter 4.

[15] See the compact statement in George C. Homans: *The Human Group*, pp. 276–80.

[16] Mirra Komarovsky: *The Unemployed Man and His Family*, The Institute of Social Research (New York: 1940), pp. xii, 24 ff.

major alteration in economic opportunity, for urban workers without property, sets off changes in the balance of reciprocal roles and expectations within the family unit.[17]

We have tried to illustrate a series of tangible functional connections between the cultural facts of kinship and the social organization of families, on the one hand, and particular features of the economic structure, on the other.

Family structure is always one of a mutually dependent set of variables in the concrete character of an economic situation. For example, in some parts of the southern Appalachians a family system developed, through the 19th and early 20th centuries, in which extended kin relations were strong, intergeneration continuity was relatively great, sex roles well defined, birth rates high. Under conditions of limited agricultural resources, comparatively limited emigration, and the dominance of the principle of equality of siblings in inheritance, the initial result was a rapid parcelization of the land. As the family system was perpetuated —in isolation from deviant cultural patterns—the subdivision of farms reached a stage at which steeper and less productive lands were cleared for cultivation. With the existing technology, this led to severe soil erosion and other depletions of agricultural resources. This threat to the standard of living developed during a period of lessened cultural isolation, which made for awareness of outside employment opportunities, as well as of new market goods obtainable only through money expenditures. One consequence of all these factors was an increase in migration of young people from the area. Migration, in turn, reacted back upon the family in a number of ways, for example: youth-parent conflict, the development of something like a system of ultimogeniture. Without following the complex sequence further, this case points to the kinds of data needed to analyze the dynamics of social interdependence in reasonably specific terms.

Kinship ties, like many other forms of established social relations, can constitute a very definite obstacle to the economic rationali-

17 Cf. E. Wight Bakke: *The Unemployed Man* (New York: 1934) and, by the same author, *Citizens Without Work* (New Haven, Conn.: 1940), esp. chaps. 8–9.

zation of production, as when in some cases, family rights and obligations have so penetrated business enterprises that inefficient relatives may be given crucial jobs, or capital needed for technological changes may be siphoned off into consumption within the extended family. We have already suggested that values or obligations developed in the family can retard economically adjustive mobility.[18] Perhaps the most striking fact about the American situation, however, is just the relatively inconsequential role of familial institutions in these respects.[19]

We also know that the family group is a basic medium for the actual definition of economic "needs" and "motives." Thus, it is now certain that older theories that found the key to economic incentive in some sort of egoistic self-interest are quite inadequate: men, in our society as well as in others, typically work not merely for themselves alone but for an actual or potential family group. The task alone does not supply the incentives for work. The values, and correlative disciplines, involved in family living are different from those of nonfamily living. This is manifest in different consumption and saving patterns; and *different* family structures similarly carry variant economic implications. In the inadequately charted field of the economics of consumption, the peculiarities of American family systems may eventually find a very tangible place. One may note such possible clues as the individualization of buying and consumption, the role of women as purchasers, the partial replacement of familial activities in the home by commercialized recreation, the budgetary and market implications of status patterns, the shifts in demand schedules with those changes in the demographic situation resulting from changes in family norms.

To continue following kinship through the institutional systems of the society, let us look briefly at a few of the more obvious connections between family and political structures. The first salient point here is that our political norms *tend* to eliminate

---

[18] R. M. Williams: "Concepts of Marginality in Rural Population Studies," *Rural Sociology*, Vol. V, no. 3 (September, 1940).

[19] A possible exception, calling for further analysis: the functions of the family in the control and transmission of wealth.

kinship as a direct basis for political power. Not ascribed status, but elective or appointive office is the dominant institutional mode [20]—for example, the commonplace rules against nepotism. However, we have seen that while our culture seems to insulate government from family, the reverse is not true—the state intervenes on a large scale in the regulation of the family.

At the basic level of personality formation, the family unit is a miniature government, as MacIver, Merriam, Lasswell and others have pointedly reminded us. The primary conceptions of authority and patterns of response to authority are initially established in parent-child relations. All parents everywhere must, by virtue of their status, demand some conformity from young children. The way in which the child responds to parental authority supplies the base upon which successively modified reactions to authority and power relations are later developed.[21] The American family system tends, broadly, to minimize parental coercion and unquestioning obedience, and to stress sibling equality. *To the degree that* this is the case, the familial norms would seem to be congruent with a democratic political system.[22] A comparative perspective wide enough to include China, Japan, and Germany, raises the hypothesis that the dominant family patterns in our society are relatively unfavorable to coercive authority. In urban middle-class families there are widespread patterns of child training which seem to encourage the questioning of suggestions or commands: the child comes to ask "why" rather than to comply "because Father says so." At the same time, it is likely that the infrequent

[20] Elements of ascription, of course, affect the achievement of political power, chiefly through the role of the family in fixing membership in ethnic, racial, or religious categories. ("No President of the United States has ever been a Negro, Catholic, or Jew.") However, this is by no means a simple case of kinship ascription—note, for instance, that the distinctions in question are *categorical* rather than a matter of specific family lines, and that even the present factual situation is very far from complete institutionalization.

[21] This does not imply a mechanical or automatic "carry-over." The notion that adult responses to political figures are simple *recapitulations* of childhood relations to parents or siblings is contradicted by the impressive evidence for the situational determination of conduct.

[22] *But* note that the basic form of the American State was laid down in a period when family structure was much more "patriarchal" than now.

use of coercive authority by parents makes it seem all the more arbitrary when it does occur. The foregoing may be described as disciplined speculation, recording at the level of hypothesis this sampling of possible intrapersonality connections between family institutions and political authority, in the absence of evidence needed to support more systematic analysis.

The relations between kinship and social stratification can not here receive much analysis beyond that given in earlier chapters. We have indicated that kinship can affect stratification positions at the one extreme by defining the actual *unit* of ranking in the stratification order, but, on the other hand, it may be given little weight as a criterion of stratification position. To the degree that kinship is minimized in the determination of ranking, the way is opened for development of stratification systems in which position is based upon the achievements and qualities of individuals.[23]

The most obvious—and most crucial—connection between kinship and stratification, as institutional systems, comes at the point of intergeneration transmission of position. The central fact here is that *in so far as family membership is a direct criterion of class position the whole effect is to perpetuate indefinitely the status quo ante;* where family determines class the result is to freeze the stratification system into rigid mold. Conversely, a system of stratification based solely upon personal achievement would be incompatible with the family as we know it. For then, there could be no hereditary transmission of status, and kinship groups would have to become atomized in this aspect. To the extent that family groups are social units they usually generate forces tending toward the use of kinship as an institutionalized criterion of position in the stratification scale. In American society the relatively slight emphasis on kinship as criterion of class position militates against family continuity—and thereby is functional for a mobile open-class system stressing personal achievement as a primary criterion.

[23] It is *not* inevitable that low stress on kinship will lead to an individualistic system of stratification. At least in the short run it is possible that membership in non-kinship groups (for example, political party organizations, cliques, etc.) could be utilized for the assignation of status, relatively apart from personal qualities and achievements of individuals.

In this aspect, the "weakness" so often deplored in the American kinship institutions is integrative with the cultural principles of upward social mobility through individual occupational achievement. This is another way of saying that a kinship system with strong intergeneration continuity would be incompatible with the fluidity of social classes that has been one of the remarkable features of America in the past. The one large-scale exception to the principle of individual achievement as the basis for ranking is that of position assigned or ascribed on the basis of membership in a distinctive racial or ethnic group. The significant thing here is precisely the tension, conflict, and moral unease that this kind of ascribed status arouses in our society—striking evidence of the difficulty of integrating an open-class system with the use of particularistic criteria of stratification.

CASE #2: ECONOMIC AND POLITICAL INSTITUTIONS—THE PROBLEM OF CONTROL

Here we confront an area of clamor, and the clash of arms. There is a "Marxian" definition, and a "Fascist" definition, and a variety of other views which clearly go beyond causal analysis to evaluate the ends or values to be served by economic and political arrangements. Here we will assume both that certain ends are attainable under all of the currently controversial systems, and that some ends that are attainable under one system are not in others. Our task is not to evaluate these alternatives, but to seek additional clarification of the evolving structural alignments in the American case. In a field where so much ideological conflict and confusion exists it may be useful to make quite explicit the elementary propositions from which we start:

1. Political power and economic activity are universal institutional systems, and the two are never completely independent.
2. Political authority never includes all social power, and nominally economic relations always have power implications.
3. Both political and the economic institutions are affected by

other institutions and operate within a wider societal framework.

4. Some normative definition and regulation of economic activity is present in every society; social controversy arises over the amount and kind of regulation—it is not a simple matter of "regimentation" versus "freedom."

During recent decades there has been an apparently widespread belief that governmental intervention is a recent innovation in American life. Although the nature and extent of the state's role in economic affairs has certainly changed drastically, even since World War I, the belief that governmental intervention—whether support or regulation—is really new is an illusion. The governments of large and complex social orders have always actively dealt with economic behavior.[24] Inevitably, under any set of conditions yet known to history, the role of the state tends to become larger as the economic system becomes more complex. The more specialization of production, the more *interdependent* an economy becomes. And the larger the units of economic production and exchange, under conditions of great specialization and technological complexity, the more crucial this interdependence is for the integration of the whole society. No state—whatever political label it may wear—can or will ignore this fact.

In present circumstances the *political* implications of economic activity have become increasingly evident. The interpenetration and mutual relations of economic activity and political power extend into levels that are not easily visible and can only be discerned by analysis of great difficulty and complexity, requiring, among other things, initial care in the specification of concepts. In chapter 6, it was found convenient to treat economic institutions as those interrelated clusters of normative rules and values which most directly govern the allocation of scarce means to alternative

---

[24] ". . . There has never been in the history of civilized nations an economic system in which governments were not used to regulate individual action and to carry on certain economic activities directly, and it is equally true that there has never been an economic system in which some reliance was not placed on the initiative of private individuals."—Lyon, Watkins, Abramson: *Government and Economic Life*, Vol. I, p. 11.

ends. Action is purely economic action in so far as it is guided by the attempt to maximize utility by applying given resources to those uses costing least in terms of their returns.

It is useful to follow Max Weber in distinguishing *economic* action, in the above sense, from *economically relevant* action and from *economically conditioned* action.

Much economically relevant behavior is not directly concerned with the production of utilities for exchange nor with the exchange process, for example, the use of time for noneconomic ends, such as recreational or religious activities that reduce the resources of a group or society for the production of economic utilities. A widely different case consists of the use of force or coercion for the direct acquisition of utilities: robbery, piracy, war-booty, reparations, and the like. Although these types of activities certainly have been of enormous relevance to the total picture of economic production and distribution, they are not economic actions *per se*. Another example here is the allocation of economic resources to political or more broadly societal ends, with relatively little consideration to ordinary criteria of cost; instead the main guiding norm may be whether this use of resources is likely to insure a given social end, such as military victory, at whatever cost.

Economically conditioned activity is also guided, in the main, by noneconomic goals and norms, although economic considerations appreciably affect the course of action. The character of the music produced in a particular society will be affected by the economic bases for composing and playing music. The religious activity of an economically deprived stratum is not likely to be identical with that of privileged groups. Similarly, the family, recreation, war, and innumerable other socio-cultural phenomena are not concretely economic activities, but all are potentially subject to variation because of economic factors playing through the total situation.

If we accept the convention of restricting *economic* activity to the peaceable allocation of scarce utilities to alternative ends, and maintain the broad distinction between this and economically *relevant* and *conditioned* activities, we have a convenient base for attacking the relation between the economic sector and the political institutions of a society. It is easy to see that the vegetable pushcart vendor is doing something different from the policeman who demands to see his peddler's license, but it is very important to see precisely what the difference is, why it occurs, and what its implications are as the scale of action and organization widens into the entire social order.

We have found the central element of political activity in the acquisition and use of power, and have seen this aspect of action emerge whenever a plurality of human beings are interacting. But the capacity to control actions of others may be fairly evenly diffused throughout a society or group, or it may be highly concentrated into one or a few strategic foci. In considering *political* power we have concentrated upon the institutional regulation of power that successfully claims legitimacy in the ultimately monopolistic use of coercion within a given territory, and especially upon the state as the association exercising this sort of power. Within the associations and groups that make up the apparatus of the state, legitimated authority eventuates in imperative control (Weber): [25] the probability that a specific command will be obeyed by a given group of persons. This is the form of authority most obvious to common-sense—but it is clear that imperative control is not confined to government, but resides also in the parent's rule in the family, the employer's command of employees, the priest's orders to the religious follower, and so on. Imperative control is most highly formalized and clearly defined in certain types of *corporate groups*— groups in which social relationships (a) are closed to outsiders (or else restricted as to admission by specific rules), and in which (b) group norms are enforced by specific individuals who are charged with this enforcement as their regular function in the group.[26]

From these distinctions several crucial conclusions follow:

1. In so far as individuals or associations engaged in overtly economic activities are able to exert power over others, their character becomes increasingly governmental. One can imagine,

[25] Max Weber: *The Theory of Social and Economic Organizations*, trans. by A. M. Henderson and Talcott Parsons (New York: 1947), pp. 152–7.

[26] Weber goes on to say that a system of order that governs corporate actions *as such* is administrative. A system that governs action outside the corporate group is then termed regulative. This will be an important point for the present discussion. Ibid., pp. 150–2.

for example, that one giant corporation came to control all manufacturing in the United States. How far would this be from a state?

2. The *internal* regulation of large economic associations involves authority and imperative control exercised in ways similar to those prevailing in administrative units that are popularly thought of as government rather than business. There is always the possibility that imperative control within the economic enterprise will be at least as rigid and severe as its opposite number in the governmental agency. The question can not safely be prejudged.

3. Even on purely theoretical grounds, it can be predicted that much political activity will be economically relevant; that much will be economically conditioned; and there is no *a priori* reason to suppose that the state may not engage in strictly economic activities. The mere existence of a specialized state means the appropriation of considerable amounts of economic utilities, which are thereby withdrawn from other potential productive uses. It is not inconceivable that large standing military forces, extensive bureaucracies, and other social apparatus relevant to war can immobilize the productive surplus of a society.

Perhaps these considerations are enough to suggest that questions centering upon economic freedom and governmental intervention are likely to be greatly confused and blurred unless certain crucial distinctions are made. The more important points may be put in the form of questions, to be answered in any analysis of the total social system:

1. *How much* power from *any quarter* is being exercised upon individuals in the society? This question is distinct from the second problem.

2. How intense is this type of control? What sanctions are utilized, and with what institutionalized regulation? At what point does taxation become confiscation, or monopoly prices lead to expropriation of the small entrepreneur, or punitive law become arbitrary persecution?

3. Is power concentrated or diffused within the social order? To what degree does any one institutionalized association or group have a monopoly of power? Is the society characterized by a pluralistic or monolithic power structure?

4. How is power distributed among the various institutional sectors? What belongs to church, to family, to industry, to labor, to the state, to something else?

5. To what extent is power institutionally regulated? This is another way of asking: To what extent has power been transmuted into legitimate authority? Still more specifically, to what degree is control exercised according to reasonably predictable universalized rules?

As we have seen,[27] the forces that shaped nineteenth century America led to the development of a limited state that was ideally to intervene as little as possible in the free play of competitively determined economic decisions being made by large numbers of formally free workers and enterprisers selling their services or goods in the open market. The state was to have a restricted and clearly defined zone of authority. It was to be a regulative rather than an administrative order, in Weber's sense. The economic arena was visualized as sharply separate from government, and as a nearly autonomous self-adjusting order.

Even while these conceptions were being systematized the real structure of American society moved rapidly to the point of negating many of the basic conditions upon which the old-style economy had rested. As the economic structure shifted toward large-scale corporative organization, the relation of government and business became a persistent focus of political tension. Stripped down to essentials, this became a running conflict over the question whether *specific* powers of various kinds were to be lodged in the corporation, the labor organization, or the state. After a period of unprecedented lack of governmental control over economic life, recent decades have shown a world-wide shift toward concentration of economic control in the State. In the United States, there had been a period of at least fifty years (say, from 1880 to 1930) when one might say that there was government of a highly imperative kind within the enterprise or firm, but relative anarchy between firms. Aside from certain state regulations and aids to be mentioned later, the control of the *total* economy was a diffuse *cultural* control, not the explicit regulation of a *definite social organization*. The

[27] See chapters 5 and 6.

great development of our day is the centralization of structure, both of business and labor organization and of the state, and this increasingly means that economic problems become political problems. It was one of the curious blind spots of *laissez-faire* theories that they failed to see how liberal capitalism depended upon a high degree of stability in the political-legal system. This very special economic system is severely strained in any society continually upset by political upheavals, or subject to unpredictable reversals of basic social rules, or to major shifts in the politically oriented allocation of resources.[28]

We are now in a position to attempt a highly condensed diagnosis of the present American situation in somewhat more specific terms. Concretely, business and government are interrelated at thousands of specific points. In the first place, the organizations and personnel of the state operate in numerous ways to *facilitate* or *implement* economic activity. Among the more important forms of implementation are:[29]

1. Development of corporation law making possible limited liability and extended life for business enterprises; 2. provision for bankruptcy and reorganization of business enterprises; 3. provision and operation of patent laws; 4. providing standard coinage, suppressing counterfeiting, maintaining redemption of currency; 5. support and regulation of banking, for example, chartering, inspection, deposit insurance; 6. regulation of stock and commodity exchange mechanisms; 7. provision of facilities, procedures, and regulations for adjusting management-labor disputes; 8. supplying essential standards: monetary standards, weights and measures, physical composition and performance of materials and products;[30]

[28] It may have been some such considerations as these which led Herbert Spencer to equate "industrial society" and peace. If industrial society—by which he meant capitalism—does not insure peace, it can at least be said that liberal capitalism is highly vulnerable to the effects of war.

[29] We shall borrow freely here from the presentation of Leverett S. Lyon, Myron W. Watkins, and Victor Abramson: *Government and Economic Life* (Washington, D. C.: 1939), drawing especially on Vol. I, pp. 41–390.

[30] For example, note this highly abbreviated list of selected statutes: Food and Drug Act (1906 and 1938), Meat Inspection Act (1907), Cotton Futures Act (1914), Commodity Exchange Act (1936), Grain Standards Act

9. undertaking research and disseminating the findings, for example, Bureau of Mines, Department of Agriculture, Public Health Service, National Bureau of Standards, military agencies, Weather Bureau; 10. collecting and disseminating information; for *producers and distributors*, for example, Departments of Commerce, State, Agriculture; on *employment*, for example, United States Employment Service, Bureau of Labor Statistics; for *consumers*, e.g., Bureau of Standards, Public Health Service, Bureau of Home Economics; for *investors*—Securities and Exchange Commission.

One could continue at great length to list the specific supportive activities of the state, at all levels, in facilitating the functioning of the economic system—even aside from such obvious things as the enforcement of property and contract norms and the provision of direct subsidies, tariffs, and a favorable legal framework. Many of the present services of the state to business represent the expansion to new functions as they have become important as a result of changes in the economic system itself. To take item #10 above for illustration: Governmental information and statistical services were established to help the individual or small organization to secure the information necessary for rational economic decisions. This had become more difficult as the economy became more complex, shifting and interdependent and the market area widened. Again, the establishment and enforcement of technical standards through the state is an economically relevant activity of an importance greater than is usually recognized.[31] For mass production in a highly specialized and interdependent economy it is essential to have a high degree of standardization of weights, measures, qualities, specifications. The wider the market and the greater the technical complexity of production and distribution, the more dependent is smooth economic adjustment upon technical precision

---

(1916), Tobacco Inspection Act (1935), Perishable Commodities Act (1930)—or even the Standard Apple Barrel Act of 1912.

[31] It is not inevitable that the state will be the agency for establishment and maintenance of such standards—the task can be, and is in part, performed by private organizations, for example, trade associations. For various definite reasons, however, the State is likely to play a major part in this field.

and upon uniformity of goods—materials, tools, devices, components.

In the above respect, then, the State serves as standard-setter and facilitating mechanism for economic action. This is one economically relevant aspect of our political structure.

The second major area of political-economic relations is the *regulation* of economic activities. This permanent and inescapable aspect of governing seems to be widely regarded in the United States both as a new development and as a *limitation* upon the activity of the business man. Realistically, however: (1) the state has always been important in the regulation of the American economy; (2) much state regulation has been the direct result of demands for regulation from the business community itself; (3) much regulation is positive in its consequences both for the profitability of particular activities and for the economy as a whole. In particular, it is essential to recognize the extent to which the state has exerted itself to *maintain competition*.[32] Free markets, we remember, do not maintain themselves. Although the Sherman Antitrust Act (1890) was followed by the greatest period of industrial combination in the national history, a long series of later legislative actions and judicial decisions shows continued efforts to maintain a competitive situation.

A major activity of American governments is the *regulation of the plane or mode of economic competition* through the establishment and enforcement of standards of market conduct. Many of these standards are very old, having been derived in large part from British common law, for example, prohibitions against misrepresentation of one's products as those of another's, misappropriation of trade secrets, inducing breach of contract, malicious interference or molestation.[33] These common-law standards were not under the charge of public officials, and required that a plaintiff prove malice in the action of the accused. As statutory legislation developed,

[32] Again we are referring to distinctions made by Lyon, Watkins, and Abramson: *Government and Economic Life*, Vol. I, chap. 3.

[33] Specific categories of action falling under this heading: attacks on the reputation of a competitor, disparaging a competitor's product or impugning his credit-worthiness, making spurious threats of litigation, intimidating employees or customers. (Ibid, pp. 312 ff.)

these limitations were partly overcome. Administrative regulation, such as that exercised by the Federal Trade Commission, is now directed against the misbranding of products; the misrepresentation of effects, of geographical origin, of value; the simulation of trade-marks and names. Special regulation of specific industries proscribes "deceptive practices" (Food and Drug Act); or requires that certain information be disclosed (obligatory grading of products, labeling of food and drugs, certain financial information concerning market securities); or it maintains minimum standards of quality or composition, for example, control of animal diseases and insect pests, composition and quality of seeds.

In the present period of American history, the reader of this book will not require any extended reminder that the state plays a major part in the *regulation of collective action of workers*. The basic labor law of the United States was initially built upon the common-law doctrines concerning "conspiracy" and "restraint of trade." The old conceptions of conspiracy as used by the courts represented strong barriers to unionization. Deriving from the doctrines regarding restraint of trade, the Supreme Court decision in the famous Danbury Hatters case (1908) held organized labor activity illegal if it retarded the "free flow of commerce between the states," even if the means used were otherwise lawful.

To these barriers to workers' concerted action, there was added the effective use of court injunctions.[34] Only with the New Deal was organized labor given legal means to carry on large-scale collective bargaining effectively. This development was in part reversed by later legislation.

Among the most important general implications emerging from our brief review are the following: (1) The central political authority has continuously had a crucial part in establishing and maintaining a stabilizing framework of rules for economic activity. (2) Much of the regulation has been indispensable to the orderly fulfillment of economic interests. (3) Economic interests and economic conflicts produce incessant political struggles. The concept of the state as umpire in the economic field is undergoing drastic

[34] These developments largely nullified the hopes of those who had regarded the Clayton Act (1914) as the "Magna Carta of Labor."

modification, both because of international pressures and because of internal changes. Instead of a clearcut capitalism of small independent units, there is a "mixed" economy including small proprietors (retail trade, agriculture, etc.), small corporations, large corporations, co-operatives, quasi-public nonprofit enterprises (educational, research, medical, etc.), traditional governmental enterprises (post office), government corporations. Due to war and the threat of war, the ends of economic production depend greatly upon political ends and wider social considerations.

The economic system is now so thoroughly intermeshed with government that a return to the limited state of 1900 vintage would require virtually complete reorganization of *both* systems. The emergence of a "welfare" state reflects, in part, the new political participation of labor, and this in turn derives from mass industrialism in the context of democratic political institutions. But the great expansion of governmental activities in such fields as social security does not make any less important the continuing supportive, facilitating, and regulative functions that will be carried out in some form under *any* political system in an industrial society.

Many other important governmental activities cannot be described in the present brief discussion. Government fiscal policy, for instance, is so important in our present society that it deserves full analysis as a sociological no less than an economic problem. The same is true of the political determination of the distribution of the national income—through taxation, tariffs, direct production of goods and services, contracts with nongovernmental businesses, and so on. Government itself is now a major segment of the whole economy.

On the side of economic influences upon the political order, nothing more can be said here beyond the analyses of chapters 5 and 6. It is enough for us to note again that organized economic associations and units continually influence government, and that economic interests always are an important factor in every area of political activity.

Out of all the thousands of points of connection between the political order and the economic, there is room for much disagreement as to the most important general features of the present

American situation. Certainly, however, *one* of the most significant is the widespread movement toward an *administrative* rather than a *regulative* order,[35] or as we have said earlier, a shift from diffuse cultural structure to definite social organization. This is occurring within business and labor as well as in the relations between government and economic organizations. The signs are numerous: large corporations, trade associations, unions, governmental organizations, price agreements, price controls, administrative allocation and "rationing" of goods. The watchwords are centralization and administrative coordination. However, these tendencies are not all-encompassing, nor do they invariably represent rigidity or constriction of the action of individuals or small groups. Yet the shift toward an administrative order is undoubtedly a central fact of the times. The crucial question is whether, and how, a pluralistic power system can be maintained under the new structural conditions. In particular, the student of social policy will now be led to consider what specific arrangements may facilitate or prevent the coalescing of economic and political elites.[36]

4. A Note on Method

In the interest of brevity we have examined illustrative material that seemed to have a large evocative or suggestive value rather than attempted anything like definitive analysis of the large and complex problems under review. The main emphasis, therefore, is to be found in the approach—the concepts, the method of thinking—rather than in the content of the analysis. Although the focus

---

[35] In the sense suggested by Weber in *Theory of Social and Economic Organization*, pp. 150 ff. A regulative political system fixes and supports the canalizing rules for economic units, but does not set the ends of economic activity nor lay down positive and mandatory courses of action. In a purely administrative order, both the economic ends and the details of action are established within a definite administrative staff which has the power to make its decisions mandatory.

[36] One might think, for instance, of the professionalization of both labor and management; of the educational system (both in its selective function and in its research and teaching functions).

has been at the macroscopic level of entire institutional systems, the underlying conceptions are applicable at the level of specific groups and individual roles. Each major set of institutional norms defines certain statuses: father, industrial worker, judge. These statuses are filled by individuals who are selected, trained, indoctrinated, and motivated in terms of *that* status. By virtue of this, the self-conceptions which individuals hold are affected by status-member-ship. There is thus a series of concepts linking analysis of broad institutional patterns to the detailed facts of individual behavior. Under certain conditions, the like-circumstanced individuals hold-ing a particular status form membership groups of workers, govern-mental officials, and so on. In a society so highly differentiated as that of the United States, there is marked specialization of statuses. Hence, individuals in their capacity of, say, educator have to orient themselves to other individuals operating in similarily specialized positions in other institutional systems. The generic twofold result is (1) that different institutions take on realistic autonomy because of the special selection, training, motivation, etc., of personnel, and the different reference and membership groups in which the indi-vidual's behavior is defined; and (2) institutions are linked to-gether in the expectations and values of individuals who are institutionally committed to deal with other role specialists. The future study of institutions and their interrelations stands to gain greatly in precision and predictive value by moving beyond the macroscopic approach to the specific investigation of *status-role problems* and *group structures*. In this way it should prove possible to bring out more specific mechanisms of structural interrelation as well as to explore the dynamic processes of institutional change.

14. The Integration of American Society

1. Introduction

No SOCIETY as a going concern is adequately defined by its institutions alone. It cannot be repeated too often that institutions constitute only the most definite systems of statuses that define expected, permissible, and obligatory interpersonal relations. But there are the additional facts of normative variability and evasion, of deviation or violation, of nonsocial factors in the situation, of relations to other societies, of noninstitutional aspects of the culture.

The interrelation of the institution reviewed in previous chapters is only one aspect of the problem of social integration. A major recent study of the problem explicitly restricted its attention to "the influence of the increasing differentiation of groups.[1] In other instances, the problem of integration has been discussed from the standpoint of class struggle, race relations, political federalism, crime, divorce, suicide, "our schizoid culture," an alleged "American character," and so ad infinitum. Evidently a term that has been turned to so many uses is sufficiently protean to require handling with care. One way to exercise such care is to first see what integration is *not*.

For sociological purposes, "integration" is not a term to be used to convey a *concealed* value-judgment.[2] When we say that one

---

[1] Robert C. Angell: *The Integration of American Society* (New York: 1941), p. 6. Angell's analysis, however, actually deals at length with the commonality of values and norms, or lack thereof, in a wide range of social structures.

[2] Although, of course, *some* values are always *implied* in the selection of the problem itself.

society is highly integrated and that another is loosely integrated, we do not necessarily imply that we think one is "better" than the other, any more than we would mean that one biological organism was better than the other because its parts were more closely interdependent. Although *social* integration represents phenomena of a quite different order than do biological organisms, there likewise occur societies in which the constituent elements are, in some real sense, mutually consistent or causally related, and there are societies loosely held together and/or abounding in inconsistencies. If one is disposed to regard the society with the greatest integration as always best, it may be useful to remember an analogy from the field of personality study: one of the best examples of high integration is the thoroughgoing paranoic personality type, whose behavior is rigidly and consistently organized in terms of conceptions of grandeur and persecution. On the other hand, if one is repelled by the term integration, because of current fears concerning the prospects for freedom and spontaneity in individual life, it may be equally useful to recall that the freest and most creative persons may not be those who give greatest rein to impulses dissociated from continuing social relations to other individuals. These problems of valuation are not intrinsic to the concept of integration as a descriptive or analytic term.

Secondly, social integration is not to be identified with the inclusiveness of highly formalized social organization. Some of the most highly integrated societies appear to have a rather slight development of formal associational structures. On the other hand, what seems on the surface to be a thoroughly integrated group or society with a developed formal organization often turns out to be a system largely organized through the coercive power of a small subgroup.

Third, integration must, for present purposes, refer to a property of societies that can be identified by definite, publicly communicable signs and then shown to vary in relation to other properties or conditions. It is *not*, therefore, considered to be a quality that can only be apprehended by direct intuition or anything of that kind.

Fourth, the integration of a society is not indexed by the mere coexistence of certain items in the same geographic area or political unit. As Sorokin has cogently insisted,[3] neither *spatial adjacency* nor the association of cultural items through a *common external factor*, such as climate or geographic conditions, tells us anything about causal or functional integration or about integration at the level of meaning. Sheer physical proximity does permit interaction through which a common life can be developed, but there are too many instances of social conflict between, or estrangement of, geographically adjacent or intermingled populations for us to expect that proximity will necessarily increase the likelihood of integration. The same consideration applies to the common influence of non-social factors: climate, geography, or physical heritage may lead to similarity of behavior, but the similarity may or may not be integrative.

Finally, integration does not mean homogeneity, or identity in all respects throughout a society. A completely homogeneous society would be, in fact, a completely unstructured "field," with nothing to give it momentum or direction. Only where there is first differentiation can there be integration: this is as true of socio-cultural systems as of any others. Children and adults differ, men and women differ, teachers and students differ—and it is the essence of their integrated roles that they are different. Societies are not integrated by being internally undifferentiated, and the cultural commonality necessary to their continued existence must be detected on a level far removed from complete unanimity in every area of activity, belief, and value.[4]

To what may "societal integration" refer? The answer is, to any category of culture or society; in the *culture*, to interests, values,

---

[3] For a conveniently concise statement of his position, see Pitirim A. Sorokin: "Forms and Problems of Culture-Integration and Methods of Their Study," *Rural Sociology*, Vol. I, no. 2 (June, 1936), pp. 128–41. Sorokin makes the important point that not all the coexisting elements in a given area or social aggregate are connected either causally or meaningfully. Contrary to all theories that postulate that every item of a culture must be interrelated, the fact is that many items are essentially unrelated.

[4] Cf. Angell: *The Integration of American Society*, pp. 19–20: "A sense of moral community does not require people to think alike on all issues. . . . The crucial question is . . . whether they concur in the ultimate values to be realized." (A further empirical question in this connection is that of just what values are ultimate for any particular situation.)

norms, beliefs, symbols and to various systems and subsystems of these; in the *society* to collectivities, groups, associations, communities, and other units of interaction. The integration of a culture is related to but not identical with the integration of a group or society. Overtly regularized and orderly interaction not infrequently occurs between individuals having relatively few beliefs and values in common. We find many examples of a broadly common culture extending over a large number of local groups or even major political entities that are either not interacting or else are in open conflict. Or, there may be an apparently unitary culture with respect to some elements (say, a religious system, or a common set of political institutions), but with great internal differentiation along lines of class and caste, or in other respects.

It seems essential to distinguish between the *factual cohesion* of a social aggregate, on the one hand, and the *societal integration* that occurs through shared values and beliefs. Factual cohesion refers merely to a human aggregate whose members interact without a disabling degree of overt conflict, regardless of the conditions upon which this state of affairs may depend.[5] There is apparently a rather wide range within which an important degree of cohesion, in the sense of co-ordinated activity, can be maintained by coercion, by the effective threat of the few over the many. Our liberal cultural bias should not lead us to suppose that all overt cohesion rests on consensus or voluntary participation. Concretely also, the co-ordination of human actions derives in considerable part from interdependent interests in the utilization of scarce and divisible values. In pure type, we would here visualize a social aggregate held together solely by a convergence of individual interests. Collective ends would consist only of those necessary to the achievement of separate individual ends. In one direction the prototype is economic exchange between persons of radically different culture; in another, the interdependence of fate in the face of a common danger. Some human interests in subsistence and safety, while not

[5] Even this statement about minimal regularity presupposes some criteria for appraising what is to be considered conflict or orderliness. From the standpoint of a purely *causal* analysis any social activity is presumably orderly, in the sense of being caused, even though it may represent normative chaos or the war of each against all.

universal, are so omnipresent as to be a major factor in the cohesion of all major human aggregates. Further, once a marked division of labor has arisen from any source, the sheer interdependence of individual interests militates against the disruption of a society, in so far as individuals recognize that interdependence.

In actual societies, however, neither coercive power nor interdependence of separate interests exists in isolation from the sharing of common goals and other normative elements—for example, cognitive standards, symbols, rules, values. At this level, the term "integration" refers to something beyond causal regularity or coordination. Integration is more than a balance-of-power situation or a symbiotic interdependence. Modern sociology seeks to find this something else by investigating the extent and kind of common-value orientations in a social system. A basic postulate is that the integration of a society can be defined in terms of the sharing of common prescriptions and proscriptions for conduct, belief, valuation. This has been expressed from time to time in various ways: that a society is a human aggregate possessing a common ultimate-value system; that a society is integrated to the degree that conformity is voluntary; that society is possible because people share "a common world of experience." It seems securely established that: (1) the continuing operation of any social aggregate does depend upon a minimal sharing of normative orientations; (2) the extent and kind of *common* orientation varies enormously among known societies; (3) integration at this level requires highly specific processes, and cannot be taken for granted as belonging to the nature of human association.[6] Integration of societies cannot be adequately explained by reducing the problem to biological and physical factors. Since societies are neither held together on the basis of a rationalistic "social contract," nor are they purely congeries of power systems, it is in the residual area of the sharing of a common culture that the sociological explanation of integration must center. This is a hard-won insight in the history of thought about society and its importance must be given every possible emphasis. At the same time "the sharing of a common culture"

[6] Talcott Parsons: "Propaganda and Social Control," *Psychiatry*, Vol. V, no. 4 (November, 1942), p. 555.

remains a vague and unproductive cliché unless it can be specified what is shared, to what extent, and through what structures or processes. The actual operation of a society as an objectively possible system, to repeat once more, depends upon the multiple interaction of a series of factors. Here we shall treat only a few aspects of the whole complex problem, without presuming that these represent either the specificity or the completeness required for a comprehensive analysis of the American situation. Integration is a concept derived by high-order abstraction, removed by several steps from the numerous concrete observations to which it is ultimately anchored. Accordingly, in what follows we will continually refer to the more detailed analyses and data already presented. In some aspects, *every* preceding chapter has dealt with problems of societal integration. The present task is thus largely one of rearranging old facts in somewhat different patterns.

2. Factors in the Cohesion of American Society

WHATEVER integration may exist in America is quite obviously not the integration of a small, stable society in which a common set of detailed standards and goals is shared by practically all members. Nor is it the integration of a society permeated with the sense of a long, slow-growing common history. Indeed, the United States constitutes something close to a crucial experiment as to the consequences of socio-cultural diversity in modern mass society. Its continued existence under essentially the same form of government through so many years when the crash of falling states has echoed through the world demonstrates, at the least, that complete cultural homogeneity is not a functional necessity for *that* much stability. To review: the total social aggregate, the United States, includes many millions of small primary groups and millions of secondary associations such as business enterprises; it is crisscrossed with incredibly long chains of indirect interaction and permeated with waves and counterwaves of mass communication;

it is segmented by lines of insulation and cleavage between massive social categories (such as racial and religious classifications); it is compartmentalized into thousands of specialized occupational statuses. We have seen that beneath these diversities there actually are many elements of widespread common-orientation, but the existing fissures in consensus are surely great enough to make the integration of the society as a whole a problematic matter rather than something to be assumed as a given fact.

If we examine the *general* bases of social cohesion—those applicable to any society—a great many different lists can be derived, each useful in terms of a certain set of data and a certain conceptual scheme. Here we shall not seek a highly refined set of analytic variables but shall work with a provisional and rather crude set of factors. The discussion will proceed in terms of these items: (1) mutual dependence and individual gains; (2) mechanisms and techniques of co-ordination and integration; (3) external pressures; (4) common-value orientations; (5) the unity of diversity: overlapping identities and multigroup membership.

These categories have all the disadvantages of remaining fairly close to a common-sense level, but the advantage of tying the discussion down to practically important structures and processes that have already received a fair amount of attention in social science research.

Let us begin by considering the place of individual gains, or the congruity and interdependence of interests. Quite aside from a community of ultimate values, it is the present contention that a major part of the cohesion of this society derives from a community of interest—that is, the *sharing* of *separate* interests to attain economic goals and any other scarce, divisible values. Congruity of interests refers to the situation in which individuals continue to interact and to avoid conflict on the basis of the gains each anticipates from perpetuation of the social framework essential to interaction. Thus, individuals mutually antagonistic in other respects often collaborate in the pursuit of their separate interests in income, power, safety, or prestige; or class-conscious industrialists and workers maintain relationships because of their economic interdependence. There is some base of value consensus in such collaboration, but it is so limited that one had best speak of dependence and interests rather than values.

Recognition of the role of common normative orientation does not mean the underestimation of the importance of mutual dependence and tangible gains of individuals. Under conditions of expanding economic opportunity, peoples of very diverse cultures have acted in America almost as if they had a tacit agreement to minimize their differences while exploiting the abundant resources. This historical "agreement," of course, implied *some* value consensus and aided the development of a broader common orientation. But for several generations strong immediate incentives for the acceptance of existing institutions, especially of property and government, were provided by widespread opportunities for economic acquisition and by a rising material level of living. Practically all classes participated in these gains, although by no means to the same extent. As noted in chapter 5, however, inequality of reward does not by itself produce social cleavage and upheaval. It does bear repeating that drastic concerted action to transform a social system seems usually to come from *powerful* groupings that feel their *legitimate aspirations systematically blocked* or their vested positions drastically threatened. This is a prime storm signal. We have previously surveyed evidence pointing to a high level of wants and aspirations in our society, as well as to considerable awareness of differential rewards. The central value-orientations of the society include a large component of divisive goals and a relatively low development of diffuse-participative values.

A social system that appeals for allegiance solely on the basis of its ability to deliver economic goods to the individual is on precarious ground in the modern world. Adherence to social institutions can never be exclusively the result of a cold-blooded calculation of specific individual advantages in acquiring scarce values. At the very least, an additional element of legitimacy is involved. It is perhaps especially crucial in a system like that just outlined that differential rewards be apportioned both according to a *common set of standards of legitimacy* and to the *effective distribution of social power*. In this way, even a consideration of such factors as the material level of living and the distribution of income, forces one eventually back to a common-value factor.

It must be added that the factors that explain the emergence or development of a certain social system are not necessarily the same as those that maintain it once it is fully established. A capitalistic economic order developed in the United States through complex historical sequences. Once developed, it contained constraining elements, relatively independent of the particular values and motivations of any one individual or partial segment of the system, for example, the necessity of making profits in business, the dependence of the propertyless worker upon wages. Around the established structures a variety of vested interests cohere. That is, these interests carry an element of customary rightness or moral claim. Therefore, vested interests always resist change in greater degree than do those interests related to temporary advantage and immediate or prospective gain. To this source of stability is added the interdependence of interests involved in an operating system that insures existing arrangements against sudden or fundamental alteration unless drastic maladjustments occur. The primary implication for the American situation seems to be that the continuation of the given economic and political structure requires that a "stake in the system" be widely held. Otherwise, the rigidity of vested interests in opposition to the claims and aspirations of nonvested interests is likely to place severe and increasing strains upon ultimate societal consensus. Goetz Briefs [7] has pointedly characterized as the "adventure of capitalism" the attempt to operate a social system in which large numbers of workers are propertyless and insecure but at the same time are personally free citizens of a democratic state. When we discussed social stratification and the role of interest groups in politics, we saw the possibly disruptive consequences of the erosion of consensus in a society of marked economic cleavages. Interests alone are not enough, and mutual dependence through the division of labor is not enough. For these factors to contribute to cohesion, two additional elements

[7] See the provocative chap. 13 of *The Proletariat* (New York: 1937), pp. 237–67.

appear essential, as *minimal* conditions: (1) congruent interests and dependencies must be linked together, and disruptive interests insulated from one another, through definite social structures; (2) there must be *procedural* agreement as to the rules under which interests may be pursued. Under the latter heading, for instance, falls the acquiescence of losers in political elections. Under the former condition, must be included all those structural arrangements and techniques of action that articulate interdependence and block conflictful interactions. Such arrangements we will call mechanisms of cohesion, if it is understood that the phrase does not connote automatism, but is being used merely to indicate structural or technical factors as distinct from other elements of societal equilibrium.

Among the mechanisms of cohesion is one that at first glance may seem wholly divisive in its implications. It consists of various types of *isolation, or insulation, of groups and statuses from other groups or statuses*. Individuals occupying certain statuses simply do not directly interact with persons in certain other statuses, or interact only minimally and in rigidly circumscribed patterns. A "map" of the interaction patterns of most American communities would unquestionably show definite clusters of frequent interaction, separated from other clusters by social voids only lightly bridged by a few individuals.[8] We have already commented on the numerous small groups and "nodes" of interaction that form in large formal organizations.

Yet, how can common understandings and common values develop under conditions of group isolation and status separation? Where is integration in this mosaic of inwardly focused social segments? The answer is that group separation is not a road to convergence upon a common-value system in anything except a procedural sense—say, an implicit agreement to differ and to remain separate. However, if groups differ radically in their values and interests, a mutually accepted insulation is one, if not necessarily the best, mechanism for at least the temporary avoidance of overt friction. The remedy can also cause the disease: groups that initially share the same values, or have the bases for developing a funda-

. See the community studies listed in chapter 5, for illustrative data.

mental commonality, will gradually diverge from one another in so far as they cease to interact meaningfully and share in common experience; the more indirect and abstract the communication, the more the mutual orientation in terms of generalized stereotypes, and the less the ability of each person fully to "take the role of the other." Consensus and empathy are not characteristic products of distance and insulation. Above all, there is a crucial difference between isolation resulting from *mutual preferences* of individuals to associate with a certain ingroup, and the separation resulting from *categorical exclusion*.

There are two major types of social insulation. One is true isolation—a lack of interaction. This occurs by virtue of physical separation of communities, within each of which people work out long-time interpersonal relations with others; it occurs by reason of systematic withdrawal from participation—as in upper-class exclusive clubs—or in the defense-avoidance behavior of repeatedly rebuffed groups, or in patterns of residential segregation, and so on. The second type of insulation involves direct person-to-person interaction, but consists of formalized and limited patterns of relationships such as the constrained interaction of superiors and subordinates in rigidly hierarchical organizations, the "racial etiquette" of parts of the South, and many functionally specific occupational roles. Such insulation is attained by numerous specific devices. It may or may not be equally accepted by the parties to the relationship. Often the relation is one of subordination-superordination, involving differential privileges defended by the one party and resented by the other. Where the relation is not too markedly asymetrical in this respect, the formalized insulation of roles and of groups sometimes permits limited interaction between persons who would come into conflict in a more inclusive and personalized relation.

Much of the separation of true *groups* in our society is basically a matter of the preferential association of persons within a broadly similar culture who share special activities and values: the occupational group, the congeniality circle, and the like. This preferential association is not necessarily rigidly exclusive, and the groups thus formed often absorb new members and shed old ones with considerable facility. In some large-scale instances, however, the separation of *groups* is preceded by, and is dependent upon, the segregation of inclusive social *categories:* Negroes, Mexicans, and so on. In these cases, individuals are assigned to generalized categories cutting across interacting groups, occupational statuses, and concrete communities. It is often said that there is a "status" of being a Negro or other minority-category individual. We prefer the term "category" because "Negro" clearly does not designate the same kind of complex of reciprocal rights and duties as appear in family, occupation, and certain other highly institutionalized systems.

Mechanisms of cohesion operate at all levels of the social structure, from the relationship of the individual in the smallest group, over to the political co-ordination of a nation or nations. We must keep always in view the apparently simple ordinary interaction of persons in their daily rounds. To participate in groups that provide regularized expectations seems to be a necessary condition for the organization of personalities as unitary systems. Thus the behavioral integration of the individual is in large measure an outcome of the integration of the groups in which he is involved. A situation in which individuals can find no stable group to which they may belong leaves the personality without the continual *reinforcement* of patterned behavior that seems essential to meaningfully integrated conduct. The discomforts and frustrations of the anomic situation —of the unsupported individuals in the midst of the "lonely crowd" [9]—are real, and result from real causes. We cannot deal here with the psychological complexities presumed in these statements. We can safely assume that there is a need for interaction, no matter how complex its sources, and that for this reason group participation necessarily means a process of reciprocal control among individuals.[10] Put in commonsense terms this means that individuals give up a considerable degree of autonomy and renounce many nonconforming tendencies in seeking group membership.

[9] David Riesman: *The Lonely Crowd* (New Haven: 1950).
[10] Compare Parson's comment that this "is one of the most important channels by which, as a dynamic process, the functional integration of the social system is maintained." "Propaganda and Social Control," p. 557.

It is in this context that the condition of the primary group in American society may be seen in something like an adequate perspective. The millions of "special areas of density" of interaction—in families, work groups, congeniality groups, neighborhoods, and so on—are still the basic matrices in which psychological security and behavioral consistency are anchored.

But the linkages of organization go much further. Above the small groups and unit-organizations are layers upon layers of more extensive organization. Individuals in our society frequently participate in a number of different groups or associations, and the smaller groups are in various way linked by communication, representation, and chain-interaction, into larger unities. If the struggle of a large union with the representatives of management in an entire industry may disrupt a larger system of co-ordination from time to time, it nevertheless represents enormously complex coordination within each of the contending aggregates. In all the major nucleated institutions, the total aggregate of individuals does not participate *directly* in the higher foci of control and communication, but is linked together by systems of representation or imperative control. As larger and larger systems of organization have spread across our society, the roles of the nodal control-points and centers of communication have become increasingly greater and increasingly invested with a public interest. Every major action at these centers of linkage throws up a moving wave of tangential effects through a labyrinth of channels. At the levels at which separate systems of interaction, imbued with different values and interests, come into contact, co-ordination is achieved (if at all) through processes of negotiation, compromise, and so on, or by reference to still *other* systems. In situations of impasse, there is either the intervention of a higher authority, as when the state enters industrial disputes, or representatives of the different parties appeal to some larger public. In these ways every long-continued struggle of large organizations tends to spread in widening circles.

Under such circumstances, the cohesion of the society as a whole depends more and more obviously upon the sheer availability of *knowledges* and *techniques* for dealing with the problems of tension and conflict in intergroup and interorganizational relations.[11] This factor is somewhat neglected in analyses of societal cohesion, but its importance seems evident from the whole of our present analysis of American society. In a discussion focusing so much upon common-value factors, it is necessary to emphasize that cohesion in a society like this is in part a strictly technical problem. The knowledges and skills adequate to the affairs of a localistic republic are simply not sufficient for the organizational demands of our present system. In recent decades, the social sciences have begun to make new attacks on the relevant problems with new research methods and increasingly sophisticated theories. We have also seen the emergence of a small but important corps of specially trained and skilled practitioners—social workers, psychiatrists and psychologists, anthropologists, economic analysts, statisticians, labor-and-management specialists, and so on. The number of skilled and motivated practitioners is still very small, and there are vast dark continents in which they can find little certified knowledge for their use. However, some useful foundations have been laid.

Under the heading of "mechanisms and techniques" we must note that mass communication is an essential factor in the present state of cohesion of American society. The relatively standardized mass information and value stimuli to which great numbers of people are being exposed, must be given its due as a pervasive factor in common responses to national and world events.[12]

It would be highly unrealistic to leave out of the present account the complex processes often characterized as *reactions to external pressures*. We have spoken earlier of the unifying consequences of external threat upon functioning groups and social systems. The specific processes involved here are becoming more exactly known, although they are still imperfectly understood.[13] In our day, of

[11] Reference may again be made to Robin M. Williams, Jr.: *The Reduction of Intergroup Tensions*, Bulletin 57, Social Science Research Council (New York: 1947), chaps 2 and 3. Note also the relevance of Robert K. Merton's article, "The Unanticipated Consequences of Purposive Social Action," *American Sociological Review*, Vol. I, no. 6 (December, 1936), pp. 894–904.

[12] See Karl Mannheim: *Man and Society in an Age of Reconstruction* (New York: 1940), esp. pp. 129 ff. and 256–9.

[13] See Otto Klineberg: *Tensions Affecting International Understanding*, Bulletin 62, Social Science Research Council (New York: 1950).

course the prime pressure is war and the threat of war.[14] The large
amount of voluntary effort and sacrifice elicited by World War II,
for instance, is documentation of a body of sentiment without
which the enormous mobilization of global conflict would be unthinkable. It may be that the mood of the men who fought that
war was more nearly that of Greek tragedy than "high-strung
patriotic emotion," [15] but it is plain that the impact of war galva-
nized into concerted action a wide range of previously discordant
segments of the society. There was the typical centralization of
authority, increase in centralized regulation, increase of intolerance
against "deviants." A previously diffuse ethnocentrism was structured and directed. As the war continued, those who felt their
sacrifices to be great pressed to have others "do their part." For
large sectors of the population, there were many immediate gains
in income, prestige, and power. Meanwhile, great numbers of
individuals continued with their accustomed tasks in terms of
previously established motives, expectations, and goals. As the
war continued there was, at least for those in military services, a
growth of common experiences—no matter how unpleasant or
distasteful at the time—which in the end left a new residue of
shared values and traditions.

Finally, it cannot be too strongly emphasized that the fact of
integration of value standards does not rest on deductions from
speculative theory, but is an observable condition that has already
been roughly indexed in some situations by empirical research. For
example, studies of American troops in Europe toward the end
of World War II showed high consensus upon the evaluation of
"combat credit" as a basis for determining the order of release of
men from the Army.[16] The agreement extended to men in non-
combat duties who were going against their own self-interest in

[14] Lest there be misunderstanding: war is not necessary to national integration, and the ultimate consequences of war may be very different indeed
from its proximate effects.

[15] The phrase is from Hugo Münsterberg: *American Patriotism and Other
Social Studies* (New York: 1913), p. 5. For extensive data on the attitudes of
American troops see *The American Soldier*, Vol. I, chap. 9 and Vol. II, chaps. 3
and 12.

[16] See the data and the description of the social context in *The American
Soldier*, Vol. II, pp. 62–4.

advocating full combat credit for front-line troops only. Although most soldiers testified to a desire to return to civilian life as soon as possible, over 70 per cent of men in rear-area units voted full combat credit to front-line troops and only 15 per cent claimed that men in the rear-area Army and corps headquarters should receive similar credit. In this case, clearly, standards of fairness and "rational appraisal" took precedence over self-interested claims. Without some such process, the operation of a highly differentiated social system without widespread recourse to force is not conceivable.

We can see again how the integration of social systems, large and small, is not a matter of everyone's doing or saying the same things, but of the *functionally strategic* convergence of the *standards* by which conduct is evaluated. It was once believed that Catholics and Protestants could not live together in the same society. They do so live in American society by reason not only of mutual insulation, and not only by virtue of the diminished intensity of traditional religious values, but also by increased sharing of a vast body of nonreligious norms and goals. To thinkers who conceive of society as an organism, it must seem incredible that a system so heterogeneous as American society can exist and function. The marked differentiation of economic levels and prestige classes has sometimes been taken to presage class conflict and basic alteration of the society. In all these cases, a neglected factor is the cohesion represented by common-value orientations extending across the many lines of social and cultural differences. Some of these common orientations are in the nature of generalized creeds: explicit, publicly communicated statements of principle that seem to serve as referents for a great variety of activities. A number of such orientations were reviewed in chapter 11, where we also saw that value uniformities are not confined to the explicit creeds of democracy, individualism, equality, and so on. There are also implicit common themes of great importance—for example, the high evaluation of activity, the stress upon conformity, the assumption that "like should associate with like," the agreement upon procedures for handling conflicts. Common-value orientations at this level do not imply agreement upon the detailed norms regulating specific behavior patterns; in the latter category there is surely great diversity, but the diversity is to a large extent assimilated by the *belief* that there is consensus upon ultimate principles that supply the generalized meanings for conduct. It is extremely important also that many of the implicit understandings that make society possible are not just *implicit* but are also resistant to statement: it is as if there is a tacit agreement not to express or to become aware of what would be dysfunctional. We greatly need careful research in this area, for observation already shows the existence of a mass of specific devices for thus suppressing disruptive elements. We suspect that a study of areas of blocked communication would often reveal conflicts that remain nondisabling only so long as they are kept from overt crystallization. The present suggestion is only that, beyond relatively conscious avoidance of conflict, there are complex latent systems of compartmentalization and insulation that are largely unrecognized but that have great functional significance. It has been indicated previously that a great deal of the "flatness" of American public discourse is probably due to the search for noncontroversial conversational pieces; if so, the implicit premise is that agreement should take priority over difference. Indeed, it is a legitimate hypothesis that one of the most pervasive and deep-rooted elements of cohesion in the heterogeneity of America is the incessant strain toward overt agreement, toward a unified public morality, signalized by external conformity.

It is hoped that certain items of our analysis have by now become thoroughly repetitious, for it is by systematic re-examination that we have our best hope of understanding the daily miracle of society in being. This is our rationale, at least, for returning once more to the role of *common symbols* in American society. It is perhaps not wholly wrong to assert that no one is yet able to demonstrate scientifically precisely what this role is. At least one provisional hypothesis, however, is sufficiently impressive to remention here. Most crudely put, it is that many of the most important symbols of national unity have so little specific ideological content that they create a common allegiance by being all things to all men.[17] "Every-

---

[17] For a suggestive example of symbolic variation see Edgar A. Schuler: "V for Victory: A Study in Symbolic Social Control," *Journal of Social Psychology*, Vol. XII, second half (May, 1944), pp. 283–99.

body" gives allegiance to the Flag, reveres the Constitution, and the Supreme Court, and knows that George Washington was an embodiment of national virtues. Unless the symbols have to be interpreted in terms of *specific* actions and values, they can constitute an overarching set of referents for enormously varied orientations throughout the society. We will totally misunderstand the fact that human behavior is symbolic if we look exclusively at the "apparent content" of creeds and icons. It is being suggested here that, within wide limits, it is precisely the amorphous, protean, and unstructured nature of the most inclusive societal symbols that gives them their enormously powerful capacity for *defining as common* that which, from other points of view, is different or even incompatible.

An important specific example of symbolic integration is afforded by the behavior of American political leaders. The role once attached to leaders of organized religion who were expected to fuse in their activities the common symbols of society has to a large extent devolved upon political figures.[18] The high governmental official is expected to stand as a symbol of the whole community and to deal with and integrate very diverse interests and values, and partly for this reason alone, he participates in and endorses the legitimacy of many different, sometimes even radically incompatible, groups and activities. In the realm of symbols no less than in the compromising of interests, political institutions form the prime focus of cohesion in the United States. The government is increasingly the focus of power struggle, and certainly could not survive in a democratic form without some compensating development of integrative patterns. The high development of national symbols, and the association of them with the top governmental offices, seems clearly to be one such reaction to the disruptive struggles of interest groupings.[19]

[18] Recall that in the study of occupational rating by North and Hatt the public placed Supreme Court judge at the top of a list of 90 occupations (chap. 5 above).

[19] It is as yet impossible to fix definite ratings to the factors of integration at this level of complexity. For a preliminary sketch of the problem see David F. Aberle *et al:* "The Functional Prerequisites of a Society," *Ethics*, Vol. LX, no. 2 (January, 1950), pp. 100–11.

A return to a small, simple, and strictly limited state in America would involve such a pyramid of improbabilities that we might as well call it impossible. If this be granted, the central role of government raises anew the eternal question: Who has custody of the custodians? Who watches the watchers? The classic American answer seems to have been: *other* custodians. The attempt has been to counter the irresponsibility of any absolute power by separate authorities, systems of checks, referrals of policy to public consent, interplay of interests—in short, the whole pattern of pluralistic balance. Enough has already been said of the consequences and limits of this pattern under current conditions. The problem does serve, however, to point to a source of cohesion not yet mentioned: *the unity coming directly from diversity.* There is no real paradox here. One outcome of diversity in this society is a multiple overlapping of groups and social categories that blurs considerably the sharp edges of potential cleavage—for example, the "cross-pressures" that operate upon individuals whose different membership and reference groups pull them toward different political alignments, or the internal heterogeneity of the major political parties.[20] Without these relatively fluid, crisscrossing allegiances it seems highly probable that conflict would be increased, assuming that class differentiation did not diminish. American society is simply riddled with cleavages. The remarkable phenomenon is the extent to which the various differences "cancel out"—are noncumulative in their incidence. There is this much realistic sociological meaning in *e pluribus unum.*[21]

The problem of value integration occurs as a problem of *meaning* —either of the actually apprehended meanings, or of the conceivable meanings that can be revealed by analysis; it also poses itself as a *causal* problem of the effects of various combinations of and alterations in values; it may be analyzed as a *functional* problem

[20] Cf. Paul F. Lazarsfeld, Bernard Berelson, and Hazel Gaudet: *The Peoples Choice* (New York: 1948). A replication and extension of this study carried out in Elmira, N. Y., has produced confirmatory evidence to be published in the near future.

[21] Cf. Williams: *The Reduction of Intergroup Tensions*, p. 59, for the hypothesis that "a society riven by many minor cleavages is in less danger of open mass conflict than a society with only one or a few cleavages."

of the interconnected consequences of different value-belief phenomena *for* selectively ordered aspects of society, culture, and personality. Our present analysis has almost wholly eschewed consideration of integration at the level of meaning. Because the materials are enormously complex and the available studies are quite rudimentary, an adequate treatment of meaningful coherence in American culture probably will have to wait for some time.[22] Here we have sought to avoid imposing external judgments regarding consistency or inconsistency in the interests of sticking as closely as possible to the most definite and clearly identifiable institutional structures. It will be noted that as a consequence the present chapter concentrates largely upon the formal aspects of integration rather than upon the content of values and interests.

3. Integration and Anomie

"AMERICAN culture" and "American society" are concepts ultimately referable to regularities observed in the behavior of individuals, each of whom, in turn, sees society as consisting largely of the regularities he encounters in the behavior of a relatively small circle of other persons. To the degree that regularity disappears in that circle, the individual is in a normless situation, no matter how firm and consistent normative regulation may be elsewhere in the society. This is *anomie* at the concrete level of its impact upon specific persons. Few things are so important in diagnosing a society as data on the stability of normative patterns in the basic units of person-to-person interaction. Thus divorce, extremely high mobility, and other forms of small-group dissolution deserve so much attention as clues to the total state of the social system.[23]

Anomie may be analyzed also in the form of various breakdowns

[22] This type of analysis, in any case, goes far beyond the bounds of any one discipline; it probably has to be achieved by a synthesis of the approaches and findings of the behavioral sciences together with major contributions from philosophy. See Susanne Langer: *Philosophy in a New Key* (Cambridge, Mass.: 1942).

[23] *Supra*, chap. 12.

in the wider normative definitions to which immediate behavior in the small situation is oriented. One of the most interesting aspects of anomie at this macroscopic level is the problem of the stress placed upon cultural goals as over against institutionalized means. This mode of stating the problem is contained in a well-known analysis by Robert K. Merton so germane to the present chapter that we will do well to recapitulate its main points. Merton's analysis [24] proceeds through the following steps, among others:

1. Deviant, nonconforming behavior is not predictable on a biological basis; the *rate* of deviance varies in different social structures, and is in part the result of definite social pressures toward nonconformity.

2. In the cultural regulation of behavior there are both legitimated *goals* and *institutionalized norms* defining prescribed or proscribed means for attaining the goals.

3. Cultural goals and the regulation of means have a range of independent variation; goals may be so stressed that normative regulation practically disappears, or the goal may be lost in an emphasis on the means-norms.

4. In American culture there is very great emphasis upon monetary success; this emphasis is systematically inculcated and reinforced; and the goal is held out to all classes of the society. There is not "a corresponding emphasis upon the legitimate avenues on which to march toward this goal." [25]

5. Innovative or deviant responses are expected to occur at different rates in various subgroups or strata of the society. For example, stress on innovation in upper economic strata leads to "white-collar crime" and sharp business practice; in lower strata, to racketeering and petty crime. Ritualism—a way of reducing level of aspiration—is expectable on a considerable scale in the respectable lower-middle strata.

6. A wide variety of beliefs and symbols in American society have the presumed function, in so far as they are effective,

---

[24] "Social Structure and Anomie: Revisions and Extensions," in *Social Theory and Social Structure* (Glencoe, Ill.: 1949).

[25] Ibid., p. 133.

of defining frustrations in individual or nonsocial terms. This is the "conservative counter-myth" as against the mythology of rebellion, which attributes mass frustration to the *status quo* system and proposes an alternative system.

7. Conformity is the dominant response in the context of the success pattern. But the value placed upon competitive success produces a strain toward deviant behavior. For the system to be stable, rewards at all positions in the scale must be proportioned to support the rules of the game and not just victory in the struggle. In the American system, *alternative* goals-means schemes remove some of the disruptive potential of the primary stress on monetary success, for example, subcultural emphases upon nonmonetary success goals.

Merton's analysis thus takes *one* aspect of normative regulation and opens up possible lines of analysis for showing the differing consequences of different means-ends emphases in variously situated groups and strata in a culture with a modal emphasis upon continuous active striving for success in a competitive occupational system. The analysis helps to specify how normative regulation can be weakened or dissolved by a strong "bombardment of interests" directed toward any scarce distributive value whatsoever. In a society so goal-centered as we have found America to be, a primary type of anomie is the corrosion of institutional norms by activistic emphases on scarce goals.

But this type of anomic condition is not the only one important for contemporary society.[26] We must not overlook the fact that rejection of norms and goals includes the phenomenon of cultural apathy with respect to standards of conduct. Qualitatively different aspects of the latter condition are variously connoted by terms such as indifference, cynicism, moral fatigue, disenchantment, withdrawal of affect, opportunism. One prominent type of apathy

---

[26] Anomie is of course a matter of degree, and to characterize a situation as anomic is to assume some standard of adequate normative development. This may be an empirical standard, for example, derived from existing modal definitions of the culture under study, or a hypothetical standard, for example, derived from an abstract model of a perfectly integrated system.

is the loss of involvement in a previously sought cultural goal,
such as occurs when continued striving results in persistent and
seemingly unavoidable frustration.[27] The loss of central life-goals
leaves the individual in a social vacuum, without focal direction
or meaning. But another crucial kind of apathy seems to emerge
from conditions of great normative complexity and/or rapid
change, when individuals are pulled this way and that by numerous
conflicting norms and goals, until the person is literally dis-oriented
and de-moralized, unable to secure a firm commitment to a set
of norms that he can feel as self-consistent. Under certain conditions, not yet understood, the result is a kind of "resignation
from responsibility": a discounting of principled conduct, a lack of
concern for the maintenance of a moral community.[28] It seems that
this lostness is *one* of the basic conditions out of which some types
of political totalitarianism emerge. The individual renounces moral
autonomy, and is subjected to an external discipline.[29]

Widespread normative apathy, however, seems to generate not
just one but several kinds of counterreaction—above all, the rise
of leaders interested in mass power, and the simultaneous demands
for conformity on the part of those who feel threatened. If these
tendencies are combined with external political and military
threats, real or presumed, one may expect an especially strong
movement toward rigid formulae of conformity and security. If
Americans are to meet the coming years with some continuity
of institutional principles, an understanding of reactions to anomie
may help in acquiring perspective on the problems of the day.

An additional central facet of normative problems in our society

[27] For example, the apathy accompanying enduring and hopeless unemployment. Cf. B. Zawadzki and Paul S. Lazarsfeld: "The Psychological Consequences of Unemployment," *Journal of Social Psychology*, Vol. VI, no. 2
(May, 1935); also the previously cited works of E. Wight Bakke.

[28] Anything that disturbs the processes of reciprocal reinforcement and
mutual corroboration of norms is, so far, a factor in anomie. Cf. Thomas D.
Eliot: "Reactions to Predictive Assumptions," *American Sociological Review*,
Vol. II, no. 4 (August, 1937), pp. 508–17.

[29] Note that a rigidly authoritarian system, if it is total, in its turn destroys individual ethical autonomy. The essence of the situation is in the familiar "we were only carrying out orders."

is, of course, the whole pattern of group solidarity and conflict, which has been treated extensively in this book and elsewhere.[30] It is enough to note here one possible connection between anomic conditions and problems of intergroup, or intercategory, relations. If individuals feel that the normative structure upon which their psychological security depends is threatened by forces they cannot identify or understand, they frequently exhibit an increased intolerance of ambiguity or differences in social relations. This is a context highly favorable to rigidly categorical definition of outgroups. If the outgroups are external to the society, one consequence is to minimize internal differences, for example, through the sense of national membership by contrast to others. But this sort of integration through heightened emphasis upon categorical group membership gives only a precarious unity, and in net balance, it seems unlikely that this will be the *main* dynamism of social cohesion in America. The institutional precipitate of the most enduring values is perhaps deeper and more commonly held than many "leaders of the people" seem to believe.

A NOTE ON THE PROBLEM OF INDEXES

We need not emphasize the fact that variation and individual differences in values and beliefs are not to be confused with *anomie*. No one individual ever experiences or knows the complete range of the value orientations current in his society; and some idiosyncratic variation always occurs. Nor can anomie be inferred from the simultaneous existence of apparently conflicting cultural orientations; the conflict may not be registered by the population, or it may be resolved or rationalized in some wider value-belief

[30] Of hundreds of excellent works, we will mention only the following for illustration: Lyman Bryson, Louis Finkelstein, and Robert M. MacIver (eds.): *Approaches to National Unity* (New York: 1945); Robert M. MacIver: *The More Perfect Union* (New York: 1948); Gunnar Myrdal: *An American Dilemma* (New York: 1944); George S. Pettee: *The Process of Revolution* (New York: 1938); Arnold Rose and Caroline Rose: *America Divided* (New York: 1948). (See the bibliography in Williams: *The Reduction of Intergroup Tensions*, pp. 135 ff.)

complex, or the different orientations may be insulated between noninteracting groups. Partly for these reasons, anomie as a social condition has to be defined independently of the psychological states thought to accompany normlessness and normative conflict. Conflict of norms, for instance, is an important fact only when two or more normative standards enjoin actions that cannot, both or all, be carried out by the same person in the same situation. Conflict or congruity may be taken as the independent variable— as a *cultural* fact to be defined by a stated degree of consensus in the group or society being examined. The *behavioral outcome* is the dependent variable. The intervening variable consists of the psy-*chological state* of individuals—for example, their anxiety or feelings of frustration. The basic model for explanatory purposes is: normative situation → psychological state → behavioral item or sequence.[31] The problem is to show how a defined *normative structure* is associated with or followed by *certain patterns of conduct* (or lack of pattern) and then to relate the two via psychological variables.

A possible model for developing indices of integration or anomie would then be as follows: First, we establish the existence of a widely accepted norm; the research techniques here range from public opinion surveys to detailed observation and interviewing. If possible we also establish indications of intensity of responses, for example, by the severity of sanctions evoked by violation. In both aspects we build up the generalized indices in terms of specific pieces of *behavior*—having children, going to college, saving money, committing suicide, voting, and so on—selecting the items of behavior on the basis of the commonly imputed meanings discoverable in the culture. Thus the commonly listed "social problems" in the United States represent the judgment of someone that an existing social condition is contrary to some norm, such as crime and delinquency, divorce and desertion, suicide, and so on. For example, *given* a widespread and intense conviction that suicide is undesirable or wrong or sinful, a high suicide rate becomes an index of malintegration, and by reason of the connection be-

[31] Strictly speaking, of course, the arrows should be written ↔ : the relations are reciprocal.

tween loss of definite normative structure and some types of suicide, it becomes a partial index of anomie.[32]

4. Integration and Change

THIS book has chosen to focus upon structure rather than process, on the premise that before we can understand change we need to see what it is that changes. Yet we have been unable to deal with any important aspect of American society or culture without considerable attention to changes and trends. In studying our own society, no one can avoid seeing that structure in the socio-cultural world is the changing fixity of a continuous process, like the contours of a whirlpool in a rapidly moving stream. A stable society is not necessarily *uneventful*, so long as the events occur in a recurrent normative framework. Social motion does not always mean social change. Change occurs when there is a shift in pattern—when new relationships emerge, new standards and goals become shared.[33] It is not necessarily social change if an individual meets a situation new to him nor if individuals vary in their behavior in given types of situations—only when the difference is shared and endures long enough to be recognizable as a new structure can we say that the culture or the society has changed. We can imagine a society full of meaningful events, rich in zest and drama, in which people over long periods live by essentially the same codes, have the same ideas and beliefs, and handle life crises by established patterns. We stress this, because of a tendency in modern American thought to equate social stability with a dull, monotonous routine.

[32] A basic work is Émile Durkheim: *Le suicide* (Paris: 1897) (New edition, 1930). Cf. Talcott Parsons: *The Structure of Social Action* (Cambridge, Mass.:) chap. 8, esp. pp. 324–38.

[33] Karl Mannheim: *Ideology and Utopia* (New York: 1936), p. 75: "By social stability we do not mean uneventfulness or the personal security of individuals, but rather the relative fixity of the existing total social structure, which guarantees the stability of the dominant values and ideas."

In line with distinctions already used throughout this volume, it is convenient to discriminate between cultural change and social change. The first has to do with changes in systems of ideas of various kinds, in beliefs, in values and norms; included also in this category are changes in the technical apparatus used for dealing with the physical world. On the other hand, *social* change refers to shifts in the ongoing interaction patterns of person-to-person relationships. In treating both categories of change, a sociological analysis gains in power as it is able to specify how and where the change occurs—in what areas of social structure, in what specific items, at what rates, through what processes. To give only one rather superficial example, it makes a great difference whether the political history of a people is that of shifts in ruling elites, that occur largely independently of the masses (palace revolutions, *coups d'etat*, and so on) or whether political changes directly involve major portions of the population and affect basic social structures other than the state itself.

The analysis of long-range social change is assuredly one of the most difficult and least-developed aspects of the scientific study of societies. Nevertheless, much valuable monographic work has accumulated during the past three generations, and many errors and inadequacies of earlier theories have been eliminated. We are now able to renounce a large part of the sweeping theories of a Comte or a Spencer, and to counsel ourselves to the disciplined patience necessary for the construction of more limited but more solidly grounded descriptions and explanations. It is a major gain, furthermore, that we can now definitely discount all theories reducing the explanation of social and cultural change to a single factor.

If we look for sources of change that permit scientific treatment, we can identify several classes of factors of the sort which served as prime movers in the earlier reductionist theories. First, there is the physical environment, in so far as it is analytically independent of human activity. No one doubts the concrete importance for human action of climate, topography, resources, location, and so on, but it can be easily shown that vast social changes occur without change in physical conditions. Likewise, granting that the biological nature of men must never be overlooked, it is not through any known alterations in that nature that we can explain the enormous and rapid changes of modern societies. In short, we do not see how one can explain a variable by a constant. If on this basis one rejects geographic or biological determinism, there is left the residual area of culture and society itself. Here again, one encounters monofactorial explanations—economic determinism, idealistic emanationism, the great man theory of history, and so on. Without taking space here to support the contention, it is the present view that all these—including Marxism—are demonstrably and seriously inadequate and misleading.[34] What are here called reductionistic explanations have in common the attempt to eliminate men's ideas and values as real causal variables—to regard them as reflections of some more basic condition. On the other hand, the present view is that *Das Kapital* has not been without influence on human history and that Einstein's $E = MC^2$ likewise made a difference, *and* that in neither of these illustrative events have subsequent developments been simple reflections of a single underlying factor.[35] Conversely, neither the present tide of world communism nor atomic weapons are emanations of the ideas to which we conventionally trace them for purposes of punctuating the continuous stream of history. In short, the explicit position of our analysis is that socio-cultural factors must be treated as primary variables in explaining change, not just for methodological convenience, but because ideas and value orientations cannot be reduced to lower orders of complexity without serious loss in understanding and predictive power. One compact way of summarizing the whole point is to say our theories of social

[34] All these closed systems are literally pseudo-scientific. But this does not imply that the remedy is an indiscriminate eclecticism, nor the easy evasion of the problem through a meaningless multiple factor approach which is unable to specify whether one thing is more important than another.

[35] Cf.: "We are made by what we have made. We project our ideas into the world of reality, and when they have taken shape and form, they shape and form us by their reaction upon us. A nation makes a system of law and government, and that system, in its measure, makes the character of that nation. We build more greatly than we know; and our acts have consequences beyond our intentions."—Ernest Barker: *National Character* (London: Methuen & Co., Ltd., 1927), p. 4.

change will make an important difference in the way in which we orient ourselves and hence in the way we will act.[36]

All too briefly, certain of the most general factors in change may be summarized as follows:

1. Changes in physical environment or biological nature, not due to the agency of cultural factors—for example, natural catastrophes, climatic changes, human genetic changes, development of new diseases.

2. Frequency and character of intercultural contact—for example, invasion, conquest, migration, trade.

3. The complexity of a given culture and social structure—for example, differentiation of subcultures, of statuses and roles.

4. The type of value orientations present in the total system for example, the relative emphasis upon tradition or innovation, upon otherworldly or this-worldly interests. Generalizing, a portion of socio-cultural changes are derived from processes internal to the system being examined.

5. Within any given socio-cultural system, certain changes emerge from the unanticipated consequences of purposive social action—for example, the secularization of a religious tradition through following out its own precepts or the precipitation of an unintended war.

6. Idiosyncratic and creative variations in individual behavior arising both from various difficulties in conformity to norms and from certain sources of indeterminancy and spontaneity in the social development of the individual human being.

Social change as a *historic* process is irreversible and concretely unique. The search for genetic or sequential explanations of change therefore leads to an infinite regression: event A was preceded by events B . . . n, and so back toward some first cause. It follows that in the attempt to establish any type of predictive generalization, the diffuse historic reality must be analyzed into repeatable categories that can be systematically related as interacting variables. This has been implicit in the whole of the present analysis,

[36] Extreme reductionism, if really taken seriously, would have us leave the crucial determination of events to those who have *other* convictions.

and it applies specifically to the problem of integration in change. Every social system is a *functioning* entity, with interdependent structures (kinship, political associations, and so on) and processes (for example, social mobility) that maintains a definite autonomy from its environment and from other social systems. The fact that American society differs from the Indian societies that once existed in the same geographic area, and from its European origins is partly the result of such relative independence.[37] The total structure of the American system up to now has been relatively favorable to social change. The social structure has been relatively free from rigidly vested status systems. The culture has been marked by strongly rationalistic elements, by an orientation away from traditionalism and toward adaptability and ingenuity in meeting new situations. Internal heterogeneity has made for an extraordinary mingling of cultures in a mobile society undergoing rapid urbanization and industrialization. The cultural focus on business activity and technological development has opened up wide segments of the system to especially rapid change.[38] The outwardly spiraling impact of scientific discovery and technological innovation, made possible by a definite and unusual cultural context, is too familiar to require description here.[39] The general picture has been one of extremely rapid advances in the application of scientific knowledge to the manipulation of physical and biological structures and processes. The social changes *partly* attrib-

[37] This is probably the place to note that any projections as to the future of American society that anyone might wish to make from the present analysis can not assume that internal changes in an interdependent world will continue to occur with the same autonomy as in the past.

[38] The "culture lag" theories, derived from the work of William F. Ogburn, maintain that technological change leads and that other changes follow. In American society, the valid element in these theories is found in the fact that the culture has been characterized by a value system that made it possible for economic and technological activities to change rapidly and hence to take on special causal significance. In other societies and in other times, the role of technology in social change is definitely minor. (See the critique of culture lag conceptions by Wilbert E. Moore in Georges Gurvitch and Wilbert E. Moore (eds.): *Twentieth Century Sociology* (New York: 1945).

[39] For a vivid summary of the situation in agriculture, often thought to be technologically "retarded," see Carl C. Taylor and associates: *Rural Life in the United States* (New York: 1949), esp. chap. 30.

utable to these developments range from the demographic revolution occasioned by lowered death rates and (more indirectly) lowered birth rates, to the mechanization and specialization of work, to the mobility and anonymity of urban life, to possible indirect repercussions upon primary value-orientations.

The central fact, almost up to the present century, was that Americans were busy at the task of opening up the social order to the relatively unrestained interplay of private economic competition and cultural diversities. The counterpoising fact is the transformation of the basic trends as the society has become an urban, industrial world-power.

Changes in social structure have been accompanied by shifts, perhaps less easily discernible, in value orientations. Even though the America of 1950 has a recognizable continuity with America of 1776, it cannot be said that the dominant beliefs and values are identical, and it is difficult to state in any brief or precise way just what the changes have been. The following appraisals of outstanding shifts in value orientations therefore stand either as *questions* or as the opinions of one observer: [40]

1. A decreased emphasis upon religious-ethical principles, correlative with increased stress upon practicality, adjustment, and conformity.

2. Increased concern with security—both with guarantees of economic security and with psychological certainties in an uncertain world. (Question: Is this attitude still one of individualism?) [41]

3. An inadequately charted and wavering movement along the two complex value-axes represented by totalistic nationalism, as over against commitment to values necessitating a less simple course of international collaboration.[42] The former is indexed by widespread attempts to establish an authoritatively defined and

[40] All the terms used here to characterize values should be read, of course, as if enclosed by quotation marks.

[41] A challenging critique of individualism in certain forms, published on the eve of World War I, is still illuminating—Herbert Croly: *The Promise of American Life* (New York: 1914).

[42] All these terms are so loaded with connotations that this short statement is certain to carry some unintended meanings.

controlled American loyalty; these attempts pose unsolved problems, and need analysis as to the cultural meaning of freedom in a nation confronted with an unforeseeably long period of external threat. On the other hand, there is much evidence of a shift from isolationism toward the kind of international order represented by some aspects of the United Nations.

4. After a long period of at least seeming loss of familistic values, in comparison to individual success and the like, some preliminary signs have appeared of a revived accent upon durable family life. Little more can be said on this matter until more research evidence appears.

5. There is continued strong emphasis upon values of humanitarianism, ethical equality, some aspects of democracy (for example, suffrage, treatment of minority groups), and certain other elements of the American Creed.

Perhaps the most important questions concerning value orientations in our society are three. First, to what extent are the traditional orientations becoming more, or less, the object of intense commitment, of strong personal involvement? Otherwise stated, how much do Americans value the values they seem to claim? It is clear that no new major creeds command any widespread public allegiance. The language of values now current would have been understandable prior to the twentieth century. But we have also to ask—and cannot answer, by evidence, because no one knows what it is crucial to know here—how intense and firm is the commitment to the value-belief systems commonly believed most characteristic of the culture.

The second question brings us again to the problem of integration: To what extent and in what ways is the consensual basis of social cohesion changing? That is, in what wise is there more or less agreement upon common values? Where is consensus fraying, and where is it being strengthened? What new syntheses and emergents can be discerned?

The third question extends the problem of integration in change beyond the permeable boundaries of American society: How far and how solidly can the value orientations herein described or suggested be extended *and* modified in a larger commonality?

545 *Integration and Change*

To the first question—value commitment—we can bring only a composite impression, suggestive rather than definitive. It is that a period of progressive disillusionment and attenuation of commitment to "principled" value orientation—perhaps most marked from the early 1920's to World War II—is drawing to a close. We at least have not as yet an "existentialist" culture. If anything, the wind is veering to other quarters.

The question as to changes in value consensus reveals a distressing lack of data and analysis. In the present study, we have worked as best we might with bits and pieces of evidence as to changes in consensus, and some light can be thus generated. Again at the level of composite judgment, it is the definite impression of this study that the unity of American value-systems is commonly and seriously *under*estimated. It is our hypothesis that commonality of values is, more than generally recognized, a matter of belief that there is consensus—not that there is agreement upon the detailed content of every norm and value. The conformity so often derided in American life has perhaps not usually been seen in its functional significance *as a pervasive signaling of a shared culture.* Furthermore, all the diversity of America that can be shown by a detached analysis is probably not so generally perceived by the majority of the people. Underneath the external flux, so this analysis suggests, there are substantial common themes and basic cultural axioms. Not even Hollywood or picture magazines entirely conceal the toughness of this web of cohesion.

The last question concerns by implication the capacity of the American people to understand *other* cultures and to work with others to create collaboratively a manageable common core of those intercultural values that seem a prerequisite to common survival. It would be a fault not to raise this question. And it would be both impossible and presumptuous here to pronounce dicta concerning it.

This work is being closed with questions, not answers; with new searches, not closed systems of interpretation. This policy is believed to be in the spirit of science. It is also believed to be in accord with the historic meaning of America.

Index of Names

Index of Subjects

A NOTE ON THE TYPE

The text of this book was set on the Monotype in Bodoni, so called after Giambattista Bodoni (1740–1813), son of a printer of Piedmont. After gaining experience and fame as superintendent of the Press of the Propaganda in Rome, Bodoni became in 1766 the head of the ducal printing house at Parma, which he soon made the foremost of its kind in Europe. His *Manuale Tipografico, completed by his widow in 1818, contains 279 pages of specimens of types, including alphabets of about thirty foreign languages. His editions of Greek, Latin, Italian, and French classics, especially his Homer, are celebrated for their typography. In type-designing he was an innovator, making his new faces rounder, wider, and lighter, with greater openness and delicacy.*

The book was composed, printed, and bound by KINGSPORT PRESS, INC., *Kingsport, Tennessee.*

Designed by HARRY FORD